ED KOCH AND THE REBUILDING OF NEW YORK CITY

COLUMBIA HISTORY OF URBAN LIFE

THE COLUMBIA HISTORY OF URBAN LIFE
KENNETH T. JACKSON, *General Editor*

ED KOCH

AND THE REBUILDING OF NEW YORK CITY

JONATHAN SOFFER

COLUMBIA UNIVERSITY PRESS / NEW YORK

Columbia University Press

Publishers Since 1893

New York   Chichester, West Sussex

Copyright © 2010 Jonathan Soffer

All rights reserved

Library of Congress Cataloging-in-Publication Data

Soffer, Jonathan M., 1956–

Ed Koch and the rebuilding of New York City / Jonathan Soffer.

p.   cm. — (The Columbia history of urban life)

Includes bibliographical references and index.

ISBN 978-0-231-15032-3 (cloth : acid-free paper) — ISBN 978-0-231-52090-4

(electronic)

1. Koch, Ed, 1924– 2. Mayors—New York (State)—New York—Biography. 3. New

York (N.Y.)—Politics and government—1951– 4. New York (N.Y.)—Social policy. 5. New

York (N.Y.)—Social conditions—20th century. I. Title.

F128.54.K63S64   2010

974.7′1043092—dc22

2009034786

[B]

To Pamela Allen Brown,
my partner, who has patiently
talked with me about
Ed Koch more than once
a day for the many years that
it took to write this book.
Her spiritual, artistic, editorial,
economic, and scholarly
contributions made this book possible.

CONTENTS

ACKNOWLEDGMENTS

First, I'd like to acknowledge Mayor Ed Koch, who has made himself, his papers, and his circle of friends available to me but has left control of the manuscript entirely in my hands and never tried to still my often critical pen. If I were the subject of a biography, I don't know if I would have as much fortitude. The many individuals I've interviewed are listed in the notes, but I am also grateful for their time. I'd also like to thank his staff, Mary Garrigan and Jody Smith, who provided me with contact details for numerous interviews, and Pat Koch Thaler, who provided family pictures and interviews. This book owes its start to Ronald Grele, former director of the Columbia University Oral History Research Office, one of my academic mentors from my first days in graduate school, who hired me back in the early 1990s as an interviewer for the original Koch oral history project, recommended me to Ed as a biographer, and has continued as a friend and adviser since his retirement. This book would not have been written if it weren't for Ron.

Scholarship depends on archives and librarians, and this book could not have been written without the help and cooperation of Kenneth Cobb, assistant commissioner of the New York City Department of Records and Information Services, and his successor as director of the Municipal Archives, Leonora Gidlund. I'd also like to particularly thank Richard Lieberman, director of the La Guardia and Wagner Archives; its archivist, Douglas DiCarlo; and its educational director, Steven Levine, for their valuable programs and facilities that ease access to primary source material on New York City for both scholars and students. Mary Marshall Clark, the current director of the Columbia University Oral History Research Office, has gone beyond simply making available the office's extensive collections on Koch and related figures to be a great friend. Her assistant director, Corie Trancho-Robie, also generously helped with permissions and other aspects of using the collection. The Village Independent Democrats also opened up their archives, which included some early Koch letters and campaign materials.

I am grateful to many Koch friends, appointees, and other knowledgeable people who donated their time and expertise in interviews, including George Arzt, Herman Badillo, Carol Bellamy, Abraham Biderman, Stanley Brezenoff, David Brown, James Capalino, Diane Coffey, Maureen Connelly, Evan Cornog, Paul Crotty, Gordon Davis, Julius Edelstein, Robert Esnard, Moe Foner, Sandy Frucher, David Garth, Stanley Geller, Ed Gold, Tom Goldstein, Victor Gotbaum, Carol Greitzer, Lee Hudson, Jane Jacobs, Sarah Kovner, Victor Kovner, John Lankenau, Nat Leventhal, Ken Lipper John LoCicero, Carl McCall, Robert J. McGuire, Ronay Menschel, Basil Paterson, Mark Penn, Richard Ravitch, Felix Rohatyn, Allen G. Schwartz, Peter J. Solomon, Gillian Sorensen, Jerry Skurnik, Al Sharpton, Norman Steisel , Henry Stern, Ed Sullivan, Pat Koch Thaler, Alair Townsend, Haskell Ward, and Miki Wolter.

M. J. Bogatin of Bogatin, Corman, and Gold was a valued friend and perspicacious legal counselor. Jess McCuan speedily and wonderfully copyedited an early draft. Stuart Schrader was an assiduous research assistant. My parents, Sanford and Miriam Soffer, gave all kinds of support and love during this long project.

Sarah T. Phillips, Richard Greenwald, Nicholas Dagen Bloom, Neal Rosendorf, David Greenberg, Jennifer Luff, Anne Kornhauser, Kim Phillips-Fein, Lara Vapnek, Jeffrey Trask, Vanessa May, Charlotte Brooks, Kristin Celello, and Daniel Katz all read chapters in my writing group, as did members of earlier writing groups, including Mary Cygan, Gunja SenGupta, and Phil Napoli. Nancy Haekyung Kwak read most of the manuscript, and Curtis Arluck read the entire book before publication. Lynda Richardson, Immy Humes, and Ella Hill also read and commented on chapters. Victor Hugo Lane and John Paul Himka helped me learn about Galicia. Pierre-Yves Saunier and Shane Ewen invited me to contribute to their volume *Another Global City: Transnational Municipal Trails in the Modern Age (1850–2000)* (New York: Palgrave, 2008) and, along with Michael Hebbert, to present my work at the European Urban History Association, a valuable experience. I would also like to thank John Belknap, Pegi Goodman, Leah Rozen, Katie Hanner, Roger Haile, Frank Van Riper, Gloria MacDarrah, Chris Hables Gray, and Fred Siegel.

The Department of Humanities and Social Sciences at New York University's Polytechnic Institute and its department heads during my tenure, Richard Wener, Harold Sjursen, and Myles Jackson, have been generous in their support with leave time and research funds. Kenneth T. Jackson encouraged me from the beginning and has been a great editor. He and cochair Lisa Keller invited me to present my work at the Columbia University Seminar on the City. Samuel K. Roberts asked me to address the Robert Wood Johnson Health & Society Scholars Working Group in African-American History and the Health and Social Sciences; Mike Wallace twice brought me to the Gotham Center for New York City History; Joel Blatt asked me to give the Estelle Feinstein Lecture at the University of Connecticut, Stamford; and Reet Sool hosted me at the University of Tartu, Estonia. I benefited greatly from these discussions and especially from comments by Judith Stein at an early stage of the project. Finally, I'd like to express appreciation to the Schoff Fund at the University Seminars at Columbia University for a grant that covered publication costs. Wilbur Rich has been a support and inspiration for my interest in urban politics since my days as an undergraduate. Jonathan Karp helped get the project started and offered valuable advice. Finally, I'd like to thank the anonymous readers for Columbia University Press and my editors there, Peter Dimock and Philip Leventhal, and my copy editor, Polly Kummel, who helped bring this project to fruition.

ED
KOCH

AND THE
REBUILDING
OF
NEW YORK CITY

1 INTRODUCTION

When Ed Koch became mayor of New York in January 1978, the city was filthy, dangerous, and nearly bankrupt. Under his predecessor, Abraham D. Beame, New York was being run by the Emergency Financial Control Board, a group of business, labor, and public officials appointed by the governor that had reduced elected officials, including Mayor Beame, to "mere spectators," according to the influential banker David Rockefeller. The *New Yorker* expected Koch, who was six feet one, to be a "tall Abe Beame," a mediocre politician who would let bankers and technocrats run the city while he looked on. Instead, he set about to become a tall Fiorello La Guardia, even moving the Little Flower's old desk into his new office.[1]

Koch revived the mayoralty as a bully pulpit, reasserted some power over the budget, restored rule by elected officials, and began to rebuild the city's credit rating. Gangly, bald, and pear-shaped, making impolitic jabs at opponents as "wackos" in his fast New York twang, Koch fashioned himself as a personification of New York, appearing on local television more than any public official except the president. His in-your-face humor and incessant flow of words reinforced his carefully cultivated reputation for candor. Reporters, hungry for a story, even followed him to the men's room, where he obligingly continued their conversation. But he was not just talk. By rebuilding New York after neglect and arson had made much of the city look like a war zone, he changed municipal politics throughout the United States.[2]

Few thought at the outset that Koch could raise New York from a nadir that its most faithful citizens found difficult to tolerate, though New Yorkers were proud of their toughness. "New York: It ain't Kansas," proclaimed the t-shirts sold in Times Square. But at the time even Kansas City, Kansas, was melting like the Wicked Witch of the West, losing 15 percent of its population between 1970 and 2006. Other cities suffered greater demographic collapse. Detroit lost more than half of its population between 1950 and 2006, and St. Louis decreased by 60 percent in the same period.[3]

New York might have suffered the same fate. Between 1970 and 1980 it lost 10 percent of its population. Unskilled workers had a hard time finding a job: New York had lost 65 percent of its manufacturing jobs between 1950 and 1989.[4] Racial tensions were growing throughout the city, exploding in riots in the summer of 1977 during a citywide blackout, with arsonists and vandals destroying hundreds of homes and stores in Bushwick, Brooklyn, in just a few days. Fires destroyed 108,000 dwelling units in the Bronx between 1970 and 1981. In one Bronx neighborhood, Hunts Point–Crotona Park East, which lost 69 percent of its population, the police station became famous as "Fort Apache." By 1980 little in that area was left to burn, and Fort Apache soon became known as "The Little House on the Prairie"—the only building left standing in a desert of rubble.[5]

Homelessness was one terrible result of the destruction of so much of the city's low-priced housing stock. State government then made a desperate situation worse by discharging thousands of mental patients from hospitals into the city's neighborhoods. At the same time low-income people were hit by high inflation that cut into welfare and disability checks as gentrification raised rents and land prices.[6] Many slept in the streets, which were often strewn with garbage and pockmarked with potholes. Mass transit deferred maintenance for years, so riders grew resigned to boarding trains that were trashy, bumpy, and often late. Schools, bridges, and government offices became dangerous; no one fixed them. Less than a year and a half before Koch took over, off-duty officers protesting layoffs rioted outside Yankee Stadium and beat up the detachment of senior officers sent to disperse them. Even Gracie Mansion, the mayor's official residence, was in danger of collapsing into the East River because the FDR Drive, which runs under it, had cracked. The city's infrastructure was like the tired shock absorbers of its vehicles—expensive to replace and unlikely to bounce back.

No mayor could solve the larger problems caused by the longer term national trends that hurt cities: subsidized suburbanization and residential segregation, rising income inequality and unemployment, deindustrialization, economic instability increased by deregulation, and the naturalization of a so-called free-market regime that was designed to camouflage the enrichment of the rich at everyone else's expense. Yet within the limits set by the federal system and the antiurban choices made by electorates nationally, Koch put New York on the road toward a precarious revival.

By the end of his first term, Koch was able to balance the city's budget, a feat that vastly exceeded expectations when he started in 1977. And by the end of his second term he could launch a locally financed $5.1 billion, ten-year program to rebuild huge areas of the city, including the South Bronx, and make them economically viable for the long term. The restoration of credit and the renewed economic growth enabled the city to borrow again and restored to elected officials the power to choose key projects, rather than leaving the decisions to unelected power brokers like Felix Rohatyn, the Lazard Frères partner who headed the Municipal Assistance Corporation.[7] By the time Koch left office in 1990, the population had increased by more than 3 percent despite a severe recession, and the burned-out "prairie" in the South Bronx was filled with newly built houses. By 2006 New York's population had soared to a record 8.2 million, 16 percent higher than in 1980, largely as a result of policies laid out by the Koch administration.[8]

This book is a biography of an extraordinary and controversial figure. Just as important, it is a history of the postwar shift in New York City's political economy, away from a manufacturing center with a welfare-state orientation to one dominated by neoliberalism, defined as the idea that "human well-being can best be advanced by liberating individual entrepreneurial freedom and skills within an institutional framework characterized by strong private property rights, free markets, and free trade." Neoliberals press to lift restraints on the private accumulation of capital (such as regulations and taxes) and to restore the power of economic elites. But neoliberalism has mainly concentrated rather than created wealth.[9] After Keynesianism failed to explain the "stagflation" that plagued the 1970s economy, intellectuals and government officials treat deindustrialization and deregulation as the inevitable result of impersonal economic forces necessary to restore America's vigor, rather than as deliberate policies that consolidated the power of financial elites. New York's late twentieth-century bourgeoisie focused on profiting from its position as a central channel for global capital while it increasingly disconnected from the national economy. Deindustrialization undermined the diversity of the city's economic base and limited the redistributive practices of city government, despite the increasing poverty of many citizens. By 1993 the profitable but unstable securities industry accounted for only 4 percent of New York's jobs but 14 percent of its wages. Developers of the downtown business district, as Robert Fitch has observed, sought to turn New York into "a kind of high-rise command center"—a modern ziggurat that made it easier to ignore the demands of the lower classes while exporting New York's once innovative and dynamic industrial economy based on crafts and small industries. This created more profit for the capitalist class than manufacturing had but restricted opportunities for most New Yorkers.[10]

Koch pioneered the Democratic Party version of neoliberalism, which allowed for government intervention to shape and subsidize private enterprise, but he remained diffident about creating new programs for redistribution or social insurance that might burden future expense budgets. The most stunning examples are Koch's multibillion-dollar housing program, which poured money into private nonprofits to construct, rehabilitate, and sell mostly middle-income housing. But Koch also poured hundreds of millions of dollars into tax abatements to subsidize construction of office buildings and luxury housing and to keep corporate headquarters from leaving the city. Such construction was one of the primary engines of growth left in New York after the long period of deindustrialization and had the side benefit of providing a significant source of minority employment. Determining whether the city ultimately got its money's worth from the tax abatement programs is difficult because few data exist that show whether the incentives actually altered the behavior of developers and corporate executives.[11]

Throughout twelve years of crisis, success, and scandal, Ed Koch maintained that he was transparent. "What you see is what you get," he liked to brag. Yet his candor was qualified by opacities and self-contradictions. Happy to discuss his prostate, he rarely mentioned those he has loved, or who have loved him, outside his immediate family. He came to office as a squeaky-clean reformer, yet he refused to acknowledge any misjudgment in making his worst hires or in forming alliances with political hacks that later proved disastrous. Voluble, brash, and self-confident, he can be reticent when he has to talk about something other than politics.

Koch was both a freewheeling showman and a hardworking policy maker, but his rhetoric and policies did not always cohere. When observers try to sum up his political ideology, for example, they often resort to paradoxes, however insufficient. For example, one historian maintains that Koch "talked like a Republican sometimes, but governed like a New Dealer."[12] More precisely, Koch's procorporate policies made the rich richer, even though he tried (though with less success) to avoid making the poor poorer. He trumpeted the death penalty and law-and-order to campaign audiences but quietly promoted liberal correctional initiatives in the city's jails. He was a reformer who deprived the Democratic machine of much of its patronage and established a nonpolitical system for appointing municipal judges, but he made deals with county leaders that he lived to regret when those leaders turned out to be crooks. He also publicly criticized some of those same judges so harshly that they feared he had compromised their independence. Koch prided himself on his ability to make alliances with Italian Catholics as mayor and with southern whites and conservative Republicans during his years in Congress, but he failed to build alliances with many black leaders in his own home town. He was tarred as a Reaganite when he blamed labor unions and overly generous pensions for much of the fiscal crisis and maintained an oppositional relationship with labor. But unlike President Ronald Reagan, Koch promoted orderly collective bargaining.

Koch's contradictions reflected the tensions inherent in governing an urban populace split along lines of geography, race, class, and ethnicity. From the start Koch's biggest political challenge could be termed the "pothole paradox." While financial and labor elites worried about selling bonds and balancing the budget, most residents experienced the crisis in terms of their ethnic loyalties and the rising levels of crime and refuse in a city that had laid off thousands of police and nearly all its street cleaners. Many police stations leaked, and some were near collapse. Patrol cars fell apart, and impossibly bumpy streets damaged them even further. Dirty streets and crime were sometimes fused in popular culture, as in the tagline for the 1991 Steven Seagal thriller *Out for Justice*, set in Brooklyn: "He's a cop. It's a dirty job . . . but somebody's got to take out the garbage."[13]

Certainly some of Koch's zigzagging was the result of being forced to play with the cards he had been dealt. The Emergency Financial Control Board, which ruled New York City from 1975 to 1978, had cut the budget deeply. Many cuts were across the board, with little regard for their effect on the city. Koch inherited agencies that barely functioned because so many experienced people had been laid off. Those who remained labored in decrepit offices because the city had no money for repairs. For the first years of his mayoralty Koch continued to cut as part of his push to restore the city's credit, but as Ester Fuchs, a leading historian of urban budgets, has noted, Koch did not fundamentally change the city's fiscal policy process or the redistributive functions of the city budget.[14]

As Mayor Michael Bloomberg observed in 2003, commenting on the stark deficit he faced on becoming mayor, "During the fiscal crisis of the 1970s, services were cut so much that crime gripped whole neighborhoods, fires gutted whole blocks, and garbage littered the streets. We haven't permitted and I won't permit that history to repeat itself." Bloomberg understood that the austerity program of the 1970s and 1980s ultimately cost far more than the budget cuts saved.[15] So Koch's greatest success—carrying out austerity, restoring the city's credit, and building a political coalition behind that policy—paradoxically contributed to the homelessness, crime, and infrastructure breakdowns that tarnished his last term. Koch tried to mitigate these problems with housing and infrastructure investments made possible by the city's renewed ability to borrow.

The direct cause of the fiscal crisis was the city's use of expensive short-term financing to cover its deficits in the early 1970s. The sources of these deficits were many, including political patronage; cuts in federal funding; increases in health, welfare, and pension spending; deindustrialization; and the credit crunch of the early 1970s and 1980s. The evaporation of federal money hurt the most. The increasing political clout of the suburbs and Sun Belt meant less federal and state money for cities, but the ultimate blame for the devastation of the city in the 1970s lies in Washington and the antiurban administrations of Presidents Gerald Ford, Jimmy Carter, and Ronald Reagan.

Of all the expenses that caused the city's budget to hemorrhage, none was more damaging than health care. The same issue that the administration of Barack Obama identified as the real culprit behind the nation's economic crisis in 2009—an out-of-control health-care system—is what brought New York City to its knees in the 1970s and 1980s. The city's fiscal crisis could have been solved if Ford, Carter, or Reagan had been able and willing to reform the U.S. health-care system. The cost of providing care to the uninsured through the city's hospital system, plus the city's 25 percent share of Medicaid expenditures—a burden that no major city outside New York State had to bear—accounted for more than half the budget gap for most of Koch's mayoralty. For four years it was responsible for more than 75 percent of the budget gap. (See chapter 11.) At the time Koch argued that the federalization of health care would allow New York City to achieve a stable and sustainable budget, a goal that has yet to be reached. He called full federal funding of Medicaid his "No. 1 priority for federal legislation," and the Democratic Party platform of 1980 called for "a universal comprehensive health insurance plan," a by-product of which would have been the stabilizing of the New York city budget. But the victor in the presidential election, Ronald Reagan, flatly (and not surprisingly) refused to assume the full cost of health care for the poor, and the state legislature in Albany would not take on the burden. As a result, Koch was never able to fully restore the city's infrastructure, security, or level of services, though he began a long process of reconstruction. After the Wall Street crash of 1987 it became evident that austerity, at least in the expense budget, would accompany any significant downturn in financial markets, because of the city's dependence on taxes from the financial services sector.[16]

For better or worse, Koch convinced most New Yorkers of the legitimacy of a new neoliberal order that subsidized Manhattan business development, particularly in the finance, insurance, and real estate sectors, privatized public space, and created huge income inequalities. He succeeded partly by using some of the fruits of growth for public development and jobs. He also decentralized city government by giving the city's fifty-nine community planning boards more power over land use, capital projects, and service delivery in their districts, though that reform was partially undone in his last year with charter reforms that made the mayor and council more powerful in the planning process. A small but important change, emblematic of the reforms in the agencies, reorganized the office that handled the mayor's correspondence, which had fallen into chaos. Koch insisted that every letter receive a response.

During his three terms he made important improvements in budgeting. City agencies began to pay their bills on time, and other reforms increased efficiency. For example, the reduction in the size of sanitation truck crews from three to two allowed the city to run many more trucks and collect more tons of garbage for the same money. Along with an enormous real estate revival in Manhattan, spurred in part by generous tax credits, Koch pushed the redevelopment of residential neighborhoods, particularly after 1985, though the program did not end New York's housing shortage. Koch's major achievements all resulted from his skill at maintaining political coalitions that mediated between popular interests and the corporate economy. As one leading scholar recognized, "It was the genius of Ed Koch to recognize that it is possible to manage the city's affairs in a way that meets with the approval of both staid investment bankers and lower middle class Jews by playing the kibitzer—the brash fellow who has an opinion on everything."[17] The kibitzer will also discuss anything with anyone, and he always is open to making a deal.

Not everyone walked away from the table happy, of course. Some are still angry. Every step on the way to recovery involved complex choices between moneyed interests and hard-pressed consumers of social services, such as hospitals and public housing. Gentrification meant fewer flophouses and low-cost hotels and drove many poor individuals and families into the street. Health-care cutbacks could mean longer waits and reduced services for the poor. Koch saw himself as a moderate and a pragmatist, trying to reconcile New York's tradition of liberalism, which used state power to mitigate economic inequality, with the new laissez-faire order. Austerity—particularly the cutbacks in drug addict rehabilitation and welfare assistance programs during the Beame period—made it harder to control the epidemics of crack, crime, and AIDS that plagued the city after 1985.[18]

Under Koch, gentrification was a deliberate policy to make the city more economically viable. Koch had inherited a city that had already deindustrialized, with little prospect of reversing that process. But New York in the age of Koch—with bistros springing up along Columbus Avenue, Wall Street fattening itself on mergers and junk bonds, and rental housing converting to co-ops or condos—became during his three mayoral terms a place that grew rather than shrank. As a mayor who had to confront the pathologies of burning neighborhoods, Koch viewed gentrification as laudable and was unapologetic about the racial implications of the process. As he said in an interview conducted in 2000 about the Newark neighborhood where he grew up: "Generally speaking, in order for a city to succeed, you need a substantial white population." After this startling statement he went on to explain: "And it isn't that whites can do more than blacks, it is that there is greater business confidence, and you will get investment which you won't normally get if the city is totally minority. [Newark] has additional problems in that it is, I think, the largest recipient of individual welfare, certainly in the state of New Jersey, maybe in the country. And that, as we know is not good for a city."[19]

The statement was quintessential Koch. An incisive orator, he had neatly encapsulated his formula for urban recovery, built on racial privilege, business confidence, and gentrification. He had also exhibited his impolitic penchant for saying what he thinks without fear of whom he might offend. Throughout his mayoralty Koch saw himself as acting "on the merits" and had little patience with those who obstructed what he believed to be the public interest. Intent on controls that would ensure that city money was well spent, Koch passed over the regular Harlem leadership and instead gave contracts to local black and Hispanic community groups outside the Democratic machine for poverty programs and housing. This practice often caused political friction in the name of efficiency and demonstrated to his opponents that Koch did not always comprehend, or seem to care much about, the problems of a black middle class in transition from a segregated society.

Some black leaders called him a racist. During the protests against the closing of Harlem's Sydenham Hospital in 1981, which proceeded nonviolently, Representative Charles B. Rangel compared the mayor to the notorious Birmingham, Alabama, public safety commissioner Eugene "Bull" Connor.[20] (Koch himself later acknowledged that the hospital closing was not worth the strife it caused.) Some of Koch's earlier pronouncements were inflammatory. During the 1977 campaign he blasted "poverty pimps" and said that the National Guard should have been called out during the 1977 blackout.[21] Such rhetoric could be indelible. Even ten years later, the president of Bronx Community College, Roscoe C. Brown, cited the "poverty pimp" remark as evidence of Koch's insensitivity to blacks, and thirty years later obituaries for Ramon C. Velez, "godfather" of New York's Puerto Rican community, mentioned that the mayor had branded him a "poverty pimp," although Velez later became Koch's political ally.[22] After 1979 many black politicians came to feel there was no place for them in a Koch coalition—not with a mayor who favored the death penalty, opposed numerical quotas for affirmative action hiring and the letting of contracts, reformed antipoverty programs, and cut welfare. For his part, Koch was cool to those African Americans whose lack of support for Israel he considered anti-Semitic. Few African American politicians packed much electoral clout. Despite the increasing minority population, black voter turnout was low. Before 1988 no black leader in New York could deliver votes as effectively as white bosses like the Brooklyn Democratic Chair Meade Esposito.

By looking at black political elites alone, however, it is easy to overstate the degree of racial polarization within the mayoral electorate, which was nothing like that within the national party system. Koch had substantial support from New York's black middle class, especially from Caribbean Americans, and in his reelection bids in 1981 and 1985 received more than 30 percent of the black vote, support he lost almost entirely by 1989. Nationally, Republican presidential candidates have received only 6 to 10 percent of the black vote since Barry Goldwater purged blacks from the Republican Party leadership in 1964. Koch remained a popular mayor only as long as he stayed popular with a large swath of New York's sizable black middle class. But its crucial support shifted for a variety of reasons when he ran for a fourth term in 1989.

Koch was arguably Israel's most prominent American advocate in the 1970s and 1980s, and he renamed many streets around the UN after Jewish heroes or Soviet dissidents. He sometimes hurt New York's international standing with his outspoken support for Israel. As he worked to extend New York's global profile, Koch turned against the United Nations for its criticisms of Israel. Though he defended the rights of Palestinians and Libyans to set up their UN missions, against neighborhood opposition, Koch provoked an outcry among the city's diplomatic community when he called the UN a cesspool because the General Assembly had voted to condemn Israel. His bluntness even provoked some grumbling that the UN should decamp, though the dissatisfaction was never taken seriously.[23]

When the campaign for an economic boycott of the apartheid regime in South Africa accelerated in the mid-1980s, Koch was so tone deaf to black constituents that he declared he would not support the boycott unless it also targeted the USSR, Iran, Libya, and Syria as a protest against their opposition to Israel. Only when advisers convinced him that this position was politically disastrous did he reverse himself and initiate a strong program for the city to divest its stocks and contracts with companies that did business in South Africa.[24]

The incident shows how important foreign relations were becoming to the reinvention of postindustrial New York's politics and economy. New York's economy has been reinvented several times but rarely by its mayor. Mayor (and governor) DeWitt Clinton spearheaded the building of the Erie Canal in the nineteenth century, turning the city's economic face from the Atlantic to the North American interior, and for nearly a century and a half New York shaped the development of the continent. By the 1980s new regional financial centers, such as Charlotte, North Carolina, and edge cities such as Stamford, Connecticut, challenged New York's preeminence within the national economy. Koch understood that New York's future lay in its role as one of the few sites that offered services to companies operating throughout the global economy. Where else in the world, save London and Tokyo, could you go in the 1980s to find a law firm with specialized knowledge of business regulations in Djakarta, Lusaka, and Malta? Foreign money buoyed the city's economy in the mid-1980s, and Koch traveled to Europe, Asia, and the Middle East, making connections to facilitate trade and investment.[25]

Koch understood, as few mayors had, that New York is a world city and that as its mayor he had a degree of power and responsibility closer to that of a head of state. The chief executive of America's media and financial hub, Ed Koch commanded a mass audience and access to the highest levels of government, business, and the media. He controlled an annual budget of more than $10 billion, at the time the eleventh-largest governmental budget in the world. He gave orders to a police force of twenty-two thousand and had direct or indirect responsibility for hospitals, welfare and schools, fire, sanitation, transportation, public housing, and more than twenty-five thousand acres of parks and playgrounds. As headquarters of the United Nations, New York hosts more diplomats than Washington, D.C., and the New York City police are responsible for their security. The mayor accredits consuls, routinely meets with world leaders, and frequently travels abroad to promote commerce.

The national economy began to improve in the mid-1980s, a stroke of luck that helped Koch win a third term in 1985. Hotels and skyscrapers began to change the city's skyline again, and a rising stock market filled the city's coffers. Having ended the fiscal crisis, he seemed to grow a bit bored in his second term. He was distracted for a year by his unsuccessful run for governor in 1982, and Koch and his administration seemed to lose direction. He regained steam in 1984 when gearing up for reelection, promoting a series of expansive liberal goals, including affordable housing to eliminate homelessness, an excellent public school system, and "a job for everyone who wants one." All still remain tantalizingly outside the city's grasp more than two decades later.[26]

The third term nearly ruined Koch's reputation. Beginning in 1986, corruption in some city agencies and among Democratic Party leaders weakened him politically. Kickbacks, fraud, and favoritism in city contracting, particularly within the machine-dominated Department of Transportation, were the first problems to surface, most graphically when Donald Manes, the borough president of Queens, was found in his car by the highway in a pool of blood from a suicide attempt. The revelation that Manes had been involved in fraud led to further investigations that slowed the processes of government. Despite the probes, Koch also racked up some impressive accomplishments in his third term that defined the mayoralties of his successors—including the housing program, antidiscrimination legislation for gays, public financing for political campaigns, and the creation of substantial programs to help AIDS sufferers. But the scandals were less damaging than the dire problems of homelessness, racial strife, the AIDS epidemic, and a spike in violence and drug crime.

Koch's political Waterloo came amid mounting racial tensions during his final two years as mayor, spurred by ugly incidents of police and vigilante violence against blacks. His remarks that Jews "would have to be crazy" to vote for the Reverend Jesse Jackson drove away some of his own supporters, both white and black. His hostility toward Jackson catalyzed the minister's formidable organization against Koch and lost him the significant minority of the black vote that he had once enjoyed. David Dinkins defeated Koch the next year to become New York's first African American mayor, receiving an astounding 97 percent of the black vote. Subsequent mayors have built on the foundation that Koch constructed. All kept Koch's basic framework of financial transparency, tax incentives to encourage construction (which some critics have called "corporate welfare"), austerity during economic downturns, and improvement of management and efficiency, for example, by computerizing management systems. Even projects halted in Koch's time, such as the redevelopment of Times Square, were structured by the basic decisions made by his administration. Despite his reservations about some of the details, the charter revision completed under Koch formally abolished the unconstitutional Board of Estimate and replaced it with a strengthened mayor and city council. Along with the system of public campaign financing for city races that he instituted, the new charter has remained the blueprint of city government. With the exception of Dinkins, all Koch's successors have followed his stance of independence from and sometimes hostility toward municipal unions.

Senator Daniel Patrick Moynihan once declared that "history will record Ed Koch as having given back New York City its morale."[27] A showman at heart who served as an unabashed civic booster, he increased spending on marketing the city as a tourist and business destination and helped publicize the state's I ♥ NY campaign, which was launched on Valentine's Day 1978, six weeks after he became mayor, and quickly caught the public imagination.[28] In his first term Koch had brought the city some of its first good fiscal news in years, but his style and sense of humor also helped New York's psychological recovery. He fearlessly courted razzes with his trademark "How'm I doing?" His satire was always blunt—he hurled the term *wackos* at his opponents while urging New Yorkers to walk to work during the 1980 transit strike, aiming to unify support and contain the costs of settling the strike. When he needed to replace the broken-down official car that he had inherited from Beame, Koch asked the public if he should be forced to go around in a "deathmobile," which eventually persuaded an embarrassed Chrysler Corporation to repair the car, shortly after a *Daily News* poll showed New Yorkers would not approve of their mayor's using a city-owned Cadillac.[29]

When Koch left office in 1989, New York still had significant problems. The city was beset by crack, AIDS, and the effects of a generation of hostile federal policies. During his three terms Koch took the city and its citizens on a ride that seemed more like the Coney Island Cyclone than a pleasant cruise on the Circle Line. Riding Koch's rollercoaster takes us to multiple vantage points on New York's shining new skyline, as well as the dirty subway platforms where homeless people sleep in cardboard boxes. To understand Koch and the reconstruction of New York City, feeling the wildness of that ride is as important as assessing the view.

2
STRUGGLING
TO BE
MIDDLE
CLASS

Ed Koch's Early Life

When Edward Irving Koch arrived in the world on December 12, 1924, his family lived in one of the nicest buildings in the Bronx, 1680 Crotona Park East.[1] From the window his mother could see the large green expanse of Crotona Park, named for the rushing waters of the old Croton Aqueduct that once ran nearby. The street was known as the "Central Park West of the Bronx," a neighborhood for Jews who had made enough money to emerge from the tenements but not enough to penetrate the bourgeois Jewish enclave on Manhattan's Upper West Side.

The family's fortunes seemed to be solid, but the Koches had only recently arrived in the middle class. For the next sixteen years they would struggle to remain there, a struggle they would almost lose. At the time being middle class in America meant education for the children and modern home conveniences, most basically, hot and cold running water. Ed Koch was not only the first member of his family to attend college, he was also the first to live his entire life in apartments equipped with hot and cold running water, so thin was the membrane that separated him from real poverty.

Ed's brother, Harold, had been born four years earlier in a cold-water flat down the hill on Jennings Street in nearby Tremont.[2] Crotona Park once formed part of one of New York's most Jewish and most "economically heterogeneous," neighborhoods.[3] Most neighbors were recent arrivals, many still linked to the Lower East Side world of the sweatshop. Like them, Louis and Joyce Koch had made their way up in the garment industry—Louis as a furrier and Joyce, before her marriage, as a blouse designer.[4]

The Jewish world around Crotona Park was a pleasant and confident world in the 1920s. Joyce and Louis Koch must have found the "modern conveniences" and the park view from their apartment a delight. They had both had much rougher childhoods, which helped prepare them for the setbacks they would face in Depression-era America. Louis Koch, known as Leib Koch before he arrived at Ellis Island, came from a poor family, inhabitants of a hamlet called Usciesko on the Dniester River in southeastern Galicia, the easternmost and poorest province of the Austro-Hungarian Empire. The nearest big city was Chernowitz, in the neighboring province of Bukovina.[5] In 1900 Galicia's 811,183 Jews comprised approximately 11 percent of the population: about 42 percent was Ukrainian, with the remainder divided principally between ethnic Poles and Germans. Most Jews (more than 70 percent) worked in the commerce and industry of the area. Nearly 77 percent of the general population and 94 percent of the ethnic Ukrainians were peasant farmers.[6]

Like many Galician Jews, Koch's paternal grandfather, Yidl Itsik, was a peddler (Yidl translates as Ed, and his grandson was named for him). As a young child, Leib began traveling among the Ukrainian peasants with Yidl and the rest of the family, exchanging manufactured goods for agricultural goods—mostly chickens, eggs, and straw—that they would then exchange with a dealer in town for cash. Sometimes Leib and his father got up at four or five in the morning because, he told his grandchildren, "the peasants, the man and the wife, used to steal one from another. The man used to tell you to come at this hour to come and buy something, and the woman used to tell you to come at this hour when the man was away in the fields. So we hadda go at the time when they wanted us to come in order to buy something from them."[7]

The family of Ed's paternal grandfather—parents, five boys, and three girls—lived in a one-room house without running water or toilets and survived off their father's meager earnings, plus a cow and a few chickens. On the sabbath the family ate meat, but the rest of the time potatoes were their mainstay. The Koches kept clean with a weekly trip to the *schvitz*—the steam baths—though in summer everyone would go swimming in the Dniester River: "The men used to bathe on one side, women bathed on the other side. The men bathed nude. The women used to put a shirt on, that's all. We didn't have bathing suits like over here," Koch's father said in an interview years later.[8]

Leib's mother, Khatschya, was a devout woman who married a rabbi after Yidl Itzik's death. Her father, Yisroel Edelstein, according to the genealogist Arthur Kurzweil, may have been a bandit—also known as Hersh Pinyas—the orthodox Jewish head of a gang of gentiles who, according to legend, would steal from Polish nobles and give to the poor.[9] Yet if young Leib's grandfather had accumulated wealth, legally or otherwise, none of it trickled down to the Koches in America.

The ethnic division of labor between Ukrainian subsistence farmers and Jewish subsistence middlemen created considerable political and economic friction, especially after the rise of the Ukrainian nationalist movement by the turn of the twentieth century.[10] Despite these tensions, Galicia, ruled from Vienna, was a more tolerant place than the Russian empire. In Russia Jews were restricted to a pale and, along with other ethnic minorities, hounded by the tsar's policy of russification—the assimilation of minorities to Russian culture. While Austria-Hungary had more than its share of anti-Semites in 1900, Ed's mother referred to its ruler as the "good Kaiser Franz Josef," a soubriquet earned when he legally emancipated Jews in 1860, giving them equal legal standing with the empire's other ethnic groups.[11]

The kaiser seemed benevolent, however, only next to the dismal tyranny and anti-Semitism of Russia. Koch's father remembered that "the tax collectors would always come on a Friday if we didn't pay taxes; they'd take the candlesticks or the bedding."[12] Perhaps the invasion of the sabbath was anti-Semitism on the part of ethnic German or Polish tax collectors; it is equally likely that the authorities merely desired to make nonpayment of taxes as unpleasant and embarrassing as possible. Mayor Koch later observed that his parents "hadn't had much to look back on" in Galicia. When Jared Thaler, Ed's nephew, asked his grandfather what he did for amusement, he replied, with a trace of sarcasm, that for fun he would chop wood to warm himself up.[13]

A TALE OF TWO BROTHERS: FROM GALICIA TO THE BRONX

Eastern Europe in the first half of the twentieth century offered many tricks of fate as to who would die and who would prosper. In 1909, when the Koch family patriarch fell ill, he ordered young Leib to New York to trade places with an older brother, Shrul, who paid his passage and returned to Galicia to head the family. A year later Yidl Itsik Koch died. Safe in New York, Leib later heard from a friend that Shrul had been shot and killed by Germans on the streets of Chernowitz when they occupied the city during World War II. After the war Shrul's surviving son, Chaim, and his family emigrated to Israel and contacted Louis. The Koches helped them out with money and periodic care packages of canned goods and clothes.

Ed's sister, Pat, met Chaim and his family on her first trip to Israel in 1953, and the families have kept in touch over the years, especially Chaim's granddaughter, who now lives in America and sees the Koch family occasionally. Ed Koch's fervent devotion to Israel can be explained in part by his own family's closeness to the Holocaust and its aftermath.[14] Koch's father never lived a life of leisure, but after he heard the news of his brother's death, he must have reflected often on how lucky he had been to board the German steamer *Cleveland,* even though he arrived in New York from Hamburg on July 26, 1909, with not a cent in his pocket. He told the Ellis Island authorities he was sixteen, though he may have been only fourteen. Other boys his age from his village traveled on the ship, and one is listed a few places ahead of him on the ship's manifest.[15]

Leib soon transformed into Louis—a self-reliant teenager who, as he told his grandson, soon "learnt a trade by pants"—that is, he became a pants maker—an entry-level occupation in the garment trade. Paid nothing for the first month, and starting at two dollars a week, he initially had to sleep in the factory. The immigration authorities listed him as only five feet six when he arrived, and the Ellis Island doctors described him as suffering from a "lack of physical development."[16] But even though he was soon laboring under sweatshop conditions, Louis managed to thrive in America, growing to six feet tall. In 1919, when he was about twenty-four, he married Yetta Silpe, an ambitious and intelligent woman who was from the Galician town of Kózlow, not far from Usciesko. They moved to the Bronx. The next year he brought over his mother, Khatschya, and his stepfather, a rabbi; they lived in a flat on Broome Street on the Lower East Side. Louis later remembered this period as one of the best of his life.[17]

Young Yetta Koch had emigrated in 1912. She had first worked for her brother, Louis Silpe, who had come eleven years earlier and had sponsored her emigration. Louis Silpe had a reputation among the Koches for meanness. The family story was that he treated Yetta more like a servant than a sister. She soon left her brother and went to school. Yetta trained as a blouse designer, which put her at the "high end" of the garment trade. Like many women at the time, she quit her job upon marriage. She also anglicized her name to Joyce.[18]

Joyce Koch embraced strong middle-class aspirations. She insisted that Louis leave the low-paying pants trade for the fur business, where he might have a chance to elevate the family's social status. She hired an English tutor, studied intensively, read voraciously, and lost even the trace of an accent. She was not a strictly observant Jew, ate nonkosher food, and insisted on speaking only English at home in front of the children.[19]

Ed Koch's family, despite his mother's middle-class impulses, was not a "typical" American nuclear family. The Koches always lived in neighborhoods near relatives.

For a time Joyce's brother Max lived with the Koches in the Crotona Park apartment. Ed and his brother were fond of Uncle Max, then a bootlegger who carried a gun and even made gin in the Koch family bathtub. Upon his marriage he took an apartment in the building next door and remained in the Bronx when the rest of the family departed for Newark. After Prohibition, Max, who was legendary for his generosity, started a coat factory (perhaps with capital accumulated in the illegal liquor trade) and, according to Ed Koch, became the "most successful" of all of the older generation of Koch's family.[20]

Joyce's brothers (and sometimes Joyce herself) were not always convinced that Louis Koch was good enough for her. The couple were very different in outlook and temperament. Louis Koch, less assimilated than his wife, remained more orthodox in religion and kept up his links with the Old World through a *landsleut verein*—an association of people from the same shtetl. He also made twice-weekly visits to the Lower East Side to help bathe his infirm mother. Characteristically, Ed most remembered the trips downtown for the delectable smells of the *grivenes* his grandmother served the boys out of the pot every week. He later compared the treat to Godiva chocolates. "My father made the trek to the Lower East Side each week out of love and filial duty, but I went for the rendered chicken fat," he wrote.[21]

Louis was much less educated than Joyce. His main formal education had been two hours a day as a child at cheder—a religious elementary school. While Louis was literate in Yiddish and Hebrew, Harold was not certain that his father was able to read English very well. Although Louis spoke fluent English (with an intonation familiar to anyone who has ever heard his son Ed talk), he never lost his heavy Yiddish accent.[22] Louis's friends knew him as a good-natured, generous man, extraordinarily devoted to hard work. "Anybody who came to him and wanted anything, he'd give them his last penny—sometimes to my mother's regret," Pat Koch Thaler observed.[23]

Joyce's warm embrace of American modernity and the ethic of upward mobility ultimately clashed with Louis's more limited horizons. All the Koch children remembered the marriage as an unhappy one, and the couple frequently argued bitterly. Ed later observed, "My mother believed Dad never rose to the success she had hoped to have with him." While Ed was always closest to his mother, he believes that "my father, not my mother, was the victim." Although she knew that Louis did not want pork in the house, Joyce would often torture him by cooking bacon and sticking the frying pan under his nose.[24] She often said they stayed together "for the sake of the children," and Ed later speculated that they were so mismatched that if they had been born into a younger generation "they ultimately would have divorced."[25]

Despite Louis's unremitting hard work with his brother Bernard to build Koch Brothers, the fur company he hoped would promote the family's prosperity, their middle-class status remained fragile, which probably exacerbated his conflict with

Joyce. No one in the family ever really understood how the business managed to survive—his father once told Ed, only half in jest, that the business generally lost money but that "we make it up in inventory."[26]

Every morning at five, Louis left for work. First, he would meet with his *khevre*, his cronies, at the Bake Oven for his daily muffin and cream cheese.[27] Louis and Bernard chose to build a nonunion shop, using their own labor and occasionally that of one or two employees. Pat later described visiting her father at the Koch Brothers fur shop, a loft in a building full of furriers in the Garment District south of Times Square. "It was just a room with a big table in it, on which they would hammer and stretch the furs to flatten and cut them, and sew them up into coats." The place was filled with chemical smells, and as they cut, the fur flew. She remembered that her father constantly sliced up his hands, which were often black from fur dye.[28]

Though Louis and Joyce never talked politics much with their kids, Ed and Harold did hear how Ben Gold and the Communist Party–dominated furriers union once busted into his shop, smashed it, and roughed Louis up because the two-man operation was nonunion. "My uncle Max had to come and get him out [of the smashed-up shop], basically because [Max] had a gun," Harold recalled. While this did not make Koch antiunion, it likely contributed to his lifelong anticommunism. As a young lawyer and reform politician, he strenuously opposed the witch-hunting activities of the House Committee on Internal Security, but throughout his career he remained critical of radicals in both the antiwar movement and the Democratic Party.[29]

DOWNWARD MOBILITY: "DON'T FORGET THE HATCHECK BOYS"

Though Louis and Bernie Koch recovered from the union raid, they could not keep their business afloat during the Depression. While the then-diverse New York City economy was not hit as badly as other places, the stock market crash killed the demand for furs and other luxury goods. Though the furriers union saw Louis as a boss, he was a self-employed artisan and quickly became as unemployed as any other worker in the downturn. After Koch Brothers failed, the family could no longer afford the rent in Crotona Park. In 1930 Louis and his family loaded a vegetable truck with furniture and moved with his brother Bernie to Newark, where seven people slept in a four-room apartment. In Newark the Koches shared the $45 monthly rent at 90 Spruce Street with Ed's uncle Bernie, aunt Mollie, and their daughter Estelle, who slept in one bedroom, with Louis and Joyce in the other. The boys, Harold and Ed, shared a foldout bed in the living room. Although Newark was a step down from Crotona Park, 90 Spruce is still today a respectable five-story townhouse, and Ed, then seven years old, feels that he was well shielded by his parents. He does not remember the move from Crotona as the trauma it was for his eleven-year-old brother Harold, who still recalled as an old man that the Koches pretended they were going to Coney Island in order to avoid losing face in the Bronx, because "everyone was so proud," he said.[30]

The Koches had to swallow their pride when they went as supplicants to Joyce's brother Louis Silpe—the same brother who had tried to make her his unpaid servant upon her arrival in America. He was the richest of their relatives and, as Harold put it, "close to being a bastard, but very smart." Louis, "a big gruff man," owned a Newark catering hall called Kruger's Auditorium, where his wife, Mary, presided over the kosher kitchen. The hall was well known and sometimes featured famous bands like Tommy Dorsey's. But Ed never remembered hearing music there, likely because he was too busy working.[31] Louis Silpe delegated the hatcheck concession to his sister's family: He did not lose a penny in the deal. Louis Koch, Joyce, and Harold would work the hatcheck counter with no salary, just tips, while Silpe pocketed the twenty-five-cent hatcheck fee. To make any money, the Koches almost had to beg. Once Ed turned ten, he too was put to work. "We often had to stand at the window box and say, 'Don't forget the hatcheck boys. We only work on tips.' And people were essentially decent, but if they'd already paid twenty-five cents, some of them wouldn't pay more, and if they did, it was generally only a dime." On Sunday mornings the family would sit around the dinner table and roll up all the week's dimes. If the labor of the whole family amounted to fifty dollars, "we would consider it pretty good," Ed recalled.[32] "We all hated him," Harold later said of his uncle Silpe. "I was just angry about everything there." According to his sister, family lore had it that Harold sometimes got his revenge by taking money out of the pockets of customers' overcoats before putting them away.[33]

Koch's father hustled to feed his family, often working the hatcheck until 2:30 A.M. and then, after two hours of sleep, schlepping in to New York to pick up whatever casual jobs he could get in the fur trade. Through it all the Koches refused to consider themselves poor. "We were working and we were eating," Harold later recalled.[34]

In 1931 Ed's sister, Pat, was born, and the family moved out of the apartment they shared with Bernie's family and into its own apartment in the same building. By 1932 their finances improved a bit, and and the Koches moved again, to 61 Milford Avenue in Newark, and soon to an even larger apartment next door. The worst of the family's fiscal crisis was over. Ed characterized the move as "several steps up" from Spruce Street: Ed and Harold now had their own bedroom with twin beds, and Pat and their parents had their own rooms.[35]

Seventy years later Koch and I traveled to Newark to see his boyhood homes. "This is Milford right here," he announced confidently as we turned onto Milford Avenue and passed his old high school. To Ed's surprise his old neighborhood on Spruce Street, which had seemed so far from Milford in terms of social distance, was less than ten blocks away.[36]

As we turned the corner onto Milford Avenue, we came upon a beautiful but decrepit Victorian house with large verandas. It was boarded up and for sale. "That was Dr. Lowenstein's house, that was the biggest house here," Koch explained. One Sunday twelve-year-old Eddie was chasing a friend during a game of tag. The friend ran out through the plate glass front door of the Koches' apartment house. The door closed behind him, and Ed could not stop in time and his hand went through the window. Blood everywhere, he ran down the block to that old Victorian, where, thankfully, the doctor was in. Lowenstein, coming in from his golf game (a rarity for eastern European Jews in the 1930s) determined that Ed had sliced through every tendon in his hand and took him immediately to the hospital for reattachment, after calling his parents at Krueger's for permission to operate. As a result of the doctor's quick action, Ed retained 80 percent of the functioning of his left hand, which remained somewhat smaller than his right hand. He was grateful to Lowenstein, because the injury, which, without surgery might have left him crippled for life, "never prevented me from doing anything."[37]

Ed's brother Harold, a precocious child four years older, was also angrier, more cynical, and rebellious. He went so far as to strike his avaricious uncle Louis, jeopardizing the whole family's livelihood. Luckily, Uncle Louis accepted Harold's apology. In contrast, Ed was far more fastidious and well behaved, a "white shoe kid," according to his brother, meaning that "if his mother sent him out in the morning in white shoes, the shoes would still be white when he returned at night." Harold was also more athletic. He often had to insist that his younger brother be included on teams, and sometimes Harold had to defend Ed with his fists. But Harold also resented being stuck with babysitting his kid brother and later recalled that he would "kick the shit out of [Ed] when my mother wasn't around." As an adult, Harold "liked women, and women liked Harold," as Ed put it in his eulogy for his brother. Ed had very different interests. He found sports a bore and in high school preferred the debate team. The accident with his hand may have made him more cautious, though his later career in the army would show that he did not lack physical ability.[38]

Ed's sister, Pat (she changed her name from Paulina when she was twelve), was eight years younger than Ed and twelve years younger than Harold. "My mother was very clear about it—I was not a planned pregnancy," Pat said. "And she was not very happy—until I was born; then she was happy because I was a girl, after two boys."[39] Though having another nonworking mouth to feed must have been a strain on the Koches' already-strained finances, both Harold and Ed took to their kid sister more than they took to each other. And the family had recovered sufficiently by 1937 to enjoy some luxuries. Ed, who was particularly close to Pat, remembered jumping into the lake at Kutscher's Country Club, a resort in the Catskills, to save the five-year-old girl who had strayed in over her head. Ed's high school, South Side High, was a tough working-class high school in a building that dominated the neighborhood. His class was about 75 percent Jewish and 25 percent black, and while some public accommodations and most neighborhoods in Newark were segregated, the high school was not. Miller Elementary School, which both Ed and Pat attended, was mostly black by the time Pat left in 1940. Yet social life was split enough that Ed remembers little contact with black students or even that his class voted a black man, Zhonta Stapleton, as "most likely to succeed."[40]

In school Koch was already "very involved politically" as an antifascist, supporting the Republicans in Spain and Haile Selassie and his followers against Mussolini's invasion of Ethiopia. More recently he has said he "was never ever radical, but I was always democratic left, and there's a big difference. I'm not going to tell you I sat down and made a careful analysis of what it means to be radical far left, and what it means not to be. But I concluded in my head, it's not where I want to be." That was not a surprising attitude for someone in his class position, scion of a hardworking liberal Jewish family grasping at the lower rung of the middle class, headed by a small boss outside the self-assured solidarity of the communist-led furriers' union.[41]

While he favored the New Deal and intervention in World War II, young Ed opposed socialist revolution; he believed in the continued vitality of capitalism. Indeed, his father's hard work seemed to be rewarded when wartime prosperity allowed him to reopen his business and bring the family to back to New York City in 1941, when Ed was sixteen. The family fortunes had improved to the point that the Koches could afford the $65 monthly rent for a pleasant and more spacious apartment on tree-lined Ocean Parkway near Church Avenue in Brooklyn. Uncle Bernie and his family were living in the building next door at 330 Ocean Parkway; Louis and Joyce moved to 320 and soon knew everybody in the building. The Koches had reached the middle class at last. They even had a family den and a living room with a blue mohair couch "for Mama's mah-jongg friends" and enough left over to sell their old furniture and buy an entirely new set, Koch recalled.[42]

The quality of life in Brooklyn was significantly better than in Newark. Ocean Parkway is a wide thoroughfare in the heart of Brooklyn; it leads from Frederick Law Olmstead's Prospect Park to Coney Island. Bounded on each side by a sidewalk and a strip of grass, with benches for visiting, and a bridle path, Ocean Parkway is (and was) one of the centers of Jewish communal life. If he liked, Ed could rent a horse and go riding on the parkway's bridle paths, and in the sultry New York summer, the family had an easy bus ride to the beach at Coney Island.[43]

As a Brooklyn resident, Ed was eligible to attend the tuition-free City College of New York, where, in September 1941, he matriculated as a freshman at age sixteen. Between the hour-and-a half subway ride every day up to the 135th Street campus and preparing for a heavy course load, Ed stuck close to home and did not become friendly with the neighbors like his mother and sister did. Soon the world war would pull him even farther away.

Koch's military career began when he was drafted in March 1943. Eager to fight Hitler, he did not reveal the injury to his hand, as his mother urged him to do. The military was his first step outside the cocoon of the almost all-Jewish world he had grown up in. The dissonance between Jewish New York and the backgrounds of the other soldiers in his unit was palpable, but Koch faced up to it better than many others. After reporting for induction, the army sent Koch to Spartanburg, South Carolina, for seventeen weeks of basic training. Americans were far less mobile in those days, and regional differences, in an era with limited national media, were far more pronounced. Anti-Semitism was raw and shocking. Jews often faced restrictive covenants that prevented them from buying property in some neighborhoods. They also were excluded from some hotels, because Jews were not really considered "white"—especially in the South. However, the army, New Deal housing, and welfare programs did not discriminate against them to the extent that they did African Americans. Koch's first platoon was about one-quarter Jewish. Most other recruits were from the South. Koch and his best friend, Jacques Lennon, a Jewish American whose family had emigrated from Luxembourg, found themselves in a borderline position.

As the only Jews who could negotiate the obstacle course at the beginning of training, Koch and Lennon were exempted from the torrents of anti-Semitic jokes and invective directed against other Jewish recruits. Non-Jews even felt free to joke about Jews in their presence. Angered, Koch vowed to build up his body, intending to defend the honor of the Jewish people. After fifteen weeks he was ready and soon found himself in the boxing ring against a big guy named LaRue, who was the best athlete in the unit. Koch later recalled: "There must have been about a hundred guys in a big circle, waiting for me and LaRue to fight. People were running around and shouting, 'They're gonna kill the Jews! Come and watch! They're gonna kill the Jews!'" LaRue knocked Koch down several times and was declared the winner. Nonetheless, Koch remembered feeling liberated for fighting, even though he lost. In a sense he had won. For the remaining two weeks of basic training no one in the battalion made any anti-Semitic comments within his hearing. Ed Koch's brief career as a pugilist is a key to understanding his character. He views anti-Semitism as a call to Jews to do battle, and he uses tropes of war when addressing the issue. Fifty years later Koch would publish a volume subtitled *My Fight against Anti-Semitism,* which opened with the declaration that "the need to confront and combat anti-Semitism is one of the greatest moral challenges facing the civilized world today."[44]

After Spartanburg, Private Koch successfully applied for the Army Specialized Training Program, which took soldiers with some college training and offered them additional studies in academic specialties useful to the army. Despite a year in high school and a year in college, in addition to his Yiddish background, he had a year of high school German plus two more semesters at City College, but could not speak proper German. While attending an academic orientation at Rollins College in Florida as part of his army training, he convinced a professor to send him on for more study, despite his deficient language skills. To his delight, the army dispatched him to Fordham University in the Bronx. The dons at Fordham diverted him to the engineering program because of his inability to speak German. For almost a year of the war he studied engineering and on the weekends took the subway home to Brooklyn.

After a year the special studies program was closed. Koch and the other participants went straight from their cushy university billets to combat infantry. He spent the summer of 1944 in an infantry refresher course in Camp Carson, Colorado, to train as a replacement for the 104th "Timberwolf" Division. Soon he found himself a member of the First Platoon of Company F, Second Battalion, 415th Infantry Regiment of that division. This company mixed together a group of special studies soldiers from colleges all over the country and a group of self-described "hillbillies" and "ridge runners," who seemed impossibly big, tan, and muscular after their return from maneuvers in the Southern California desert. The college guys exercised as much as possible to catch up. During these years Ed went from being a pale and thin city boy to being well built and handsome, with a shock of dark wavy hair.[45]

The groups, which were more professional after months in the army than the raw recruits in basic training, came to largely cooperate and respect each other, regardless of regional or ethnic differences, though Ed tended to hang out with his fellow college students, like Al Milwid, the son of a butcher from Bayonne, New Jersey. An infantryman in the outfit, Mike Berrigan, passed the time with Koch discussing the differences between Judaism and Catholicism. This proved an important introduction for Koch, who would, from the beginning of his political career, depend on building Catholic-Jewish coalitions and on a common identity as "white ethnics."[46]

Koch, Milwid, Berrigan, and the rest of Company F embarked for Europe on a former passenger liner, the *Cristobal,* from a pier in south Brooklyn (not two miles from the Koch family abode) on August 27, 1944, disembarking in peaceful Cherbourg on September 7, 1944. By this time France had been liberated. Allied armies on both fronts were advancing steadily toward Germany. Pfc. Edward J. Apple of the division later wrote:

> We many not have entered Normandy while bayonets were drawn;
> It was only D plus 90 and the Jerry foe had gone.
> Our only present danger lay within the hedge and field
> 'Twas Nazi booby traps and mines—ingeniously concealed.[47]

George Greenburg, a sergeant in Koch's regiment, recalled: "We saw no Paris beauties or glamour here." Instead, Koch and his buddies bedded down in tents in the apple orchards, surrounded by Normandy's infamous high green hedgerows. As the fall cold set in, the soldiers learned that "Calvados, the French firewater, would keep you warm all night. It worked pretty well in your cigarette lighter too," the division historians recalled.[48] After a few weeks of guarding supply trains between Normandy and Versailles, the Timberwolves were declared combat ready and joined the Allied drive through the Low Countries and into Germany.[49]

Ed became known for his foraging abilities after he made friends with a local family and traded a few supplies for cider and stories about the German occupation. On his back he often carried extra food and equipment that might be useful in the field. For Koch, the unit's "designated scrounger," many of his later memories of the war were food related—eating his first fresh-slaughtered pig; negotiating with local families for chicken and Calvados—anything to supplement the dreary C and K rations proffered by the army.[50] If the secure and decisive Ed Koch was ever haunted by anything, it may have been the story of the devout Walter Bolechowski, a soldier from Philadelphia. Ed had discovered the abandoned stores of a Dutch family, but Bolechowski feared that he'd be punished by God if he shared in the feast. Koch and the others persuaded him to eat, but Bolechowski lamented having done so. Later that night a mortar struck and killed him in his foxhole. The others in the squad, who were lucky to survive, "all felt responsible for his death."[51]

By the end of October, Company F had fought in the drive to clear the Scheldt estuary of Germans in order to open up the port of Antwerp and increase the flow of supplies to troops driving west. Soon after, Company F came under heavy fire while advancing toward the Siegfried Line at Aachen, and Koch saw many of his comrades wounded or killed by enemy fire. Koch vividly recalls one who was struck by an artillery fragment, another who stepped on a mine. After Mike Berrigan stepped on a shoe mine, Ed, who had been standing about twenty feet away, walked right into the minefield to hold his friend's hand, comfort him, and to call for the medics, who took Berrigan to a field hospital. Berrigan later claimed that Koch had saved his life, though Koch modestly denies it. As his unit entered Aachen in November 1944, Koch, laden with heavy gear, fell down the cellar stairs of a building he was searching and was sent to the hospital in with an injured knee and sprained foot. The injuries might well have saved his life, as he missed the heavy fighting of early December 1944, during the Battle of the Bulge, when the Timberwolves, according to their official history, experienced the "heaviest artillery concentration ever experienced by American troops."[52]

After the war in Europe ended, the army needed soldiers who spoke German. The shortage was so great that no one questioned Koch's language ability when Ed, now a sergeant, volunteered for the European Civil Affairs Division (ECAD). He became the interpreter for a detachment of ten or twelve soldiers. Their assignment was to help "de-nazify" a small town in Bavaria—by removing the local officials and replacing them with officials who were less notoriously pro-Nazi. He quickly learned passable German on the job—fortunately, the local Bavarian dialect was more compatible with Yiddish than were dialects in other parts of Germany. Occupied Germany gave Ed Koch his first real experience in politics and compromise. Most of the candidates to run the village had some Nazi activities in their past. The best the Americans could do was to try to choose people whom they believed were unlikely to act like Nazis in the future.[53]

After a few months in civil administration, Sergeant Koch returned stateside with two battle stars, a combat infantry badge, an honorable discharge, and a Bavarian dog named Boxer that the army had somehow allowed him to ship across the Atlantic.[54] He moved back home to Ocean Parkway—he did not even think of living anywhere else, as sons in Jewish families would customarily stay at home until they were married.[55]

After three years in the army, Ed, like many other returning veterans, was eager to get on with his future, and he had the GI Bill of Rights to help pay for it. The army had helped Koch assimilate into an America beyond the confines of Jewish New York, giving him a new physical confidence and even some political experience. The GI bill made him part of a new generation of young professionals, children of a generation of European immigrants. In New York the amalgamation of Jewish and Catholic ethnics into the American mainstream anticipated the coalition that would become Mayor Koch's base of support.

Though he only had three and a half semesters of college, Koch hoped to go directly into law school—the GI bill would pay his tuition at New York University, and waivers of college degrees were common. Like many American vets, Koch wanted a professional degree that would enable him to earn a living, and he wanted it as soon as possible. The first NYU law professor Koch approached told him to go back and finish his undergraduate degree at City College of New York (CCNY). Another professor, Paul Kauffman, a CCNY alumnus, came by and joined the conversation. Kauffman asked the young veteran where he had gone to school and what his average had been. Koch replied that he had had a B average at CCNY. Kauffman told the other professor that "a B average at CCNY was like an A anywhere else" and persuaded him to admit Koch without a bachelor's degree.

A SOAPBOX AND A SHINGLE: BECOMING A VILLAGER

After a brief stint as a busboy at the Adler Hotel in the Catskills, Koch entered NYU's law program. He began to hang out in Greenwich Village, staying late to play in a weekly poker game with his classmates. The Village was becoming a college town because of the postwar expansion of New York University, which, like Ed Koch's legal education, was financed by the GI bill.[56] Federal money, the growth of the city, and the increasing fortunes of NYU alumni after 1945 would later turn the university from a provincial school into a multibillion-dollar institution. The law school was a vehicle of upward mobility for first- and second-generation children of immigrants like Ed; it had yet to transform itself into a hard-driving competitor of Columbia and Harvard.

By attending summers, Koch was able to finish law school in two years. Now twenty-four years old, he had reached the threshold of a long and difficult transition into Manhattan's professional classes.[57] Koch graduated in the middle of his class, which was, in itself, an achievement: he lacked the final two years of undergraduate school, when so many students polish their skills, and he was the first member of his family to study beyond high school. Young Ed was an outsider to the professional world and faced daunting obstacles. After he passed the New York State Bar exam on his second try in the spring of 1949, he found that applying to the character committee was a humbling experience. Most young applicants knew other lawyers who could serve as their references, but Ed was such an outsider to what was then a much smaller, tight-knit legal profession that he "had to really dig to find somebody who knew somebody on the committee" to vouch for his character.[58]

Once admitted to the bar, young lawyers like Koch found it was not easy to get jobs. Without any contacts in the political or legal world, he had to make cold calls. Again, the City College network helped him most. One benevolent CCNY alumnus referred him to a lawyer named Joe Finkelstein at 38 Park Row, a building across from city hall. Finkelstein was Ed Koch's first mentor. He paid Ed fifteen dollars per week plus office space, which was not even enough to enable him to have regular lunches out with his friends. Koch proved himself a hard worker and parlayed his job with Finkelstein into a sixty-dollar-a-week job at the law firm of Regosin and Edwards.

In postwar New York, sixty dollars was barely a living wage if you had a family, but it was more than enough for a young man who was still living with his parents on Ocean Parkway. The young lawyer was able to buy an old green Plymouth, which the whole family considered a milestone, especially Pat, whom he soon taught to drive.[59] Koch spent two years at Regosin and Edwards but found the research-oriented job too quiet and sedentary. Ed Koch loved to talk. He wanted to talk for a living. He wanted to orate, to wow his listeners, to win. In 1952 he decided to start his own practice.

Koch later shrugged off as low risk his decision to go it alone—he had no dependents, and the GI bill paid him $100 per month for a year to start a business. The kindly Finkelstein helped him once again by giving him some free space at the Park Row offices—though as soon as Ed could afford it he moved to spartan offices at 52 Wall Street. He remained there until he gave up practicing law when he was elected to Congress in 1968.

Working as a lawyer involves more than hanging out a sign. And being a solo practitioner means scrounging enough work every month to live on, pay office rent, and meet expenses. Koch had no mentor on a day-to-day basis to teach him the techniques of trial, and he had to do all his typing, telephoning, and scheduling himself. "I really didn't like it," he recalled.[60] Koch took whatever work he could get—for his first trial his client was his father, Louis, who had sued one Milton Wiener, who had promised to get Koch's brother, Harold, a Teamsters union card in exchange for $500. Wiener disappeared with Louis Koch's money and about $10,000 hard earned by people on Milford Avenue who had desperately wanted to get themselves or their children a secure job at the tail end of the Depression. A decade later Harold spotted Wiener on a Manhattan street corner and had him arrested. Ed did his family proud and won the case. In a turn of events that would have made a good episode of Koch's 1990s TV show, *People's Court,* Ed used the old judgment to garnish Wiener's wages for ten dollars a week to pay the judgment.

As an ambitious young attorney Koch, a man of tremendous energy like his father, never needed much sleep. He'd start work in his office at 6 or 7 A.M. and quit a little after 5, then go for a full night of meetings, social activities, or political work.[61] At one point he even tried his hand at being an inventor. Ed Koch's first and only invention, officially called the "Simulated Vehicle Toy," received U.S. Patent No. 3,009,443, granted July 30, 1963. The Boxmobile was a set of decals that could be put on any box to make it look like a toy automobile, at least to a child. "While the parent may not receive the direct satisfaction of achievement since assembly is so simple, there will be considerable satisfaction resulting from the child's statement to the effect 'see what Daddy built for me.'" Ed printed up a few boxes of the decals, and his father tried to help market them, but they never sold much. Soon Koch was back to hustling for clients.[62]

His social world continued to revolve around Brooklyn and the Young People's League (YPL) of his family synagogue, the Flatbush Jewish Center, which he joined with his sister, Pat, a politically active student at Brooklyn College until 1953. YPL was a Jewish cultural group, the predecessor of United Synagogue Youth, organized in 1951. Although Koch today attends the Orthodox Park East Synagogue, he is "not Orthodox," and his early experience with Conservative Judaism was important in defining his Jewish identity. Conservative Judaism might be defined by its core belief in the continuity of Jewish law and tradition balanced with modernity, for example permitting men and women to sit together in the synagogue, while encouraging the use of Hebrew as the language of prayer and the observance of dietary laws. The Conservative movement emphasizes social justice, and an ecumenical sense of Jewish community that includes all Jews, be they Orthodox, Hasidic, Reform, or even secular. Conservatives allow local rabbis discretion in many matters and reinterpretations of tradition.[63]

Koch threw himself into his evening activities, partly as a way to build contacts for his law business. He soon became president of YPL, the synagogue group, which "became a very successful operation raising money for the synagogue," though it never produced much business for his firm. Eventually, Koch worked on the YPL's national governing body. The core of five or six young people planned retreats, parties, and amateur theatricals. The YPL's activities were cultural and political as well as social. Pat and Ed went for weekends to Camp Ramah, the Conservative movement's summer camp, for "Zionist experiences—a lot of Hebrew song singing and Israeli dancing," Pat recalled. In the months leading up to Israel's independence in 1948, she remembers a drive to collect "army discards" like "bayonets, helmets, daggers, and other useful equipment" that the organization forwarded to Israel. Koch became acquainted with Israeli culture through the YPL, which cemented his identification with Judaism and the Jewish state, both of which would become central to his political career.[64]

The young lawyer also began to get more involved in politics, though today he does not remember which organizations he actually joined. He attended meetings of the American Veterans Committee, the liberal veterans organization that later became controlled by Communists. According to Koch, he abandoned the organization as the Communists took it over. At one point Koch considered joining the National Lawyers Guild, attracted by its campaign to compel the all-white American Bar Association to accept African American members, but says he shied away because of false rumors that the NLG, which did not exclude Communists, was "a communist front."[65]

Koch yearned to draw crowds and engage them. In a political culture not yet monopolized by television, all he needed was a soapbox and a busy corner. He set himself up on a soapbox as a lunchtime street speaker for Adlai Stevenson in 1952. Against the background of an American flag, then required by state election law for political speakers, he charged deep into Republican country, near the steps of Federal Hall at Broad and Wall, a few steps from the New York Stock Exchange.[66] One afternoon a burly Irish cop walked up to Koch and demanded that he stop speaking, even though the election laws allowed him to talk to a crowd without a permit. Koch, who did not want to lose his crowd, tried to debate with the cop. Ed pointed out that the police never interfered with the evangelist who always addressed crowds across the street. "He's different," the cop replied. "He's a fanatic."[67] Koch always told this story in later years to emphasize that he was *not,* and never had been, a radical, which he equated with fanaticism. Before the civil rights revolution of the 1960s, cities invested enormous discretion in individual police officers to regulate public space. Even in liberal and relatively tolerant New York, a single police officer could stop a speaker from campaigning for a major presidential candidate.

As much as Koch enjoyed his soapbox, politics was not yet his obsession. But in 1953 he exercised his speaking talents on behalf of City Council President Rudolph Halley, the Liberal candidate for mayor and a former prosecutor famous for his crackdown on the mob. Koch's rhetoric was even less subtle in his early days. He told listeners at a Jewish Community Center not far from his Brooklyn home that Robert

F. Wagner (soon to be elected mayor) was "a tool of the Democratic leaders and racketeers."[68] Wagner was the candidate of the Tammany leader Carmine De Sapio but was certainly not mobbed up, and Wagner's son Robert would become one of Koch's closest friends and aides. Former mayor Wagner would even head one of Koch's congressional campaign committees. Koch's remarks at the start of his legal and political career demonstrate both the shrill certainty of his inexperience and his distance from the centers of power.

3 IT TAKES A VILLAGE (1949–58)

In 1952 Koch never thought that he would become a national political figure. For one thing, few lived at home with their parents. Koch would not move out from under the constant bickering of his parents until he was thirty-two years old. In the summer of 1956 Pat Koch, who had become an administrator at the Jewish Theological Seminary in New York City, heard that a coworker's friends were renting a house together at Fair Harbor on Fire Island. Ed, who did not know anyone in the group, joined Pat's friends and had a such a great time on the sandbar, far from the strictures of his parents' home, that he decided to move out. His father threatened to never speak to him again if he left before Pat was married later in the year (for reasons unclear even to Ed). Pat says it was considered a *shande* (a disgrace) for an unmarried son to live apart from his parents. His parents had pressured him to marry, but, as Koch put it, "it just never happened." It was time to leave for a freer environment.[1]

Greenwich Village was the Manhattan residential neighborhood that Koch knew best from his law school years at NYU, and in the fall of 1956 he rented an apartment at 81 Bedford Street with a roommate, Bill Sommer, one of his Fair Harbor housemates. Bedford Street was a comfortable billet for a young lawyer. Even in the 1920s his neighborhood was one of the most rapidly gentrifying areas of the Village.[2] Despite threats of a cutoff, he and his father continued to talk. Ed's practice was by then generating a modest income, so he could afford half the $145 monthly rent; he took over the whole apartment after Sommer got married and moved out a few months later.[3]

Koch's move to the Village coincided with the 1956 presidential election. Almost as soon as he arrived at Bedford Street, he again took to the soapboxes for Stevenson, this time working with the Stevenson organization in the Village. It sprung up outside the regular Democratic organization and would evolve into the reform-minded Village Independent Democrats. On Sheridan Square, in Washington Square Park, in the twisting streets to the West, and in the apartment towers of Fifth Avenue, where he would eventually retire, Ed Koch had found his own neighborhood, his political and even spiritual home, Greenwich Village. Koch relished the spontaneity of the Village scene, where "you could always go to hangouts like the Limelight, which offered a three-course meal for $2.50, and run into friends." Koch's Village life revolved around friends, movies, politics, and his law practice.[4]

The difficult task of building a law practice occupied much of his time, although he was not much of a rainmaker. He liked to have people around him, and tried early on to find a law partner, but for years he did not have enough clients to make splitting the practice profitable. Politics, he thought, might drum up more business. It was also more fun than the daily humdrum of law practice—and holding elective office promised a potential alternative career. In both realms he faced a similar barrier. The upper reaches of both reform politics and law were dominated by graduates of elite, mostly Ivy League, institutions. They not only formed a powerful network, but many judged people based on their polish and pedigree. It was not strictly a matter of ethnicity—by the 1950s a number of Jewish firms and lawyers were located on Wall Street, once a WASP haven. A Brooklyn Jewish kid with just three semesters at City College and who finished in the middle of his class at NYU Law (as it was then) simply lacked the connections that came from an education at Harvard. Koch's catch-as-catch-can law practice of wills, divorces, and slip-and-falls put him outside the pale of "serious" New York lawyers. John Lankenau, a former partner from the corporate legal world, recalled that Koch had "a kind of a small town small city practice of a sort that is common upstate," quite unlike the practices of Wall Street types who toiled in the loftier realms of securities regulations and corporate contracts.[5] In the vocabulary of reformers of the time, Koch faced the daunting challenge of demonstrating he was "a man of stature." He also had to earn his keep in a solo law practice without working so hard that he had no time for politics.[6] The great question of Koch's life between 1956 and 1963 was whether he could overcome his own invisibility in the eyes of those he needed to impress. In a very real sense it took a village to make Koch into a contender.

Greenwich Village is famous as a place where visitors always get lost. The twisted streets are named, not numbered, for the residents had gotten the city to exempt their quarter from the 1811 grid that defined Manhattan's street pattern north of Canal. For years the isolation of the so-called American ward (no Catholics or Jews welcome) made the Village the sort of Yankee island that Henry James described in his novel *Washington Square* (1881). By the 1890s, however, the mostly Italian and Irish immigrants who worked in factories and docks at the western and southern ends of the neighborhood had moved in. Some, but not all, of the "Americans" fled north, their once-grand houses sometimes subdivided into rooming houses or replaced by crowded tenements. The Italian immigrants also pushed out the significant African American population that had inhabited the area near the docks since colonial times. Plunging real estate values and rents in the early twentieth century attracted artists, radicals, and bohemians, who made the neighborhood famous for unconventionality and the avant-garde by 1912. Caroline Ware, writing in the twenties, was the first to name the new breed "Villagers."[7] By the 1950s when Ed moved in, residents had become more ethnically diverse. Blue-collar Italians and Jews lived life cheek by jowl with artists, mystics, and intellectuals, and the neighborhood attracted the Beats, the last wave of talented bohemia in the West Village. After the publication of *On the Road* in 1957, Jack Kerouac returned to the Village as a literary lion, joining Allen Ginsberg, Gregory Corso, and many other important Beats who helped make the Village a center of the avant-garde. This heady cultural mix would not last long. Village rents were spiraling beyond the means of most real bohemians. In the 1960s and 1970s the counterculture pushed out to the margins of former slum neighborhoods once called the Lower East Side and the South Village; real estate agents soon reinvented these areas as the "East Village" and "SoHo," short for "South of Houston Street."

Ed Koch was never a bohemian, which made him a more typical "Villager" than Corso or Kerouac. Ed remembered spending his days wearing Brooks Brothers suits, though a reporter later described him as "sitting in his cluttered law office, clad in shirtsleeves and cord trousers."[8] He never developed his childhood interest in writing poetry, but he was influenced by the Village counterculture. In the late fifties he took guitar lessons and became an amateur folksinger. A picture taken by his brother-in-law, Al Thaler, shortly after Ed moved to the Village, shows a thin young man with close-cropped hair strumming his guitar as sensitively as any participant at a hootenanny.[9] He later moderated the "Hall of Issues," a controversial series on sex, art, and politics sponsored by a group of pop and avant-garde artists at Judson Memorial Church.[10]

The Village in the 1950s was one of the few places in the country where homosexual practices might be debated instead of treated with knee-jerk disgust. Like the streets of the Village, many inhabitants were neither square nor straight. The Village was a magnet for gay people from all over the country. No place was truly safe, however. Before the Stonewall uprising of 1969, the police could harass gay people at will, through bar raids, entrapment, and disorderly conduct arrests, just as they could arbitrarily order political speakers to move on. While the phrase "gay culture," already in use by the 1950s, did not derive its name from the Village's Gay Street, many Villagers believed that it did. Although the rise of the gay liberation movement is often traced to Stonewall, the idea of gay liberation began much earlier. Seymour Krim, editor of the noted anthology *The Beats* (1960), published a pioneering essay in 1959 declaring that homosexuals "have been the great unrecognized minority . . . . We want recognition for our simple human rights, just like Negroes, Jews and women."[11]

"EGGHEADS OF THE WORLD, UNITE!"

Unlike gays and women, African Americans were a tiny minority in the Village, and their quest did not loom large in most residents' minds. On a national level too, civil rights was not at the forefront of most white liberal agendas in the 1950s. Many signaled as much by fervently supporting Adlai Stevenson for president in 1952, 1956, and 1960. Stevenson was no champion of civil rights: in 1954, after the Supreme Court ruled in *Brown v. Board of Education*, he said he favored slow and gradual desegregation in deference to "tradition"—a bid to preserve his support among southerners.

After he moved to the Village in 1956, Koch had become an avid Stevenson supporter. Stevenson volunteers adored their candidate and deplored the perfunctory presidential campaign of the regular Democratic clubs, such as Carmine De Sapio's Tamawa club in the Village. De Sapio correctly perceived Stevenson as a lost cause. Stevenson volunteers, many of them young professionals with elite educations, perceived the regulars' disinterest in their hero as a sign of moral degradation.

So what might have inspired an idealistic Villager like Ed Koch to an almost evangelical fervor for a balding midwestern governor whom Koch today assesses as "ineffective and incompetent"?[12] In a word, *wit*. Stevenson had a quality that they recognized (or desired) in themselves. The other candidates were far from scintillating. Averell Harriman, the other leading Democratic candidate in New York, was known as a rather dull diplomat and businessman. . The Republicans had Eisenhower, a man who deliberately assumed an underwhelming style in public while deftly manipulating behind the scenes—a winning strategy that resulted in the so-called hidden hand presidency.[13] Stevenson, on the other hand, reminded his idealistic young supporters of the gracious and eloquent Franklin Delano Roosevelt, an association strengthened by the support of Eleanor Roosevelt, who was among Stevenson's greatest boosters. Stevenson actually took time off from campaigning to write his own speeches and could respond to the devastating charge that he was an egghead by declaring, "Eggheads of the world, unite! You have nothing to lose but your yolks!"[14] At that time pre-Vietnam liberals applauded his lofty rhetoric of universalism, an emancipatory vision that justified cold war imperialism around the world. The challenge facing the United States, he declared, was "to encourage, aid and inspire the aspirations of half of mankind for a better life, to guide these aspirations into paths that lead to freedom"—in other words, to remake the world in America's image. [15]

Koch still praises Stevenson as "an intellectual, a man whose speeches were of a high order," though he now believes that given the softness of Stevenson's support for Israel and civil rights, he "would have been a terrible president."[16] Koch's view is not shared by all former Stevenson volunteers who went on to become active in reform politics in the Village. Activist Miki Wolter remembered the Illinois governor as "an idealist" who would have promoted freedom of speech and opposed McCarthyism as president. To Ed Gold, Stevenson, though supported by the Chicago boss Jacob Arvey, was "the anti-boss politician," an "alternative to the one-man rule" of party officials like Carmine De Sapio. "We were much more focused on everybody having a right to participate in decision making," Gold recalled.[17]

After Stevenson's defeat, Citizens for Stevenson met in December 1956 and debated whether to form an insurgent political club, the Village Independent Democrats (VID) to challenge Carmine De Sapio for district leader and democratize the procedures of the Democratic Party. This was no easy task, and the stakes were high. De Sapio was one of the most powerful party leaders in recent New York City history.

The reformers of the 1950s, many of them veterans of Adlai Stevenson's 1956 presidential campaign, built their organization in reaction to a regular club that was literally patriarchal and based largely on seniority, blocking both women and a generation of young World War II veterans from power. Two of the reformers' main goals were "to encourage the participation of all people in the affairs of the Democratic Party" and to eliminate political patronage, which they defined as the use of "services, favors, or contributions to a political party" as a factor in appointment to public office.[18]

The insurgents waged a fierce war against the regulars, which amounted to an internecine battle between liberals. Koch and his friends tried to dismiss De Sapio as hopelessly conservative, but the truth was that he often supported candidates who were to the left of the VID. His candidate for president, New York governor Averell Harriman, was significantly more liberal than Adlai Stevenson, particularly on civil rights. The reformers charged after the election that the De Sapio machine had devoted more effort to electing cronies to judgeships than to the great crusade for Stevenson in the general election. While De Sapio did not divulge why he failed to go all-out for Stevenson, his reasons were unlikely to have been rooted in conservative ideology. Most likely, the regulars discerned the hopelessness of the Stevenson cause (he lost by a landslide) and decided to push for local candidates whom they could elect. VID members had their own theories. Most intriguing is the one advanced by Gold, but not substantiated by any contemporary evidence, that some South Village Italians disliked Stevenson's running mate, Senator Estes Kefauver of Tennessee, perceiving his televised hearings on racketeering as a "direct attack against Italians."[19] None of these seemed like valid reasons to the Stevenson volunteers, who called a meeting (which Ed Koch attended) to convert the old campaign organization into an insurgent political club.

Koch was far from the center of the charismatic leadership of that group. He felt that if he joined the new Village Independent Democrats he would be in the unenviable position of being "an insurgent within an insurgent club" and, what's more, a club then dominated by Richard Kuh, a magna cum laude graduate of Harvard Law and principal deputy to Manhattan District Attorney Frank Hogan. Kuh would become notorious seven years later for his prosecution of the comedian Lenny Bruce. The puritanical Kuh did not see nonelite lawyers like Koch as the stuff candidates were made of. Koch recalls that "Everything I seemed to want to do . . . always placed me in conflict with Dick Kuh, and so I decided to leave" the VID before it got off the ground.[20]

Koch left politics for almost a year. Then, late in 1957, some young lawyers recruited him for the Tamawa club, one of the many New York County political clubs that elected the regular assembly district leaders who made up the executive committee of the New York County Democratic Party, better known as Tammany Hall. De Sapio, the leader of Tamawa, was also the leader of Tammany. For a struggling young lawyer, joining the regular Democratic organization seemed to promise more legal work, and perhaps a political career, and his friends promised that Tamawa was going to reform from within, allowing a younger generation to take over. In contrast, VID's insurgency seemed like a long shot. But after a few months at Tamawa, Koch realized that the prospect of a reformed Tammany was an illusion. His law practice did improve, perhaps because his name was getting out more, but he never received any business that he attributed to Tamawa.[21] He later recalled that the club, located in a dingy upstairs loft at 88 Seventh Avenue South, "was run like an Orthodox synagogue," with men and women segregated on opposite sides of the room. De Sapio and his lieutenants literally did the club's business in a closed back room.[22] Koch never dealt with De Sapio directly but with an outer circle of club veterans, Judge Thomas Chimera; Thomas I. Fitzgerald, the club secretary; and De Sapio's uncle, George Tombini, a tough ex-stevedore who later became Ed's next door neighbor.

Robert Fine, another lawyer in Tamawa, recalled that Ed approached Tombini and Chimera one day and asked them outright what the path of his advancement could be. Fine remembers overhearing Chimera's sage advice: "You come down here and give neighborhood advice, you help the people. If you do what I did and meet people, someday you can become a judge." When Koch asked how long that would take, Chimera replied, "Twenty years." Koch did not want to be a judge and probably had no intention of waiting until his fifties to hold political office. With no promise of reform or participation, Koch quit after several months, never to return.[23]

While Tamawa stagnated, VID blossomed, with more than three hundred contentious members and twenty committees. Koch rejoined the expanding club, which held weekly meetings that often lasted past midnight, debating politics and resolutions on issues ranging from the pushcarts on Bleecker Street to the bleak prospects for world peace. Kuh, rather than Koch, soon found himself at odds with the spirit of VID, whose constitution declared, "The true direction of political activity is the ceaseless examination and evaluation of local and national goals."[24] When the club passed a resolution calling for repeal of the sodomy laws—Koch fully supported the repeal—Kuh took umbrage. When the club called for legalization of marijuana and adoption of the English system for supplying free heroin plus treatment for drug addicts, the prosecutor stormed out of a meeting and resigned his membership in mid-1957.[25]

THE BOSS TO BEAT: CARMINE DE SAPIO

The politics of VID could be fractious and competitive, but the club was united on one thing: Carmine De Sapio had to go. When the VID formed in his home district in 1957, with the express goal of toppling him, the boss of Tammany was at the top of his game in New York politics. He controlled almost all state and city patronage as New York secretary of state and through his close relationship with Mayor Robert F. Wagner. At the apex, as the Democratic national committeeman in control of New York's huge block of convention delegates, he could be a presidential kingmaker. De Sapio's local leadership in Greenwich Village was, however, the foundation of his empire. The races in which his candidates were challenged by VID members were of national interest because if De Sapio lost the district leadership, the pyramid that had taken so long to build would topple because he would lose most of his higher party offices and could no longer serve as the leader of Tammany Hall.

De Sapio, though often labeled a boss, differed significantly from his predecessors, who preferred to operate behind the scenes. He craved publicity and used persistence rather than connections to launch his career. De Sapio began as an insurgent in early 1939, displacing Dan Finn, the scion of an old Irish Tammany family, in a series of hard-fought elections. Tammany simply refused to seat him until 1943, after he won his third election. After that he advanced rapidly in alliance with the Bronx chairman, Ed Flynn, FDR's closest ally in New York's Democratic party.

De Sapio suffered a major setback as leader in 1950 when his choice for mayor, Ferdinand Pecora, was beaten by the political neophyte Vincent Impellitteri. "Impy," as he was widely known to the public, had no political experience and little visible ability: "I got no ideas, you got any?" he asked the Board of Estimate when its members tackled difficult issues. Mayor William O'Dwyer, who left office to become ambassador to Mexico, added Impy to the Democratic ticket on the advice of Representative Vito Marcantonio of New York, but the real force behind Impellitteri's candidacy was Thomas "Three-Finger Brown" Lucchese, head of a major crime family. When, a few months after the election, evidence emerged of O'Dwyer's ties to another mob boss, Frank Costello, speculation was widespread that O'Dwyer had resigned for that reason. However, historians point out that he was never indicted and probably just wanted to spend more time with his new wife, the socialite Sloan Simpson, who was twenty-five years his junior.[26]

De Sapio seemed to be in danger of losing his leadership as a result of Impellitteri's victory. But in 1953 the Tammany leader consolidated his power base by getting Robert F. Wagner elected as mayor. Wagner, the son of New York's famous senator, trounced Impellitteri 2–1 citywide and carried every borough except Staten Island. It was a big victory for the cleaner faction of Tammany: De Sapio, Bronx County Chairman Ed Flynn, and his successor, Charles Buckley.[27] As a result, Carmine De Sapio became the undisputed leader of the Democratic Party.[28] The next year he broadened his control statewide by getting banker and diplomat W. Averell Harriman elected governor of New York State.

The new leader understood that by the 1950s, most of Tammany's traditional power bases had evaporated. Civil service laws had vastly reduced patronage. After the New Deal, welfare became a largely a government function, reducing one source of Tammany power. The strengthening of the state and its independent law enforcement powers had also made corruption much less profitable and more politically hazardous. Immigration restrictions reduced the traditional flow of fresh blood into the machine. Finally, the passage of state-sponsored primary laws and the enormous expansion of a liberal New York City electorate energized by FDR and the New Deal, made nominations much more difficult to control. In these circumstances De Sapio believed that Tammany could win only if it supported competent candidates who stood on the "right side" of the issues, which generally meant the liberal side.[29]

Governor Harriman appointed the Democratic leader as New York's secretary of state, a position that gave De Sapio some direct patronage power and enabled him to sponsor various electoral reforms. His targets were the kinds of tactics that his predecessor, "Sheriff Dan" Finn, had used against De Sapio a decade earlier. De Sapio replaced paper ballots with mechanical voting machines and instituted permanent personal registration, allowing voters to stay registered so long as they kept voting, which substantially increased voter turnout. Declaring that "any man who can't carry his own assembly district with his name on the ballot should not be leader," De Sapio also instituted direct election of district leaders, the reform that would eventually do him in.[30] But at that time it was inconceivable that the popular and successful De Sapio could be touched within his own bailiwick.

By 1956 De Sapio had accomplished all that a party leader could, except to select a president. So he set out to do that, too. As a national committeeman from New York, De Sapio, with help from Harry Truman, tried to push Harriman for president by withholding New York's delegates from frontrunners Stevenson and Kefauver. The strategy did not work, and it came at a price—the alienation of the Stevenson Democrats, which led to the formation of independent clubs like the Village Independent Democrats right in his backyard.

De Sapio easily held off the VID challenge to his leadership in 1957, with a little help from William Randolph Hearst whose papers spread the false rumor that De Sapio's opponent, Herman Greitzer, was a communist. (Dan Finn had made the same charge against De Sapio in his insurgent bid.) But that year De Sapio's power base began to erode. In July 1957 a taxi driver found an envelope containing $11,200 in moldy currency on the backseat of his cab. The cabdriver turned the money in to the police, and it got into the papers that his last passenger had been the highly recognizable Carmine De Sapio. He denied that the money belonged to him, but no one else claimed it, and after one year the taxi driver received what must be one of the largest tips in New York City history. The association was particularly damaging in people's minds. A decade earlier the reputed mafia don Frank Costello had similarly enriched a cabdriver by $27,000 in cash. While De Sapio maintained his close ties to both Governor Harriman and Mayor Wagner, the highly publicized incident added weight to the reformers' accusations.[31]

De Sapio's handling of the statewide ticket for 1958 proved an even bigger disaster. At the state convention that year in Buffalo, De Sapio brokered a disastrous deal to run Manhattan DA Frank Hogan for the U.S. Senate, incurring the wrath of Governor Harriman and Senator Herbert Lehman. Lehman, a former governor who firmly believed party officials should be subordinate to elected officials, repeatedly accused De Sapio of bossism for not following Harriman's instructions. Privately, Lehman vowed to dump the Tammany leader.[32] De Sapio might have resolved the clash had the Democratic ticket won in November, but in a recession year when Democrats elsewhere swept America, the party lost every statewide office except comptroller to the Republicans. Nelson A. Rockefeller defeated Harriman for governor, and Kenneth Keating beat Hogan for senator. The election results that year called the Tammany leader's competence and usefulness into question.

Lehman, not known for his forgiving disposition, proved a dangerous enemy to De Sapio. He set up the citywide Committee for Democratic Voters (CDV), which raised $500,000 that the CDV channeled to local clubs. This helped coordinate their efforts and gave them a source of professional campaign advice.[33] De Sapio had already alienated New York's most prominent Democrat, Eleanor Roosevelt when he supported Harriman over her son Franklin Jr. in the 1954 governor's race. The Lehman-Roosevelt defection made a significant difference. In the 1959 primary the VID candidate Charles McGuinness, running for district leader with Lehman's aid, nearly defeated De Sapio, who won by only 619 votes. VID won a majority of the local Democratic county committee seats, suggesting that an upset of De Sapio was only a matter of time.[34]

Now politically vulnerable, De Sapio should have sought to mollify his opponents and solidify his support within the party. Instead De Sapio's handpicked state Democratic chair, Michael H. Prendergast, got into a political battle with the already-incensed Lehman, denying the five-term governor and two-term senator a spot in the state's delegation to the 1960 Democratic National Convention. This lack of proper deference to an important party elder outraged Mayor Wagner, himself the scion of a prominent New Deal family. Wagner personally traveled to Albany and, in a private meeting with De Sapio and Prendergast, forced the latter to give up his own seat at the convention to Lehman. Wagner intended the decision to be private, but it leaked to a UPI reporter who overhead the three men in the elevator. This incident also marked the first rift in the hitherto easy friendship between Wagner and De Sapio.[35]

Prendergast and De Sapio's vendetta against Lehman deepened in ways that seriously undercut their position. In a futile attempt to play kingmaker, De Sapio had once again tried to withhold support from the eventual nominee, John F. Kennedy, who had used his Irish connections to organize much of upstate New York behind the Tammany leader's back. In New York the Kennedys remained closer to Bronx boss Charlie Buckley than to the Tammany leader.[36]

During the presidential campaign Senator Lehman and Eleanor Roosevelt agreed to appear on a platform with Senator John F. Kennedy at a rally at Columbus Circle but only if they were regular speakers—they did not want to just decorate the stage. At the outset liberal Jews distrusted an Irish nominee whom they perceived as less than liberal.(Kennedy had been the sole Democrat to abstain from the censure of Joseph McCarthy, for example.) The appearance of Lehman and Eleanor Roosevelt with Kennedy was vital to convince Jews to support the relatively conservative candidate at the head of the ticket. Nonetheless, Prendergast refused to allow Lehman to speak, agreeing only after Kennedy himself telephoned to make the request. Prendergast went back on his word, and Lehman was not allowed to speak at the rally. After Kennedy finished his speech, Lehman confronted the nominee, declaring he had been "double-crossed." Kennedy replied, "You weren't double-crossed, I was. And I'll get the dirty son of a bitch bastard who did it if it's that last thing I do." Democratic National Chair John Bailey informed De Sapio that he would get patronage from the administration only if he immediately fired Prendergast as state chair. De Sapio declined, and while the administration did not openly declare war against him, neither did it give him the extra help he needed to hold on. Tellingly, De Sapio tried to repair relations with the Kennedys and avoid any charges of short-changing the national ticket; he met with the VID activist Stanley Geller to coordinate the neighborhood's efforts for Kennedy.[37]

A KEY UPSET

Perhaps the most significant event in the contest for control of the party in 1960 was reform district leader William Fitts Ryan's upset victory against incumbent Representative Ludwig Teller in the Democratic primary. Teller, an NYU law professor whose voting record was nearly as liberal as Ryan's, had opened up his club for an unprecedented measure of democracy—so class and ideology played minimal parts. Ryan had won largely by closely associating himself with Lehman and by slapping a sticker on Teller's posters throughout the district that read, "Candidate of Carmine De Sapio."[38] *De Sapio* had become an epithet like *Boss Tweed*.

Koch had stayed out of politics for almost a year after he quit Tamawa but returned sometime in 1958. On a quiet Thursday night he had gone to a regular meeting of the reform club and found a surprisingly warm welcome (though some members saw him as tarnished by Tammany). In fact, Koch, a man keenly aware of social dissonance, said that he was surprised at how nice people were to him, though Miki Wolter remembered that at first some people were paranoid about Tamawa spies. Koch overcame their suspicions by a combination of hard work and a hard reform line; he became dedicated to the destruction of De Sapio and the patronage system. According to Stanley Geller, it was clear from the start that Koch was someone who wanted a political career, but "no one particularly held that against him."[39]

It took time, however, for the young lawyer to become a leader in the club. In 1959 he ran for both the presidency and vice presidency of the club and lost, to the longtime VID activist, Howard Moody, pastor of Judson Memorial Church. Koch's speech, according to Gold, another defeated candidate for one of VID's three vice-presidential slots, consisted of a weak apology for his time in Tamawa, and Koch lost badly.

If this defeat soured Koch on the VID, he did not let the rejection fester. More probably it was a trial run, an attempt to identify himself as a leader. And the open democratic environment of the club allowed him to distinguish himself in other ways. Almost immediately, he became head of the speakers' bureau, in charge of soapbox oratory. His unstinting efforts on behalf of the club's 1959 slate of Charles McGuinness and Gwen Worth for district leader (male) and district leader (female) dispelled the fears of skeptics.[40] But Koch wanted an office, and he now faced the challenge of convincing the other club members, many of whom were Ivy Leaguers, that he had the stature of a great reform politician who could beat the boss.

4 "RHYMES WITH NOTCH" (1959–64)

Family crisis interrupted Koch's political career in 1960, when surgeons performing a routine gall bladder operation on his mother discovered that she had metastasized cancer. The surgeon estimated that she had three months to live. The word *cancer* in those days was almost unmentionable, and to Ed's later regret the doctors never informed her of her diagnosis, though she must have known from the nature of the treatments she had to undergo. When alone with his mother, Ed put a brave face on the situation and tried to give her hope of recovery. When he left her to drive home at night, he found himself in tears. Ed had to bear primary responsibility for his mother's care. His father lacked the background to deal with the doctors. Pat was married and living in Rockland County; her second child had been born premature on the same day as her mother's operation. Harold was in New Jersey. He and Pat came to Brooklyn to help when they could.[1]

Ed lived the closest to Brooklyn and had the most flexible schedule, so he took his mother to appointments and to radiation treatments. There were no hospices in those days, and hospitals would not admit a terminally ill patient. Instead, a doctor came by the apartment every day to administer pain medication. A few weeks later Ed and Joyce visited another doctor, at a small hospital on the Upper East Side, who claimed that he could cure her with injections of a horse serum. The supposed cancer cure was nonsense, but at least he put Joyce Koch in the hospital, where she could get constant care. After periods of terrific pain, Joyce Silpe Koch died in Trafalgar Hospital on October 25, 1960, at 8:02 P.M., three months after her original surgery.[2] She was sixty-three. One of the biggest regrets of Koch's life was that he and the rest of the family chose not to be frank with Joyce about her condition and treatment. After a period of mourning his father remarried. Rose Klein, a widow who did not have Joyce's intellectual spark, got along with Louis far better than Joyce had. Ed could not help commenting that Rose, unlike his mother, was "the antithesis of sophistication," but the Koch children were grateful that she took good care of their father.[3]

After Joyce's death Ed threw himself into political and social activities of the Village Independent Democrats (VID), though he was known as one of the club's most conservative members—"the Senator Taft of the VID," according to William Honan, then a VID activist. Honan remembers debating with him about the execution of Caryl Chessman, a convicted rapist who became a published author and expert in U.S. law, with Koch supporting the death penalty.[4]

VID's main primary race in 1960 was a contest for seats on the state Democratic Committee that pitted its members James I. Lanigan and Sarah Schoenkopf against two moderate reformers backed by De Sapio. Koch played a major role in the state committee campaign, even though he knew and respected the opposition candidates and harbored deep misgivings about Lanigan.[5] Koch concentrated on attacking De Sapio and bossism rather than praising Lanigan. This was not hard—Koch was terrified that Tamawa would use foul means to win, like breaking in and stealing the bound petitions before they were filed, thus knocking the club's candidates off the ballot. Taking no chances, he stayed up all night guarding the bound green sheets of paper with a baseball bat. But while some regulars were said to have committed a certain number of irregularities, like busing in former residents to vote, no enforcers arrived to snatch the irreplaceable documents or clunk Ed Koch on the head.[6] Lanigan and Schoenkopf went on to win decisively. Their victory suggested that the club was ready for an effective challenge to Carmine De Sapio himself.[7]

As Mayor Wagner contemplated both his low standing in the polls and his bid for a third term as mayor in the 1961 election, the lessons of Lanigan, Schoenkopf, and Ryan's victories against regular candidates like Ludwig Teller—who should have attracted liberal voters—were not lost on him. In a meeting with his closest aides, Wagner remarked, "After what happened to Lou Teller, what I want to know is how anyone can win if he has De Sapio's support."[8] Always slow to make a decision, the mayor had settled things in his own mind: De Sapio would have to go; the mayor could no longer afford to be identified with him. Instead, he would run for reelection with the support of the reformers. Wagner, who was famous for avoiding conflict, never confronted De Sapio. He simply stopped taking his phone calls.[9]

The Wagner family had always prospered under Tammany, so this rejection was a break with tradition. The mayor's father had become a U.S. senator with the political blessings of Tammany boss Charles Francis Murphy. The mayor himself owed his career to De Sapio, who acidly observed: "We are faced with the spectacle of a candidate who seeks reelection on a platform of cleaning up the mess that he himself has created."[10] Wagner's treachery outraged outer borough leaders, who rejected the mayor's candidacy for reelection. All would be crushed in the wake of Wagner's victory over the regular candidate, New York State Controller Arthur Levitt. Wagner carried all boroughs except heavily Italian Staten Island, in part because rank-and-file Irish voters supported the Irish-German Wagner.[11] He then easily defeated Republican Louis Lefkowitz in the general election.

While De Sapio fell from favor with Gracie Mansion, the leaders of the VID found themselves being courted by Wagner himself. Suddenly, the club and its leaders tasted real power. "I was just so impressed with us being in Wagner's office, and his obviously wanting our support, probably more than we wanted his, though I think we wanted his, too. It wasn't acrimonious," Miki Wolter recalled. The mayor, widely known for his reluctance to commit himself, avoided specific promises but made it clear that he would help Koch and Greitzer get credit for resolving some major community issues.[12]

The VID, which now claimed seven hundred paid members, chose the state committeeman James I. Lanigan to run for the district leadership against De Sapio in 1961.[13] A Harvard-educated developer, Lanigan was Mr. Young Democrat, as much an insider as Ed Koch was an outsider. "When Jim dropped a name, it was Hubert, Averell, Adlai," recalled Carol Greitzer, a former club president who later became a member of the New York City Council.[14] Back then, if anyone had looked at the VID membership and asked who might become mayor, senator, or president, few would have mentioned the rather obscure Ed Koch. Despite Lanigan's alcoholism and self-absorption, many might have answered "Jim Lanigan." But those weaknesses proved greater than his political assets. Within two years Lanigan would wreck his own political career, then fade into obscurity. Ed Koch would take his place on the path to power.

Lanigan received crucial support within the club from his Harvard classmate Stanley Geller, a VID founder and officer who had also considered running for district leader. Geller remembered Lanigan as "one of the best orators I had ever heard as a young man." He continued to support Lanigan, though it soon became apparent to Geller that Lanigan "had lost quite a bit of that talent by then, probably because of his drinking."[15] As the leader of the faction known for its ideological purity on reform matters, especially internal party democracy, Geller was also wary of the Democratic Party hierarchy that Lanigan represented. Nonetheless, Geller praised Lanigan after his state committee victory for leading "a revolution that has completely changed the reform movement."[16] The club also designated Carol Greitzer to face Tamawa incumbent Elsie Gleason Mattura for the female district leader position. (A unique New York law, still in effect today, divides each party position between two candidates, one male and one female.)[17] Now that Wagner had shown his hand, delivering the independent-minded VID to the mayor was Lanigan's and Greitzer's biggest challenge. Wagner was a difficult sell even to the more conservative reform clubs, and VID was among the toughest, given Wagner's past as a De Sapio candidate and a record they considered mediocre. The VID had even passed a resolution opposing Wagner's renomination and deriding the mayor for "laxity and ineffectiveness."

One major controversy, about the right to sing in Washington Square Park, almost killed the VID-Wagner deal. Ed Koch was in the middle of that particular dispute, representing a group of musicians arrested late in April 1961 for singing in defiance of a singing ban by the parks commissioner, Newbold Morris. The folksingers had gathered in Washington Square on weekends since 1944.[18] The core of opposition to singing came from South Village Italians and from the De Sapio–controlled Greenwich Village Association and community planning board. The WASP-dominated Washington Square Civic Association, real estate interests, and NYU probably all played a part as well. The opponents of singing claimed that the hootenannies had attracted unsavory people from outside the neighborhood, making the park unsuitable for children.[19]

What had changed since 1944, when the tradition began? The addition of African Americans to the crowd.[20] On Sunday, April 9, police dispersed an integrated crowd of folksingers who had gathered to protest Morris's denial of their permit. What the *New York Times* characterized as a battle with police ensued, though a film of the incident shows that it consisted of little more than a refusal to leave or to stop singing, followed by arrests. The *New York Mirror,* the most sensational and conservative of the tabloids, claimed that "3,000 beatniks" tore up the park, though the true number was about three hundred, and there was little property damage. All the demonstrators were eventually cleared, except for the outspoken novelist Harold "Doc" Humes, who was given a suspended sentence for speaking in the park without a permit.[21]

By early May the folksingers planned an "Oust Wagner" rally. That got the mayor's attention, as it could jeopardize his fragile relations with VID just as he was trying to woo them. The day before the rally, the mayor reversed his parks commissioner's rule and decreed the park open to singing without a permit.[22] Two months later VID finally endorsed the mayor by a vote of 63 to 33, after a tense two-and-a-half-hour de-bate that made the club's lack of enthusiasm obvious. Purist Herman Greitzer left the club for good after the Wagner endorsement. His wife, Carol, remained and ran for district leader.[23]

The club endorsement of Wagner paid off almost immediately for the reform slate and its would-be constituents. One of the reformers' beefs was that Wagner ig-nored their complaints about Robert Moses. In a variety of formal positions Moses had been responsible for the planning and construction of many of New York's high-ways, parks, and other public works since the 1920s. The VID was dead set against Moses's plan to demolish portions of the Village for the Lower Manhattan Express-way. Now the mayor personally visited the largely Italian tenants of Downing Street who were opposing demolition of their homes for Moses's expressway. Flanked by the VID candidates for district leader, James Lanigan and Carol Greitzer, Wagner inspected the homes to see that they were not slums and patiently listened to argu-ments against demolition. Previously indifferent, he soon killed the project that his own administration had planned. Village community activists reaped other divi-dends. The mayor threw his support behind a plan to turn the old Jefferson Market Courthouse into a public library. To at least the few Italians in the neighborhood who switched their votes, and even to the majority of Italians who did not, it was clear that the reformers had clout, and De Sapio could not deliver.[24]

On election night Greitzer-Lanigan supporters gathered at the Limelight to watch the results come in. Tamawa gathered at its clubhouse directly across Seventh Avenue South. Turnout was high, and it soon became clear that the reformers had swept to victory. Lanigan beat De Sapio by a solid vote of 5,972 to 4,666, outpolling Mayor Wagner, who carried the district by only 5,788 to 4,960. De Sapio held his home area, the South Village. He lost mostly because of the West Village, where La-nigan and Greitzer had gained popularity from their effective support for residents whose homes were slated for demolition. There the Tammany leader's 1959 showing of 59 percent was reduced to 42.5 percent. He even suffered the ignominy of losing his own election district in the race for county committeeman, coming in sixth out of six candidates.[25]

Lanigan and Greitzer basked in media attention. At midnight Adlai Stevenson showed up to predict that Lanigan, his "old and dear and valued friend," would "be-come a great leader in the Democratic Party." Carol Greitzer remembered Ed Koch's face that night: "He looked wistful. It was almost as if he were thinking, 'Someday, this is going to be me.'"[26] Lanigan's head now swelled to zeppelin-like proportions. Less than two weeks after the election, he went on television and declared his candi-dacy for county leader, without checking with either the club or Wagner, who now controlled the party machinery. "We were all stunned," Ed Koch remembered, say-ing that Lanigan made himself and the club look foolish by announcing his ambi-tions so soon after the election.[27]

The election of Stanley Geller as president of VID had great import for Ed Koch. A prominent constitutional lawyer who would soon win *Engel v. Vitale,* the U.S. Supreme Court case that banned most organized prayer in public schools, Geller believed in those days that the club should "fight, fight, fight until the last vestige of opposition is gone." That meant that he thought the club should run a candidate against the liberal, but pro–De Sapio, state assemblyman William Passannante. Koch wanted very much to be that candidate.[28]

More moderate club members thought Passannante was unbeatable and that fielding a VID candidate would needlessly antagonize an acceptable representative of the Village. Moreover, Wagner and Lehman supported the incumbent—after their fight with De Sapio, they did not want to appear anti-Italian by opposing a liberal Italian. At the time all Ed Koch could see was the possibility of finally having a shot at public office, even in a race no one else wanted to invest time and money in because of Passannante's popularity. Koch thought that if he worked hard enough, he could win. "In retrospect, it was foolish," Koch later commented.[29]

Passannante, young, dark-haired, handsome, and famous for his brightly colored neckties, openly admired De Sapio, who was literally his godfather at his baptism. Passannante was a Harvard Law School graduate, which, along with his liberal voting record, gave him an in with other young Village professionals, who usually took their cues from VID. The proven vote getter had defeated a Republican incumbent. And at the grassroots level, which the reformers so idealized, no one had campaigned around the neighborhood more. Carol Greitzer recalled: "He knew a lot of people. You'd see him walking around and talking to shopkeepers. He spent a lot of time just wandering around the Village." VID itself had backed Passannante for reelection in 1958, in an ad that declared, "Bill Passannante has been an independent thinking Assemblyman, unique in a boss-ruled club."[30]

In contrast, Koch was so little known that the *Village Voice* felt obliged to explain that he was a tenants' lawyer whose name "rhymes with 'notch.'"[31] The campaign was the biggest electoral disaster of Koch's political career and nearly ended it for good. After a spat with VID over a minor political favor, Senator Lehman refused to endorse Koch, which amounted to tacit support for Passannante.[32] As a result, Koch was a goner, reduced to faulting Passannante on the very minor issues that divided them, such as his votes for bills that would have taken away the driver's licenses of communists convicted under the Smith Act and narcotics addicts. According to Greitzer, "Ed was a terrible candidate. He really learned a lot from that campaign. He was really awful. But he came out with some good positions. You know, he was for gay rights; he was for abortion, way-out things. But he was a good speaker on the stump for other people. He just didn't know how to do it for himself yet, but he later learned to be a great campaigner."[33]

Koch, with wry humor, dubbed his failed bid the "SAD campaign," because he advocated repeal of laws banning consensual sodomy, abortion, and divorce. He also favored more low- and middle-income housing, a more stringent ethics code for state legislators, maintaining free tuition at City College, and the elimination of patronage. The campaign also reflected Koch's own pugnaciousness and martial ardor: "He will fight for you every time your interests are at stake—regardless of whom he must oppose, what the odds are for victory. This is not a man out to build a paper record . . . this is a man out to fight for you!"[34]

Koch had moved too far from the center, and the establishment united to squash him. By August the Citizens' Union, one of the city's leading reform groups, had endorsed Passannante, dismissing Koch as "an intelligent, community-minded and articulate lawyer with no comparable experience or demonstrated legislative capacity."[35] Koch, described by one reporter as "in love with reform," was devastated by this rejection. The *Village Voice* endorsed the young lawyer, but of the city's major political figures, only Eleanor Roosevelt stuck with Koch.[36] She was the only one who really sympathized with the VID's efforts to democratize party politics. But in the last months of her life, her ability to campaign had diminished. Stanley Geller remembered helping her onto a speaker's platform on the northwest corner of Washington Square Park as the former first lady asked him, "What is the name of our candidate?" Geller replied: "Ed Koch, Ed Koch, Mrs. Roosevelt." Then she mounted the platform and addressed the crowd of about one hundred people: "I've come to speak for our candidate, and my friend, Ed Koch."[37] Even if Eleanor Roosevelt had been twenty years younger or twenty times more committed, she could not have saved the Koch campaign. A week before the primary Lehman and Mayor Wagner both attacked Koch. So did Jim Lanigan, who soon quit VID.[38]

"MILITANT, PUGNACIOUS, AND INTRANSIGENT"

When the election results came in, Passannante had crushed Koch with 57.7 percent of the vote—5,048–3,703.[39] Koch took the defeat hard. Not usually a big drinker, he reportedly got smashed on election night after the returns came in and talked of quitting politics for good. The day after the election Koch sent Eleanor Roosevelt a somewhat bitter letter, thanking her for sticking with him "even when it must have been a great source of embarrassment for you." Koch confided in her that his "feelings in defeat are mixed. I am disconsolate that a victory predicted by most in the 1st Assembly District ten days ago was savagely wrested from the VID by forces which included Carmine De Sapio, Mayor Wagner, and Senator Herbert H. Lehman; yet I am proud that in defeat the VID remained militant, pugnacious and intransigent on the philosophy of Reform."[40]

Passannante's victory led Lanigan to underestimate the power of reform grass-roots politics. Lanigan thought that he could remain as district leader while ditching VID if he had elite support. After the election he met with Passannante and Edward Costikyan, the county leader, to talk about forming a new club in the district to take the leadership away from the VID.[41] Costikyan, who thought the VID members were somewhat crazy, remained officially neutral but sympathetic to Lanigan, while Passannante stayed aloof as he jockeyed unsuccessfully for the position of Democratic leader in the state assembly. Soon after, Lanigan thumbed his nose at the most basic principle of VID by accepting a patronage job with the Wagner administration, a clear sign of the mayor's intent to derail the club. At the time Koch commented that Wagner and Costikyan were trying "to blackjack us into being good boys" if they did not obey Lanigan. From the perspective of many VID members, Lanigan was no better than De Sapio once he took Wagner's patronage and demanded that they adhere to party discipline.[42]

VID prepared for both war with Lanigan and a potential De Sapio comeback. Most professional politicians underestimated the power of VID's grassroots organization and assumed that the club was too weak to defend his turf. The club was $5,000 in debt from Koch's state assembly campaign. In addition to the split with Lanigan, the club was divided internally between the moderate faction and the hard-nosed faction led by Geller and Koch. Despite his very real clashes with those who had not helped with his campaign, Koch managed to get elected president of VID, promising not to run for district leader.

At the time most expected that Koch's pugnacity, self-righteousness, and desire for revenge would worsen the split within the club. Koch and the other hard-nosers wanted to ban members from taking any appointed government jobs. Their antipatronage policy was at the very center of their project to create a grassroots political movement of disinterested citizens. The real problem between the two factions was that Koch "had denounced some of us," recalled Ed Gold.[43] President Koch at first seemed to confirm moderate fears of his factionalism, by declaring that the VID's endorsement of Mayor Wagner in 1961 had been "a horrendous mistake."[44] Then he did something no one had expected. "It happened in a flash," Ed Gold recalled. "As soon as he won that thing, he brightened up and immediately tried to unify the club" by appointing his former political enemies to important committee chairmanships and by reaching out to the moderates.[45] He knew he could not go on to higher office without their support, and he made a conscious decision to woo them. Koch's efforts at bridging the divide in the club seemed to work. It was one of the few times that Koch would forgive people who had opposed him in an election. Without that pragmatic act of forgiveness, foreign to his own temperament, Koch might never have made a political career. At last, he was "a man of stature." Despite the surface unity, said Carol Greitzer: "You still identified people for a couple of years later as though they were on this side or that side of the fight [over the VID presidency]. Even though you were all together against a common enemy."[46]

Forgiveness might have been in Koch's character, but forgetfulness was not. Stephen Berger, a moderate VID member who did work hard on Koch's behalf, reconciled with Koch and later served as an appointee in his city administration. But Berger believed that although Koch did renew their friendship, he never completely got over their ancient factional dispute.[47] Forty years later Koch minced no words about his gut-level reaction to his treatment by some in the VID. He had suffered "a betrayal in some cases. If you're an old friend, and I'm in need of your help and support, fuck you, you're lucky if I ever talk to you again. I mean I talk to them, I'm civil, but I'll never forgive them for walking away from me."[48]

Painful as it was, his failed campaign was more influential than Koch could have predicted, as Passannante became well known for crafting pioneering reform legislation on gay rights, abortion, and divorce.[49] The 1962 campaign for the First District assembly seat proved, moreover, that once De Sapio was defeated, reform candidates would need more than opposition to bossism to run against equally liberal regulars and win.[50] As the Tamawa club planned to destroy the VID, the reform club hunted for a candidate for district leader to oppose a De Sapio comeback. Possibilities included Theodore Bikel, then starring as Baron Von Trapp in the original production of the *Sound of Music,* and Adrian DeWind, a lawyer who much later would chair the board of the environmentalist Natural Resources Defense Council.[51] Neither man would make the run. Finally, in early June, with time running out, the club reluctantly turned to Ed Koch. He hardly looked like their strongest candidate against De Sapio, given Koch's poor showing against Passannante and his narrow margin in the race for president of VID. But the club unified behind him, and Miki Wolter, a leading moderate, seconded his nomination.[52]

Koch negotiated a rapprochement with Wagner, Lehman, and Costikyan, who were mad at him for his sharp tongue and refusal to recognize their authority in the party. Fearful of a De Sapio comeback that would have threatened Wagner's control of the party, and even his ability to function as mayor, the three politicians nonetheless fell in line behind Koch in his quest for the job of district leader. But Koch still had to show public contrition. On a radio program he publicly recanted his earlier accusations that Mayor Wagner and Senator Lehman were bosses, an extreme insult to two icons of New York's New Deal. Even after apologizing, Koch refused to endorse a Wagner-backed judicial candidate, and acidly explained that he did not think the mayor wanted a "sycophantic" club.[53] Lehman, though still outraged that Stanley Geller had accused him of "buying up little reform clubs around Manhattan," reluctantly accepted Koch's apology, but kept him sweating until mid-August for his crucial endorsement. Wagner, who had more to worry about, was more supportive.[54]

In an off-off-year election Carmine's comeback would be the sexiest media story of the campaign. This time it would be fought along somewhat different lines. De

Sapio attacked the reformers as "cold-eyed strangers" who "have suddenly turned fatherly and decided to solve our problems for us." He also made the clash between residents and nightlife on MacDougal Street the prime issue of the campaign.[55] De Sapio also turned to one other important group of community activists—the Village Humane League, whose director declared that "if all the cats and kittens could speak, they would join me in saying God bless you . . . God bless you, Mr. De Sapio."[56] The lesson was not lost on Koch, who assiduously courted pet owners and nonviolent animal rights groups for the rest of his career—smart politics with one of the most active constituencies.

Koch and Greitzer significantly changed their strategy from the 1961 and 1962 reform campaigns, heeding a poll commissioned by the suddenly friendly county chair, Costikyan, and paid for by *New York Law Journal* publisher Jerry Finkelstein. According to the survey, most people cared little about the war of reform against bossism. Most, however, wanted district leaders who participated actively in community affairs. Koch had seemed like a narrow-minded political apparatchik, concerned only with internal democracy. He surprised Costikyan by shifting the emphasis of the campaign: "Instead of patronage he talked potholes," the county leader recalled.[57]

WOOING ITALIANS AWAY FROM DE SAPIO

De Sapio perceived the salience of community issues early on, roasting the reformers in a campaign ad that complained of "the mess on MacDougal Street," which he exaggerated into "a human cesspool . . . over-run with motley throngs of exhibitionists, disorderly characters, and drunken vagrants."[58] Instead of defending the counterculture, Koch and Greitzer formed an emergency committee with neighborhood residents to remedy the "mess." When De Sapio met with several deputy commissioners from police, sanitation, and other agencies who promised stronger enforcement, Koch and Greitzer countered, using their influence with Wagner to make a dramatic series of moves. They obtained a nighttime parking ban on both sides of MacDougal Street and a release of funds for a middle-income housing project that had been on the back burner. They ended an eight-year struggle to win a ban on motor vehicles in Washington Square Park—which included the buses that used the space around the arch as a turnaround, a practice that Robert Moses had instituted as a prelude to his plan to extend Fifth Avenue through the park to improve traffic flow. Koch and Greitzer persuaded the mayor to take all these actions in the last week before the election, even though city traffic officials had previously claimed it could not be done for another two months. Wagner, in characteristically cautious fashion, did not endorse Koch but sent a telegram that credited him for the banishment of buses from the park.[59]

Koch and Greitzer also ran on their record of the last two years, from the effort of Koch and others to improve housing code enforcement to the VID program that provided more than two thousand polio shots. At the end of the campaign they staged a motorcade through the Village and held a primary eve rally in the center of the Village, at the corner of West Fourth and Tenth Streets. In their final campaign ads, defeating bossism was the last item on the list, after rent control, more low- and middle-income housing, and relief of public school overcrowding without jeopardizing integration. They supported more cops on the beat to preserve public order while insisting that homeless people and "addicts must be treated as the victims of a disease and not criminals." They reminded all and sundry that they had stopped Moses's expressway, saving the homes of the largely Italian tenants.[60]

Koch was vulnerable in part because of voters' identification of him with the folksingers who had demanded the right to sing. He could not afford to be seen as exclusively on the side of the NYU professors and the beatniks. In his first run for district leader, however, Koch's record reflected his civil liberties concerns and not his sensitivity to the culture of the South Village Italians. In fact, he did not yet have much of a public record at all. Carol Greitzer, the incumbent district leader, was responsible for most of VID's accomplishments in the district between 1961 and 1963, when she was coleader with the ineffectual Lanigan. Greitzer recalled that "I had lots of clippings and Ed didn't have so many clippings. And he resolved at that point, never to be without clippings again." Some of Koch's stiffness in the previous campaign started to melt away, and he became more charming in public. Greitzer thought Koch improved significantly during the 1963 campaign. "Ed was good to campaign with. He would come back to the club and give a report on what we had done, and he would embellish stories beautifully. It wasn't inaccurate. But he would add little details. . . . I learned that if you can do that, and make a better story out of it, that's something to do."[61]

Jane Jacobs, the author and West Village activist, remembered that at first Koch "was still learning and [Greitzer] was the savvy one."[62] This was an unusual change for the New York County Democratic Committee—better known as Tammany Hall—where women had traditionally been kept in the background, even though by party rules, party committees were comprised of one man and one woman from each district. Nonetheless, by the summer of 1963 Koch had begun to get more press attention than Greitzer, his running mate, because he was the challenger to De Sapio and had a tight race.[63] Greitzer was considered a shoo-in because of her strong presence in the community, though on paper her opponent seemed formidable. Political "neophyte" Diana Halle, a Jewish attorney with an undergraduate degree from Cornell, might appeal to some older Jewish regular voters. She also lived in Stewart House, one of the largest buildings in the district, which gave her a significant base.

The rigors of the campaign did not eclipse Ed Koch's work on civil rights. Koch even took time off during the last week of the primary campaign to attend the March on Washington on August 28, 1963. The growing prominence of civil rights as an issue for VID contrasted with its total absence from De Sapio's campaign literature. Local organizers in the Village even held their own prefatory rally six days before the March on Washington. A crowd of several thousand came to hear NAACP leaders Herbert Hill, James Yates, Myrtle Turner, and the actor Ruby Dee, who shared the platform with Greenwich Village Association president Anthony DaPolito and Ed Koch, who called for a "change in the moral climate to end racial discrimination once and for all."[64] Even during the campaign, Koch worked as a "participating attorney" for the Congress on Racial Equality (CORE), successfully mediated a dispute between the NAACP and the Howard Johnson restaurant chain about racially discriminatory hiring policies, intervened in school integration issues, and called for open housing. On school integration, though, he was somewhat more cautious about white sensibilities than were some other liberals of the time. Integration, he argued in a letter to the *Villager,* should be supported by busing minority students to "decent schools in our own Village" rather than sending kids from the Village to bad schools in minority neighborhoods.[65]

Still, politics and participatory democracy remained at the core of Koch's interests. "A district leader is one who helps formulate policy," Koch told a reporter. "His position gives him the opportunity to speak to enrolled Democrats of the club indicating to them what his opinion is; on the other hand a leader should not impose his will on others. He should participate in a discussion to get the benefit of the views of other Democrats, then a position should be hammered out—a position which represents a majority of Democrats is then decided by a vote." Such a model seemed completely anarchistic to his opponent, Carmine De Sapio, who complained that "the Democrats in the district have seen their community torn apart by dissidence and bickering." "Self-styled reformers," he remarked, could not "point to a single genuine reform which they have achieved since September 1961."[66]

On election day both sides realized the race was close. Things at first looked bad for Koch. Turnout was unusually low in the reform-minded North Village, and VID had to make a special effort at the end of the day to get its voters out. According to an urban legend, some VID voters showed up in pajamas just before the 10 P.M. poll closing. Actually, Koch "rang a woman's doorbell at 15 Washington Place at about 9:45 P.M. and asked her to vote." He convinced her to come out, and "she put a coat over her nightgown" and ran to the closing polling place.[67] In contrast, the Tamawa organization in the South Village was able to marshal its troops and voters efficiently, and De Sapio did better than expected in the West Village portion of the district, where VID had lavished much of its community efforts.

Election night was tense at both clubs, whose members realized that a few votes either way might decide the outcome. The reformers feared that the regulars, who still controlled most of the election inspectors, might steal the election. Ed Gold recalled, "We always knew they gave the cops money, which was standard procedure, but we thought it was underhanded." In addition, "we knew they had some dummy voters they gave a couple bucks to come in and vote." One building, owned by a family in the cement and paving business, had "room for seven or eight people," but as many as fifty people registered as living there. "That was just one of the realities we had to live with," Gold said.[68]

As the results came in district by district, even the local experts could not determine the outcome. At VID "people joked nervously about a 'mixed marriage'" between De Sapio and Greitzer, who had clearly won her race. The last election district to go up on the board was Stewart House (by itself a whole election district), which was the home of De Sapio's running mate, Diana Halle, and which Tamawa was expected to carry. When the results showed that Koch had carried the building 165–77, everyone knew he had won the election. The final results gave Koch a margin of 41 votes; Greitzer won by more than 650, out of roughly 8,000 cast. VID activists scrambled off to impound the voting machines to prevent fraud.[69]

An ecstatic crowd mobbed VID headquarters. Former VID president Ed Gold added to the uproar by announcing, "There are De Sapio people living inside three polling places" and urging captains to get back to their precincts.[70] At Tamawa the reaction was more subdued. De Sapio listened to the results in his back room, along with his business partner and public relations guru Sidney Baron. The numbers filtered out to the outer room and the overflow crowd in the street. When the last election district was in, De Sapio addressed the crowd: "No one can forget what you have done in our behalf," he said. "If we have not measured up to your expectations, it is not because you did not try."[71] De Sapio would never hold elective office again.

In the first Koch–De Sapio rematch, held in 1964 as a result of De Sapio's court challenge of the 1963 election results, Koch enlarged his margin to 164 votes. The next time he stood for election, in the regular 1965 primary, which gave him his first chance to run the same year as a mayoral election, he defeated De Sapio by a solid majority of more than 500 votes, and the old boss finally gave up. Koch, rising from bitter and overwhelming defeat, was now the Villager with the brightest political future. His life became a permanent political campaign.

The grassroots democracy of reform politics profoundly influenced Koch's later career. Most important, he learned the basic techniques of politics and campaigning. He also learned how to integrate his conservative instincts with friendships with liberal supporters, and when to pragmatically modify his natural instinct to divide the world into political friend and foe. Conversely, his experience with grassroots politics and community organizing made him much more sympathetic to the use of public space for protest and political speech than many other New York politicians, and it committed him to one of his most important goals as mayor—to regain democratic control of the government from the state appointees on the Emergency Financial Control Board. The question in 1965 was where would he go next?

5 THE MAN WHO BEAT CARMINE DE SAPIO

Koch's life changed fundamentally when he became assembly district leader in January 1964. For the first time he felt the thrill of making banner headlines, becoming an instant hero to liberal voters who barely knew how to pronounce his name. To his admirers the tall, rangy Koch was the Man Who Beat Carmine De Sapio—a Jewish version of the character, played by Jimmy Stewart, who vanquished a local political boss in *The Man Who Shot Liberty Valance*. Another, less obvious, parallel was that in the movie Jimmy Stewart confesses that he really owed his victory to the gun power of rancher John Wayne. Koch understood from the beginning that his political muscle really came from the Village Independent Democrats and his other community supporters. Given how narrow his victory was, he was determined to expand that base and run for higher office at the first opportunity.

Koch found his first taste of fame exhilarating; fortune did not preoccupy him unduly. Nor did De Sapio's continuing challenge to Koch's 41-vote margin in court. In the sweet days before the Vietnam War fragmented American liberalism, Koch soon found himself courted by the first lady, Lady Bird Johnson, who had come to the Village for the preview of Arthur Miller's new play, *After the Fall*. A shrewd political operator, Lady Bird wanted to ensure friendly relations with the reformers so that De Sapio's early backing of her husband would not create an early enmity in reaction. In her presence Koch was shy and awestruck, stumbling over his words and nervously repeating himself. "She's a wonderfully warm, a wonderfully gracious woman," Koch told reporters after the meeting.[1]

Hobnobbing with the first lady must have been heady indeed to a former hatcheck clerk from Newark, but Koch still faced the problem of material subsistence as a lawyer. His growing political prominence brought in clients, but few were wealthy. The *Village Voice,* which retained him for $600 a year, was his only major corporate client. As a reformer, he refused to market his newfound political influence. Not counting election-law cases, only five of his cases made the published law reports. All were decided between 1958 and 1962. Perhaps after 1962, when he started running for office, he simply did not have time for that kind of litigation and referred his appeals to other lawyers. Most of these cases were divorces; one was a foreclosure. And he won most of them. Life in politics meant that he had to spend much of his time away from the law. Koch needed a partner on whom he could depend to share both the work and the profits, and the moderate increase in clients that his new fame brought him made that possible.

His first attempt at partnership failed. The new partner, Lester Evens (later a civil court judge who had to answer complaints about his brusque manner), was also active in reform politics and tenant organizing.[2] The firm, however, needed more attention than Koch could give; it could not support two lawyers whose primary interest was politics. Koch was bringing in all the clients but sharing the profits 50–50, a poor arrangement that he terminated after one year. What he really needed was a skilled nonpolitical lawyer with few steady clients, with whom Koch could share the work as well as the profits.

He found both in Allen G. Schwartz, a corporate lawyer and former prosecutor who was ten years younger. Schwartz, who joined Koch's firm at the beginning of 1965, recalled years later that "Ed Koch and I never had an argument and we never had an uncomfortable day with each other." Schwartz became Koch's closest friend. Part of understanding Koch is understanding his relationship with his very bright, but much less splashy, alter ego. Schwartz, like Koch, was a Brooklyn kid who had gone to City College, but Schwartz had gone on to make law review at the University of Pennsylvania. At Penn, Schwartz participated in a program run by Mayor Wagner's commissioner of corrections, Anna Cross. She recruited law students at top schools to serve as corrections officers in the Tombs and other jails during their summer vacations. "We did all the things that any officer would have done," he remembered. Schwartz and six others all worked in some capacity in the criminal justice system at different stages of their careers. After a stint in the army, Schwartz's close friend, Leonard Sandler, persuaded him to apply for a job with the New York County District Attorney's Office, considered at that time to be the finest prosecutorial outfit in the nation. After a few years as an assistant DA, Schwartz joined a midtown law firm that eventually merged with the white-shoe White and Case. Sandler later took Schwartz out to dinner with Ed Koch, who was looking for a new law partner. The two men hit it off immediately, and Koch offered him the partnership. But Schwartz had other plans.[3]

In 1964 he took a leave from life as a corporate lawyer, intending to write a musical. Instead, he became defense counsel in one of the great causes célèbres of the 1960s, the prosecution of the comedian Lenny Bruce. Schwartz became "good friends" with Bruce and, at his request, represented Bruce's codefendants, Howard and Alice Solomon, who owned the nightclub where Bruce was performing when he was arrested. The prosecutor was the same Richard Kuh who had put the lid on Ed Koch's ambitions with VID back in 1956 and who broke with the reformers (before Koch rejoined the club) over their calls for the legalization of homosexuality and some drugs.[4]

Bruce's jokes about gays and venereal disease were more scatological than pornographic. He got laughs out of the audience's discomfort with his material. According to Schwartz, who had worked closely with Kuh in the DA's office, prosecutors aggressively pursued Bruce because of the Jewish comedian's satiric remarks about the Catholic church and the Kennedys, not because of the sexual content of his routine.[5]

Schwartz, who thought Kuh was "out of control," went out to dinner with his old friend one night to try to settle the case in a reasonable fashion. How, he asked, could you hold the nightclub owners responsible when much of Bruce's act was improvised? They could not know what he was going to say in advance. Kuh dismissed Schwartz's objections and grew apoplectic in recounting how Bruce had mocked Jackie Kennedy for trying to leap out of the limo during her husband's assassination: "Do you know what Lenny Bruce said in his act? He said that she hauled ass to save her own ass. They that live by the sword die by the sword."[6] To Kuh, Bruce's travesty against the sacred Kennedys was really the worst thing he had done. Bruce was convicted by a three-judge panel dominated by John Murtagh, a judge with strong connections to the archdiocese, but the conviction was overturned in 1967, after Bruce's death.[7] Engrossed in the drama of the Bruce case, Schwartz never wrote his musical comedy. He returned briefly to his white-shoe law firm, which now seemed infinitely boring. He remembered Koch's offer, and they formed the firm of Koch and Schwartz on January 1, 1965.

Schwartz and Koch matched each other well. Koch was comfortable with Schwartz as a City College kid who'd made good in the Ivies. The younger lawyer bridged Koch's neighborhood practice and the corporate legal world. Koch brought in clients; Schwartz handled most of the litigation and legal research and managed the firm's money, which they split evenly. Koch was a "good trial lawyer" and a tenacious negotiator, but his main contribution was lining up a virtual parade of political figures as clients, according to Schwartz. The arrangement with Schwartz, who had few of his own clients, allowed Koch to spend more time at politics, especially after his election to the city council in 1966. Both Schwartz and Koch were early risers, arriving at the office at 7:30 A.M., eating lunch together, and leaving at 5:00. Often at night Koch would go out with Schwartz and his wife, and he even found them an apartment in his building, 72 Barrow Street.[8]

One real test of their relationship came after Koch won his seat on the city council. An old friend from Newark, a bookmaker, wanted to go legit and build parking garages. He offered Koch $25,000 to lobby for a change in the laws regulating garages that would allow the ex-bookie to operate. After hearing the offer Koch walked into Schwartz's office, closed the door, and asked him if he thought they should take it. At the time, according to Schwartz, they were each pulling about $7,500 out of the partnership. Nonetheless, he advised Koch to decline because the bookie wanted him to do political, not legal, work. And "a great grin" broke out on Koch's face because he did not want to do it, either. "I've never known him to do anything [political] because money was involved," Schwartz recalled.

The firm of Koch and Schwartz soon expanded. John Lankenau and Victor Kovner, two prominent lawyers with connections to the reform Democrats, joined the firm in 1966. As mayor, Koch later appointed Allen Schwartz to be the city's corporation counsel, and President Clinton appointed Schwartz to the federal district court. Victor Kovner became corporation counsel under Mayor David Dinkins. Kovner and his wife, Sarah, one of the founders of VID, have remained for decades among New York's most prominent liberal Democrats.

For much of his involvement with the firm, Lankenau, a former assistant U.S. attorney, was under contract to the major firm of Winthrop, Stimson, working to sort out a famous salad oil scandal: a vegetable oil dealer had collected tens of millions of dollars in fraudulent warehouse receipts for salad oil that was not, in fact, sitting in tanks in New Jersey. This lucrative legal contract was an occasion for negotiation among Koch and his partners. According to Lankenau, Schwartz thought Lankenau should contribute one-third of his fees to Koch and Schwartz, an arrangement that Lankenau opposed because the work would all be done at Winthrop, Stimson and would not cost Koch and Schwartz a dime. But he agreed to give the firm 25 percent cut of the fees as an investment to build up Koch and Schwartz, which had made only modest profits.[9]

The firm's paltry profits were not surprising, as Koch did little lawyering and ran an almost permanent campaign in those years—first for city council, then for Congress. Once Koch departed in 1969, after he was elected to the House of Representatives, so did Schwartz, though Lankenau and Kovner, who had not known each other at the outset, remained partners for many years.[10]

Of Koch's three partners, only Schwartz remained Koch's friend. Lankenau thought that Koch might have worked harder at making money for the firm, but he and Kovner continued to support Koch politically for years. They broke off their relations with Koch when they became disenchanted by the scandals of his third term and what they saw as Koch's contribution to the increasing racial polarization of the city. In fact, Kovner helped put together Dinkins's successful bid to unseat Koch in 1989. Lankenau stopped supporting Koch because he felt that the mayor had ignored the African American community.[11]

Ed Koch wanted to rise in politics more than he wanted to be a successful lawyer, and he was willing to work as hard as he could to achieve office. When asked on a congressional questionnaire what he would do if he lost his seat, Koch answered, "I don't know," which suggests that he was not terribly interested in returning to law.[12] His mayoral ambitions began surprisingly early in his career. Soon after Allen Schwartz's son, David, was born in 1965, Koch promised that he would hold the boy's bar mitzvah in Gracie Mansion. Schwartz thought then that Koch was out of his mind, but when David's bar mitzvah came around, Koch delivered on his promise.[13]

Twice he announced a campaign for higher office, only to promptly withdraw it because he had to defend his district leadership. Koch had very briefly hoped to run against the powerful Republican state senator MacNeill Mitchell in 1964; then, in 1965, Koch planned to run for an at-large seat on the city council—a Manhattan-wide election that might have put Koch in line to become borough president, then mayor.[14] Both times, Carmine De Sapio blocked Koch's ambition by threatening to emerge from his political grave. As The Man Who Beat De Sapio, Koch's political career was worth little if De Sapio returned to power. Koch would have to slay the old dragon twice more before he could capture the treasure of public office.

In Koch's first narrow win for the district leadership in 1963, De Sapio's lawyers documented sixty-five cases of voters who had failed to properly sign the registration books. The lower court had upheld Koch's election, finding that thirty of the sixty-five voters who did not sign were entitled to vote anyway. The Court of Appeals, New York's highest court, held that all sixty-five voters who did not sign the register had cast invalid votes and on May 7, 1964, ordered a new election.[15]

At the time Koch had been outraged by the challenge to the election results— how could he, an ultrareformer, be accused of irregularities? "I was incensed," he remembered. After De Sapio publicly accused him of voter fraud, Koch turned his back on him: "'You can't shake my hand after you called me a crook and you said I opened up the graves to vote people,'" Koch remembered telling his opponent. In fact, he'd given De Sapio ammunition. The boss went on television and declared (as Koch relates it) "'something un-American happened out there. Koch refused to shake hands with me.' It was front-page news in the *New York Times*, and I learned a lesson, because the *Times* denounced me for being unsportsmanlike and not shaking hands. I decided, from this point on, I'll shake hands with the devil." Though many stories about the Koch–De Sapio race did reach the front page, the handshaking story actually ran on page 22 of the *Times*, a revealing example of how small mistakes can loom large in a politician's mind. At the time he was still sufficiently unknown that R.W. Apple of the *Times*, like a *Voice* reporter a couple of years before, found it necessary to inform readers once again that "Koch rhymes with notch."[16]

The incident added to Koch's firecracker image but did not hurt him very much. In the perpetual campaign that his life had become, he recovered quickly. Almost every evening in those days he could be found at the Sheridan Square subway station, the VID clubhouse, or holding court at the Limelight. "Koch is a regular guy," commented one longshoreman, "he hangs out on Sheridan Square."[17] Koch's hard work at the Limelight and other local haunts increased his margin to 164 votes in the court-ordered rerun against De Sapio. Even before the court decision came down, Koch tried his best to reach out to the Italian community, bringing in city agencies to defend it from encroachments by the burgeoning downtown Manhattan nightlife. He also made a name in the more affluent, reform-oriented areas of the Village for his militant defense of the neighborhood from encroachment by city agencies that wanted to plant high-rises and highways there. Politically, this also meant a rapprochement with Passannante, who joined the VID in March 1964 and was cordially welcomed into the club by his former opponent, Koch, who called Passannante's decision to join the club "an act of courage."[18] But most important, Koch fought for neighborhood control of Greenwich Village's public spaces.

THE MESS ON MACDOUGAL

One of the knottiest problems for Koch was the commercialization of MacDougal Street, the major issue of his 1963 campaign for district leader. Koch became the leading political champion of the MacDougal residents. They, in turn, eventually became more than an important part of his political base—they showed Koch how he could reach out to Catholic voters more effectively than other liberal politicians by selectively countering the counterculture—a basic recipe of his future political success.

Once a residential tenement neighborhood with social clubs and other locally owned businesses, MacDougal Street had sprouted coffeehouses and cabarets that operated all night long, offering entertainment to increasingly noisy crowds. Barkers corralled passers-by and harassed the neighbors. The local neighborhood way of life seemed to be slipping into the muck as the bar zone became a downtown version of Times Square, every weekend full of noisy drunken teenagers until dawn. Young people, often underage, gravitated to the Village "from all over the city and they had no regard for the neighborhood, and they would piss in the doorways," Koch later wrote.[19] Panhandlers, drug dealers, and prostitutes of both sexes increasingly hassled park pedestrians with solicitations, making use of the park acutely uncomfortable for families with children. This was the famous "mess on MacDougal Street" that Carmine De Sapio's newspaper ads had tried to lay on the doorstep of the VID, which was vulnerable because of Koch's activities on behalf of the right to sing in Washington Square Park. Soon after De Sapio raised the issue in the 1963 campaign, Koch helped form the MacDougal Street Neighborhood Association (MANA), along with two important leaders in the Italian community—Dina Nolan, a Republican precinct captain, and a young attorney, Emmanuel "Wally" Popolizio. Popolizio was a Village native and one-time Kiwanis Man of the Year. Because of his connections to the numerous community organizations that made up the political and cultural fabric of the Italian South Village, he became the chair of MANA. Nolan, Popolizio, and a few of their neighbors joined at first because they were desperate to do something about the conversion of their neighborhood into a crowded amusement area. One night Koch and his friends counted "ten thousand people in front of Harry Rissetto's liquor store, in the space of maybe an hour, walking back and forth on MacDougal Street."[20]

Ed Koch soon inspired devotion in MANA's members because of his indefatigable energy for saving their neighborhood. But trust and devotion were not yet in the picture at the first community meeting. First, the trustees of Our Lady of Pompeii Church blocked him from reserving their meeting hall, probably at the behest of Carmine De Sapio or his supporters. When Koch arrived at NYU's Education Center as temporary chair of the first meeting, he was greeted by several African American picketers carrying "Down with Koch" signs. John A. D'Apolito, owner of Tony's restaurant on Bleecker Street, had hired the pickets to make Koch look bad because D'Apolito was angered by Koch's proposal to regulate restaurant canopies. Meeting with the MacDougal community was Koch's "obvious attempt to get the Italian vote," D'Apolito told a reporter, "but he won't get it anyway because it's a prejudiced thing."[21]

Koch used his skills as a soapbox orator to win over the mostly Italian crowd. When one non-Italian "hippie type" rose to complain about Bill Passannante, Koch ruled him out of order—political attacks would not be germane to the meeting. Ed appealed to the crowd—which identified the hippie with the outsiders besieging their neighborhood. They supported Koch, shouting "Sit down! Sit down! He's the chairman."[22] This was the turning point at the meeting, as the locals began to see that Koch, politically motivated or not, did not want just a front group for the VID but an effective grassroots lobby for the neighborhood.

With Mayor Wagner aiming to undermine De Sapio's support, Wagner helped Koch out by sending senior city officials to the MacDougal Street meetings; they outlined their approach to the problem, including taking some of the night clubs to court for zoning violations. The crowd applauded those who offered the harshest remedies. Yet MacDougal residents were not deaf to all moderate voices. Carol Greitzer pointed out that the only thing that kept landlords from selling their rent-controlled buildings to developers was the money they got from commercial tenants; the neighborhood had to solve the problem of the rowdy night scene without harming local business. The crowd applauded with approval when the poet Allen Ginsberg got up to speak for noncommercial coffeehouses, where people could put on plays without charging admission. "If you make a law banning all coffeehouses, then you will close down a lot of valuable artistic enterprises," Ginsberg warned.[23]

By the end of that first of many MANA meetings, Koch had won respect but few votes, as his next two elections against De Sapio would show. But the South Villagers no longer hated him, and once De Sapio was gone for good, many became staunch supporters of Koch. He helped them construct an intellectually honest organization, run according to participatory democratic tenets by the concerned residents themselves and headed by Wally Popolizio, one of their own. Working together, they had a measure of success. Ultimately, MANA claimed a thousand members. Koch gained credit and credibility as the organization embraced even strong De Sapio supporters, which meant that Koch could not use it as a political launching pad against the former Tammany leader. The bars did not go away, but after a year of agitation, MANA and Koch got city hall to ban parking on MacDougal Street, divert sightseeing buses from the area, and to seek injunctions that would padlock illegal nightclubs.[24] But Koch also convinced the city to devote more police to "clean up" the Village, including "plans to increase surveillance of Greenwich Village to curtail loitering and solicitation by homosexuals." Koch boasted that "more effective" measures would be taken to arrest alleged homosexual solicitors in Village Square at Eighth Street and Sixth Avenue. Gay activists at the time complained that these measures led to an increase in unfair entrapment arrests and harassment of gay men in the Village.[25]

Washington Square Park remained another area of conflict. The parks commissioner, Newbold Morris, offered a design by the architect Gilmore Clarke that would have reconfigured the park radically, with walkways between the arch, a hexagonal fountain, and a Greek-style colonnade connecting two "comfort stations."[26] Clarke also proposed surrounding the park with a two-foot masonry fence. All this "Beaux Arts" redrawing ran directly contrary to a thirty-one-point plan suggested by the community, which called for renovation rather than a redesign. The architect Robert Jacobs, husband of the famous urbanist Jane Jacobs, blasted Clarke as "Robert Moses' favorite designer," claiming that he had simply revived Moses's old plans for the park, which "cut off the corners and erected a temple to urination to balance the temple to George Washington."[27] Mayor Wagner's priority was supporting Koch in order to prevent a De Sapio comeback, and in a meeting with Commissioner Morris, Koch, and Greitzer, Wagner overruled his parks commissioner and stopped the renovation plan.[28] This made Morris—an old Moses warhorse who had once run for mayor himself—even less cooperative on small matters, such as Koch and Greitzer's request to set an area of the park aside for women with children, similar to Coram Fields in London. Morris dismissed the idea as silly, until it turned out that he had agreed to it in a previous letter.[29]

"I WILL NOT JOIN THOSE WHO PATRONIZE THE NEGRO"

Back at VID, the summer of 1964 was a period of rising expectations and frustration. At the moment of Barry Goldwater's presidential nomination, right-wing terror in the South was not an abstraction. As the Republican delegates met at San Francisco's Cow Palace, Marine Corps frogmen, working at the request of the Federal Bureau of Investigation, were searching the Pearl River in Neshoba County, Mississippi, for the bodies of the civil rights workers James Chaney, Michael Schwerner, and Andrew Goodman, all murdered by segregationists. Later in his career Koch frequently referred to their deaths. For him it was a defining moment of injustice within American society, and it remained at the core of his liberal ideology, in part because it linked Jews and blacks as victims.

Violence wracked New York as well as the South that July. Fifteen-year-old James Powell was shot and killed by an off-duty New York City police lieutenant on July 16, 1964. Powell was attending remedial reading classes in summer school on the Upper East Side. A building superintendent on East Seventy-sixth Street sprayed a group of African American students hanging out in front of the school with a hose to quiet them down. To the students the hose evoked the hoses used against civil rights demonstrators in Birmingham by Sheriff Bull Connor the year before. The kids pelted the super with trash from a garbage can. Powell allegedly went after the super with a knife and then struggled with an off-duty officer. The officer first tried to stop Powell, fired a warning shot, and then shot him dead. A week later Harlem was beset by riots and looting, stopped only after concerted action of local community leaders and the police.[30] Ultimately, black politicians and activists worked to stop the riots, which some referred to as "Goldwater rallies" because they thought the violence only aided the enemies of equality.[31]

In the Village issues of police brutality came dramatically into relief that winter when James Yates, the chair of the local NAACP, was cursed and kicked by hospital personnel and a city police officer after being brought by ambulance to St. Vincent's Hospital for medical treatment.[32] Ed Koch said that Yates's case showed the need for legislation he had drafted on behalf of council member Theodore Weiss in 1964 that would require formal evaluation of allegations of police brutality.[33] The bill, which would have created the Civilian Complaint Review Board, a joint board of civilians and police to review brutality complaints, had languished in the conservative city council. Two years later, when the measure was resurrected by Mayor John Lindsay, it became a major landmark in the moderation of Koch's liberalism. In a showdown with the mayor, political forces sympathetic to the Irish-dominated police department, which believed that any civilian review would be unfair to the cops, overwhelmingly defeated the board in an unusual November 1966 referendum. More than 80 percent of Catholic voters went against the board, a higher percentage than voted for John F. Kennedy, a statistic of note to Koch, a young Jewish politician courting a Catholic constituency.[34]

This was a major political setback for Lindsay. Some of Koch's Italian supporters urged him to repudiate the civilian complaint board, even though he had helped draft the original proposal in 1964. He refused, and the Italian American community stuck with him nonetheless, even though the city's conservative Catholics overwhelmingly opposed civilian review of complaints against the police. As mayor, Koch praised the willingness of the Italians in those days to support him despite urging him to change his mind about the Civilian Review Board, which he contrasted with the ideological purity allegedly demanded by liberals of their candidates.[35] The Civilian Review Board issue was the exception that proved the rule. After a few years Koch often differed more with his VID friends than with his Italian supporters in matters involving race and crime.

One contretemps in 1964 eerily foreshadowed some of the racial controversies of Koch's mayoralty. Wilbert Tatum, one of the few African American members of the VID, introduced a resolution calling for VID members to circulate petitions asking President Lyndon B. Johnson to send federal troops to the South to enforce the Civil Rights Act. The debate about Tatum's resolution was disturbingly petty. Some VID members wanted to strengthen the resolution to "demand" that Johnson send troops. Koch and others worried that such a petition, in any form, would stimulate "white backlash" and help elect Goldwater. Tatum, frustrated by the lengthy debate about what he saw as a fairly simple issue, challenged: "I wonder what action this club would take if Jews were being beaten and killed in wholesale lots. There would not be a 2½-hour debate on language. All of you here would insist on hammering out the most radical petition that your collective minds could conceive."[36]

Koch replied publicly the next night at an NAACP rally held to protest the disappearance of civil rights workers James Chaney, Michael Schwerner, and Andrew Goodman, whose bodies were found eight days later. Noting that two were Jewish, Koch retorted, "I'm not going to be read out of the civil rights movement by those who think the best position must be the most extreme one." He once again insisted that, in a "tough election," "extremism" on racial issues might drive moderates to Goldwater. Koch continued by lashing out at the "unconscionable attacks" on New York Mayor Robert F. Wagner, such as the recent attempt by the civil rights worker

Herb Callender to make a citizen's arrest of the mayor for failing to crack down on racial discrimination in construction unions. The crowd applauded weakly, then cheered the NAACP labor secretary Herbert Hill, who replied that nobody had to read Koch out of the civil rights movement because "that eminent ward heeler" was doing it on his own.[37]

Koch made a partial retreat the next night at the VID, acquiescing to the call for federal troops. But he tried to insist that VID send a telegram to the White House rather than circulating a petition, which he felt would waste the club's organizing resources. Koch seemed extraordinarily keen to restrain the least hint of radicalism. The club, always at its proudest when overruling its own leadership, did not agree, and the petition resolution carried 44–27.[38]

The matter did not end there, as Koch tried to set things right in a letter to the *Voice*, declaring, "I support militancy in the struggle for equal rights in housing, education, employment, and every other area where any Americans are denied their due." Then he denounced the violence of the Harlem riots. If he had stopped there, he might have repaired the damage, but he could not resist turning the knife a bit on the radicals, adding, "I will not join those who patronize the Negro and explain away the criminal acts of a few out of millions of law-abiding Negroes by referring to aggressions against the Negro over the past three hundred years."[39] A letter signed "Reader from Harlem" mocked him: "I wish Mr. Koch would not patronize the Caucasian and try to ignore or explain away the criminal acts of a few out of millions of law-abiding Caucasians."[40] Twenty-four years later Tatum became the editor of the *New York Amsterdam News*, where he published his famous weekly editorials all headlined "Koch Must Resign." Tatum challenged Koch to a radio debate in 1988, and to his surprise the mayor accepted, renewing the debate about civil rights that they had started so long before.

EYES ON THE PRIZE: KOCH GOES SOUTH

In August 1964 Koch went to Mississippi for eight days to defend civil rights workers who had been registering voters. He made no bones about his political motivations, by his own account rejecting an assignment in Tennessee that would not have seemed as dangerous to his constituents (though it was) and asking to be sent to Mississippi. When he arrived in Jackson, the coordinators for the Lawyers' Constitutional Defense Committee, Marion Wright and Peter Edelman, sent him out with a young civil rights worker named Perlman to Laurel, Mississippi, to defend a group of white and black college students who had been charged with assault after a lunch counter sit-in at the local Kress's.[41]

After the sheriff brought the defendants into the courtroom, a white farmer stood up and assaulted one of the accused. Despite Koch's entreaties, the sheriff refused to intervene. After the arraignment Koch and Perlman set out for the county clerk's office to pick up some transcripts of earlier trials. A crowd of ten or fifteen white farmers menacingly clapped their hands in unison and followed the two around town, threatening to put them through a shivaree—an ancient and violent ritual of humiliation that might end in beating or death. Perlman had been beaten up in Hattiesburg and recognized the signs, so the two suddenly turned about, walked sharply through the surprised crowd, and headed back to the courthouse.[42]

At first the local prosecutor would not lift a finger to protect them but then helped Koch to a phone, which he used to call the Laurel office of the FBI. Someone picked up the phone and said in a thick drawl, "Federal Bureau of Investigation, Robert E. Lee speaking." The FBI refused to protect Koch and Perlman, so Koch left his name and told "Lee," "I'll give you my itinerary so that'll make it easier to find the bodies. We're going back to Jackson if we get out of this building." Then the prosecutor helped them slip through a side door to their car, and they returned to Jackson. Koch returned the next day to try the assault case. He even got the judge to order integrated seating in the courtroom. Though all the defendants were convicted, the judge suspended their sentences, suggesting that he "was aware that we were right" that the protesters should not have been convicted at all. On Koch's last day there a group of racist whites from Mississippi attacked an integrated picnic of civil rights workers and beat up some of them.[43]

Intent on publicizing this outrage to a national audience, Koch flew to Atlantic City, where the 1964 Democratic National Convention was about to reject the claim of Fannie Lou Hamer and Mississippi Freedom Democrats to be seated in place of the white-dominated Mississippi delegation. Koch found Joseph Rauh, a Washington insider who headed the liberal Americans for Democratic Action, and told him all about the riot. When Rauh asked the color of the students who were beaten up at the picnic, Koch said, "They were white." According to Koch, Rauh replied, "Can't use it." Koch has insisted that Rauh meant that he was not interested in bringing stories about beatings of whites before the credentials committee, but Rauh said that if he said "can't use it," "it could only have been because I already had the evidence I needed for my case—and *not*, as the Mayor would now have it, because I wasn't interested in such evidence." Rauh further pointed out that he actually did present evidence of violence against whites at the credentials committee hearing on seating the integrated Mississippi Freedom delegation. But Koch, who later asserted that the incident "had a profound impact on me," remained wary of what he called a "double standard" between the suffering of whites and that of blacks in the civil rights movement. He came to believe that all kinds of injustices against whites and the suffering of whites, especially Jews, were often understated and underrated.[44]

Koch's views put him at odds with liberals, radicals, and African American activists, who argued that African Americans had suffered more than whites and should be compensated for centuries of slavery and discrimination in order to surmount past injustices, demands that eventually resulted in affirmative action programs. From these early civil rights days Koch came to believe in color blindness, rather than reparation or affirmative action of any kind for African Americans. To Koch affirmative action evoked the ethnic quotas that Ivy League colleges and others had used to deny Jews admission to top institutions until the fifties, when many instituted test scores and merit as the main criteria for admission. As a result, he opposed quotas in almost any form.

While Koch acknowledged the horrors of racism, he rarely recognized its corollary—white privilege. His unbending opposition to quotas and his lack of sensitivity to the special damage wreaked by the history of slavery and racism would cause a widening schism with many of his closest friends and associates. Helping blacks reach the middle class seemed only fair to many of Koch's cohort who had gotten a leg up (like Koch himself) from the GI bill and Mayor Fiorello La Guardia's integration of Jews and Italians into formerly Irish preserves in the New York City civil service.[45] But this divide occurred early on—Koch never transformed into a conservative upon becoming mayor, as some scholars have suggested. His liberalism and its limits were both remarkably consistent.

Koch returned to the South in 1965. He and a group of VID members took a one-day trip to Alabama to join about thirty thousand blacks and ten thousand whites for a march on George Wallace's capitol in Montgomery in support of the Voting Rights Act. Koch told Jack Newfield, who covered the Montgomery demonstration for the *Village Voice,* that "walking through the Negro section [of the city] made me feel like I was marching through Paris again with the liberation army. The white section was what it must have been like marching through Germany." As Newfield described it, "the symbolism of the scene was inescapable. At the spot where Jefferson Davis was inaugurated, where George Wallace shouted in his inaugural speech in 1961 'Segregation now, segregation tomorrow, segregation forever,' the largest civil-rights demonstration in the history of the South sang 'We Shall Overcome'—black and white together."[46] Koch revealingly interpreted the events of the civil rights movement in terms of the Second World War—a sort of replay of the Jews' struggle against fascism, an interpretation that remains at the core of much misunderstanding between blacks and Jews. From the beginning of his career, he participated in the civil rights movement, but he always believed that legal equality should be the primary tool to end racial inequality.

DE SAPIO COMEBACK?

The civil rights revolution almost ended Ed Koch's political career but not because of his forays into the South. The Supreme Court gave federal district courts the green light to order reapportionments of state legislative and congressional districts to allow equal representation for each citizen, in the 1962 case of *Baker v. Carr*. It took a few years for the principle to be implemented, but by 1965 VID was faced with reapportionment plans that would split up its original district. This was no coincidence. Louis DeSalvio, a regular from the adjacent district who was close to Carmine De Sapio, chaired the state assembly committee in charge of reapportionment.

At the same time Mayor Wagner named city council member J. Raymond Jones, known as "the Harlem Fox," to chair the New York County Democratic Party. Jones, an independent but dedicated regular, helped start the careers of many prominent black New York politicians, including three of Koch's future mayoral opponents: Percy E. Sutton, Herman D. Farrell, and David N. Dinkins. Jones disliked the reformers on general principles, and the Village Independent Democrats had particularly annoyed him by opposing Constance Baker Motley, a young black attorney, for Manhattan borough president. According to one account, Koch had inadvertently insulted Jones, who then decided to try to cut him off at the knees politically.[47]

The new reapportionment plan split the Village at Sixth Avenue and put Koch and Greitzer's residences in separate districts. These lines made a De Sapio comeback a real possibility, especially after a federal court threw out a VID challenge to the scheme.[48] Worse yet for Koch, Ray Jones accused him in the *New York Times* of telling district leaders at a reapportionment meeting, "I can't win with all those Italians in my [new] district. I want them out."[49] Years later Jones stuck by his story. Koch denied it with "the courage of a kamikaze pilot," but the damage was done, and Koch believed that it might be the end of his political career.[50]

Miki Wolter, one of Koch's closest friends and political advisers at the time, thought that Jones had set him up—telling Koch something like "you don't want so many Italians in your district" and then quoting him based on any sign of assent he may have given to the proposition. If there was such a ruse, it worked because "Ed was quite naive politically," Wolter added.[51] Wolter was walking around the Village with a dejected Koch as he contemplated the end of his political career, when they decided spontaneously that the best thing to do was just walk right down to the South Village and talk to people. The pair walked "along the streets, just saying hello to people," telling them that Koch did not say the terrible things Jones accused him of. "It worked much better than if we had planned it. He was recognized. There was a bit of grumbling, some hostile comments, while others shook his hand and said, 'Glad to see you down here,' and a crowd developed, and they walked with us," she said.[52] His friends in MANA, the neighborhood organization he had set up, continued to trust him. A few days after the election De Sapio loyalist Pete Canevari told Koch he ought to resign from MANA "for what you did." Referring to the comment about Italians, and denying it once again, Koch submitted his resignation to the board, saying the work and nonpartisan nature of the organization were more important. He then left the room while the board deliberated. But then Wally Popolizio came out and told Koch that the board, including some strong De Sapio loyalists, had voted unanimously to ask him to stay.[53]

In 1965 Koch had had his eye on an at-large seat on the city council; this council member was elected by voters throughout Manhattan. Instead he faced another, very chancy run for his political life against Carmine De Sapio for district leader.[54] De Sapio began a well-financed campaign and hit Koch for pushing VID to endorse Koch's close friend Leonard Sandler for a judgeship after a screening panel had recommended another candidate. De Sapio also faulted Koch for opposing the war in Vietnam, telling a reporter that a district leader should not "have a Vietnam position different from the President's."[55]

Koch told reporters less than a month before the primary that he was seriously worried about his third contest in as many years. The new district split the Village and added new, heavily Italian, territory in the South Village, where De Sapio could expect 70 percent of the vote. And there was a slice of "terra incognita" that ran along the West Side waterfront as far north as Forty-fifth Street.[56] In the end the new northern territory helped Koch, who finally beat De Sapio by the solid margin of more than 500 votes.

De Sapio, who for years had been a huge obstacle for Koch, was now cast off for good. But before Koch could run for anything, he and the reformers would have to deal with the uncomfortable results of the mayoral primary. They viewed the nominee, Abraham D. Beame, the city's comptroller, as a colorless product of the Brooklyn machine. Beame, a diminutive accountant then in his mid-sixties, had risen through the civil service to be budget director and then ran for the comptroller's job. He was surprisingly liberal, certainly more committed to the municipal welfare state than Koch. But many reformers thought Beame embodied Mayor Wagner's blandness without the incumbent's considerable talents for negotiation. "I didn't like what he stood for, and I didn't think he could lead the city effectively," Koch later wrote of Beame.[57] The Democratic victor in the primary for comptroller was Mario Procaccino, who seemed to the reformers to be ideologically closer to Barry Goldwater than to LBJ.[58] The combination of Beame and Procaccino put many reformers in a ticket-switching mood.

To some Manhattan-centric VID members, Beame seemed like a political throwback from the hierarchical Brooklyn clubhouse. In contrast, the Republican-Liberal mayoral nominee, John V. Lindsay, was a handsome, dashing, Yale-educated lawyer. As their member of Congress, he was well known and generally liked in Village reform circles. In Washington Lindsay had replaced a lion of the Old Right, Frederick Coudert. Unlike his McCarthyite predecessor, Lindsay had strongly opposed continuation of the House Un-American Activities Committee and had made a reputation as a strong civil libertarian. No single phrase can better encapsulate the energetic image he tried to cultivate than his campaign slogan: "He is fresh and everyone else is tired."[59]

Faced with what they saw as clubhouse blandness, Koch and VID opted out, refused to endorse the Democratic candidate, and took the most radical anti-Beame position of any Democratic club in the city. Even the Riverside Democrats on the Upper West Side, one of the closest politically to VID, toed the Democratic line and backed Beame. Most reformers had chafed at the very cautious pace of change under Wagner. The reformers justifiably feared that the city was decaying as crime increased, and the effects of redlining, white flight, and deindustrialization had become painfully visible. Lindsay's energy and finesse seemed to them more like what the city needed. They saw little prospect that Beame could do anything about the city's problems.

ANOTHER "TRAINED MONKEY" FOR LINDSAY

Koch, Carol Greitzer, and Martin Berger, the president of VID, called a press conference two days before the election and, without a club vote, personally endorsed John Lindsay for mayor—an act that Koch remembers as "political heresy." He had defied both the city's Democratic Party and the participatory democratic principles of the reform movement.[60] The club never voted to endorse Lindsay, though in a vote after the fact, its members overwhelmingly ratified their leaders' action.[61] No one expected the explosion of publicity that the VID leaders' endorsement generated. On election day the *New York Daily News* ran a huge headline: "LBJ and Humphrey Push Beame; Reform Dem Koch Backs Lindsay." At a live televised event to publicize Lindsay, Koch was confounded by the scions of conservative wealth and privilege: "All I can say to myself is, these are terrible people. I wouldn't associate with these people. These are all the richies, all the people who are dilettantes. These are not the people who would ever be supportive of me. I don't like them politically, and I don't like them socially. What the hell am I doing here?" Koch, who was capable of unexpected bouts of shyness, said he felt like a "trained monkey" and turned down the offer of Lindsay's campaign manager to put Koch on television to repeat his endorsement.[62] The ease and empathy that Koch later achieved with the rich, the famous, and the television camera, compared with the discomfort he felt at the beginning of his career, was one of the greatest differences between the young "liberal" Koch of the 1960s and the neoliberal Koch of the 1980s.

Koch and Greitzer's endorsement of Lindsay enraged the regular Democrats. If they had had the power to do so, some district leaders probably would have hanged and quartered Koch and Greitzer. As it was, the worst they could do was expel them from the county executive committee, a futile gesture. Tammany chair J. Raymond Jones put Koch and Greitzer through a savage tongue lashing in the Binnacle Room of the Commodore Hotel in midtown Manhattan. But the boisterous session, in which East Side leaders P. Vincent "Duke" Viggiano and Louis DeSalvio called Koch and Greitzer traitors and bums, ended with only a slap on the wrist.[63]

Koch continued to argue with regular leaders as the imbroglio spilled out into Forty-second Street during rush hour; he nearly started a fistfight in front of television cameras with District Leader Mitch Bloom, who was nursing a broken leg. *Village Voice* reporter Mary Perot Nichols told her readers that as passers-by stopped to watch, goggle-eyed Koch taunted the old-line leader: "I know why you're mad—because you're going to lose your job" under Lindsay. Bloom, who was also a deputy highway commissioner, waved his cane in Koch's face and shouted, "I'm a Democrat! I wouldn't work under a Republican administration! You—you would take any dog-catcher's job if you could get it." Koch turned toward the cameras and explained that he supported Lindsay because he was against patronage and thought it was wrong for any district leader to hold a city job. As Nichols reported:

> Bloom hollered, "I got a broken leg, but I could take you on without a leg." "What's going on?" asked a bystander. "Oh, it's just a Tammany Hall meeting," replied another. "It's about Koch supporting Lindsay." "They ought to keep him on," said the first man, "he's the hottest thing they've got."[64]

6 A REBEL WITH REASON

Koch did not stay district leader for long after Lindsay's election in the fall of 1965, as he won a seat on the New York City Council the next year. At his swearing-in ceremony, Lindsay's parks commissioner, Thomas Hoving, called him "a rebel with reason," a moniker that Koch, many years later, changed to "a liberal with sanity" as he moved to the right and positioned himself to run for mayor.

Despite Koch's crucial endorsement of Lindsay, the new mayor had appointed a conservative Republican banker, Woodward Kingman, to fill the vacancy on the city council created when the incumbent took over Lindsay's seat in Congress. Kingman then had had to run in a special election against the Democratic candidate—Ed

Koch. The real contest was one of personality: Koch, the brash New Yorker, and Kingman, the staid banker, could hardly have been more different.

Koch moved swiftly to organize a campaign as soon as he heard of the vacancy, proclaiming that his candidacy would "reflect the concerns" of his campaign's co-chairs, Michael Harrington and Jane Jacobs. Harrington was the author of the famous 1962 study of poverty *The Other America*, and Jacobs's *Life and Death of Great American Cities* had revolutionized thinking about city planning. Koch also got enthusiastic support from MANA activists, who appreciated his three years of work to clean up the "mess on MacDougal," though the MacDougal neighborhood continued to become less residential and more entertainment oriented throughout this period.[1] "I don't give a damn whether he moved mountains or not, he tried," said MANA chair Wally Popolizio.[2] He and another MANA activist, Dina Nolan, opened an independent "Koch for Council" storefront at 83 MacDougal Street. Nolan, who was a Republican precinct captain, reportedly turned down an offer of $1,000 from a Republican state senator, to quit the Koch campaign.[3] The South Village had voted solidly for De Sapio; in the three district leader races Koch had been the "outsider." Now he united all but the diehards among the feuding factions in the Village.

Through the help of his close friend Henry Stern, Koch secured the crucial early support of the Liberal Party, which, unlike the mayor himself, was grateful for Koch's endorsement of Lindsay. Democrats, allergic to pulling a Republican lever, often voted for liberal Republicans such as Senator Jacob Javits or Lindsay on the Liberal line. Conversely, the party's endorsement made it easier for a reform Democrat like Koch to attract liberal Republican voters. The Liberals, as it turned out, provided Koch's margin of victory, but they also forestalled any serious Democratic primary challengers, by guaranteeing Koch's position on the November ballot as a spoiler. With Koch splitting the general election vote as a Liberal, no other Democrat could hope to win the seat.[4] After four straight years of political campaigns and community activism, Koch was far better known than Kingman. A private poll cited by Newfield in the *Village Voice* showed Koch behind only President Johnson and Senator Robert F. Kennedy in voter recognition in the district. And strong editorial support from the *Voice* helped assure big majorities in the Village and Chelsea.[5]

Lindsay endorsed his appointee, Kingman, but permitted Hoving, who was a popular parks commissioner, to endorse Koch a few days before the election. Koch thought that because he was the overwhelming favorite to win and had crossed parties to support the mayor, the mayor should return the favor and endorse him. In the end, Koch won by a comfortable margin of about 3 percent.[6] He carried all but two of the election districts in the Village and all ten of its Italian districts. Koch recalls his first taste of victory in a race for public office as surpassingly sweet. On election night Koch took a cab from VID headquarters to the MacDougal Street storefront opened by Popolizio and Nolan. When he arrived, the crowd outside the store filled the street. Many people held up candles, and the street thumped with cries of joy at his election victory. Tom Hoving leaped onto an office table and began to dance a jig. Then the crowd, chanting, lifted Hoving and Koch up on their shoulders. "It was a night like no other I'll ever go through—just sheer joy and love and affection came from these people. I'll never forget it as long as I live," Koch later wrote.[7] The most important lesson of his city council victory was that cheers from conservative Catholics as well liberal reformers were the key to his advancement.[8]

LINDSAY STRIKES OUT ON MACDOUGAL

Winning conservative support did not require Koch to abandon liberalism, and he did not. Courting conservatives did require him to show respect for the organic and hierarchical political values of conservative communities. He modified his priorities in light of their political needs. For example, without reversing his position on the right to sing, he went from being the defender of the Washington Square Park folksingers to an apostle of order on MacDougal Street.

Both MANA and Koch initially hoped for much from the Lindsay administration. Lindsay seemed committed to the same kind of decentralized politics as Koch and Jane Jacobs. But for white ethnics much of Lindsay's promise of more power for neighborhoods proved empty and provided Koch with a primer on how not to be mayor. While Wagner had been infuriatingly cautious about making commitments, keeping expectations low, the Lindsay administration tended to raise hopes that would soon be dashed. MacDougal Street is a good case study. At first Lindsay's deputy mayor, Robert Price, met with cheers when he promised a MANA meeting that the city would begin cleaning up the area within thirty days and said he was designating a special mayoral assistant to supervise it. "The audience was in such high spirits that little business could be transacted after he departed," the *Voice* reported.[9]

Unfortunately, the man Lindsay appointed to clean up MacDougal Street was James Marcus, a socialite-turned-compulsive-gambler. Marcus was later indicted on charges that he received kickbacks as water commissioner and used the money to pay back his gambling debts to Tony "Ducks" Corallo (cited by the FBI as an organized crime figure). Carmine De Sapio was also fingered in the Marcus case and was convicted in 1969 in a bribery conspiracy that stemmed from a scheme to get kickbacks from Consolidated Edison.[10]

Marcus's bright idea for MacDougal Street, a police-enforced curfew, caused a small riot. The *Daily News* headline read "Village Horde Foils Cleanup: Cops Yield to 1,500 Beatniks." The sport of dodging the curfew attracted even larger crowds of young people.[11] Koch had predicted the failure of the curfew and suggested more sensibly that instead of arresting crowds of minors, the police should simply check their IDs and notify their parents.[12]

Lindsay himself showed up later that spring at the Village Gate nightclub for a meeting with both MANA and the various MacDougal Street nightclub owners. Almost all factions applauded his pledges to direct the police not to entrap homosexuals or censure the avant-garde. As the discussion progressed, the mayor revealed his superficial knowledge of the neighborhood's problems, which angered activists. While a mayor normally would not be expected to know all the issues in every neighborhood (though as mayor Koch tried his best), Lindsay had represented the area in Congress less than a year before and should have been an expert. The neighborhood people insisted that their problem was not with the avant-garde counterculture; they favored broad civil liberties and free noncommercial culture. Their problem was with the nightclub operators, who created noise that repeatedly disturbed their sleep.[13] While Lindsay assured MANA chair Wally Popolizio that the city would enforce noise and zoning laws, the mayor made it clear that he was really more interested in protecting the avant-garde than local residents. Moreover, he seemed unable to distinguish the drunken teenage tourists, who made the residents miserable, from the avant-garde itself. Many artists and the remaining bohemians were also residents who did not appreciate fifteen-year-old boys urinating on their doorsteps any more than the local Italian grocer did.

A year later Lindsay had accomplished almost nothing for MacDougal Street, except to demonstrate his lack of concern, in contrast to the days when Mayor Wagner overruled commissioners, even on big issues like the use of Washington Square Park, in order to please the community. Koch grew increasingly irritated with Lindsay because he believed that the mayor had treated him with disrespect and that the mayor's inaction had hurt the neighborhood. The mayor's opposition to Koch's political ambitions soon hardened into hostility to Koch himself and made it difficult for the council member to deliver to his constituents. The old party structure that Koch had worked so hard to bring down had actually served neighborhoods better than he realized. Lindsay, elected independent of any party organization, owed little to anyone, except the people who had paid for his television ads. Koch, in turn, was angered by Lindsay's failure to assist him politically and began to treat the mayor as a political enemy, denouncing him ever more stridently.

Koch's response was to step up community organizing. MANA turned the former grocery that had served as the Koch campaign storefront into a community center, and Councilman Koch kept office hours there on Wednesday nights. The office was staffed afternoons, about twenty-five hours a week. Koch had managed to recruit local Italians as volunteers to work alongside VID members, creating precisely the sort of face-to-face community effort that fit with VID's vision of participatory democracy.[14]

MANA even borrowed the tactics of the civil rights movement. The association, which had gotten tour buses banned from MacDougal, hired its own buses and trooped, five hundred strong, including Koch, to Gracie Mansion, where members picketed with signs such as "Good Night Sweet Prince. Keep until tomorrow. You can. You don't live on MacDougal Street"; "Everybody needs a scene. Does the Village have to serve the whole metropolitan area?"; "We Want a Mayor, Not Peter Pan" (a reference to the mayor's seeming absorption in Never-Never Land, not his sexuality). The group also made a reference to the mayor's peculiar response to council member Ed Koch's role in organizing the demonstration. Lindsay had exclaimed lamely that "Koch is so weak, he will probably fall down after walking around the Mansion once." Ed's constituents roared back from the picket lines: "Mayor is weak, Koch is strong."[15]

Koch's "weakness" stemmed from the fecklessness of the New York City Council, a weak body that usually doomed to oblivion bills from first-year reformers. Koch found the council a "gaggle of clowns" that did little more than change the names of streets. But he proved a wiz at getting the press to cover him.[16] He hung out in the press room and touted new and interesting ideas in an age that demanded them. Almost immediately, he introduced high-profile legislation that made headlines, though it had no chance of passage. No legislation moved without the permission of Majority Leader David Ross, who sometimes consigned bills to committees that met triennially.[17]

Council members were paid only $10,000 a year, which explains part of the body's docility. As part-time legislators, most members concentrated on earning a living. In addition to the city salary, each council member got $5,000 "in lieu of expenses," without having to account for the money. Council members and state legislators (who received similar benefits) generally pocketed these "lulus," as they are still known in New York politics. During the campaign Koch pledged to use his lulu to hire young policy analysts to suggest new legislation and areas for political action. Soon after the election he received two hundred applications from a variety of professionals with experience in law, government, business, and academia.[18] The people he hired during his two-year stint on the city council, many of them young corporate lawyers, became part of a permanent brain trust that served Koch for the rest of his career. These advisers met every Monday evening at Koch's apartment, helping the council member soak up information about public policy from urban to foreign affairs. He even took lessons on becoming more telegenic. The seminars began his transformation from a small-time lawyer to a big-time politician.

From the beginning Koch proved sensitive to the radical changes taking place in neighborhoods in the outer boroughs. Throughout the 1960s and '70s "redlining" was pushing white families into the suburbs. This was the collusion of banks, developers, and federal mortgage agencies to deny financing to areas with older housing stock, particularly if the neighborhood had even a few nonwhite residents. The Federal Home Loan Corporation actually sent out surveyors to determine the precise racial composition and condition of housing stock in each neighborhood, mapping in red areas considered unsuitable for financing. The lenders wanted to force whites out of older housing stock in the city and into new construction in all-white neighborhoods or suburbs for the benefit of developers and banks. Redliners devalued many homes in urban neighborhoods, especially in the outer boroughs, forcing residents to sell and flee or face losing the life savings they had put into a house.[19]

"Blockbusters" also destabilized white neighborhoods. These unscrupulous real estate agents sold houses in white neighborhoods to African American clients, which often led to redlining by the home loan system, which tightened the availability of credit in neighborhoods with even a small number of black residents. Then the agents would prey upon white residents' racism and fear of financial loss, setting off a stampede of whites to sell their homes. These agents profited from their commissions on the resulting transactions as white and middle-class black families unloaded their houses, turning integrated neighborhoods into segregated ghettos.[20]

Koch proposed an unusual scheme to stop blockbusting: government-sponsored insurance against declines in property values stemming from a change in the racial or ethnic composition of a neighborhood. He claimed that the program would "offer the Negro family genuine choice of satisfactory housing in any urban or suburban neighborhood." In addition, Koch's bill called for a task force to promote the rehabilitation of housing in black neighborhoods. The proposal went nowhere—the submissive city council was not one to take on the powerful real estate and banking industry, and claims under his proposed insurance would have been difficult to adjudicate. But Koch did not stop offering new ideas to his moribund colleagues.[21]

He continued his crusade against the automobile in New York City, urging the elimination of commuter discounts for autos on the bridges and tunnels into the city and introducing a bill to take the Lower Manhattan Expressway off the city's planning maps.[22] The expressway, a Moses project, would have ravaged a swath of the Lower East Side, Little Italy, and the South Village so that big trucks could get from Brooklyn to New Jersey twenty minutes faster. The project had popped up again when the Lindsay administration approved a plan to bury the western part of the road, which would then emerge above ground to bisect Little Italy. Along with allies like Jane Jacobs, who was arrested while protesting at the Board of Estimate hearing that approved the project, Koch continued to fight the plan in the city council and in Congress. The highway was never built, saving what are now SoHo and the northern part of Chinatown from destruction.[23]

Koch's anti-auto program was not simply a reflection of his subway-bound constituency. Jane Jacobs's insight that crowded city streets generate a safe, productive, and interesting city society intrigued him because Koch loved the streets—he loved campaigning, talking to people, and trying to do justice. From the beginning of his campaign for city council, he became a fixture on the streets of his district, leafleting in the mornings at subway stops and shaking hands with hundreds of passers-by on the crowded New York avenues. He did not stop just because he won elections. Throughout his career Ed Koch spent as much time as he could on the sidewalks of New York.

KOCH FOR CONGRESS

Frustrated by the political irrelevance of city council, Koch determined to move up to a job with some real power. "This is not where I'm ending up," he told David Brown, one of his aides.[24] He did not waste much time. After only a year on the council, Koch declared his candidacy for Lindsay's old House seat in the 1968 election, and it looked like a very good bet. The incumbent, liberal Republican Theodore Kupferman, had won the February 1966 special election by the narrow margin of 995 votes.[25] The district, though Republican for the previous thirty-one years, was becoming more Democratic and seemed ripe for picking, especially when Kupferman took a judgeship and left the seat without an incumbent. Koch had won his council seat in almost the same district by more than 2,000 votes against a slightly more conservative Republican.

Koch announced that he would run as a peace candidate and as a supporter of Senator Eugene McCarthy's. McCarthy, the Minnesota Democrat, had challenged President Johnson's renomination and nearly defeated the president in the New Hampshire primary because of the unpopularity of the war. Declaring urban affairs and Vietnam to be the most important issues of the campaign, Koch called for a halt to the bombing of North Vietnam and a step-by-step deescalation of the war.[26] By March, Koch had won the backing of the VID over Allard K. Lowenstein, the impresario of the McCarthy campaign, by a lopsided vote of 88–11. Koch also got the Liberal designation, crucial to attracting Liberal Republican crossovers and even more important to deny Democratic crossovers to any liberal Republican opponent.[27]

After LBJ quit the presidential race on March 31, 1968, Robert F. Kennedy announced his candidacy.[28] Koch unhesitatingly threw his support behind the New York senator, because he felt Kennedy had a better chance than McCarthy or Hubert Humphrey of defeating the Republicans and preferred Kennedy's muscular brand of liberalism and strong anticommunist credentials. But VID remained stubbornly unbossed. Some VID members mistrusted RFK's famous toughness and his intensely competitive demeanor; to many he was just another macho opportunist who had toadied to Joe McCarthy. They often used the word *ruthless* to describe him, implying that he was a Democratic Nixon. RFK's cult of personality, moreover, was anathema to many believers in participatory democracy.[29] Eugene McCarthy, known for his dreamy indifference to ambition, catalyzed the idealists, but he had less appeal for the pragmatists.[30] Koch and Stanley Geller, both Kennedy supporters, found themselves in a minority of 108 to 8, as the club overwhelmingly reendorsed McCarthy.[31]

For the first time but not the last, Koch found himself to the right of his home club. Despite some fierce arguments, Koch would maintain ties with VID well into his first term as mayor. But after he became a Kennedy backer, he was politically not quite one of them, despite his nearly consistent 100 percent rating from the liberal Americans for Democratic Action. Koch had to cater to a congressional district that was more conservative than his home area in the Village. Although he came out against the war in 1966, making him among the earliest Democratic doves, Koch embraced the basic validity of cold war doctrines such as containment and anticommunism, distancing himself from much of the antiwar movement by 1968 on these issues. Yet, despite his continuing commitment to the cold war, Koch retained the peace movement's support because he insisted that the United States should withdraw from Vietnam and because he championed the movement's use of public space for public protest.

On April 4, 1968, Martin Luther King was assassinated in Memphis, followed by widespread rioting across the United States. Mayor Lindsay took credit for New York's emerging unscathed. Koch had to delay the opening of his campaign office, out of respect. A few days later he began to engage his two opponents in the Democratic congressional primary, Paul Rao, a Tammany Democrat who had served as the citywide chair of the Beame campaign. Rao was out to avenge Koch's endorsement of Lindsay for mayor in 1965. Koch's other opponent, the real estate executive John McKean, advertised his support for McCarthy, though he had supported LBJ until the president's withdrawal.

All three were doves though not of a feather. Koch had the most elaborate position. He favored unconditional cessation of the bombing of North Vietnam, a negotiated settlement with the National Liberation Front (derogatively called the Viet Cong) and, after negotiations, withdrawal of U.S. troops from Vietnam. Rao and McKean merely wanted to refer the matter to the UN General Assembly. Koch supported rent control and the Ford Foundation's proposals for decentralizing the New York City school system. McKean favored subsidies for low-interest mortgages instead of rent control. All the candidates raised the issue of New York's rising crime rate.[32]

The central issue of the primary race, however, was "dissent." Did citizens have the right to condemn U.S. foreign policy? Was it right to engage in protest marches and civil disobedience against the administration? Koch answered in the affirmative. His opponents, particularly Rao, believed, in line with the hierarchical philosophy of the regular Democrats, that patriotism required deference to executive elites and party leadership. Deference was never Ed Koch's strong suit, which is what many voters liked about him. Koch was usually willing to argue and think, and he believed in protest as a legitimate and necessary part of the political system.

Koch's constant attention to his district paid dividends; he received 62 percent of the primary vote, defeating Rao with more than 15,000 votes out of the 25,000 cast, and McKean came in a distant third. The Republican primary augured ill for Koch's Republican opponent, state senator Whitney North Seymour Jr., a descendant of one of New York's most prominent families, who—in contrast to Koch's massive primary victory—barely edged out, 12,291–10,851, Assemblyman S. William Green, the scion of the Grand Union supermarket chain (who would eventually succeed Koch in the seat).[33]

In the primary McCarthy captured almost half the state's delegates to the Democratic National Convention, and McCarthy backer Paul O'Dwyer, the younger brother of former mayor William O'Dwyer, won the Democratic nomination to challenge incumbent Republican senator Jacob K. Javits. In the wake of the assassination of RFK, Koch had reendorsed McCarthy, telling the press, "The war in Vietnam must end. Poverty in the country must no longer be tolerated." McCarthy later reciprocated by endorsing Koch, despite the congressional candidate's temporary defection.[34]

The violence of the August 1968 Democratic convention in Chicago shocked the country and particularly liberal Democrats like Koch. He refused to support Hubert Humphrey, because the vice president "would not call off Mayor Daley's Gestapo."[35] Koch had watched Daley's police clubbing demonstrators on television, and, as the New Yorker saw it, "the overwhelming number of demonstrators were decent human beings, students for the most part. And in many cases, pedestrians and onlookers were caught up in the melee and bullied by the police. You saw that on television. You saw Alex Rosenberg, district leader from the 19th Congressional district, whom I know, pulled out of the hall. You saw Paul O'Dwyer pulled out of the hall." Humphrey was at fault because "he is not his own man. He had obligations to President Johnson and Mayor Daley which prevented him from criticizing the president's policies and the use of excessive police force," Koch declared. Nonetheless, as the election of Richard Nixon grew more likely, Koch began telling people to vote for Humphrey. Even VID finally embraced the Humphrey campaign though so sullenly that it seemed to mock Humphrey's declaration that he represented "the politics of joy."[36]

Through all this Koch stayed on message. David Brown wrote John Lankenau, Koch's campaign manager, on September 1 that "the premises of the campaign plan agreed to in early July appear to be still valid."[37] These called for Koch to run as "a new kind of Congressman," who, in Brown's words, would "speak out for radical change in our nation's priorities" and "publicly question the long-held assumptions of [his] own political party."[38]

So how radical was Koch in 1968? He pledged to support repeal of the 1964 Tonkin Gulf Resolution, cited by the president as congressional authorization to deploy combat troops to Indochina. Koch also called for a cutting off Defense Department funding to stop both the bombing of North Vietnam and the escalation of the war in South Vietnam. But Koch favored a redefinition of national security that was closer to Eisenhower's than Abbie Hoffman's. Koch synthesized Democratic and Republican positions of the 1950s. Like Ike, he felt that domestic concerns and the health of the civilian economy should enter into calculations of the value of military spending, but as a good liberal Democrat, he hoped to create a peace dividend that could free up money for a "significant shift" to domestic spending, especially for cities.[39]

Koch called for a new "GI bill" for workers and the poor that would subsidize their job training, just as Koch had gotten a year of salary from the GI bill to start his law practice, and he called for massive sharing of federal income-tax revenues with localities to fight poverty and reverse the decay of cities. Some other important Koch proposals included creation of a federal ombudsman's office and allowing citizens access to their own FBI files.[40] Finally, Koch tried to address the issue of crime, calling for stringent gun control, including registration and a ban on the mail-order sale of guns, and rehabilitative programs, such as increased funding for drug treatment and methadone programs. He later voted for the death penalty but did not advertise it, as much of his liberal base would have been outraged.[41]

Koch's district reached from the Village across Manhattan and up the wealthy East Side, known for generations as the Silk Stocking District, though its population was becoming more middle class. The differences in Koch's and Seymour's styles, which reflected their class and ethnicity, separated them far more than their differences on the issues. The willingness to press flesh and mount soapboxes on the public streets marked the most important distinction between Edward Irving Koch, the son of struggling Galitzianers, and Whitney North Seymour, a scion of New York's Gilded Age bourgeoisie. Both were conscious of this. During the campaign Koch proudly picketed a supermarket that was selling grapes in violation of the national boycott called by César Chávez and the United Farm Workers, and Koch pointed to his record of demonstrating at the "plaza of lost causes"—UN Plaza—against both the Vietnam War and the Soviet invasion of Czechoslovakia. Seymour offered up his own idea of the space in which politics should be transacted: "I've never joined any kind of protest march or demonstration" (except for one to ban automobiles from Central Park, which Koch said he also attended "at the head of the march"). "That's the difference between Ed Koch and me—he demonstrates and I get work done." Seymour often trumpeted his almost-perfect attendance record in the state senate (he sacrificed many important primary campaign appearances in order to keep it near perfect; it was marred only when Governor Rockefeller asked him to attend the funeral of Martin Luther King). Seymour claimed sponsorship of "more than 125 bills" that were enacted into law, compared with what he said was Koch's lackluster legislative record on the city council. The figure is somewhat deceptive, as Mayor Lindsay made Seymour the official conduit in the legislature for the city's bills, many of which were passed as a matter of routine, and most did not originate with the Silk

Stocking state senator.[42] Lindsay's endorsement of Seymour enraged Koch, who still felt that he deserved at least neutrality in return for his election-eve endorsement of Lindsay. According to Koch, Lindsay's subsequent statement that Koch's election was a catastrophe for New York made the new U.S. representative a permanent and dangerous adversary of the mayor's.[43]

Seymour's disdain for street politics may have cost him the election. He spent his ample campaign funds on mailings, paid staff, and trying to attract organizational support. Koch relied on about three hundred volunteer canvassers and his personal presence on the street. Seymour had simply not understood the fundamental importance of pressing the flesh, particularly in densely populated Manhattan, where a local candidate can still meet an appreciable percentage of the electorate on the street.

One day, while Koch was meeting voters at the Stuyvesant Town subway stop at Fourteenth Street and First Avenue, Seymour pulled up in a car bedecked with campaign signs and offered Koch a ride. "When did you get here?" the Republican asked. "Seven o'clock," Koch replied. "How long have you been doing this?" Seymour asked again. Koch told him, "About a year." According to Koch, "There was a pregnant silence, and I believe it sunk in that he was facing a real problem." Seymour was only beginning to understand what Koch had long since mastered—the power of performing in the city's public spaces. Seymour even took a vacation in the middle of the campaign. Koch, who had been campaigning almost continuously for six years, kept on shaking hands.[44]

When the results came in, they were surprisingly close. Koch won with 48 percent, or 74,627 votes (16,499 on the Liberal Party line), to 45 percent (70,086 votes) for Seymour and 5.8 percent (9,030 votes) for the Conservative Party candidate, Richard J. Callahan.[45] Koch now had the potential to gain a citywide, even a national, audience. He had been sold as a "new" kind of representative. He had become a purveyor of programs, committed to taking the schemes of his wonky associates off the drawing board and putting them into action. But though Koch was legislatively ambitious, getting his ideas through the minefields of Congress would require patience. New members are legendarily powerless. That Koch could parlay his House seat into the mayoralty of New York City still seemed fantastic to almost everyone but the unshakably persistent member of Congress from the East Side.

7 KOCH'S CORRIDOR (1969–76)

When Ed Koch arrived in Congress, the vitality of the Democratic leadership was embodied in the dozing form of Speaker John W. McCormack, who slept in his chair as Nixon addressed the nation. To the old bulls who ruled Congress in January 1969, Koch seemed like a man from outer space. He was one of only fourteen Jewish members for most of the time that he served in Congress, and when he arrived, none of the others had reached the most senior levels.[1] Anti-Semitism still flourished on the Hill in those days, sometimes manifesting itself as intense rural and suburban resistance to anything desired by the good citizens of New York. Sometimes it was hard to miss. As late as 1977, Koch's last year in the House, Senator James O. Eastland of

Mississippi could sneer openly at Senator Jacob Javits, saying, "I don't like you or your kind," because Javits was Jewish.[2]

Since Koch came from what seemed to be another universe—Greenwich Village—he was assigned to the panel least appropriate to his interests, the Committee on Science and Astronautics, for his first year in the House. His meager power there was limited to blasting the rocketry budget, for the National Aeronautics and Space Administration spent nary a penny in Manhattan: "I cannot justify approving monies to find out whether or not there is some microbe on Mars, when in fact I know there are rats in Harlem apartments."[3]

Many liberal members of Congress in those days were condemned to a political vacuum, quarantined permanently on the back benches. But Koch had a knack, as during his stint in the army, for making friends who were very different from him. Koch may have preferred the cosmopolitan Jewish world of New York to provincial, WASPish Washington, D.C., and sports bored him to death, but from his days with the Timberwolves he knew how to hang out with guys from North Texas and South Dakota. And, most important, he learned the rules fast. After some gaffes in the first few months, such as writing Speaker McCormack to reproach him for the arrest of antiwar protesters on the Capitol steps, Koch became "very respectful of the leadership, and that was certainly something that was greatly appreciated," former staffer Ronay Arlt Menschel recalled.[4] Respect in those days meant keeping quiet, learning House business, and accepting the guidance of senior members.

After only a year he had made some friends in Congress and convinced the Democratic leadership of his reliability. The leaders reassigned him to his first choice, Wright Patman's Banking and Currency Committee. This was valuable to Koch's constituents—his district held perhaps the greatest concentration of financial industry executives in the United States. More important to Koch, the committee had jurisdiction over housing programs, one of the issues closest to his heart.

The congressional years were lonely for Koch, who never felt quite at home in the capital city. The House in those days provided no orientation to show new members around town or even how to navigate the vast corridors of the Capitol Building. From the perspective of a New York foodie, the fare in Washington (long before the arrival of Salvadorans and Ethiopians) was expensive and mediocre. Koch dined occasionally at the famous Duke Ziebert's, and sometimes he'd take prominent constituents like the journalist Mary Perot Nichols and the Reverend H. Carl McCall to the House restaurant for lunch. He ate a lot of steak at business luncheons. The corridors of power had a definite lack of schmaltz.[5]

THE BAR MITZVAH BOY AND THE BAPTISTS

Koch responded to his alienation from the Washington scene by making his Jewishness and commitment to Israel central to his identity, in a way that he had not stressed earlier in his political career. The real watershed was the 1973 vote on the $2.2 billion appropriation to replenish Israel's arms supply during and after the Yom Kippur War. The House in those days was rife with open anti-Semitism, as well as questions about whether supporting Israel was in America's national interest. Koch tended to equate one with the other. During the vote Koch overheard a conversation he termed revolting. The participants were Clarence Long, the Maryland Democrat then number two on the foreign operations subcommittee of the Appropriations Committee; and its chair, Otto Passman, Democrat of Louisiana, and Julia Hansen, Democrat from Washington State. Though Long and Passman were both generally supporters of Israel, Long complained to the others that he was voting for the measure despite his sympathy for the Egyptians, because he had many Jews in his district and no Arabs. Passman said he was neutral but that the Jews always asked for more than they should. But he too (in Koch's words) "didn't want trouble in his district," showing that his support was not philosophical but "came probably as the result of campaign contributions from Jewish organizations." Hansen then went off on a bizarre tangent, saying, "You know, I was once cheated by a Jew," and launching into a diatribe about how she did not like Jews.[6]

Koch had always been a fairly secular Jew.[7] As a law school student in 1948 he had cheered when the UN General Assembly pushed the Partition Resolution (recommending the division of Palestine into two provisional states, one Jewish, one Arab) over the top, and he had carried the little *pushka*, the blue and white box for Keren Kayemet (the Jewish National Fund) that was distributed to Jewish households all over the world to raise money for planting trees in Israel. He had family in Israel, ties kept up since his sister, Pat, visited there in the 50s. As a law student he had even collected war surplus bayonets for the Haganah, the main Jewish army in Palestine. But he had never joined any of the numerous Zionist organizations active in New York in the 1940s and 1950s.[8] When he first was elected to Congress, Israel had been less of a concern than the Vietnam War, both to him and his constituents. But by his first year in Congress, Koch had become a kind of Jewish exemplar—in part a reaction to his alienation from, and desire for, acceptance in the white male Christian-dominated House. But Koch also found that his own deeply held beliefs dovetailed with his interests in gaining political support citywide through advocacy of the national causes of Jews, Greeks, and other diasporic communities in New York.

After Sonny Montgomery, a powerful House member from Mississippi, asked Koch to come to a Thursday morning prayer breakfast to talk about Judaism to southern Democrats (they'd had a cancellation), Koch readily agreed. The invitation "brought home to me that I was not only a Congressman, but a Jewish Congressman." Like many American Jews, Koch had never had much formal Jewish education, just what he needed for a bar mitzvah—pronouncing Hebrew characters and what he had picked up from growing up in Jewish neighborhoods. Israel's champion in the House did not know its language and had not even memorized the kaddish, the prayer for the dead. With only four days before the prayer breakfast, Koch rushed to the library and made some notes on a variety of Jewish topics.

His twenty-minute talk at the prayer breakfast explained the difference between the three major branches of Judaism (Reform, Conservative, and Orthodox) and described the Hasidim, whom he compared to the Amish. Koch started the question period himself, citing one query that he believed that his colleagues "might hesitate to ask": "Do Jews have dual loyalty?" Koch answered emphatically that "you wouldn't ask that of a Member who was of French, German, or Irish extraction and whose love of the culture and the country of his antecedents was as strong as that of mine for mine. But in your minds you do ask it of Jews." Then, disarmingly, he "raised his right hand" and promised, "If Israel ever invades America, I shall stand with America." By Koch's account this declaration delighted the prayer breakfasters.[9]

Koch's hurried researches into Judaism became a defining intellectual moment. His typed notes for the talk included "interesting quotes" from the Talmud, two of which became staples:

> If I am not for myself, who is for me? If I am only for myself, what am I? And if not now, when?[10]
>
> Justice and only justice shall you follow.[11]

He even got in a few political licks as a supporter of Nixon's price controls, then one of the dominant issues in Washington, while countering some stereotypes: "The Rabbis taught that the following persons are to be chastised: They who hoard produce in order to corner the market and cause prices to rise; or those who practice usury, or those who inflate prices."[12]

Koch also told the southerners about Masada, the Roman fortress captured by Jewish zealots that the Romans recaptured in 70 C.E. The commander ordered all 960 men, women, and children to commit suicide rather than become slaves. Both the Talmud and Maimonides, according to Koch's notes, disapproved of this mass suicide, which was contrary to Jewish law. Maimonides advocated Jewish adaptation to local conditions, saying, "You should live with them." The Holocaust had changed all that, Koch told the Baptists. The Masada story of zealots standing to the last was taken to heart: "The philosophy changed to one of 'Ein Breirah—we have no choice.' To a large extent that characterizes the feeling of most Israeli leaders today—we no longer have the luxury of relying on other people's good intentions; we have to do the job ourselves. Hitler took away the last choice we had to 'Live with them.'"[13]

Though some often imagine Jewish members of Congress as being in constant contact with the American Israel Public Affairs Committee (AIPAC), Koch said he had relatively little. Like most lawmakers, he got AIPAC mailings but maintains that AIPAC never lobbied him "because they didn't have to." AIPAC expended its efforts on swing votes.[14] Moreover, as a leading pro-Israel legislator, Koch had much more direct sources of information and support within the Jewish community and Israel itself. Many of his Israeli contacts and friendships developed during the three trips he took to Israel while he was in Congress.

Koch made his first trip to Israel in 1971 at the invitation of the Israeli government, which provided a guide, though Koch paid for the trip. Though he was still just a second-term member of Congress with little power, the Israelis treated him as a VIP. He met with Prime Minister Golda Meir, who became so engrossed in their conversation that they wandered out of her office as her security detail scrambled to keep up.[15]

David Ben Gurion, Israel's first president, also met with the young American member of Congress. Koch remembered him as "a tiny man," senile by then but still "a living patriarch," with his trademark halo of white hair jutting back from a long forehead.[16] Koch met Israel's future leaders, as well: Yigal Allon, who would become prime minister; Abba Eban, who would serve as foreign minister; and Pinchas Sapir, who would become finance minister.

On this trip Koch began a lifelong friendship with Teddy Kollek, the energetic Labor Party mayor of Jerusalem from 1965 to 1993 (which coincided with Koch's stint as mayor of New York). Kollek was an unusual figure in Israeli politics, known for his openness to Jerusalem's Arabs. Kollek tried to mitigate the negative impact on the city's Arab citizens of Israeli-sponsored redevelopment and modernization of Jerusalem (with less success after the expansionist Likud Party took over the national government). Koch remembered that even during the First Intifada, Kollek refused any security detail that might inhibit Palestinian citizens of the city from approaching him.[17]

Koch experienced the Israeli victory in the Six Day War of 1967 as an exhilarating liberation for both Arabs and Jews, a perspective few Arabs shared. His optimism reflected Kollek's idealistic multicultural vision and mirrored Koch's own then-liberal ideals: "The entire city of Jerusalem is united and people of all faiths . . . come to Jerusalem to walk and pray in their respective holy places. . . . The West Bank has daily communications and travel with Jordan," and Israeli trade with Arab countries was increasing. In contrast, before the war, borders had been closed and a Jewish cemetery was desecrated while Jordan controlled East Jerusalem. Terrorism, Koch reported, was diminishing, and Arab students crossed the border at Al Quintara to attend Egyptian universities.[18] Later Koch would propose to give Jerusalem a binational city administration, with Palestinians voting in national elections for their own national government, while Israelis did the same. "If I can live with Howie Golden as the borough president of Brooklyn, Teddy Kollek can live with a borough president who's Palestinian in East Jerusalem," Koch later quipped.[19]

That Koch could interpret the occupation of Gaza and the West Bank as emancipatory for Arabs reflects his apparent failure to have met or talked to any Arabs on his first two trips. He acknowledged, however, that Israel, like the United States, did have its problems. He highlighted for his constituents his meetings with the "Black Pantherim" (a hebraized version of the Black Panthers), an organization of North African Jews combating discrimination by the European majority.[20] Koch made his second trip to Israel soon after the 1973 Yom Kippur War as part of a House delegation that included his close friend Benjamin S. Rosenthal, a member of the House Foreign Affairs Committee, and representatives Bella Abzug, Joseph P. Addabbo, and Lester Wolff, all from New York City, as well as Koch's close friend Charles Wilson, Democrat of Texas, and Roy A. Taylor, Democrat of North Carolina.[21] These House members seem to have followed separate itineraries on the trip.

Koch and Wilson toured the Sinai so soon after the war that Russian tanks were still burning in the desert. Wilson would go on to become one of the architects of the anti-Soviet guerrilla war in Afghanistan. Famous for his womanizing and foreign policy antics, Wilson is portrayed by the actor Tom Hanks in the film *Charlie Wilson's War* (2007). Koch later recalled that Wilson became enchanted with the beautiful Israeli captain who was their guide. When her commanding officer, concerned about Wilson's intentions, tried to reassign the captain, Koch took the commanding officer aside and told him, "Are you crazy? This woman is 21, let her take care of herself." Nothing happened between the two, but Wilson became one of Israel's biggest boosters in Congress, unusual for an oil-state representative with almost no Jews in his district. He loved the romance of Israel as an underdog and that supporters of Israel filled his campaign coffers. "The AIPAC people loved me because here I was, a cowboy from Texas, hysterical about their cause," Wilson recalled. He eventually managed to get a seat on the Appropriations Committee over the objections of his own delegation. Wilson was investigated in 1982–83 by the House Ethics Committee and the Justice Department and cleared of allegations that he used drugs. Despite his exoneration, Wilson faced a tough primary in 1984 as a result of the accusations, so Mayor Koch organized a fundraiser, telling donors, "This is a man who has less than ten Jewish constituents, but he helps Israel because he believes in it." The donors responded with an estimated $100,000, which helped Wilson stay in office.[22]

Koch and Rosenthal later joined Abzug in a meeting with Prime Minister Golda Meir, who briefed them on alleged Syrian atrocities against Israelis on the Golan front. Abzug then held her own press conference, displaying the photos and grabbing all the glory, which infuriated Koch and Rosenthal. They described her maneuver to the *New York Times* as a "surreptitious, devious mischievous act." In private, Rosenthal was even more scathing, referring to Abzug as "the Beast of Belsen," a notorious concentration camp guard.[23]

On the 1973 trip, as in 1971, Koch did not stop in any Arab countries. Koch did visit Syria or Jordan on his next Mideast trip, in 1975, a ten-day junket with two other members of the Appropriations Subcommittee on Foreign Operations. Syrian President Hafez al-Assad, busy with another visiting leader, declined to meet with the delegation. Uninterested in lower-level contacts that he viewed as propagandistic, Koch insisted that the U.S. embassy arrange a trip for him to a Syrian synagogue. The trip seemed to upset the embassy more than it did the Syrians, until their diplomats read Koch's account in the Travel and Resorts section of the *Times*.

Koch was inexperienced in the Middle East—he'd never been to an Arab country before, and he and his companion, Representative Joe Early, a Massachusetts Democrat, even joked to each other about being murdered on the streets of Damascus— more fear than reality for two U.S. congressmen visiting as honored guests of a police state in a city with a murder rate far lower than Washington's. Accompanied by a driver and a guide from the Syrian Foreign Ministry, Early and Koch set off for three synagogues in Damascus's ancient Jewish quarter, trailed by the official guide and three Palestinian refugees. Koch believed that this hostile entourage inhibited frank conversations with local Jews, which were limited to "such questions as whether a cure for cancer had been found in the United States," and he feared that anyone he talked to about politics might later be subjected to punishment.[24]

The trip did, however, spark his first serious conversation with an Arab politician. Syrian ambassador Sabah Kabbani protested to the *Times* that Syrian Jews suffered no discrimination and that Koch's Travel and Resorts article had reinforced negative stereotypes of Arabs by claiming that they did, though Koch's article made such a charge only implicitly. Koch met Kabbani for lunch soon after and later enlisted his help to reunify thirteen Syrian Jews with their American relatives.[25]

Koch had more fun on the 1975 trip when he reached Israel and continued to expand his powerful circle of friends—that's when he first met Ariel Sharon, then the victorious general of the 1973 war who had enveloped and defeated Egyptian forces that had crossed the Suez Canal. Sharon took the House members on a tour of the Sinai and explained the campaign. Koch was eventually a guest in Sharon's home in the Negev. At the time Koch disagreed with the general that the West Bank should be annexed to Israel.[26]

This new emphasis on Israel and his Jewish identity refocused aspects of Koch's personality that were there from the beginning. In his early political days he had separated his political world into those for and against Ed Koch, with little gray area between. While Koch was prepared to argue about Israel, and would even on occasion rile Israeli leaders with his advice, support for the existence of a Jewish national state became his new litmus test for whether a politician was friend or foe.[27] This, even more than his long-standing anticommunism, separated him from those New Leftists and left liberals who questioned the basic premises of Zionism.

His support for Israel also brought him into conflict with many African American members of Congress. Koch was extremely conscious that many of his black colleagues, including John Conyers, Shirley Chisholm, and Yvonne Braithwaite Burke, sometimes voted against U.S. support for Israel. In a private 1972 letter Koch said that he was both "distressed and angered" that despite Jewish support (including his own) for the civil rights movement, some black leaders and groups were trying to "elevate their own people by standing on the necks of the Jews." He declared, "I will not sit back and tolerate that so long as there is a breath in my body."[28] His concern intensified in 1975 after the UN General Assembly passed Resolution 3379 declaring that Zionism "is a form of racism."

Koch's support for Israel was deeply rooted in his history, emotions, and sense of justice, but it also fit with his later basic strategy of building coalitions between moderate Manhattan liberals and more conservative Jews in the outer boroughs as a path to the mayoralty. Koch also courted other ethnic groups, expressing his empathy for their nationalist causes, attending their events, and wooing their leaders: some journalists later labeled him "Ethnic Ed," though he said and did far less on foreign policy issues that concerned African Americans, probably a reaction to the shakiness of black support for Israel.[29]

Representative Koch furthered his mayoral ambitions by intervening in matters important to white ethnic voters in the outer boroughs as well as some of his own East Side constituents: He highlighted human rights abuses in Hungary, voting against selling a submarine to the Greek dictatorship; he voted to block aid to Turkey to please the city's Greeks, and he supported holding a referendum on independence for Puerto Rico.[30] Liberals cheered when he denounced the Nicaraguan dictator Anastasio Somoza, and the Uruguayan secret police even threatened Koch's life was when he tried to cut off military aid to Uruguay.[31]

It is easy to see these votes as crass attempts to get ethnic votes—during Koch's 1977 mayoral race, his campaign ran ads featuring Italian, Hungarian, and Greek supporters—but this union of ethnic causes ran deeply in a man whose most visceral political belief was support for Israel. He saw other ethnic national causes as analogous and therefore deserving of his support.

"Today I'm Italian. Last week I was Polish. And the week before I was Ukrainian. But every day I'm Jewish. I love the parades. I go to all of them," Koch once declared.[32] Of course, Koch's family came from Galicia, which in the twentieth century was Austrian, Polish, Soviet, and Ukrainian; Italian and Greek were more of a stretch. But Koch thought that stretching his identity was a healthy exercise among New York's diverse populations: "There's nothing wrong with ethnic politics. A lot of people like to talk about the melting pot. It's all bullshit. There is ethnic politics in this country and in this city in particular, and it's okay. More Jews will vote for me than for an ordinary non-Jewish candidate."[33]

He maintained, however, that a better-qualified candidate can overcome an ethnic disadvantage. If no Greek was running for mayor, he wanted to be the Greeks' second choice—a non-Greek whom they knew and trusted. The same principle applied to his hard work on MacDougal Street, where he made himself the second choice of many of the Italians in the neighborhood, who embraced him once Carmine De Sapio left the political scene.

Religion was the key to this strategy, particularly the relationships Koch developed with religious leaders. He assiduously courted rabbis from New York's polymorphous Jewish communities, a forest of ethnicities and political views ranging from radical feminist women rabbis to the most reactionary ultraorthodox men. During his 1973 mayoral bid he even visited the inscrutable Lubavitcher rebbe, Menachem Schneerson, who remained silent throughout the entire interview while Koch talked. When he emerged, he praised the rebbe's brilliance to his followers: "My God, what that man knows about politics!"[34]

Koch's relationship with the Greek Orthodox primate of the Americas, Archbishop Iakovos, was livelier. He helped the archbishop get through to a high State Department official during the 1974 Turkish invasion of Cyprus. Koch was in awe of the Greek primate: "There are some people who exuded saintliness, and he's one of them. I hadn't met anyone else like him, not even my rabbi."[35] Koch became committed to the Greek Cypriot cause, working to cut off military aid to Turkey with Democratic representatives Ben Rosenthal, who represented heavily Greek Astoria, Queens, Paul Sarbanes of Maryland, and John Brademas of Indiana, the latter both Greek Americans. Koch dismissed the arguments of friends who warned him that the Turkish side of the issue had some merit. Assessing the matter in light of Turkey's near alliance with Israel, he later admitted that he may have swung too far against Turkey.[36] But at the time it was local politics that mattered. Koch's close relationship to Archbishop Iakovos was a taste of the much closer ties he would forge as mayor with the Roman Catholic hierarchy.[37]

CONGRESSMAN RISING

In 1970 first-term representatives had but two paths to power. They could climb up the ranks of seniority and reach great heights if their party stayed in the majority, or they could run for higher office. Koch pursued both routes. If he had stayed in the House, his career might have paralleled that of Charles Rangel, who was elected one term after Koch and became chair of the House Ways and Means Committee with power over all spending and tax legislation, but it took Rangel thirty-six years to get there. Koch might have been chair of appropriations, the committee to which he was appointed in 1974; that committee has jurisdiction over all government spending, which makes its chair one of the most powerful individuals in the entire nation.

Alone most of the time, the bachelor House member threw himself into work and gained a reputation for diligence. He gravitated to others who never stopped working. Frequently he'd dine with Ronay Menschel, the brilliant head of his Washington office—she said they were both workaholics. He first met House staffer Diane Coffey, later the manager of both his congressional and mayoral offices, because they both rose early and used to sit together drinking coffee in the early mornings in the almost empty House cafeteria before plunging into a twelve-hour workday. Koch was far more introverted in those days than in his later years. "He was very shy and used to welcome the company," Coffey recalled. When Koch became more influential, he got Wayne Hays, chair of the House Administration Committee, to open the door to the House cafeteria even earlier so members and staffers could get coffee to start the day. Hays dubbed it "Koch's Corridor."[38]

Koch's Corridor was emblematic of his connection to food. He understood the value of lunch more than most members of Congress. He used lunch to promote opposition to the Vietnam War and to unify the New York delegation. Though first-year members were to be seen and not heard, Koch made it his business to eat lunch in the members' dining room every day to find out who was wavering on the war. He soon reached out to Robert Giaimo, an important five-term Democrat from Connecticut who had developed serious doubts about the war but feared a reversal would look bad to his constituents. Koch proposed that he and Giaimo cosponsor a resolution "saying that whether we are for or against the war, the fact is we cannot win the war, and without expressing a moral judgment, we the undersigned believe it is now in the best interests of the United States to withdraw." Eventually, Giaimo, whose seniority made him far more credible to House Democrats than most other antiwar liberals, led the fight to cut off funding for the war and counted it among his greatest accomplishments.[39]

As time went on, Koch learned to put his extraordinary capacity for political schmoozing to good use, though he was bad with small talk and hated cocktail parties. As a regular at the House pool after his first term, he hung out in the locker room, laughing and swapping stories with macho members, showing that he was more than a bookish Jewish kid in an institution that was almost all male.[40]

New York's congressional delegation had generally been fractious and unable to unite behind the state's interests, as other large delegations, like California's, did. The city's fiscal crisis in the 1970s made unity vital. But Abzug and Koch got into a fuss over what was supposed to be a joint news conference and did not speak to each other for eight months during one of the most crucial phases of the crisis. By 1976 even conservative upstate Republicans had a strong interest in getting federal aid to the city because its problems were affecting the credit and budget of the entire state. Koch became secretary of the New York delegation and unified it by upgrading the food at the delegation's lunch meetings, including offering an unlimited ice cream bar. The New York delegation also provided support that was crucial to Koch's career in Congress, especially in getting him appointed to the Appropriations Committee in 1974, which marked him as one of the House's future leaders.[41]

Koch's consensus building paid off in other ways, and though his politics were on the left of Congress's limited political spectrum, he remained well liked, even by conservatives. In September 1969, soon after the death of Ho Chi Minh, Koch went on the floor and called on the U.S. government to intensify its peace overtures to the

North Vietnamese in the wake of the loss of their "George Washington." The conservative Ohio Democrat Wayne Hays responded by calling Koch virtually "an emissary from Hanoi." Koch reprinted the exchange and urged his constituents to write to Hays, who was promptly deluged with letters. A week later a smiling Hays walked up to Koch on the House floor and told him to desist. Laughing together with Hays, Koch felt the exchange was a "signal that I was finally accepted."[42]

Koch's antiwar stance put him in league with a small group of liberal Democrats called the "new politics" faction. Their influence proved almost nil, Koch learned from experience. He and Brooklyn representative Bertram Podell opposed a Republican amendment to a supplemental appropriations bill requiring universities to take away the financial aid of student rioters or face the loss of federal construction loans. The amendment, supported by Appropriations Committee chair George H. Mahon, showed how conservative the House could be on such issues—it passed 329–61. An antiwar amendment by Upper West Side representative William F. Ryan to delete $1.2 billion from the supplemental appropriation bill for the Vietnam War attracted only 25 votes, which showed how tiny the "new politics" faction really was in the House of Representatives in 1969.[43] Koch's proposals to broaden the draft exemption for conscientious objectors to the Vietnam War received little more support.[44]

Some of Koch's proposals went nowhere, but they raised his profile; and some proved to be ahead of their time. Koch attracted wide attention when he traveled to Canada in January 1970, hearing testimony from some of the estimated fifty thousand draft resisters who had emigrated there. Again, seeking consensus on even the most controversial and sensitive subjects, he argued that even for proponents of the war, support for amnesty made sense. "Canada is delighted to have these people," Koch argued, insisting that amnesty would help bring Americans together and bring talented young people back to the United States.[45] Eventually, President Jimmy Carter would implement amnesty through a very unpopular presidential pardon.

Koch also called for lighter penalties for smoking marijuana. When, shortly after his election in 1969, he called for a commission to study decriminalization of the drug, his colleagues treated the idea as political poison. Two years later, responding to growing concern by parents with "the criminal records their children were being saddled with," President Richard Nixon appointed a commission that later recommended decriminalization.[46]

Koch believed that his "biggest accomplishment" during his congressional career was his successful effort to increase funding for mass transit, a more traditional liberal issue. The $89 million in additional grants for the New York City subways obviously squared with the interests of his thousands of subway-riding constituents and showed his increasing clout. It also reflected a vision of the city that demanded that people, not automobiles, should dominate the landscape and that a move away from massive highway and auto subsidies might make the rest of the country more like

New York—densely populated, efficient, and, contrary to popular opinion, relatively safe.[47]

KOCH, GAY RIGHTS, AND PRIVACY RIGHTS

One of Koch's most important causes was privacy—the deregulation of private space. Koch supported gay rights early on with a comfort and a passion not seen in many straight politicians in the 1960s and 1970s. Koch never avowed any particular orientation and maintained that his sexuality was an entirely private matter. Koch's position must be seen within the context of the emerging gay rights movement, which was literally born in his district, forged in the heat of the police raid of the Stonewall Inn on Christopher Street during his first year in Congress. He had supported the cause of sexual freedom since his first race in 1962. After a police raid on a gay bar called the Snake Pit in the spring of 1970, Koch became "one of the first elected officials to publicly lobby on behalf of the homosexuals of Greenwich Village." After Stonewall, Koch reminded Police Commissioner Howard Leary that "it is not a violation of the law to be homosexual or heterosexual, and the law should never be used to harass either," and Koch repeatedly testified in favor of the antidiscrimination bill introduced into the New York City Council.[48]

Koch found other ways to benefit gay constituents from his post in Congress, cosponsoring national antidiscrimination legislation in 1974 with Los Angeles Representative Henry Waxman. Koch also tried to eliminate the income tax provisions that then taxed single taxpayers more than married ones (56 percent of the population of his district was single, widowed, or divorced).[49] He discovered that military discharge papers, even if they were honorable, contained "separation program numbers," codes that tipped employers off to veterans whom the Pentagon suspected of madness, "homosexual tendencies," or even bed wetting. Koch eventually got the Department of Defense to stop this practice.[50] Even more important was a piece of general legislation that would help gay people, the Privacy Act of 1971. Koch was proud of the partnership he had forged to create the bill with Representative Barry M. Goldwater Jr., a conservative Republican from Arizona. The Privacy Act basically required that federal agencies notify people of files maintained on them and allow citizens to inspect and correct their records.[51]

Koch was undoubtedly one of Congress's most progressive members on Vietnam. Indeed, his social liberalism put him not too far from a conservative epithet, hurled by supporters of Richard Nixon at Democratic presidential candidate George McGovern in 1972. McGovern, they said, was in favor of "acid, amnesty, and abortion." But just as Koch, as a young liberal reformer, had courted Italian Republicans in the Village, so he tried to form relationships with both more conservative members of the New York House delegation and, more pointedly, with conservative and rural member of the House. During the early stages of the fiscal crisis in 1975, New York desperately needed votes for loan guarantees. So Koch invited a delegation of South Dakota cattle ranchers to New York City, accompanied by Larry Pressler, their extremely conservative Republican representative. A photo shows Pressler, Koch, and the other cattle barons standing tall in their Stetsons as they walked past the Red Apple Supermarket at Second Avenue and Seventy-fifth Street. Declaring that a city default would create major financial problems for their own state, Pressler and the ranchers rallied to New York's cause. Indeed, Pressler eventually moved to New York City and endorsed Barack Obama for president in 2008.[52]

THE PERMANENT CAMPAIGN

Koch's only administrative experience before running for mayor was running his congressional office. But he created a reputation on Capitol Hill for unusual diligence and efficiency, which helped carry him into Gracie Mansion. He inspired his staff with a tremendous sense of loyalty and remained close to Coffey and Menschel, his original House staffers. Even though he was a first-termer, Koch ran "one of the busiest offices around" because of his iron-clad rule that required a response to any contact with his office within two weeks—no small task for a small operation processing more than fifty thousand letters, telegrams, and phone calls a year.[53]

The representative who had learned how to heckle the hecklers on a soapbox especially relished answering hate mail. One Upper East Side constituent slammed Koch's ardent support for Israel in a mailgram that read: "Koch, if I ever see your name on a ballet [sic] again I will donate $350,000 to your opponent. Why don't you Jews stop trying to run America?"[54]

Koch replied, "I have your nice telegram. I'm sure you were delighted that I got 77.6% of the vote in the last election. You must have jumped for joy. Again, thanks for your congratulations. Do give my best to the others living under the rock with you."[55] That turned the trick; the Upper East Sider wrote back that he was delighted with Koch's response, as "it was the funniest damned piece of mail I've had for months," adding that "if we didn't seem so diametrically opposed, I might even vote for you again sometime."[56]

New York is the one city in the United States where the sidewalks are so crowded that a politician can shake the hands of hundreds of voters in a day without any media or mediation. That's one reason Koch loved it. The city lends itself to a measure of grassroots democracy unknown in most of the rest of the country, and Koch made the most of this—for years he waged a permanent campaign.

When Congress broke on Thursday afternoons, Ed rushed home, often attending some evening function back in New York. By 7 A.M. he'd be campaigning at the subway, handing constituents copies of his latest statements along with a detachable form so that they could write the president or cabinet members in support of his position. A head higher than most of the crowd rushing into the trains, he became so well known that he did not have to introduce himself. He'd just stick out his hand and ask the question that he had discovered was the one phrase that would get harried New Yorkers to stop: "I'm Ed Koch, your congressman. How'm I doin'?" He recalled, "Sometimes they'd tell me I was doing lousy, but they always stopped, and they talked to me and I listened."[57]

After the morning subway he'd go to his New York office near city hall at 26 Federal Plaza and work some more. He'd spend the weekends going to political functions or to his "traveling office," where he'd sit at a desk and meet voters at announced locations throughout the district. And he held town meetings in various parts of his district every three months.[58] These frequent trips home only increased his sense of cultural isolation when he headed south to Washington.

Ethnic politics and transnational relations within New York City, as well as his own enthusiasm, drove Koch into extensive engagement with U.S. foreign policy in his first two terms in Congress, which coincided with Richard Nixon's first term. Koch's own sense of alienation in a Congress with more anti-Semites than multiculturalists, and increased identification with the cause of the Jewish state after the 1967 and 1973 wars, led him to more urgent advocacy for Israel and strengthened his sense of Jewish identity.

Despite this sense of alienation, Koch was brilliant at assembling unexpected, and often bipartisan alliances with conservatives such as his work on privacy with Barry Goldwater Jr. or his friendship with Charlie Wilson—unusual for a liberal representative from New York, which presaged the kinds of center-right coalitions Koch would forge as mayor.

8 "A LIBERAL WITH SANITY"

Koch as the Anti-Bella

As early as 1969, a time one might consider the most freethinking in Koch's career—he was devoted to amnesty for draft resisters, liberalization of marijuana laws, mass transit aid, and ending the war in Vietnam—Koch showed definite limits to his liberalism. During a 1971 demonstration, when more radical members of Congress allowed demonstrators affiliated with Vietnam Veterans Against the War to sleep on their office floor, Koch refused. More significantly, the left-liberal columnist Jack Newfield accused him of red-baiting, after an incident at a rally at Hunter College on November 13, 1969.

During a rowdy meeting—nihilists with a laughter machine forced U.S. Representative Leonard Farbstein off the stage—Koch got into a shouting match with some of the Hunter College demonstrators. When one shouted, "Why don't you endorse the March on Washington?" Koch replied, "I won't endorse any march called by the Fifth Avenue Peace Committee so long as they have communists on their steering committee." The audience erupted in anger. The refusal to exclude communists was one of the founding principles of the New Left and much of the antiwar movement. As early as 1969 Koch drew an anticommunist line between himself and a significant and growing segment of the Democratic Party that identified with the Left—a line that would be reinforced as some Democratic leftists challenged Israel's policies.

That day at Hunter College, Koch shared the podium with Bella Abzug, who would soon come to define the Democratic Left, such as it was in the United States. Abzug would burst onto the scene in 1970 as America's leading feminist member of Congress, a short, heavy-set, tanned figure famous for her enormous hat and abrupt manner. As she herself put it: "There are those who say I'm impatient, impetuous, uppity, rude, profane, brash and overbearing. Whether I'm any of these things, or all of them . . . I'm a very serious woman."[1]

When Koch called himself "a liberal with sanity," he knew well that many of his listeners thought of Bella Abzug as the liberal who lacked it. Craziness, in the eyes of Koch and moderate liberals, meant those like Abzug who believed in a radical transformation of capitalism and patriarchy. The sharp lines of differentiation would of course influence the outcome of the 1977 mayoral race, the only time Koch and Abzug ran against each other. But this case study also exposes fissures in post-McGovern liberalism, amplified in the national media arena of New York City. Abzug became an icon of liberalism; Koch, who has defined himself as a "Henry Jackson–Joe Lieberman Democrat" (though he is more socially liberal than Lieberman), belongs in the genealogy of the Democratic Party's right—the common ancestor of both neoconservatism and the Clintonist Democratic Leadership Council.

Abzug, like Koch, was ultimately pragmatic. But while Koch was the sort of liberal who saw problems with the system and wanted to reform it, Abzug held to broader, more radical aims. Koch's attempts to marginalize her as a congressional colleague and later, when they were rival mayoral aspirants, infuriated her. One of the most visible leaders of the emerging women's movement, Abzug came from an Old Left political background, though she was never a member of the Communist Party and often disputed with it. In retirement Abzug and Koch wound up living on different floors of the same building—but their rivalry was so bitter and ingrained that, after her death in 1998, Koch stunned many of her friends when he went downstairs to pay his respects at her shiva.[2] Later he even advocated erecting a statue to her memory in Washington Square Park, which their apartments overlooked.[3]

Ed and Bella both had 100 percent liberal voting records during their time in Congress according to the liberal rating organization Americans for Democratic Action, and often it was what they had in common politically, combined with their different temperaments, that made them such rivals. Born in 1920, Abzug was four years older, the age of Koch's older brother, Harold, and possessed a similarly combative spirit. Both were the children of Jewish immigrants who lived in New York and owned small businesses. Koch and Abzug both found support among Manhattan liberals and reformers. Both passionately opposed the war in Vietnam and found themselves drawn to politics by ambition, combined with a certainty that the things they believed in were just.[4]

The similarities ended there. Koch had grown up in a well-informed, but not passionately political household. He was a solid but not spectacular student who always had an interest in politics but had not really devoted himself to it fully until he was a young lawyer in his thirties. His parents focused primarily on hard work and economic advancement. He was an obedient child and had grown up anticommunist. Finally, he was a good boss—hard driving, yes, but he inspired such loyalty that staff from his earliest days in politics stuck with him through twelve years of mayoralty. Most are still his friends.

Abzug was more radical, less obedient, and more intellectual. In 1917 Bella Savitsky's father, Emmanuel, had renamed his Chelsea butcher shop "The Live and Let Live Meat Market" as a protest against American involvement in World War I, at a time when antiwar protesters might suffer jail or deportation. Bella was known as a neighborhood prodigy in Hebrew school and excelled academically. When her father died, just as she was entering high school, she showed up at the synagogue and said kaddish as if she were a man, a degree of transgression that would be unimaginable for Koch as a youngster. From the age of eleven Bella joined the socialist-Zionist Hashomer Hatzair (The Young Watchmen).[5] Hashomer, affiliated with the left-wing Mapam Party in Israel, had alienated more conservative Zionists because it opposed partition of the Palestine Mandate in 1948, advocating instead a binational state rather than an exclusively Jewish one. Although it was independent of the American Communist Party, Mapam belonged to the Communist Third International until the 1950s, when it was kicked out for being too independent of Moscow and too supportive of Israel.[6]

At Hunter College she became student council president and fought the Rapp-Coudert committee of the state legislature, which sought to expose and fire communist teachers and professors. At Hunter she met a core group of friends who joined her as lifelong political activists. Rejected from Harvard Law (which then refused to accept women), Bella attended Columbia University Law School during World War II. She met Martin Abzug, her future husband, on a bus trip to a Yehudi Menuhin fund-raising concert for war relief for the Soviet Union. Martin supported

Bella's political activities throughout their forty-two-year marriage. She became a labor lawyer, and when male lawyers, management, and union officials tried to pretend that she was not even in the room, she started wearing large hats so that she could not be ignored.[7]

Though too much of an individualist to join the Communist Party, her politics anticipated the "anti-anticommunism" of the New Left—the policy of refusing to exclude communists from noncommunist organizations and coalitions. Abzug became "one of the very few independent attorneys willing to take 'Communist cases,'" and represented many victims of McCarthy-era blacklisting.[8] Later in her career her relationship with the Communist Party became a worrisome issue. One former member of her staff remembered that when a constituent asked whether she had communist affiliations, "she just turned red. But she knew she had to be very careful about the way she responded to the guy. Because she didn't want to get trapped in a denial that wasn't truthful. So she very skillfully changed the subject."[9]

While pregnant for the first time, she traveled to Mississippi to defend Willie McGee, an African American falsely accused of raping a white woman. Refused a hotel room on her arrival in Jackson and fearing the worst from the Ku Klux Klan when a taxi driver offered to take her fifteen miles into the country to find a place to sleep, the pregnant Abzug stayed up all night, locked in the toilet of the Jackson bus station, and fearlessly appeared in court the next morning to defend her client. She lost the baby. Despite repeated appeals and two stays from the U.S. Supreme Court, she lost McGee too, when Mississippi executed him in 1951.[10]

In 1961 Abzug and a group of close friends started the Women Strike for Peace, first dedicated to obtaining a ban on nuclear testing and later to organizing protests against the Indochina wars. She gained recognition as a fiery protest orator, which led her to mount a successful challenge to one of the last Tammany members of the House in Manhattan, Leonard Farbstein.[11]

Farbstein was not a hack. He had been sufficiently liberal to deflect two previous challenges from reformers that had been based on discrediting his political affiliations with Tammany, rather than on his politics or voting record. But his margins were becoming thinner and thinner in the Nineteenth Congressional District, which snaked through Manhattan from the Upper West Side across a part of southern Greenwich Village to the still heavily Jewish Lower East Side. Sixty-seven years old, he was increasingly out of step with the bulge of baby-boomer voters who had entered the electorate. As a regular Democrat, he was naturally inclined to support President Johnson and was a late convert to the anti–Vietnam War cause. In contrast, Abzug had helped to found the antiwar movement.

Her campaign, on new issues like women's liberation and gay liberation, as well as an antiwar platform, bewildered the old New Deal Democrat. Abzug campaigned with the slogan "A Woman's Place Is in the House, and in the Senate." The decisive difference in the campaign was the larger-than-life persona of Abzug herself. Unlike the pale male reformers whom Farbstein had previously dispatched, Bella Abzug was the most instantly recognizable New York political figure since Fiorello La Guardia, with her bright-colored dress and flamboyant trademark hats. Another icon of Jewish and gay New York, Barbra Streisand, became her friend and supporter, attracting huge crowds in the district and raising sums of money for Abzug "in five figures."[12]

When Farbstein forces spread the rumor that she was against selling jets to Israel, Abzug confronted the him in public, declaring: "Lennie, this is one Jew you're not going to out-Jew." If voters sensed any ambivalence on her part toward Israel, her demonstrated fluency in Yiddish and Hebrew often came in handy in overcoming it.[13] The issue of jet sales to Israel was political dynamite in the overwhelmingly Jewish district, and Abzug had initially told the VID that she opposed the sale, then repudiated that position and denied she had ever said that. Koch later maintained that she had actually opposed the sale of the Phantom jets, citing a 1972 letter by Jack Newfield in which the reporter acknowledged that he had heard her say in 1970 at VID that she was against the jets. Newfield had earlier supported her denials. Though Abzug dutifully took scrupulously pro-Israel positions ever after, it was easy to question her commitment—any coolness toward Israel would be a big part of the perceived difference between her and Ed Koch and a significant political liability.[14] Abzug wrote a long letter to the *Village Voice* asserting her unequivocal support for the sale of the Phantoms to Israel, but she protested that she had been forced into it: "The question of sale of jets to Israel has become the issue—an exclusive litmus test for all political leaders. Granted that Israel needs and should get the jets, what next? Does anyone think that Israel's future lies with perpetual warfare?" she asked, adding that "a viable solution does not lie in continuing the arms race in the Middle East ad infinitum."[15] Those who supported Israel without qualification blanched at the suggestion that she might not favor future arms sales and accused her of "trying to satisfy Arab imperialism on the one hand while paying lip service to Israeli democracy on the other."[16] Abzug decisively beat Farbstein in the primary but barely nosed out her Republican-Liberal opponent, the talk show host Barry Farber, in the generally safe Democratic district in the 1970 general election; the raucous campaign had seen militants from the Jewish Defense League picketing her campaign headquarters, shouting, "Israel, yes, Bella, no!" and "A vote for Bella is a vote for communism." Ed Koch then defended her against Farber's accusations that she had been linked to the Communist Party, charges that both Abzug and Koch considered red-baiting.[17]

Abzug hit the House like a ton of bricks, and her supporters loved every minute of it. "From day one she was determined to rock the timbers of the institution," remembered James Capalino, who joined her staff as her first intern in 1971 and later went to work for Koch.[18] When the Democratic leadership assigned her to the lackluster government operations committee (instead of her choice, armed services), she branded the assignment an outrage in the *New York Times*. This was in contrast to Koch, who had acquiesced to an even worse initial appointment and soon got his first choice. When William "Fishbait" Miller, the House doorkeeper (a powerful administrator), asked her to take off her trademark hat the first time she walked onto the House floor, she told him to "go fuck yourself," though Miller later told *Time* that it was a joke and that he and Abzug are "big buddies."[19] About this and other reports that she used profanity, Abzug wrote in her diary: "I suppose I should deny [them] but who would believe me? I'm a very spontaneous and excitable and emotional person, and I do have a way of expressing myself pretty strongly sometimes . . . . All that matters is that I say what I feel, and I always do *that*."[20]

After her formal swearing-in in January 1971, Abzug walked out to the steps of the Capitol to meet a crowd of six hundred cheering supporters from Women's Strike for Peace and the gay liberation movement. With Ed Koch and Father Robert Drinan, the Massachusetts Democrat, standing behind her, Representative Shirley Chisholm of Brooklyn administered the oath once more. Then, to more cheers, Abzug announced through a bullhorn that she was introducing a bill to order President Nixon to fix a date for ending the war.[21] With a raspy voice that Norman Mailer once said "could boil the fat off a taxi driver's neck," Abzug created a political spectacle unequalled on Capitol Hill. She was a first-rate lawyer and had mastered parliamentary procedure, and because of her unique national audience and constituency in the women's movement, she was eventually accepted by her colleagues. In her three terms she achieved a modest level of power in the House out of proportion to her lack of seniority. Abzug struck hard, not only on the issue of the war but in support of the Equal Rights Amendment and feminist issues such as twenty-four-hour day care.[22]

Her celebrity was unrivaled on the Hill, even by the unassuming Speaker, Carl Albert, who consequently handled her with kid gloves. "There were days, just to give you an illustration, where we had over a thousand visitors to the office. The line used to form in the Longworth House Office Building for people to just sign her guestbook and hope they'd meet her. I mean, the management of the tourism alone was a full-time job, let alone dealing with Bella's personality," said former Abzug staffer Jim Capalino.[23]

She was hell to work for. Capalino, who had joined her as a twenty-year-old intern in January 1971 while a junior at Colgate, recalled that "by March 1 the entire staff had quit and Bella made me her administrative assistant."[24] And she soon became "completely paranoid about Ed Koch"—especially when she felt he was stealing her thunder:

> Literally, the staff would tremble when she came into the office. It was really sad. So she closes the door, and the next thing I hear—I thought she was being attacked. I thought seriously there was a mugging going on in the office. So she starts screaming at the top of her lungs. And she starts screaming, *'Capalino, get the fuck in here.'* So I walk into the office.

I said, 'Yes, Congresswoman?' and she is in a *rage*. And she's looking at the Metropolitan section of the *Times*, and I can't even remember what the issue was, but Ed had released a statement about something and she was seething.

"Why weren't we on top of this?" I'd seen the article. And I said, "Well first of all, Congresswoman, it is an issue in his district." And then she said, "I can't abide this guy. He's like a caterpillar. He's got a thousand arms that are always in motion." And she starts flailing her arms. . . . And she went on for five minutes. Just this download of sort of paranoia about Ed. And I went back to my desk, and I said, oh, my god, this is a new sign of mental illness. And from that day on, you could not mention his name in her midst. If you said "Congressman Koch," if anybody said, "Congressman Koch," she'd chop their head off. She said, "You're to refer to him as 'the other congressman.'"[25]

Abzug was also hard for the staff to manage. "You couldn't keep Bella on message or on schedule to save her life," said Capalino.[26] Whereas Koch's staff methodically replied to every constituent who contacted the office, Abzug's constituent office diverted much of its energy to organizing the national peace movement.

In her first term the office was run by a friend since childhood, Mim Kelber, of whom Abzug wrote, "We share the same political reflexes."[27] Kelber wrote a statement that Abzug (read over Capalino's objections), calling for Speaker Carl Albert's resignation because he had refused to "calendar" a resolution against the war. About three hours later "the Speaker's chief of staff calls and says in his slowest Oklahoma drawl: 'Jeem, the congresswoman has not only written her death certificate, she has signed it too.' Click."[28] The next day Abzug met with the Speaker, and "he read her the riot act," telling her, according to Capalino, who was with her, that her behavior was "inexcusable . . . We have to be able to disagree agreeably." Despite the warning, Abzug kept on being Abzug, and Albert never actually punished her.[29]

Koch did not yet have Abzug's knack for national publicity, and he lacked the national constituency that underwrote it. But he had already developed a talent for talking in pithy sound bites, which the media lapped up like stray cats in a dairy. He was not, like Abzug, at the head of a great popular movement like feminism, and he was far from being New York's most recognizable figure. He drove his staff hard, but he was also considerate. Koch concentrated on moving up the conventional way in Congress, hunting for advancement through his contacts in the New York delegation. Koch became fairly powerful, but he disgusted Abzug, who thought he was toadying to a prowar leadership.[30] Between his constant campaigning at the subways and the high standards he set for constituent service, Koch was spectacularly well liked in his own district by the time he ran for reelection in 1970 as Abzug was eking out a win against Farbstein across town.

In that year, the old conservative wing of the party, including the Tamawa club, ran the perennial candidate Paul Rao, who tried rather pathetically to red-bait Koch during the primary campaign. Rao declared that the congressman was "not a Democrat, not a Republican, but a Liberal. He is a radical."[31] In the June primary Koch showed himself to be well within mainstream opinion in the district, dispatching Rao 83 percent to 17 percent of the vote. In his home area of the district, around the West Village/VID area, Koch got 89 percent, and in even relatively conservative Stuyvesant Town beat Rao 65–35, with Koch doubling his 1968 primary vote throughout the district.[32] Koch's victory in the primary surprised no one, but the magnitude of his victory was a political triumph, showing the sort of overwhelming strength in his district that might allow him to take the same path that Lindsay had taken—a Manhattan expressway to Gracie Mansion.

In the 1970 general election Koch won 62 percent of the vote against a young patrician electronics millionaire, Peter Sprague, who outspent him 3 to 1, flipping what had been a Republican seat into a Democratic one, safe as long as Koch wished to hold it.[33]

Abzug soon became a very direct rival. New York State had lost congressional seats in the 1970 census, and that meant a bloody redistricting. In 1972 Abzug's enemies in the state legislature (both Democrats and Republicans) eliminated her district by dividing it into three parts. When Governor Nelson Rockefeller intervened at the last minute, adding even more hostile territory to Abzug's new district, she alienated Democratic leaders who were supposed to be negotiating on her behalf by yelling at them in late-night phone calls.[34] The final redistricting plan left her with no safe district in which to run in 1972. It lumped much of the West Village in with conservative Catholic Staten Island, where Abzug did not have a prayer against the incumbent Democrat John Murphy. Abzug's tireless opposition to patriarchy appealed little to the conservative Catholic voters whom Koch had carefully wooed since he won his first district coleadership race. Even if Abzug had beaten Murphy in a primary, the district was political poison: she would have likely lost to a Republican that November.

Short of winning a difficult run against John Rooney, a very senior conservative from Brooklyn, Abzug could hold on to her seat only if she ran against a another reformer—either Ed Koch on the East Side or the beloved member of the House from the West Side, William Fitts Ryan, the first of the postwar reformers elected to the House. Neither alternative was appetizing: "Eddie Koch is studying Karate, and Bella is studying cannibalism," remarked Hugh Carey, the representative from Park Slope in Brooklyn, suggesting how nasty a Koch-Abzug race might be. The Republicans may have wanted to help Abzug get the nomination, hoping to regain the seat in the general election. Such a strategy might have worked—when Koch went on to the mayoralty in 1977, Abzug ran for his seat and narrowly lost to Republican William Green. But in 1972 Koch managed to keep Abzug from running in his district by getting early endorsements from eighteen of the twenty-two Democratic district leaders—both reformers and regulars. Even Abzug could not buck such a show of party unity.[35]

She chose instead to run on the West Side against Ryan in one of the most bitter and nasty races in the history of New York politics. Ryan, dying of cancer, was deeply revered by many of his constituents, which added to the drama. Abzug's decision to run against him, one reformer wrote to the *Village Voice,* was "indecent and inhuman."[36] "No wonder Ron Dellums has called her a 'white elite motherfucker'—too bad she sees Bill Ryan as the nigger of Manhattan," one reader wrote to the *Voice*.[37] Abzug always maintained that Dellums was only jesting when he said that. Koch, who witnessed the exchange, believed that Dellums was in earnest, after Abzug berated him for being late for a vote. Dellums later remarked that he had reacted in anger, "because punctuality is very significant to me. Going back to my childhood it was a value instilled in me as a countermeasure to a stereotype," so Koch was right that Dellums was earnest. Still, the minute he said it, Dellums recalls saying to himself, "Oh why did I say that?" The next day he went to her office and made up.[38]

Ryan won the primary by a 2–1 margin but died before the election. Some of Ryan's supporters believed that the strain of the primary race killed him and blamed Abzug.[39] So deep was the acrimony between the Ryan and Abzug forces that Ryan's widow, Priscilla, unsuccessfully contested Abzug's claim to the Democratic nomination, and then ran for her late husband's seat in the general election, on the Liberal line. Priscilla Ryan lost but posed a serious threat because of strong backing from Albert Shanker, president of the United Federation of Teachers, and from the Liberal Party leader Alex Rose, both strong, liberal anticommunists who detested Abzug for her Old Left roots and radical politics.[40]

Koch lost any sympathy that he might have had for Abzug after she considered running against him. The McGovern campaign, which he supported with grave reservations and later criticized as "socialist," accentuated the difference between them, as Koch began to move to the right in response to the disastrous results of that campaign. They were "ground glass in each other's coffee," according to the journalist Mary Perot Nichols. Abzug returned the sentiment—she was "extra mad at Koch for being unbeatable in his own district." For Koch there was, to use the critic Harold Bloom's phrase, a certain anxiety of influence. Abzug pioneered the politics of blunt and sometimes outrageous statements that made Koch famous as mayor.[41] And Koch copied her in other ways. When Abzug wrote an autobiography that was a big hit in 1971, Koch started proposing books to publishers, but his work was rejected until he became mayor. When he was in Congress, he was never the national figure that Abzug was.

Koch later recalled, "Bella and I just dislike one another intensely, personally as well as politically," and he often saw Abzug's support as a way to rally opponents to a position. Yet the antipathy between Abzug and Koch was more than political competitiveness. Their differences were seemingly minor if you look at their voting records alone. But Koch saw Abzug as a radical who wanted to destroy the capitalist system, while he wanted to "remove the inequities without destroying the system."

That meant that he was significantly more sympathetic to management, even if he did not oppose the existence of unions. Abzug, one of the founders of the Women's Strike for Peace, also unambiguously challenged U.S. imperialism.[42]

Koch, a self-described "Henry Jackson Democrat," despite his ardent opposition to the Vietnam War, believed that a strong American empire confronting the Soviets at every turn was the best hope for both the prosperity and security of the United States and the survival of the Jewish state and the best guarantee of universal human rights. This pro–cold war stance formed part of Koch's basic appeal to the more nationalist Jews and Catholics and to other ethnic minorities with nationalist causes, such as the Irish and the Greeks.

Abzug saw anti-imperialism as integral to both peace and feminism. A mirror of Koch's notion that supporting the cold war was sanity was Abzug's opinion that the cold war was expensive paranoia that hurt families and jobs back home. In keeping with her earlier prepartition belief in a binational state in Palestine, by the 1970s Abzug opposed the territorial expansion of Israel, believing that a compromise with the Palestinians was a precondition to the continued existence of a Jewish state. Her coalition was a progressive coalition: feminists, the peace movement, and the Left. She tended to identify more with ideology than ethnicity. The fissure between the two New York liberals was one of the primary divides within the Democratic Party itself, one that would cut the party into three factions through the 1970s. One was the antiwar, social democratic Left associated with Abzug. Koch would tack to the right wing on foreign policy issues—toward neoconservatism—and on domestic issues pioneered a neoliberal, so-called free-market approach that anticipated that of the Democratic Leadership Council and the Clinton administration.

9 NEW YORK
Divided and Broke (1973–77)

Ed Koch set his sights on the mayoralty after a mere eighteen months in Washington, although seven years would pass before he attained it. Running for higher office is a far chancier route to real power than waiting out the seniority system, but Koch quickly tired of the D.C.–New York shuttle. For a member of Congress, New York's mayoralty is the only elective office worth having that does not require a current office holder to resign in order to run.

Koch's 1970 reelection to the House by a huge majority, then unheard-of for a Democrat in his historically Republican district, fueled his mayoral ambitions. Shortly afterward he and one of his long-time aides, David Brown, talked about a plan that Brown had drawn up for a run in the next mayoral election, then three years away. Brown was the adviser who had urged Koch to "speak out for radical change" in his first congressional campaign, in 1968. Two years later Brown had told Koch to move to the center, because it was "unlikely that he would ever be the first choice of either the New Left or the Old Right."[1]

Anticipating a difficult campaign, Brown counseled Koch to tone down his brash personality. He urged Koch to forgo "the understandable pleasure that comes from telling off a special interest group that seeks a favor; having your revenge on some potential ally who opposed you in the past; making an impulsive decision without the benefit of friends' advice; or viewing almost every other politician as your natural enemy." Koch would never abandon his view of politics as his personal battlefield. Ironically, his failure to establish a definite persona outside his district proved the biggest obstacle in his first try at the mayoralty, in 1973.[2]

Koch worked hard at becoming more mediagenic: he even took speech lessons to round his shrill, nasal speech into tones that would be more pleasing to television and radio listeners. "The brown ground soggy bogs of oozing mud. Skies became black masses of angry clouds," he repeated endlessly as part of a "tonal drill."[3] None of this made any difference. Koch's first mayoralty outing was a disaster, according to his close political confidant John LoCicero. Having kept the idea of running secret for almost two years, Koch sprang the final decision on friends and advisers late in 1972. That delay meant a late start, and amateurishness and naïvêté marred his campaign. His fund-raising effort stalled out after pulling in about $100,000, a fraction of the money necessary for a citywide race. Koch had always been a street campaigner, and he underestimated the power of television to sway primary voters, which is why he and Brown, who became his campaign manager, did not raise or spend money on media. They were more interested in building a field organization and used their funding to pay staff.[4]

Most damagingly, Koch failed to distinguish himself from all the other candidates. He did stand out from the two regular outer-borough candidates, Abe Beame from Brooklyn and the conservative Mario Biaggi from the Bronx. But Koch was eclipsed by two other Jewish reformers from Manhattan, Jerome Kretchmer, a former Lindsay environmental commissioner, and the powerful state assembly majority leader, Al Blumenthal, both of whom were better known citywide than Koch. When Koch began to use law-and-order rhetoric, "it just wasn't believable from him," recalled LoCicero, who at the time advocated that the campaign focus on good government.[5] The voters didn't buy the law-and-order approach, and Koch's rightward shift rankled some old friends back in his Manhattan base.

When Blumenthal clinched the endorsement of the citywide reform organization, the left-liberal New Democratic Coalition, Koch withdrew from the race. His first run had self-destructed after only three months. Koch did not even get the endorsement of his own club, the Village Independent Democrats. The only time the editorial page of the *New York Times* mentioned Koch was when he dropped out. *The Almanac of American Politics for 1974* wrote that Koch would "undoubtedly" stay in Washington "for many years to come."[6]

If ability to come back after a bad defeat is the hallmark of the successful politician, Koch had grit to spare. As a member of Congress, Koch kept harping on the need to be tough on crime, but he also called for good government in a time of economic crisis. Both issues reflected the tensions created by postwar government policies on housing and labor. In the 1950s white ethnics had far more access to mortgages, education loans, craft union cards, and government patronage jobs than African Americans. By the 1970s the barriers to minority employment and housing had begun to break down just as deindustrialization made the position and social status of white ethnics more precarious.[7] In the 1950s and 1960s the well-documented decline in manufacturing jobs had been counterbalanced by the creation of white-collar jobs. If a fur cutter's daughter became a secretary, her family might perceive her as occupying a higher rung on the ladder, even if the pay and benefits were not as good as those for a union job.

The painful economic realignment of the early 1970s threw both blue- and white-collar American workers out of their jobs. Double-digit inflation threatened their living standards. The stagnation in social mobility intensified competition among New York's different ethnic groups for shrinking resources. Optimism that blacks and whites could integrate deteriorated in the face of these pressures—along with outer-borough housing stocks: disinvestment and manipulation by banks and real estate agents encouraged white flight to the suburbs. New York City in the 1970s, especially in the outer boroughs, became a checkerboard of ethnic enclaves, fraught with explosive racial and class tensions.

Koch realized that his political future would depend on his ability to appeal to the most powerful bloc of voters in the city: disgruntled white ethnics. Though their share of their electorate would decline by 25 percent by the 1980s, in 1969 non-Latino whites comprised 79 percent of the electorate for the general election for mayor and a preponderance of the primary electors. The proportion of white voters participating in mayoral elections steadily declined through 1989, one of the principal reasons that Koch lost his bid for a fourth term.[8]

New York's electorate in the 1970s seemingly validated the conventional political wisdom of the day, encapsulated in *The Real Majority,* a book by the political consultant Richard Scammon and the former LBJ White House staffer Ben Wattenberg. Scammon and Wattenberg argued that the majority of voters were "un-young, un-poor, and un-black," and the authors believed that the liberalism of the 1960s had encouraged crime and pornography and discouraged patriotism, what they called "the Social Issue." The Social Issue had replaced the economy as the primary motivation of the majority of American voters, turning U.S. politics in a conservative direction.[9] Left liberals made exactly the opposite argument. Bella Abzug, for example, wrote that she would "organize a new political coalition of the women, the minorities and the young people, along with the poor, the elderly, the workers and the unemployed, which is going to turn this country upside down and inside out." Richard Nixon explicitly embraced *The Real Majority,* and his landslide victory in 1972 on a law-and-order platform seemed to confirm its thesis, as did Koch's 1977 defeat of Abzug.[10]

Koch did not need any polls or experts to tell him where to expand his base outside his congressional district. His first priority was outer-borough Jews, many of whom were increasingly conservative. After 1972 Koch increasingly referred to Jewish grievances rather than those of African Americans: Jewish teachers and principals in predominantly black school districts were being judged by their race, not their merit; some communities were attempting to hold elections for the boards of antipoverty agencies on Saturday, when religious Jews could not vote, and some black politicians, he believed, were increasingly hostile toward Israel.[11]

Koch was completely at home talking politics with housewives on Ocean Parkway, in the heart of Jewish Brooklyn, where he had lived with his parents until he was thirty. His secondary base would be working- and middle-class Catholics, a group that he had successfully courted after the defeat of Carmine De Sapio. Koch was adept at ethnic appeals to Italian and Greek voters, both important groups in Queens. With increasing white flight from the city, Catholic power was waning. With the exception of the almost impossibly multiethnic La Guardia (an Italian Episcopalian with a Jewish mother and a large Italian Catholic constituency), every mayor from 1914 to 1965 had been Catholic. (For more than twenty-five years, from the mayoralty of Robert F. Wagner to that of Rudolph Giuliani, no Catholic won.) Koch wanted to be the Jewish candidate that white Catholics felt most comfortable with. But the price he had to pay for white ethnic support was estrangement from the left wing of the reform movement that had nurtured Koch's political career. Crime was a hot-button issue to these voters, and in the early seventies U.S. Representative Koch played directly to his new targets.

JEWS, BLACKS, AND FOREST HILLS: KOCH'S RUBICON

After he became mayor, Koch would characterize the Forest Hills controversy about public housing as his "political Rubicon." Koch's version of Caesar's pivotal decision to advance on Rome occurred during a Sunday drive in 1972 to a construction site in Queens, where residents had been fighting a proposed public housing development since early in 1971. More than a thousand residents, arrayed around a huge hole dug for the foundations of three 24-story buildings, were protesting the New York City Housing Authority's plans to create 840 low-income housing units there. The plan had begun as a vision of neighborhood integration through small-scale "scatter-site" residential development, which the U.S. Department of Housing and Urban Development had replaced with the large-scale towers.[12] Forest Hills was overwhelmingly white and Jewish, with a small Hispanic population (5.6 percent). While blacks made up almost 15 percent of New York City's population, in Forest Hills only 0.05 percent of the population was black. Median income in Forest Hills in 1970 was $14,368, considerably higher than the $9,682 median income for the five boroughs, yet almost one-third of Forest Hills residents were foreign born, more than twice the percentage for the city as a whole. Some of the project's most vocal opponents were Orthodox Jews, many originally from neighborhoods such as Brownsville that had recently become African American ghettos.[13]

The Forest Hills demonstrations marked the end of the tolerant pluralism of the Wagner years, described in Wallace Sayre and Herbert Kaufman's classic *Governing New York City*.[14] Pluralism was succeeded by an archipelago of decentralized powers—including the Great Society poverty programs and decentralized school districts—that weakened the central authority of the mayor and the central city government. Sometimes this fragmentation manifested as single-issue politics, defined as "the mobilization of angry citizens around an issue that becomes so emotionally charged that those mobilized treat that one issue as a litmus test for elected officials." The Forest Hills housing controversy ushered in an ugly new brand of urban politics filled with rage and racism, a history that may have drawn Koch to visit the project. At a demonstration in November 1971 protesters had hurled torches and rocks over the chain link fence that surrounded the construction site for the Forest Hills project. The torches went out, without causing damage, but one protester yelled, "If this were Harlem, those trailers would have burned long ago."[15]

According to Koch, curiosity—not opportunism—spurred him to go to Forest Hills early in 1972 to check out the construction site. He had previously discussed the matter with Ben Rosenthal, who represented Forest Hills in Congress and was a close friend. Rosenthal tried to discourage Koch from getting involved, so the Sunday drive was not entirely spontaneous.[16] Koch claimed he had no idea there would be a demonstration, so the sight of "two thousand people circling the hole in the ground with signs and yelling and screaming" surprised him. According to Koch, when a member of the crowd pulled him to a microphone and asked him to speak, he spontaneously offered his support for the protesters in an address broadcast over WCBS radio. The tenor of Koch's speech, which was not recorded, might be gleaned from a controversial interview he gave to reporters a few weeks later: "Two traditions are in conflict. The first is an old, very American tradition. . . . You save your money and move to Forest Hills. Work hard, be thrifty and you'll be rewarded. The second tradition is that everyone has a right to the opportunity for a better life and some people, because of historical circumstances beyond their control, can't get that better life unless the government assists them, literally picks them up and moves them there."[17]

Koch's words strongly implied that people who lived in projects were not "hard working" (never mind that many were employed) and that they were hopelessly passive and dependent on government handouts. His remarks pleased Forest Hills residents but raised howls among his reform-minded supporters and in the pages of the *Village Voice*. Sarah Schoenkopf Kovner, once one of his closest supporters and confidants, stopped talking to him.[18] *Voice* columnists Nat Hentoff and Jack Newfield, usually strong Koch backers in those days, censured him, though Hentoff privately assured him of his continued friendship. Newfield wrote that the controversy "has brought out the worst in many people, especially Manhattan Congressman Ed Koch," whom Newfield accused of being motivated by opportunism and his own mayoral ambitions. Koch's own home club, the VID, endorsed the full-scale Forest Hills project by a 10–1 margin and passed a resolution suggesting a site for a low-income housing project at Seventh Avenue and Eleventh Street.[19]

Harsh as it was, Koch's rhetoric was moderate compared with that of many protesters. *Village Voice* reporter Paul Cowan, touring Forest Hills to report on the controversy, tried to present the residents' positions fairly, but he also heard and reported frequent and virulent expressions of racism. Roger Starr, writing in the neoconservative journal *Commentary,* acknowledged the intense racism of some of the project's foes. Even Rabbi Meir Kahane, leader of the right-wing Jewish Defense League (JDL), professed that he was shocked at the racism of some protesters: "Suddenly all these Jews that used to get up in the Forest Hills Jewish Center and say that J.D.L. uses violence and that they're bad, come over to me and say, 'Listen, if that housing project goes up, can you blow it up?' It happened to me. Incredible. . . . When we go into Forest Hills now on this low-income housing project, we will say, 'If you people think that we're going to march for Jewish racism any more than for non-Jewish racism, you're wrong.'"[20]

Herman Badillo, a man whose conservative instincts on some social issues were similar to Koch's, was appalled at the paranoid arguments of the protesters: "Linking the size of the proposed Forest Hills project to the fear about too many poor tipping [the balance in] the neighborhood, for example, is the worst form of exaggerated fear-mongering when the facts of the situation are closely analyzed." Badillo, a former city housing commissioner, argued that the project as conceived would have "less than 35% minority families." He claimed that "they would be carefully screened," though screening regulations did not always survive constitutional challenge.[21] Proponents of the project, like Hentoff, claimed that the numbers of low-income blacks, at most 2 percent of the population of the neighborhood, were too small to result in mass sell-offs by whites. Hentoff believed that if the Forest Hills project were canceled, low-income housing would be built only inside black ghettoes, thereby subsidizing segregation. That prospect made some reformers bitter about Koch's defection.[22]

Koch was having none of it. In a private letter he called Badillo's criticism "an outrage." He continued to defend the Forest Hills activists, telling one reporter, "These people moved out of the slums because of fear and worked all their lives to do it. This project would turn into a slum in no time. They have a rational fear of increased crime and loss of property values, and I bitterly resent anyone who labels them racist."[23] As combative as Koch sounded, he spent considerable efforts working toward a compromise. After ostentatiously refusing to alter the project for a few months, the Lindsay administration adopted the solution favored by Koch and Mario Cuomo, who had been appointed by the mayor as mediator. The revised project had to have mixed income levels, and the number of units was almost halved, as was the size of the towers. The apartment complex became subsidized co-ops instead of rentals, with 40 percent set aside for the elderly. Cuomo was widely lauded for the deal, but Koch also later claimed credit.[24] Looking back on the project almost a quarter-century later, the *Times* reported that "opponents' fear of crime and other social ills proved unwarranted." Just as Badillo had predicted, whites eventually occupied more than 60 percent of the units. But the 40 percent of co-op residents who were minorities meant that the project had successfully achieved integration.[25]

Forest Hills raised Koch's profile while it damaged his relationships with old friends and supporters. His partisanship also paid some unexpected political dividends. One was his new relationship with Brooklyn district leader Anthony J. Genovesi, a power in the regular organization of Brooklyn Democratic chair Meade Esposito. A mutual friend took Koch and Genovesi to the Amato Opera in the early 1970s, and the pair soon struck up a warm relationship. After Forest Hills, Koch accepted Genovesi's invitation to protest a 904-unit housing development sponsored by the United Autoworkers in Flatbush that protesters said looked like "a prison compound." Genovesi so appreciated Koch's efforts to stop the project that he carried Koch's petitions for mayor in 1973, despite Genovesi's ostensible support of Abe Beame for mayor. And once Beame was defeated in 1977, Genovesi helped arrange Esposito's support for Koch in the mayoral runoff.[26]

GETTING PRESS BY ACTING TOUGH

White fear of crime fueled the Forest Hills affair, and Koch's actions outdid his earlier efforts to style himself as tough on crime. The episode also taught him more about how to attract the attention of reporters. Before his first mayoral run, Koch had already distributed more than fifteen hundred whistles to neighborhood groups in his district as part of a high-profile campaign against crime. Koch also introduced legislation to provide federal money for improved street lighting, a bill that drew national attention.[27]

In 1972 Koch pressed a complaint against a panhandler who had threatened to hit him if he did not hand over some money. The story highlighted the difficulty that citizens faced in dealing with street harassment. Koch spent almost two hours at a police station while the arrest was processed. An assistant district attorney told Koch that if he wanted the man to be charged with a felony, it would take three more hours. Koch declined and asked the district attorney's office to prosecute the man for misdemeanors—intoxication, loitering, and harassment—then attended court at 8:15 P.M. The panhandler, who was never publicly identified, was fined $50 and released. Koch told the *Times* that he checked with the city three months later and the fine was never paid, so his assailant had escaped even the minimal penalty. New Yorkers, he said, "are outraged at the way our courts are administering the justice system."[28]

While some friends recoiled at the spectacle of an increasingly conservative-sounding Koch, his strong legalistic bent and liberal roots also led him to champion prisoners' rights. He was probably influenced in this direction by his former law partner and close friend Allen G. Schwartz, who had a long-standing interest in prison reform. Also, Koch's policy of answering all constituent letters meant his office dealt with a flood of correspondence from prisoners that most other offices would ignore. In 1970 Koch had submitted a survey to inmates at the Tombs, as the New York County jail in downtown Manhattan has been called for more than a century, and used the results to prepare a report to the House Judiciary Committee recommending that Congress set minimum prison standards. He eventually introduced a bill to accompany the report.[29] Koch already knew about overcrowding—the Tombs then operated at 209 percent of capacity. But the survey, answered by 907 prisoners, half the population, revealed severe failures of sanitation—vermin infestation and a shortage of soap—and complaints about beatings by guards. One prisoner called the Tombs "a dungeon of fear." The bill did not pass, but a federal judge eventually ordered improvements at the Tombs. Whatever else he might say about crime, Koch continued to monitor New York prison conditions throughout his time in Congress and made corrections reform a priority of his mayoral administration.[30]

As he prepared to run for mayor in 1977, Koch seemed a very different man politically than when he had entered Congress. He had absorbed many conservative positions oriented toward a white urban working class that felt increasingly insecure. His willingness to work with conservatives was not always matched by a willingness to compromise with politicians to his left, especially African American members of Congress who lacked enthusiasm for Israel. While Koch could tolerate ambivalence from white members of the House, he interpreted any sign of hesitation about the U.S. alliance with Israel, especially if came from black politicians, more as a personal affront than a political disagreement. As a result, he tended to view blacks as competitors for power rather than as victims of discrimination.

Koch sought citywide support by reinforcing his old identity as a postwar lower-middle-class Brooklynite while assiduously cultivating his constituency—Silk

Stocking Manhattan—in his quest for a smashing 1976 reelection victory. In Manhattan he retained much liberal support with his 100 percent voting record approval from the Americans for Democratic Action—the arbiter of liberal voting records—along with his opposition to the Vietnam War, his technical competence as a legislator, and his excellent credentials on civil liberties issues. He had supported George McGovern but three years after McGovern's defeat criticized him for his supposed "militant elitism that seeks revolutionary economic change."[31] But if McGovern, as his critics charged, supported acid, amnesty for draft resisters and deserters, and abortion, it could be said that Koch supported marijuana decriminalization, amnesty, and choice. Thus Koch remained liberal enough for the general satisfaction of the East Side and Greenwich Village. For the increasingly anxious outer-borough whites, he also favored capital punishment without regard to its disproportionate impact on blacks, and he opposed busing, affirmative action, and scatter-site housing, all of which were intended to benefit blacks.

But these positions did not seem to disrupt the political consensus in his district. Republican opponents charged that Koch was not serious about crime (because of his whistle distribution stunt) and that he had left the House Banking and Currency Committee, where he had accumulated seniority, for Appropriations, where he supposedly had less power. But the appointment to the Appropriations Committee carried *more* power. Koch won the 1976 general election for his House seat with 76 percent of the vote.[32]

THE ONSET OF NEW YORK CITY'S FISCAL CRISIS, 1975–77

Koch faced his greatest challenges in the House in his last two terms. As a member of the influential Appropriations Committee, he held significant power for the first time—and he had a much stronger base for a mayoral run than he had had in 1973. New York needed federal aid to stay afloat, and he was in a pivotal position to keep money flowing.[33]

The causes of the fiscal crisis were as tangled as the roots of a mangrove. New York was not the only U.S. city with fiscal and social problems. Indeed, during the Ford, Carter, and Reagan administrations, critics of aid to New York invariably objected that if they helped New York, they would have to help other cities that were in even worse shape, as if reconstructing Cleveland or St. Louis would have been impossible or reprehensible. And this stance ignored the federal investment in suburbanization that had greatly contributed to the urban crisis.[34]

The worst global recession since the thirties was particularly acute in 1973–74. The weakness in the United States had several causes: the resurgence of the economies of Europe and Japan had created new competition and eroded U.S. economic dominance. As Judith Stein has pointed out in her study of the steel industry, the ascendancy of cold war foreign policy goals had led successive U.S. governments to pursue policies that effectively deindustrialized the United States in order to promote its foreign policy goals. During the 1950s and 1960s the United States invested in the development of steel industries in Europe and Japan while cutting tariff barriers to the importation of steel from those countries, in the hope that their economic development would help their economies and thereby contain communism. Ultimately, this reduced the market for U.S. steel and worsened the U.S. balance of payments. By the 1970s the outflow of gold and dollars to pay for the Vietnam War and suddenly expensive oil imports contributed to a drastically worsening balance of trade for the United States and ultimately stagflation—a toxic combination of high inflation and high unemployment.[35]

The sudden rise of oil prices in 1973 also depressed the economies of developing countries, jeopardizing their ability to pay back loans. Many of those loans were held by New York banks, and the crisis endangered their liquidity. The same banks had been marketing New York's burgeoning debt. Lindsay and Beame financed deficits irresponsibly, particularly after 1970, using expensive short-term borrowing that rose from $26 million under Wagner to almost $7.6 billion by 1975. The city's debt service more than quadrupled in the same period. And excessive state borrowing, using what would later be called junk bonds, led to the default of some state agencies, further frightening the bond market.[36]

At the time the capitalization of expense items—selling bonds to cover recurring expenses, that is, items in the city's operating budget—was taken for granted as a staple of municipal finance, and it seemed to work so long as credit was inexpensive and revenues were increasing. By the fall of 1974 the market for city securities was tightening, spurred by an embarrassing public squabble between Comptroller Harrison J. Goldin and Mayor Beame about the actual size of the city's deficit. The cost of borrowing increased. New York had an increasingly difficult time meeting its obligations. By February 1975 its credit had begun to collapse, with demands for its bonds clearly slowing. Three months later the banks refused to market any more New York City bonds.[37]

Why did New York accumulate so much debt? At the time the conventional wisdom was that New York was a lavish spender on welfare, overly generous to its employees, and had hired too many of them. "The only realistic course," the *New York Times* editorialized in May 1975, "is to cut spending to levels that the city can afford—and that means reducing personnel and services far more drastically than the Mayor has so far suggested," including a hiring freeze and the suspension of wage and benefit increases already negotiated with the unions.[38]

Beame tried to resist cutbacks, pretending that the city was not bankrupt but only facing a short-term "cash-flow" problem caused by the timing of state and federal aid. This was transparent nonsense and further undermined the city's credit. Beame's obduracy gave ammunition to conservative Republicans. Treasury Secretary William Simon, a leading conservative ideologue, opposed federal aid to New York. He hoped to eliminate New York's social democracy and bust its public employee unions, never mind the effects on the city. Simon especially wanted an end to free tuition at City University, which was more an ideological imperative than a financial one. He was not the only strong opponent of an aid program. White House Chief of Staff Donald Rumsfeld, a former U.S. representative from Illinois, reportedly hoped that New York's troubles would leave Chicago as the nation's leading financial center.[39]

PINK SLIPS AND "BLOOD DAYS"

By the end of May 1975 Mayor Beame had prepared two budgets—one that he called an "austerity budget" that called for laying off thirty thousand employees, the other a doomsday crisis budget that eliminated sixty thousand jobs, in the event that increases in state aid were not forthcoming. He issued more than sixteen thousand pink slips the next day. Ultimately, the city laid off forty-seven thousand municipal employees between June 1975 and April 30, 1976, including 20 percent of the police force and 20 percent of elementary school teachers.[40]

There was a grain of truth to the conventional narrative that New York's fiscal crisis resulted from bad management and bloated union contracts. Even before the fiscal crisis began, Lindsay and Beame had invested little in computerization and had failed to improve budget and information systems, which led to loose management, then disastrous inefficiency, when departments had to lay off the people who did the work that computers should have been doing—and the city still had no money to computerize. Some union work rules and pension provisions were outrageous, such as "blood days," which gave police officers an entire day off if they donated blood. Moreover, mayors had a conflict of interest when they bargained on behalf of the taxpayers with unions that supported the mayors for reelection.

But the solution that Washington forced on New York made its problems worse. Drastic budget cuts and layoffs destroyed the ability of city agencies to perform basic services or to respond to new crises, such as an arson epidemic in Brooklyn and the Bronx. (See chapter 13). The cuts also interrupted the normal transfer of knowledge and experience within agencies. And much of the traditional fiscal crisis narrative, which focuses on the faults of New York City rather than those of federal policy, does not explain why so many other cities had fiscal crises at the same time.[41] Fiscal insufficiency was structural, inherent in the peculiar burdens that federalism places on municipalities in general and New York in particular.[42]

Throughout much of New York's history, increased spending was a typical response to rising unemployment and disorder during downturns in the business cycle or structural changes in the local economy. In the 1970s New York lacked sufficient resources to cope with the emergency. Unemployment was aggravated by the flight of the middle classes to the suburbs and the Sun Belt—a matter of changing tastes but also subsidized by federal tax, housing, and transportation policies, as well as the construction of water projects and other infrastructure that made Sun Belt cities habitable.[43]

When the increasing power of suburban constituencies put a series of antiurban administrations in Washington—Nixon, Ford, and Carter—federal funding for the increasingly poor and segregated central cities dried up. And many continuing federal programs, such as Medicaid, obligated New York to unsustainable levels of matching funds. Lindsay and Beame compensated by putting recurring expense items, normally paid for out of current tax revenue, into the capital budget, which was financed by debt. In effect, they were buying groceries with the city's credit card. Eventually, this necessitated short-term credits at high interest and an eventual default. Overly generous municipal employment contracts had little to do with pushing New York into fiscal crisis. The compensation of city employees in New York was not substantially higher than in fiscally sound Chicago.[44] Moreover, from 1971 to 1975 labor costs actually fell as a percentage of New York's budget, from 56.4 percent to 47.4 percent.[45]

But the governmental structure of New York made the city pay for many functions, such as education and hospitals, that in Chicago were paid for by Cook County or other state and municipal entities. Under Mayor Lindsay those extra functions grew from 56 percent to 73 percent of the budget Chicago's strong, machine-backed mayor was able to cut budgets and capital expenditures without the motivation of an extreme crisis, which seemed to be the precondition for cuts in New York, where huge portions of the city budget went to agencies, such as the Board of Education and the Health and Hospitals Corporation, that the mayor did not directly control and that had strong independent constituencies.[46]

Pork barrel politicking also contributed to New York's budgetary woes. The contracts, supplies, and equipment budget grew a phenomenal 620 percent from 1961 to 1975, when it amounted to $1.3 billion—more than twice the entire budget of CUNY. The other item that grew at a phenomenal rate was debt service, as a result of shifting expenses to the capital budget and short-term borrowing on anticipated revenues.[47] As interest rates rose in response to the inflationary pressures and higher investment risks of the early 1970s, borrowing became unaffordable. The biggest drag on revenues was the failure to assess property at its true market value. Assessments dropped from an average of 82 percent of market value in 1961 to only 48 percent of market value in 1975. If all taxable property had been fully assessed in accordance with rulings of the New York Court of Appeals, the city would have generated enough revenue to avoid the crisis.[48] At the time opponents of taxation claimed that raising property taxes would raise rents and chase more companies out, yet the decline in services and the lack of affordable housing were arguably more likely to push businesses out than a modest tax increase.

With the private market not interested in refinancing New York City's debt, the federal government was the first place to turn. But the administration of Gerald R. Ford was decidedly unsympathetic—so much so that the *Daily News* famously (and accurately) characterized his reaction as "Drop Dead." A *Times* reporter observed that President Ford's position was a product of "his feeling that his own natural constituency is rural, conservative, and geographically far removed" from New York. He also feared that if he helped New York, other cities that were falling into even worse ruin might also demand aid.[49]

Ford's antipathy toward saving the city was part of a larger elite movement of business conservatives. The historian Kim Phillips-Fein has detailed how a group of business people and conservative intellectuals, including William Simon, organized politically to attack social democratic institutions, which they saw as debilitating to the economy and demoralizing to the labor force. Simon, who believed in the radical free-market conservatism of Ayn Rand, did his utmost to drive New York into bankruptcy, hoping to end its social democratic aspirations.[50]

He also influenced some of the men who formed the junta that ran New York's new austerity regime. For example, Governor Hugh Carey appointed Citibank CEO Walter Wriston to the two new state agencies that took over New York's municipal government: the Municipal Assistance Corporation, charged with refinancing the city's bonds, and the Emergency Financial Control Board, which was given total power to collect and disburse city funds. Wriston later joined Simon in the Executive Advisory Group, the group that sought to implement Simon's call for "a massive and unprecedented mobilization" of capitalists for a social order based on Rand's ideas. They also worked on strategies to elect Ronald Reagan as president.[51]

"TRUST ME?"

International pressure and a growing realization that the bankruptcy of the nation's largest city would undermine confidence in the dollar and the U.S. economy, as well as implementation of the control board's fiscal and management reforms and destructive across-the-board budget cuts, led Congress to pass a "rescue" package of so-called seasonal loans. Seasonal loans are loans to farmers or other businesses "with seasonal business patterns as well as to other customers with temporary needs," which perhaps made them more palatable to rural representatives in Congress. They were designed to meet the city's short-term need for cash as revenues ran out. As the political scientist Ester Fuchs has noted, however, the federal loans merely created "the opportunity to borrow funds at what might be characterized as 'loan shark' rates." The program failed to provide New York with a path back to solvency by restructuring its debt.[52]

That was left to the considerably more limited resources of New York State. Governor Carey's first response to the city's impending bankruptcy had been to create the Municipal Assistance Corporation in June 1975. "Big MAC" refinanced municipal debt with bonds secured by a first lien on the city's stock transfer tax and sales tax receipts. It then exchanged short-term city bonds for longer-term municipal bonds. Selling these bonds was not easy, and the cost of borrowing was high. Donna Shalala, who was a MAC board member, recalled her experience in trying to sell MAC bonds to a group of investors in Texas: "The questions I got were so incredibly hostile, they shook me. 'How do you expect me to buy bonds for a city that doesn't even know how many city workers it has?' asked one. What do you say to these guys—'Trust me?'"[53] MAC was also granted power over the budget, but those powers proved insufficient as Mayor Beame resisted some of the cuts it ordered and rehired laid-off workers.

Beame's intransigence prompted Carey to create the control board, which held the city's purse strings. The unions, which had at the outset resisted cutbacks with slogans like "They say cut-back, we say fight-back," were co-opted into the process because union leaders feared that bankruptcy would nullify the contracts that they had negotiated and threaten the unions' existence. So union leaders formed a de facto partnership with the banks, purchasing a large share of MAC's otherwise unmarketable bonds with union pension funds, in exchange for a seat at the table where the city's budget was being slashed. In doing so they risked their members' retirement funds, gambling that their conservative antagonists would be able to save the city, and that as a major creditor they would be able to maintain collective bargaining and limit cuts that would hurt city workers.

The collapse of union opposition cemented the power of the unelected boards of MAC and the Emergency Financial Control Board to impose austerity. New York's elected officials had so completely lost control that the EFCB forced Beame to fire his closest confidant, First Deputy Mayor James A. Cavanagh, in favor of the establishment insider John Zuccotti, who became de facto mayor. This was probably a sensible measure. Cavanagh was an old-school La Guardia–era civil servant who had risen through the ranks with Abe Beame by passing city exams; he had not actually completed his bachelor's degree until he was sixty-one and serving as first deputy mayor.[54]

Cavanagh was not interested in computers or modern management techniques. Instead he managed with small white slips of paper. Koch's parks commissioner, Gordon Davis, who started out in the Lindsay administration's budget bureau, recalled how Cavanaugh used to balance the budget: "All us new-fangled program budget types, hot shits from Harvard, we'd sit there and do our program analysis and when we were done, there was a huge gap still there. Jim Cavanaugh would get on the phone with the comptroller's office and he never had anything on his desk but these little white notepads." Cavanagh and the comptroller "would say this and that, and then they'd do something like—well, a standard technique was to re-estimate the welfare."[55]

Cavanagh was not the only one fired. By 1976 the control board had reduced the workforce by nearly 100,000 from its 1974 peak—a 27 percent reduction. Capital spending was slashed almost 75 percent, and maintenance, repair, and replacement of city facilities came to a halt without rhyme or reason. The crisis even stopped nearly completed projects, such as the fully equipped Woodhull Hospital, which remained closed for another five years. It also realized Simon's ideological crusade by imposing tuition at City University.[56]

The consequences of these cuts were devastating, creating a city in which almost nothing was maintained or repaired for a decade. Proponents of austerity claimed, like Margaret Thatcher, that "there is no alternative." It is true that the local or state government could do little to raise more money from private sources. Ford, Simon, and Congress bear much of the responsibility for the thousands of people who lost their homes, jobs, or health or even their lives as a consequence of the budget cuts. The vast sums that had to be spent to repair the damage to New York's infrastructure would have been unnecessary if the federal government had guaranteed a much smaller sum over a long term to fund the capital budget. Indeed, making management more efficient and modernizing methods of control, such as computerization, required capital investment.

The fiscal crisis led Koch to make a second run for mayor in 1977. He wanted to save his beloved city. He became an ex-officio member of the control board and gained the support of EFCB and MAC directors like William Ellinghaus of AT&T and David Margolis of Colt Industries, who became one of his closest friends. Yet Koch remained curiously disengaged from the board's work, making it clear that membership on the board did not mean that he was endorsing its views. He had little to say about his role, perhaps because he was no fiscal expert.[57]

He did manage to offend the black president of the Health and Hospitals Corporation, which runs the city's public hospitals. Koch and his congressional colleague Herman Badillo, concerned that HHC was hemorrhaging tax revenues, called for the resignation of its president, Dr. John L. S. Holloman Jr. Holloman was already under fire from Mayor Beame, but Koch made it more personal, reportedly branding Holloman as incompetent, which could be interpreted as a racist code word. Testifying at a subsequent hearing called by Koch and Badillo, Holloman denounced Koch as a racist, then stormed out of the hearing, according to the *New York Amsterdam News*. The call for Holloman's resignation made many in the Harlem establishment bitter about Koch; they perceived Badillo and Koch's position as a betrayal by public officials "once recognized by the Black community on the race issue." While Koch and Badillo saw themselves as reformers acting on merit, the *Amsterdam News* perceived the attacks as racially motivated attempts "aimed at firing Holloman from the position that makes him, a Black man, the highest paid public servant in New York City." That mistrust would continue when, as mayor, Koch made unpopular decisions to close hospitals and reform the HHC, a key to balancing the budget.[58]

Although Koch agreed with many of the control board's management goals, such as improving HHC management, he was outraged at the idea of giving control to the city's creditors (as represented by the MAC and the control board directors) instead of elected officials. He even sued to have control board declared unconstitutional, later insisting that "if I were the Mayor, I would never have gone along with it: I don't think I could have accepted a state of affairs that made me one-seventh of a mayor."[59]

10 THE 1977 MAYORAL ELECTION

I didn't get my job through the *New York Times*.

—ED KOCH

The indefatigable Ed Koch shivered and shook hands at subway entrances, an early-morning routine that went back to his first days in politics almost two decades earlier. It was January 1977, and his mayoral prospects seemed chillier than the winter air. He was polling at 2 percent, and his campaign had little cash on hand. Despite his successes in Washington and among his own constituents, some pundits and political pros dismissed Koch as a bohemian representative from Greenwich Village, a lightweight with little clout outside Manhattan, known for issuing blizzards of statements nobody ever read. Koch kept shaking hands. This election was his last chance—his failed 1973 campaign had branded him as a laughable also-ran.

Koch was fully aware that he'd have to offer voters much more than a handshake at the subway. His mistakes had taught him the two keys to victory: money and television. He also had to set himself off from the pack. For this he came up with a brilliant political stunt: a faux romance with the first Jewish Miss America, Bess Myerson. Myerson was a tall brunette with a memorable smile and political ambitions of her own. Before the end of her one-year reign in 1945, she had toured the country speaking for religious and racial tolerance, sponsored by the B'nai B'rith Anti-Defamation League, and had given a solo piano concert at Carnegie Hall. Myerson was a symbol of America's acceptance of Jews, and she stayed in the public eye through the 1950s with appearances on quiz shows and in the 1960s as Mayor John V. Lindsay's commissioner of consumer affairs. Why help Koch? He was the candidate who needed her most and whose fortunes she could most influence. And in 1977 it was clear that the first Jewish Miss America had strong ambitions of her own, perhaps extending all the way to the White House. Putting Koch in the mayoralty could be the first step to the Senate and beyond, and indeed Koch, along with Governor Carey and Senator Daniel P. Moynihan, supported Myerson's unsuccessful bid for the U.S. Senate in 1980. And Koch definitely needed Myerson. Associating with her would "brand" him and set him apart in a crowded field (at one point there were eight other potential candidates). Koch was not born with charisma but acquired it later as success brought self-confidence. At this point, however, out in Brooklyn or Queens he was just another Jewish member of Congress, practically invisible. But when Koch and Myerson appeared together, no one could take their eyes off them. Koch was just learning the art of making love to the television camera, while Myerson was a past mistress of the medium. In a time when *bachelorhood* carried a homophobic stigma, she provided the bald, unromantic, politics-obsessed bachelor with a storybook narrative—he must be manly if he was wooing Miss America.

The attractive fiction came at a heavy price. In private there was nothing between them, but she "added a dimension of credibility" for those voters concerned about Koch's sexual preference, according to Jim Capalino, the campaign's field coordinator. Sometimes Myerson seemed to forget that it was Koch who was running for mayor. Capalino recalled that while Myerson's contribution was immense and her schedule was grueling, "a huge amount of time and effort was spent constantly playing to her ego."[1]

Despite being high maintenance, Myerson made many thrilling appearances at the beginning of the campaign, which helped Koch attract notice. Although at one point Bess almost quit, "when she was getting good press, she loved it," and she stopped complaining.[2] After a summer break, during which Koch trudged sidewalks so hot they could fry the proverbial egg, she came back for the final round, chiding Koch's runoff opponent, Mario Cuomo, for his negative campaigning. Koch was happy to benefit from Myerson's glamour until he became glamorous in his own right as New York's celebrity mayor, and after his election they appeared in public together less and less.[3]

Meyerson's public support was vital to Koch's victory. But he owed Myerson even more for connecting him with the media consultant David Garth, who had master-minded Hugh Carey's come-from-behind win in the 1974 gubernatorial contest. Koch supporters Steve Berger and John LoCicero had chatted Garth up about the mayoral race on the beach at Fire Island in the summer of 1976. Garth mentioned Koch, along with Cuomo, then the New York secretary of state, and State Attorney General Robert Abrams as candidates the voters were likely to find appealing. LoCicero, the campaign manager, reported to Koch, "You know, David Garth really likes you." So Koch asked Myerson, another mutual friend, to arrange dinner.[4] Garth's chief researcher, Maureen Connelly, confirmed that Koch had some considerable strengths, specifically his reputation as a hardworking congressman who was more conservative and pragmatic than one might expect. He had developed relationships with a number of ethnic constituencies in the outer boroughs, fragmentary pockets of support that could be stitched together with that of moderately liberal Jewish voters in Manhattan and more conservative voters in the outer boroughs to secure the 20 percent of the electorate necessary to get into the runoff.[5]

GARTH PUTS KOCH ON MESSAGE

Garth signed on with Koch after Cuomo assured Garth he would not run.[6] Garth then began to transform the gangly stentorian Koch into a standout who would eclipse his more famous rivals. In 1974 Garth's brilliant television campaign had made Carey, then another obscure New York congressman, famous enough to become New York's first Democratic governor in sixteen years. "He can do the same for me," Koch told contributors in a fund-raising letter.[7] Though Koch appeared lackluster, pundits began to declare that any candidate who could raise enough money to pay for Garth's considerable talents "is automatically moved a square ahead on the chessboard."[8]

In private Garth was less optimistic, telling the candidate, "Ed, you're a 20-to-1 shot." Though the media touted Garth's invincibility, he avoided such complacencies in managing the campaign and closely controlled Koch's most intense personal impulses: to talk and to eat. Garth's most important stricture was message discipline. When Garth had anything to say about it, every declaration and appearance was designed to communicate the idea that Edward I. Koch would be a competent mayor.[9]

Projecting an image of competence required Koch to be absolutely serious, despite his penchant for quips and sarcasm. When Koch asked, "How'm I doing?" Garth growled: "I'll tell you how you're doing, you son of a bitch: you're really pissing me off. Stop asking that question."[10] For the duration of the 1977 primary campaign, Koch obeyed and convinced pundits that he was a colorless technocrat. Just before he took office, Andy Logan wrote in the *New Yorker* that "the assumption is that [Koch's] mayoral style will be low-key, unpretentious, and resolutely unhistrionic," recalling another reporter's description of the mayor-elect as "a tall Abe Beame." Ed Koch, the future "mayatollah," was still under wraps.[11]

Garth did allow one exception to his ban on humor—a commercial launched soon after Beame announced his candidacy for reelection, though the ad was strictly scripted. Beame had told the press that he wanted to run again so he could "finish the job." In the commercial Koch told voters: "Four years ago, Abe Beame told us he knew the buck. And two years later we didn't have any bucks. Then he told us he made the tough decisions. He must have forgotten Felix Rohatyn, Steve Berger, Governor Carey and Big Mac. Now Mayor Beame is asking for four more years to finish the job. Finish the job? Hasn't he done enough?"[12]

Koch loved to eat and hated to call contributors. But at the beginning Garth gave the candidate "two commandments: number one—lose weight, and number two—raise money." Specifically, Koch had to lose fifteen pounds and raise $250,000 before declaring his candidacy to prove that he could afford Garth's services.[13] Koch forced himself to work the phones while sweating out the weight. Garth, a heavy guy himself, explained his theory that candidates need to be healthy and energetic in order to tame their tongues: "If you can control your weight—something happens in the psyche. Goddamn, I can control something. And there's a little bit of a feeling that maybe I am master of my fate." Garth was remaking a shy, starchy Jewish representative into a media genius in his own right.[14]

Control of the candidate's mind and body was not enough. Garth also demanded (and got) control of the campaign budget—the vast majority of which would go to television, with a field operation so shoestring that Koch's petitions barely had enough signatures to qualify him for the ballot. Jerry Skurnik, a member of the campaign staff, recalled that the economies on petitioning amounted to a calculated risk that none of the other candidates, for their own reasons, would sue to get Koch off the ballot, a move that was actively contemplated by the Beame campaign.[15] Garth's candidates were largely independent of traditional sources of grassroots political power. He was among the first to understand that television was largely replacing political parties as the medium between candidates and voters. Television required simple repetitive messages like "competence"—a hard sell for a small-time-lawyer-turned congressman with no executive experience.[16]

In the context of that election, however, competence meant embracing the rhetoric of fiscal crisis—the subordination of all other interests to policies designed to increase the tax base through deregulation and budgetary austerity.[17] The history of the 1977 mayoral campaign suggests that even severe crises may be represented in electoral campaigns as incremental, business-as-usual politics. Koch's success with a pro-austerity platform was surprising, given the fate of the other candidates who favored austerity: First Deputy Mayor John Zuccotti, the developer Richard Ravitch, the attorney Edward N. Costikyan, and Joel Harnett, president of the City Club, a government watchdog. Zuccotti never got started. Ravitch and Costikyan quickly found that Manhattanites peddling austerity could find precious little traction outside their own political circles. Harnett stayed the course and performed so poorly that he provoked the laughter of the chattering classes.

U.S. Representative Herman Badillo, a Puerto Rican orphan who had worked his way through City College and Brooklyn Law School, had initially seemed to have a better shot than Koch. Badillo had as much congressional seniority as Koch and far more executive experience as a Wagner administration commissioner and as Bronx Borough president; Badillo's views on the fiscal crisis and social issues like the death penalty were similar to Koch's. But Badillo did not have Garth or money, and by 1977 he already had the taint of the perennial candidate.

Badillo's advocacy of austerity whipsawed his candidacy. The city's elite expected that if he won, he would owe too many debts to the minority community, which probably precluded Badillo from picking up the money and support of establishment types like Governor Carey and Felix Rohatyn, who were committed to the austerity regime. At the same time African American politicos correctly took Badillo's fiscal prudence as a threat to their own jobs and patronage. So instead of helping Badillo to build a minority coalition that might have been far out in the lead, most black politicians supported Percy Sutton, the Manhattan Borough president.

Tall and suave, Sutton was the biggest name on the Harlem political scene. He had been one of the Tuskegee airmen in World War II and a lawyer for Malcolm X. Sutton hoped to add enough votes to his base to get the 18 to 20 percent of the electorate necessary to make the runoff. Other candidates criticized the austerity regime but none as unequivocally as Sutton. In his kickoff speech he called on New York to "liberate itself from the banks." His campaign stressed the need for New Deal–style jobs programs to stimulate New York's struggling economy, and he alone proposed to increase the tax base and tourism through legalized gambling.[18] The Sutton campaign concentrated on promoting the idea of a black mayor on the explicit assumption that Sutton would drastically increase both patronage and respect for the black community. Though he tended to blame his lack of success on a lack of campaign funds, the real problem was that his support in the black community was too weak to put him in contention. Two other candidates—Bella Abzug and Mayor Beame—took many black votes away from Sutton.

Abzug was the biggest star in the field, and she had considerable backing from other stars, such as Barbra Streisand, Lily Tomlin, Shirley MacLaine, Woody Allen, Mary Travers, and Gloria Steinem. Though Abzug was one of Congress's most progressive members, her 1977 campaign was strangely ambivalent, reflecting the difficulty that New York's Left had in responding effectively to the rising neoliberal order.[19] Abzug denounced what she called the "New York Times-EFCB-Wall Street-Steve Berger vision of New York, a New York of diminishing expectations." At the same time she inconsistently embraced austerity, declaring that New York needed a mayor who could "tell people 'No' and make it stick." Given her calls for the restoration of free tuition at City University, repeal of the Taylor Law to allow public employees to strike, and other expansions of city spending, it was not clear to whom she was going to say no.[20]

Her slogan, "Bella Means Business," contradicted both her socialist past and her criticisms of the austerity regime. Instead, she used business boosterism, declaring, without a trace of irony, that "reducing taxes will be a top priority of my administration together with improving essential city services"—anticipating one of the most questionable arguments of Reaganomics—that reducing taxes would increase revenues.[21] This was a far cry from her 1972 congressional race when she laid a much greater emphasis on redistributive policies and macroeconomic issues, calling for "an end to militarism and domination of our society by the corporate power structure."[22] The inconsistencies in Abzug's rhetoric and her failure to articulate a coherent social democratic alternative, along with her reputation as a poor manager of her congressional staff, raised questions about her competence to be mayor, even among many who sent her to Congress and backed her nearly successful 1976 bid for the Democratic nomination for the U.S. Senate. Her television ads touting her as a fighter did nothing to ease such doubts.

Of all the candidates, the fiscal crisis was the most bitter reality for the incumbent mayor, Abraham D. Beame. Because he had served as city comptroller when much of the debt ballooned, many voters held him responsible. Beame also had to overcome the impression, largely accurate, that the Emergency Financial Control Board had reduced him to a figurehead. Surprisingly, he remained a viable candidate for reelection. As the first Jewish mayor, Beame had a leg up with the largest ethnic group voting in the Democratic primary and considerable support from old-line labor leaders like Harry Van Arsdale of the Central Labor Council, Albert Shanker of the United Federation of Teachers, and Sol C. Chaikin of the International Ladies Garment Workers' Union. Beame also got his share of money and support from real estate interests.[23]

Many voters did not connect rising crime and decreasing services to the abstract issues of the fiscal crisis. And thousands of city workers felt that Beame had tried to save their jobs. The media visibility of incumbency was Beame's greatest strength. Losing power over the budget did not matter so much when, as mayor, he was the only candidate to get advance notice from the police of the capture of the serial killer David Berkowitz—who called himself "Son of Sam." Beame was able to call television camera crews to police headquarters at 1:40 A.M. on a hot August night to film him taking partial credit for cracking the case, highlighting his newfound support for the death penalty.[24]

The death penalty's most visible opponent in the race was Cuomo, who had been a prominent lawyer in Queens and had negotiated the compromise over public housing in Forest Hills. His most famous supporter was Jackie Onassis, and he got a large contributions from David Geffen and the liquor king Edgar M. Bronfman. Much of Cuomo's support was conferred on him by Governor Carey, and most of it came from the Democratic establishment of the 1950s—the former governor W. Averell Harriman, the former mayor Robert F. Wagner, and Truman-era warhorses like former air force secretary Thomas K. Finletter and former secretary of labor Anna Rosenberg. But real estate moguls and quite a few private carters also ponied up for Cuomo, who raised the most money among the primary candidates. And he had significant labor support, including the backing of the Communications Workers and the Seafarers Union.[25]

Cuomo adroitly took liberal positions that addressed conservative concerns. He talked about the administrative reorganization of the welfare and criminal justice systems, promising to be "mayor of the law."[26] Cuomo's liberal version of law-and-order rhetoric managed to appeal to his core constituency of outer-borough Italians, who loved his ethnicity more than his politics and perceived him as an anti-Manhattan candidate. Although his liberal brand of Catholicism and opposition to the death penalty would eventually allow Cuomo to build political bridges to Manhattan, in 1977 he was far from the liberal icon he would become in the 1980s. His principal weakness was his inexperience as a candidate—he was "not as forceful and persuasive with prepared speeches as in person-to-person contact and in off-the-cuff talks," the New York Times declared of the man who would later gain a reputation as a great orator.[27] Cuomo sought the support of labor by pushing for the construction of Westway, an expensive, partly underground highway and development project on the Lower West Side of Manhattan that succeeded the defeated Lower Manhattan Expressway. He also tried to soft-pedal his identification with an austerity system, although it had been the price of his strong backing from Carey. Indeed, the governor had pushed Cuomo into the race so hard that he almost appeared to be running against his will, and the Times even wrote that Cuomo was "regarded as a puppet" of the governor. But Carey's support was a much bigger asset than a liability. Because of the governor Cuomo raised more than $700,000 for the first primary campaign.[28]

Except for Bess Myerson, Koch's campaign was startlingly lacking in support from celebrities. The composer Richard Rodgers and the pornographer Al Goldstein were perhaps Koch's next-most-famous backers, but neither had a high profile in the campaign. Nor did Koch sup at labor's table. But Richard Nixon had pegged Koch's political potential as far back as 1969 when he first met the new representative of New York's Upper East Side. "Lotta money in that district," Nixon told Koch. Koch's district connections meant that he could raise money from old New York names like Whitney and Havemeyer, and from members of the Emergency Financial Control Board like William Ellinghaus, vice chair of AT&T and a member of Koch's finance committee, and David Margolis of Colt Industries, one of Koch's closest buddies.[29] Mostly, Koch's campaign money came from wealthy personal friends like Margolis; Bernard Rome, a self-made millionaire; Antonio G. Olivieri, a member of the state assembly for the East Side; and Robert Menschel, a partner in Goldman Sachs who was married to the long-time Koch aide Ronay Menschel. Robert Menschel brought in several other Goldman partners as contributors, including Robert E. Rubin, who would serve as secretary of the treasury under President Bill Clinton.[30]

Koch used his long-time support for the death penalty, unusual for a liberal Jew from Manhattan, to reach for more conservative outer-borough voters. Anticipating the strategy of Bill Clinton, Koch believed that a nominally liberal candidate could favor the death penalty and attract working-class conservatives while retaining the votes of liberal voters, although the strategy made Garth nervous. Garth saw the death penalty as a distraction from message discipline: the Koch campaign was alone in its focus on the fiscal crisis, portraying Ed as the competent candidate who would solve the financial mess. As Garth, who crafted the message, observed, "Nothing about it was subtle, because there was nothing about Ed Koch that was subtle."[31] Even the campaign's specific policy proposals were variations on the fiscal crisis theme. For example, Koch called for reforms of the Health and Hospitals Corporation, the police, and other city agencies, not so much to improve services as to return to a firm financial footing.

For most of the campaign Koch stayed "on message," with the exception of his periodic zingers about the death penalty. At the press conference announcing his candidacy, he told reporters that New York was "facing its darkest hour—with the continued threat of bankruptcy, the loss of more and more jobs, and the steadily increasing crime rate"—and criticized Beame for having to be "dragged kicking and screaming to every decision" by the EFCB. Koch, in contrast, billed himself as the candidate who would find a way out of the austerity regime and restore financial health.[32] Yet Koch did not entirely reject his liberal origins, opposing Westway (a position he reversed as mayor) and strongly supporting rent control.[33]

While not even Garth could prevent Koch from talking about the death penalty, he did put a stop to other detours from Koch's main message about competence. Garth convinced Koch that the fiscal crisis was the elephant in the room and that voters would support the only viable candidate willing to tell them straight that the elephant was there and that he intended to look it in the eye. Of all the candidates,

Koch used the harshest rhetoric, blaming the crisis on unions, leftists, and "poverty pimps," but he also made more specific management proposals, including changes in work rules to increase the productivity of city workers, bringing the Board of Education under mayoral control, and the introduction of zero-based budgeting. All these were geared to an austerity approach and restoring municipal credit.[34]

Koch also got significant boosts in May and June 1977, when Costikyan pulled out of the race and became Koch's campaign cochair, which enhanced the liberal congressman's reputation for fiscal soundness, as Costikyan was a pillar of the establishment. Then Garth's first media blitz, complete with radio and television spots, began to make Koch a household name. Still, at the end of May the two frontrunners were Beame and Abzug, by far the two best-known candidates, although Abzug had not yet officially declared her candidacy.[35]

BLACKOUT AND BACKLASH

Until mid-July 1977 it seemed like an ordinary summer campaign. Koch had been driving all over in a rented Winnebago with "Koch for Mayor" plastered on the side and an ice cream truck sound system playing "N.Y.C."—not the more famous Sinatra number, "New York, New York" but a paen to the city from the musical *Annie* that the composer Charles Strouse gave him the right to use. Koch had been tirelessly traveling the five boroughs for weeks, meeting voters in hundreds of neighborhoods, while Garth's television spots established his identity.[36]

Meanwhile, Bella Abzug, the frontrunner, began to self-destruct. In a moment of politically foolish labor dogmatism, she declared that, notwithstanding state law, police and fire fighters had a "constitutional right-to-strike," which fueled fears that she would be a poor administrator. Beame accused her of interfering in his negotiations with the uniformed services and then cemented police support for himself with a sweetheart labor settlement.[37]

On July 13 everything changed. The lights went out all over New York. That night was either a carnival or a Walpurgisnacht, depending on your class status and attitude toward private property. As long as the sun was up, the mood was festive on that long, warm summer evening. In Harlem and up and down the West Side, people crowded on the sidewalks, drinking beer that remained cool and catching news from passing car radios. As the sun went down, more people went indoors to candlelit apartments. Tens of thousands broke into stores and made off with merchandise. If you lived on Broadway or in Bushwick or Harlem, you could hear the sound of glass breaking in the darkened streets. The police arrested more than four thousand people for looting, but many more made it home with the swag.[38]

In Harlem the *Amsterdam News* reported reactions to the looting that ranged from those who saw the looters as animals to those who thought they were "victims of joblessness and oppression who saw a chance to strike back at their oppressors." The paper itself blamed a lack of black leadership and invoked New Deal solutions, specifically, jobs programs—the era was still sufficiently liberal that people believed that the federal government should guarantee full employment by becoming the employer of last resort.[39]

The widespread looting clearly set back the campaigns of Badillo and Sutton. Sutton tried his best to prevent the racial polarization of voters, taking the pulpit at the Abyssinian Baptist Church to denounce the looters for "dragging an entire people backward and downward into the primeval ooze and slime of riot and disorder," insisting that the problem of looting had been "misperceived" as racial rather than criminal. Sutton also noted out that he and Badillo were the only candidates willing to walk the streets during the riots and try (vainly) to calm the crowds. Even Sutton's own campaign aides conceded that the small political space for electing a black mayor had contracted as a result of the blackout looting. The racial fears the looting engendered also diminished Abzug's support.[40] Some white voters made little distinction between blacks and looters, and the looting put them in the mood for revenge.[41]

Koch knew it was a breakthrough moment, and it thrilled him. He became the chief exponent of the "blackout backlash," charging that Beame had "lost control of city services to the municipal unions and now has lost control of the streets."[42] Throwing common sense aside, he blamed Beame for failing to mobilize the National Guard to halt the looters, though it was not even logistically possible to get the Guard into the streets that night. Koch's militancy appealed to lower-income white voters, and he would run second only to Beame among them.[43] But a crowd of black shoppers who recognized the dangers of his call to deploy soldiers heckled Koch at a campaign stop in Jamaica, Queens. One member of the crowd, Bob Davis, an unemployed chef, likened Koch's proposed tactics to throwing gasoline on a fire: "They would have shot up just everybody."[44]

The conventional wisdom at the time was that Beame benefited most from the blackout, under the theory that New Yorkers rally to the mayor in a disaster, just as they rallied to the previously unpopular Rudolph Giuliani after 9/11.[45] As mayor Beame was on television daily, trying to calm the citizenry and appealing to his good friend president Jimmy Carter for help. For several days Beame's opponents were relegated to the occasional carping sound bite.

Though pundits assumed that the blackout publicity would help the mayor, it did not. Instead, the increasing disorder of an already-chaotic city seemed to increase many voters' wish for new leadership. Carter, who had pledged help for the city while running for president, refused to declare New York a disaster area, which would have qualified it for massive federal funds. He handed the mayor a check for a paltry $11 million, a drop in the bucket given the damage wrought by the looters.

Koch attacked Carter and, by implication, Beame for failing to make good on the 1976 presidential campaign promise.[46]

Blackout backlash forced the New York mayoral race to the right, and for the first time polls showed Koch as a contender, in a statistical dead heat with Cuomo and Beame for the second-place position that would get him into the runoff. Abzug still held first place, but her star was fading. The good news for Koch was that by early August, 11 percent of voters were still undecided. Beame and Abzug were well known; undecided voters had probably already rejected them.[47]

Enter Rupert Murdoch, who had bought the sleepy liberal *New York Post* that summer and used it to reshape New York's public space and political discourse. New Yorkers read their papers in public. On the subways, park benches, in New York's newly emerging sidewalk cafés, even in the transparent steel-net trash bins that grace New York's sidewalks, Murdoch's *Post* invaded people's imaginations—even those who refused to buy it—because of its lurid headlines that broadcast sex, violence, and celebrity gossip of the Studio 54 era.

While the *Times* took little notice of "Son of Sam," who had killed five people and wounded six others in a year, the *Post* and its higher-quality rival, the *Daily News,* filled New York with fearful headlines. In the media whirlpool around the ".44-caliber killer," people even forgot about the bombing of several buildings by Puerto Rican nationalists. Murdoch's hijacking of New York's popular culture, spreading both terror and horror with headlines like "Sam Sleeps" (over a photo smuggled from the killer's cell), coincided with the deaths of several of the greatest figures in American postwar popular culture—Elvis Presley, Groucho Marx, and Bing Crosby, all memorialized by Murdoch's huge headlines.[48]

Governor Carey and the Democratic establishment had taken it for granted that Murdoch would back Cuomo. But Murdoch wanted a mayor of his own making, and when the *Times* made an early endorsement of Cuomo, Murdoch lurched toward Koch. The media mogul's only doubts were about Koch's administrative competence. Apparently, Garth's messaging did not impress him. So he called up Koch, arranged a meeting, and told him that the *Post* would endorse him if he would appoint attorney Ed Costikyan as first deputy mayor. Koch eagerly agreed.[49]

On August 19 the *Post* trumpeted its endorsement of Koch with the first of several front- page editorials touting him: "Koch has not only demonstrated competence and dogged determination to face the most unpopular problems, but also has shown that he is a decent man who cares for the people of this great community." Murdoch also praised him for "the courage to make the really tough decisions that will face any new mayor." That meant that the conservative press magnate was satisfied with Koch's commitment to continue the austerity regime and give it political cover.[50] The paper, which until then, had virtually ignored Koch, now covered his doings with so little pretense of objectivity that several reporters resigned in protest.

A few days after the endorsement the paper described Mario Cuomo as brooding and presented Bella Abzug, who had been endorsed by Barbra Streisand and other film stars, as the "celebrity entry of Campaign '77," in contrast to Koch, whom it had dubbed "Give 'em hell Ed." A profile of Koch that ran in the *Post* ended with this quote from the candidate: "You don't have to be rich and handsome to become mayor."[51] When New York's other major tabloid, the *Daily News,* endorsed Koch four days later, the *Post* continued its bashing of Hollywood liberals with a cartoon showing a tiny sad Beame on a huge couch listening to an aide read the paper. The caption read, "The *News* has jumped on the Koch bandwagon. I hear *Variety* is endorsing Bella. . . . How about *Playboy*?"[52] Koch was gaining, but Beame, who had nosed out Abzug in recent days, remained in the lead. But then Joel Harnett, the businessman candidate who would get less than 1 percent of the vote, wrecked the mayor's momentum. Harnett had sued the Securities and Exchange Commission to force it to release its report on New York's fiscal crisis, which the agency had tried to withhold until after the election. He won on August 26. The report accused Beame and Comptroller Harrison J. Goldin of misleading investors about New York's financial condition. Beame denounced the report as a "vicious document" and a "hatchet job." But the damage was done, especially after Murdoch flooded New York with the headline "Beame Conned the City."[53]

Koch glided into the last three weeks of the campaign with his popularity growing while Beame and Abzug were losing traction. The hapless Beame, already reeling from the SEC revelations, was sitting on stage at a candidates' forum when he was smeared with an apple-crumb pie hurled by Aron Kay, the legendary Yippie known as the Pieman, as a protest against the mayor's candidacy for reelection. "Yeah, it's Kay," Bella Abzug told Beame sympathetically. "He threw a pie at me awhile ago." Kay was taken to the police station and released without being charged. The image of a big apple all over the mayor's blue suit increased some New Yorkers' sense that Beame was passive and pathetic, especially when he laughed it off and declined to prosecute.[54]

While Beame became an object of increasing ridicule, Koch kept up a brutal campaign schedule, catnapping where he could, sometimes ignoring Garth's injunctions about humor or speaking off the cuff. Koch tried to use Cuomo's advantage in campaign funds against him, tying his opponent to the establishment in general and the governor in particular: "I don't have [Carey] breaking arms for me. He's like Idi Amin. They bring him in on a chair and carry him around the room."[55]

The next week the campaign got harder and harder to call, and the candidates got even edgier, slipping "into finger-jabbing shouting matches" at their last debate, just a week before the election Surprisingly, little of their choler had anything to do with the fiscal crisis, a topic only for the also-rans. Most of the jabbing was aimed at Koch, a sure sign that he was winning. Koch enjoyed every minute of his rivals' attention, telling the audience: "I like to be known by my enemies."[56]

In that last debate Koch labored to express white ethnic anger and fear of blacks without descending to racism—by arguing that class, not race, was the real issue. But many African Americans did not read his language as racially neutral. In debate, Percy Sutton attacked Koch for using "frightening terms" like "poverty pimps" when discussing the poor. These, Sutton said, were racist "code terms." Sutton thus left Koch, now seen as the man to beat, with an aura of conservatism, even racism.[57]

On September 8 the turnout was painfully small and the election was excruciatingly close. In a city of 7.5 million souls, a mere 7,000 votes allowed Mario Cuomo to knock Mayor Beame out of the runoff, and fewer than 50,000 votes separated first place finisher Ed Koch from fifth place finisher Percy Sutton—a mere 4.3 percent of the vote. The runoff promised to be a horse race—Cuomo and Koch were less than 10,000 votes apart, a mere 1.2 percent.

TABLE 1

Democratic Mayoral Primary Results, 1977

CANDIDATE	VOTES	% OF VOTE
Koch	180,348	19.8
Cuomo	170,560	18.7
Beame	163,810	18
Abzug	150,719	16.6
Sutton	131,197	14.4
Badillo	99,809	11
Harnett	13,927	1.5
Total	910,370	

Source: *New York Times*, September 10, 1977.

THE RUNOFF

Koch went full tilt into runoff mode and refused to rest. Cuomo took a day off and brooded about coming in second. He had expected to win, and when he didn't, according to his biographer, "he became irritable. His usual persuasive verbal skills gave way to a style of 'slashing attack' that Koch later observed 'did not reflect Cuomo's regular persona.' "[58] Koch was tougher because campaigning had been his regular routine for more than twenty years.

At his victory party Koch introduced Bess Myerson as "the most important person of the campaign," followed by cheers from the crowd of "First Lady Bess!"[59] Yet Koch could not afford to revel in his win. With the runoff only two weeks away, speed meant everything. Three hours after he left his victory party, he showed up at the Sheepshead Bay subway station to shake hands and thank his supporters. "Hey, Eddie, you're terrific!" yelled one Brooklyn passerby.[60] Koch turned all his energy to fighting Cuomo. The Koch camp viewed Cuomo with "very deep trepidation" because it seemed likely that the Cuomo campaign would continue attacks, "very much *sotto voce,* on Ed's sexuality," Capalino recalled. Koch would have preferred to run against the more polite Abe Beame, who was widely discredited outside his base.[61]

Garth had been planning and polling for the runoff in the last few weeks of the primary campaign. On the night of the primary he sprang into action even earlier than Koch, meeting with LoCicero and Capalino at 2:30 A.M. to discuss runoff strategy. After Koch won the runoff, "the money cascaded in." Both the Koch and Cuomo campaigns would have enough money to saturate the airwaves with commercials during the short interval before the runoff, so field operations would be key. That meant getting endorsements from people who could field political organizations on short notice.[62]

Garth pointed out to his non-Jewish colleagues that Rosh Hashanah, Yom Kippur (which followed unusually close-after that year), and the sabbath all fell during the nine-day runoff period, give them only two full days of field campaigning. He outlined a strategy: get the support of Beame and of every other elected official and party leader they could gather before Cuomo knew what hit him. In particular, this strategy aimed to counter Cuomo's base in Queens and among Italian voters in Brooklyn and on Staten Island. Koch would build a coalition of Bronx Hispanics through the endorsement of Badillo, Brooklyn regulars through the endorsement of Beame and Esposito, and the Harlem political establishment, which would shore up Koch's liberal Manhattan base and offset questions there about his liberalism. Polling showed that the victor in the runoff would be the inheritor of the Beame vote. Beame's endorsement would reassure his voters that Koch was not a kook from Greenwich Village or a Lindsayite from the elite East Side but a solid outer-borough Jew like most of them. The party leaders were key. Garth, who usually put his faith in television ads, recognized that television could not do the job alone because both campaigns would saturate the airwaves. Koch had virtually no field operation, and, under the circumstances, only the party machinery with its block captains in place could turn out voters on such short notice.[63]

The strategy worked. Deputy Mayor Stanley Friedman, who gave his endorsement to Koch in the first round of phone calls, acted as one of his most important conduits to Mayor Beame and accumulated considerable capital with the future administration. Koch would help Friedman become Bronx County Democratic chair after an incumbent, Patrick Cunningham, resigned under indictment. Queens County chair Donald Manes played a double game, officially supporting favorite son Mario Cuomo but allowing, even encouraging, local leaders—especially in Jewish areas like Forest Hills—to support Koch. After years of being an outsider to the county organizations, Koch reveled in making deals with the regular pols.

Brooklyn's county leader, Meade Esposito, an Italian with a heavily Jewish constituency, came on board more quickly than expected. So did Kenneth Shapiro, a prominent Brooklyn regular and counsel to state assembly Speaker Stanley Steingut, a Brooklynite. Esposito had considered resigning rather than work with Koch, whom he assumed, in LoCicero's words, was a "*pazzo* from Greenwich Village." But Shapiro and Tony Genovesi kept repeating Koch's overtures, in contrast to Cuomo, who feared that allying with Esposito might tarnish Cuomo's reputation.[64] Moreover, Koch had bought significant credit with the Brooklyn machine years earlier by testifying as a character witness in the trials of two members of Congress from Brooklyn, Frank Brasco and Bert Podell, who were subsequently convicted of corruption. This may have suggested to Esposito a flexibility in such matters that Koch did not intend and would live to regret. At that moment, though, this old political debt was an indispensable benefit to Koch, who desperately needed Esposito's campaign troops.[65]

On the Sunday after the primary Koch, Garth, and LoCicero drove out to Esposito's mother's house in Brooklyn, with Garth screaming at the driver, who got so lost that they were an hour late. Even if his mother's famous meatballs had to stew, Esposito showed no sign of anger. LoCicero recalled: "As soon as we walk in he says, 'I don't want anything. You're my man. Have some meatballs.'"[66] Esposito also agreed to keep his endorsement secret, as Garth feared it might do some political harm. Koch's old friend Tony Genovesi and Esposito's close friend Milton Mollen, presiding justice of the Supreme Court, joined them for lunch. The Brooklyn county leader could not have been more cordial, or clever—he asked for nothing but access to the new mayor and his administration in return for the support of his extensive electoral organization. Koch probably felt more gratitude than if Esposito had asked for specific favors and put him on the spot. And Koch would show that gratitude. Esposito was magnetic, a likable guy. Their handshake sealed a bond that Fiorello La Guardia would never have made with a Brooklyn boss, but Koch kvelled as county leaders leaped onto his bandwagon.

Esposito's support did not deliver Brooklyn. Koch still needed Mayor Beame, not a natural ally. The defeated mayor's pride was stung by his narrow loss, by Koch's criticisms during the campaign, and perhaps even by the old wound of Koch's 1965 endorsement of Lindsay in Beame's first run for mayor. Though the mayor had trouble making up his mind, his son Bernard (Buddy) Beame and publicist Howard Rubenstein maintained constant contact with the Koch campaign. Buddy Beame actively helped Koch by keeping his father away from Cuomo. The mayor kept his options open but finally endorsed Koch on Friday, September 16. Koch had scheduled a giant rally on a big stage set up in Trump/Warbasse Houses, a huge housing project on

Coney Island, "the heart of Jewish South Brooklyn," the next Sunday.[67] Much of Koch's credibility in south Brooklyn hung on whether Beame would show up and announce his wholehearted support, as the crowd had been told. Beame never liked to be early and would often sit in his limousine at political events until the last minute. With thousands, many of them campaign workers, in the huge plaza on Coney Island, Koch's campaign aides waited tensely for the mayor to arrive. They needed his active blessing if Koch was to carry the relatively conservative areas of south Brooklyn.

Beame made the rally the last drama of his mayoralty. A crowd of five to ten thousand people waited impatiently for him to show up. Minutes ticked by. No mayor. Jim Capalino ordered the band to play more music. Still no mayor. The crowd grew agitated. Capalino got local pols to start giving short speeches. No mayor. Capalino recalled: "This is was pre–cell phone, and we have beepers but no cell phones. So we're trying to reach Buddy [Beame]. He's not returning any telephone calls. . . . Garth's going nuts in his office. I'm out in the field. LoCicero's there. We're all going nuts."

The crowd grew even more restless and, despite Capalino's worry about starting without the mayor, Koch overruled him: "Stop it. He's not going to come, forget it, it's not going to happen."[68] So they started the program, and in the background people could hear a faint siren that was growing louder and louder. A police car advanced through the crowd, getting closer and closer to the stage.

It had to be the mayor. As Capalino recalled,

> Suddenly they can't get any farther. Two bodyguards pop out of the front door, open up the back door. The mayor—if you could appreciate it, you couldn't see the mayor to save your life, five foot what, one, two?—and suddenly the crowd goes apeshit because they realize that Abe is showing up to do the endorsement. And I said to myself privately that night, "Unless we fuck it up, we'll win." Because . . . for hard core—not only Jewish, but even Italo-American—voters, Abe's willingness to pass the baton to Ed just completely took away any doubts. Any—Ed's a little nutty, Ed's a little this, Ed's a little that, you know what I mean, always a 5 percent not completely certain about Ed. All that just completely went away.[69]

Horse-trading in Harlem Koch had no time to glory in Beame's endorsement. With Brooklyn secured by Beame and Esposito, the campaign turned to the Harlem establishment, whose leaders were reeling from what state senator Carl McCall called "a shocking defeat."[70] Percy Sutton had finished fifth in the mayoral race, and for the first time in more than two decades Harlem leaders had lost control of the borough presidency of Manhattan. Koch quickly offered to negotiate. Cuomo, in contrast, thought blacks had nowhere else to go, and the *Amsterdam News* characterized his refusal to deal as "self-righteous, arrogant, sarcastic, and unyielding."[71] Worse, Cuomo inadvertently insulted the Harlem leaders by spreading rumors that they had already endorsed Koch. Then Cuomo got his own black supporters in Brooklyn to endorse him without consulting their colleagues from Manhattan. This embarrassed Sutton, David Dinkins, Basil Paterson (the first African American to run for statewide office in New York), and Representative Charles Rangel, who had not yet decided whom to support and hoped that black politicians could increase their waning clout by making a unified endorsement.[72]

Koch, while far from a natural ally of black leaders, was eager to do business, even though it would have been a *shande* if it leaked out that he was making deals during the Jewish High Holidays. So he sneaked over to a low-profile meeting with fifteen black leaders in David Garth's office on the eve of Rosh Hashanah. The unprecedented meeting showed how this election broke up the usual alliances, dividing reform, regular, and minority Democrats "almost down the middle," as the *Times* noted.[73] Koch's desire to centralize power and patronage in the mayoralty, along with his support for austerity, was fundamentally opposed to the interests of many black leaders. But during his campaign Koch courted them assiduously, promising publicly to "appoint more blacks than the Lindsay and Beame administrations combined," to appoint a black deputy mayor (presumably former state senator Basil Patterson), and to refrain from using "code words" such as "poverty pimp" in the campaign. According to McCall and Paterson, who were at the Rosh Hashanah eve meeting, Koch also promised not to abolish the antipoverty agencies that were the financial mainstay of a portion of the black political elite and vowed to provide jobs to the black community. During the campaign he also pledged that Sydenham Hospital in Harlem would remain open.[74] Most of the Harlem leadership—Rangel, Patterson, the *Amsterdam News*, McCall, and City Clerk David N. Dinkins—were satisfied and gave him their backing. While Koch kept most of those promises, the broken ones rankled, none more so than Sydenham.

A candidate could hope to communicate only one or two things in a nine-day campaign. Message discipline was even more important than in the primary. During the runoff and general election campaigns, Koch pursued a message that was pleasing to the Manhattan establishment and white ethnics alike: that he would "make tough decisions and say no," reinforcing the hard-line image that had made him stand out during the summer. At the same time he portrayed Cuomo as a weak and vacillating "conciliator and compromiser," a theme that (not coincidentally) asserted that Koch would be the more masculine mayor.[75]

In a media environment in which both candidates could saturate the airwaves, Gerald Rafshoon, Cuomo's media man, tried to portray Koch as an elitist, perhaps an effeminate Manhattanite. One Cuomo ad pictured Koch's face dissolving into that of Lindsay, who was to some voters emblematic of softness on crime. Another depicted Koch as a weathercock, shifting with the political wind. Garth responded with a commercial featuring Bess Myerson "looking fabulous in a red dress" and confronting the opposition: "Whatever happened to character, Mr. Cuomo? We thought you were better than that."[76]

Cuomo, who badly needed to expand beyond his Catholic base, called for "unity" and wooed the support of labor—a constituency Koch had blamed for New York's fiscal troubles.[77] Cuomo also fished for feminist votes by hinting that Bella Abzug would play a major role in a Cuomo administration. Cuomo seems not to have understood the need for speed, as Garth and Koch did. Abzug endorsed Cuomo, though too late to do much good. The reformers were split. Cuomo's liberal credentials were far from established in those days, as he had alienated many West Side liberals through his support of the multibillion-dollar Westway project. Most West Side liberals stuck with Koch, a Manhattanite who seemed much more part of their universe.

QUEER-BAITING IN QUEENS

Homosexuals are not men who sleep with other men. Homosexuals are men who in fifteen years of trying cannot get a pissant antidiscrimination bill through City Council. A homosexual is somebody who knows nobody and who nobody knows. Who has zero clout. Does this sound like me, Henry?

—ROY COHN IN TONY KUSHNER'S *ANGELS IN AMERICA*

Rumors about Koch's sexual preference had dogged the candidate from the time of his first race in 1962. Koch later recalled that because he was not married, "I don't think I was ever in any campaign where my adversaries wouldn't engage in an underground smear, Koch is gay, VID is gay, and in the beginning I must say, it's very searing." The rumors were particularly damaging to a candidate courting a socially conservative outer-borough constituency. Even a seemingly innocent story on Koch's apartment in the Home section of the *New York Times* mentioning his copy of Arthur Bell's *Dancing the Gay Lib Blues* caused a furor.[78]

Stereotyped by the code words *Greenwich Village bachelor,* a characterization used in a debate by his opponent Mario Cuomo, Koch categorically denied rumors of his homosexuality, telling WNEW News just before the 1977 general election: "I don't happen to be homosexual, but if I were, I would hope that I wouldn't be ashamed of it. God makes you whatever you are."[79] Such a reasoned and tolerant answer was atypical for straight politicians at the time, even liberal ones. Koch never embraced homophobic positions to confirm his heterosexuality, a tactic used by many closeted politicians. Although Koch did not construct himself as gay, neither did he create an unambiguously straight family man persona like that of Mario Cuomo in 1977 or claim the privilege that accompanies that role.

Openly gay politicians were then virtually nonexistent outside San Francisco. In the oppressive, but changing, climate of the 1970s, heterosexuality was compulsory for politicians, and conventional political wisdom often discounted the unmarried. *Voice* columnists Alexander Cockburn and James Ridgeway perceptively noted that the election of Koch, Carol Bellamy, Andrew Stein, Hugh Carey, and Mary Anne Krupsak suggested that the public was at long last willing to accept politicians "with no visible spouse."[80]

The only prominent openly gay elected official in the United States at that time was San Francisco supervisor Harvey Milk. Along with Mayor George Moscone, he would be assassinated on the steps of San Francisco's city hall by Dan White, ex-cop and former county supervisor, a year after Koch's election. And, incredibly, those murders were tolerated by the legal system. White escaped a life sentence with his notorious "Twinkie defense," convincing a jury that he had become crazed by eating too much sugar and therefore lacked the intent requisite for first-degree murder. If, hypothetically, Koch was gay and had come out, or had been outed, he probably would have lost the election. In the violently homophobic climate of the times, false rumors even had the potential to threaten his life.

Bess Myerson's unusual role in the campaign—hand in hand with Koch at every appearance—also gave rise to exactly the speculation it was designed to quiet. Their platonic friendship has been called an "immaculate deception." Garth himself sometimes called Koch and Myerson the "Smith Brothers—two beards," alluding to the two nineteenth-century gentlemen pictured on a brand of cough drops.[81]

In this charged atmosphere rumors started up at lightning speed. Koch's supporters long suspected Cuomo of generating some of them, but Cuomo vehemently denies it and says that he threw people out of his office who came to him with derogatory information about Koch.[82] Nonetheless, commercials and appearances emphasized that Cuomo was "a family man," in implicit contrast to the unmarried Koch. Reporters did not miss the implication. Cuomo also held a press conference just before the election complaining that gay rights groups had criticized him and endorsed Koch. When Koch proved that those groups did not exist, Cuomo's complaints seemed groundless and designed to insinuate Koch was queer.[83] And while Cuomo may have had nothing to do with spreading rumors, Michael Dowd, the manager of Cuomo's primary campaign, hired a private detective to check out Koch's sex life. The detective reported directly to Cuomo's Brooklyn campaign coordinator, Thomas Chardavoyne. Dowd lamely claimed that he was looking into the charges "on my own with a few friends" because he feared that Koch might be blackmailed if he were elected.[84]

In other words, Koch was not paranoid: he did have enemies seeking to destroy him. One suspect was Cuomo's son Andrew. His supporters raged for years against the young Cuomo, then twenty years old, for allegedly plastering Queens with "Vote for Cuomo, Not the Homo" stickers. (Both Cuomos have always denied the charge.) According to Capalino, the Koch campaign shrugged the stickers off at first, until they became a persistent feature in Italian neighborhoods where they would do the most damage to Koch. Capalino finally detailed some campaign workers to watch a street, and they got the license plate of the man who was putting them up. Garth found out it belonged to someone who worked under Andrew Cuomo in the campaign, though there was no direct link. When Garth complained the postering stopped for a while, and the Cuomo campaign issued "oceans of denial" that it had anything to do with "Vote for Cuomo, Not the Homo," which only made the malicious rhyme better known.[85]

THE SCANDAL THAT NEVER HAPPENED

A much bigger potential scandal was averted when Sam DeMilia, president of the Police Benevolent Association, visited Garth to make a deal for the PBA's endorsement of Koch, as rumors swirled that DeMilia had learned that a male visitor had beaten Koch up in his apartment. When he heard this, Garth called LoCicero. As LoCicero recalled, Garth said to him, "'What the fuck did you do? You never told me this happened.'" "I said, 'Look—I had lunch with Koch every Saturday, I saw him every week. I never saw a mark on his face. But you'll have to talk to him. I can't say.'"[86] As Koch walked out of the last debate before the general election, he saw Garth and told him, "It's not true. Never happened." Garth, who later stressed that "as long as I've known Ed, I was never blindsided by him on this issue," showed remarkable cool and complete trust in his candidate.[87]

When DeMilia arrived at Koch's campaign headquarters, Garth asked him what he wanted "and he said approval of transfers/precincts, approvals of hours/shifts, that kind of stuff," Garth said. Then Koch, who had been waiting outside, came in, and Garth told him what DeMilia wanted. "And Ed said, 'As far as access to the mayor, you have it because any union leader is going to have that. As far as the rest of the stuff, baloney. Nothing. And I want to make that very clear. Nothing.'"[88]

At that point, Garth said, DeMilia pointed to a file in his hand, claiming he had an affidavit from a former officer substantiating rumors that the police had come to Koch's apartment after he had been beaten up and that Koch had declined to prosecute—a story designed to feed rumors that Koch was queer. Garth said that to call the union leader's bluff, he started dialing the number for Frank Lynn, a political reporter for the *New York Times*. "And Sam's going, 'No, no.' He never said anything to me. He just got up. Took the file he had, which I had never looked at, and walked out." In a subsequent probe by the New York City Department of Investigation, DeMilia later denied under oath that he ever tried to smear or blackmail Koch, or that he had any derogatory information about him. Yet a story similar to the one DeMilia proffered to Garth surfaced on the AP wire a few days after the DeMilia-Garth meeting, and one week before the election, with a "hold for confirmation." Both campaigns saw copies of the story, but in a rare display of editorial restraint the newspapers did not run it. No record of the alleged visit to Koch's apartment was ever recorded in precinct daybooks or court records.[89]

In the rushed atmosphere of the runoff, queer-baiting tactics seem to have had little effect. Koch won a smashing victory, defeating Cuomo 432,000 to 355,000, or 55.3 percent to 44.7 percent. Koch gained votes in liberal districts that had gone for Sutton, Badillo, and Abzug, which contributed mightily to his victory. In addition to doing well with those relatively few liberal Jews who bothered to vote, the Koch campaign was able—with help from Esposito and Beame—to stimulate a relatively heavy turnout in conservative Jewish areas and take two-thirds of the vote there. The Cuomo campaign did an excellent job of turning out its voters in the areas that their candidate had carried in the primary. But Cuomo's Catholic constituency was not large enough by itself to carry a Democratic runoff, especially with the Harlem leaders backing Koch.[90]

CUOMO'S LAST STAND

The grueling selection process was not yet over, though for a day or two it seemed that the election might be a shoo-in for Koch. Governor Carey urged Cuomo to quit the race, but a few days after the runoff he decided to resume full-scale political warfare on the Liberal line.[91] "The guy's a conservative," Cuomo told the press, pointing to Koch's establishment and party machine endorsements, although elements of Cuomo's coalition were just as conservative. Koch quipped that "as Mr. Cuomo sees it, if a politician endorses Cuomo, 'It's because God told him to,' while if the same politician endorses me, 'it's a deal.'"[92]

Although Koch was likely to win—indeed, by the end of the campaign fundraising for all other candidates almost halted—he could not take the election for granted. Cuomo, who still had considerable support from Italians and unions, was more of a threat in the general election than he had been in the runoff because many Catholics were registered Republicans and now could pull the lever for him.[93] The Republican state senator Roy Goodman and the Conservative Party's Barry Farber, a talk-show host, were weak—they would together receive only a little more than 8 percent of the vote. Although Cuomo's candidacy was still very much alive, Koch and his tired organization coasted at the beginning of the general election campaign. Even their media buys were down, despite access to plenty of money. In the runoff Koch spent $600,000 but only $200,000 in the much longer general election campaign.[94] He received the endorsement of almost every prominent Democrat in the state, including that of Governor Hugh Carey, who broke his earlier promise to the Liberals to help Cuomo. Even Democrats who loathed Koch, like Percy Sutton and Bella Abzug, reluctantly swung behind the Democratic nominee.[95]

Garth's tight rein had made Koch seem boring and predictable. But Koch, especially a cranky, tired Koch, could not keep from bucking his handler. With Garth taking a brief break, Koch gave in to his deepest passions: the defense of Israel and massive national publicity. Koch wanted a public showdown with Jimmy Carter when the president came to New York to endorse him in October 1977. Koch believed that Carter had made "a complete sellout of Israel" by pursuing a joint declaration with the Soviet Union that called for a multilateral Middle East peace conference in Geneva, with the goal of creating a Palestinian state. As Carter disembarked at the La Guardia heliport to meet the press, Ed Koch was there with a surprise: a letter that he had already distributed to the reporters who were on hand.[96] Photos of the event show Koch eye to eye with the much shorter Carter, who was standing on a platform. The incumbent mayor Beame, who was famously orthodox when it came to political manners, looked up at them uneasily, his eyes focused on the letter. Koch had been scheduled to drive into Manhattan with Carter and then go to the south Bronx for dramatic photo-ops and pledges of support for Koch's efforts to reconstruct the area. Instead, Carter stranded Koch on the tarmac after he read the letter. They would later patch things up, but the Carter-Koch relationship remained contentious.[97]

Koch's display of chutzpah helped him keep the votes of some conservative outer-borough Jews who had been slowly moving toward Cuomo. Before the incident at the heliport, Cuomo vied with Koch to make the strongest criticism of Carter's policy on Israel.[98] Koch's crass but canny confrontation of Carter showed him as tough and countered Cuomo's attempt to raise questions about Koch's masculinity.[99] Nevertheless, Cuomo gained on Koch steadily as the November election neared.

Election day saw low turnout, with a memorable downpour and floods that challenged Koch's get-out-the-vote effort.[100] When the results came in, Koch had won a bare majority in the four-way race, but he enjoyed a large margin over Cuomo—712,976 (50.3 percent) to 587,257 (41.4 percent) for Cuomo, with only 119,093 (8.3 percent) votes for the Republican Goodman and Conservative Farber. Cuomo had succeeded in turning out the white Catholic vote (a significant portion of it Republican). He cut down Koch's margin in the outer-borough assembly districts (carried by Beame in the primary), likely by vastly increasing the non-Jewish turnout in those areas. Despite continuing low turnouts of liberals, blacks, and Hispanics, Koch owed his election to his significant margins (more than 60 percent) in assembly districts that had supported Abzug, Sutton, and Badillo. Instead of paying back the liberals who supported him, however, Koch would put his greatest efforts into seducing those Italian, Irish, and Hispanic Catholics who had voted against him. His decision to build a coalition with outer-borough Catholics through regular party organizations would have grave consequences. But all that was far in the future.[101]

THE TRANSITION

Koch suddenly found himself in charge of a city that was a physical, financial, and administrative wreck. After election day's heavy rains, a cartoon on page six of the

Post portrayed Koch in a mask and snorkel, standing on the roof of Gracie Mansion, ready to dive into the floodwaters of a drowning and disordered city. As mayor-elect Koch confronted headlines like "W. Side IRT Still Running Despite Peril of Derailment" and "Rikers Guards Warn Koch of a 'New Attica.'"[102] Though he looked "tired and somewhat rumpled" the day after the election, he ebulliently promised to "confront the fiscal crisis, the quality of our schools, the need to protect our citizens, the declining conditions in our neighborhoods—not with the words of an election campaign, but with the actions that those problems and so many others demand."[103]

As everyone awaited the first signs of managerial ability, the interregnum was marked instead by chaos. The interminable election campaign meant Koch got little help from a tired, defeated, and generally ineffectual Beame team. Taking over a city in such bad shape placed enormous pressure on Koch's inner circle, the members of which had already been working more than sixty hours a week during an abnormally lengthy campaign. Few New Yorkers really believed that Koch would succeed where Beame had clearly failed.

A tour of city agencies shocked Jim Capalino, who served as transition director. The drastic deterioration of city agencies as a result of years of fiscal austerity had cost more than it saved. Agency offices were of "third world quality," and almost all agencies lacked adequate office supplies. "Things that had been broken hadn't been fixed in months," Capalino recalled. Whole rooms were "uninhabitable because of unrepaired leaks and water damage."[104] Governing seemed impossible.

The fiscal crisis also created a more direct pressure—the federal seasonal loan guarantee program that had allowed New York to pay its pending bills was due to expire in June. Congress wanted a plan for a return to private credit markets before it would even consider extending the program. This would require much of Koch's attention before he even assumed the mayoralty. Koch wanted to show those congressional committees that he was in charge and that the city's government was no longer weak, leaderless, and unmanaged, as it had been under his predecessor.

The goal was worthy, but the reality was that Koch's staff was afflicted by internal dramas—the result of making his first cabinet a team of rivals, many with their own constituencies. Ed Costikyan, slated to be a major player in both the transition and the administration, quit in a fit of pique during the transition when Koch, despite his promise to Rupert Murdoch, withdrew the title of first deputy mayor.[105] Koch made several appointments of friends and associates, such as his former partner, Allen G. Schwartz, whom Koch named corporation counsel. Koch attempted to build a multiethnic coalition, naming Basil Paterson as deputy mayor for labor relations and Herman Badillo as deputy mayor for operations. Koch also appointed some neoconservatives, including the economist Blanche Bernstein, who was the new commissioner of human resources. The left-liberal *Village Voice* immediately criticized her, alleging that her previous activities "seem to have consisted of devising new strategies to cut the welfare budget."[106]

The transition, while not a disaster, was not a particularly promising start to the Koch administration. Beame did little to help. Mary Beame even called Koch to ask if she and Abe could stay for a few more days at Gracie Mansion. Koch immediately released the story to the press, announcing that the Beames could stay but that he "was also moving in on January first, and I don't know who is going to be whose guest." Goading the Beames into leaving by embarrassing them in the press was not especially smooth or gracious, but it was pure Koch. For the first time but not the last, he flexed his muscles as mayor of New York City, and he reveled in it.[107]

11
THE CRITICAL FIRST TERM (1978–81)

Ed Koch ostentatiously rode a city bus to his inauguration. Robert Allison, the driver of the M-6 bus that took the mayor-elect from his home on West Fourth Street to city hall on Inauguration Day, told him: "Do a good job for us." According to a New York Times/Channel 2 News poll, 59 percent of New Yorkers believed Koch would make the city government more "competent and effective," in contrast to the worn-out image of the outgoing Beame administration.[1]

Koch's role model was Fiorello H. La Guardia, the "Little Flower," who has been called the "inventor of the modern mayoralty" for his hands-on style. Koch saw his own first day in office as "the moment the people took over City Hall," and he immediately reclaimed La Guardia's desk from a staffer who was using it.[2] Since the Little Flower was only five feet two, the six-one Koch could not fit without making the desk a lot taller. He sent it out to the city's carpenters, but they made the desk too high. Koch kept the desk in his office but gave up trying to sit at it.[3]

Size was not the only difference between the two mayors. La Guardia had eschewed inauguration festivities—there was too much work to be done. He had driven to the headquarters of each major agency to swear in and delineate the missions of each of his commissioners.[4] Koch reveled in his inauguration and spent much of the day at four celebrations, each in a different borough. Like La Guardia, he was determined to be a great mayor. He talked so much and so compulsively that day, especially about his idées fixes, that few onlookers could have realized that he would prove himself able to listen as well as talk. He loved debate, and on most issues was unusually willing to listen to an ideologically (if not always ethnically) diverse group of advisers, as well as to dispute with citizens at the hundreds of neighborhood meetings he would hold as mayor.

Koch's inaugural speech, which was more subtle than brilliant and received only tepid applause, reflected a neoliberalism that was far more concerned with "business confidence" than with affirmative action. Koch was aware that he was departing from the norms that dominated New York politics from the time of La Guardia.[5] Opening with a trite reference to John F. Kennedy's "Ask not what your country can do for you," Koch told all New Yorkers who loved their city that they would have to sacrifice to save it. He paid homage to the social democratic traditions of the city: "I do not exaggerate when I say that New York is unique in the history of human kindness. New York is not a problem. New York is a stroke of genius. From its earliest days, this city has been a lifeboat for the homeless, a larder for the hungry, a living library to the intellectually starved, a refuge not only for the oppressed but also for the creative."[6]

But the city had been too altruistic for its own good, leading to mistakes "of the heart," Koch concluded. By painting New York's welfare state as an overindulgent mother, the new mayor implied that a strict father had now taken over.[7] The leaders of poverty programs, most of whom were black and Hispanic, were the chief targets of his ire, though he did not name names: "In the past programs that were meant to help the needy ended up as bonanzas for the greedy. All too often those who were charged with caring for the disadvantaged turned the generosity of New Yorkers into a form of folly."[8] While Koch promised to stand by poor New Yorkers ("The money that is appropriated for the poor must directly benefit the poor"), he closed his address with an appeal to the well-off. Gentrification was the key to his program for New York's revival, and Koch called for an influx of "urban pioneers" to reinvigorate the city's neighborhoods. Koch gave priority to the interests of revenue providers, not service consumers, and appealed for people with capital—a category that, in

1977, mostly meant white people—to come to New York to rehabilitate and rebuild the city's housing stock, create jobs, and make it economically viable again.[9]

Ed Koch intended to continue the austerity program, but he hoped to retain the confidence of both fiscal watchdogs and the citizens of New York who continued to suffer from the extremes of neoliberal fiscal discipline. He wanted to control the city's budget and, in doing so, return power to the mayoralty. In total devotion to his work he would surpass La Guardia, who had routinely worked ten-hour days.[10] Koch, a man with little life outside politics, "was determined to devote practically every minute, including breakfasts, to solving the problems of the city."[11] Like his father, Koch could imagine no life other than one of unremitting hard work, and he believed that by working eighteen hours a day he could manage both austerity and improvement.

After the swearing-in Koch entered city hall to sign a sheaf of executive orders structuring his administration. One controversial measure raised the salaries of managers so that they were significantly higher than those of their employees, infuriating union employees who had deferred wages and forgone raises for years. The most dramatic executive order banned discrimination on the basis of sexual orientation in employment, housing, credit, provision of city services, and by city contractors.[12] Koch's new decree of equality for a whole class of citizens was momentous, even if it riled social conservatives. "Gays Laud Koch, Cops Can't Agree," complained Rupert Murdoch's conservative *New York Post*.[13]

Not all New Yorkers subscribed to Koch's version of liberalism. He preached a gospel of efficiency and argued that such intervention should primarily benefit the interests of business and a broad middle class. Some of New York's poor were ready to push back as early as the night of the inauguration. The first four inaugural celebrations for the new mayor went without a hitch, but at the fifth, on Eastern Parkway in the large plaza in front of the Brooklyn Museum, marchers led by the Reverend Herbert Daughtry drove away Koch's well-wishers. The marchers were protesting the acquittal of a police officer who had shot and killed a teenager at point-blank range on Thanksgiving Day 1976, the latest in a series of police shootings of black children in Crown Heights.[14] With Koch's security in some confusion, Daughtry seized the microphone. He wanted to get Koch's attention because, as a lame duck, Beame had refused to seek a federal investigation of the shooting.[15]

The new mayor listened to Daughtry and then addressed the crowd, and the night ended without great trouble. But later, speaking to the press, Koch set a combative tone, declaring, "I'm never going to be silenced by demonstrators," before leaving for Gracie Mansion.[16] Koch did set up a meeting with Daughtry on January 12, just a few days into his new administration, and agreed to write U.S. Attorney David Trager to request an investigation of whether the officer had violated the dead teenager's civil rights.[17] But continued killings by the police, and tensions between the black and Hasidic communities, meant that Daughtry would remain one of the mayor's harshest critics.

When he got home to Gracie Mansion after his first long day as mayor, Koch was wide-eyed at the sumptuous trappings of his new office. He spent his first night there with members of his family and marveled that it was possible to go from hatcheck boy to mayor of a world city. His brother, Harold, remembered sitting with Ed in their undershorts on that first night in Gracie Mansion, drinking soda and watching television: "Would you fucking believe it? That a nice Jewish kid like my brother and me, his brother, could be sitting in Gracie Mansion? Beyond anything you could dream up."[18]

Koch's new life included duties that ranged from welcoming the empress of Iran to worrying about the discharge of raw sewage.[19] Emulating La Guardia, Koch visited city agencies almost every day to see how they were operating. Unlike Beame, who had given a one-on-one interview once a year to each of the major papers, Koch talked to reporters so incessantly—sometimes even in the men's room—that a wag at the *Times* dubbed him "unavoidably available for comment." Koch's chattiness proved a nightmare for his press secretary, Maureen Connelly. "He didn't need a spokesman—he needed a muzzle," she later observed. Nearly every appointment he made was leaked to the press, and he usually turned out to be the leaker.[20]

In his first term the mayor traveled to public meetings all over the city and often took lumps from the crowd. But his populist grandstanding wore off as he became accustomed to fame. He had originally planned to take the subway regularly and spend weekends in his spartan three-room Greenwich Village apartment, where he could still run out the door to Murray's for some stinky cheese. The *Times* said that it was important for the mayor to live in the mansion because it was a public space "unattached to any constituency" and accused Koch of hypocrisy for supporting a new law requiring city employees to reside in the city while refusing to move himself.[21] He began to take the limousine more and the subway less, and he largely abandoned his apartment for Gracie Mansion. He even got used to being accompanied everywhere by police. But he never abandoned his constant devotion to work.

STEP ONE: RESTORE THE CITY'S CREDIT

During his campaign Koch treated the fiscal crisis as "the elephant in the room" that he alone had the guts to take on. Now it was time for him to prove it. New York had been shut out of the credit market because analysts believed that the cost of the city's debt service had become too large a percentage of its revenues to guarantee that its debts would be paid. The impact was severe: money to replace equipment and repair infrastructure dried up, and maintenance was deferred so long that some systems were beyond repair. Landlords were burning down acres of the south Bronx for the insurance money, and entire blocks came off the tax rolls because owners found it less expensive to abandon their buildings than to pay the accrued property taxes.

For the first six months of his mayoralty Koch's top priority was seeking federal guarantees of New York's bonds that would enable the city to finance critical repairs and give him breathing room to bring New York back into private credit markets. "It was more a political crisis than just a fiscal crisis. When you lose your credibility you lose the chance to borrow from people and to gain confidence," said David Brown, who served as deputy mayor for administration. Koch's mission was to reassure Washington and Albany that "we were doing things differently."[22] Regaining trust meant convincing doubters at the highest levels. On the day Koch took office, a Carter administration official (probably Jack Watson, the White House staffer in charge of urban issues) told the *Daily News* that "a long-term loan or guarantee has almost no chance in Congress" and that he'd heard from "a congressman who is considered a big friend" of New York's that if the city insisted on long-term aid, it would damage its chances of getting any aid at all.[23]

Koch knew that to convince anyone, he had to establish his mastery of the city's byzantine finances. How much money did the city need to dig itself out, for example? Shockingly, no one seemed to know. Beame's estimate of the deficit jumped from $110 million before the election to more than $240 million after his defeat. Koch, whose knowledge of municipal finance was almost nil, had to learn how to decipher the city's budget practically overnight. Jim Brigham, Koch's budget director, became Koch's teacher, spending hours with him, going through the budget line by line to explain where the money came from and how it was spent. Koch had an especially hard time grasping that a budget was only a prediction, always subject to change because of changes in revenues and expenses. At first Koch thought that "if you put a number out, that's got to be it. That's the number you're going to live with," Brigham recalled. So when Brigham was able to show that the city had unexpectedly collected enough money to allow Koch to raise employees' pay, the mayor was furious, because he had been touting numbers that showed that the city had no money for a raise: "He thought he had lost credibility." After awhile "he finally began to realize that a budget is only an expectation," Brigham said. "You can't predict the future with a hundred percent accuracy."[24]

The new mayor assembled a task force of senior officials who gathered every night to craft the four-year financial plan required by Congress and the state's Emergency Financial Control Board. Their dedication was remarkable: serving meant working two jobs, and meeting in a city building at 250 Broadway that had little heat. They did without the basics. "No one was allowed to have dinner until 11:00 at night, because Phil Toia, who was the Deputy Mayor of Finance, felt that if you were hungry it would make you stay awake, but if you ate something you'd be sleepy."[25]

Koch began to show some talent for fiscal planning, and he and his advisers developed an overall strategy that was admirably clearcut:

- Balance the books with calculations based on recognizably conservative and sober estimates.
- Reform and improve management while making careful capital investments that would improve productivity (such as computerization, so the city could accurately count the number of its employees) and in infrastructure—literally, to rebuild things before they fell down.
- Adopt subsidies for business and cut red tape in order to convince David Rockefeller and the rest of the business community, such as the Business Roundtable, that Koch was going to run a probusiness administration. This strategy panned out: Rockefeller, who as a young man had worked for La Guardia at city hall, became a preeminent partner of the mayor's in re-establishing business confidence. Many other business leaders, particularly from the financial sector, including Felix Rohatyn of Lazard Frères and Walter Wriston of Citicorp, played key roles.[26]

THE HEALTH-CARE HEMORRHAGE

Koch continued the city's austerity program to reestablish its credit, which made sense on a local level. The root problem—the cost of health care—was intractable, beyond his power to fix without a massive realignment of political interests on a national scale. Providing health care for the uninsured was eating up a huge part of the city's budget each year, and the city suffered deeply not because of too much social democracy at home but from far too little participation by the federal government. While deficits in a budget as large as New York City's may be overdetermined by the continuation of many different expenditures, health care stands out as a category where the failures of the federal and state governments to enact reforms were direct causes of New York City's long-term fiscal instability.

The failure of the Ford and Carter administrations to federalize health-care spending and establish a system for caring for the uninsured was, by itself, the cause of nearly half of New York's budget gap for all but three years of Koch's twelve-year mayoralty. (See table 2). Approximately 35 percent of the city's population that was younger than sixty-five was uninsured or on Medicaid in 1985, according to a city study.[27] When Koch took over as mayor, the cost of caring for the uninsured was 106 percent of the city's total budget gap, in part because of New York State required that all local governments pick up 25 percent of the tab for Medicaid (which insures the poorest people), a burden that no other major city in the country had to carry. While Koch was temporarily able to trim these costs through improved collection practices and processing of patient insurance from 1980 to 1983, after that health-care costs ballooned to 60 percent or more of the budget gap, climbing to a whopping 109 percent during the 1987 Wall Street crash. If Washington had taken over these expenses, New York City would not have had a fiscal crisis, it would not have had to cut services, and city government would have been in a far better position to deal with the public health–related problems of homelessness, AIDS, and drugs that plagued Koch's last term in office. Democrats generally supported such measures in their 1980 platform, but Carter did little to move them forward, one reason he was challenged for re-nomination by Senator Edward M. Kennedy.[28]

TABLE 2

Cost of Health-Care Subsidies for Uninsured New Yorkers as a Percentage of the Budget Gap, 1978–89

YEAR	HHC SUBSIDY FOR UNINSURED (MILLIONS)	MEDICAID, CITY SHARE (MILLIONS)	TOTAL (MILLIONS)	CITY BUDGET GAP* (MILLIONS)	PERCENTAGE OF BUDGET GAP
1978	$234	$138	$372	$763	49%
1979	234	404	638	600	106
1980	210	130	340	1,104	30
1981	166	134	300	1,063	28
1982	183	187	370	954	39
1983	207	217	425	854	50
1984	237	250	487	1,022	48
1985	272	253	525	870	60
1986	273	279	552	735	75
1987	332	300	632	577	109
1988	409	347	756	1,149	65
1989	409	465	874	1,018	85

*As set out in the annual financial plan submitted to the Emergency Financial Control Board each January.

Sources: Office of the Mayor, City of New York, Executive Budgets for the City of New York, 1979–89, New York City Municipal Library; Charles Brecher and Raymond D. Horton, with Robert A. Cropf and Dean Michael Mead, *Power Failure: New York City Politics and Policy since 1960* (New York: Oxford University Press, 1993), table 15.2, 336; Citizens Budget Commission, "Managing the Budget in the Bloomberg Administration," December 7, 2001, www.cbcny.org/NYC_Fiscal_Outlook.pdf (April 27, 2008); Office of Strategic Planning, Health and Hospitals Corporation, "NYC Medically Uninsured Summary Data," December 1988, City Hall Library, 27.

But health care reform that would put the city back on an even keel was at best a long-term prospect. Instead, Koch tried the more conventional route of seeking long-term financial guarantees from Congress so that the city could raise private capital to restructure its debt. He faced some ferocious opposition, even though the loan guarantees would ultimately net the federal government a profit. The rhetoric deployed against New York was old as the Bible.[29] Gothamites (whom some Americans could not distinguish from Sodomites) had to suffer because of their sin. Neoliberals and conservatives all offered their own explanations of the fiscal crisis, charging that the profligate excesses of an overly generous welfare state and union demands had led to the budgetary downfall. Republican Utah senator Jake Garn said that New York's officials were liars when they claimed that the city would go bankrupt without federal loans and guarantees. Representative Richard Kelly, Republican from Florida, explained, "The unions have forced industry out of the city. The uniformed services are the highest-paid in the U.S. of A. And welfare? City politicians keep jacking up the rates to get the ghetto vote. No doubt about it."[30]

New York's "worst enemy," according to Koch, was the quirky senator William Proxmire, the Wisconsin Democrat who chaired the Senate Banking Committee.[31] A gadfly who had made a career of publicizing waste in the federal government, Proxmire attacked New York so often that the *New Yorker* declared, "Some consideration has been given here to see if he could be prosecuted as a common scold."[32] Proxmire's skepticism about providing aid to New York City had some justification. New York's government was full of corrupt sinecures. In one of the most blatant examples, Abe Beame gave Bronx Democratic chair Stanley Friedman, a midnight appointment for life to the Board of Water Supply. The part-time job came with secretary, limousine, and a salary of $25,000 per year (the equivalent of $89,000 in 2009 dollars).

But Koch fought graft, which helped his case with the senators. When Beame's appointments became public, Koch had called for the abolition of the water board, and as soon as he took over as mayor, he obliged Friedman to resign for the good of the city before the Senate hearings began.[33] Koch lobbied Albany to repeal the "Heart Law," which allowed cops with coronary ailments to retire at three-quarters pay, whether their illness resulted from the stress of the job or from donuts. He shared Proxmire's outrage about the Lindsay administration's sweetheart deal for Yankee Stadium. Although Beame had opposed the project when he was comptroller—it required the city to pay for the approximately $100 million renovation of Yankee Stadium, four times the original price tag of $24 million—he had continued the project even after the fiscal crisis forced him to freeze almost every other city construction project, abandoned plans to renovate the surrounding neighborhood, and shifted $300,000 originally budgeted for the neighborhood to the Yankees to buy equipment for the team. Two days after Koch's inauguration, Proxmire and Edward Brooke, the Massachusetts Republican who was the ranking minority member of the Senate Banking Committee, publicized an ominous letter they had sent to Treasury Secretary Michael Blumenthal declaring that "they are yet to be convinced" that the federal government should lend New York City any more money after the seasonal loan program expired on June 30. In response, the *Daily News* tried to do its civic duty. Hoping that a headline like its famous "Ford to New York: Drop Dead," which had goaded Ford to grant the city federal loans, would spur Proxmire to drop his opposition, it dubbed him "Senator Scrooge."[34] Unfortunately, he co-opted the moniker and even wore a Senator Scrooge nametag to his office Christmas party. Koch dedicated the next six months to persuading Congress that it was "a matter for equity and justice" while putting into place an elaborate set of laws and agreements to meet the preconditions for obtaining federal aid.[35]

Proxmire wanted the city to meet four requirements before he would even schedule hearings on the loan guarantees:

1. A financial plan detailing how New York would reach a balanced budget by 1982, according to generally accepted accounting principles
2. A package of increased state aid to prove that local remedies had been exhausted
3. Settlement of a three-year contract (later reduced to two years) with the unions
4. Persuade city unions to support federal legislation permitting additional investment in city bonds by the city's employee pension funds, even though they had already put 35 percent of their holdings in such investments. The investments were clearly below the standards of prudence demanded by existing federal regulations, which prohibited all other pension funds from taking the kind of risks with employee money that Proxmire tried to mandate for city pension funds.

Koch tried but could not meet all those conditions. Ultimately, under the pressure of the expiration of the seasonal loan program on June 30, Proxmire relented and scheduled the hearings.

Koch understood that he had to show the Senate Banking Committee that he could make credible budgets. He understood that producing an honest and accurate accounting of the city's money was the first step to restoring its credit in Washington and elsewhere. A budget is simply a series of complex predictions about the future. Koch agreed with those who wanted the city's budget to be as realistic as possible. As a result the first budgetary news out of city hall was not good. The true deficit, Koch reported, would be almost $500 million, not $243 million, as Beame had predicted after the election, and far, far larger than the $110 million that Beame had predicted before the election. Though Koch based his number almost entirely on Beame's figures, he chose to eliminate a financial pathology—paying for recurring but unaffordable expenses by placing them in the capital budget—in effect, the city had been paying for its groceries with a credit card and paying only the minimum balance. Some of these expenditures were so essential that they could not simply be eliminated. But generally accepted accounting principles required that the capital budget be reserved for specific kinds of expenses, usually construction and significant repairs and improvements to the infrastructure, and distinct from operating expenses, especially if they were recurring. Beame acknowledged the need to stop borrowing for expenses, but he had said that it would take until fiscal year 1986 to make the switchover. Koch promised to do it by FY 1982 if he got the loan guarantees, a forthright move calculated to please both bondholders and Congress and to impress upon them that the city's true problems were too big for the city and state to handle on their own.[36]

Proxmire and Brooke had argued that the state should do more. The city had heavily invested its pension funds in bonds issued by a state agency, the Municipal Assistance Corporation (Big MAC), which borrowed money by issuing municipal bonds secured by a first lien on particular city tax revenues. But New York State's $9.2 billion pension fund, administered by long-time State Comptroller Arthur Levitt, had not bought significant quantities of Big MAC's paper and was one of the last sources of wealth that the state had left untapped.

Koch went to Albany on January 15 to change Levitt's mind about investing pension funds in MAC or other city bonds. The comptroller saw these as imprudent investments that would compromise his fiduciary duty to the state's pensioners. Albany was snowy, camouflaging the cold expanses of the new state office building complex—alabaster and marble temples of 1960s modernism erected by Nelson A. Rockefeller at a cost of $1 billion. At Koch's first sighting of the monstrosity known as the Empire State Plaza, he compared it to Brasilia or "something built by the Pharaohs of Egypt." Even native Albanians often complained of Rockefeller's "edifice complex."[37]

Arthur Levitt seemed to be chiseled out of marble, too. He was a legendary figure in state government—a product of the Brooklyn regulars, he had been the state comptroller since the 1950s. He had seen mayors come and go and in 1961 had even run a futile campaign against Wagner out of loyalty to Carmine De Sapio.[38]

The seventy-seven-year-old Levitt was little prepared for Koch's condescension. The mayor brusquely declared at the outset that their meeting was "a waste of time" unless Levitt was willing to commit to purchasing city bonds with state pension funds. Levitt categorically refused to compromise. "No power on earth is going to make me violate those responsibilities," Levitt declared in private, as he had in public. Koch reached no compromise but baited Levitt by satirically repeating the comptroller's oath of office. At the time Koch seemed totally childish, but there was a method to his madness. Koch generated headlines that made one point crystal clear at the Senate Banking Committee hearings: Levitt would buy no New York

City bonds without passage of the federal aid program, despite Proxmire's attempts to force Levitt to do so.[39]

On January 20 Koch sent the city's four-year financial plan to Treasury Secretary Blumenthal. The mayor proposed a combination of cuts, increased aid from Washington and Albany, and the continuation of federal seasonal loans to keep cash flowing. In addition, he asked for a new program of long-term federally guaranteed loans to allow the city to borrow financing for its capital construction needs and help restructure its debt—vital to saving a city whose sidewalks, bridges, and water and gas mains were crumbling. The Ford administration, during the 1975 crisis, had granted only short-term loans on the ground that the program could be terminated quickly (he also was no doubt influenced by Treasury Secretary William Simon's punitive attitude). The seasonal loans had failed because of the city's chronically weak economy, shortage of revenues, and continuing enormous mandated expenditures like Medicaid.

In return for all the additional help, Koch proposed to bring the city's budget into true balance by 1982. He would reduce city spending by $174 million through "a partial hiring freeze, improvements in productivity, reduced welfare eligibility and [welfare] overpayments, and an across the board cut of 3% per year in all non-labor related city expenses, such as supplies and electricity for a total cut of 12% over the course of the four-year plan." He also postulated somewhat quixotically that the city would peg employees' raises to increases in their productivity—though his assumption of a 6 percent annual inflation rate suggests that he thought he could get the unions to accept further cuts in the real wages of their members. The plan also made the somewhat risky assumption that subsidies to the Health and Hospitals Corporation (HHC) and the Transit Authority would remain static, but Koch would later expend considerable political capital to reduce the size of the HHC to fit the financial plan.[40]

In the four years between 1978 and 1982, Koch would cut twenty thousand jobs by attrition, imposing a hiring freeze in all departments except police, fire, corrections, sanitation, and education. These cuts came on top of the sixty-one thousand city jobs eliminated since the crisis began in 1975. The Koch plan also proposed an increase of $283 million in annual state and federal aid to help fund a laundry list projects totaling $657 million. Reportedly, Koch did trim some items that Beame had proposed and that had met with considerable derision in Washington, such as federal funding of fire control in New York Harbor. The state, Koch hoped, would make its revenue-sharing formula more generous, taking over the program called Aid to Families with Dependent Children (AFDC) and all costs of the senior colleges of the City University.

The most contentious element of the plan was new borrowing. New York's capital needs were enormous. Years of austerity had made New York hazardous and leaky. Water main breaks and gas explosions had become more frequent, and significant construction and maintenance were urgently needed in other areas. Koch proposed a $5.1 billion budget for capital improvements during the four-year term of the financial plan. He hoped, long before the term was over, to sell a small proportion of bonds at high interest to private investors as a way of gradually reentering the normal market for municipal bonds. Most of the rest of the financing would come from bonds sold to city and state pension funds, with federal guarantees and a continuing waiver of federal regulations to allow them to invest a larger proportion of their holdings in city securities than was normally permissible.

In February, Koch, Carey, and their subordinates hammered out a plan that would give the city approximately $200 million in increased aid from New York State. That spring they shepherded the enabling legislation through the state legislature. In Washington the Senate Banking Committee initially voted a preliminary resolution opposing federal aid, a major setback.[41] Koch managed to offset the bad news from the Senate by obtaining a firm declaration of support from President Carter, although the mayor had had to push hard to get it.[42]

CUTBACKS, LAYOFFS, AND GIVEBACKS

Koch geared up to win over the Senate Banking Committee. Planning for that vote was part of a sophisticated Washington strategy. Koch first brought a somewhat hostile Carter administration on board, promising that aid to New York could be a victory for a president who had been labeled as bad at working with Congress. And to win that victory, Koch understood what was not obvious, given Democratic majorities in both houses: Republican votes were the key to success. A big margin in the House would help push the measure through a reluctant Senate. Koch also had an insider's advantage as a former member of the House Banking and Currency Committee; this became clear on April 26, when the House committee's subcommittee on economic stabilization approved the loan guarantee program by a lopsided 12–2 vote. On May 3 the committee surprised even its chair in approving the loan guarantees with a bipartisan vote of 32 to 8. The committee vote built momentum. But, artfully, the House leaders delayed a vote on the floor until it would have the most impact on the reluctant Senate committee.[43]

Despite this good news, the remaining hurdles were considerable. On May 23 Proxmire derailed the whole process, canceling the Senate loan hearings "in view of the fact that no agreement has been reached on the labor contracts or on any of the other outstanding issues in the New York City financing situation." Koch was able to convince him to reschedule for June 6 only by promising to get a labor agreement by that date.[44]

One of the key preconditions for the federal loans was the conclusion of multi-year labor agreements that the city could afford. New labor agreements were also a priority for Koch, who came into the labor negotiations naively hoping for significant givebacks, such as increased managerial flexibility. He blamed the municipal unions for running up wages and causing deficits, and he spoke grandiosely of a "no-cost" settlement that would be paid for entirely in givebacks—agreements by unions to ease work rules.

Koch prided himself on his negotiating skills, but his style was that of a confrontational divorce lawyer. Municipal labor negotiation is generally a process of conciliation rather than conflict. His first foray into the field did not add to his luster, though he was smart enough to avoid the catastrophic transit strike that gave John Lindsay's administration such a poor start. Koch's adversarial stance probably saved some money, but his boast that he could achieve a labor settlement without raising wages was empty.

At the outset the unions held some significant cards as important creditors. Koch needed them to get the loan guarantees through Congress and to keep buying bonds with their members' pension fund money. Union leaders were strongly unified and assigned a union head to court each of the seven deputy mayors and other major figures in the administration.[45] With the high inflation of the 1970s, union members had suffered real losses because of deferred cost-of-living increases (COLAs) and layoffs. Union leaders could point to a membership that had already made sacrifices and was expecting results. Proxmire unwittingly gave the unions a tremendous advantage by holding the loan guarantee hearings hostage to a settlement.[46] Moreover, the unions had vastly more staff resources than the city for fact-finding and negotiation. An interviewer for the *Fiscal Observer* commented that "the City of New York is a little twerp up against big-time, experienced unions—the office of Municipal Labor Relations has an annual budget of $750,000, which happens to equal the fee that that the PBA [Police Benevolent Association] is paying its new lawyer."[47]

The transit workers' contract would expire first. Negotiating their contract is always a difficult proposition. A transit strike shuts down the whole city, costing billions. Any increases granted to the transit workers would set a precedent for all other city labor contracts, and an overly generous settlement could require a politically unpopular fare hike, particularly galling to a riding public that had become accustomed to the worst service in living memory. But Koch had only indirect control of the negotiations conducted by the Metropolitan Transportation Authority (MTA), a state agency run by a board jointly appointed by the mayor and the governor.

The final settlement cost the transit authority about $100 million (with the potential for an additional $16 million in COLAs), with a 6 percent raise spread over twenty-one months. That amount was feasible under the Koch financial plan, but the prospect of similar settlements with other city unions meant the city would be paying its workers $715 to $800 million more than it had been, which produced howls from Washington.[48] Proxmire denounced the transit deal as outrageous, although his insistence on a fast settlement had undermined the city's bargaining position. However, the wage package remained in line with national averages.[49]

By the time the transit settlement was in hand, revised budget estimates had begun to reveal revenues in FY 1978 sufficient to give city workers a raise. The unexpected surplus eventually rose to $610 million.[50] Negotiations with the municipal unions began in earnest on June 2, after Proxmire agreed to hold hearings four days later. Koch retreated from his initial refusal to grant raises. After a twenty-five-hour negotiating session, the talks dramatically deadlocked over the return of $200 million in deferred wages that the workers had given up in their 1975 contract to help out with the fiscal crisis and that Beame had promised to pay back in the next settlement.[51] Koch and Felix Rohatyn, however, asserted they had no obligation to pay until the city could afford to do so. Finally, late on June 3, under pressure of the upcoming Proxmire hearings, Koch and Victor Gotbaum, the head of the American Federation of State, County and Municipal Employees (AFSCME), the largest public employee union, agreed to send the matter to arbitration, which eventually awarded most of the money to the workers.[52]

The day before the Proxmire hearings, the city and AFSCME reached agreement on a settlement that would cost $757 million—a bit less than the transit workers', but significantly more than the initial offer. The same day the city council and the Board of Estimate passed the $13.5 billion budget.[53] Negotiator David Margolis, no friend of the unions, considered it a good deal. So did Gotbaum, who, despite his difficult personal relations with the mayor, saw that first contract in positive terms: "We began to get some decent settlements. We really were able to go back to standard collective bargaining when Koch took over."[54]

SHOWDOWN WITH SENATOR SCROOGE

With not one day to spare, Mayor Koch was ready to take on Senator Scrooge as the federal loan guarantee hearings began on June 6, 1978. The hearings opened with Proxmire stating his misgivings: "It troubles me greatly that the committee will be confronting, in these 4 days, the same pleas for financial aid to prevent a New York City bankruptcy that we heard 3 years ago in 1975—and from many of the same people as well." Giving New York needed long-term financing for capital improvements would entangle Washington in the city's affairs for a generation, Proxmire warned, and guarantees would "remove the pressures on the city and keep it from making the tough decisions" needed to revive its credit, turning it into a "guarantee junkie." Finally, he worried that other cities would be inspired to spend irresponsibly in the belief that the federal government would come to their rescue.[55]

One might have expected Koch's testimony to follow the initial presentations by New York's two senators, Daniel Patrick Moynihan, a Democrat, and Jacob K. Javits, a Republican, but instead Koch arranged that the first witnesses would be two Republican congressmen, J. William Stanton of Ohio, the ranking Republican on the House Banking Committee, and Stewart B. McKinney of Connecticut, who was the ranking minority member of the House banking subcommittee that had already approved the guarantee bill. Stanton declared that he had spoken with the House Minority Leader and had been told, "'There is no Republican party position on this particular legislation.'" Both testified to their faith in Ed Koch to solve New York's problems. "He's extremely well liked, loved on both sides of the political aisle; and I'm here to ask for more continued aid to a great degree because of him. I just have great confidence that he can do the job and no matter what program you come up with it's gong to be up to him to do it," Stanton told the more skeptical senators.[56] He was followed by Richard Kelly, a conservative Florida Republican (later convicted of bribery in the 1980 Abscam scandal) who argued rather simplistically for bankruptcy, accusing Koch of capitulating to the unions: "The people that run that town must quit spending so much money. There is no other solution."[57]

Koch was determined not to be intimidated. He stood his ground, arguing that the labor settlement was a relatively small proportion of spending. Union givebacks on work rules were insignificant, but Koch pledged to fight for reforms in the future, denouncing the practice of giving a whole day off to police officers who donated blood. Then he started ticking off the measures he was taking to see that New York was better managed:

Committing to a budget strictly balanced according to generally accepted accounting principles. This involved not only a balance of expenditures and revenues but removing all expense items from the capital budget.

- Guaranteeing independent audits of city finances.
- Strengthening the Office of Operations.
- Instituting a computerized integrated financial management system.
- Expanding economic development efforts.
- Keeping a tighter rein on employees, with commissioners disciplining employees for taking excessive sick leave and other abuses.
- Better scrutinizing the reliability and performance of city contractors.
- Evaluating poverty and model cities programs and terminating contracts with those that failed to pay adequate benefits to their employees.

Koch knew that these proposals were politically popular but pledged to implement them even if they were not. "What happens when I do these things?" he asked the committee rhetorically. "There are picket lines around City Hall and in front of Gracie Mansion, but those things—the measures that I take—won't be deterred simply because there are people who get upset that there is a change going on because the change is intended to use our city dollars, our state dollars and our federal dollars to a far better extent than ever before and to remove the incompetence." That was the clincher that helped to win over some of the initially hostile senators.[58]

Proxmire went on the offensive, harping on a familiar theme: Why didn't New York go to the Wall Street bankers who had lavished loans on Third World countries in the sixties and seventies? He thought New York banks should "invest at least as substantial a percentage in New York City as they do in some of those African and South American countries." The trouble with this idea was that many debtor nations had defaulted on their loans and the banks had little cash to spare. Koch, well acquainted with foreign aid from his time on the House Appropriations Committee, replied that the federal government should also be as generous to U.S. cities as it was to foreign nations: "If you would only do for us what you do for the Latin American and African countries, we would not ask for more, but we are not even asking for that. . . . What we are asking for is a guarantee where the federal government is going to make money as a result."[59]

The Wisconsin senator insisted that short-term seasonal loans directly from the federal treasury were preferable to President Carter's proposal for long-term loan guarantees, even though, as Koch pointed out, seasonal loans required cash outlays, whereas loan guarantees would actually benefit the U.S. Treasury. "Guarantees are cheaper, less risky, involve less cash on the part of the federal government, and will get you and us out of this exercise faster," the financier Felix Rohatyn told the committee.[60] The seasonal program proposed by Chairman Proxmire "would assure [that] the city is a permanent fiscal cripple, without access to the private credit markets," insisted Harrison J. Goldin, the city's comptroller.[61] In response to Proxmire's proposal to require the New York banks to invest 1 percent of their assets in propping up the city government, David Rockefeller and Edward L. Palmer, who chaired the executive committee of Citibank, argued that they were already meeting their responsibilities to both New York and their stockholders, and Palmer accused Proxmire of favoring a socialistic system of "credit allocation."[62]

The hearings were a tremendous success for Koch and for New York. On June 9 the House voted 247 to 155, a margin Koch termed overwhelming, in favor of a $2 billion guarantee. The magnitude of this accomplishment contrasts with the 10-vote margin in the House that had approved the bailout in 1975. Senator Proxmire declared that the vote was "a tribute to Mayor Koch, who is highly respected in the House."[63]

Even New York's supporters were surprised when, a week later, the Senate Banking Committee voted 12–3 to send its bill for $1.65 billion in long-term loan guarantees to the Senate floor, and days after the House passed the compromise on the lower figure, the final bill passed the Senate on July 27. In any case, in a high-profile ceremony on the steps of New York City Hall, Carter, in a rare moment of harmony with New York politicians, praised Koch for his fiscal discipline.[64] Even Senator Proxmire was impressed with the new mayor, describing Koch as a star.[65]

12 THE POLITICS OF RACE AND PARTY

As a new mayor Koch had to meet the demands for reform and increased efficiency while forging alliances with the leaders of the regular county Democratic machines: Donald Manes of Queens, Stanley Friedman of the Bronx, and Meade Esposito of Brooklyn. These demands were not always compatible, but as one of his closest friends observed, Koch had no choice "because you can't govern otherwise. . . . You don't deal with the Borough of Queens unless you can figure out how to live with Donny Manes."[1]

Koch had spent his political youth fighting the regulars, but he owed the Brooklyn, Bronx, and Queens leaders to varying degrees for supporting his campaign, and he still needed them. The county leaders had three sources of power in addition to their ability to deliver votes. One stemmed from the peculiar structure of New York City government (eventually declared unconstitutional toward the end of Koch's time in office), which vested enormous powers in the Board of Estimate, consisting of the mayor, comptroller, city council president, and the five borough presidents. Manes, the Queens borough president, was also a county leader. The makeup of the board meant that the majority of votes was controlled or heavily influenced by county leaders. In addition, the county leaders more or less controlled the sheeplike majority on the city council. The third source of county leaders' power was their ability to control who ran for judgeships and who received patronage in the state court system, including the State Supreme Court (a trial court in New York), the Appellate Division, and Surrogate's Court, which appoints lawyers to administer estates and serve as guardians—lucrative sinecures in a city like New York where wealthy people die intestate or become incompetent or orphaned with surprising frequency.

The new mayor knew he had to compromise with the county leaders, but he did set limits on their influence. His most important act was to reform the process for appointing city judges. For decades county leaders had recommended candidates to mayors. Koch set up an independent screening committee that sent him lists of candidates. Political parties were completely removed from the process for the first time in city history, and incumbency no longer trumped competence. And to maintain political independence, Koch would appoint or reappoint based only on the committee's recommendation, regardless of his own opinion or even public denunciation of a judge. Of all the reforms that Koch instituted, he was proudest of this one, which deprived the county leaders of one of their prime sources of power. (State judgeships continue to be controlled under the old system, and county leaders have been known to sell nominations for judgeships—a Kings County Democratic chair was convicted of doing so in 2007.)[2]

At a meeting at Gracie Mansion early in his term, Koch warned the party leaders that "it will injure someone to be perceived as recommended by a county leader" for a judgeship. But the mayor tempered the blow with assurances that he still wanted to work with them. Koch pledged to support the county leaders' candidates for local offices, "provided they're not crooks," and to show up for fundraisers for their party organizations. And, he told them, "you'll come in the front door and not the back door. . . . I'm not ashamed to be seen with you."[3]

If politics is all about give and take, time has shown that Koch gave a little too much credibility to Esposito. Two of Koch's most controversial appointments were Beame holdovers with ties to Esposito's Brooklyn machine. Anthony T. Vaccarello, the sanitation commissioner, was not recommended by the Koch transition team's screening panel, but Koch was impressed as the two men traveled around monitoring snow removal during a huge blizzard that hit New York in the middle of January 1978.

Only nine months later Koch replaced Vaccarello when he proved unable to reorganize the sanitation department to pick up more garbage with fewer employees.[4]

Esposito did not intervene to protect Vaccarello, but he did play a pivotal role in Koch's ultimately disastrous decision to appoint another Beame holdover, Anthony Ameruso, as his new commissioner of transportation. Ameruso looked good on paper, having won an award from John Zuccotti, Beame's first deputy mayor, for his performance as head of the highways department. The award provided Koch with a cover for one of the few appointments requested, albeit indirectly, by a party boss. In an interview in 2004 Koch recalled the county leader's pitch: "Meade Esposito said, 'I have to tell you something.' That was always his way of talking, his style, which was more like *The Sopranos*. Nothing lethal about him. I don't know that he was in any way mob-connected. I had no way of knowing that." Esposito had a bone to pick, Koch said.

> "Listen, Mayor, there are no Italians in your administration." I hadn't even thought about it. I said, "Of course, there must be." He said, "There are no Italians in your administration who are commissioners or deputy mayors. It's not right." I said, if that's true, it's not right. The Italians are a large section of the population. And I checked and there weren't any.
>
> And so I decided, since the position of transportation commissioner was still open, I said, I'm taking Tony Ameruso.[5]

Both men were choosing to ignore one inconvenient fact, and both knew it. Koch *had* appointed Italians to high-level positions in the administration, including Philip Toia, who was deputy mayor for finance, and John LoCicero, Koch's main political adviser. But Koch realized Esposito did not mean *any* Italian—he meant more Italians like Vaccarello from the Brooklyn Democratic organization. When black leaders complained that there were no blacks at high levels in the administration, Koch would point to numerous appointments, few of whom had come up through their clubhouses. He did not dream of playing this game with the white regulars because they had institutional power that their African American counterparts lacked.

Ameruso appeared to know he was protected. According to transition staffer Jim Capalino, Ameruso "treated the interview with the screening panel as a joke." The panel, which was a citizens' committee created by Koch, rejected him as unqualified and publicly protested the appointment of a party hack.[6] The next day Koch disbanded the panel in a fit of rage. Almost three decades later Koch would still bridle at the good-government types for doing what they were supposed to do in what had been billed as a reform administration: "I said to myself, fuck you. What you've now done means I'll never have another citizens' committee to do what I asked you to do. In almost every other case, if not every other case, I took their recommendation. I'm not taking it in your case, because he's good and I don't have any Italians and he's

Italian. I don't regret it except for the fact that he ultimately went to jail. But he didn't go to jail for stealing, he went to jail for lying."[7]

What seems to have made him angriest was that time proved the critics right. The committee had not yet chosen candidates for chair of the Taxi and Limousine Commission, so for good measure Koch appointed Jay Turoff, a Brooklyn party hack who eventually turned out to be a crook. And during Koch's third term Ameruso was convicted of perjury, and Esposito was found guilty of giving an illegal gratuity to Biaggi.

To put it mildly, Koch seems to have overcompensated for having been a hard-nosed reformer once upon a time in the Village Independent Democrats. Early in his first term as mayor Koch was already looking ahead to his next race, according to David Brown, and he was keen on building bridges to those he had once attacked: "Ed, being a reformer from the Village, was suspect to the regular party organization in the outer boroughs, and he was determined, looking ahead as all politicians do to reelection, to not have to go through that schism in the primary in 1981, so he wanted a working relationship with the regulars."[8]

Mayor Koch began to characterize Manhattanites who rejected the regulars as either elitists or holier-than-thou goo-goos (activists for good government). While Koch was always ready to judge minority leaders of community action agencies as suspicious and perhaps corrupt, he treated the white regulars as average people you could do business with. From the vantage of old age Koch could toss off joking references to Esposito's *Sopranos* manner, but as a new mayor Koch treated the county leaders as likable guys from the outer boroughs who happened to be successful politicians, just like he was. He dismissed as overstated romantic nonsense the idea that some county leaders were crooks. In fact it was Koch, not the reformers, who proved to be naive, but that fact would not emerge until the indictments were handed up eight years later, tarnishing his cherished reputation.[9]

The mayor told his commissioners that they had to keep the county leaders in the loop. "You don't have to take their advice. But meet them. Don't let them read in the paper tomorrow about things that you could tell them about," Koch told Haskell Ward, his community development commissioner.[10] Maureen Connelly did her part by meeting with Esposito over dinner at the venerable Tiro a Segno restaurant on MacDougal Street to talk about firing an incompetent mayoral counsel. It didn't take long to cover all the issues: "He said, 'Have the liver and onions.' I said, 'Meade, he's a nincompoop.' Meade said, 'OK.'"[11]

Koch's newfound friendliness with the regulars bore a tinge of willful ignorance. After all, even his most reform-minded commissioners had to deal with entrenched machine influence in the upper levels of the bureaucracy. "There was a general sense that senior officials in the government had rabbis, that someone was protecting the most senior civil servants," Haskell Ward recalled. Brown, then Koch's deputy mayor of administration, corroborated the existence of political rabbis, usually county leaders, who protected people at the top of the bureaucracy.[12] Two agency heads in the Koch inner circle, Robert F. Wagner Jr. and James Capalino, were offered a bribe or had to deal with attempted extortion. Wagner said that when he chaired the city planning commission, he once took a hard line against a Manhattan building project by an influential Brooklyn political family. When a member of that family then began to drop hints about helping Wagner to retire his campaign debts, Wagner admonished: "Stop! Don't say anything more or I'll have to call the Department of Investigation."[13] Capalino, according to the Department of Investigation, refused to give a raise to a subordinate who also worked for Herbert S. Bauch, publisher of the *Sentinel*, the newspaper of the Civil Service Retired Employees Association. When Bauch threatened Capalino with bad publicity, Capalino reported him, and Bauch eventually pleaded guilty to attempted larceny by extortion, though he was only fined $500. According to both Bauch and Capalino, this was the way business had been done at the General Services Administration before Capalino took control.[14]

Koch's management style was to decentralize control, which produced mixed results. Koch allowed commissioners to hire and fire whomever they wanted, without even notifying him in advance, and in most cases he did not interfere in their policies and administrative decisions. So long as no illegal discrimination was involved, he would back his commissioners, regardless of what the county leaders said, and every commissioner whom I interviewed praised Koch for never wavering in his support in these cases. On the negative side he gave too much power and not enough oversight to weak machine regulars, like Ameruso. Koch's most successful clubhouse appointment was Anthony Gliedman, who served as ports and terminals commissioner. He was a Columbia Law graduate and member of Esposito's Jefferson Democratic Club. Gliedman did well enough to deserve promotion to housing commissioner, but he was a rarity, both a Columbia-educated technocrat and a regular.[15]

KOCH AND AFRICAN AMERICANS, 1978

By the end of his first week in office, Koch had made thirty appointments, only two of blacks. The *Amsterdam News* termed this "a poor beginning." He then appointed two black commissioners the next week but also made Blanche Bernstein, an academic who had flirted with idea of abolishing Aid to Families with Dependent Children (AFDC), his human resources administrator. Her mandate was to cut the welfare caseload, and though her ideas were little different from the welfare reforms that Bill Clinton would advocate, at the time she was viewed as a conservative, in part because of her self-righteous manner.

State senator Carl McCall, then a prominent Harlem political leader, charged that Bernstein was "anti-poor."[16] The issue of Bernstein came up in the spring of 1978, when Koch held a huge meeting of black leaders from across the spectrum.

"Everybody from Charlie Rangel to Calvin Butts to the black members of the City Council, like Wendell Foster, Mary Pinkett, Percy Sutton, and others were in Gracie Mansion that morning," recalled Allen G. Schwartz, then serving as corporation counsel (the city's chief lawyer), who attended, along with Wagner, Brown, Basil Paterson, Herman Badillo, and Bernstein herself.

The black politicians at the meeting angrily attacked Bernstein and her welfare policies. Koch stood up, looked at the group, and said, "You shouldn't be pointing your finger at Blanche Bernstein; you should be talking about me because she's doing exactly what I'm telling her to do." With an "almost audible gasp," even on the administration's side of the room, "everyone pulled back." Paterson, at the time the only black deputy mayor, got up and left the table. Schwartz and Wagner gave each other an "uh-oh" look, recognizing the gravity of the situation. Schwartz believed that "it was the moment at which Ed Koch moved away almost irrevocably from the black community, and his relationship with them was never the same."[17] U.S. Representative Charles Rangel complained, amid reports of a "deep and growing antagonism" with black leaders, that "none of us was able to get through to the mayor on the problems he was having in the black community. . . . Knowing Ed, I'd wouldn't say he is a racist. There isn't any group he hasn't told to go to hell. His arrogance is unbiased."[18] Bernstein proved so combative and impolitic that Koch had to fire her only a few months later, so he derived no particular political benefit from defending her.

The incident did reveal his underlying attitudes toward the black political establishment. As his press secretary, Maureen Connelly, observed, "Ed is a master of communications, but he just didn't have the knack to communicate to the black community."[19] Bobby Wagner Jr., son of another New York mayor, recalled that the political style of Harlem politicians "was alien to him," so Koch never grasped "the politics of real poverty, as opposed to the sort of relative poverty that you discover in the Italian parts of his [former Congressional] district." When Wagner's father was mayor (1954–65), Adam Clayton Powell Jr. and J. Raymond Jones were alive and there was "a much greater strength among black political leadership, and I think that was helpful." In the late 1970s no black politician had the power of Powell or Jones, who were figures as crucial to Mayor Wagner as Esposito and Manes were to Mayor Koch.[20]

Badillo remarked that though Koch had good relations with Hispanics throughout his mayoralty, he "never really got along very well with blacks. I mean, that was one of his problems, which went on all through his mayoralty." Badillo said when he would set up meetings with black leaders, and set up "the right atmosphere . . . the moment Koch walked in there was tension in the room."[21] Asked if Ed Koch was "uncomfortable" with blacks, former deputy mayor Basil Paterson replied diplomatically that he "didn't know how comfortable Koch was, but he was no different from most white elected officials or politicians. He got along very well initially with black elected officials. . . . I think as he got along, he had problems. Ed didn't brook criticism too well, and if there's one thing about black politicians and black community leaders, they will not bite their tongues."[22] In the opinion of Bobby Wagner, Koch worsened his political relationships with black leaders by answering such attacks with anger and "sort of implying that when Charlie [Rangel] went after him or [the Reverend] Daughtry went after him, it was all blacks going after him, and he was at war with all blacks."[23]

Koch stepped up his recruitment of blacks to city hall, but his efforts did not smooth over his relations with black politicians, despite an uneasy truce for the year that Basil Paterson remained in the administration. Some were put off by the lack of black faces in Koch's inner circle, but it also rankled when Koch bypassed the black power brokers in making his appointments, according to Koch confidant David Margolis, who was on the conservative side of Koch's brace of advisers.[24] One black politician, who insisted on anonymity, remarked to the *Soho Weekly News* that Koch's black appointees "may be talented people who do good work, but they are simply not relevant to the community. They don't live in it, they don't work in it."[25] In a similar vein Carl McCall commented that the split between the mayor and black political leaders began because Koch's "appointments were not people who had come up through the political ranks. . . . He seemed to be going out of his way to find people who did not have those relationships." McCall cited the appointment of Haskell Ward as an example. Community Development Commissioner Haskell Ward was the African American appointee closest to Ed Koch, and frequently traveled all over with the mayor and Dan Wolf, the former publisher of the *Village Voice*, Koch's closest confidant. According to Ward, the three became pretty close.[26] Ward was a Georgian who had worked in New York for the Ford Foundation and on the State Department's policy planning staff. He had not risen through the political clubhouse of J. Raymond Jones, as Percy Sutton and David Dinkins had, but was identified instead with the Atlanta elite. But the issue of appointments was only part of the reason for the schism, added McCall—Koch "seemed to be opposed to affirmative action and more inclusion of minorities of government. The message that we thought we were getting was a message against inclusion and diversity."[27]

Koch's failure to deal with the Harlem regulars reflected both their political weakness and Koch's underlying preference for a predominantly white and Hispanic coalition, which became clear by Koch's second year in office.[28] Sutton and Dinkins had proved in the 1977 primaries for mayor and Manhattan Borough president that they could not control Harlem, where turnout had been low and Abzug and Beame had made heavy inroads. The long-time rivalry between the black leadership of Harlem and Brooklyn also greatly diminished their power, while the usually united front of Esposito, Manes, and Friedman gave them a huge advantage in their ability to deliver votes that Koch needed. As Brown put it, the mayor "had to do a whole lot of bridgework to the outer boroughs" to ensure his reelection. And from watching the career of the last East Side congressman who had become mayor, John V. Lindsay,

Koch learned that deference to black leaders could come at the cost of conservative white votes. Thus Koch felt free to ignore Harlem politicians and strengthen ties to some African American allies in other boroughs—such as the African Methodist Episcopal minister Floyd H. Flake in Queens—while bolstering his ties to white regulars.[29]

Connelly believed that Koch gave his critics credibility by whacking them rhetorically. "I think Ed Koch made Reverend Herbert Daughtry. For better or for worse, he was not a very well-known minister. But Ed—if he perceived that someone was trying to intimidate him, he would get his back up and lash out. I mean, his line was: 'I'm not a punching bag. I'm not a pillow. I give as good as I get.' I think that damaged his standing in the black community."[30] Brown put it this way: "Ed would quarrel with anybody, no matter what race or ethnicity. He wasn't going to yield when he thought he was right."[31] An exchange of letters between Koch and Mary Pinckett, a member of the city council, illustrates how little he was willing to give even after she claimed he had told her "shut up, I've heard your big mouth before." Instead of making an outright apology, Koch wrote that he did not recall saying that to her, and neither did Brooklyn Borough president Howard Golden or Herman Badillo. Pinkett did remember it that way and knew others at their meeting who did as well. Grudgingly, Koch apologized: "Although I do not believe that I used the words that you recall, if that is your recollection, I regret it. If you had mentioned the incident at any point since that meeting, I would have immediately apologized." They would eventually make up, and Pinkett had warmer relations with the mayor than many other black politicians, but Koch treated few other potential allies so shabbily.[32]

Koch's bluntness may have been the spark for some of the anti-Koch, anti-Semitic graffiti that began to appear in Harlem six months into his administration. Koch provoked stronger reactions than his predecessor had. Fred Samuel, also a city council member, aptly observed, "Abe Beame was Jewish, but he was never viewed as 'the Jewish Mayor.' He knew how to reach out to the black community. But because of [Koch's] appointment of so many Jewish commissioners—Basil Paterson is the only black in the high councils of the administration and he is in a 'nonblack' job—and tightening up on the poverty board and on Model Cities, Koch is viewed as 'the Jewish Mayor.'"[33] Being known as "the Jewish mayor" did not faze Koch, who continued to defend Israel and attack the welfare state. Some in the black community saw Koch's stance on Israel as special pleading for his own ethnic group and his newfound neoliberalism as a discriminatory attack on poor blacks, who relied on government assistance for survival and as a stepping stone to the middle class. But Koch showed little sign of being willing to understand black points of view on the subject of discrimination. He assumed that the difficulties African Americans faced in ascending to the middle class in the 1970s and 1980s were the same difficulties that Jews had faced in the 1950s and 1960s; he discounted the considerable government assistance that he had received; and he assumed that legal changes had effectively wiped out the problem of discrimination.

A chance remark in 1980 illustrates Koch's attitude. In 1980, when U.S. Representative Elizabeth Holtzman was running against Bess Myerson for the Democratic nomination for U.S. Senate, he faulted Holtzman for failing to make friends with neo-Confederate legislators:

> She's very smart and able, but she could never get anybody to vote for something they were neutral on, on the basis of "Do me a favor, will you, I need your vote." She's not as bad as Bella . . . not as abrasive . . . but the same number of people would say no. You want an example? Robert E. Lee. They wanted to give him back his citizenship. She voted no. Is it really that terrible to give him that honor? It means so much to the Southerners as a symbol. You wouldn't vote yes? What does it cost, right? I'll tell you what it costs. It costs goodwill if you vote no, and it's senseless.[34]

The remark is telling in terms of how heedless Koch could be of black (and liberal white) sensibilities, implying that fond memories of Robert E. Lee have nothing to do with racism. It is fair to speculate that if Lee had been a notorious anti-Semite, instead of a defender of a slave republic, Koch would never have voted for the resolution. The message seemed to be, if you alienate southerners, it's foolish. Alienating blacks is another story.

THE WAR ON THE WAR ON POVERTY

Why did Koch specify only two goals by name in his short inaugural speech: boosting gentrification and reforming community service agencies? They were hardly more urgent than the city's quest for federal loans and its desperate need for capital to maintain the most basic city services. Koch ignored the issues on most voters' minds, namely, increasing police protection, preventing crime, collecting garbage, and repairing the streets. Koch did not highlight the antipoverty programs because of their fiscal significance, either—they represented only $35 to $40 million in a budget of more than $4 billion, and most of the funding was federal. Yet he moved quickly to prioritize gentrification and agency reform, generating lawsuits and even a recall effort by black leaders who had run the old system.

Koch insisted on resuming direct mayoral authority over all contracts, effectively depriving local boards of the power to spend money.[35] City hall later also took direct control of other formerly decentralized entities such as the Model Cities program. Taking control of the antipoverty agencies served several purposes. First and foremost, Koch argued, it was good government. By the time of his inauguration Koch's eye was on Washington, where he had to demonstrate his commitment to rooting out bad management, waste, and corruption in order to win the federal guarantee of New York's bonds.[36]

But his urgent need to get control of the poverty agencies also had a more local political dimension, although he downplayed that aspect. His policy removed a huge amount of patronage from potential and declared political opponents and gave it to his administration, which kept the money in the communities but spent it Koch's way. "It wasn't about the power; it was about the corruption," he was still insisting thirty years later.[37] Thirty-five million dollars may have been a tiny portion of a multibillion-dollar budget, but it was money that leaders of poverty agencies dipped into for patronage. Thirty-five million dollars was more than all nine mayoral candidates combined had spent in the 1977 campaign. And the effectiveness of the reformed and newly formed community action agencies would prove critical to the success of the housing program that Koch began to implement in 1985.

The reforms undoubtedly made the system more efficient and canceled contracts that smelled of fraud, referring numerous cases to the Department of Investigation and the U.S. Attorney's Office to determine whether administrators had hired "no-show employees; paid double salaries, and paid political kickbacks."[38] At the time Koch administration officials seemed dedicated to establishing the administration's reputation for fiscal probity, crucial for getting increased federal and state aid. Deputy Mayor Phil Trimble noted that even after the reorganization of the antipoverty agencies was completed, audit and control functions remained at city hall. "We've got to establish fiscal discipline," he told the press at the time, adding that the administration was implementing the first real check to see whether the antipoverty programs were actually doing business at the addresses they listed, something that the Beame administration apparently never did.[39]

According to Haskell Ward, who enforced these changes as head of the Community Development Administration, Koch went after these relatively small agencies because their management had gone radically wrong and he was trying to establish performance standards that would lower their overhead, improve their efficiency, and get more money to poor people in the neighborhoods. When Ward took over, black employees would come to him "as a normal order of things about jobs that they considered their jobs, and practices that they considered perfectly legitimate, that were just really verging on illegal . . . and they thought that everybody did the same thing and that it was just their agency that was being singled out because everybody else was behaving the same way."[40]

Ward began implementing Koch's policies within three weeks of the inauguration. The Koch administration quickly suspended a jobs program in Jamaica, Queens, and canceled lucrative city contracts with the Fort Greene Community Corporation until it removed a board member, David Billings III, who chaired the citywide umbrella group of poverty organizations and had been convicted two years earlier of using federal poverty money for a down payment on a house in Brooklyn. Ward tried to neutralize charges of racism by terminating contracts with Jewish agencies such as the B'nai Torah Institute, an antipoverty organization serving Russian immigrants (sometimes with spoiled food) that had been the target of three federal investigations; some of its chief administrators were convicted of perjury and conspiracy.[41]

Koch did not care whether his policies for reforming the poverty programs angered black political elites, though he hoped the move would have some appeal to middle-class blacks. Rangel, McCall, and others filed suit to block the changes, but this may not have been as strongly in their political interest as they thought.[42] In Ward's view, by the time he became commissioner, "the poverty programs had lost favor with the black middle class, the educated, and the achiever class among blacks. No really competent African American of any standing or educational background, no first-class African Americans, wanted to head poverty programs."[43]

This revealing statement explains some of the hostility Ward encountered from people who were not part of the older black bourgeoisie, who were not what he called "first-class African Americans." But, Ward added, "it was also one of the reasons that I thought it was important for someone of my background to take that kind of job. Because African Americans were among the first to say that they were embarrassed by the aura of corruption."[44] Local black political elites saw it differently. "There is deep concern that Koch will exploit the image (and reality) of ineffectiveness as a means of reducing the funding into black anti-poverty areas and redirecting some of those funds to white areas of poverty," Bryant Rollins editorialized in the *Amsterdam News*.[45]

The community action agencies grew out of Lyndon Johnson's War on Poverty and were designed to decentralize power and empower the poor. Title II of the Economic Opportunity Act of 1964 set up the Office of Economic Opportunity and mandated that the new antipoverty agencies be "developed, conducted, and administered with the maximum feasible participation of residents of the area and members of the groups served."[46] The goal was to create programs to promote upward mobility without paternalism, bureaucracy, or old-fashioned political patronage brokered through big-city machines. The programs did enable some people in poor communities to join the middle class by taking control of the agencies (whose leadership was selected in special antipoverty agency elections) just as global economic realignment was causing the disappearance of factory jobs in the United States. During the late 1970s government jobs remained one of the surest paths into the middle class for African Americans. Yet the funding for the antipoverty agencies was too meager to send more than a few blacks to the middle class. These agencies were often inefficient and wasteful and did not always get money to the poor who most needed it.[47]

But the antipoverty programs had some successes. They "taught a whole generation of people how to work in an office," after generations of blacks had been excluded from white-collar jobs, observed Edward C. Sullivan, a white state assemblyman who represented West Harlem during and after Koch's mayoralty. Roger Wilkins observed that the agencies "nurtured a level of leadership in the black community that enriched the next two decades of our national life" and "brought more life and self-help activity to the black ghettos than I've ever seen before or since."[48] Sullivan said, "Koch always looked at the inefficiencies, but he didn't look at— because he wasn't interested in, I'll assert—the uplifting of people from children of sharecroppers and of menial servants to become office workers and managers, creating a managerial class or a civil service class."[49]

This creation of independent, federally financed political machines was hardly the intent of the legislation, but many big-city mayors, including Robert F. Wagner and Richard J. Daley, feared that the act would create federally funded power bases for the poor to demand additional services, independent of the mayor or political parties. The cost of these services, they feared, could be borne only by taxing middle-class voters. While Wagner generally was in favor of federal aid to fight poverty, he testified at a 1965 hearing held by Adam Clayton Powell's House Education and Labor Committee that "governing bodies, through their chief executives or otherwise, should have the ultimate authority, as they have the ultimate responsibility for the . . . conduct and operations of the poverty program." In "perhaps the bitterest of the local feuds" stirred by the War on Poverty, Powell tried to hold back action on New York's application for antipoverty funds until the mayor, who had centralized control of the funds in city hall, provided for more direct participation by the poor. Faced by a "revolt of the mayors," the White House dispatched Vice President Hubert Humphrey to the 1965 meeting of the U.S. Conference of Mayors to assuage angry mayors who were threatening to pass a resolution accusing the director of the Office of Economic Opportunity, Sargent Shriver, of "fostering class struggle" by supporting local empowerment of the poor.[50]

John Lindsay did not face the same political dilemma as Wagner and Daley. He was elected in 1965 with the support of liberals and some conservative Republicans and liberal reform Democrats, including, in that first election, Ed Koch. Lindsay's original coalition was, as his Conservative Party opponent William F. Buckley put it, an oxymoron, a self-contradictory ambiguity. A tepidly liberal Republican, Lindsay needed either the traditionally Democratic middle- and working-class white ethnic voters who had been the backbone of the Wagner administration or to develop a new constituency combining liberal professional elites and a newly mobilized constituency of poor minority voters. He chose the latter, appointing new poverty program leaders from the poor neighborhoods, such as the Brownsville librarian Major Owens, who was later elected to the state senate and to Congress. Lindsay, reversing

Wagner's stance, also allowed neighborhood elections for boards of directors of programs that would appeal to the unaffiliated poor.[51]

As the political scientist Martin Shefter has pointed out, it was "only a slight simplification to say that centralization was a technique with which the [Lindsay] administration sought to enhance the influence of its upper- and upper-middle-class allies and decentralization was a technique for enhancing the influence of its non-white allies. The Lindsay administration, however, was unable to control the political forces that decentralization unleashed."[52] Paradoxically, Charles V. Hamilton, a leading expert on black politics, has argued that poverty programs depressed black voter turnout by disrupting the old political machines and their "patron-client relationships," which depended on getting their clients to vote. The new community action agencies and Model Cities programs created "patron-recipient relationships," more like charity without the recipient's undertaking any reciprocal obligation. Hamilton argues that this trend may have prevented Percy Sutton from making a successful mayoral bid. If Hamilton is correct, Koch's reforms, combined with Reagan's later severe cuts in antipoverty programs, may have aided the African American political mobilization of the 1980s that eventually made David Dinkins Koch's successor.[53]

RANGEL'S END RUN: "LET HIM SPEAK!"

New alliances were forged, and new enemies made, in the battle over the antipoverty agencies. As deputy mayor Herman Badillo initially had partial responsibility for the poverty reforms, which divided the Hispanic community—in part because Badillo used the occasion to temporarily deprive council member Ramon Velez, often held up as the archetypal poverty program boss, of his power base. "We've got to stop the stealing," Badillo declared. But by 1979, a few months before he was fired by Koch, Badillo was at odds with Ward, who wanted to close down the Puerto Rican Community Development Project and build a new program, while Badillo campaigned to retain the organization but reform it.[54]

At the height of the internal conflict more than one thousand poverty agency employees went to Albany to lobby against centralization. But the Koch administration, though it ultimately won, handled the issue clumsily. Haskell Ward allowed himself to be set up by an offended Rangel, who opposed some of the reforms, at a public meeting. Ward had lunched with Rangel before the meeting and explained to him that he had prevented Representative Stephen Solarz from speaking at a similar hearing in Brooklyn because he was not on the list, so Ward asked Rangel to sign up beforehand. Rangel replied: "I don't even know if I'm coming, Haskell, but I will tell you this: I won't create a problem." But Rangel did show up late to speak, and Ward refused to recognize both Rangel and political reality. The crowd, restless with chants of "Let him speak, let him speak," stormed the stage. Ward had to end the meeting. Rangel got headlines about the protests while Ward had to sneak out of the building under police escort. Koch, recognizing that Ward had been had by the much wilier Rangel, asked Ward, "Why didn't you let him speak?"[55] But Ward persevered, and the antipoverty programs came under mayoral control within a year.

The state senate's Black and Puerto Rican Caucus, chaired by Vander Beatty, even tried to start a recall campaign against Koch, though New York State does not allow recall elections. Beatty had benefited greatly from the system: through jobs in the agencies themselves, summer jobs programs that they administered, and community action funds available to their boards, Beatty, like other political figures from impoverished neighborhoods, had built a formidable political empire and had gotten rich doing it, until federal prosecutors ended his career. But the poverty programs also sustained hundreds of people for whom poverty agency jobs were tickets to the middle class and who were not essentially corrupt. The anxiety and precariousness of their class position was what led to charges by "speaker after speaker" at a public hearing that the Koch reorganization was genocide.[56]

Beatty offered a measure that would have added the ability to hold recall elections to the city charter. Ultimately, most major black politicians, including Charles Rangel, Shirley Chisholm, and Carl McCall, rejected the recall strategy, charging that it was likely "to result in an overwhelming vote of confidence in the mayor." After that the Beatty petition lost steam. When David Dinkins, the city clerk, refused to certify that the petitions had enough signatures to put the measure on the ballot, Beatty charged that Dinkins was "a tool of Koch."[57]

Eventually, despite lawsuits, the recall attempt, and challenges in Washington, the poverty programs were reformed. Many were cut out of existence anyway by the Reagan budgets of the 1980s. But while the reforms at first hurt Koch politically, and while he would later embrace some of the so-called poverty pimps he initially denounced, the resurgence of accountable community organizations later became a key to the successful redevelopment of poor neighborhoods (see chapter 19).

13

SHAKE-UP (1979–80)

The year 1978, the shakedown cruise for Koch's new activist regime, was a whirl-wind of appointments and budget and labor negotiations. But 1979 supposedly was the year when "nothing happened"—or, at any rate, when little of importance changed from the way things had been the year before, according to veteran city hall reporter Andy Logan. The mayor continued his frenetic pace. He kept constant company with the press, complete with unmissable photo opportunities: "Koch hugging a giant Paddington Bear, Koch with his chin out announcing that he will not be intimidated by some group of demonstrators, who, like more amenable New Yorkers, are also his constituents."[1] Despite Koch's energetic style, city services had not shown much improvement. It was too early to see the effects of the trickle of capital spending he had resumed, and his seven deputy mayors crossed wires on occasion, sometimes delivering minor shocks to the political system. Despite these problems Koch remained confident that he could get New York back on a steady course. If nothing was happening, he would reshuffle his government so that something would happen.

Optimism distinguished Koch from other politicians in the dismal climate of the late 1970s. While Jimmy Carter whined in the summer of 1979 that "the erosion of our confidence in the future is threatening to destroy the social and the political fabric of America," the mayor's public persona combined activism, confidence, and even entertainment, and most New Yorkers forgave the need for even greater austerity.[2] No wonder he would soon recognize a kindred spirit in Ronald Reagan, who performed a middle American version of the same shtick. Koch, unlike Reagan, emphasized government activism to promote the private sector and to aid the middle class and, to some extent, the poor.[3]

Koch's activism placed him "in stunning contrast to Carter, as one of the few public officials whose activities are covered by a major national paper as closely and constantly as the President's," according to one local reporter in 1979. "The often quotable, rarely informative Mr. Koch" stood in contrast to Carter "because [Koch] hasn't lost his sense of outrage."[4] Koch was not in politics for the money, and he gained tremendous credit for turning back a $20,000 salary increase voted by the city council. Koch thought that the raise might weaken his position in the 1980 labor contract negotiations.[5]

Not everyone warmed to his act. Koch's exchanges of invective often amused a public too long accustomed to the colorlessness of mayors like Beame and Wagner and the patrician manners of Lindsay. But liberal journalist Douglas Ireland warned that the mayor had begun a "cult of personality," a hyperbole implicitly comparing Koch with Stalin, Mao Zedong, and Kim Il Sung.[6]

Koch had based his whole political career on being a Jew with an uncommon affinity for Catholics. Once Cuomo was out of the picture, Koch assiduously cultivated New York's Catholic hierarchy and laity. The October 1979 visit of pope John Paul II provided an unprecedented opportunity. Koch made him the first pope to be welcomed with a ticker-tape parade.[7] Invited or not, the mayor traveled by car, helicopter, and boat to participate in all the pope's public appearances, and even gave the Holy Father a gold medal. Hanging with the pope was smart politics; for some Catholic voters it made Koch the next best thing to actually being Catholic. For many years Catholic voters were an important and loyal part of Koch's political base. Herman Badillo asserted that Koch reorganized his government in 1979 because of his rejection of the liberal multiracial coalition that had originally elected him. The reorganization was designed to curry favor with a revamped coalition of Jews, Catholics, and relatively conservative middle-class blacks and Hispanics, and that coalition re-elected him twice. While Badillo's point of view was undoubtedly influenced by his firing, his general conclusion seems valid.[8]

Koch's intense attentiveness to the Catholic hierarchy paradoxically gave the mayor political leeway for his strong support of gay rights. Staying close to the church was the best possible antidote to queer baiting, which disappeared as an issue for nearly ten years until another strong Catholic candidate, U.S. Attorney Rudolph Giuliani, became a potential mayoral candidate.

THEY DON'T CRY WOLF IN THE BRONX

Some of the most haunting images in New York's history were filmed in late 1979 for the horror movie *Wolfen,* hailed as the biggest Hollywood filming project in New York for some time, a consequence of Deputy Mayor Peter Solomon's strong efforts to promote New York City as a set for films and television. *Wolfen* presented the Bronx in the starkest possible terms. Starring Albert Finney and Edward James Olmos, the film's premise was that the destruction of the south Bronx had raised the ghosts of Native American wolf spirits. The film was shot in the desolate area south of Charlotte Street that Jimmy Carter had promised to rebuild, and the filmmakers made it even scarier by building an abandoned church on the site. The *wolfen* themselves were corporeal enough to maul the throats of developers who threatened their home.[9] But in 1979 the south Bronx would have been *lucky* to have developers. *Wolfen* was not the neighborhood's only film portrayal. Some German filmmakers also used it as a location for a film about the bombing of Dresden.[10]

Jimmy Carter had made Charlotte Street both a benchmark and a myth. Its career as a symbol, according to Bobby Wagner, "leads to reflection on the power of television on how decisions get made. [Carter's] advance men picked Charlotte Street because it is incredibly dramatic. I mean, you could find almost equally devastated areas in central Brooklyn or Lower East Side or Central Harlem, but they're flat, and this one had a slope to it so it made the drama of abandonment all the greater." The Beame administration had responded with a plan, expressly drawn up for Carter's press conference by Victor Marrero, chair of the city planning commission, to build a "town within a town."[11] Carter had excluded Koch from the 1977 Charlotte Street photo-op because of the letter critical of Carter's Middle East policy that Koch had handed him at the airport. (See chapter 10). In the long run the most important effect of Carter's trip was that it focused international attention on the south Bronx, prompting a stream of what Jill Jonnes referred to as "urban disaster tourists," with little more effect on the neighborhood's future than the spectres and spectators of *Wolfen.*[12] But it would also focus Koch's attention on the rebuilding of the Bronx as one of the principal legacies of his administration. The redevelopment got off to a slow start, but by the time Koch left office he had proved that government intervention could save neighborhoods.

The burning of the Bronx in the 1970s and early 1980s occurred for a number of reasons. One was that apartment living went out of fashion for middle- and lower-middle class families who could now afford a single-family home in the suburbs. Many children of immigrants had lost the desire to live in a dense, European village–style environment. They no longer wanted to hear their aunt Bessie screaming the latest gossip across the air shaft.[13]

After the 1950s the federal government subsidized and promoted the desire for the privacy of a detached single-family home. Banks and real estate interests made it more difficult to get loans to fix up old buildings because they wanted to make money from selling new ones. Thousands who simply wanted a more modern high-rise Jewish village with splendid views of the water moved to Co-op City, located in the marshes on eastern edge of the Bronx. The development retained some of the left-wing feistiness of the old Jewish Bronx. These buildings were so huge that in 1975 an increase in maintenance charges to residents prompted one of the largest rent strikes in U.S. history. The migration to the suburbs and Co-op City left thousands of older apartments vacant.[14] The biggest problem was transience. As the long-time and more established residents left, they were replaced by poorer people who were often more likely to move from apartment to apartment, especially in areas like the south Bronx that had the oldest housing. All these factors produced a wave of friction fires—the kind that start when the pages of insurance policies are rubbed together.

When the landlord Albert Epstein and his former tenant Benjamin Warren were indicted in February 1970 for the murder of three boys whom they had hired to torch Epstein's building at 1132 Kelly Street in the Morrisania section of the Bronx, the case was labeled bizarre.[15] Few realized that the lurid tale was the new normal. By 1974 the Bronx had seen more than four hundred cases of arson, and they seemed to be methodical attempts to force tenants to vacate: an initial small fire, followed by a conflagration, after which crews would strip the buildings of valuable plumbing and other metal fixtures. These fires damaged the morale of fire fighters and caused injuries to New York's bravest as they entered dangerously weakened vacant buildings to put out the flames.[16]

While there was a shortage of affordable housing throughout the city, between 1950 and 1980 the population of the south Bronx declined 57 percent, from 436,923 to 167,370. At the same time crime spiraled across the borough. Between 1960 and 1969 assaults rose from 998 to 4,256; burglaries went from 1,765 to 29,276.[17]

As the Bronx historian Evelyn Gonzalez notes, "The social collapse of the South Bronx occurred before its physical destruction. Poverty and old buildings do not inevitably lead to crime, abandonment and arson, for there had always been slums in the city." Other boroughs suffered abandonment, but the Bronx had the youngest, poorest, and most transient population, and that made it hard to find tenants. According to Gonzalez, "The problem was not rent control but finding any tenant at all."[18]

Landlords abandoned properties that had no rent-paying tenants. Buildings began to burn down. Landlords destroyed them for the insurance money. Gangs and addicts stripped buildings of metal and fixtures; sometimes residents torched their apartments to get high priority for public housing.[19] Lindsay and Beame did almost nothing to stop the fires, and the situation was made worse after the Lindsay administration established an ineffective fire alarm system and started to close firehouses, management decisions based on junk social science. Reductions in service in minority neighborhoods became even more severe with the budget cuts ordered by the Emergency Financial Control Board after 1975.[20] Longer response times by the fire department increased the damage done by each fire.

By May 1975, just as the fiscal crisis began, fires in the south Bronx rose by 20 percent, now more than 12,300 fires a year, more than 30 percent of them arson. Yet the Beame administration did almost nothing to investigate or deter the burning of the Bronx, and the Ford administration's Justice Department did not investigate the interstate insurance frauds involved in many fires.

Police and fire officials had only the vaguest idea of who might be setting the blazes, though many of those apprehended were landlords. The sheer number of cases overwhelmed the small force of fire marshals assigned to the Bronx. Not surprisingly, their investigations did not make much progress. Of the five marshals assigned to a task force in the largely Hispanic south Bronx in 1975, only one spoke Spanish. Deputy Mayor Stanley Friedman, a Bronx politician who had enormous influence in the Beame administration and who was himself convicted of fraud and corruption in the late 1980s (see chapter 23), waited a year to order the police to investigate, but the police units assigned lacked basic equipment, such as radios and unmarked cars, or any real intelligence operation to find out who was setting the blazes. They arrested mostly small fry.[21]

The highly ideological claim that the Bronx burned down because of rent control does not explain the increasing incidence of arson nationally, mostly in localities that lacked rent control.[22] As Michael Jacobsen and Phillip Kasinitz have pointed out, economic conditions in the early 1970s provided fertile ground for arson and insurance fraud. In a deregulated insurance industry the increasing use of derivatives transferred risk from the original parties to distant investors. Rising interest rates created an incentive for insurance brokers to write policies in risky areas, invest their fees at the prevailing high rates of interest, and pass the actual risks on to someone else. Like the subprime mortgage problems that surfaced in 2008, the biggest losses were suffered by the buyers of derivatives of the original fire insurance policies, an investment that only appeared to be low risk. Exacerbating the problem was a state program that unwittingly assisted the crooks: its purpose was to help areas that previously had been redlined by making low-cost fire insurance more readily available. Buyers of reinsurance contracts were far removed from the scene of the actual damage. The Sasse syndicate of Lloyds of London absorbed many of the losses. Sasse gave a Florida company, DenHar Underwriters, blanket authorization to write policies in the United States. DenHar, in turn, sold policies through the Columbian Brokerage in the Bronx. Columbian, the people on the ground in the Bronx, did little to filter out landlords who had had many fires in the past or to do much else to assess the risks of the policies they were writing. The people who were actually liable were an ocean away when the properties they had insured in the Bronx started to burn to the ground.[23] Sasse lost $45 million of the personal fortunes of Lloyds' "names." The names in turn sued both Lloyds and its reinsurer, a Brazilian government company, I.R.B., which refused to pay the claims. Thus the south Bronx arson crisis precipitated one of the largest insurance scandals in British history and even put Brazilian taxpayers at risk. The full dimension of the financial loss was not detected for years. The frauds were hard to trace because the Bronx policies had passed through many different corporations, some formed to conceal the identities of landlords with repeated losses from fire.[24]

WHAT WAS TO BE DONE?

When Koch took office, he had a two-front war on his hands, stopping arson and rebuilding the areas that had been destroyed. Initially, he had little success with either. Despite the indictments of fifteen people, including a former community planning board chair, arson continued to increase "at a record rate." Koch then fired his fire commissioner, Augustus Beekman, and replaced him with the well-regarded prosecutor, Charles Hynes, who vowed to make fighting arson his top priority. Koch and Police Commissioner Robert McGuire also gave the police more authority to investigate fires. They created the Arson Strike Force in August 1978, with twenty-five detectives, eleven fire marshals, representatives of the Bronx district attorney's office, and Herbert Sturz, the mayor's criminal justice coordinator. The task force began to seek funding from the federal Law Enforcement Assistance Administration and talked to insurance industry organizations about improving their practices.[25] Once again, computers, data, and crime proved important. The task force identified the biggest problems as a lack of research and data processing of public records. The poor recordkeeping of city agencies allowed landlords to hide behind dummy corporations and thwarted prosecutions. The Arson Strike Force received federal funding for a project to hire senior citizens to comb through the records to find landlords who had a pattern of fire-prone buildings, data that proved to be an important component of later prosecutions. Despite the federal money, the head of the Arson Strike

Force in 1980 cited continuing problems. The police department and fire marshals continued to argue over jurisdiction, and city and federal funding still did not provide the task force with sufficient scientific and technical resources, including sufficient funding to maintain and test the Arson Risk Prediction Index, a computerized tool for predicting which buildings might be the next to burn.[26]

By 1981 insurance became more difficult to acquire, thanks to stronger regulation and declining interest rates that made it less attractive for insurance companies to tolerate arson and phony policies. Despite these changes, Wilfredo E. Morales of the determined Bronx community group Don't Move Improve wrote the mayor that "with an arrest rate for arson now looming at about .75% and a conviction rate in the area of .3%, it becomes evident that at the moment the law-abiding system is waging a losing battle against arson."[27]

In 1981 the city inaugurated a program that sent fire marshals, who worked in teams of fifty and were known as "red caps," into the burning neighborhoods. The red caps took their name from "the conspicuous headgear they sometimes wear, are based in a distinctive trailer, drive marked cars and saturate a small area, responding to every fire, night or day. They make their presence known not only to residents, whose help they cultivate and rely on, but also to the drug dealers, addicts, squatters and scavengers who cause much of the problem."[28] The city's Department of Housing Preservation and Development also embarked on a program to seal up vacant buildings, to make them harder to torch and loot. Within a year the arson epidemic began to subside. The total number of fires that year decreased by 7 percent from the year before and was more than a third lower than 1977 levels.[29] The red caps were so successful that the administration restored full charge of arson investigation to the fire marshals, halting the experiment that had given joint jurisdiction to the police. At the same time the city created the Arson Major Case Squad, a joint effort of the fire and police departments that focused on major arson cases and organized arson-for-profit schemes.[30] Between 1970 and 1981 the Bronx lost more than 20 percent of its housing stock—108,000 units, more than enough to house everyone in a city the size of Albany.[31] By 1985 the administration was able to declare partial victory, as arson declined to levels not seen since 1967.[32]

Stopping arson was only half the answer. Rebuilding was the other half. The Koch administration started with Herman Badillo's grand vision for rebuilding first the south Bronx and then the other ghettoes of America.[33] The former New York City Housing commissioner and Bronx borough president gave up a congressional seat in the hope of implementing, as a deputy mayor, his ideas for rebuilding the Bronx. Badillo met many times with President Jimmy Carter to discuss the south Bronx, telling the president that "the easiest thing we can do in this country is to rebuild the slums because . . . you have the streets, you have the sewers, you have the police stations, fire stations, all those facilities, all that has happened is that the housing has burned down." Badillo proposed to build low-density housing hooked up to that infrastructure and pay for it with mortgages subsidized by the State of New York, with the new homeowners putting little or no money down. Private homeowners, not the government, would ultimately pay for the new housing, as they paid down their mortgages, so "you will find that it is very cheap to rebuild the South Bronx," Badillo told the president. Carter was unimpressed, and the White House continued to press for a paltry $55 million appropriation to fund several conventional programs it claimed would promote economic development—like more employment programs and building a new federal building—instead of the $1.5 billion housing program that Badillo believed was necessary and that in many respects was the blueprint for the $5.1 billion housing program that Koch instituted seven years later.[34]

From his new job in city hall, Badillo hired Edward J. Logue, a lawyer and public developer who had headed Boston's Redevelopment Authority and had built huge projects in Boston and New Haven, Connecticut. Logue was often compared with Robert Moses, though Moses had far better architectural taste. Government Center in Boston, one of Logue's biggest projects, is an ugly, empty, bleak place that represents modernism at its worst. Even Logue's obituary in the *Boston Globe* noted that "few of Logue's projects are heralded for warmth or urban intimacy." The best the obituarist could do was credit Logue with raising real estate values in the areas he developed. When Logue came to the South Bronx Project, his reputation had been damaged by the near-bankruptcy of a public corporation he had run, the Urban Development Corporation. He wanted to rebuild his reputation. Despite these negatives and many setbacks, Logue held on in the Bronx until the city saw substantial results, though he would not play the central role that he and Badillo initially envisioned.[35] Instead, community organizations would take the initiative, with help from the Koch administration and downtown philanthropists, especially David Rockefeller, now concerned that "planned shrinkage" might shrivel the city to nothing.[36] The term refers to the urban renewal doctrine espoused by Beame's city housing administrator, Roger Starr, who advocated cutting services and slowing housing rehabilitation in poor neighborhoods to accelerate their depopulation. Starr claimed that this would allow New York to concentrate its resources on saving what was left.

Some Bronx residents had responded to the attention they received from Carter's visit (and the private donations it brought) by organizing numerous community groups, such as the Banana Kelly Improvement Association, a group of mostly African American tenants who organized themselves as urban homesteaders and obtained money from the city to rehabilitate buildings scheduled for demolition on a bend in Kelly Street known as "the Banana." The group became a model for other nonprofit developers and ultimately provided a range of social services designed to stabilize the neighborhood.[37]

Though often painted as conservative, the Koch administration encouraged grassroots housing activism. After years of double-talk and inaction from Beame administration officials, Nat Leventhal, Koch's first commissioner of housing preservation and development, provided "the first real tools to fight abandonment and to rehabilitate buildings."[38] Some community groups that began to rebuild included the Mid-Bronx Desperadoes, which, as the MBD Development Corporation, would eventually market the houses on the rebuilt Charlotte Street in 1983–84. The oldest of the community organizations was the People's Development Corporation, originally founded in 1974, which for a time acquired a staff of 250 but faded by 1982 because its funding and ambition to redevelop forty blocks exceeded its skill in executing plans.[39]

Some groups pioneered green economics almost literally at the grassroots level. The People's Development Corporation was working on using garbage to start a worm farm as an alternative form of economic development. Another group, Bronx Frontier, composted waste from the Bronx Zoo and marketed it as "ZooDoo." It also transformed vacant lots into small parks. Bronx 2000, another nonprofit, set about organizing tenants and merchants in the Tremont business district, clearing lots for parkland and even setting up a mushroom farm that supplied specialized fungi to fancy restaurants.[40] Even Logue, encouraged by the administration, broke with his past as a technocrat who imposed decisions on neighborhoods and encouraged community groups to increase their participation in development projects.

In Koch's first year Badillo ran the main redevelopment effort from the top down. Robert F. Wagner, then chair of the city planning commission, became one of the strongest critics of the plan that resulted. He recalled a city hall briefing with Deputy Mayor David Brown at which "they had these maps up there. And somebody would say, 'Well, why is that space over there empty? Let's put housing there.' And somebody else would say, 'Why is that transportation ramp not built? Let's build it.'" As Wagner recalled, "David said to me he now knew how the war in Vietnam was operating. You put 60 people in a room with lots of maps. They make decisions."[41]

Wagner was even more skeptical of the plan that emerged to build seven hundred units of co-ops on Charlotte Street, the location chosen because Carter had made it a symbol, not because it was the best site for a sustainable development. Wagner believed that new development needed to be at the edges of blighted areas, expanding viable neighborhoods, rather than starting "with the area of greatest devastation." In contrast, Badillo and Logue made large-scale plans for the whole borough on the dubious assumption that more and more federal money would be forthcoming once they rebuilt the area Carter had helped make into an international emblem of urban decay. Wagner and other officials remained keenly aware that there were many competing, dire needs for capital funding throughout the five boroughs.

When Koch invested large sums in the Bronx in the mid- and late 1980s, the investment paid off over the long term. Rebuilding the Bronx, as Badillo believed, might have been the greatest success of Carter's presidency if the president had had the wisdom to invest the money. But Wagner read the harsh political reality correctly, that Carter would make only a token gesture to the south Bronx despite his grandstanding. As the city was not yet financially able to step in, the Charlotte Street Project as proposed would fail—a half-built island of construction in a sea of devastation.[42]

Badillo and Wagner began to wage open warfare over the Charlotte Street project almost from the beginning of the administration in 1978 and fought for more than a year. Koch decided to settle the matter by going up to the Bronx with Badillo and Wagner to talk the projects over, but their dispute was so heated that it literally nearly killed them. Badillo, who was driving, began to argue with Wagner, who was sitting in the back seat. Badillo got so angry that he kept turning around to face his opponent while "switching lanes and running stop signs." Somehow, they made it safely to Charlotte Street.[43] Koch told Wagner and Badillo that he very much hoped that Wagner would support the plan as "a leap of faith," and the city planning commission subsequently issued a qualified endorsement.[44]

Meanwhile, a variety of political forces built up against the plan, as politicians began to see it as a ploy to grab the lion's share of scarce capital funding for the Bronx to the detriment of the other boroughs. Badillo and Phil Trimble, the deputy mayor for intergovernmental operations, did not notice. They insisted on seeking an early Board of Estimate vote on a mapping change to allow the Charlotte Street project to be built. Badillo hoped to embarrass the board into consensus, insisting on pushing it through in one meeting, which would require a three-quarters vote instead of the simple majority if proposal went through the regular process of presentation at two meetings. If Badillo had won, the city would have made a firm commitment to build the Charlotte Street project. Koch, who earnestly wanted the project, played his part, winning a commitment from the White House that the federal government would fund 26,500 housing units in the Bronx, though it did not commit a specific dollar amount. And the mayor personally attended the Board of Estimate meeting, declaring that a negative vote would end the South Bronx project forever.[45]

Badillo and Trimble had not bothered to count votes. The Charlotte Street project was defeated 7–4, as only the mayor, who had two votes, and the borough presidents of Staten Island and the Bronx voted for the project. The borough presidents from Brooklyn, Manhattan, and Queens questioned Carter's commitment and, because they mistrusted Carter, feared that the huge project would drain what little city money there was for the development in their own boroughs. The project's isolation from functioning neighborhoods made it easy to ridicule: "Seven hundred apartments in the middle of an advanced wasteland, what's the sense of that?" observed Queens Borough President Donald Manes.[46] Harrison J. "Jay" Goldin, the city's comptroller, supported Charlotte Street in the first Board of Estimate vote, because Badillo had endorsed him for state comptroller. Badillo had hoped that Goldin would win so that Badillo could run for city comptroller. But Goldin had lost the race. Now Badillo was openly planning to run against him, so Goldin switched sides, declaring that the booklet containing Badillo's plan was just "a press release and not an economic development program."[47]

The White House, having gone out on what it considered a limb, was stunned by the Board of Estimate's rejection of the project. Koch, who had lobbied hard for the project in Washington, was livid. He declared that the vote would put an end to all future development plans for the south Bronx during his administration. When Bobby Wagner asked him in a telephone conversation on a Friday afternoon how he could write off an entire borough, Koch hung up on him.[48] By Monday the mayor had publicly retreated from this position, declaring that "while some people eat crow, he was at least prepared to eat turkey," the *Times* reported, and put Wagner in charge of a much less ambitious plan, a quarter of the size of the first one, that concentrated on rehabilitating existing housing rather than building new towers. In 1983 he would attend completion ceremonies for a raft of suburban-style prefab houses erected on Charlotte Street that sold to private owners for $47,800 apiece (having a basement cost an additional $6,000).[49] Koch would later cackle that at the ceremony "it was nice to be with Jay Goldin, so that I could recall for everyone that he, along with Carol Bellamy [the city council president], had been the one who had let the feds walk away from their commitments to that area."[50]

When the low-rise, suburban-style Charlotte Gardens houses were finally completed in 1983, Koch could justifiably point to the development with pride. But Charlotte Gardens had also disproved one of the central premises of the Badillo plan, that the presence of existing infrastructure would make construction less expensive. Each house had required a $10,000 subsidy to prepare the ground because the foundations for the apartment buildings that had occupied the site were set so much deeper in the ground than those for ranch houses. This requirement delayed construction for three years. In the years since the houses have appreciated to more than triple the cost of construction. Even during the 2009 recession, houses in the formerly desolate neighborhood held much of their increased value, selling for $150,000 to 395,000, considerably more than the original $53,800 (see chapter 18).[51] The green lawns of Charlotte Gardens, once the barren backdrop of *Wolfen*, now look more like those in Amityville.

THE GREAT SHAKE-UP

After the 1979 Charlotte Street debacle at the Board of Estimate, the mayor and his closest aides decided that the coalition style of government was not working. Koch originally wanted a large number of deputy mayors, to reflect his diverse electoral coalition. He had refused to appoint a first deputy mayor. He wanted authority and responsibility to flow directly to and from the mayor, in contrast to the Beame administration, where First Deputy Mayor John Zuccotti had supplanted the authority of an incapable mayor.

Until 1979 Koch had tried to maintain control of this system by requiring the commissioners of the various city departments to send him bimonthly reports. "There are now three big growth industries in New York: fast-food joints, massage parlors, and deputy mayors," Robert F. Wagner Jr. quipped after Koch had been on the job for three months.[52] Deputy Mayor David Brown, one of Koch's most trusted lieutenants, held Herman Badillo responsible for some of the problems with the system and leaked his doubts about the competence of Badillo's staff.[53] Brown recalled that the "first eighteen months of any administration is a trial-and-error period. There are political obligations, and some of those choices just don't work out." He warned Koch in writing after the Board of Estimate vote that he did not think that Badillo would work out as deputy mayor.[54]

Early in Koch's first administration, with seven deputy mayors talking to the press, and Koch maintaining his constant chatter to reporters, there was little message discipline. Instead, seven increasingly competitive bureaucracies were stepping all over each other's toes and sometimes bruising the mayor's foot. Koch also blamed defeat of the Charlotte Street project on Trimble, who was in charge of lobbying for it, as well as on Badillo. At that point Koch "realized that what I had done was create a monster," particularly after the departure of Brown, who had reined the barons in.[55] "People were deputy-mayor shopping" for the official who would be most sympathetic to their cause, commented Bellamy, who approved the reshuffle.[56]

Koch had become increasingly dissatisfied with the huge city hall staffs that each deputy mayor had amassed. Perhaps the turning point was the question from the reporter Joyce Purnick, who asked Koch what, precisely, Herman Badillo's job was—and the mayor had no answer.[57] Badillo had remained petulantly without portfolio after he refused to participate in new plans for the south Bronx.[58] Though the problems with Badillo were clear by the middle of February 1979, it was several months before Koch put a concrete plan for reform into place. He delayed until summer, when he settled on asking Nat Leventhal to take Brown's place and promoted Wagner to the post of deputy mayor for policy.

Leventhal, then housing commissioner, was deeply skeptical about taking the deputy mayor job. He insisted that the number of deputy mayors be reduced to two and that he be "first among equals."[59] Just before the Fourth of July weekend, Koch issued a memo requiring biweekly reports from all deputy mayors, so that he could see exactly what each was doing and make intelligent reassignments.[60] Koch had second thoughts and approached Allen G. Schwartz, his former law partner who was now corporation counsel, to offer him one of the deputy mayor jobs, which Schwartz, who had little political experience, turned down. Moreover, Leventhal and Wagner had agreed that neither would take the job unless the other did.[61]

On the last weekend of July 1979, the day after Schwartz rejected the job, Koch began meeting secretly at Schwartz's house in Rye, New York, with the new deputy mayors, Leventhal and Wagner, to plan a sweeping reorganization of the administration.[62] Koch then moved swiftly and fired or demoted almost all the deputy mayors and most of their staffs. Haskell Ward would be gone within the month.[63] Only Peter J. Solomon, deputy mayor for economic development, was untouched by the changes. Solomon argued successfully that demotion would hurt his ability to do his job and that, unlike the other positions, economic development had been a deputy mayoral position since the Lindsay administration.[64]

One by one Koch called in his top associates for conversations that were among the most painful of his mayoralty. Many of those fired or demoted were old friends. Some cried. Others needed considerable persuasion to stay on at a lower level, but long-time Koch staffers like Ronay Menschel loyally remained, though with less prestigious titles.

Koch "was tightening the chain of command," as Schwartz explained the new structure.[65] Leventhal, the new deputy mayor for operations, would police the agencies, locating trouble spots and pressuring commissioners to improve.[66] He was a graduate of Queens College and Columbia Law and had started in government right out of law school as an aide to Senator Robert F. Kennedy. Then Leventhal became a prodigy in city government. After he served a stint as chief of staff at city hall, Lindsay appointed the twenty-nine-year-old to be commissioner of rent and housing maintenance.[67] As Koch's housing commissioner, Leventhal had made a reputation as one of the administration's most effective figures, improving the lives of thousands of people living in housing units taken over by his department, most often after the owners failed to pay their taxes.

Leventhal understood how the agencies worked, how to demand a high level of improvement without demanding the impossible, and how to govern and make policy without unduly interfering with the commissioners. He had originally met Koch while serving as Lindsay's rent commissioner. Koch had tried to have him arrested for neglecting city-owned buildings in his district. Leventhal appeased the angry congressman, explaining that the buildings were not actually owned by the city, but nevertheless ordered contractors in to fix the heat immediately.[68]

Much of Leventhal's job, no matter what his title was, was to be a counterbalance to Koch. "Where Koch often speaks before he thinks, Leventhal is guarded and careful. Where Koch enjoys the spotlight, Leventhal works hard at being self-effacing. Where Koch courts controversy, Leventhal treads lightly and diplomatically," observed one columnist.[69] Leventhal's principal responsibility was overseeing the operation and management of city services. He was the first of Koch's deputies who required the commissioners to report to him, "which was noticed, because Koch had promised [his commissioners] that that would never happen." They had signed on with the understanding that they would report directly to the mayor. But Leventhal convinced Koch that he did not have time to keep tabs on each commissioner and had to rely on a deputy to coordinate their efforts: "You can't have the mayor being the public spokesperson and being out there all the time and still supervising each commissioner," he said.[70] Commissioners, Leventhal observed, "have to feel pressure. They perform better. If they know the Deputy Mayor is going to remember, that's pressure to perform." Leventhal would sit at his desk all day, calling the agencies to follow up on the reports he received from their commissioners, taking only a five-minute lunch, typically "a fruit drink and a hamburger with ketchup," to get a handle on what city government was actually doing.[71]

In a typical memo Leventhal reported on his work to Koch in the fall of 1979: "The water cooler in the file room, long broken, has been fixed at least temporarily by my direct order. Now on to the less important stuff, " which included evaluating the records of commissioners in "fulfilling the mayor's campaign promises" and "checking deep into the operations of the sanitation department," after the Board of Estimate blocked an administration move to hire 562 more sanitation workers. The board demanded both more attention from the mayor before he asked it to make decisions and more productivity from sanitation employees, whom some board members saw as loafers.[72]

Leventhal responded to the Board of Estimate by sending out his own managers from city hall to improve productivity reporting and targets in the sanitation department and end the "constant warfare" between Sanitation Commissioner Norman Steisel and the sanitation men's union about extending collection routes. He may have been tough on Steisel, but Leventhal also recalled defending Steisel's record in disciplining workers who were not diligent after a *Daily News* editorial made unfavorable comparisons between New York and Chicago.[73]

Leventhal did not just try to clean up the sanitation problem of the moment; he tried to fix the systemic problems behind it: Koch's poor relationship with the Board of Estimate, which included several members who wanted to replace Koch as mayor. "As of now, we deal almost exclusively with [Board of Estimate] staff until the day of the executive session, and even then principals are frequently not involved. On an issue as important as sanitation hirings, I believe we should involve both you and the other principal members of the Board of Estimate more directly and as far in advance as is reasonable," Leventhal wrote Koch. The new deputy mayor hoped to restructure meetings with council president Carol Bellamy and Comptroller Jay Goldin so Koch could use them "to start lobbying directly for your priorities." Manhattan Borough president Andrew Stein noted that before Leventhal's reforms, "the mayor never briefed any of us on the plan, and we were treated cavalierly, " but the early briefings helped garner votes in advance. Leventhal also addressed other reasons that had been given for denying the budget increase for sanitation—concern about the deficits of the agencies not under direct mayoral control, such as the Board of Education and the Health and Hospitals Corporation.[74]

Wagner became deputy mayor for policy and would continue for a time as chair of the city planning commission. He had an encyclopedic knowledge of city planning, and few people had clearer ideas about how to save New York. Wagner had tried to follow in the footsteps of his grandfather, the senator, and of his father, the mayor, but in temperament he was more scholar than politician, more of a creative type than an administrator. But like his dad he also had a talent for reconciling political conflicts. Cautious, and skilled at promoting ambiguity, he was a welcome counterpoint to Koch's tendency to slash at every Gordian knot in his path.

After serving as council member-at-large for Manhattan, Wagner had run for Manhattan borough president, the office his father had held before becoming mayor. But the younger Wagner was defeated by the wealthy Andrew Stein—Stein had the good looks and the money, and Wagner had the brains and the backing of most of the Democratic establishment. Stein, who eventually earned the respect of many politicians, was then considered a dim bulb but brilliant at glad-handing. Wagner maintained his father's tradition of perpetual tardiness for campaign rallies and tended to overschedule, "as if he was exempt from the laws of physics," according to a close friend.[75] While working the crowd at a West Side block party, he was likely to stop campaigning to read a book he saw on a sale table.

Koch was a man who still marveled that he had landed in Gracie Mansion. Wagner had grown up there, and in his father's last term (after his mother's death) he served as Mayor Wagner's adviser and confidant. He had gone to the best schools and loved learning, but he also knew where the bodies were buried in New York politics, and he had the wisdom to analyze brilliantly the political and policy problems of the day. While he was serving as city planning chair, a report that crossed his desk claimed that the FDR Drive was structurally sound. Wagner's father had once warned him that La Guardia had hastened construction of the highway so that it would open before an election and that the work on it had been shoddy. Wagner sent the engineers back. They determined that Gracie Mansion itself was literally in danger of falling into the East River if corrective action was not taken. "He was history in City Hall," recalled Schwartz. "Bobby would remember, and so he would be there to help you not to make the same mistake that had been made somewhere else, or to direct you into an area that had been more successful."[76]

When he was deputy mayor, Wagner's top priority was to attract desperately needed capital from private bond markets. Repairing New York's battered infrastructure, he believed, was more important than major new projects. This brought him into conflict with Badillo, who wanted large projects immediately and who oversimplified Wagner's recommendation as planned shrinkage.[77]

Although Wagner modestly described himself as "the deputy mayor for rhetoric," Koch had given him broad powers as deputy mayor for policy.[78] In addition to being the mayor's top policy adviser, Wagner supervised the Board of Education and the Health and Hospitals Corporation and served as principal liaison to MAC and the Emergency Financial Control Board.[79] Wagner's family roots in the New Deal (his grandfather wrote the National Labor Relations Act) and his liberal record on the city council gave him bridges to the Left, although some of his work for the Koch administration tarnished his liberal image. Certainly, Wagner's mild manner served as an important balm, but it must have been difficult for someone who inherited his father's trait of avoiding conflict and unpleasantness to embroil himself in some of the bloodiest political fights of the day. His desire for consensus sometimes played out as paralysis and indecision.

Wagner could be "a very strange person in many ways and I think he had many personal problems," noted his close collaborator Nat Leventhal. "I mean, there were times that he would disappear for several days."[80] Wagner could indeed behave erratically, and he may have suffered from depression.[81] But, as Leventhal put it, "you forgive a lot with Bob because he [was] so great."[82]

Leventhal and Wagner had such different personalities and interests that they were able to divide authority without stepping on each other's toes. "Bob was a very thoughtful policy-oriented guy who really didn't care about managing anything. And I was a roll-up-your-sleeves manager. I loved to take problems with seven commissioners in the room and work it out, whether it's implementing the dog shit law or two-man sanitation trucks," Leventhal said. The two men who had such a close working relationship rarely socialized together, but Leventhal said, "I felt a real kinship with him."[83]

After only a couple of months the administration began to emerge from the malaise that Koch's ebullience had concealed. "Leventhal-Wagner Blend Adds More Zip to the City," the *Times* reported a little more than a year after the shake-up. While the pair had hardly solved the city services crisis or blunted Koch's sharp tongue, the consensus was that "things seemed to get done, where before they did not." In part this was because Wagner's diplomatic skills defused conflicts in labor and budget negotiations before Koch managed to make them confrontational, and Leventhal soothed members of the council and Board of Estimate by providing them with more details about agency operations.[84] That meant that Koch was going into the year before his reelection campaign with a city that was still broken but with an administration that was the best run in decades. Koch tried to push progress along by making decisions on the merits. But sometimes actions that made good management sense were disastrous politically.

CLOSING SYDENHAM HOSPITAL: EFFICIENCY VERSUS PRACTICAL POLITICS

The closing of Sydenham Hospital in Harlem was one of the biggest political mistakes of Koch's mayoralty. Koch himself has called it "his greatest racial controversy."[85] He was planning to close the hospital because experts had advised him that the hospital provided poor care, wasted money, and was not accessible to the disabled. But closing the hospital broke a promise that Koch had made to moderate black politicians, who would never trust him again, and it infuriated their rank-and-file supporters. Despite the strong case for closing the hospital on the merits, the economic savings were small and the political fallout was enormous.[86] Two years into his first term, Koch had so squandered his credibility among black leaders that some even accused the mayor of plotting the deaths of black people.

"Koch Kicks Poor," screamed the *Amsterdam News* in June, after the mayor announced plans to close Sydenham, Metropolitan, and two hospitals in Brooklyn.[87] Because no hospitals in white areas were slated to close, Harlem congressman Charles Rangel asked federal agencies to investigate whether the closings involved intentional racial bias, and on the same ground he sought an injunction to prevent the closing. The U.S. Department of Health, Education and Welfare required that the city conduct a special census of the entire city hospitals system to prove that the closings would not have a discriminatory impact. The closings were finalized only in September 1980, after the Civil Rights Office of HEW cleared the plan as having no discriminatory impact.[88]

The reorganization of the Health and Hospitals Corporation (HHC) proved the most controversial political drama of Koch's first term, particularly the protests of the closing of Sydenham Hospital. To many Harlemites, Sydenham, in the heart of Harlem at 124th Street and Manhattan Avenue, was a monument to African American accomplishments in the face of segregation. In 1943 Sydenham became the first fully integrated private hospital in the United States and the first to give staff privileges to black attending physicians. Because of that tradition, of which many residents of the 1970s were aware, the closing of Sydenham was one of the most conspicuous budget cuts in Harlem during the Koch era.[89]

Restructuring the Health and Hospitals Corporation was one of the central problems of the fiscal crisis, aggravated by the failure of President Jimmy Carter or the Democratic Congress to even attempt an overhaul of the U.S. health-care system. As Bobby Wagner later observed, at the time of Sydenham's closing there was "tremendous concern within the Koch administration about the HHC, being the one agency that could plunge us back into a fiscal crisis, push us over the abyss, and the need to deal with the financial issues there."[90] Koch had promised during the mayoral campaign to make enormous changes to the huge municipal hospital system. The mayor saw closing Sydenham as a step toward gaining control of an intractable financial headache. He viewed the closing as a good government measure that would allow him to redirect some of its operating budget to more modern facilities. What others saw as a broken campaign promise to the black community, Koch considered a noble sacrifice of his own political interests for the public good.[91]

The Health and Hospitals Corporation had once been a wonder of New York's social democracy, providing (in part because of poor billing procedures) virtually free care to the uninsured. As the city grew more dependent on Washington in the late 1970s, senators from states that did not have equally comprehensive health care systems criticized it as an expensive and profligate welfare burden that the federal government should not have to subsidize. Never mind that neither Carter nor Democratic critics of New York had taken any significant steps toward ensuring Americans had access to comprehensive and reasonably priced health insurance.[92] New York's problems in the late 1970s were not necessarily the result of too much social democracy but too little. National reform of the health care system might have wiped out New York's budget gap while improving the lives of the urban poor throughout the United States.

On the merits Health and Hospitals was an easy target: Many white voters were predisposed to believe that its underpaid managers, many of them members of minority groups, were incompetent—a prejudice that was reinforced when it discovered that the agency had not been paying social security taxes for more than seven thousand of its employees.[93] Doubtless, the agency was poorly run, but after the years of layoffs and attrition that accompanied the fiscal crisis, few city agencies were well run, no matter which ethnic group predominated in their offices.

The vast majority of the hospital agency's costs were financed like those of other hospitals: from payments by Medicare, Medicaid, and private third-party insurers. New York City was the only municipal government (as opposed to state government) that had to pick up 25 percent of its own Medicaid costs—a mandated expenditure of about $404 million in 1979. The largely unsuccessful effort to get the state to take over those costs was one of the great sagas of the fiscal crisis, and the requirement remains a drag on New York City's budget today. (See chapter 11.)[94] Before the fiscal crisis the social-democratic ethos of the city humanely militated against pressing the uninsured too hard. But combined with the $404 million local Medicaid share, New York spent $638 million on insurance for the poor and health care for the uninsured in 1979, more than the $600 million budget gap that year. Such subsidies were no longer affordable. (See chapter 11.)[95]

High fixed costs also contributed to the huge HHC deficits. Approximately five thousand beds were empty citywide, at both public and private hospitals. A 1976 study showed that eliminating those beds would save only $96.4 million, while closing entire hospitals might save as much as $233 million. As Ed Koch put it: "In a voluntary hospital, when you don't pay your bills the hospital goes broke. In a municipal, the city comes in with a subsidy over and above the funds that were originally planned, and then it is the city that goes broke."[96] But plugging the health and hospitals hole in the budget was not an easy task. The mayor lacked direct control over the agency, which made it even more difficult to implement unpopular measures, such as hospital closings.

HHC was a public corporation with its own board of directors and president, not a mayoral agency. The mayor could exert considerable power over the agency but only indirectly. One of New York City's greatest structural problems is that the mayor does not directly control large portions of the budget. The political scientist Ester Fuchs compared New York's setup with the centralized mayoral control of all spending in Chicago and has argued that the degree of mayoral control was the primary reason for Chicago's balanced budget in the 1970s and New York's continued financial instability.[97]

For years Koch proved incapable of hiring effective administrators to run the agency and exacerbated the problems by appointing a series of white, often Jewish, administrators who often were received poorly in the largely minority-staffed agency. Koch's health adviser, Dr. Martin Cherkasky, the president of Montefiore, a Jewish voluntary hospital, enraged union leaders (and the mayor) with his Christmas Eve suggestion that Koch intended to cut the agency in half. He left the administration just before the ethics board ruled on whether his role as an adviser to the city conflicted with his post at Montefiore.[98]

The real storm over Health and Hospitals began in 1979 when Haskell Ward, then the new deputy mayor for human services, formed a task force and charged it with reducing the city's subsidy to HHC by $80 million over three years.[99] The task force decided in June 1979 to close four municipal hospitals: Sydenham in Harlem, Metropolitan in East Harlem, and Cumberland and Greenpoint hospitals in Brooklyn. The Brooklyn closings were relatively uncontroversial because those hospitals would be replaced by a brand new facility, Woodhull Hospital. Woodhull had been finished almost five years earlier, but the fiscal crisis meant that HHC had lacked the funds to open it.

Ward and other administration officials believed that the case for closing Metropolitan was the weakest.[100] Closing Metropolitan and Sydenham put Ward in a very difficult political position. Koch himself described Ward as a "lightning rod" for criticism of the administration, from both the black community and from liberals. As city council member Fred Samuel put it, much of the African American political elite saw Ward "not as the voice for the poor, but the hatchet man for the mayor," a characterization that Ward deeply resented.[101]

Hospital closing was a particularly sensitive issue in Harlem, which had lost a hospital just months before. Arthur C. Logan Memorial Hospital, founded in the 1870s, was the only African American voluntary hospital in New York. It had gone bankrupt in 1976 but limped along until it closed three years later. Rev. Wyatt T. Walker, one of Martin Luther King's closest aides and a trustee of the hospital, described Logan Memorial's bankruptcy as "a catastrophe for our community."[102] Although the unions, notably District Council 37 of AFSCME, opposed the closing of Sydenham, they also accepted the Koch administration's offer, part of the closing plan, to guarantee jobs within the HHC system to Sydenham's union employees.[103] White liberals, like Alexander "Pete" Grannis, a Democrat who represented the Upper East Side in the state assembly, also protested the plan. Grannis warned that the

Ward task force report "misleads the public into thinking that there is an excess of health services in the city. The fact that the report completely ignores long term care, care for the elderly, prenatal, alcoholism, and mental hygiene services, just to name a few, invalidates its conclusions regarding excess capacity."[104]

The closing of these historically black hospitals was part of a national phenomenon arising from the passage of Medicare in 1965, which made most public and private hospitals dependent on federal funding and therefore subject to the antidiscrimination provisions of the Civil Rights Act of 1964. Most hospitals were integrated within six months of the passage of Medicare. While many black physicians thought integration would bring whites into black hospitals as well as blacks into white hospitals, they underestimated the stigma that segregation had attached to separate black institutions. When black physicians gained admitting privileges at white hospitals, black patients increasingly patronized the white hospitals that had formerly excluded them, especially as Medicare and Medicaid gave them more choice. But the converse was not true. White patients did not patronize historically black hospitals, and the number of historically black hospitals declined from 124 in 1944 to just ten in 1989. The decline of black hospitals accompanied "a well documented improvement in access to health care for the poor and for blacks."[105] Some African American health professionals saw it coming: "The Negro Hospital is dead. The Civil Rights Act killed it," observed Hiram Sibley, the executive director of the Hospital Planning Council of Metropolitan Chicago, as early as 1967.[106]

Debates among African Americans about the implications of these closings, indeed, about Sydenham itself, reflected long-standing divisions in the black community. This was the famous debate between the accommodationist approach of Booker T. Washington, which focused on the development of separate black institutions, such as segregated hospitals and medical schools, and the integrationist goals of W. E. B. Du Bois and the NAACP. This controversy was mirrored in the 1930s and 1940s by a schism among African American physicians in Harlem. Louis Wright, a Harvard Medical School graduate, favored integrated hospitals where black and white physicians would compete as equals. Another group of African American doctors in Harlem, mostly graduates of black medical schools such as Howard and Meharry, who wanted separate black private hospitals. Wright was accused of being a tool of Tammany for excluding some black physicians from Harlem Hospital after its 1930 reorganization. By 1933 only four of twenty-seven African American physicians on the hospital's inpatient staff were graduates of historically black medical schools. However, W. E. B. Du Bois defended him, arguing that "to fill Harlem Hospital with such dead weight was to play into the hands of every 'Nigger hater' in the land, [and] 'prove' the inability of the Negro physician to measure up to modern, exacting standards." Needless to say, physicians who had graduated from black medical schools took umbrage.[107] Four decades later some of this history had a role in the acrimony over the closing of Sydenham. The anthropologist Ebun Akinwayo Adelona, a participant-observer, explained the hospital struggle as an attempt to wrest "local control" of health care from the white-dominated metropolitan government and develop it as "a model of ethnic pride."[108]

The Health Care Subcommittee of the organization 100 Black Men, including health care executives from Harlem and Sydenham Hospitals, expressed deep concerns about the closings, highlighting some of the difficulties for black professionals who, in the 1970s, were still in transition from a segregated world to an integrated one. Ward, himself a pillar of the black bourgeoisie, described them as "a sort of kindred spirit." The 100 Black Men told Ward they were concerned that health-care executives in HHC, many of them black, were paid 40 percent of the salaries in the private sector and saw this as a form of racial discrimination. They disliked that Sydenham's physicians and inpatient services were being shunted to the nearby Hospital for Joint Diseases, which "was felt to have a history of discriminatory behavior itself and not viewed as a community hospital." Finally, they told Ward that they believed the closings of historically black institutions, such as Logan and Sydenham, would severely limit the ability of black doctors "to practice medicine in Harlem," by limiting their access to hospitals in the neighborhood.[109]

To these black professionals the closing of Sydenham threatened what little was left of the protective shell of their preintegration community. Koch had failed to understand this history when he remarked dismissively that Sydenham had been kept open merely "as a cultural landmark." He failed to grasp the degree to which the thinking of many black professionals remained in a pre–civil rights world. Despite increased legal protections in the sluggish economy of the 1970s, good private-sector jobs were slower to open, particularly to older black professionals of the segregation era. Koch's legalistic liberalism discounted these practical problems for black professionals in transition, assuming that civil rights legislation would guarantee equal opportunities. He also failed to understand the long history in the black community of mistrust and even fear of the white medical establishment.

Even before the closings of Sydenham and Metropolitan hospitals were officially announced, there was a large demonstration at city hall against the rumored hospital closings.[110] "If any bed has to be eliminated," thundered Rangel, "it will have to be that of the Mayor's at Gracie Mansion."[111] Al Vann, a member of the state assembly who had previously been close enough to Ward to ask for patronage, insisted that Koch was "trying to play God," deciding who would live or die.[112]

Koch believed, above all, that he was acting on the merits of good policy arguments. "Nothing was being done at Sydenham that couldn't be done more efficiently and with better equipment at Harlem Hospital or St. Luke's or Mount Sinai, each of which was within a four-minute ambulance ride," the mayor argued. Closing Sydenham and other hospitals had been recommended by Dr. John L.S. Holloman, the African American doctor who had led the HHC under the Beame administration, a fact often cited by Koch.[113]

Invoking Holloman, who had been ousted from his position and replaced by a white technocrat, may have only fanned the widespread fears that blacks were losing control of the health-care system in Harlem. The entire municipal health-care system would be dismantled, Harlem residents feared, and, like so many other city services in Harlem in the 1970s, the quality of health care services would suffer. In 1980 Holloman himself condemned the closings. State senator H. Carl McCall did not see municipal hospitals as second rate and argued that while voluntary hospitals may have had higher general standards, "poor people simply do not get the same treatment as rich people in voluntary hospitals." McCall and other Sydenham advocates argued that statistics tended to conceal that poor African American patients often fared better at African American hospitals because minority staff and doctors "tend to treat minority group and poor patients as brothers and sisters rather than as audio-visual material in a medical school curriculum."[114]

Wagner, whom Koch designated to supervise the hospital closings, was devastated by the way the Sydenham closing severed his relationship with black leaders whom he and his father had known as personal and political friends for years. At the time the younger Wagner had pressed for a compromise.[115] Yet a decade later he still felt that "the truth is that we were absolutely right in what we were doing" by closing the hospital. Wagner pointed out that every independent report since 1964 had argued for closing, that Sydenham was the most expensive hospital per patient in the system, yet it was the only city hospital not affiliated with a medical school and was not even wheelchair accessible. The facilities, mostly used for inpatient drug rehabilitation, were so poor that "if you were shot or stabbed right outside the hospital, under federal and state guidelines, you could not be taken to Sydenham.... Its medical board was chaired by a dentist, which is a remarkable thing for what is supposed to be a major medical provider," Wagner said.[116]

But these arguments meant little to many in Harlem. "After 32 years of working as a dietary aide here [at Sydenham], and two children and grandchildren born to me here, I know in a deeply personal way that this is a good hospital and that we need its acute-care and emergency medical services in the Harlem community. Anyone who says we don't doesn't know a thing about our needs and doesn't care a bit about our health," declared a dietician who worked in the hospital.[117] This was not a self-serving comment, as the closing plan provided that all employees would be given jobs at other institutions.

Koch's real hatchet man on health care issues was not Haskell Ward but the imperious mayoral assistant Victor Botnick, who made the case to the mayor for closing Sydenham as soon as possible. Sydenham was small potatoes—132 beds and budget of less than $13 million. But Botnick characterized it as a "problem hospital," operating on a year-to-year accreditation because of "administrative, operational and physical plant deficiencies." He continued to argue that "the facility is obsolete in many areas, especially the operating rooms, laboratories, and radiology suites. There are major life safety code violations." Botnick thought that bringing the hospital up to code would cost $4 to $6 million.[118]

The administration's strategy, which ultimately succeeded, was to insist on closing Metropolitan until the Carter administration felt sufficient pressure to fund its continuance. Wagner and Ward strenuously opposed closing Metropolitan Hospital, while Botnick, who pushed for closing both hospitals, recalled that Metropolitan "was a tool to get more Federal aid."[119] After weeks of abuse from the black community Ward desperately wanted to give Harlem residents some good news and leaked the Koch strategy to the media, which led the mayor—who had already cooled toward Ward because he had accidentally leaked the resignation of Blanche Bernstein, the human resources commissioner—to ask for his resignation.[120]

Though Ward did not criticize Koch publicly, his resignation damaged the administration, as Ward was the only African American in Koch's inner circle. Ward was not a sophisticated political infighter, certainly no match for Botnick, who had convinced Koch that Ward was disloyal and a leaker. Nevertheless, Ward's departure "demonstrated to many that Koch couldn't even keep a black that he liked, let alone one that Rangel and the others liked," Koch biographers reported.[121] The departure of Badillo around the same time and the ascendancy of Leventhal, Solomon, and Wagner bleached the public face of a Koch administration that had already come under criticism for its racial homogeneity. In response to the criticisms Koch released statistics compiled by the employment commissioner, Ronald Gault, one of the senior African Americans in the administration, showing that while Koch had not met his campaign promise to appoint more blacks to top-level positions than had Beame, Wagner, and Lindsay combined, Koch had exceeded the percentages of black appointees in each of those administrations, with 18.4 percent of top-level appointments going to blacks, compared with 4.9 percent for Wagner, 10.5 percent for Lindsay, and 12.1 percent for Beame. Koch, pushing back against the idea that less patronage for black politicians meant fewer jobs for blacks, also pointed to increasing minority employment in summer jobs, from 76 percent of all city summer jobs in 1978 to 92 percent in 1979; an increase in Model Cities Scholarships from 2,000 to 5,000; and a shift of resources to improve city-owned housing.[122] The issue was not purely one of ethnic patronage, but of patronage to particular political networks. And while there might be a certain number of black commissioners, Koch's inner circle in city hall and his kitchen cabinet looked heavily white and Jewish, particularly after Ward's departure and the summer reorganization. Policy, practice, and rhetoric made Koch seem unsympathetic to blacks, and he was beginning to realize that he had a political problem: "A negative feeling that I have to correct" among blacks, a change in tone that reporters found striking.[123]

This mea culpa was prompted by polls in the summer of 1979 that showed that Koch was viewed unfavorably by 55 percent of blacks and favorably by only 38 percent.[124] But these numbers grew worse within days, after the *New Yorker* published

Ken Auletta's generally sympathetic profile of the mayor, which quoted the transcript of an oral history interview that Koch had done while he was still in Congress. (The mayor had given Auletta a copy.) Blacks were "basically anti-Semitic," Koch said. He continued, "Now I want to be fair about it, I think whites are basically anti-black."[125] City council member Fred Samuel, one of the black officials most willing to deal with Koch in his first year as mayor, said his remarks were "a stereotype that is unbecoming for a mayor," and council member Wendell Foster suggested that Koch "doesn't know anyone of any significance in the black community." Even the *Times* editorial page, which was generally sympathetic to Koch, asked "whether a man who seems to have such little faith in good racial relations can in fact improve them."[126]

As the bad publicity from the profile mounted, Koch met with Rangel to apologize, set up a series of meetings with black leaders, and declare that he was listening. Rangel upped the ante by accusing Koch of saying that blacks were "biologically anti-semitic." Rangel began his breakfast with Koch by saying, "I wish you had told me ten years ago that you believed that, genetically, blacks don't like Jews." Koch replied that he thought black anti-Semitism resulted from ethnic succession in neighborhoods, not biological causes. He told Rangel he thought that when blacks move to formerly Jewish neighborhoods and "the Jews still continue to do business, and they are the landlords to a great extent, and the blacks dislike them for that reason." Rangel replied, "Well, I am glad that you say that that is not what it is. It is not genetic."[127]

The two men left to face the reporters massed outside, and Rangel remained aloof, saying the incident showed that "obviously the mayor hasn't met many black folks and doesn't know us." He met Koch's ham-handed attempts at apology by interjecting: "What the Mayor is trying to say is that it was *dumb*." Koch recalls: "I laughed, and it was a genuine laugh, and said, 'You say things so nicely, Charlie.'" The papers reported that Koch was uncharacteristically contrite.[128] "Then," Koch recalled, "we walked to the car and I put my arm on his shoulder. And that was really a first-class picture on the front page of the *New York Times*."[129]

Koch inaugurated a series of weekly meetings during the summer of 1979 with Rangel and five black city council members, and that somewhat calmed hostilities. But these meetings, as it turned out, merely set the stage for future controversy. Rev. Herbert Daughtry, the leader of the Black United Front, who was excluded from the meetings, declared that he was "still very unhappy" with the mayor. But the *Times* showed a big photo of Koch kissing a smiling city council member Mary Pinkett of Brooklyn on the cheek—suggesting a huge improvement in relations since the dispute about whether he had told her to shut up the year before.

But the main reason for the cordiality was that Koch seemed to be making concessions. Rangel told the press that "the mayor said for the third time that the rhetoric of closing hospitals would end," pointing out that both Sydenham and Metropolitan were in his district, a big hit for any politician. The two men had also discussed the lack of black representation on the Board of Estimate. Fred Samuel told the press that "the mayor said that there would not be any arbitrary single act on his part [to close Sydenham]—that there would be discussions."[130] If Koch had followed through on either of these fronts, he might have significantly improved relations with black politicians and with some of the 55 percent of blacks who disapproved of his performance. Instead, he would enrage them by raising their expectations of cooperation and then changing his mind.

Koch's temporary détente with the black political establishment began to unravel as the date for the closing of Sydenham Hospital grew closer. Sydenham became a symbol of the disempowerment of the black community far out of proportion to its importance as a health-care facility. As it became apparent that the administration was determined to close it, Rangel, angry that both hospitals Koch was closing were in his district, abandoned his usually genial persona and began to compare Koch with such notorious racists as Birmingham Police Commissioner Eugene "Bull" Connor and Philadelphia mayor Frank Rizzo.[131] Privately, Rangel was furious with Koch for forcing him to focus on local issues, telling Bobby Wagner, "You made me a district leader again, and I don't want to be a district leader. . . . I'm much more valuable to the city down in Ways and Means."[132]

Rangel, who was trying to reach a compromise to fund the Sydenham facility, reluctantly acquiesced to a plan to close the hospital that was signed in the White House rose garden by city and federal officials. The next step was to convert Sydenham, which already treated many drug addicts, into a drug treatment center. Rangel understood the complexity of his position, and his remarks seemed calculated to create an illusion of unity with more radical critics who focused on rebuilding Sydenham as a an acute care hospital. But Rangel was less focused than they on keeping the hospital open. From his perspective his job was to bring home the bacon, and he was open to compromise on where federal monies would go.[133]

After the White House rose garden deal, the legal obstacles to closing the facility were removed one by one. Patricia Harris, the secretary of the U.S. Department of Health and Human Services (successor to HEW), called Koch to tell him that the closing plan had cleared its last hurdle, an assessment by her agency's Office of Civil Rights that the closings would not violate the constitutional or statutory rights of Harlem residents.[134]

On September 11 the Ad Hoc Committee to Save Sydenham, a new community group that included a number of activist ministers, announced it would physically oppose the closing of the hospital: "The community has rejected the 'JUNKIE JOINT' that the government wants to force on us. We are trying to keep Sydenham as a hospital, with an Emergency Room and in-patient beds."[135] The sit-in began on Monday, September 15. Two days later Sydenham's emergency room closed, and the hospital stopped admitting new patients. The plan was to close when the last patient was discharged at the end of the month. Twenty minutes after city officials shuttered the emergency room, a group of demonstrators, including Reverend Daughtry and the Reverend Timothy Mitchell, burst into the locked emergency room through a side door, declaring, "We'll stay here forever if that's what it takes." The demonstrators settled into the office of the hospital's sympathetic executive director, Carl Carter, and declared themselves "the People's administration." Outside, protesters, many of them from Local 420 of AFSCME, carried signs that read, "Koch Kuts Kill" and "Mayor Koch Has Harlem's Blood on His Hands." Upstairs were sixty-nine patients, eight of them undergoing surgery that day. Eventually, the demonstrators "set up housekeeping" and hung an effigy of Koch.[136] The next day police locked the protesters in the administrative offices. They were allowed, even encouraged, to leave, but once gone they could not get back inside to rejoin the protest.[137] The Sydenham closing "became a citywide issue and a focus of a sense on the part of the black community that this was an administration that opposed their real needs," Wagner later recalled.[138]

At the beginning of the protest Koch sounded belligerent: "The worst thing in the world we could do is talk with people engaged in an illegal action," he declared. Later he told the press: "I am not a racist and I will not be deterred by false charges designed to cow me and drive me away. I am interested in better medical care and they are interested in confrontation."[139] The mayor's response to Sydenham was partially modeled on his popular get-tough policy during the transit strike that spring. The mayor sought injunctions against the hospital protesters and refused to negotiate, but he did seek to limit the conflict, particularly at the physical level. The mayor carefully declared that he was not going to order "anyone dragged out" at that point in the sit-in. Perhaps he realized that, as Edward C. Sullivan, a member of the state assembly, later observed, any fatalities or injuries might have led to a riot.[140]

Koch undoubtedly realized the delicacy of the situation, which is why he put the very discreet Wagner in charge of the situation.[141] But somehow either Koch or Wagner allowed Botnick to give orders to the police massed in front of the hospital. Botnick was an intelligent but deeply stubborn and officious political operative. Then in his mid-twenties, he was given increasing responsibility for health care throughout his tenure in the administration. He was a long-time loyalist, having started out as a teenager driving Congressman Koch around his district, and Botnick had quickly developed a fierce personal bond with the mayor. John LoCicero described Botnick's relationship to the mayor: "You know the story of when the king says, 'Will no one get rid of this troublesome priest?'—and so the guy goes out and kills the bishop? Well, Victor would take a machine gun and shoot everybody. That's the kind of guy he was, he would go out and do a thousand percent of what Ed Koch wanted him to do."[142] As the mayor's man and the mayor's man only, Botnick was vulnerable to Koch's enemies and alienated potential allies with his offensive and intimidating style.

Botnick's intransigence infuriated opponents of the hospital closings. To state assembly member Sullivan, Botnick's confrontational style and utter loyalty to the mayor exacerbated racial polarization, giving the impression that "health decisions were being made not on the basis of what was good for the people of the city but what their political impact would be."[143]

On the eve of Yom Kippur, September 19, Botnick was the ranking official on the scene of the Sydenham protest. Though he was in charge of the police, who were out in force, Botnick grew unnerved at seeing a chanting crowd of several hundred mostly black people. According to Botnick's diary, state assembly member George Miller said to him, "Tomorrow is your holiday and we are going to destroy that holiday." Botnick grew tense and fearful and said later, "I said to myself, thank God I am here with a hundred cops." Then he spotted the effigy of Koch. Infuriated, he pointed it out to Police Chief Martin Duffy, commander of Manhattan North. The effigy dangled from the third floor of the occupied hospital. Though Duffy said he feared risking a riot on such a vain pretext, Botnick ordered him to march his men up there and take the Koch doll down immediately—and to separate the demonstrators from the occupiers by adding trucks to the barricades, which greatly increased the tension around the hospital. Botnick was lucky. His meddling caused no riot that day, in part because the police resisted imposing the strict control of demonstrators that Botnick would have preferred. "It's been very peaceful. It seems the best offense is no defense," said one officer on the line who seemed to have more street smarts than an appetite for confrontation.[144]

The next day, Yom Kippur, thirty people were injured in a half-hour fracas. That afternoon Rangel, state senator Leon Bogues, Miller, and Sullivan were allowed in to talk to the protesters. While Sullivan and the others were inside, Botnick heard from the police that "organized groups of males" were pushing to the front with plans to knock down the barricades. The crowd, frustrated by the police barriers that Botnick had ordered, began to chant, "The walls of Jericho must come down."[145] Sullivan said he was visiting the Twenty-eighth Precinct just before the police waded in to disperse the crowd, and "the police inspector was talking to the men who were about to go in. And he was saying, 'Look, there's going to be action. But you're used to that, you guys are strong,' as any commander might buck up his troops." Eventually, "the billyclubs came to [clear] the square. Nobody was badly hurt, or was killed, but people were hurt. I'm not saying that everyone in the crowd was behaving themselves, because that would not be true. Bottles were thrown." Sullivan feared that if the violence escalated, it could easily turn into a citywide riot. Koch insisted that "the police are trying very hard not to give [demonstrators] what they want—overreaction."[146]

The occupation lasted for ten days and remained mostly nonviolent. On Monday night about a thousand people demonstrated peacefully. Koch even extended the closing date by two weeks to allow time for a group of doctors try to convert Sydenham into a voluntary hospital, a plan that was ultimately unsuccessful.[147] Koch also offered amnesty if the demonstrators, reduced in number to nine, would leave, an offer they rejected, maintaining their demands that Koch reopen the emergency room and that they meet with President Carter and Governor Carey on the issue. Demonstrators initially called for a six-month delay in the closing, which they shortened to six weeks as the mayor's deadline for final closure of the hospital approached.[148] Finally, in the wee hours of September 26 the police went in and carried out the protesters. They were released without charges.[149] Sydenham Hospital closed its doors for good on November 21, 1980.[150] The building remained open for two years (at a cost of $2 million) and was eventually converted into Mannie Wilson Towers, a senior citizen housing complex by a group associated with Fred Samuel. The conversion cost $6 million, as much as Victor Botnick had estimated would be necessary to modernize Sydenham as a hospital. In 2000 the Columbia University School of Dentistry opened a health-care clinic in the basement (the morgue of the old hospital) at a cost to Columbia of $4 million.[151]

Closing Sydenham was a pyrrhic victory for Koch, who undoubtedly shaved a few dollars from the expense budget and who believed he had acted on the merits in closing a poor-quality health-care facility. But Koch, never popular with black politicians and activists, had so completely burned his bridges that he could not even visit Harlem or Bedford Stuyvesant for months.[152] And that made it much harder for him to gain widespread confidence from the larger African American community later in his term, when there were ugly incidents of violence against blacks.

The administration continued to make clumsy missteps that increased African Americans' mistrust of the Koch administration's health-care policy. Five months after the Sydenham closing the new president of the Health and Hospitals Corporation, Dr. Abraham Kauvar, made a comment that Samuel characterized as "more than dumb, it was ugly." Kauvar had complained in a public meeting that government critics "were always looking for a nigger in woodpile." Koch fired him immediately, a move praised by moderate black leaders, including Samuel, but the incident did not increase faith in the administration of the HHC. The agency's problems were far from solved, but at least Koch's quick action salvaged his relations with the few black leaders who were still talking to him.[153]

While local politics, and especially the Koch administration's confrontational style, increased the rancor surrounding Sydenham, the decision to close it was part of a larger national story. The Civil Rights Acts, it had been assumed, would bring African Americans integration, greater political power, and prosperity. But as Judith Stein has pointed out, legal solutions provided only limited economic advancement in the face of the economic crisis of the 1970s, although many liberals, notably Ed Koch, believed that legislation alone would be enough.[154] And while in many places African Americans did increase their political power in the 1970s and 1980s, in the microclimate of New York City politics from 1978 to 1987, black political power was in decline, a casualty of the neoliberal consensus.

If Koch had been a more patient man, he could have found more palatable ways to close Sydenham. Stan Brezenoff, later president of HHC, observed that though policy arguments for keeping Sydenham open were few, "the timing of it was wrong," and the closing should have been held in abeyance until the administration could show the community that "there are other things of a more positive nature going on, and then they're more prepared to accept a good will determination, a good faith determination."[155] But the mayor was willing to brave strong opposition to closing Sydenham Hospital. It was not just about money, because the money saved was trivial. Koch thought of himself as standing on principle, making the decision to close the hospital based on hard numbers and bottom lines. To some extent he probably also sensed that confrontations with blacks made him more popular with certain groups of white voters. But Koch could not comprehend, until after he left office, that to the activists and professionals at Sydenham, he had posed an unacceptable choice between unequal institutions and institutions in which they had little power or community stake.

14

CONTROLLED FUSION

Or, to Koch or Not to Koch

(1980–81)

In January 1980, with reelection on his horizon, Koch wanted more than reelection. He wanted a landslide.[1] Such a goal required the subtlety to sail between incumbent president Jimmy Carter and challenger Ronald Reagan toward the mayoral nomination of both major parties, which was possible because of New York's unique tradition of cross-endorsement. Carter's primary challenger, Senator Edward M. Kennedy, had the unofficial backing of his fellow Irishmen Governor Hugh Carey and Senator Daniel Patrick Moynihan, which made Koch the most important elected official supporting Carter in New York. Kennedy seemed unlikely to win the presidency, though his policy positions, particularly on health care, were vastly better for

New York than Carter's. So Koch held his nose and endorsed the president, hoping to milk him for every federal aid dollar he could. At the same time Koch was courting local Republican politicians, and eventually Ronald Reagan, whom Koch believed would be the next president, and for whom he had considerably more respect and affection than he did for Carter.

Normally, mayors promote their popularity with generous preelection settlements with the unions and other forms of lavish spending. Koch did the opposite. He made himself wildly popular by cutting services and expenditures and announcing a leaner-than-normal budget for fiscal 1981, all while he was facing contract negotiations. He balanced the budget according to generally accepted accounting principles (GAAP) by FY 1981, one year earlier than he had originally promised in the financial plan he presented to Congress when he took office. Soon even machine pols not known for their facility with math were talking knowingly about "GAAP balance."

The idea to balance the budget early came from a *Wall Street Journal* reporter who suggested to Nat Leventhal that New York's budget gap numbers had put the goal within reach. "It was like an atomic bomb that dropped," Leventhal recalled.[2] The economic elite was ecstatic, for Koch had fulfilled a promise that many people believed no mayor would ever deliver on.[3] While in the short term this meant more cuts, in the long term it was the first sign that after five difficult years austerity might eventually end, and it demonstrated to the credit markets that New York City was once again in control of its spending.

This abstract fiscal goal, designed to save millions in interest by bringing the city back into the private credit market ahead of schedule, meant that the city would have to raise an additional $278 million in revenue or from budget cuts. That raised the total projected gap to $677 million in FY1981. Koch still managed to eliminate the last $150 million in expense items from the capital budget and move them to the operating budget. He ponied up $128 million more to make timely payments to pension plans. Both moves were necessary to reach GAAP balance and were largely financed by budget cuts. He managed to do this without any layoffs of city workers, though city agencies would continue to shrink by attrition. He would also have to keep an eye on the future, because New York City's budget shortfall was expected to grow to $1.139 billion in FY1982.[4]

Part of the challenge was to make cuts with the least possible impact on New York's already-compromised operations, so Nat Leventhal, deputy mayor for operations, was heavily involved in the budget process. He actually constructed a "parallel organization" to the budget bureau, so that "whenever there was a budgetary discussion in the mayor's office, instead of just having the OMB people there, I would be there, and I would have my operations people, who knew that area expertly. So that we weren't going to let the mayor be guided by OMB, who would say: "'Oh you can cut the $50 million dollars there, no problem.'" For example, Leventhal carefully examined the effect of across-the-board cutbacks on overtime and concluded that it would be a costly mistake to cut the overtime of the uniformed services, where staffing needs are difficult to predict. In the uniformed services overtime actually saved money by helping "hold the line on fulltime hires."[5]

The state laws enacted at the outset of the fiscal crisis required the mayor to file a "Plan to Eliminate the Gap" with the Emergency Financial Control Board (EFCB) in January. It was supposed to predict the size of the deficit and explaining the measures he planned to take to raise cash and cut expenditures to prevent a deficit. As the state's fiscal watchdog, Special Deputy Comptroller Sidney Schwartz explained, "A budget *gap* is an estimate that expenditures will likely exceed revenues unless corrections are made; a *deficit* is an actual excess of expenditures over revenues."[6] To get the EFCB first to approve the gap elimination proposal and then, in June, the budget, Koch either had to demonstrate that his predictions of revenue were likely to come true or he had to order compensatory cuts.

As with previous gap elimination proposals, Koch hoped for increased state and federal aid and higher tax revenues—a dubious assumption in the political climate of the time. California voters had approved Proposition 13 in 1978; it capped property taxes and was billed as a "taxpayer revolt," though it primarily benefited large corporations. Carter, seeking reelection in 1980, was intent on cutting the federal budget, despite signs of an economic slowdown. While Koch benefited from his fiscal conservatism in the context of the New York fiscal crisis (though he did raise taxes when necessary), Carter's budget cutting probably hurt his reelection chances because it did not, as he had expected, slow inflation, which was caused mostly by high energy prices, and it failed to counteract recession.[7] Meanwhile, Governor Carey, worried that New York City's problems were beginning to affect the state's fiscal integrity, was cautious about increasing state aid to the city.

But this time Koch had other sources of money. Undaunted by the post-Proposition 13 rhetoric, he called for a tax increase. Despite the national slowdown, New York City's economy was improving, and city revenues had finally stopped sliding. Koch could get away with tax increases because he also promised to make even deeper cuts. Most of the reductions were in the education budget, which had shrunk anyway after a post–Baby Boom slump in enrollment. But the education budget was the area for which the state legislature, often strongly influenced by the United Federation of Teachers, was most likely to find new funds to restore cuts. Indeed, Koch later restored about $91 million of $111 million in cuts.[8] Additional plans for closing the gap included funds generated by better billing practices at the Health and Hospitals Corporation, losing as many as ten thousand city employees through attrition, and the abolition of several small mayoral agencies, including the departments of ports and terminals, and cultural affairs. The latter was saved, though with a greatly reduced budget.[9]

Both labor leaders and the control board criticized Koch's "Plan to Eliminate the Gap" as unrealistic because it posited only a 4 percent increase in salaries for municipal wage settlements—far below the rise in the cost of living and even below President Carter's guidelines, which were designed to limit inflationary wage increases. In 1978 Koch had tried talking tough to the unions and then agreed to a larger settlement; critics simply did not believe that he could hold wages down. Although the transit workers would bargain with the Metropolitan Transportation Authority, not directly with the tough-minded mayor, their contract would set the pattern for a final settlement between the city and the municipal unions, whose contracts expired three months later, so the transit workers' contract had enormous budgetary implications for the city. Koch would have to reach a contract with Victor Gotbaum of District Council 37 of the American Federation of State, County and Municipal Employees (AFSCME), who would argue that municipal employees deserved as much as the transit workers.[10] Then Koch would face talks with the uniformed services, police, fire, and sanitation, which always argued that they deserved more than other city workers. Despite Koch's usual commitment to honesty in budgeting, he also feared that any figure he put in the budget for a wage increase might be seen as the starting point for negotiations. If the control board had let him, he'd have submitted an increase of zero.[11]

Despite suspicions that some of his assumptions were too optimistic, the plan was a political coup for Koch. "Mayor Koch has now shown his courage in spectacular fashion, asking the public to accept higher taxes, reduced services, and a sizable reduction in the city work force," the *Times* editorial page declared.[12] In contrast, the unions were generally wary of the budget plan, and City Council President Carol Bellamy, while praising Koch's fiscal goals, criticized his tax package as regressive.[13] One part of Koch's plan was, however, covertly progressive: reassessing for tax purposes the values of co-ops in midtown Manhattan despite the protests of their wealthy occupants.[14]

Both the Carter administration and critics of city spending, such as senators William Proxmire and Jake Garn, praised Koch's efforts.[15] At a Senate hearing Garn, the deeply conservative former mayor of Salt Lake City, complimented Koch for "courage and candor" and compared him favorably with Mayor Beame.[16] Even the conservative Republican presidential contender, Ronald Reagan, had cautious praise for Koch, assuring the mayor that if the Californian were elected president, federal loan guarantees would continue uninterrupted, although Reagan opposed any increases. That assurance bolstered the credibility of Koch's budget plan because its most important assumptions would be valid no matter who won the presidential election.[17] Koch appreciated Reagan's help, and moved closer to the Republicans as the year wore on.

After five months of work to produce a final budget Koch, focused and determined, faced reporters in the Blue Room of Gracie Mansion. He pounded his fist on the table, maintaining that the budget was balanced.[18] Nevertheless, Comer Coppie, the executive director of the Emergency Financial Control Board, told Koch he had serious questions about whether the budget was, in fact, balanced because Koch proposed drawing on some one-time funds—though not borrowing—to pay for recurring expenses.[19]

Meanwhile, relations between the mayor and the governor were heating up. Carey's budget cutting had made Koch's budget balancing act all the more difficult. Instead of counterproductively striking out at Carey, Koch settled his anger on a softer target—the state senate's minority leader, Manfred Ohrenstein, a Democratic reformer from the West Side of Manhattan. When Carey vetoed a $70 million addition to the city's package of state aid that Koch had requested as part of his budget plan, the mayor persuaded the assembly Democrats and the Republican majority in the state senate to vote to override the veto. Senate Republicans went along. All he needed were the votes of the Democratic state senators from New York City. The deal ought to have been easy to pull off because it was in the best interests of the state senators' constituents, whose services would otherwise be cut. But Ohrenstein threw a tantrum because Koch had endorsed Republican state senator John Marchi of Staten Island for reelection. Koch later endorsed two more Republican state senators.[20] The minority leader, more concerned about his own power than about the city's fiscal well-being, forced the Democratic senators to sustain the governor's veto, knocking one of the legs out from under Koch's attempts to balance the budget.[21]

Koch held a press conference to denounce Ohrenstein and, as an early adopter of the VCR, debated a video recording of the senate minority leader, commonplace in the era of YouTube but a political novelty at the time. After Ohrenstein explained the vote to override the governor's veto of aid to the city, Koch stopped the tape and told the press, "Regrettably I lost." When Ohrenstein complained about Koch's vilification of state senate Democrats, the mayor declared that he should have been even tougher on them. In the end he shamed the Democratic legislators into giving the city money.[22]

Despite all the obstacles, Koch's budget remained in balance, thanks to revenues that were coming in higher than expected and greater success in reducing city subsidies to the Health and Hospitals Corporation than the monitoring agencies had expected. These were direct dividends of Nat Leventhal's careful monitoring of the budget and of moderate labor settlements. By December 1980 the city's budget gap for fiscal 1982 was down to $421 million, quite a bit less than the $830 million the financial control board had estimated in June.[23] But the crucial conflict with labor still loomed.

THE TRANSIT STRIKE

Perhaps more than any other event of his mayoralty, the 1980 transit strike revealed the political weakness of the unions. They might sit at the table of New York's creditors and provide financial support to political campaigns, but unions had lost popular support, particularly for strike action. Years of losing manufacturing jobs had reduced New York's status as one of America's premier union towns. The transit strike would significantly reduce the power of the public employee unions, which would never again receive the kind of public support they had enjoyed in the past.[24]

The 1980 transit strike was to the municipal unions what the air traffic controllers' strike—when President Reagan fired and replaced the strikers—was to the union movement nationally. Koch's attitudes and actions in the transit strike, like many of his actions in the crucial political turning point of 1980, reveal much about his relationship to conservatism. His hard line in the transit strike and the public support he received for it certainly reflected a tougher stance toward city unions than he or his predecessors had ever taken. Koch believed that management and labor had competing interests, in contrast to the collaborative approach to labor relations that had characterized the Wagner and Beame administrations—"a sea change for how a Democrat dealt with city labor unions," according to Meyer S. "Sandy" Frucher, then Carey's director of employee relations.

Koch, well aware that state law prohibited strikes by public employees, relished using harsh rhetoric and every legal tool at his disposal against strikers. During the transit stoppage Ed Koch, more than any other Democratic officeholder in America, mobilized popular support against unionism and touted his success as one of greatest moments of his mayoralty. He often enjoyed sounding like a Republican, as when he refused to throw his weight behind the boycott of the J. P. Stevens Company that led to the organization of southern textile workers, a drive depicted in the film *Norma Rae* (1979). However, unlike Reagan, Koch was not a union buster. He embraced collective bargaining and used technically skilled negotiators to reach labor agreements, and worked hard with the unions to avoid additional layoffs by limiting the budgetary impact of wage increases. According to Victor Gotbaum, the leader of the city's largest public employee union, much of harshest rhetoric on both sides was for show. Nonetheless, Koch's adversarial tone marked the end of an era of labor-management collaboration.[25]

Despite his move toward the right, Koch kept faith with the basic New Deal proposition that government regulations and programs could benefit the American people, and his business-friendly measures returned to the New Deal tenet that economic growth was the predicate to any redistribution of wealth. But he never embraced privatization for its own sake. For example, he resisted selling the municipal radio station, WNYC, when Peter Solomon urged him to unload it.[26] Still, he tended, especially in his rhetoric, to move toward conservative positions that he found both popular and palatable.

The transit strike was a contest that all sides saw as having broader implications for the municipal union contracts set to expire that spring. New York's public employees were fed up with years of stagnant wages in the face of double-digit inflation.

They could, with justification, point to their unions' cooperation during the fiscal crisis. Not only had the union pension funds financed a substantial portion of MAC bonds, but the workers themselves had kept New York afloat with decreases in their real wages for five years.

Union leaders had been cooperative with the austerity regime, in return for a seat at the table. But by 1980 the-rank and-file was dissatisfied—especially with pay. As a result the heads of the uniformed unions—police, fire, and sanitation, as well as the transit union—all faced significant leadership challenges. Unlike the redoubtable labor leaders of the 1960s and 1970s such as John De Lury of the sanitation workers and Mike Quill of the Transport Workers Union, most survived by narrow margins. Edward T. Ostrowski, for example, the president of the sanitationmen's union in 1980, won election by plurality of 97 votes in a union with seventy-five hundred members.[27]

City workers who wanted increased wages faced powerful opposition that supported Koch's hard line, including the Emergency Financial Control Board, which had the power to veto any union contract it found too expensive. Proxmire, who still headed the Senate committee in charge of federal loan guarantees, and his GOP counterpart, Garn, urged a modest labor settlement, similar to previous contract negotiations, when the unions had accepted 4 percent annual raises, substantially less than the rate of inflation. Albert Shanker of the teachers' union and Gotbaum of AFSCME, the two largest municipal unions, were quick to denounce the senators for outside interference in the collective bargaining process, while Koch told city residents that New York could afford to give 4 percent raises but no more without widening its budget gap. No one believed that the unions could settle for so little.[28]

A coalition of all municipal unions broached initial proposals early in 1980 that appeared to cost as much as $500 million, which might double the budget gap and probably would lead to massive layoffs. Union leaders were caught in a difficult position—if they won a wage increase that was too big, some of their members might lose their jobs. If they settled for too little, some labor leaders might lose their jobs to challengers.

The contract of the Transport Workers Union (TWU) was the first to come up and was perhaps the most volatile, because of its history of militancy. The TWU had won a difficult strike in 1965 and had the most militant tradition of any of the municipal unions. Its contract was with the Metropolitan Transportation Authority (MTA). As an independent regional authority funded by riders, with considerable subsidies from state and city governments, the MTA had deeper pockets than the financially strapped New York City.

The TWU was also volatile because ethnic succession had made John Lawe's future as union president precarious. Lawe was a relic of Irish domination of the transit union, which by 1980 had mostly black and Hispanic members. His executive board was controlled by members of two other factions that had been unable to unify to oppose him in the December 1979 elections. He had won with 9,781 votes. But more than thirteen thousand members had voted for one of his three opponents. Lawe was considered a sell-out by some of his members for even trying to reach agreement with MTA Chair Richard Ravitch.[29]

As the contract deadline loomed, Koch's implacably opposed any wage settlement of more than 8 percent over two years. The union proposed 30 percent pay increases and improvements in pensions and health care. "A transit strike is terrible. Paying salaries you can't afford is terrible. It's the horns of a dilemma," Koch remarked, even though Carey had already guaranteed that the state would pick up the tab for any wage settlement.[30] Koch would likely have dissociated himself from almost any settlement acceptable to the members of the TWU in order to prevent it from becoming a pattern for contracts for other municipal workers.[31] "Thus," remarked the veteran labor negotiator Theodore Kheel, "an irresistible force is colliding with an immovable object and only chaos can result."[32]

The Koch administration began to make plans to deal with a total transit shutdown that would disrupt the lives of millions. Some plans were generic, like setting up a phone number for traffic information, reversing lanes on the river crossings at rush hour, encouraging the use of commuter railroads not on strike, and requiring people to carpool to and from Manhattan at rush hour. Some measures had Koch's stamp. On a trip to China earlier in the year, Koch had applauded the widespread use of bicycles in Beijing and on his return instituted more experimental bike lanes in Manhattan, though he later reversed himself and even tried to ban bikes. The transit strike emergency plan put bike lanes on all the bridges, and Koch personally urged New Yorkers to fill the streets with bikes. Biking remained at higher levels even after the strike.[33] He also appointed Eugene Connell, an executive on loan from AT&T, to coordinate an emergency plan.[34]

The timing of the strike was no coincidence. After weathering a January transit strike in 1966, Mayor John V. Lindsay had negotiated an April expiration date for future TWU contracts. In 1980 the city negotiators were even luckier because city schools and parochial schools, as well as the City University, were on Passover/Easter break when the strike started, significantly lessening traffic.

The two principals, MTA chair Ravitch and TWU president Lawe, tried their best to avoid a strike. At the urging of Kheel, who had been hired as a consultant by the Central Labor Council, the two negotiators met at the Boardroom, a midtown club, and worked out what they thought was a script that the most contentious parties on each side (Mayor Koch for management and the TWU executive board for the union) could be persuaded to accept. Union officials would agree only to an offer that originated with the union, so, according to Frucher, Lawe was supposed to take Ravitch's initial offer of a 6 percent annual raise for the term of the contract and get authorization from his executive board for a 7 percent counterproposal, which Ravitch would then sign.[35]

But the pent-up frustration among members of the executive board, some of whom were, according to Ravitch, "a little drunk," had built considerable momentum toward a strike.[36] No 7 percent solution could slow this momentum, and board members shouted down an 8 percent proposal offered by the mediator Walter Gellhorn. Why didn't Lawe come back with a 9 percent counteroffer? Perhaps he thought it necessary to strike to maintain his leadership. A "senior union official" told the press at the beginning of the strike that board members had felt that Ravitch had "broken faith" by presenting 6 percent as his last offer and then upping it. "Once that slippage occurred, how did we know when they might stop?" the official asked.[37]

Carey announced that he would enforce the full penalties of the Taylor Law prohibiting strikes by public employees—a fine for workers of two days' pay for every strike day and contempt fines for the union amounting to $1 million if its leaders told their members to ignore court injunctions to return to work.[38] Lawe's more famous predecessor, Michael Quill, had had a heart attack after he was jailed during the 1966 transit strike and died soon after—when the judge jailed Quill, he had declared in his thick Irish brogue, "The judge can drop dead in his black robes and we would not call off the strike."[39]

Mediator Gellhorn had a long night of prestrike negotiations at the Sheraton Centre Hotel in midtown. He had tried in vain to convince the TWU executive board to accept, or at least make, a counteroffer. At 2:05 A.M. on April 1 Gellhorn announced: "There is a strike." Lawe confirmed it: "That's it. The strike is on."[40] Koch was in the catbird seat: by unilaterally breaking off negotiations, the union had declared that "it was their strike," meaning New Yorkers would blame the union when they had to walk to work.[41]

At a meeting with Police Commissioner Robert McGuire at One Police Plaza, the mayor looked out the window on April 1 and saw thousands of commuters pouring into the financial district. With typical hyperbole he recalled: "It was like the Russian Army coming over frozen Lake Ladoga to save Leningrad," though it was actually a nice spring morning.[42] The mayor instinctively went to the Brooklyn Bridge and the Staten Island ferry terminal to greet commuters, a gesture he repeated daily during the strike. He managed to unify public opposition to the strike, in what had been one of America's strongest union towns, where it had been unthinkable to cross a picket line.[43] New York was a union town no longer.

As Koch stood on the bridge, his big figure and bald pate were as unmistakable from afar as his blue windbreaker with the word *Mayor* written in big white letters on the back. "Hi, Hiya. Just wanted to say hello. Just wanted to thank you for helping," he told commuters that brilliant spring morning. "I have a proclamation: No rain for the duration," he said with a smile. Those few individuals who approached him to say they supported the union he dismissed to the press as "wackos," a word he practically trademarked. Even Koch could not halt a few April showers, but the generally good spring weather hurt the union enormously.[44] Most mayors would find only political misfortune in a lengthy transit strike. Koch adored the battle: "The adrenalines are flowing. . . . I think there's no life comparable to mine, none. There is never a boring day, Never!" He wanted nothing less than a union capitulation, but he wanted to mobilize citizens to win the strike, rather than relying on governmental power alone.[45]

Koch turned the strike into one of the high points of his political popularity, as he correctly calculated that New Yorkers, like other Americans, had become more individualistic and were less likely to reflexively support the union. At the same time he believed that they could be convinced to act together as citizens for what he saw as the common good. Strangely, he mixed Depression and biblical metaphors, telling one voter: "The worst fear is fear itself, now Roosevelt said that better. But what I mean is that the unthinkable has happened, and now we have to show that we can live through it. This is not Armageddon."[46] And New Yorkers did display their flair for hurdling even extraordinary obstacles that city life put in their way.

Traffic was relatively light the first day, though it would become increasingly frustrating as the eleven days of strike wore on. Leventhal remembered the transit strike as "one of the great moments of the Koch administration. . . . Every morning at six, seven A.M., we were in the police headquarters. I'd be looking at the Brooklyn Bridge, and the traffic would be stopped, standstill. and I'd turn to [traffic engineer] Sam Schwartz. I'd say, Sam, nothing's moving. It's OK, he'd say, it's acting as a regulator. Everything's going perfectly."[47] Most people encountering Koch that morning supported his stand. "You know what happened under Mayor Lindsay in 1966? He said don't come into work. Wasn't that dumb?" Koch told a caller to the emergency center, where he periodically went to personally answer the phone. When this quote hit the papers, a furious John Lindsay complained that Koch had fabricated "a wholly false, outrageous and demagogic piece of political buck-passing at its worst."[48]

Koch's strategy for the transit strike was threefold: to resist settlement in order to demonstrate to the municipal employee unions that they would not have the support of the public if they walked out; to make clear that strict application of injunctions and penalties under the Taylor Law would cancel out any concessions the unions might win; and to establish a wage-increase pattern for the contracts at 8 percent or less.

Victor Gotbaum complained that "what [Koch is] doing is undercutting negotiations. Every action he takes prolongs the strike. While he maintains he will not involve himself in the strike, he's using a magnificent manipulative technique. He's involved himself with the straphangers and has made himself a victim instead of looking for some kind of solution. I think going to all the bridges is fine. But he's avoiding responsibility." This was a pretty moderate comment for a labor leader, who might have denounced the mayor as a scab. But Gotbaum shrewdly recognized the new political climate and that the mayor's role had changed. Leventhal asked: "What in the world is the mayor supposed to do? He's supposed to rally the city and get [citizens] to do business as usual and not let them be beaten to a pulp by an illegal strike."[49]

As Frucher, one of the state's negotiators, put it, "where you stand is where you sit," and from the governor's chair the picture looked considerably different than from the mayor's perspective. Carey, a more traditional pro-labor Democrat than Koch, was just recovering from years of difficult labor relations with zero-increase contracts for the state employee unions. He was far more eager than Koch to improve relations with the unions, more willing to forgive penalties, and he was more skeptical about the costs of refusing to settle. The chief negotiator, Ravitch, though a Carey appointee, had mayoral ambitions of his own and tended to act independently of both Koch and the governor. Ravitch was a well-known developer who "had his own lines to the editorial boards," and, as Frucher observed, "sometimes governors and mayors develop tensions with people that are independent."[50]

By April 4 it was clear that there would be no quick settlement before the schools went back into session. This was the third day, and the strike was starting to take its toll. Motorists had avoided New York for two days, keeping traffic at reasonable levels. On the third day the streets were jammed, with traffic 40 percent above normal, despite a high occupancy rate for each car.[51]

Perhaps the most enduring consequence of the 1980 strike was that the word *gridlock* escaped from the jargon of traffic engineering into common parlance.[52] To reduce traffic Koch asked for temporary increases in auto tolls and asked businesses to institute a four-day workweek with staggered hours for workers to return home, which cut traffic in the evening. The morning rush hour remained hellish, especially after the Long Island Rail Road also went on strike. Business was down 30 percent in Manhattan and Brooklyn department stores. Despite estimates that the strike cost New York's business leaders $1 billion, they maintained class solidarity, strongly supporting Koch's challenge to the unions.[53]

Koch also gridlocked negotiations by pursuing contempt citations against Lawe and other TWU leaders for breaking the Taylor Law. The MTA stopped striking workers' paychecks and put them in escrow to pay Taylor Law fines. While Koch may have been content to leave the negotiations to the MTA, he asked corporation counsel Allen G. Schwartz to sue the union to recover additional damages caused by the strike's impact on the city, claimed to be between $1 and $2 million per day. Koch declared: "You have two philosophies—One is to lay down and let them run over you; the other is to say we will respond with all our defenses. You cannot lay down." He and Schwartz concluded at the beginning of the strike that they would seek to impose on the strikers every penalty that the law allowed and resist attempts to provide amnesty or pay increases to offset the fines.[54]

Koch recognized that he might lose this fight, as he was a "minority stockholder" in the MTA, but he wanted to make it crystal clear to the municipal unions that, in any contract negotiation, the legal penalties for striking would be financially prohibi-

tive. But there were limits to how far even Koch would go. Although the MTA probably could have withheld the strikers' paychecks for work done before the strike and
forced them to sue for the money, the mayor rejected this approach, which he said
was not "sensible as a matter of equity or public relations."[55]

By the weekend the MTA had gone to court and secured the maximum penalties
against the strikers; Koch then pressured a reluctant Ravitch to move to the Sheraton and declare himself ready to negotiate any and all issues whenever Lawe wished
to show up. Ravitch refused. He saw this as an empty gesture, as he and Lawe had
never had any problems reaching each other or appearing together in public. Koch,
however, was playing a blame game. He saw Ravitch's perch in the hotel room as an
important symbol that the MTA was waiting to talk while the union stalled.[56]

Easter Sunday, April 6, brought the annual Central Park egg roll, but no one was
able to get there by subway. The negotiators progressed on the secondary issue of
givebacks, such as reducing paid wash-up and toilet time and mandated coffee
breaks, and rollbacks of generous sick leave and overtime pay. No one would yet
touch the main gap between the two sides—the union's demand for a 15 percent
raise the first year of the contract and a 10 percent raise the second year, and the
counterproposal for 6 percent each year.[57] New rifts appeared, as Lawe asked for amnesty from the Taylor Law penalties if the TWU returned to work, and Ravitch categorically ruled that out. Reaching a settlement would take five more days.[58]

By Monday there were signs that the public's patience was wearing thin. "You're
starting to get horn-blowing again—you didn't hear that last week," observed police
officer Anthony Cichon, who was directing traffic at Forty-second Street and Ninth
Avenue. But Mayor Koch did not lose his joviality, gaily urging motorists to fill their
radiators with water to avoid breakdowns in the still-long traffic jams.[59] As the public
became more discontented, so did Governor Carey, who began to push harder for a
settlement. In contrast to Koch's statement that "we're not going to sell out this city,"
Carey remarked: "We want to make sure that people aren't just looking at the number," referring to the size of the wage increase.[60]

The governor "felt that the damage that was done in a transit strike fell dispropor-
tionately on the low end, people of color, people who were poor . . . and we were
watching the unemployment numbers go zooming up. The hourly employees were
getting killed," Frucher recalled. When Koch's people noted that the mayor was "still
being cheered on the Brooklyn Bridge," despite the mounting evidence that the
poor were the worst hurt by the strike, Frucher rejoined that "they cheered Hitler in
Berlin too." He only meant that cheering alone was not what should determine public policy, but the remark infuriated the mayor. More than twenty-five years later,
Koch met Frucher's son at a public function, put his arm around him, and announced: "Your father called me Hitler, but I have forgiven him."[61]

Carey urged Koch to allow his own former deputy mayor for labor relations, Basil A. Paterson, to mediate in the hope that he could make a bridge to dissident black

unionists, as well as Paterson's fellow Catholics, in the heavily Catholic union.[62] Fearing that Paterson would exert pressure on the MTA for a higher wage increase than Koch wanted, the mayor rejected the plan—the only bridges he was interested in were the ones that New Yorkers had to walk across because of the strike, and he feared that Paterson's intervention would be perceived as conciliatory toward the strikers.[63] But the tie-ups on Tuesday, April 8, "were the worst yet," with the heaviest traffic volume since the strike began, and City University cancelled classes because attendance was so low. The costs to the economy were beginning to mount, with garment shipments down 25 percent and general truck traffic down 11 percent.[64]

During a press conference on Wednesday, April 9, Koch reiterated his commitment to negotiate round-the-clock, and a reporter asked, "Have you called John Lawe to tell him this?" Koch called Lawe right after the press conference. According to the mayor, Ravitch had refused to move to the Sheraton the previous weekend, which still was where negotiations were supposed to take place. Koch told Lawe to blame Ravitch, who had wanted to go home to his family during Passover, if no one showed up to negotiate. After this appeared in the papers, Ravitch agreed to meet.[65] Then Carey and Koch decided that Ravitch and Lawe should not settle matters on their own. They asked the MTA and TWU boards to meet together in hopes of breaking the impasse.[66]

Koch persisted in his hard line in the face of rain and flooded roads, which caused the worst traffic jams of the strike and headlines such as "Feet Ache—and So Does the Psyche." In Hollis, Queens, he even addressed a group of one hundred striking transit workers who showed up when he made a prescheduled appearance at a synagogue there. When a transit worker, Ronald T. Morabito, asked, "Why do you treat us as second-class citizens?" Koch replied that a big raise would require a fare increase or more state or federal money because it was not coming out of his budget. The people from the synagogue cheered his response, while the transit workers jeered and walked off. Like the controversy about Paterson, the incident at the synagogue suggested the strike had an ethnic subtext, with Jews out of sympathy with the transit workers' union, which was heavily Catholic—both its white and minority members. Though it was not Koch's doing, to some extent the strike also became racialized, as some media pointed to "black and Hispanic militants" as the cause of the dispute.[67]

As of the night of April 10 Koch still thought the public would stay solidly behind him and that there was no need to give in. The mayor's Office of Economic Development estimated that the damage to the economy was limited. Most worrying was the slump in the apparel industry, "with one-half of surveyed firms reporting production losses of 10%–75%," perhaps because many of the poorest workers in the garment industry, who lived in faraway outer-borough neighborhoods, had the most trouble getting to work. For the wealthy the effects were less pronounced. The strike had no effect on floor activity on the stock exchange, the hotels were full, retail food sales were normal, and most Fortune 500 companies were open for business. But department store sales were off 25 to 30 percent, restaurant business was down about 20 percent, and Broadway had taken a bad hit.[68]

The next morning Koch showed up at city hall after only a few hours of sleep. He had traveled out to Far Rockaway, where a police officer had been shot—not an easy trip at any time of day during the strike. Koch's will seemed to dominate even the traffic. Budget director Jim Brigham recalled: "The mayor had a driver—I can't remember his name—who could get us through the worst traffic jams imaginable. You know, the streets of the city were just almost gridlocked all over the place, and this guy could get us uptown through that traffic . . . [by] putting a little light on top of the car, in a matter of twenty minutes. . . . He could make that car go through the smallest spaces imaginable."[69] By then it was plain that the deal that Ravitch was going to offer would exceed the 16 percent Koch insisted upon and might climb as high as 21 percent spread over two years. According to Koch, Carey understood in advance that the mayor would have to blast almost any agreement that was reached. Carey claimed he was told that, with the givebacks the union had conceded, the real cost of the settlement was only 5.5 percent. Still, the tension between the governor's people and the mayor was considerable. The governor's people did not want to alienate the unions any more than they had to and were genuinely concerned about the strike-caused jump in unemployment among poorer, and especially hourly, workers. Koch fought with Carey's chief of staff, Robert Morgado, who at one point told Koch, "I don't care what you think." "You will care what I think," Koch replied. The mayor later labeled Morgado duplicitous, asserting that he tried to conceal the full cost of the final settlement.[70]

The final agreement was 9 percent in year 1 and 8 percent in year 2, with a cost-of-living adjustment that would probably cost 3.7 percent in the last six months of the contract—for a total of 21 percent—but given what the union members would have to pay in Taylor Law penalties, this was only a trivial amount above the 8 percent and 8 percent proposal Ravitch had offered before the strike. Koch nevertheless thought that Ravitch, a once and future rival for the mayoralty, should have done better and bitterly criticized him. This was not personal; Ravitch, like Carey, understood why Koch had to distance himself from the settlement because of the future negotiations with the other municipal unions. Later they would work together to finance the billions of dollars needed to renovate the decayed subway system.[71]

Koch thought New Yorkers were willing to keep walking and that, with unions harried by the mounting Taylor Law fines, time was on his side. Though he despised the settlement, the mayor declared victory. Even two years later it was clear that Koch's unprecedented hard line on imposing and collecting the Taylor Law fines, which had often in the past been forgiven as part of strike settlements, had been a blow to all the municipal unions. Gotbaum observed: "The [Transport Workers] union is not weak, but it's not in a strong position either. They're still paying off the fines."[72]

The settlement was approved despite intense resistance on both sides, suggesting that it was actually as close a compromise as could be expected. While to Koch the 21 percent seemed too high, the bottom line was that with lost pay and Taylor Law penalties, workers got little more in their paychecks than they would have gotten had they not gone on strike. The TWU executive committee, in a tie vote, failed to endorse the agreement, but Lawe was able to secure enough board votes to end the strike, pending a vote by the unpredictable membership, which eventually did ratify.

Mayor Koch's four appointees on the MTA board planned to vote against the contract. Also set to vote no were Carol Bellamy—who, according to Koch, called it a "shitty agreement"—Stephen Berger, the former financial control board director; and one independent member, leaving Ravitch to join Governor Carey's appointees to break a tie.[73] This would have greatly undermined the MTA's credibility. Carey called Bellamy, who decided to vote in favor, and Berger, who offered to resign but was persuaded to abstain. Berger explained, "We did not obtain the kinds of productivity pieces I cared about. But I didn't vote 'no' because I didn't think our turkeys out there for another week could get one more inch from John Lawe, who already got their pants and underwear and everything else. If I had liked the package at all, I would not have abstained."[74]

Koch immediately called a press conference to denounce the settlement: "The city won the battle in the streets, the Metropolitan Transportation Authority lost it at the bargaining table. For almost two weeks, New Yorkers showed that they could withstand what many said was the worst that could happen to the city—and withstand it with grace, spirit, patience, and courage." He insisted that he would never accept the TWU contract as a precedent for municipal negotiations, intimating that he was willing to brave even police, fire, and garbage strikes to limit labor costs.[75]

The *New York Times* praised Koch as a "scrappy cheerleader" and declared that "the reputation for toughness that he built up in the strike and emphasized at its end will be tested soon enough. His passion is purposeful, not narrowly self-serving."[76] Albert Shanker accused Koch of "trying to perpetuate some sort of class struggle," and that was not far off the mark. Koch had turned the public against the public employee unions, which was surely more in the long-term interests of the city's bourgeoisie than its working class. Koch's stance gained even more credibility with the public as it became evident that the givebacks that were supposed to reduce the cost of the settlement had been grossly overestimated during the negotiations and that the 50-cent fare was in grave danger.[77] Within three months the fare would be raised to 60 cents.[78]

Koch would next face down other municipal unions, winning settlements of 8 percent for each of two years (16 percent) from Gotbaum and 9 percent the first year and 8 percent the second year (17 percent) from the uniformed workers' unions (police, fire, corrections, and sanitation).[79] "Koch was clearly prepared to take them all on. They knew he would impose the maximum sanctions, or he was threatening to do so and they took him at his word," Leventhal recalled.[80] He beat the police, fire, and sanitation workers at a game of chicken, settling only five hours before a threatened walkout that might have resulted in calling out the National Guard to pick up the garbage and patrol the streets.

The year after the transit strike President Ronald Reagan fired striking air traffic controllers and busted their union, the Professional Air Traffic Controllers Organization (perhaps better known as PATCO). Koch was clearly more liberal in his approach. He never abandoned collective bargaining with the municipal unions, even if he used tough tactics in strikes. But he had turned public sentiment against the unions and abandoned a traditional Democratic constituency—labor—for a coalition with Republicans.

KOCHING CARTER

After the 1980 presidential election, the Kings County Republican chair George L. Clark suggested a new verb: *to Koch,* based on Koch's conduct toward Jimmy Carter. According to Andy Logan, "it would define anyone who has endorsed a politician of his party but then savaged him throughout the campaign while at the same time heaping praise on the candidate's opponent, helping him to win."[81] Koch denied that he was helping Reagan and bristled at the idea that he was in any way disloyal to the president.

Carter's handling of Koch is an example of the bad judgment and lack of savvy that cost the Georgian the election. Koch had made contingency plans for either a win or a loss by Carter. If he won, Koch could still claim to be one of his earliest endorsers in New York (though Teddy Kennedy still won the New York primary). If Carter lost, Koch was the Democratic big-city mayor who was closest to and friendliest with Ronald Reagan. Meanwhile Koch was pushing hard for the Republican endorsement for New York mayor in 1981, a powerful incentive to help Reagan.

It is a cliché but not an exaggeration: with friends like Koch, Carter did not need enemies. Koch later told a reporter: "My support of President Carter doesn't mean that I will be silent when he says things that are wrong." Still, Koch did defend the president at times, as at a springtime rally for Soviet Jews.[82]

In August 1980, during Democratic National Convention at Madison Square Garden, Carey and Moynihan called for a vote on a resolution for an open convention—one that would release the delegates from voting for the candidate to whom they were pledged in the primaries. Carey and Moynihan figured that Democratic discontent with Carter was so profound that the resolution had a chance—and if it passed, the convention might turn to a more electable candidate than either Kennedy or Carter. Carey endorsed Carter only after the convention and after a personal meeting.[83]

Koch did little to help the Carter camp. He refused to take a position on the open convention resolution, noting that if it did pass, Carter would lose the nomination. Koch had no trouble rattling off the names of four people whom he would prefer to see as the Democratic presidential candidate. He had previously declared that Carter looked increasingly unlikely to carry New York because his record on aid to the city was lousy and because Jewish voters were unhappy about Billy Carter's having accepted a $200,000 loan from representatives of the Libyan dictator Colonel Muammar Gadhafi. Billy Carter, Koch told the press, "happens to be a wacko." Koch criticized the president for sending his brother to represent the United States at the tenth anniversary celebration of Muammar Gaddafi's reign as dictator. The mayor even publicly predicted Carter's defeat in the general election.[84] Indeed, the nicest thing Koch said about any Democratic presidential candidate at the convention was to praise Ted Kennedy for dropping out before the roll call: "This way, instead of having a bloodletting, with veins and arteries, all we did was cut a little capillary," he quipped.[85]

In his speech to the convention, however, Koch went for the jugular, pointing out that if, as promised in the Democratic platform, the federal government assumed the city's costs for Medicaid and welfare, "we would have no trouble balancing our budget. We could lend money to Chrysler." This was a theme he had hammered on throughout the primary campaign, and it echoed a principal demand of the Republicans: an end to the "mandate millstone"—actions the federal government required of local governments without providing them any money to carry the mandates out. Finally, he slammed the low priority that Carter and Congress assigned to cities: "When Mount St. Helens exploded, Congress appropriated $850 million. . . . But while New York's South Bronx or Los Angeles's Watts or Boston's Roxbury crumbles and decays, there is no similar response."[86]

Koch kept heavy pressure on the federal government, which was crucial to the success of his budget plan. When Treasury Secretary G. William Miller delayed approval of $300 million in loan guarantees, Koch went on the offensive. The mayor declared that New York had received "zilch" from Carter and warned him that he was not "going to be the next President" if he broke his promises. Koch's dislike of Carter was genuine, but the attacks were part of a two-pronged strategy to squeeze more money out of the administration and demonstrate Koch's independence to the Republicans, whom he praised for denouncing the unfunded federal mandates.[87] Within a month the Carter administration released the guarantees. Vice President Walter Mondale and then Carter himself declared it a priority to defeat a Proxmire amendment that would have blocked the money.[88]

But the other half of the strategy worked too, suggesting that Koch was playing Carter for a sucker. As early as April, Koch had predicted that Reagan would carry New York City.[89] Koch had found a new friend: Reagan, who announced his confidence in Koch, declared his support for the loan guarantees, and opposed the Proxmire amendment, inducing the Wisconsin Democrat to shelve it.[90] Given the opposition from both Reagan and Carter, the amendment clearly had no future. "Thank God for the two-party system," Koch declared, an ironic remark for someone seeking the nomination of both parties.[91]

Yet the two-party system did make Carter more generous than he might have been otherwise. With the election just three weeks away, the president finally reversed his position and said the federal government should assume all Medicaid costs, which was Koch's "No. 1 priority for federal legislation" and would have gone a long way toward restoring the city's long-term fiscal stability.[92] But Carter's responsiveness only made Koch more aware of his political leverage.

Koch did not let up on his criticism of Carter, refusing to appear with him at a synagogue in Forest Hills, Queens, and disassociating himself from Carter's policy on the Middle East, declaring just a month before the election, "I will not go as an emissary to a synagogue to take up the subject of Carter's position on Israel," even as Koch continued to weakly reiterate his endorsement.[93]

With the election just days away Carter pledged to support Israel in the Security Council with the veto of any resolutions condemning it, not to participate in the General Assembly if it tried to throw Israel out of the UN, and not to sell fighter planes with offensive capabilities to Saudi Arabia. Koch then agreed to campaign for Carter in Florida and Philadelphia.[94] In Florida crowds were sparse. According to *Times* reporter Joyce Purnick, "while [Koch] managed at all stops to cite his support for President Carter, he spoke more often about himself." And even then he did not much praise Carter. On the crucial issue of Mideast policy, Koch's endorsement of the president sounded like an open threat: "I don't know if he will keep his commitments after he is elected. If he doesn't, he should rot in hell." Koch now says that the *New York Post* quoted him out of context, but the "rot in hell" comment remained the most memorable of his pronouncements on Carter. He did not withdraw his statement, although he did say years later that he accepted Carter's pronouncements on Israel "as those of an honorable man."[95]

That Koch could get away with such slights to a sitting president of his party is a measure of Carter's lack of resolve, a microcosm of the larger problems with Carter's presidency. Imagine if the roles had been reversed and some other politician—great or small—had acted toward Koch as he acted toward Carter. Koch's revenge would have been swift, relentless, and enduring, whether he won the election or not. Instead, Carter chose to ignore Koch, arrogantly assuming that Koch had nowhere else to go. "What's Koch going to do?" joked Detroit mayor Coleman Young at the convention, "support Reagan?"[96]

Despite his formal endorsement of Carter, Koch supported Reagan quite effectively, delighting thousands of "Reagan Democrats," the very constituency that Koch assiduously courted in the outer boroughs. Though the mayor claimed that he honored his commitments to Carter, Koch also liked Reagan personally and calculated that he was more likely to stick to his promises, perhaps because of Carter's oft-mocked declaration that he would never lie. Reagan seemed far more sympa-thetic to Israel and even to the Israeli Right. Most important, Koch probably consid-ered that the former California governor was overwhelmingly likely to win. Reagan would cut billions of dollars in federal money, but Koch would be paid in coin that he could use to restore New York's fiscal stability—continuation of loan guarantees and reduction of unfunded mandates. Koch also stood to gain the Republican desig-nation for mayor, which he had been seeking openly since January and required the consent of Republican Party leaders.[97]

Amazingly, Koch delivered the support of the Democratic county leaders of Staten Island, the Bronx, and Queens to conservative Republican state senators John Marchi, John Calandra, and Frank Padavan.[98] On the national level Koch assumed a glamour of conservatism. He took the extraordinary step of addressing the Republi-can platform committee to call for federal block grants to cities and an end to un-funded federally mandated programs, a key issue for the Republicans. The Republi-cans treated Koch to a lovefest compared with his contentious meetings with Carter and the Democrats. "You're singing our song," commented Representative Trent Lott of Alabama. Nevertheless, Koch "respectfully declined" when Republican Na-tional Chair Bill Brock invited him to join the Republican Party.[99]

The day before the platform committee meeting, William E. Simon, policy chair of the Reagan campaign, volunteered to organize Republican Citizens for Koch. Si-mon's endorsement was particularly significant. Simon was one of the most impor-tant organizers of the ideological offensive of big business in the 1970s. As treasury secretary in 1975, he had been singularly responsible for the human and capital costs of the fiscal crisis by denying a bailout that would have enabled New York to restruc-ture without destroying its organizational and physical infrastructure. (See chapter 9).[100] Koch's willingness to cut services in the name of fiscal integrity, balancing the budget a year ahead of time, and his friendly political overtures convinced Simon he "was the best mayor since Fiorello La Guardia." Koch, the *Times* wrote, "has carved himself out a niche as a fiscal conservative close to Reagan's philosophy."[101]

Koch was a godsend to New York Republicans; their party had received only 4 percent of the mayoral vote in 1977. Two of the three mayors elected after Koch were Republicans—in part because Koch legitimized New York City's Republican Party in 1980–81. Through his friendly attitude toward Reagan, and his run on the Repub-lican line in 1981, he made it easier for thousands of increasingly conservative but traditionally Democratic Jewish voters to support Republicans for years afterward. Koch's gestures to Reagan also gained him favorable notice from conservative Cath-olic voters, who had gone largely for Cuomo in 1977 and strongly supported Reagan in 1980.

Does this mean that Koch had become a conservative? At the time cordial Re-publicans overstated Koch's actual embrace of conservatism—after all, he was criti-cizing Carter simultaneously for not giving cities more money and for failing to nationalize health insurance. On questions of foreign policy, Koch greatly preferred Reagan to Carter because of the Californian's tough anti-Soviet rhetoric, his nationalistic distrust of the United Nations, and his strong endorsement of the Jewish state.

Koch had always reveled in conservative praise, as when William F. Buckley endorsed him over Cuomo in the 1977 runoff. Koch received more of it when he invited Reagan to Gracie Mansion for a cordial briefing the day after Koch criticized Carter on Israel. That meeting, just three weeks before the election, had been arranged by Rupert Murdoch.[102] "You're killing us. Why are you doing this?" Democratic National chair Robert Strauss asked after the invitation was announced. The mayor replied, "Hey, this guy might be the next president of the United States and there are some things that the city needs, and I can't put a political interest ahead of what I need to get for the city."[103] Meeting with Reagan was very much in Koch's political interest, given his calculation that the Republican could, and should, win.

Reagan praised the mayor and practically endorsed him for reelection, saying, "I don't care what line [he runs on] as long as he continues to be mayor and is doing what he's doing." Reagan also agreed to continue to help with federal loan guarantees and reduce unfunded mandates, though he declined to federalize Medicaid, as Koch pressed him to do.[104] This visit was just before the annual Alfred E. Smith dinner, at which both Carter and Reagan were to speak, and Koch, in tux and tails, had his studs pop out just as he was leaving for the dinner with the Reagans. Nancy Reagan fixed them for the bachelor mayor, and the next day Ronald Reagan joked, "Any time you have trouble with your studs, Nancy says you can call her.[105]

Just after the election Koch was quick to declare that he did not "fear for the country" as a result of Reagan's election. Voters for Reagan, he insisted to a student audience at Princeton University, were not endorsing a hierarchical conservatism but were saying instead: "'I've had enough. Government has got to take a step back. The pendulum has gone too far.' . . . This is not conservatism or liberalism, it is just a rational approach to life. . . . They really believe in local government. Is that conservative? I happen to think that is liberal."[106] And after the election of the conservative Republican Alfonse M. D'Amato to the U.S. Senate from New York, Koch quickly met with the senator-elect, praising him as a "conservative with sanity." This kicked off a lifelong friendship with the Long Island machine politician known as "Senator Pothole," in part for the copious federal funding he brought back to the region.[107]

Despite New York's overwhelmingly Democratic registration, Koch's flirtations with the Republican Party enhanced his popularity. A poll taken just after the Democratic Convention in August showed that 59 percent, "including a majority of Republicans," planned to vote for Koch for reelection. His coalition was predominantly white—his popularity among Jews, Italians, and the Irish was 75 percent, while 60 percent of blacks and 50 percent of Hispanics said they disapproved of Koch. But they still liked Koch better than they did Republican presidential candidates. Only 50 percent of blacks said they would definitely vote against the mayor, whereas 90 percent or more of African American voters opposed Republican presidential candidates in every election after 1960.[108]

Ronald Reagan's election did bring on a new era of neoliberalism—tax reductions and increases in defense spending, vastly reduced expectations of government, with vastly increased expectations for individual self-discipline and hard labor, unprotected by unions, for the average American. The funeral for John Lennon, a few weeks before Reagan's inauguration, also marked the death of a more gentle social ideal, summed up by Lennon's lyric: "All you need is love." A few days before his murder the artist had told an interviewer: "The thing the '60s did was to show us the possibilities and the responsibility that we all had. It wasn't the answer. It just gave us a glimpse of the possibility."[109] Mayor Koch organized a tribute to Lennon attended by 150,000 people on a cold December day at the Central Park band shell, just across the park from where Lennon was murdered. A simple tribute, no speeches, just Lennon's music playing over loudspeakers, ended an era.[110]

"SUPERLANDSLIDE": THE 1981 MAYORAL ELECTION

Ed Koch flashed a broad smile as he entered city hall's Blue Room to deliver his budget message for fiscal year 1982. Thunderstorms darkened the skies over the Empire State Building that afternoon, but the fiscal predictions were bright. Revenue projections were up, and the economy had picked up, though some studies warned that the improvement would not last. Koch expected a surplus big enough to absorb the aid cuts planned by the new Reagan administration; the city would even be able to expand some services, and for the second consecutive year it would balance the budget according to generally accepted accounting principles.[111]

Koch was up in the polls and his likelihood of reelection seemed nearly certain. "I know a balanced budget is a bore," he observed with a chuckle to the assembled press corps.[112] Certainly it was less exciting than a movie made that year called *Fort Apache: The Bronx* or the public boycott of that movie called by a group of city council members who charged that it unfairly stereotyped residents of the Forty-first Police Precinct, where the film is set.[113] Much of the debate about the budget was a scramble for credit. Felix Rohatyn needled Koch, suggesting that most of the work had been done in 1975–76 and that most of the credit belonged to Governor Carey (and therefore to Rohatyn himself) for creating the Municipal Assistance Corporation and Emergency Financial Control Board. Even Abe Beame tried to claim credit for the recovery in an unseemly exchange of letters in the *Times* with Koch. Beame noted that he had borne the brunt of reducing the workforce by almost fifty thousand between 1974 and 1977.[114]

Koch declared with characteristic modesty, "Somebody has to take credit. It might as well be me."[115] But the consensus among more neutral observers was that the mayor really had gotten New York back on its feet. Reporter Clyde Haberman observed, "Even those who think [Koch] is too quick at times to praise himself say that he took many key measures to restore fiscal order."[116] Marilyn Rubin, a professor at the New School for Social Research, suggested that Koch deserved credit for maintaining tight spending controls, improving cash management, and increasing city revenues through imposition of user fees on such commodities as water. His fiscal prudence enabled the city to reduce income taxes, from 10.8 percent of personal income when he took office to 9.3 percent of personal income at the end of his first term.[117]

Koch acknowledged that his 1981 budget was an election-year budget, spending to please voters with expanded city services. But it was an extraordinarily prudent election-year budget—Koch's whole reputation rested on his fiscal reliability, and he was trying to ease back into credit markets, so he did not want to spend too much. The budget surplus, he told the press, "does not mean that the days of wine and roses have returned or that fiscal discipline can be relaxed. It does mean, though, that the worst pain is behind us, that cutting can be balanced with some new initiatives."[118]

His initial budget plan, which was adopted with minor revisions, made hiring new police officers its priority. As passed by the city council and the Board of Estimate, the budget included money to hire a few hundred more officers than Koch's original plan of more than twenty-three hundred, who were needed to supplement the city police force, as well as the Transit Police and Housing Authority Police. He also added more than three hundred corrections officers as well as new beds in the prison system.[119]

Sanitation got $10 million to continue implementation of two-man trucks and other productivity improvements, money for 445 more sanitation workers, and a "flying squad" of seventy-five employees to target the biggest messes. Some teachers would be rehired, along with three hundred school crossing guards and 375 firefighters.[120] After crime, dirt, and education the biggest concern of most New Yorkers was the deterioration of the subways. Koch put $35 million in the capital budget for purchase of subway cars and replacement of the defective undercarriages in some new cars. And he pledged that the subways would be reliable at times of peak demand by 1983. Somehow the budget even absorbed Reagan's budget cuts, which diminished federal aid by an estimated $350 million in just the first year of the Reagan administration.[121]

Despite the cuts, Koch found the new president friendlier and more accessible than Carter, if less forthcoming. "I like him. He's a man of character," Koch told the press, even while objecting to Reagan's cuts in mass transit subsidies, food stamps, and social service programs.[122] Koch noted that the budget process was relatively boring without the drama of Garn or Proxmire bashing New York. But Garn and Proxmire, along with Senator D'Amato, did try to prohibit rent control, a move Reagan eventually blocked at Koch's request. Koch himself had qualms about rent control but did not want to subject himself to the wrath of New York's numerous tenants, especially in an election year.[123]

The 1981 mayoral election was a complicated affair though never in doubt. The only question was the size of Koch's majority. After discussions with the Conservative Party, Koch withdrew from attempts to run on that line; the Liberals had become his enemies and would run council member Mary Codd, a Staten Island Liberal, against him in the general election. Koch ran in the Republican primary, having obtained support of four of the five Republican county chairs. The most cautious of these was George L. Clark of Brooklyn, who was about to become state chair and who later asserted that Koch promised him that he would not run for statewide office if reelected as mayor. Koch insists that he merely said that he "wanted to be mayor forever" and never made any specific promises not to run for governor or any other higher office.[124]

Endorsing Koch was especially difficult for conservatives who had been trying to Reaganize the New York Republican Party—one of the most liberal in the nation during the Rockefeller and Lindsay years. Only Reagan's personal support of Koch could overcome the conservative New Yorkers' objections, and still many conservatives balked. Republican assemblyman John Esposito declared his intention to run, and the county leaders were in the awkward position of backing a liberal Democrat who was certain to win the Republican primary against a conservative. Esposito, wary of a return of the party to Lindsayism, declared that the cross-endorsement of Koch "threatens the existence of the Republican Party in the U.S."[125]

Koch beat Esposito in the Republican primary 66 percent to 33 percent, holding all but two assembly districts against the conservative assemblyman. In the Democratic primary Koch beat his principal opponent, the liberal assemblyman Frank Barbaro, by the lopsided margin of 59 percent to 36 percent, with 4 percent going to minor candidate Melvin Klenetsky. Koch claimed that his Republican cross-endorsement would help in Albany and in Washington: "That it's something that no other mayor has done—maybe it's not like climbing Mount Everest, but maybe like climbing the World Trade Center," which seemed perfectly in tune with Koch's character.[126]

Koch was still very much a Democrat, and Republicans in the victory ballroom that election night must have been dismayed, as Koch immediately swung to the left and stepped up his hitherto muted criticism of Ronald Reagan's budget.[127] Friends said he was miffed that the White House did not include Koch in the delegation to Anwar Sadat's funeral. Koch began to participate in strategy sessions on how to revitalize the Democratic Party.[128]

Koch called his general election victory a superlandslide. He carried every assembly district. Koch received an astounding 914,943 votes, 79 percent, to 161, 676 (14 percent) for Barbaro, who was running as an independent; 42,271 (3.5 percent) for Esposito on the Conservative line, and 43,392 (3.5 percent) for the Liberal Mary Codd. Although Koch's percentage was unmatched by any modern mayor, the turnout was low and the raw number of votes Koch took in the election was less than Lindsay received in 1969 or than Beame had gotten without incumbency in 1973.[129]

Koch's coalition with the Republicans was uneasy. A year later Clark, the Brooklyn Republican chair, bitterly regretted the endorsement, which had cost him credibility with the conservative wing of the party. Koch drifted back to liberal positions on domestic issues. By December 1981 he was calling President Reagan's domestic programs "a sham and a shame," in an effort, he later said, to influence congressional races in the 1982 elections.[130]

After the 1981 election Koch shifted emphasis to rebuilding the Democratic Party. He wanted to move the party away from social democracy, though the spending he advocated implied shifting welfare burdens from localities to the federal government, implicitly using the federal income tax to redistribute income from rich to poor and from suburbs to city, a decidedly liberal position. He argued that "the federal role should be one of focused intervention on problems that are in the national interest to resolve—and essentially beyond the capacities of the localities to support alone. These problems are often highly concentrated in particular areas," that is, welfare, indigent medical care, job training, and the education of the deprived and disabled.[131]

In an address to a Democratic Party strategy conference, Koch declared that the Democrats' problem was that they had become the "party of the status quo." The problem was not that Democrats favored helping the poor, disadvantaged, and unemployed but that they had become committed to specific programs, interests, and bureaucracies that in the maelstrom of the economic and social crises of the 1970s and 1980s no longer accomplished their intended purpose.

Koch's real beef with liberals was foreign policy. Though he frequently denounced political "litmus tests," his own litmus test was whether a politician or party "supports Israel's security."[132] This had been one of his greatest sources of friction with Carter, who was otherwise a more conservative Democrat than Koch. But in these speeches to Democratic groups, such as the strategy conference, the mayor barely mentioned foreign policy issues though he urged Democrats to "recapture the center" on both domestic issues and defense.[133]

15 GOVERNOR KOCH? (1982–83)

After his smashing victory Koch had achieved everything he had been aiming for politically for the past four years, although city services and infrastructure remained inadequate. Despite the landslide, his second inauguration on a rainy New Year's Day was far more low key than his first. Held in the dramatic and sumptuous marble rotunda of the Surrogate's Court building across from city hall, Koch did not even buy a new suit for the occasion and read his speech "phlegmatically," according the *Times*. "What can I say? The first time can never be fully matched," Koch declared. Even the metaphors of his inaugural speech seemed to reflect an existentialist preoccupation with boredom and absurdity. Koch may never have read Albert Camus' *The*

Myth of Sisyphus, an essay in which Camus examines the myth of the king who was condemned to roll a stone up a mountain, only to see it roll back to the bottom again and again, leaving him to start again. Camus's essay argues that we must learn to live with the absurdity of life. "If this were a Greek myth," Koch said, "there would be nothing to do except step aside and watch our four years of sweat and sacrifice roll back down that mountain." While Camus suggests that acceptance of the absurdity is the only way to enjoy brief moments of both consciousness and happiness, Koch, not surprisingly, took the more religious and conventional route, the leap of faith: "But New York is not a myth. New York is a miracle. This is the greatest city in the world, a city of winners, and we are not stepping aside for anybody."[1] Given Koch's talent for ridicule and invective, he might have appreciated Camus' remark: "There is no fate that cannot be surmounted by scorn."[2]

With a moderately scornful sense of the absurdity of Koch's situation, city council president Carol Bellamy presented the mayor at the inauguration with a copy of Dr. Seuss's *Yertle the Turtle,* slyly countering his appeal to continue the leap of faith that New Yorkers had already granted him for four years. *Yertle,* oddly similar to the *Myth of Sisyphus,* is the story of an authoritarian turtle who convinces all the other turtles to pile on each other so that Yertle can be at the top—until the turtle at the bottom burps, sending Yertle falling back into the mud.[3] This was a satiric exaggeration, but the election had consolidated Koch's celebrity and power. Still, it was not clear to him or anyone else how he could solve the city's problems.

Koch tried to give some credit for New York's fiscal and economic turnaround to the sacrifices of the city's citizens, declaring, "We did it together." The challenges of running New York were still daunting: the Reagan administration's proposed cuts in federal aid to cities would, he said, "turn back the clock." Reagan was completely opposed to a federal takeover of Medicaid, despite a mandated 70 percent rise in costs for that program. The Federal Reserve's tight money policy, aimed at reducing inflation, was also strangling tax receipts. So the policies of the president whom Koch had done so much to elect threatened his greatest achievement—New York's hard-won balanced budget. Koch pointed with pride to improvements in the economy, the reform of public space, and the increase in real estate development in the city and promised improvements in city services at a slow but "accelerating pace."[4]

Soon after the inaugural Koch took his January break in Spain. He met with King Juan Carlos, who had recently played a crucial role in his country's transition to parliamentary democracy.[5] In Andalusia, Koch played tourist at the Alhambra and the Alcazar palaces, with a long and cordial stop in Jerez, where Pedro Domecq gave Koch a personal tour of his sherry winery and treated him as an honored guest.[6] Finally, Koch and his friends headed north to Barcelona, took in the spectacular views from the top of Montjuïc, and the beautiful, outlandish architecture of Antoni Gaudí. Koch also made a stop off the usual tourist itinerary, the fifth-century C.E. cellars of the Shlomo Ben Adret synagogue, then being restored.[7]

While Koch was traveling, New York was swirling with a move to nominate him for governor. *New York Post* publisher Rupert Murdoch flooded the city with the words *DRAFT KOCH* in large type on the front page and invited tabloid readers to submit a tear-off coupon if they wanted Koch to run. Thousands did. By the time Koch walked off the airplane in New York, he was already fueling the speculation and of course reveling in the attention. "I think I have thirty days to enjoy this," he told reporters.[8]

Koch's father died the next day, January 28. He was eighty-nine. Ed Koch sat shiva in the Orthodox manner, without shaving or wearing shoes, but only for the Reform Jewish period—three days instead of seven. But after the period of mourning, the nonpoliticians in Koch's entourage, his closest personal friends, pushed him to take the plunge. These included former corporation counsel Allen Schwartz and Koch adviser Dan Wolf, businessman David Margolis, and restaurateur Peter Aschkenazy, along with political bosses like Stanley Friedman, who wanted to be Koch's De Sapio, with visions of patronage plums dancing in his head.

If, as Koch claimed, he never thought that a Jewish guy from New York City could be president, some of his friends did—but they were amateurs. The whole thing was a fantasy. Most professional politicos close to Koch thought running for governor was a foolhardy move. At that point the poll numbers were still good. But they realized that being governor did not fit with the story Koch had written about his own life, the story of a man devoted to serving his city. Not surprisingly, Koch's most politically experienced friends strongly opposed the run and expected him to lose. These included John LoCicero, Miriam Bockman, Maureen Connelly, Deputy Mayor Robert F. Wagner, and media adviser David Garth, who had agreed to work for Mario Cuomo if Koch did not run. They understood that the 20 percent lead over Cuomo that the polls showed for a gubernatorial race could melt overnight. "It will be a very tough, very nasty campaign—it won't be a cakewalk," Garth told a reporter. Koch himself later described the decision to run as a lark.[9]

Garth believed that he had averted disaster by pledging to Koch that he would turn down Cuomo's bid for his services and $250,000 in fees if Koch would agree not to run. Garth keenly understood that Koch was incapable of formulating a coherent narrative about why he should be governor. "We sat on the porch at Gracie Mansion one day. I asked him: Why the hell do you want to be governor? There was a big pause. I said I knew all the mental reasons, but what do you want it for? He couldn't answer."[10] Koch's personal friends persuaded him otherwise, and the best explanation is that, turning around the city's finances and improving its management structures, without really having the money to make the city safer and cleaner, was frustratingly Sisyphean. As governor, he might have the power to move forward. Koch ran to satisfy his ambition, as well as to promote the interests of New York City. Such motives proved very difficult to sell upstate.

If New York was Sisyphean, for Koch upstate New York was a slightly different kind of hell. His preparations for running included a public apology to Albany mayor Erastus Corning for saying that living in Albany was "a fate worse than death" because it had no decent restaurants.[11] The mayor announced his candidacy for governor on February 22, claiming that Reagan's "New Federalism," which shifted responsibility for social service programs from the federal government to the states, was his prime reason for running, and that his successful management of the city qualified him to be governor.[12] These were not strong arguments, but initially he had significant prospects of winning, despite the evidently cool reception of cynical reporters, who informed readers that Koch had solemnly pledged at the Western Wall in Jerusalem to serve out his term for mayor.[13]

Even his frontrunner status was something of a liability. The gubernatorial campaign tarnished Koch's reform image when he declared his candidacy on the steps of city hall surrounded by the five New York county leaders. With Rupert Murdoch's tear-off coupons and other propaganda, the campaign seemed like a caricature of machine politics straight out of a Frank Capra film. Koch raised lots of money—but not as much as the conservative Republican candidate Louis Lehrman, who spent more than $7 million of his Rite-Aid drugstore fortune to get the Republican nomination, defeating veteran Rockefeller Republican Paul Curran, a former prosecutor. In October 1982 Koch reported having spent $3.6 million on the primary, and Cuomo reported $1.7 million.[14]

Koch's chances declined precipitously the day after he announced his candidacy, when reports surfaced that Koch had told an interviewer for *Playboy* that living in the suburbs was "sterile, it's nothing, it's wasting your life." In response to a question about "life in the country," Koch replied: "The country? Rural America? That is a joke! [*Laughs*]." Later he commented, "Let's leave out rural America, with the cows." When the interviewer, intent on cracking Koch's defense of the city, asked about the "the loss of time because of lousy city services, late subways?" Hizzoner replied, "As opposed to wasting time in a car? Or, out in the country, wasting time in a pickup truck? [*Laughs*] When you have to drive 20 miles to buy a gingham dress or [*laughs louder*] a Sears Roebuck suit? [*Cracks up*]. This rural America thing—I'm telling you, it's a joke."[15]

Koch's jocularity about the boredom of living north of the Bronx can be explained by its timing: he had clearly not yet decided to run at the time of the interview, telling *Playboy*, "Anyone who suggests that I run for governor is no friend of mine. It's a terrible position, and besides it requires living in Albany, which is small town life at its worst. I wouldn't even consider it."[16] The *Playboy* interviewer later acknowledged he was determined to badger Koch into admitting that life in New York

City might not be ideal: "There was a lot of interrupting, laughing and occasional yelling as I tried to persuade him, or provoke him, to comment on the difficulties of living in a big city today. But no, Ed Koch remained adamant: New York is terrific, second only to Xanadu."[17]

Thus Koch, not yet in gubernatorial mode, was convinced that he had not cracked in the way the reporter sought, and Koch clearly had not been thinking about state-wide office several months earlier. So when Garth asked him if there was "anything hot in" the interview, Koch replied no, that "it went well."[18] Indeed, Evan Cornog, then assistant press secretary, who sat in for the entire eighteen hours of the interview, thought that Koch had said nothing that he had not said many times before.[19]

Though Koch remained ahead in the polls, the first poll Garth took a few days after news of the *Playboy* interview hit the stands shocked the hardened campaign veteran. Koch was still in the lead, but his positive rating had plummeted 25 percent, and his negative rating had soared to 28 percent, "the biggest, fastest plunge Garth had ever seen in politics."[20] Koch's snide remarks compounded the ugly, naked butt of ambition he had displayed when he announced his candidacy. He had become upstaters' worst nightmare of a New York City candidate. As one upstate editorial writer asked rhetorically, did Koch know "the difference between Cayuga and Keuka Lakes? Oswego and Owego? The Genesee and the Oswegathia? Can he locate the Southern Tier? The Blue Line? Tug Hill?"[21] Koch made clear that he would not learn and did not care which were lakes and which were counties. Koch was spending every night in New York City while following an exhausting schedule of appearances by helicopter upstate. It soon was apparent that Koch knew and cared little about anything upstate.

The energy he normally put into perfect staff work and excellent briefing for any situation vanished. It was a sloppiness seen only in Koch's bad campaigns, like the 1973 mayoral campaign, when he had no real idea how citywide politics worked. After a Rotary dinner at which he had nothing to say about the club or its service work, he advised his scheduler, Jerry Skurnik, that the only rotary he wanted to see was the one on his helicopter. Asked by a reporter in Cooperstown what county he was in, he replied, "Oneonta." He was in fact in Otsego County, and New York has no county named Oneonta, which is a city. A news story about Koch going upstate to get photographed feeding a goat provoked derisive laughter. As lieutenant governor, Cuomo had campaigned upstate before and knew the territory better, which extended his solid lead north and west of Westchester.[22]

Instead of promoting New York's cosmopolitanism—the desired image of the world city—Koch seemed to project its parochialism and provoked a rhetorical backlash against the city: "Those of us who wasted half our lives there, before escaping to upstate areas, know best where the pits really are . . . . Despite all the 'excitement' of the big city, most Gotham residents pass their lives in fear and forced loneliness," opined an editorial writer in sleepy Syracuse.[23]

Koch's candidacy for governor hurt the city. Some aides thought there was "a notable decline in activity in City Hall," as the mayor directed his attention elsewhere.[24] With Koch confused in Cooperstown and exhausted when he returned to Gracie Mansion at night, city government ran on routine. It is hard to point to one significant initiative taken by city government during Koch's gubernatorial campaign, which lasted from February to September 1982.

Koch tended to do better in the New York suburbs, which were full of former city dwellers who watched television news broadcasts from Manhattan and knew him better than Albanians, as residents of the state capital are called. But even here he had a conflict of interest, because as mayor he wanted suburbanites to contribute more money to the city, where many of them worked. Koch favored a commuter tax to help improve city services, which Cuomo, as lieutenant governor, opposed. Similar conflicts of interest came out in debates and editorial meetings as the candidates discussed what they would do with the state budget.[25] And back home in New York City his support was weak. Many voters who liked Koch preferred to keep him as mayor, rather than sending him up the river to Albany. By the August polls he was doing better in the 'burbs than in the city.[26] Moreover, Cuomo successfully appealed to a liberal primary electorate by denouncing the pro–death penalty Koch as engaging in "the politics of electocution" (sic).[27] Cuomo also taunted him with commercials pointing out that New York City had seen 115,524 more crimes in 1981 than in 1977, when Koch was first elected mayor.[28]

Koch was still fending off questions about the *Playboy* interview through the summer. His poll numbers were moving ever downward, despite intensive campaigning. Koch's double-digit lead had shrunk to 8 points, and among likely voters, he was 3 points behind Cuomo and sinking.[29] The next month did not bring much better news. The mayor was uncharacteristically ill prepared in his first debate with Cuomo and conceded that his opponent had won the first encounter.

Polls showed Cuomo with a 12-point lead upstate, despite Koch's exhausting efforts to campaign there. Koch maintained a wide lead in the suburbs. But the mayor had lost his runaway frontrunner status by August.[30] The upstate vote for Cuomo proved decisive in the September primary. By carrying numerous small upstate counties like Fulton by huge margins (1,228–440), and larger upstate cities like Albany with leads greater than 3–1, Cuomo won 67 percent of the vote upstate, piling up a lead of 108,374—more than enough to offset Koch's narrow win by 27,934 votes in the New York City suburbs. But it was in New York City, where less than a year before Koch had received 75.2 percent of the vote for mayor in the general election and just under 60 percent in the 1981 Democratic primary, that Koch had truly lost the election. In the city he beat Cuomo by a humiliatingly small margin of 3,886 votes, 50.25 percent to 49.75 percent.[31]

"I'm still the mayor. And that's not bad. In fact, it's good. I love the city of New York and all the people in it. And tomorrow I'll be out at City Hall working as hard as I always have," Koch told the crowd that gathered to hear his concession. He clearly was relieved that he didn't have to move to Albany and devote his career to expanding cheese production in Washington County. And he made amends with Cuomo, with whom he'd have to work for the good of the city, by immediately endorsing him for governor in the general election.[32] Koch had made himself look ridiculous by running for governor; even many of the people who loved him as mayor knew it. Now he would have to work even harder to recoup.

On both the political and fiscal fronts, Koch's run for governor marked something of a tack to the left. He denounced Reagan's abandonment of the cities and made a budget and a labor settlement sufficiently generous that the fiscal monitors were not entirely happy.

The mayor's fiscal 1983 budget, which took effect in July 1982, in the middle of the gubernatorial campaign, tried to hold the line by choosing cuts that Koch claimed would not endanger the modest improvements in services he was able to offer while avoiding the "false economies" of across-the-board cuts. "Service reductions, beyond the modest cuts we are proposing, and coming on top of substantial Federal cuts, would be disastrous for the city's future," Koch declared. But for the first time since 1978, in the face of a sharp economic downturn, a Koch budget might not pass muster with the Emergency Financial Control Board, whose director, Comer S. Coppie, called for Koch to cut ten thousand city jobs to balance the budget.[33]

By July critics from both inside and outside government were beginning to question whether Koch's budget was as forthright and conservative as his past budgets had been. Charles Brecher and Raymond D. Horton of the Citizens Budget Commission held their annual conference on the city budget and charged that Koch's 1982 budget, released as he was running for reelection as mayor, had "deviated sharply from principles of sound fiscal policy" by creating six thousand municipal jobs for that fiscal year through one-shot budgetary gimmickry.[34] This enraged Koch. The mayor had previously barred all city officials from taking part in the annual gathering of academics, government officials, bankers, politicians, and civic activists held by professors Brecher and Horton. The ban came after a *Daily News* headline characterized a study issued by the two academics as an accusation that Koch had "balanced the budget on the backs of the poor." When the *News* headline had first hit, the mayor had asked Brecher and Horton to accompany him immediately to the city hall press room for an impromptu press conference rebutting the charge. They refused. Although Brecher and Horton publicly declared in a subsequent *Times* op-ed piece that the phrase "inaccurately describes the way Mayor Koch has used his budgetary authority," Koch was not mollified. He had wanted more immediate and personal contrition. Koch felt that Brecher and Horton had contributed to the spate of rumors about the budget and he viewed what they had said as an assault on his integrity.[35]

The degree of alarm over whether Koch would abandon the goal of balancing the budget without gimmicks was exaggerated. A few months before the Brecher and

Horton op-ed, a skeptical control board had approved the administration's plan to plug the annual budget gap only after Budget Director Alair Townsend promised a program of cuts that would be triggered if revenues did not match the budget's projections. Many of those cuts had to be implemented after the fall election season, when it became clear the city was not taking in enough cash to balance the budget.[36]

Koch met with a group of minority politicians and acknowledged that budget cuts would hurt minority neighborhoods more than wealthier ones, which could use private money to compensate for the lack of services in their neighborhoods. The meeting was cordial. Former deputy mayor Herman Badillo suggested that taxes be raised and cuts reduced, but the mayor could offer little but sympathy: the power to raise taxes largely resided in Albany.[37]

Koch ultimately called for across-the-board budget cuts totaling 7.5 percent and contemplated laying off as many as thirty-three hundred employees, along with achieving reductions in the city workforce of fifty-three hundred jobs through attrition.[38] Koch, who had deep misgivings about the rise in crime and filth that would result from layoffs, needed to both satisfy the credit markets and motivate labor leaders to press the state government for additional aid, which might forestall the contingency layoff program. Once again, it seemed that there was no escape from austerity, but Koch was a lucky man. By April 1983 critics were accusing him of crying wolf with his prognosis for devastating cuts. More state and federal aid that the control board had ordered not be counted had actually materialized, and city revenues ran ahead of projections, as New York unexpectedly recovered from the recession faster than the rest of the country. While conservative budgeting prevented the city from incurring deficits based on excessively generous revenue predictions, the city budget remained insufficiently stable to guarantee a solid base of services, given how closely tied it was to the fortunes of the financial and real estate industries.[39]

1983: MAKEOVER AT CITY HALL

Normally, a year like 1983 is a sleeper for political history, an off-off-election year in New York, with nothing at stake but a few judgeships, gubernatorial races in far-off states, and general boredom. But Koch's race for governor had delayed and displaced much of the cabinet shuffling that would usually occur after winning a second term. He now began to consider how to give his administration a new direction and focus.

Staff and cabinet-level jobs in an administration are not for the fainthearted. Most require at least some attention around the clock. Staffers generally considered Koch to be a considerate but demanding boss. Koch may have run for governor because he had burned out in the mayor's job, which is a lot harder than being governor. Governors get blamed directly for very little, but when the snow is not plowed or the garbage picked up, or when people get mugged, they hold the mayor responsible. Deputy Mayor Nat Leventhal, who undoubtedly understood the ways in which the administration had stalled, had been considering leaving office since the gubernatorial primary, though he stayed on for another year and a half, when he resigned to become president of Lincoln Center.[40]

Some new appointments had long-term effects, such as the appointment of Henry Stern as parks commissioner; he would serve nearly six years under Koch, skip a term under Dinkins, and serve another eight years under Giuliani. Others, like the appointments of a new police commissioner and schools chancellor, were racially charged. Just as Jews had been trying to break through the Irish-dominated system in the 1930s, African Americans now vied for positions as top teachers and administrators. This meant that the leading candidate for schools chancellor of many African American political and education groups was Dr. Thomas Minter, a former high school music teacher who held a Harvard Ph.D. and had served as an assistant secretary of education in the Carter administration, for the position of schools chancellor.

Mayor Koch had other plans. He had little confidence in either the African American groups or the United Federation of Teachers to make decisions outside their own self-interest. He hoped to get more direct control of the school system, which represented a major chunk of his budget over which he had no control, by engineering the appointment by the city's Board of Education of his key troubleshooter and trusted former deputy mayor, Robert F. Wagner, as chancellor. Koch's support for Wagner precipitated a "street-fight" for the post as Minter's supporters accused Koch of racism for rejecting a qualified black candidate in favor of his own pick, a politician without formal credentials in the field. "This issue shows that instead of taking advantage of an opportunity to reach out and repair his relations with minorities, he has taken a position that will do more to damage race relations between the Mayor and the minority community than anything I can imagine," said state senator Carl McCall.[41] Koch vehemently denied the charge, insisting that he opposed "racial quotas" but would search especially hard for minorities whom he could appoint because of their merit. Koch cited his past appointments as evidence that he was paying attention to the problem.[42]

When the Board of Education, prompted by the mayor, voted 6–1 to offer Wagner the job, Brooklyn assemblyman Al Vann, a teacher and veteran advocate of a greater African American presence in the school system, termed it "a raw display of political power on the part of the Mayor."[43] But the street fight was not over yet. State law required Wagner to get a waiver from the state commissioner of education because of Wagner did not have a doctoral degree. Possibly on Cuomo's instructions, the state refused the waiver.[44] Not that this ended the story. Koch appointed Wagner to a seat on the Board of Education in 1985; he became its president the next year.

Ironically, in this new role he worked to make the board more active and independent and less of a rubber stamp for the chancellor.[45]

But Koch still vetoed Minter. The job went instead to Anthony G. Alvarado, a phenomenally successful district superintendent. Alvarado was forced to resign after allegations surfaced that he had taken thousands of dollars in loans from his subordinates at the Board of Education and had falsified documents to get bank loans. He stepped down just five months after his appointment and was eventually replaced by Nathan Quinones, a Board of Education official seen as more of a conciliator.[46]

The period of 1983–84 also brought a new senior leadership into the Koch administration. Stan Brezenoff succeeded Nat Leventhal as deputy mayor for policy and eventually became first deputy mayor. Brezenoff, who had been one of Koch's chief troubleshooters before moving to city hall, often has described how his radical past and sensitivity to working in an integrated environment helped him to make Koch's neoliberal policies more palatable. In the difficult and divided agencies in which Brezenoff worked in—the Department of Employment, the Human Resources Administration (a Lindsay-era euphemism for the welfare department), and the Health and Hospitals Corporation—he displayed unusual tact and diplomacy.[47] Brezenoff's ties to New York's grassroots civil rights organizations were unusual for someone in his position. He grew up in a "left-wing household" in East New York—a part of town built as modest housing that has gone through block busting, ghettoization, and a degree of recovery but never gentrification.[48] He was not especially political at first, but his friends and family looked up to Koch's generation, "bemoaning the poor timing of our existence, so that we weren't in Spain, or couldn't fight the war against fascism." Brezenoff majored in philosophy at Brooklyn College, which at the time featured a notable group of analytic philosophers, joined the army reserve to avoid the draft and then tried graduate school in philosophy at Cornell.

Academia did not appeal to him, so he took full-time jobs with the Customs Bureau and Norelco. Then he "got caught up in the civil rights movement." In 1963 he joined the Brooklyn chapter of the Congress of Racial Equality (CORE) after hearing news reports of white teenagers in the Bronx who were hurling eggs, pieces of brick, and Molotov cocktails at protesters who were demanding an end to whites-only hiring at local White Castle hamburger joints.[49] Ultimately, Brezenoff quit his job at Norelco to work for three years with the Reverend Milton Galamison on his campaign to integrate the Brooklyn schools. Brezenoff was a full-time activist. He had been arrested at sit-ins and identified in news reports as "Galamison's white henchman." He'd been close to CORE director Sonny Carson and was CORE's last white staffer, but the civil rights movement became a black-led movement, and he left in 1966.[50]

After Brezenoff got married, he needed to find better-paying work. Though he had never been convicted on any of the charges lodged against him, his arrest record meant he could not get a license to drive a cab and disqualified him from many other positions. A friend in Adam Clayton Powell's office got him a job as a parks department recreation worker, working with Italian kids in Bushwick. Then, during the Lindsay administration, Brezenoff joined the War on Poverty, eventually working his way up to head the community corporations section of the Community Development Agency, a subagency of the city's Human Resources Administration. Brezenoff soon attracted the attention of his boss, Mitchell I. Sviridoff, who eventually brought Brezenoff along with him to the Ford Foundation, where Brezenoff polished his administrative skills and added elite contacts to his grassroots ones.[51]

Because of his earlier relationships with the largely minority bureaucrats in the Human Resources Administration and the other city agencies he worked in, during the Koch administration Brezenoff implemented management reforms and neoliberal policies such as welfare eligibility controls, agency accountability, and caseload reduction without raising hackles within the agency the way his predecessor Blanche Bernstein had done. "I think there was some astonishment [at] how I appeared to be able to walk amongst what they must have regarded as real minefields. They really missed the point. It wasn't so much that I had any special skills, it was just that I knew everybody," he recalled.[52] He was able to repeat that success at the Health and Hospitals Corporation, an agency to which Koch appointed a series of failed administrators. Though happy at the Human Resources Administration, Brezenoff took over at the Health and Hospitals Corporation (HHC), discovering almost immediately that the agency "was a wasteland." The board was notoriously unruly, and the agency did not pay its bills. In order to conceal the size of the agency's debt and make the books balance at the end of the year, HHC administrators would "just stuff bills in the drawer and wait until the next year," Brezenoff recalled, noting that the agency had no chief financial officer and no systemwide financial controls in place—the records were kept separately at each hospital.[53]

The day he took over, the doctors went out on strike to protest the quality of care in city hospitals. Brezenoff saw quickly that improving the administration, and particularly the agency's cash flow, was the prerequisite to any increase in services. He appointed Ed Burke, a "tough chief financial officer," to build an accountable financial system, and Brezenoff completely reformed top hospital management. "Within a year I had changed every senior position, most of the hospital directors were gone, and within two years I think only a handful of hospital directors were left," he recalled.[54]

Brezenoff continued to rise in Ed Koch's estimation for succeeding where three other appointees had failed. In 1984, when Koch faced a delicate bid for reelection to a third term, one in which racial issues were key, he picked Brezenoff as his chief deputy, a man with significant civil rights credentials and a greater understanding of the history and aspirations of African Americans than almost any other white man the mayor could have chosen. In addition, Brezenoff had proved many times over that he had the administrative abilities to keep the city afloat.

The second member of the administration's senior triumvirate was Bob Esnard, a plain-spoken architect of Puerto Rican and Cuban descent. When he was elevated to the rank of deputy mayor, from commissioner of buildings, the *Times*'s "Man in the News" profile bore the headline "Enforcer Moves Up," a reference to Esnard's willingness to go to the mat to enforce building regulations. He sent twenty-eight landlords to jail shortly after he arrived at the department.[55]

The third member of Koch's management team, Alair Townsend, who had been budget director, was "a surprise appointment" to the difficult position of deputy mayor for economic development. She had served as an assistant secretary for management and budget at the Department of Health and Human Services in the Carter administration and was the first economic development deputy mayor to come from government instead of private industry—Koch had previously favored investment bankers, such as Peter J. Solomon and Kenneth Lipper. Townsend took to the business world and eventually became the publisher of *Crain's New York Business*, one of several publications about the financial, fashion, and media worlds that started up in the New York of the 1980s. She too was probably more liberal than Koch. Brezenoff thought of her as "quite a socially conscious person," with whom he often allied on social welfare issues within the administration. Brezenoff, Townsend, and Esnard would preside over a new governmental activism made possible by the city's improved financial condition.[56]

Hoping to dispel the mood of Sisyphean futility, in the spring of 1983 Koch ordered all his principal subordinates to write him memoranda on both general goals for the administration and specific actions that would aid their agencies and jurisdictions.[57] He called a meeting for June 16 to discuss the reports. It was clear that a new direction was needed, as the new corporation counsel, F. A. O. "Fritz" Schwarz (great-grandson of the founder of the famed toy store and not to be confused with his predecessor, Allen G. Schwartz), put it: "You have conquered the fiscal crisis, brought good management to the City, and restored our joie de vivre. These are fantastic contributions—but the voter may begin to say so what else is new."[58]

Some of the most important suggestions included Stan Brezenoff's idea that all city agencies should divest their holdings in companies doing business with South Africa, something already under consideration at the Health and Hospitals Corporation but not something that Koch, more interested in Israel and anticommunism, was ready to pursue. Brezenoff, who was already thought likely to succeed Leventhal as deputy mayor for operations, had enormous prestige, and within the next two years divestment would become a linchpin of Koch's reelection strategy. Instead of tolerating divestment, Brezenoff counseled, the mayor should spearhead it—and then reap the political credit. Brezenoff also suggested another major goal of the administration for the reelection cycle of 1985—housing homeless families. The new city housing program, as released to the public two years later, would not be so explicitly linked to the homeless.[59] Although Brezenoff's suggestions were fundamental to shaping a new liberal direction for the administration, Koch's favorite memo, drafted by Alair Townsend, proposed that the administration concentrate on cost containment (and especially holding labor costs down), long-term planning, economic development, and "improving our image in serving the public."[60]

These goals were not necessarily in conflict with Brezenoff's more traditional liberalism, and Townsend and Brezenoff would cooperate as a kind of liberal axis, shifting Koch away from the his frequent conservative impulses. Liberal empathy and recognition of the need for governmental reform—what Townsend called "improving our image in serving the public"—would be cornerstones of the resurgent Clintonian liberalism of the 1990s, presaged by the Koch administration of the 1980s.

16 LARGER THAN LIFE (1984–85)

The Dow Jones Industrial Average began one of its longest rises in history from late in 1983 until it dropped like a rock in October 1987. In those four years people who had doubted that the economy of the United States could ever be free of stagflation began to recover their confidence. And the boom meant more money to rebuild and to alleviate distress, with lots of loose change left over for the campaigns of politicians like Ed Koch. Koch rode the wave of jubilation brilliantly, emerging as a household name. He became America's Mayor long before the 9/11 attacks propelled Rudolph Giuliani to international fame.

While Koch's failed bid for the governorship had stilled his ambition for higher office, he had not lost his interest in national politics. He wanted to be a kingmaker in the presidential election and to strengthen the probusiness wing of the Democratic Party. The mayor argued that Democratic candidates had to acknowledge that "the panaceas of the 1930s, 1940s, 1950s and 1960s will not work in the 1980s and 1990s."[1] His program anticipated that of the "New Democrats," such as Bill Clinton. Koch, like Clinton, built his appeal on such conservative causes as slashing deficits, promoting the death penalty, and reducing welfare benefits. Koch also constructed a volunteer service program that presaged Clinton's AmeriCorps.[2] The resemblance between Koch and Clinton was more than coincidence. They shared a vision of the Democrats' future, and Clinton's chief pollster was Mark Penn, who began his career with Koch in 1973 and remained one of his key strategists. Both politicians sought to attract the support of the so-called Reagan Democrats—the blue-collar, largely Catholic voters who had jumped ship to the Republican Party in the 1980 election but who had largely returned to vote for a bipartisan Koch in 1981.

Koch's appeal to Catholics was a delicate balancing act. Koch never fully embraced social conservatism. Though he flirted with disapproval of abortion, his support for gay rights never wavered. The mayor cultivated close relations with the Catholic hierarchy, especially John J. O'Connor, and attended his installation as archbishop of New York on March 19, 1984.[3] Koch and O'Connor later traveled together to Rome to attend the archbishop's investiture as a cardinal in 1985. Koch frequently attended mass at St. Patrick's Cathedral, sitting in the front pew, a position noted from the pulpit by O'Connor, who sometimes declared, "I see that Mayor Koch is in place, so let the Mass begin!" Koch's law partner Jim Gill, who was also close to the cardinal, says, "They were like brothers."[4]

When Koch was mayor, he would dine with O'Connor "about six times a year, half at Gracie Mansion, half at the rectory."[5] Because of his own moral certainty, the moral certainties of Catholic doctrine appealed to Koch. The relationship coincided as much with Koch's political habits and history as with his political interests. Fascinated with Catholicism since his army days—the first time he was not surrounded by a predominantly Jewish world—Koch had built his political career on his ability to win over Greenwich Village's Italians and Irish. Koch once asked Gill, a prominent Catholic, why the cardinal stayed so friendly despite their differences on gay rights and abortion, while O'Connor criticized Mario Cuomo and other politicians severely for the same positions. Gill responded that the cardinal had to be tougher on them than on Koch because, the church considered Koch, a non-Catholic, to be "invincibly ignorant"—a reply that made the cardinal laugh uproariously when Gill related it.[6] Friendship did not stop O'Connor from challenging Koch's Executive Order 50, banning discrimination against homosexuals by government contractors, which included Catholic social agencies. The state Court of Appeals eventually overturned Koch's order, on the ground that the power to enact such a ban belonged to the city council, not the mayor. [7]

After 1983 the administration's liberalism increased along with its revenue, part of the brief Reagan-era financial boom. The new cadre of senior leaders nudged city hall slightly to the left. According to early polls in 1983, Koch's reelection was not a foregone conclusion, and by the end of the year his political advisers had plotted a multilayer strategy. The early polling revealed "cracks in his image, some constituencies not as strong, his having his highest ratings among more Republican and Independent voters." White working-class voters who had swung to Ronald Reagan, the so-called Reagan Democrats, were also key. They might have been expected to be more conservative, but in a local context theirs was not small-government conservatism. They principally desired improved city services. In addition, New York was becoming more black and Hispanic, and minority voters might unite around a credible black candidate, such as Basil Paterson. Caulking the cracks in the Koch coalition took considerable money, effort, and acumen.[8]

While campaign staff and consultants spent much of 1984 and 1985 working on the more technical aspects of the campaign, such as mailing and polling, Brezenoff and Garth were positioning Koch for the race. Part of the problem was that Koch, because of his outspoken nature, often sounded more like a critic of the government than the guy who was running it. But as Brezenoff pointed out, "at some point the government becomes yours, sort of, unless you're really good at maintaining not only a sense of outrage, which Ed really was quite good at, but at helping the public to understand what can be changed, what can't be changed, what constitutes change."[9]

David Garth's publicly advised Koch to run a sober campaign on his record (likely Garth's private advice, too). Mayoral advisers tried to make Koch look more governmental, reviving a discarded tradition of giving an annual "State of the City" speech. In January 1984 he delivered mostly good news, as New York was coming out of the Reagan recession faster than many other places, but the speech was uncharacteristically colorless, and some found it boring. Full of statistics designed to demonstrate that New Yorkers were better off than they were when Koch took office, the speech employed unabashedly neoliberal rhetoric. Business tax cuts and downtown development were Koch's campaign kickoff priorities, and continuing fiscal austerity meant that despite an improving revenue stream, Koch could not return the size of the police force or number of street cleaners to precrisis levels.[10]

Koch did not ignore liberal causes altogether. New York's restored credit, the raison d'être of the austerity regime, would be used to rebuild crumbling infrastructure and increase employment. But Koch did not mention social justice until the very end of his speech, when he demanded more state money from Governor Cuomo to house the homeless. Toward the end of the speech Koch added a few paragraphs to dispel the view that had emerged in some polls and focus groups, that he had become a conservative Republican or a neocon. He attacked the Reagan administration for "sacrificing domestic stability on the altar of national defense" and declared that "New York has always been a haven for the poor—our harbor beckoned them, our residents embraced them, our government and social agencies fed and clothed them. *We have and will continue to maintain these traditions*" (the emphasis was Koch's). He went on to call for a fight against discrimination and greater opportunities for minorities and the unemployed, sounding quite like a traditional New Deal Democrat.[11]

Although 1984 was a presidential election year, Koch made as big a splash in the national news as any of the candidates for the Democratic nomination. "He's overexposed," Garth observed a year later while launching a series of television commercials that showed other people commenting on Koch but did not picture the mayor himself. Beneath the talking heads ran the pedestrian slogan "Ed Koch Works for All New Yorkers."[12] Koch may have followed Garth's advice to play it straight during the "State of the City" address, but the mayor's next big move turned into a public relations coup beyond anyone's expectations. He had long been dubious about Garth's low-key strategy, which he was convinced had lost him the governorship.[13]

KOCH WRITES A LOVE STORY

In the winter of 1984, with the presidential campaign season underway, Koch opted for theatricality over message discipline by publishing a memoir that redefined chutzpah. His friend and adviser Dan Wolf described *Mayor: An Autobiography* as "the best love story since *Tristan and Isolde,* only Ed Koch plays both parts."[14] Despite harboring literary ambitions since his rival Bella Abzug published her memoir in the early 1970s, Koch could never interest a publisher in a book about his days in Congress. No one anticipated *Mayor*'s popularity—within three weeks of its release it had hit the *New York Times* best-seller list and stayed there for twenty-one weeks, vying to retain first place with *The March of Folly* by Barbara Tuchman. *Motherhood: The Oldest Profession,* by the humorist Erma Bombeck, ultimately displaced *Mayor* on the list. Koch reported on his tax return that he earned $136,587 in royalties from it in 1984.[15]

Why did this book enjoy so much more success than, say, Mario Cuomo's *Campaign Diaries,* published a few months later? For one thing, Cuomo's book is detailed and deadly serious. Koch's memoir is little more than a string of insults and anecdotes, and he makes no effort to impress his reader as a literary stylist—in his days as a lawyer, he said, he always hated writing. Koch on the printed page sounds like Koch talking into a tape recorder, which is exactly what it was. The mayor entertained and piqued readers by creating a comically inflated persona, a bit like a Macy's

Thanksgiving Day balloon, and he was playing the dangerous game of hurling sharp arrows at his enemies. Both inspired and appalling, his creation was reminiscent of Warren Beatty's Senator Bullworth—constitutionally incapable of normal political dissimilation or even manners. The book was controversial because Koch revealed private conversations unflattering to friend and foe alike. Americans are always starved for politicians who have not been homogenized by consultants. City hall reporter Sam Roberts succinctly catalogued the injured parties: "Mr. Koch writes that he made Mr. Carter turn gray, Representative Charles Rangel sweat, former Deputy Mayor Herman Badillo twitch. The Mayor says he even made two people cry."[16] His targets and betrayed allies included former secretary of state Cyrus Vance, who told Koch that Carter would "sell out" Israel after the 1980 election, according to *Mayor*. *New York Times* columnist William Safire complained that Koch gave him the story about Vance and Carter shortly after it occurred, then told him not to run it. Safire, sounding a little like Koch himself, called the mayor "the Soupy Sellout."

Koch also railed against Basil Paterson, whom Koch claimed failed to defend him from anti-Semitic jibes hurled at the mayor in a Harlem church. (Paterson's version of this story differed, as did newspaper accounts at the time.) Even as readers flocked to buy the book, critics had so much fun panning its self-absorption that they probably helped its sales. Koch "so exuberantly labels other people wackos that it is tempting to think that he is one," wrote the conservative columnist George Will, who claimed that the mayor "gave candor a bad name."[17]

Not everyone thought that Koch was quite as honest and guileless as the book made him out to be. Bella Abzug, for example, claimed that Koch falsely accused her of failing to support the sale of jets to Israel. Koch, in response, pointed to journalist Jack Newfield's admission in print that he had heard her say that she opposed the sale and that Newfield had initially suppressed the statement to protect her.[10] Abzug also argued that "Koch's pose of candor in his book *Mayor* is fraudulent" and produced details and witnesses to corroborate her claim that she had been maligned.

Koch's new celebrity transcended genre and medium. In the 1985 Ricky Skaggs video *Country Boy*, shot in Times Square, Koch plays alongside Skaggs and bluegrass icon Bill Monroe as a bagel-eating, sheepskin-clad New York taxi driver who reveals that, deep down, he is a country boy, too. Perhaps the casting was prompted by photos of Koch in cowboy hat and boots while on a speaking engagement in Houston. The video, the second music video shown on the brand new cable channel VH1, gained instant fame. Koch's celebrity was popping so fast, he even made it into the comic books, shown calling Governor Cuomo for national guard troops to deal with the depredations of the Incredible Hulk, a bizarre reflection of Koch's call for such troops as a candidate during the 1977 blackout and riots.[19]

The year after *Mayor* was published, Koch convinced Charles Strouse, whose works included the musical *Annie,* to do an election-year musical based on Koch's autobiography. He hoped to outdo La Guardia—the musical *Fiorello!* was staged in

1959 after its subject had been dead for fourteen years. *Fiorello!* won a Pulitzer and tied *The Sound of Music* for four Tonys. *Mayor,* an off-Broadway cabaret show, won no awards but proved durable enough to reissue on CD in 2001, sixteen years after the show closed.

Strouse insisted that the work could not lionize the mayor, and Koch agreed. "We won't show Ed Koch taking money from builders and putting it in his pockets. But we will show him at dinner with the builders," Strouse explained. Koch did not have any direct participation in the script. Instead, the writer and actors spent time with Koch and many of the pols portrayed in the book, including Carol Bellamy, Victor Gotbaum, and Herman D. "Denny" Farrell, a state assembly member. Jay Goldin, then New York City's comptroller, approached Strouse after he heard that the composer was talking to other politicians to get material. The result was the song "I Want to Be the Mayor"—a wicked send-up of Goldin's frustrated ambition—complete with a scene in which Goldin signs a pact with the devil and still can't get elected mayor of New York.[20]

Some of the other numbers included "Hootspa," the "March of the Yuppies," and "What You See Is What You Get," a reference to Koch's claim that he said say the same things and held the same opinions in private as in public. *New York Times* critic Frank Rich thought the show "will offend no one (with the possible exceptions of Harry and Leona Helmsley the comic villains)."[21] One song, "How'm I doin'?" still resonates, because it cuts to the central dilemma of Koch's neoliberalism. In a nightmare patterned on Dickens's *A Christmas Carol,* the ghost of Fiorello La Guardia dresses down a Scrooge-like Koch and, referring to his State of the City message, tells him that statistics don't make a city great nor do the rich—"It's the people that count." The nightmare makes the character "Koch" recant his neoliberalism and return to the old-time liberalism of the La Guardia era.[22]

KOCH TO JACKSON: DROP OUT!

Koch provided enough showmanship that, for New Yorkers, the dreariness of the 1984 campaign for the Democratic presidential nomination was almost relegated to the background. Koch belatedly endorsed Walter Mondale in his contest with Gary Hart, whom Koch perceived as the weaker supporter of Israel.[23] Soon after, Mondale hired Garth to do his New York ads, which helped cement Mondale's relationship with the mayor, who also gained from his support for Geraldine Ferraro, the eventual vice-presidential nominee.[24]

While Koch attracted lots of attention, it did not always bring applause. He fought with Jesse Jackson about Middle East issues just as Koch's reelection campaign was seeking African American votes. Jackson's ties to Arab leaders offended Koch. The civil rights leader had called for an independent Palestinian state and pushed for changes in U.S. policy toward Israel and for opening contacts with the Palestine Liberation Organization. Most alarming to Koch was Jackson's insistent questioning of whether continued support for Israel was in America's national interest.[25]

A scandal erupted when Milton Coleman, an African American reporter for the *Washington Post*, reported that he had heard Jackson, who was seeking the Democratic presidential nomination, refer to Jews as "Hymies" and New York City as "Hymietown" in a private conversation. Jackson, after an initial denial, later acknowledged Coleman's report to be true.[26] Louis Farrakhan, the Black Muslim leader, allegedly threatened Coleman's life, and while Jackson condemned the threat, he refused to repudiate Farrakhan as a supporter.[27] Indeed, Jackson tried to mediate between reporter and minister, claiming that they were ""two very able professionals caught in a cycle that could be damaging to their careers."[28] Walter Mondale and Gary Hart both came down hard on Jackson in debates.[29] After Farrakhan called Hitler a "great man," Koch declared that the presence of Farrakhan on Jackson's bandwagon "was an issue of fundamental integrity that has cast a chilling shadow across the 1984 campaign" and called for Jackson to drop out of the race if he would not repudiate Farrakhan.[30]

As the presidential campaign continued, Koch went out of his way to savage the first major black presidential candidate. Speculating about to why Jackson would not drop Farrakhan from his campaign, Koch told a television audience, "I believe that Farrakhan knows something about Jackson. You know what I think he knows? I think he knows where Jesse Jackson's money has come from. I think it comes from Libya." Operation PUSH, Jackson's community organizing operation, did receive $200,000 from the Arab League and $350,000 from an anonymous donor.[31] According to the *Washington Post*, Jackson acknowledged receiving a $10,000 contribution to Operation PUSH from the Libyan chargé d'affaires Ali Houderi in December 1979. The contribution triggered a preliminary inquiry by the Department of Justice, to determine whether Jackson had failed to register as a foreign agent, but the department took no further action.[32]

Koch decided to confront the problem of his relationship with the black community head-on. *Amsterdam News* editor Wilbert Tatum was "surprised as hell" when Mayor Koch offered to debate him on television, after the paper ran an editorial repudiating Farrakhan headlined "Who Will Repudiate Koch?" The debate reprised a rivalry from 1964 when Tatum debated Koch for hours at the Village Independent Democrats about a civil rights resolution that Koch thought was too radical (see chapter 5).[33]

Charges and countercharges filled the air, with Tatum making reference to the segregationist Alabama governor George Wallace, and Koch charging that "some black leaders are using Jews as scapegoats." Koch, much like his caricature in the musical *Mayor!* dropped blizzards of memorized statistics to support his contention that he'd improved health care in Harlem despite the closing of Sydenham Hospital, appointed more minorities than any other mayor, and eased black unemployment. Tatum, recalling a line of Ronald Reagan's, replied, "There you go again with figures, Ed." "Don't smear," Koch rejoined, later asking, "Tell me where I've been unfair." Tatum replied, "Mr. Mayor, your book is outrageous," additionally citing his criticism of black officials as "poverty pimps," rhetoric that Tatum thought just as inflammatory as Farrakhan's.[34]

The presidential primary results contained some potentially bad news for Koch's reelection campaign. While Mondale had won the primary, Jackson had unified the black vote. He managed to get a stunning 34 percent of the vote citywide and 26 percent of the statewide vote, far more than expected, and only one point behind second-place finisher Gary Hart. Democratic representative Major R. Owens predicted that the opposition to Koch would "go into the 1985 mayoral race with at least 300,000 black voters. With a candidate with a rainbow appeal, we are confident we can win." But Jackson got only 7 percent of the white vote in the city, suggesting that he had alienated even most liberal Jews.[35]

Koch was favored for reelection by 51 percent of Democrats in the presidential primary exit polls, with only 36 percent saying that they were definitely against the mayor. But because the number of black voters was increasing, the primary exit poll showed that Koch's support among blacks had slipped to 17 percent, a little more than half the black support that he had gotten in 1981. A black candidate who was unimpeachably pro-Israel and anti-Farrakhan might be able to build on Jackson's 7 percent of New York's white voters.[36]

While, as David Garth observed, it was "a little bit premature to read Koch's death knell," the primary results suggested that a black moderate, such as former deputy mayor Basil Paterson, might be able to build a coalition of white liberals and unseat the incumbent mayor, much as Harold Washington had in Chicago.[37] And Koch now had to share the national political stage with a fellow New Yorker. His long-time rival Mario Cuomo had stunned the nation with a brilliant keynote address at the 1984 Democratic National Convention. The speech made Cuomo a potential president or Supreme Court justice, a level of politics that Koch would never reach.

WHAT INSENSITIVITY?

Once the convention was out of the way, the mayoral election topped the agenda of New York's politicians. After a successful fund-raiser and enhanced prospects in the wake of Jackson's primary showing, Paterson pulled out of the race because of a heart condition, though unfavorable polls may have played a role in his decision. This left the fractious black leadership without a candidate that both Brooklyn and Manhattan could agree on, indeed without any candidate of Paterson's stature.[38]

Nor could they unite behind a white liberal candidate, such as city council president Carol Bellamy. Instead, the Harlem leaders did their utmost to undercut her and help Koch by running Herman D. "Denny" Farrell, who, as New York County (Manhattan) Democratic chair and a member of the state assembly, was well known among politicians but unknown to the general public. With both in the race, neither candidate could hope to win, even if they could catch up to Koch's daunting media and financial advantages among city elites: by January the Koch campaign had taken in $2.8 million as opposed to only $147,323 for Paterson.[39] Bellamy came off as wonky. She disparaged Koch's theatricality but went too far in the other direction. Much of her campaign centered on learned, detailed policy papers that bored people outside the government. Bellamy later said that she "would have liked to have been perceived as more positive in recommending rather than complaining."[40]

Though Bellamy had plenty to criticize in a city that was still ridden with dirt and crime, she was never able to get traction because her detailed policy prescriptions sounded pettifogging in a city hungry for heroics. Koch, in contrast, managed to combine a formidable command of policy with a sense of fun.

As the election year of 1985 began, Koch still played primarily to white voters by reversing his stand and endorsing a grand jury's decision to decline homicide charges for subway vigilante Bernhard Goetz, who had shot and wounded four African American men who he claimed had threatened him on a train. And he defended the grand jury's decision not to indict the police officer who killed Eleanor Bumpurs, an emotionally disturbed woman who was being evicted from her apartment (see chapter 22).[41] Then, for fiscal reasons, Koch opposed making Martin Luther King Day a city holiday, though he favored it as a federal holiday. From Koch's perspective he was saving $17 million a year, the cost of a paid holiday, and continuing his program to get higher productivity. But the decision made him look like he was in league with racist conservatives who opposed the King holiday because they abhorred the civil rights movement. When Bellamy in protest told her staff to observe the holiday, Koch vindictively pursued her with a bill for several thousand dollars for the lost staff time as she was leaving office after losing the mayoral primary. Even the *Times* thought he was being outrageously nasty.[42]

Koch tried to back away from the charge that he was divisive. In a *Times* op-ed entitled "What Insensitivity to Minority Concerns?" Koch, who had done so much finger-pointing at black anti-Semitism, tried to refocus the debate "on the tension between blacks and whites" and called for President Reagan to appoint a commission on racism in American society to update the findings of the Kerner Commission, which had been an important motivation for John V. Lindsay's liberal policies. Koch also pressed his commissioners to find ways to hire and promote more minorities without using quotas, which he vehemently opposed, pointing to an initiative by the sanitation commissioner, Norman Steisel. Steisel had "found a way to make supervisory positions more available to minority personnel in his department 'by eliminating the traditional seniority requirements and allowing all sanitation workers, regardless of their time on the job, to file for the exam."[43]

Despite these shifts, Jim Harding, Koch's hard-working assistant for minority affairs, warned in the first months of Koch's third term that "there is perception in the community, that qualified Blacks are being overlooked for the top level positions that have become vacant recently in this administration. . . . It would be quite a shame if all our gains are withered away because of this perception." Later Harding claimed that since the beginning of Ed Koch's mayoralty, overall minority employment by the city had increased by 70 percent.[44]

At the beginning of his campaign, despite the advantages of money and a divided opposition, Koch was still vulnerable. He had been denied the Republican line because Kings County party chair George Clark believed that Koch had broken a personal promise to him, made when he received the Republican nod in 1981, by running for governor, though Koch denied that he had made that commitment. The Liberals were divided, and eventually the courts awarded Carol Bellamy their ballot line. So Koch had to win the Democratic primary. A January newspaper poll showed that Democrats favored his reelection by only 52 percent to 40 percent (compared with 68 percent to 31 percent among the city's relatively few Republicans). The encouraging number was that Koch still retained the support of 31 percent of blacks, down only a tad from 1981.[45] Koch could expect to mine the black community for tens of thousands of voters who were weakly committed to his opponents. With a budget more flush with cash, Koch was able to consider new programs. He tacked to the left once again and pulled together a domestic and a foreign policy initiative calculated to appeal to blacks and liberals.

A mayor running for a third term cannot just promise more of the same, so Koch made two bold moves. He proposed a $4.4 billion, five-year housing program to build or renovate 100,000 apartments and to double the size of the housing program, all with clever leveraging of city and state money.[46] The mayor tended to be reactive, responding with pragmatism to daily crises, but the housing program was atypically strategic (see chapter 18). The other switch came in the field of international relations. Koch discovered the movement to divest government and corporate investments in South Africa. While Koch had always opposed apartheid, he had not previously supported divestment.[47] Koch waffled on South Africa issues until 1984, after his increasingly strong denunciations of presidential candidate Jesse Jackson had significantly sharpened racial tensions. During the 1984 presidential campaign Koch had criticized Jackson for taking contributions from the Arab League for Operation PUSH. At the time Koch said it would be equally unacceptable had Jackson's rival for the nomination, Vice President Walter Mondale, taken money from South Africans. Dumisani Kumalo, project director of the American Committee on Africa, an organization promoting the economic boycott of South Africa, then disclosed that Koch had taken a $2,000 campaign contribution from Baskin and Sears, a Washington law firm that Kumalo termed the apartheid government's "chief lobbyist." Koch, who was very hard to embarrass, stoutly refused to return the money, maintaining that it was defensible because he took money from a legitimate law firm, not from the government of South Africa itself. New York governor Mario Cuomo took a similar position.[48] Around that time Koch also declared that he would not favor an international economic boycott of South Africa by Western democracies and their allies unless they also boycotted the Soviet Union, Iran, Libya, and Syria.[49]

Two months later Koch reversed his position and named a panel to study how to sever New York's relations with companies that traded with South Africa. Political pressures forced the change. He made the announcement the day mayoral rivals Bellamy and Goldin, both trustees of New York's employee pension fund, announced a much more sweeping plan. Bellamy and Goldin, along with a controlling faction of the trustees of the multibillion-dollar fund, called for divestiture of all South Africa–related stocks within five years, "except for those firms which meet a strict standard of active opposition to apartheid."[50] Koch probably judged the political fallout from opposing divestment could harm his reelection chances. The *New York Times*'s editorial board commented that "it's hard to avoid a wan smile over New York's City Hall auction of the high ground from which to denounce such racism."[51]

That view may be accurate, but it is too limited. Koch also finally realized that the Reagan administration's policy of "constructive engagement" with the Afrikaner nationalist government was on the wrong side of history.[52] The panel Koch assembled to study New York's ties to South Africa, consisting of high-level administration officials, reported in mid-July and called for divestment of pension fund investments in some companies doing business in South Africa, estimated at $2 billion of the $23 billion in assets held by New York City's five pension funds. The committee also called for modification of city contracting practices to ban purchases from South Africa, and from some companies doing business there, and to "'look for other ways to express solidarity' with black South Africans who were trying to end Pretoria's policy of apartheid."[53] Koch endorsed its recommendations. Characteristically, he used his power over public space to demonstrate the new policy, renaming the corner in front of the South African mission to the UN at Forty-second Street and Second Avenue after Nelson and Winnie Mandela.

Koch jumped into the antiapartheid fight with energy, and he reaped the benefits of national publicity in photo opportunities with Coretta Scott King, Andrew Young, Jesse Jackson, and other black leaders before his 1985 run for reelection against Bellamy and Denny Farrell, an African American. Divestment is one of the clearest cases in which Koch used municipal foreign policy to further his own cause with New York voters, in this case African Americans and liberals. In August 1985 the city council passed Local Law 19, which, among other provisions, prohibited the city from depositing money with banks if they sold Krugerrands, underwrote South African government securities, or made most types of loans to the South African government. Municipal divestment had a quick effect: companies, including banks, took the boycott legislation "very seriously," wrote city housing commissioner Paul Crotty in an internal memo to the mayor's office.[54]

Although economists dispute the effectiveness of South Africa divestment, New York's decision spurred twenty-eight other municipalities and the state of Maryland to follow suit. The boycott forced numerous companies to reassess their links to South Africa. AT&T, Bell and Howell, and General Electric withdrew in early 1986, in response to a new wave of municipal laws, including one in New York City that would have cost them millions in sales by prohibiting city agencies to purchase goods from companies doing business in South Africa.[55]

Koch continued these efforts to stop apartheid even after he overwhelmingly defeated his opponents in the September 10, 1985, primary, working with Dr. Benjamin Hooks, executive director of the NAACP, to organize a "national day of mourning" for South Africa. Then Koch almost blew it all with a cranky outburst of anticommunism when invited to a UN panel on apartheid. Questioned by Soviet and Bulgarian members of the panel about what the United States and New York were doing to end apartheid, he responded by denouncing the Soviet Union for being "as bad as South Africa" and Bulgaria for mistreatment of ethnic Turks within its borders. Such self-indulgence received unfavorable press as far away as Australia. He seemed to have abandoned the idea of a broad front against the South African regime.[56]

The mayoral campaign of 1985 was something of an anticlimax. Koch kicked it off with the warmest of optimism, justified by the first solid recovery of the U.S. economy in fifteen years: "The rosy glow on the horizon is real," he declared.[57] While Basil Paterson had been a real threat, Bellamy and Farrell were not. The game had changed from consolidating Koch's white base to obtaining a "mandate" with the largest majority possible, including as large a slice of the minority vote as Koch could manage. While earlier campaigns had followed Garth in declaring television the primary medium of campaigns, leaving field operations to a shoestring, Koch had enough money in 1985 for closely targeted mail operations. He had already used these to promote white registration to offset the increase in black registration. Two computer technologies were key—the computerization of voter lists and the novel use of the first laser printers, which produced mail that looked personalized, in contrast to the block letters of old-style computer printouts.

This proved critical, according to campaign consultant Mark Penn: "We used these techniques of writing to people. Setting up direct communications between Koch and people in the city. Doing Italian things in Italian," as well as using the copious campaign treasury to set up a more traditional New York block-by-block and building-by-building organization. Penn remembered that he "got into a cab one day, and a cabdriver started telling me about the mail he got from Ed Koch. It's not that often that people start telling me about the mail they got. . . . We did it up in a very expensive-looking way. But at that time personalized mail like that was just totally new."[58]

Bellamy and Farrell could not get traction, though they tried hitting Koch for his ties to real estate and big business—unimpressive in the middle of the Reagan-era boom, a time when big business was reasserting itself ideologically. Bellamy charged that the Koch administration was "outrageous and immoral" and had put the government up "for sale" to developers, which might have been a stronger message at another time. In the ebullient environment of 1985, Koch shrugged her off, pointing out that in previous campaigns Bellamy had accepted contributions from some of the same developers, though he had by that point raised a total of $6 million to Bellamy's $615,000.[59]

Koch expanded his sophisticated, well-financed field and mail operations to the black community and spotlighted his effort to get as many black votes as possible. His going over the head of black leaders underlined the notion that the malice dividing New York did not emanate from Koch, or from the average black voter, but from the black political elites that he sought to short-circuit. "The basic concept was, if the black vote is going to be the most difficult for him, you make a conscious effort to go after it rather than go away from it," David Garth explained.[60] Forty percent of the Koch television commercials had a predominantly "black emphasis," according to Garth, who noted that "it used to be a general fear that if you put blacks in commercials, it was going to cost you a certain amount of white support. I think those days have passed. I think there's been general acceptance. The highest-rated TV show is Bill Cosby, O.K.?"[61]

Koch, who had sewn up most other voters, except for a few white liberals on the Upper West Side and the Village, had nowhere to go but up with the black vote. Koch made numerous appearances in black areas, where he risked getting booed but generally was not. Koch campaign money and patronage began to flow into black and Hispanic neighborhoods as the campaign opened storefront offices in neighborhoods that had seen no citywide mayoral campaign with a permanent presence for decades. The campaign sometimes worked with local leaders whom the mayor had previously denounced. "Poverticians make good campaign workers," remarked the columnist Sydney Schanberg, noting that Bronx Democratic chair Stanley Friedman had brought the much-denounced Ramon Velez, who had received $200,000 in salaries from various antipoverty programs, back into the Koch fold.[62] Campaign aides estimated that they spent about a quarter of their field operation money in minority neighborhoods.

By August Koch's reelection was so inevitable that even Mario Cuomo virtually endorsed him for reelection. Koch's primary victory was overwhelming: 63.3 percent of the primary vote. And that included substantial minority support—41 percent of the black vote and 62.4 percent of the Latino vote. Among white Catholics,

Koch earned a solid 69.3 percent margin and a runaway 77.6 percent of outer-borough Jews, the largest voting group. He carried all but four of sixty assembly districts, Farrell won his own district and two other black districts; Bellamy carried only the liberal Sixty-ninth Assembly District, which included Morningside Heights and parts of the Upper West Side. Koch's reelection appeared assured.[63]

The ensuing general election campaign against Bellamy; Republican candidate Diane McGrath, a minor patronage employee; and the Right-to-Life candidate, Rabbi Lew Y. Levin, was a farce, though Koch took seriously the need to build the biggest majority possible. Its only enduring image was a major Catholic Charities fund-raiser just before the election, where Koch sat at the top of a five-tiered dais, and McGrath sat at table 218. Koch got 78 percent of the scant turnout of 1.1 million; his nearest opponent, Bellamy, running on the Liberal line, got 10 percent. McGrath came in third with 9 percent.[64] Hours later Koch reiterated his call for a business tax cut, but he also began to spend money on education, housing, and infrastructure.[65] But just as things were looking up, Koch had to confront several severe new problems: homelessness that had become far more widespread, the AIDS epidemic, and the emergence of crack, a new highly addictive form of cocaine that spawned a culture of crime and violence.

Louis and Joyce Silpe Koch, Ed Koch's parents, in the 1940s.

Sergeant Koch returns from Germany, 1946.

Koch at age thirty-two, relaxing with friends on Fire Island, July 1956.
LA GUARDIA AND WAGNER ARCHIVES

Mayor Robert F. Wagner has a friendly drink with former Democratic party leader Carmine De Sapio, October 11, 1963. De Sapio had just been narrowly defeated by Ed Koch and would try for a comeback, to no avail.
LA GUARDIA AND WAGNER ARCHIVES, WAGNER COLLECTION

New York Representatives Shirley Chisholm and Edward I. Koch demonstrate against the Vietnam War on the Capitol steps with the Quaker Action Group during its weekly Wednesday vigil on June 18, 1969. Capitol Police routinely arrested the demonstrators (though not Koch and Chisholm). . Koch protested the arrests to Speaker John W. McCormack, who took no action, but a court ruled the protests legal the next day.
J. B. SINGLETON

Ed Koch and Bella Abzug at a hearing in 1974. Although his voting record was similar to Abzug's, Koch identified himself as a "liberal with sanity," implying that Abzug had none. Abzug hated Koch so much that she would not allow aides to mention his name in her presence.
RONAY MENSCHEL

Koch campaigning during his 1977 mayoral race.

©HARVEY WANG

A happy warrior on the mayoral campaign trail, 1977.
©HARVEY WANG

Ed Koch wins the runoff for the Democratic mayoral nomination, September 19, 1977. Bess
Myerson and David Garth are at his right.
©JEROME LIEBLING

The condo building once known as Harlem's Sydenham Hospital, 2009. In 1980 protesters occupied Sydenham, demanding that Koch keep it open. Koch's intransigence on the issue damaged his relationships with African American leaders. The hospital became a condominium complex, and Columbia University operates a clinic in the basement, formerly the hospital's morgue.
JONATHAN SOFFER

Mayor Koch talks to skeptical constituents on Merrick Boulevard in Queens, September 26, 1983, a week after Representative John Conyers held public hearings that detailed abuses by New York police against African Americans.

DAILY NEWS/ANTHONY PESCATORE

Mayor Ed Koch dressed as a matador with Twiggy (left) and Tommy Tune (right) and the cast of the Broadway musical *My One and Only* during the Inner Circle performance at the Hilton, late April 1984. Koch, one of the most theatrical politicians in the country, initially balked at the hat but decided that "the likelihood is that I will be perceived, as I hope it will be, as going along with an outrageous joke."

DAILY NEWS/WILLIE ANDERSON

A Hasidic Jew blocks Mayor Koch's limousine in protest against Koch's support of gay rights, May 5, 1985. A bill prohibiting discrimination based on sexual orientation passed the city council the following year.
DAILY NEWS/ANTHONY PESCATORE

LEFT PAGE

As the Incredible Hulk ravages New York, Mayor Koch telephones Governor Mario Cuomo, requesting that he call out the National Guard. Originally published in 1984 at the height of Koch's national celebrity, the cartoon recalls Koch's demand that Mayor Beame call out the guard to stop looting during 1977 blackout. While Beame ignored him, his showy demand set him apart as a "law and order candidate" (see page 245).
PERMISSION OF MARVEL COMICS

Civil rights protesters in Bensonhurst, September 17, 1989, after Yusuf Hawkins was murdered by a gang of white teens. Koch, who had already been defeated for reelection, angered
the Reverend Al Sharpton and other activists by pleading with them not to march because of
the potential for riots. Sharpton countered that African Americans had to assert their right to
travel in any neighborhood in New York. The tense demonstrations continued for months, and
there were no riots.

DAILY NEWS/DENNIS CARUSO

The funeral of Yusuf K. Hawkins, a young African American who was murdered in Benson-hurst, Brooklyn, where he had gone to shop for a used car. He was slain just days before the 1989 mayoral primary between Ed Koch and David Dinkins. The funeral was held on September 30, after Dinkins won.

Squatters demonstrate in December 1989 for their right to live in Tompkins Square Park. A year earlier police violently evicted them from the park, igniting a riot and heightening tensions between gentrifiers and the Lower East Side counterculture.

Koch appalled many of his friends by endorsing President George W. Bush for reelection and then by speaking at the Republican National Convention held in New York in 2004.

17

A NEW SPATIAL ORDER

Gentrification, the Parks, Times Square

The Koch administration created a new spatial order for New York City in the 1980s by promoting gentrification and privatizing public space, the latter accomplished through the creation of private groups that raised money and ultimately took over management of significant parts of the park system. A controversial system of tax incentives encouraged office building construction and subsidized big companies to keep their headquarters in Manhattan. City hall also carried out redevelopment of seamy areas of the city, notably Times Square, in an effort to attract tourists and improve those spaces for residents. While each of these initiatives had drawbacks, as well as promised advantages, Koch's policies set the pattern for such development policies for a generation.

GENTRIFICATION OR RENAISSANCE?

"People often snicker when they hear of it. A renaissance in New York City? The rich moving in and the poor moving out? The mind boggles at the very notion," wrote Blake Fleetwood in the *New York Times Magazine* in 1979, at the end of Koch's first year as mayor.[1] Fleetwood's incredulity now seems quaint. Koch had made gentrification one of his primary goals, announcing it in his first inaugural speech. New York City today, with its high housing prices, increasingly scarce vacant land and buildings, and its newly chic outer-borough neighborhoods, is in large part the result of economic development strategies that his administration created and put in place three decades ago. These policies continued to bear fruit as they were maintained by subsequent administrations.[2]

Although the term *gentrification* dates to the 1960s, when the British sociologist Ruth Glass noted the movement of upper-middle-class professionals into working-class neighborhoods in central London, the word did not really enter the popular American lexicon until 1978.[3] The geographer Neil Smith defines gentrification as the "process . . . by which poor and working-class neighborhoods are refurbished via an influx of private capital and middle-class homebuyers and renters—neighborhoods that had previously experienced disinvestment and a middle-class exodus." While many on the left blame the inmigration of an urban gentry for causing dislocation, homelessness, and increased poverty, few go so far as to call gentrification revanchist, as Smith does, seeing it as the political revenge of the "haves" against the "have-nots."[4]

Koch saw gentrification as a way to revitalize the city by taking advantage of economic forces much larger than the city government. Chief among them was the emergence of New York as an information economy and as a world city that functioned as a node within the global economy. The old working-class New York of Koch's youth—the New York of small unionized industry, of social democratic aspiration—was never coming back, and its demise could not be resisted. "If we try, we will be fighting against forces that are so profound we will be doomed to fail," observed Robert F. Wagner Jr., one of the main intellectual forces behind Koch's development policy.[5] Only the reinvention of the city within the context of the new neoliberal global economy could save it, Wagner believed. Subsidies for the upgrading of tenements to luxury housing; expansion of services to gentrified neighborhoods; tax abatements for downtown office expansion; promotion of tourism; and the "rebranding" of the city as both exciting and safe encouraged the concentration of specialized financial and legal services in the city. The Koch administration rode, and encouraged, the trend of expanding specialized services, making it part of its strategy to create a gentrified world city.[6]

Though Koch and his administration tried hard to stimulate gentrification, they did not invent or even initiate it. Indeed, New York had seen an increase in gentrification in the late 1970s despite the budget crisis and the recession. The vacancy rate for rental apartments fell 30 percent, from 2.95 percent to 2.15 percent, between 1978 and 1981. Only forty-two thousand of New York's 1.9 million apartments became available, and lower-priced apartments were even scarcer, with a vacancy rate below 2 percent. At the same time the median rent rose 26 percent.[7] This made it very difficult for even stable middle-class families to find an affordable place to live in New York. Then some landlords used tax breaks to convert flophouses into luxury housing, making finding a place to live extremely difficult for all but the wealthy. Housing for people with problems—alcoholism, drug dependence, or mental health problems—became all but nonexistent. Some of the poorest and most vulnerable residents of the city were undoubtedly hurt by the drive toward gentrification. For those living in single-room-occupancy hotels (SROs) in particular, Koch's policies may have seemed draconian. Thousands lost their rooms or apartments because of the city's tax policies of the late 1970s (see chapter 18).

Gentrification can be lucrative and seductive, if you have the money to participate. While Realtors were fond of the phrase "urban renaissance," buyers used the rhetoric of the Wild West frontier. Self-styled pioneers braved the dirt and crime of rundown neighborhoods where, in the early 1980s, they could buy as much as five thousand square feet in a dilapidated brownstone for as little as $25,000. Repairing fixer-uppers had its rewards: new owners watched prices quintuple as people like them, and then even wealthier people, moved in. By 1981 Park Slope, a Brooklyn neighborhood where gentrification had already begun by the early 1970s, was no longer a quarter of toughs and welfare recipients coexisting with hippie co-ops. The *New York Times* reported that "laundromats and grocery stores have been displaced by boutiques, parking spaces are suddenly hard to find. . . . The buzz word for the latest arrivals is 'lawyers from Manhattan.'"[8] Eventually, the housing market globalized. Park Slope, which also is home to a movie studio, would be filmed and displayed all over the world. By the late 1990s a cocktail party guest in Istanbul might discuss the host's plan to buy a condo in Park Slope, citing the neighborhood by name.

One of the most spectacular metamorphoses came on Manhattan's Upper West Side. Back in the late 1970s, when Koch took office, the area was hardly the priciest neighborhood in New York, although it was one of the most liberal and diverse. One of its thoroughfares, Columbus Avenue, was among the first to see gentrification. Historically, Columbus Avenue was the slum behind Central Park West that servants and carriage horses called home, "a street of simple neighborhood service shops, side-street rooming houses and occasional pockets of crime."[9] By 1979 it had become the a playground of yuppies in their twenties and thirties, a place for strolling past boutiques and eating places with names like Sedutto, Mythology, Non Sequitur, Jezebel, and Genghis Khan's Bicycle.[10] This veneer of exoticism reflected the acceleration of globalization and had the tasty effect of adding to the city's already dizzying choice of ethnic eateries. Koch promoted the hundreds of restaurants that sprang up by eating in every one—or so it seemed in those years, when it was impossible to grab a bite anywhere without seeing his photo in the window, smiling broadly, with the owner under his arm.

During the 1970s and 1980s New York, London, and Tokyo became the three main nodes of information, analysis, and coordination for the global economy. Despite advances in electronic communication, which were expected to decentralize business, world cities generated jobs in specialized financial and legal services. To staff their expanding media, world cities also required armies of writers, editors, artists, filmmakers, photographers, and other highly skilled information professionals. All these professionals often worked long irregular hours, which created myriad service jobs, from dog walkers to waiters to housecleaners, often low paid and offering little chance for advancement.[11] Some analysts have called this the "hourglass economy" with jobs for the highly educated at one end and service workers at the other, with few jobs in the middle.[12] Not all media jobs were highly paid, either: in book publishing, for example, fresh recruits from the Ivy League started at $18,000 or even less in the late 1970s and into the 1980s.

Clearly, something more than jobs was pulling the information elite back to urban life. Tastes were changing, especially among ambitious young people, who were graduating from college only to find their suburban hometowns immensely stultifying. Commuting to the city was difficult, home ownership expensive. Sensing a market, city real estate agents did their best to sell people on returning to New York, reversing their tactics of just a decade before, when they had despoiled and disinvested in city neighborhoods to push people to the suburbs.[13] More and more landlords took their dilapidated buildings in Manhattan out of the rental market, spruced them up, and sold off apartments to individual owners as co-ops or condominiums. Sometimes speculators bought up the apartments of elderly renters at discount prices, on the grim hope of huge profits after their tenants died. Small city apartments could replace the family house because families had become significantly smaller. The factor that was perhaps most important, and least explicable, was the growing perception that city living was fashionable again. Strolling down Columbus Avenue looking fine and looking at those who looked fine was far more fun than going to bed at night in unspectacular bedroom communities like Scarsdale or Stamford.[14]

With so many new people flooding the city's housing market, gentrification began to accelerate. Denunciations of gentrification are often couched in racial terms, with white newcomers blamed for ousting blacks and for changing tight-knit communities for the worse. Yet in many places the overall effect was not always complete displacement but rather integration. A study of gentrification in two African American neighborhoods, Harlem and Brooklyn's Clinton Hill, argues that the integration of neighborhoods often benefits many original residents, who shop at newly opened stores and enjoy improved city services without necessarily being displaced. Gentrification's "revanchist" aspects often manifest instead as new limitations on the behavior of the poor, such as crackdowns on public drunkenness.[15]

THE FIRST TRUMP: FALLING TAXES AND RISING TOWERS (1978–82)

Despite dirty streets and other symptoms of continuing austerity, Koch campaigned for a second term on the theme that New York was "coming back." This was more than a campaign slogan: the city economy's really was reviving. After a long slump, the real estate business "is in high gear," wrote *New York Times* architecture critic Ada Louise Huxtable during the summer of 1980.[16]

Koch's mayoralty has even been labeled "the era of big development" because of his efforts to use what amounted to off-budget expenditures—such as tax abatements and land-use policies to subsidize new construction.[17] "Ed Koch was a pro-development mayor," recalled former deputy mayor Robert Esnard. "He would joke with people that the taller the building, the more taxes there are. He would see in these tall buildings policemen and firemen and parks and schools. . . . That made him a hero in the real estate industry and in the business community and that was because he was able to stand up. It made sense to do a particular thing, and to have this building built and get all these new taxes and get all these new jobs, and get the income from all this activity. . . . He reveled in it."[18] But it is also arguable that the taller the building, the greater the city's need for more affordable housing for the people who will work there.

The number of major construction projects increased dramatically during 1981. Only six small office buildings rose in New York from 1978 to 1981, only about 880,000 square feet of office space all told. Between 1981 and 1990 developers increased office stock by fifty-three million square feet, a 22 percent increase. At first the bulk of new construction rose on the already-dense East Side, so the administration expanded zoning and tax incentives to promote development on the West Side.[19]

Tax abatements, which reduced real estate taxes for a period of years in return for particular kinds of development, were the most controversial subsidies, totaling more than $1 billion in lost revenues. Critics of abatements regard them as corporate welfare and as a vast subsidy that shrank the stock of low-cost housing by an estimated 100,000 units.[20] What abatements cost is difficult to determine, because it is impossible to tell whether the buildings would have been built without the incentive, and the cost has to be balanced against income taxes and other unabated taxes collected from people working to build the building and those who live or work inside them when they are built. Abatements are particularly attractive to a government lacking credit, as it is one of the few ways to leverage its future income.

The Koch administration used three types of tax abatements: the first, J-51, subsidized the renovation of existing housing and originally was approved by the city council in 1955 as a way to cushion landlords' outlays for bringing hot water to cold-water flats. By the 1980s, landlords used J-51 abatements for loft conversions and gentrification. The subsidies had some negative consequences, spurring the exodus of small manufacturing operations, which were forced out by lucrative residential conversions. It also led to the upgrading of thousands of units of SRO housing and the eviction of thousands of economically and socially marginal residents (see chapter 18).[21]

The second type, section 421, was designed to ease New York's housing shortage, providing a twelve-year tax reduction for new apartment construction on vacant or underused sites. Scholars and other critics have disputed the value of the 421 abatements because they initially applied to luxury buildings and by some estimates constituted a tax expenditure of $551 million between 1976 and 1987. The lower taxes allowed builders or rental agents to get 5 to 10 percent more income from the rent, which in turn allowed developers to finance a bigger percentage of the construction and required less direct investment by the developer. Proponents of the subsidy argue that the city did not really lose revenue, because the buildings would not have been built otherwise, and over the long term the new buildings would substantially increase the tax base.[22]

The most controversial subsidies were individually negotiated tax reductions, estimated to cost between $233 and $600 million in lost taxes by between 1977 and 1981. In a city where tens of thousands were desperately poor, these tax deals subsidized large corporations in order to get them to stay. For example, in 1978 AT&T, a company that realized $5.7 billion in profits the following year, was granted a $20 million tax exemption to build a new headquarters in an overbuilt area of Manhattan.[23] Critics of such programs argue that the practice allows companies that are not thinking of moving to apply for subsidies by pretending they are. Others complained that some New York subsidies were a giveaway to powerful interests; in Manhattan real estate had revived sufficiently that no reward was needed to get people to build, they argued.

"I don't know if they would have pulled out without a tax abatement, but I didn't feel we wanted to put them to that test," countered Karen N. Gerard, deputy mayor for economic development, when challenged on the tax breaks given to the developer Olympia and York to build the commercial part of Battery Park City, a neighborhood built on landfill from the World Trade Center excavation site. Nonetheless, this deal followed on the heels of a Koch administration attempt to limit abatements in the most lucrative zones—Manhattan from Thirty-fourth Street to Ninety-sixth Street from the East River to Sixth Avenue, and everything south of Fulton Street.[24]

Gerard's predecessor, Peter Solomon, had tried to restructure the system to curb some of the worst abuses and loopholes, and called for reform, but he defended the overall system, arguing that it generated far more than the value of the tax reductions in greater construction activity and more than eight-six thousand permanent jobs. Solomon pointed out that the abatement "applies solely to the *increase* in value that results" from the construction of the project, and therefore increased net tax revenues. They are, he argued, an incentive, but not the equivalent of an expenditure of tax funds, as his critics argued.[25]

In 1981, as Koch was running for reelection, two splashy new midtown hotels epitomized the revival. They were the first to open up in midtown in a long time. Both projects made their owners' names synonymous with the glittering greed of the roaring eighties: Leona Helmsley, developer of the Helmsley Palace Hotel, and Donald J. Trump, who converted the old Commodore Hotel next to Grand Central Station into the Grand Hyatt, creating a much-acclaimed luxury spot in a degenerating section of midtown. In the process Trump not only reshaped the skyline but turned himself into a celebrity.

Architecture critic Paul Goldberger praised the Hyatt as "new and pleasant . . . the most spectacular large convention hotel New York . . . in more than a generation—a building that thrusts aside the banality and triviality of the designs of structures like the New York Hilton and the Sheraton Centre in favor of a kind of glittery, cosmopolitan elegance new York has not seen in a big new hotel building since the Waldorf-Astoria."[26] And Huxtable lauded Trump personally for pursuing "a complex and risky investment at a time when New York, and 42d Street, were in the deepest doldrums."[27]

Trump the developer and Koch the pro-development mayor, both geniuses at self-promotion, helped revive New York as a center of glitz and glamour. They soon developed a mutual dislike so intense that even New York was barely big enough for the both of them. Koch saw himself as a reformer, promoting the public interest. Trump aggressively asserted his own private interests. According to his biographer, he looked back on the dedication ceremony of the Verrazano-Narrows Bridge, which he had attended as a boy, as a formative experience. Politicians, some of whom had opposed the bridge, took center stage while everyone ignored the bridge's brilliant designer, Othmar Ammann. The young Donald drew the moral: "If you let people treat you how they want, you'll be made a fool. I realized then and there something I would never forget: I don't want to be made anybody's sucker." A thoroughgoing individualist, Trump was a protégé of attorney Roy Cohn, a wily self-centered fixer and the former counsel to Senator Joseph McCarthy.[28]

Trump had assembled a tract for the planned Thirty-fourth Street Convention Center, but Koch balked at letting him develop it and rejected his offer to waive a

$500,000 brokerage fee if the center were named after his father, developer Fred Trump Sr.[29] Then housing commissioner Anthony Gliedman reversed the Beame administration's decision to give a 421 tax abatement to the huge Trump Tower skyscraper on the ground that the tax break was designed to promote development in "marginal neighborhoods," not a project at its blatantly central location of Fifth Avenue and Fifty-seventh Street. Trump eventually won his tax abatement in the Court of Appeals, surprising many legal experts, but dropped the suit he had filed against Gliedman personally and offered him a job when he left government.[30] The fight over the tax abatement for Trump Tower inaugurated "a long, simmering feud between Donald and Mayor Koch. The animosity between the two men eventually escalated into a tragicomic war," according to Donald Trump's biographer.[31] After he left the mayoralty, Koch called Trump "a blowhard" and "a supreme, egotistical lightweight," though "he did build some good quality buildings."[32]

When parks department plans to rebuild the Wollman skating rink in Central Park came to a standstill in 1986, Trump had an opening to embarrass Koch. The rink had been closed since 1980 for reconstruction. Disastrously, the parks commissioner, Gordon Davis, had decided on an untried energy-efficient technology to make ice that circulated freon gas instead of brine.[33] Unexpectedly, a galvanic reaction of the freon, the tubing that held it, and the iron rebar in the rink's concrete slab had caused pinholes to develop, allowing the ozone-damaging gas to escape. Of course, the system would not freeze water. Worse, the leaks were invisible and required special technology to repair, whereas a brine leak was obvious and could be fixed by regular plumbers.[34]

The administration went to the Board of Estimate with a proposal to bypass the usual lengthy contracting process and create a special committee to build a new brine rink by the next skating season for $3.5 million. But the rink stink came during the high point of the Manes/Friedman corruption scandals. Comptroller Jay Goldin, a perennial mayoral candidate, and Brooklyn borough president Howard Golden, a regular opponent of Koch's, had a field day, calling the Koch administration incompetent and inefficient. When they blocked the proposal, the newspapers slammed the parks department for being too inept to build even an ice-skating rink.[35]

Trump, whose apartment looked down on the rink, saw a shining opportunity to garner respect as a benefactor—and to win international fame as New York's premier developer. A keen neoliberal, he also saw a way to communicate an ideological message, that the private sector was more efficient than government, and offered to take charge of rebuilding the rink.[36] Koch was aware that Trump's offer could be bad for government and politically embarrassing to him. He tried to turn Trump down. The Board of Estimate accepted basically the same sort of project that Esnard had proposed as a public work and at the same cost.[37]

Trump called in favors from companies that expected huge future contracts from him, which helped keep the rink project's cost down. Though unexpected difficulties arose—the rink's drainage system was not connected to the sewer system, for instance—he finished the rink on budget and on time. Not content to bask in civic glory, Trump asked Koch to rename the rink in his honor, which Koch was willing to do if Trump ponied up the $3 million that the renovation cost the city. "Foolishly, he rejected my offer," Koch recalled.[38] But Trump had scored an ideological point, seeming to prove that well-run private enterprises were more efficient than government agencies, and he damaged Koch's claim to be a good manager, even though the condition of the parks had begun a long, slow improvement, and the Trump project would be coordinated by Koch's recently resigned housing commissioner, Anthony Gliedman.[39]

REFORMING THE PARKS

New York's great parks—which deserve to be called true works of art—were turning into sandlots and mud when Koch took over in 1978. Parts of Central Park had been reduced to a "sea of dust."[40] Lesser parks were in even worse shape. Monuments and park buildings were festooned with ugly spray-painted graffiti, and angry vandals routinely punched the slats off park benches. Recreational equipment was often broken and unusable—and when it was replaced, the parks department bought cheap steel versions of swing sets and jungle gyms that made playgrounds look like penitentiaries. Some parks had even degenerated into dumps for illegal auto chop shops. The lack of a capital budget had nearly destroyed the park system. Even as limited capital funds became available in the early 1980s, they were far from sufficient to erase the damage of years of neglect.

Gordon Davis, who served as parks commissioner from 1978 to 1983, hoped to bring in private money and management without painting government out of the picture. A tall, gregarious African American, educated at Williams and Harvard Law, Davis's enthusiasm was reminiscent of Progressive-era reformers'. His father, W. Allison Davis, was the John Dewey Distinguished Professor of Education at the University of Chicago. Perhaps something of the old pragmatist's spirit rubbed off on the son.

The parks department's budget had been cut more severely than those of most city agencies because it was funded almost entirely with city tax money. So while a $100,000 cut from a social welfare agency that received 70 percent of its funds from the federal government might reduce the budget deficit by $30,000, a $100,000 cut from parks budget would reduce the deficit by $100,000. Mayors Lindsay and Beame had worsened the situation by appointing a new commissioner every year between 1973 and 1978. "Each one of them was different, and each one had their own approach to things. It was a sad situation," Davis recalled.[41] "The Parks Department, after Robert Moses, was a sitting duck. It didn't have the political power or clout or stature to prevent the kind of bloodletting that occurred" during the fiscal crisis. The result was that when Davis took office, only 16 percent of parks were in good condition. By 1980 he had that figure up to 26 percent, but it would take twenty years for the department to recover.[42]

Davis inherited an agency with a reputation for a slack workforce. Junior people were fired first (and replaced to some extent with temporary and chronically unemployed workers from President Carter's Comprehensive Employment and Training Act (better known by its acronym, CETA) program, part of a stimulus package designed to reduce municipal layoffs by hiring the poor). By the early 1980s the agency had few experienced supervisors.[43] The formal structure of the parks department when Davis arrived in 1978 was still that created by Moses, but the middle managers who had made Moses's department function were long gone. It was up to Davis to reorganize the entire department to conform with contemporary reality.

His first response was to reassert control over the use of Central Park, canceling a big annual food festival called "Taste of the Big Apple." The previous five commissioners had freely issued permits for big events, but Davis thought that many overloaded the park's ecosystem with people, garbage, and discarded food. "We needed to restore a balance," Davis recalled. The park had powerful private interests on its side; it is surrounded by a wealthy community that wanted the park fixed. But under the old regime the department had no way of using private donors' money effectively. The agency rarely completed projects, and, according to Davis, "when sometimes they got done, they were awful."[44]

Davis proceeded with a relatively small project, reconstruction of a building called the Central Park Dairy to demonstrate that his department could spend money efficiently. Davis realized that "this is the key to everything. If you can build something, if you can change something, if you can use private money or even city money to do something good with it, people will give you more money, and that's exactly what happened." He knew, however, that private funding would not be enough to rebuild his organization and the whole park system. His hope was that visible improvements would win the agency more funding from the budget.[45]

In the meantime financiers Richard Gilder and George Soros funded and presented to Davis a management study that recommended appointment of an independent administrator for Central Park, bypassing the boroughwide parks bureaucracy. "Soros and Gilder seemed a bit pushy to me, and my first reaction was no. I had no idea who George Soros was," Davis said.[46] A few months later he changed his mind about the management plan but shocked the donors by appointing Elizabeth Barlow, the head of a rival parks group, to run Central Park. Barlow was the first in a series of charismatic and well-connected administrators whom Davis appointed from outside the civil service to run the major parks. Her first move was to set up the Central Park Conservancy, a foundation that would take over private fund raising and management of Central Park.[47]

Davis and Barlow believed the only way to save the park was to insulate it from the fiscal uncertainty of the political system, which they believed had betrayed the parks. Although they were using a combination of public and private funds, Davis said their hope was that the new Central Park administration would achieve "institutional continuity" modeled on "the Port Authority, or Con Edison." During Koch's mayoralty the conservancy would spend approximately $31 million, largely on restoration and maintenance projects.[48]

By 1980, Davis had secured $500,000 in state funding, supplemented by $60,000 from a James Taylor concert, to restore Sheep Meadow. The conservancy also restored Bethesda Terrace, including Bethesda Fountain, which is topped by the towering Bethesda Angel, its wings outstretched against the sky. The sculpture symbolizes the succor that the park offers to harassed New Yorkers, and playwright Tony Kushner later made it emblematic of 1980s New York in his Pulitzer Prize–winning play, *Angels in America*.

The restoration of Bethesda Terrace reflected a new view of the park as one of New York's great museums, deserving of both private and public support, rather than simply a tax-funded city service. "Central Park is one of the greatest artistic achievements of American civilization, clearly in the same category as *Moby Dick* or the invention of jazz," Commissioner Davis declared, but it is also "the city's most public place." The commissioner insisted that the public-private partnership would also "reflect the park . . . as a democracy, with room for walkers, joggers, cyclists, Frisbee players and other users as well as for those who think of it as an outdoor museum."[49] Barlow estimated that it would take $100 million and ten years to get the park back in shape, an unthinkable sum in a city budget that still could not pay for adequate street cleaning or police protection. She also argued that private funding would go farther, by avoiding many costly requirements for public construction.[50]

Nevertheless, two groups criticized the conservancy. One argued that Barlow and Davis were too innovative, that by adapting Central Park to contemporary use they departed too much from their duty to preserve the original design of Frederick Law Olmsted and Calvert Vaux. Other critics objected to privatization itself on the ground that it "eroded the historical definition of public space as public property," as private groups and money took over more and more maintenance, rebuilding, and rules.[51] Elizabeth Blackmar, who cowrote a history of Central Park, argued that by privatizing management of the park the city abdicated functions that should be financed by the taxpayer. She traced the public-private partnership to a group of economists called public choice theorists, who "applied the logic of the market to governments, arguing that rational wealth-maximizing individual citizens expected and were entitled to a strict quid pro quo for their taxes. . . . Broad conceptions of public space as government-owned and managed institutions or resources open to all, as a sum larger than its parts or as the product of collective effort had no place in such analyses."[52]

Privatization delegated management and restoration functions to nonprofits such as the conservancy, aiming to make as much money as possible from park concessions such as boathouses and restaurants or from corporate events held in the park. These enterprises were meant to plow money back into restoration and maintenance. The downside was that privatization could lead to the overuse of park resources, and it could endanger the very concept of city parks as shared democratic public spaces created as pastoral refuges from the commercial and consumerist cares of daily city life.

Davis avoided those pitfalls throughout his commissionership, pointing out that the majority of park development would always remain public and reiterating that he was committed to maintaining the parks as a public forum.[53] A test came when he agreed to allow a giant rally against nuclear weapons in Central Park on June 12, 1982, with estimates of attendance going as high as one million. "I loved it," Davis recalled. The rally was peaceful and orderly, and a triumph for free speech in the city, in contrast to the more restrictive policies of later administrations.[54]

HENRY STERN: PARKS COMMISSIONER FOR ALL SEASONS

Koch's first reaction was, "You gotta be crazy," when aides mentioned Henry J. Stern as a possible successor to Gordon Davis, who decided to leave the administration in 1983. Koch feared that his close friend's quixotic eccentricities might not play well with the public. But Moses himself was parks commissioner longer than Stern, who would serve for fourteen years under mayors Koch and Giuliani.[55]

Stern was a slight man with a dark beard that grayed as he presided over the parks. Like his predecessor, he had attended Harvard Law but had gotten there through Bronx Science and City College. With the backing of the Liberal Party, he had worked in appointed jobs since the early 1960s and in 1973 became the party's only elected official, beating the Republican in an at-large boroughwide election in Manhattan, a system that was declared unconstitutional shortly before his appointment as parks commissioner in 1983.[56]

Stern made it clear soon after his appointment that he was no ordinary official but "a man for all species" who saw himself as the "commissioner for fun." He mostly followed and developed the basic structure of promoting public-private partnerships, such as the Central Park Conservancy, inherited from his predecessor. In transforming the culture of the parks department, he also caused a split with some of the older employees by hiring young, often Ivy League–educated, staff.[57] Stern made a splash almost immediately. Faced with immediate cuts in his operating budget, he declared that unless two hundred swimmers turned up at an underused city pool on Fifth-ninth Street, it would be closed. They showed up and the pool stayed open.[58]

Stern delighted in wit and wordplay to a degree unusual even in a New York City official. Admirers, such as his successor, Adrian Benepe, described him as a "combination of Woody Allen and Groucho Marx," though he added that "there are things he has said that have offended people, particularly in the age of political correctness."[59] Stern also championed some controversial causes. Despite vocal opposition from conservatives on the city council, he created a memorial to John Lennon in Central Park, known as Strawberry Fields, using money donated by Yoko Ono.

Stern's close relationship with Koch, plus the greater availability of capital funds, allowed Stern to undertake an almost unprecedented reconstruction of the parks. He did not stop there, reversing a policy of Davis's by acquiring additional parkland. Davis had felt that the more than twenty-six thousand acres were more than the parks department could care for and had halted acquisitions. Stern felt that "land is land, land is forever. You may not have enough money to fix it now, but you will later. On the other hand, if you lose it, it's forever."[60] From 1983 to 2009 the parks system added more than three thousand acres, growing to 14 percent of New York's land area. The department had to manage its parks with only thirty-nine hundred employees (expanded to forty-eight hundred by 1988), compared with the more than five thousand parks workers in the years just before the fiscal crisis. But these numbers were small compared with the forces Robert Moses had at his disposal when he created the parks system in its modern form. In 1934 alone Moses had an army of thirty to sixty thousand temporary employees from federal relief at his disposal. That year they completed more than seventeen hundred park-related construction projects, including a major renovation of Bryant Park.[61]

The capital improvements made under Stern were noticeable everywhere. Stern persuaded Koch to use capital funds to restore the Minton china mosaics at the entrance to Bethesda Terrace and to rebuild Belvedere Castle, a focal point of Central Park. Bryant Park, City Hall Park, Union Square, Flushing Meadow, and the Crotona Park Pool in the south Bronx, where Ed Koch used to swim as a young child, were all renovated. The Parachute Jump at Coney Island gained city landmark status, and the Parks Department overhauled it. The "commissioner for all species" also became the leading defender of trees against what he called arboricide. Stern promulgated new regulations for tree replacement, vastly multiplying the number of trees that were replanted. And he enforced the regulations stringently.[62]

Stern had his share of disasters on his watch—a Diana Ross concert was rained out, leaving the Great Lawn a sea of mud. Worse, at the rain-check concert the next night groups of "marauding youth" attacked concertgoers—the city received as many as two hundred complaints of "robberies and jewelry and purse snatchings." Stern responded by reducing the number of popular music concerts in the Park.[63]

In 1983 Donald Manes, the corrupt borough president of Queens, managed to secure the mayor's support for a Grand Prix racetrack in Flushing Meadows. Koch ordinarily allowed his commissioners to decide such matters on their merits, so his decision to interfere illustrates how much he was willing to bend the rules for the Democratic county leaders. Forced to support an environmental nightmare, Stern did his best behind the scenes to delay it, declaring it dead with some alacrity after Manes's exposure and suicide.[64] The Grand Prix affair damaged Koch politically, and Stern got little credit for his efforts against it. "How many of City Hall's earnest arguments masked a cynical agenda?" asked the *Times* editorial board.[65]

Manes's attempt to invade Flushing Meadows with the Grand Prix and the Diana Ross incident were minor, compared with some real tragedies in the parks that marred Koch's last term. An eleven-year-old boy died after he sneaked into the Prospect Park zoo after hours and climbed into the polar bear enclosure. When the police arrived, they saw the bears pulling at the boy's body and shot them in an effort to rescue the child, who was already dead.[66]

Two years later a twenty-eight-year-old investment banker, who had been jogging near 102d Street in Central Park on April 19, 1989, was badly beaten and raped. Police concluded that the woman, who came to be known as the "Central Park jogger," had been the victim of what they called a "wilding" by a group of African American teens. Five boys, fifteen and sixteen years old, were convicted of the rape on the basis of confessions they made while in police custody. Although most black leaders denounced the boys, the case had disturbing echoes of past false charges of rape against black men, such as the Scottsboro Boys case. Defense lawyers pointed to the prosecution's lack of forensic evidence and reliance on confessions obtained in custody.[67] They were right. In 2002 a convicted serial rapist, who was already serving a life sentence, confessed that he had raped the jogger. After DNA evidence corroborated his statement, prosecutors vacated the boys' convictions.[68]

The Central Park jogger case touched a nerve and divided New York racially in a way few crimes had ever done, producing screaming headlines such as the *Post's* "None of Us Is Safe." Koch and Stern struggled to reassure park users, especially women. Responding to the headline, Stern commented, "It's difficult to say it in the aftermath of a tragedy, but the fact is, by the numbers, the park is safe." He pointed out that the streets outside the park were far more dangerous: Central Park had seen only 537 felonies in 1988, compared with more than twenty-five thousand in the neighboring Midtown South Precinct. But statistics could not contain an emotionally charged political situation, especially when those statistics suggested that on average one and a half *felonies* were committed in the park every day. A few days later Stern announced plans to increase Central Park's security. Two years later Central Park was the site of only 368 felonies a year, a figure that had dropped to ninety-seven by 2008.[69]

When Koch left office in 1989, Henry Stern received mostly plaudits. But his term under Giuliani was not as smooth. Most seriously, the city paid $12 million to settle a lawsuit brought by parks department employees. They complained that Stern had promoted inexperienced white Ivy Leaguers over more experienced minority workers and that he had paid whites more for doing the same jobs. The plaintiffs also alleged that Stern's jokes were sometimes racist and created a hostile work environment. Even his attempts to protect trees came under criticism, after officials tried to fine a Brooklyn homeowner $42,000 for cutting down a single seventy-year-old tree.[70]

Nonetheless, Stern and Davis placed the parks on a path to recovery by the end of Koch's mayoralty. Although the Koch administration laid the groundwork for partial privatization, it also increased public funding for parks from 1984 to 1987 and maintained a spending level of 0.7 to 0.8 percent of the total city operating budget even in the lean years of 1987–89.[71] But the parks had a long way to go. When Stern left office in 1990, only 25 percent of the parks were rated as acceptable, according to the Citizen's Budget Commission, about the same as when Davis left office in 1983. Despite significant investment, the parks had fallen so far into disrepair that it was apparently impossible to maintain more than a quarter of the system without a long period of additional capital investment. The real improvement came during Stern's second eight-year stint, with 89 percent rated acceptable by 2000. Reaching that point took a combination of $60 million in private money, volunteer labor, and some productivity increases, as well as investment from the capital budget. Mayors Dinkins and Giuliani continued to reduce the parks department's operating budget, however. By 2000 funding was down to 0.5 percent of the budget, and staff was about 30 percent the size of prefiscal crisis levels. The parks department is another example of basic structures put in place during the Koch administration that paid dividends in subsequent decades, but it is also an example of an agency that was forced to privatize and continued to suffer severe cuts because of the city's continuing financial difficulties.[72]

Koch's successors used private investment as an excuse to close parks to demonstrators, turning them from public forums into semiprivate gardens.[73] In 2000, for example, Mayor Michael Bloomberg, then a Republican, refused permits for a Central Park rally to protest the Republican National Convention, which was being held in New York. Part of Bloomberg's reasoning was that the protest might disrupt delicate restorations and irrigation systems installed with private money. A more politically sympathetic administration might have found a way, as Gordon Davis had in 1982. Indeed, Davis protested the Bloomberg administration's decision to deny protesters use of the park. Though private financing and management restored Central Park to its original glory, privatization eventually slid down the slippery slope that Blackmar and other critics had feared, as the parks department's duty to maintain parks as a public forum was preempted by the need to protect expensive privately funded sod.[74]

Tapping the wealthy was not the only method of privatizing the maintenance of parks and streets. Another was to shift some of the burden for maintaining the parks to citizens through regulation. Reform state assemblyman Ed Lehner, who represented Washington Heights, and state senator Franz Leichter, who represented Morningside Heights and Washington Heights, introduced and convinced the state legislature to pass the "pooper-scooper law," which makes dog owners liable for fines up to $100 for failing to pick up after their animals. New York's streets, Leichter charged, had become a "one big dog latrine," with dogs depositing an estimated 125 tons of poop a day.[75]

Koch prioritized poop scooping, announcing on television that "cleaning up after your dog is no longer a courtesy—it's the law." He even demonstrated the latest in pooper-scooper technology. It was a small step toward making hiking around New York a less slippery experience. Posted signs declared, "It's the Law: Clean up After Your Dog."[76] Both Macy's and Gimbels soon sold out of scoops, and Toto, canine star of the musical *The Wiz,* pawprinted himself to dedicate Manhattan's first public dog loo but refused to use it after sniffing at the hole.[77] In 1984 the *Times* applauded the dog law, estimating that 60 percent of the dog waste deposited was scooped up. A column called "The Worm and the Apple" awarded the sanitation and parks departments an apple for their successful enforcement of the pooper-scooper law. Three years later they got a worm after enforcement declined.[78] The long-term results of the law were mixed, reflecting Koch's tendency to crack down on matters that came to his attention, with enforcement subsiding when his interest moved on. The removal of dog waste from the sidewalks was a simple matter, however, compared with the complexities of revamping the "crossroads of the world," Times Square.

TIMES SQUARE REDEVELOPMENT

Sure there are hustlers, thieves, prostitutes, cripples, derelicts, winos, molesters, monsters, droolers, accosters. I'm not denying it. Would you prefer to cement over the whole beehive with a dipsy-doodle exhibition hall and kick out those people so they'll congregate on another block and make a new heaven and hell somewhere else, maybe not as bright and never as satisfyingly central?[79]

—PHILLIP LOPATE

Mythologized in the thirties and forties as the place where lowlife rubbed shoulders (and more) with high society, Times Square was for most Americans a film icon, a confection of flashing signs and night clubs. Within its cabarets and bars swells in top hats mixed with comic rogues and floozies straight out of Damon Runyon. After

1945 the dominant image was that of the exuberant thousands who rushed into the square to embrace each other after the defeat of Hitler. But by the 1969 release of *Midnight Cowboy*, Forty-second Street had become synonymous with hustlers like Joe Buck (Jon Voight) or insane loners such as Travis Bickle (Robert De Niro), who tries to protect a twelve-year-old hooker played by Jodie Foster by killing all her customers, in Martin Scorsese's *Taxi Driver* (1976).

In the Times Square of the seventies and eighties, sex was explicit everywhere and in just about every form known to any taste. Many still flocked to the area for other attractions, however. Broadway theater, always financially volatile, still had its good years as well as its nosedives. In those days it was still possible to see a play, or eat a greasy steak and baked potato at Tad's, for five dollars. Second-run movie houses catered to New York's thousands of college students with all-night showings of B movies for a dollar. Entertainment by the local pickpockets, thieves, and addicts was free. Outside, the more gullible could lose their money in a version of the shell game, which, like some of the other professions practiced in the square, had been part of civilization at least since ancient Babylon.

Times Square was not so dangerous that New Yorkers could not enjoy it; indeed the frisson was the fun. But Forty-second Street did scare the fainthearted, and not without reason. By the time Koch became mayor, the neighborhood had more felony and crime complaints than any other, despite, or perhaps because of, being targeted again and again by law enforcement.

Times Square was the apotheosis of free-market economics, answering the demand for cheap and easy access to drugs, porn, and prostitution. Since the time of Queen Elizabeth I public order had been enforced by giving the authorities almost unfettered discretion to decide who should be removed from the streets. By the time Koch became mayor, that power was gone, and the police and politicians had failed to formulate and implement alternative strategies for regulating porn, prostitution, and drug dealing.[80]

The de facto decriminalization of vagrancy and similar "status" crimes, came as a result of the U.S. Supreme Court decision in *Papachristou v. Jacksonville* (1972), which held that people could be arrested only for their conduct, not for their status, as a known pickpocket, prostitute, or pimp, for example. And it led to a reduction of policing of minor crimes. One of the draft environmental impact statements for Times Square's renewal noted: "The police cannot arrest people simply because they are standing around—and this is a good deal of what takes places on 42nd Street.... The crowds provide the market and the screen for the hustlers and pushers—the market in the sense of potential customers and the screen in the sense that those hanging around are often indistinguishable from criminals."[81]

Other judicial decisions virtually legalized pornography, at least in cities like New York, where community standards were tolerant. Scores of strip joints, massage parlors, and X-rated theaters dotted the area. The economic incentives for porn were considerable. A study by social scientists at City University of New York estimated that the weekly gross of a single peep show ranged from $74,000 to $106,000, amounting to $5 million a year. And that was only the licit portion of the profits.[82]

Because it was still a transit and entertainment center, Times Square was a hugely appealing prospect for redevelopment. Developers and the city, starting with the Beame administration, realized that a grand plan was necessary. It would have to be financed by the construction of revenue-producing office towers, as Beame had no direct funds to offer. The first major plan for redesigning Forty-second Street since the early 60s came from the 42nd Street Development Corporation, spearheaded by Fred Papert, a former president of the Municipal Art Society and former chair of the city planning commission. Although the plan aimed to preserve Forty-second Street's historic theaters, it included three office towers and a huge fashion mart of debatable utility, and it proposed to demolish the Times Tower and its world-famous illuminated signs. Suburbanites could arrive by bus at Port Authority and walk by bridge over Eighth Avenue to a two-story shopping mall–theme park, complete with a then-futuristic IMAX theater, without ever touching the ground. The plan also envisioned tourists peering into radio and television studios and watching shows being made. Other exhibits would charge a $4 admission fee and were supposed to provide a strange simulacrum of the gritty city neighborhood that the entire project proposed to erase.[83]

Robert F. Wagner Jr., the planning commission chair, disliked the plan for the social-spatial stratification of Times Square, telling developers that the administration would at best give lukewarm support. Behind the scenes Wagner was more candid in voicing his objections to the mayor. Huxtable, the influential *Times* architecture critic, also heavily criticized the plan.[84] The most effective critic was Ed Koch, who was outraged when he attended the developers' presentation, which he termed "Disneyland on 42nd Street."[85] Even years later he bluntly exclaimed: "'Their exhibit included a *Ferris wheel* on Forty-second Street! It was shit, to put it bluntly. I don't pretend to be a city planner, but I know dross from gold. So I said, 'We're not going to do this.'" Koch knew how to use ridicule to stop multibillion-dollar programs, and this time he used all the subtlety one would use to flatten a cockroach. He railed against the plan in the press, calling it "orange juice" when "what New York needs is seltzer."[86]

The next year, to keep Times Square from descending into a bland parody of itself, the administration brought in the design firm of Cooper and Eckstut to issue guidelines for new designs for Forty-second Street redevelopment. The firm was credited with a successful redesign of Battery Park City that, in the words of Sandy Frucher, who chaired the Battery Park City Authority, "made the project part of New York City" instead of a futuristic Le Corbusier-style ghetto.[87] The goal of the design firm was to preserve the unique visual spectacle and social diversity of Times Square while making it a more pleasant place for pedestrians.[88]

The new design firm recommended preserving the Times Tower, theaters, and entertainment as the focal point, protecting its historical identity, and ensuring the area was full of "prominent signage" and lighting. Requiring new office towers to be clad in shiny reflective materials would ramp up the brilliance even more. Many details concentrated on maintaining the human scale of walking through the square by prohibiting shiny cladding below the fifth floor and requiring that the towers be set back from the sidewalks. The visible cornices of the buildings would remain at five stories, giving the illusion that the street had not changed.[89]

After the Cooper-Eckstut guidelines were published, Wagner, now deputy mayor for policy, and Herbert Sturz, the new chair of the city planning commission, made the crucial decisions that structured the Times Square project for the next sixteen years. They were keenly aware that, because of the fiscal crisis, city departments had fired most of the engineers capable of building huge public projects. It would take years to restore that capability. But they also realized it was vital to keep the project public and under city control. So they turned to a public partner, the Urban Development Corporation, an independent state authority with condemnation and other wide powers that also had long experience in large-scale development.

To build the crucial office towers city planners chose George Klein, a relatively low-profile but eminently respectable developer, who offered a design by Philip Johnson and his partner John Burgee, the most prestigious architects of the day. Faced with the challenge of designing office buildings for Times Square, the pair replaced Disney-style sterility with insipidity and corporate sterility. Johnson and Burgee's model was Rockefeller Center, but instead of having tourists walk through the elevated conduits of an intubated Forty-second Street, as in Papert's plan, the troglodytes doomed to work in their buildings could avoid the mean streets by walking through underground concourses into bland granite slabs reaching up as high as fifty-six stories with no setback from the street. To lay a claim to postmodernity, Johnson and Burgee covered their towers with dull pink granite sheaths and crowned them with glass mansards and decorative iron finials. Huxtable mocked them as "enormous pop-up buildings with fancy hats." Looking at the designs years later, Johnson himself declared, "I must have been out of my mind," because the designs were so mediocre.[90]

Johnson and Burgee's plan disregarded the Cooper-Eckstut guidelines almost entirely. The architects wanted to demolish the Times Tower and replace it with a laser light display similar to the ones used to memorialize the Twin Towers a few months after 9/11—eliminating Times Square's entire history and the rationale for its name. Thomas Bender, an urban historian, pointed out that the designers were "contemptuous of the public character of the street" by ignoring guidelines for setting the towers back to preserve a more human dimension for the area. "We could acknowledge its privatization and rename it Klein's Square," Bender quipped.[91] The mayor, however, refused to acknowledge that the seltzer had lost its fizz. Impatient by 1983 to get the project done while he was still mayor, he snapped, "I, for one have never felt it necessary to explain why we improve something," when asked why his administration had adopted a program that violated its own architectural guidelines.[92]

An onslaught of well-orchestrated criticism helped change the mayor's mind. The first sign was the overwhelmingly negative reaction to construction of the Portman/Marriott Hotel in 1982, the first of the renewal projects to be constructed. The hotel project entailed the destruction of the historic Helen Hayes and Morosco theaters, which, after two years of litigation and public protests, were finally torn down in 1982. Koch always tried to appeal to important cultural interests and the theater industry. The Portman Hotel protests embarrassed him into preserving the rest of the area's theaters and its entertainment sector.[93]

The coup de grace for the Klein-Johnson-Burgee design, despite its approval by the Board of Estimate in 1984, was a clever campaign by Hugh Hardy and the Municipal Arts Society. First, they sponsored a contest for alternative designs that demonstrated that most architects thought that the Times Tower should stay. Then, on a fall evening in 1984 with the streets full of theatergoers, Hardy arranged for all the lights in the square to be turned off, "except for a lone light on a sign that said: 'Hey Mr. Mayor! It's Dark Out Here! Help Keep the Bright Lights in Times Square.'" Hardy followed up with a film narrated by Jason Robards, who declared that "instead of a bowl of light, we would be offered canyon walls."[94]

Koch got the message. With architecture critics turning even more against the plan, the planning commission hired a leading lighting designer, Paul Marantz, who designed special machines for measuring the light in Times Square. Based on his study, the commission drafted an innovative new zoning law, approved by the Board of Estimate in 1987, that required buildings through signage, art, or other means to pour a certain amount of light into the square, as measured by Marantz's machines. The law also required 16,800 square feet of lighted signage for every block of building, which is about as bright as the brightest block on the Square at that time.[95]

Times Square would not be redeveloped until the end of the 1990s, almost a decade after Koch left office. The local landlords, canny New York real estate moguls, tied the project up with litigation from 1984 until 1990—they were making lots of money out of the sleazy status quo and wanted to make sure they got paid top dollar for their holdings. The landlords resented their exclusion from the redevelopment process and wanted to challenge the legitimacy of public power in the form of eminent domain to convey benefits on rival developers. When the litigation finally was settled in 1990, New York was mired in recession, and the real estate market was in the dumps. The administration of Mayor David Dinkins kept the project alive, but Klein had, after all those years of litigation, lost most of the prospective tenants he'd lined up for the towers and pulled out. And in the glut of office space, few developers would take on four new office towers.

When the project was finally built in the late 1990s, Mayor Rudy Giuliani claimed credit. Giuliani had played a leading role in bringing Disney and other corporate sponsors into the redevelopment of Times Square. But according to the leading scholar of Times Square redevelopment, Lynne Sagalyn, these companies were merely buying into an attractive investment, given the improving economy. "While it did take a bold mayor to face the political risks of pushing through such a large-scale public project, that mayor was Edward I. Koch," she concludes.[96]

Not Giuliani but Koch, says Sagalyn, established the basic structural parameters for the project—rejection of the theme park model, public control through the city planning commission and the UDC, the requirement that the city's financial contribution would be completely off-budget, hewing to the Cooper-Eckstut guidelines, and the unprecedented 1987 zoning law requiring buildings to provide lighted signage to keep Times Square bright. Ultimately, Koch's team recognized that Times Square should remain one of the world's major spectacles and entertainment centers—and that reforming it into an clean and bland extension of the midtown corporate office district would only diminish New York's luster.

Times Square today is a mosaic of corporate logos, but, as Rebecca Robertson has observed, "what populism means now is a corporate culture, whether you like it or not."[97] Disney and other familiar brands have replaced the underground economy, which has moved on to other areas of city, but the new consumers who shop Times Square have helped fill the pricey seats of Broadway theaters. Global corporations have helped preserve Times Square as one of the most lively areas for regular folks to go for a jolt of glitter. More brilliant than ever, the signage overwhelms the senses with pulsing light, information, purity, danger—orange juice *and* fizz.

18 HOMELESSNESS

Ed Koch always tried to exceed Fiorello La Guardia, but in the case of homelessness, the comparison is sad. Koch, though he surely tried as hard, had less success in reducing homelessness than his predecessor did in the depths of the Depression. Of course, La Guardia had Franklin Roosevelt to work with—a president committed to freedom from fear and freedom from want throughout the world. New York's homeless got little comfort from Ronald Reagan, who claimed that "one problem that we've had, even in the best of times, and that is the people who are sleeping on the grates, the homeless who are homeless, you might say, by choice."[1]

Reagan's mid-1980s "prosperity" was among the worst of times for those many New Yorkers who lived outside the charmed circles of finance and real estate. The appearance of more and more street people was the flip side of gentrification. In 1986 the number of people regularly housed in city shelters rose to ten thousand, a level not reached since the middle of the Great Depression in 1936. But during the Depression the numbers of homeless in New York peaked at that level and diminished as the New Deal took root. Reaganomics meant more and more people were out on the street.[2]

Ed Koch could boast that his administration had done more for the homeless than any other municipal government, but without the kind of federal help La Guardia had, Koch could not stem the tide. La Guardia worked with a president who began the first federal jobs and public housing programs and bolstered unions committed to providing affordable housing. Reagan virtually stopped construction of public housing and many other forms of social spending, fostering the myth that his administration was preserving a "safety net." Koch tried to do everything he could within that framework to help people. In 1988, during a period of retrenchment, Koch spent $375 million in city money and $382 million more in state and federal funds to house the homeless—sixteen times more than Philadelphia, even though New York is nearly five times larger.[3] Temporary shelter for the homeless obviously would not solve the problem of homelessness. The administration initially modeled its response on the Depression, understandably hoping that, as in the 1930s, economic revival would alleviate what it understood to be a temporary situation.

But, paradoxically, Koch's success in restoring city neighborhoods and promoting business confidence was a principal cause of homelessness, a situation worsened by the drastic reduction of the state-run in-patient mental facilities that had housed and cared for tens of thousands before the 1970s. The displacement of poor long-time residents, though not his goal, was inherent in his strategy for economic development, which raised real estate values through tax abatements and incentives.[4] As housing prices rose, the number of empty apartments at the bottom of the housing scale sank dangerously close to zero.[5] Well-adjusted and educated people who could no longer afford to live in New York City could move to the Sun Belt or the suburbs and get new jobs. But those who had mental or substance abuse problems and little or no education lacked the flexibility to adjust to new economic conditions in a laissez-faire society. The geographer Neil Smith theorizes that gentrification occurs when the value of ground rent (the cost of renting just the land) exceeds the value of the improvements on the property. Then developers can buy structures inexpensively, renovate them, and sell them profitably at a bargain price. During the 1980s this process proceeded apace (see chapter 17).[6]

THE VAGRANT CRISIS

By 1979 the streets were beginning to fill up with bums—older alcoholic men who had been turned out of their traditional skid row haunts. The population on the streets also swelled with newcomers: young black men, "shopping bag ladies," people who had been released from state mental institutions, and an increasing number of homeless families that had never before been a significant part of the homeless population One of the Koch administration's first responses to homelessness was to set up what Stanley Brezenoff, the commissioner of the Human Resources Administration, termed a storefront "crash pad" for bag ladies. "They generally refuse services, but we're going to make an attempt to help them," he declared.[7]

But the shortage in the traditional flophouses that have provided housing for New York's most marginally competent citizens made it harder to help. The conversion of many single-room-occupancy hotels (SROs) into luxury housing began early in Koch's first term. The tax incentives for the rehabilitation of these buildings meant that New York lost an estimated 100,000 units of its cheapest housing—hotel housing that could be rented for little money without complicated applications or expensive security deposits. Even though most of the SRO tenants moved elsewhere, rather than joining the ranks of the homeless, the SRO crisis contributed significantly to the housing shortage.[8] Koch appointed the conscientious Laurence Klein to work on the SRO issue, inviting him to communicate directly through biweekly reports.[9] Klein inaugurated an interagency approach to support SRO residents, lobbying the state for changes in policies "which affect this vulnerable service-needy population and protect the rights of the community-at-large which has been inundated by an inequitable saturation of problem individuals."[10]

Klein first tried to improve conditions in SROs through a program of code enforcement, with big fines for hotels that refused to comply. He proclaimed that "this administration is not going to tolerate sleazy run-down SRO hotels to continue business-as-usual." In one case, the city buildings department fined the Westsider Hotel $37,500.[11] But Klein warned the mayor that code enforcement and fines, which made it less profitable to run welfare hotels, simply increased landlords' incentives to evict the tenants and use J-51 tax breaks to gut the buildings and turn them into luxury housing. The J-51 program gave developers a credit in the form of a tax exemption, against increases in their future property taxes for up to ten years for the amount of money they spent upgrading a building. SROs in prime locations like the Upper West Side were likely candidates for such upgrades.

The poor and filthy addicts, drunks, and crazy people hanging out in front of the hotels seemed threatening to middle-class residents, who were not happy when they or their children were approached by drug dealers or prostitutes. Even many of the most tolerant, politically progressive middle-class residents were not terribly sorry to see the hotels renovated as middle-class apartments. But these hotels provided a refuge to those who needed it most. Klein called for curbs on J-51 incentives to contain the problem and prevent the harassment and eviction of SRO residents.[12]

As the weather got warmer in the summer of 1979, Klein warned the mayor that "the wholesale conversion of former SRO hotels in Manhattan, regardless of the salutary benefits of the gentrification process, would inevitably lead us into a potential relocation crisis with scores of homeless poor requiring emergency shelter in armories." Klein had worked with some SRO property redevelopers like Columbia University and Jerome Kretchmer, a former city environmental protection commissioner, trying to relocate people caught in SRO conversions. But these efforts were unsuccessful, and Klein informed the mayor that "it is painfully obvious from these relocation attempts that there is no empty low-income housing anywhere, including the city's in-rem housing stock [housing owned by the city because the owners defaulted on taxes] available to properly locate the thousands of displaced tenants."[13]

The SRO coordinator called for a complete moratorium on J-51 conversions of SROs until the system for granting them could be reformed. The city then granted J-51 property tax exemptions as of right to anyone who applied and met the program's criteria, even before construction began. There was no control on the quality of the work that the city was subsidizing. Often landlords used the renovation process to harass their tenants into quitting the premises. Klein proposed reforms, to be passed during the moratorium, that would delay the grant of the J-51 tax break until construction was completed. He said tax breaks should be denied if repairs were shoddy or if tenants were harassed, in order to halt subsidies for repairs that would lead to the even worse problem of evictions. Klein accused then-housing commissioner Nat Leventhal of obstructing such a moratorium.[14] But Leventhal and Koch were so focused on rehabilitating housing that they failed to perceive the harm in SRO conversions. The renewal of the J-51 program that passed the city council in November 1979 did little to address the concerns that tax-subsidized renovation would throw thousands of SRO tenants from poorly maintained, but low-rent, housing and onto the streets.[15]

About a month after Klein wrote him, Koch ordered a reconsideration of administration policy on J-51. But top officials remained confident that they could solve the problem, and the administration did little more for more than a year. They belatedly began to regulate SRO conversions, with Koch signing a bill just after the 1981 election that provided tax incentives to owners to upgrade the hotels rather than convert them to co-ops or condominiums. But by that time the number of rooms renting for less than $50 a week had dropped from fifty thousand in 1975 to fourteen thousand.[16]

Klein understood that the problem went well beyond the question of SROs. He warned the mayor that, "without exaggeration, we are creating in Manhattan a class of homeless people who should rival the Vietnamese boat people for our attention and sympathy."[17] His dire predictions soon became a reality. In early 1981, with the mayor running for reelection, a *Times* headline proclaimed, "New York Is Facing a 'Crisis' on Vagrants." "Touching almost every neighborhood in the city, they are becoming the brunt of everybody's negative feelings and they are presenting this society with one of its greatest challenges," Sarah Connell, regional director of the New York State Office of Mental Health, told the paper.[18]

Within a few short years the elderly, mostly white, men of skid row had been replaced by a new population that was much more heavily African American, sometimes dubbed "the New Homeless." This population had developed addiction at a much earlier age than older homeless populations. Later in the 1980s crack addiction drove many men and women into homelessness. The "New Homeless" were in worse shape than the older alcoholics. Their addiction at a young age meant they had less education or training than the traditional Skid Row bums. Even if they could get over their drug problem, they were virtually unemployable. And some used violence against the older generation of homeless people.[19]

The first explosion in homelessness coincided with a time of increased unemployment, especially during the severe recession induced by Federal Reserve chair Paul Volcker in 1981–82 in a successful bid to tame double-digit inflation. Volcker raised interest rates to nearly 20 percent and revalued the dollar. While New York was hurt less than some other regions, it had few jobs for marginal and unskilled people. Poverty rose with interest rates, and for the first time large numbers of families were homeless. And poverty was increasing nationally. From 1978 to 1985 the number of households living below the poverty line increased 25 percent, and the average poor family lost $600 in income. Though much of the economy improved after 1983, the number of homeless families continued to increase through the 1980s. And the expanding financial sector increased demand for high-end housing.[20]

The shortage of low-cost housing in the city is only half the story. Declining social services and the increasing drug addiction and anomie of Reagan-era America swelled the numbers of men and women sleeping outdoors. At the time the causes of homelessness were not well understood, but later studies suggest that homeless people often have high rates of "personal disability" and high levels of "family estrangement." Generally the poorest of the poor, they often have no private safety net to compensate for the low level of social services in the United States.[21]

Former mental patients made up perhaps as much as a third of the homeless population after the late 1970s. Tens of thousands of mental patients who had been cared for, sometimes for life, in state hospitals were deinstitutionalized in a well-intentioned and ostensibly humanitarian effort to safeguard their civil rights. Those previously hospitalized for mental illness made up somewhere between 11 percent and 33 percent of New York's homeless population, and they were among the most visible street people.[22]

Advocates for deinstitutionalization, such as Dr. Allan Miller, New York's commissioner of mental hygiene, tried to fund community-based outpatient care with the savings the state realized after it closed two-thirds of the beds in its mental hospitals. But that did not happen. In 1979 alone six thousand patients were released from the five state mental hospitals in New York City, with little provision made for their housing or for outpatient care to help them function in society. With a full-blown fiscal crisis in both city and state, officials were reluctant to create new programs of any size. At the same time the state institutions kept patient populations low by ratcheting up standards for admission, accepting only the most severely incapacitated patients.[23]

Meanwhile, the political system aimed what money there was at the wrong target. Unionized employees in depressed upstate areas and their powerful protectors in Albany were able to prevent cuts in jobs at the mental hospitals in those areas, despite a drastic decline in the institutionalized population. For those who remained as inpatients, this probably meant better care, but tens of thousands of people found themselves out on the mean streets of New York, trying to earn a living with no psychiatric or social support.[24]

THE RIGHT TO SHELTER—AND THE RIGHT TO REFUSE

The most consequential event in the history of homelessness during the Koch administration was a lawsuit, *Callahan v. Carey* (1979), brought by Robert M. Hayes, originally a lawyer associated with the white-shoe firm of Sullivan and Cromwell. He subsequently founded the Coalition for the Homeless. On behalf of six clients from the Bowery, Hayes obtained a state court injunction ordering the Koch administration to provide 750 more beds for homeless single men. State Supreme Court Justice Andrew R. Tyler held that the New York State constitution gave homeless men a right to "adequate shelter," a holding later extended to homeless women and families.[25] As one scholar explained, the *Callahan* decision began "a tortuous process of grudging compliance with and exacting monitoring of what would become a slew of court orders."[26] The Koch administration initially thought that providing additional beds in a new shelter on Ward's Island would solve the problem, but as Stan Brezenoff observed, "it handled it for about a year."[27]

The administration eventually settled the case by signing a 1981 consent decree that placed efforts to help the homeless under a judge's supervision, in effect giving Hayes and the Coalition for the Homeless the power to supervise every detail.[28] Corporation Counsel Allen G. Schwartz persuaded Koch to agree because the administration seemed likely to lose the court case, and because city hall thought the problem would be solved by adding a few more shelter beds, a gross underestimation. By the end of Koch's term the shelters had ten thousand residents.[29]

The *Callahan* decision has also been severely criticized because it allowed homeless advocates and a judge to take over management of the shelters to the most minute detail and, ironically, constrained political debate and limited spending to building more and better emergency shelters instead of experimenting with more permanent alternatives. "Elemental decencies were spelled out in obsessive fashion—space between beds, quality of food, ratio of men to toilet facilities, arrangement of storage for belongings—not only because of the threat of institutional neglect but because that was where the legal leverage lay."[30] This locked in a system that required spending $18,000 to $20,000 per person per year on huge shelters, some of which housed hundreds of men in huge rooms.

"It's not exactly a palace, but it's nice," Koch declared in early 1980 while inspecting the new Keener Building, a renovated mental hospital on Ward's Island originally designed to provide 180 additional beds to homeless men and replace the horrible makeshift "Big Room" at the Third Street Men's Shelter.[31] By the time of the 1981 consent decree, the Ward's Island facility had been expanded to house 450 men but was actually housing 526, and the overflow meant that the "Big Room" had to be reopened.[32] The Keener facility was nice only when it was new and unused. City officials wanted to keep it sufficiently uncomfortable to deter new clients, some of whom had been prematurely discharged from the same building when it was a hospital. Yet city officials also wanted the shelter system to be good enough so that people would choose the shelters over living on the street. Kim Hopper, an ethnographer of homelessness in New York City, describes the Ward Island shelter as "a paragon of institutional thrift. It was run by a limited and overworked staff. Bedding was rudimentary; light mattresses on metal frames. Walls were bereft of any ornament but graffiti," and there was little in the way of recreation, reading material, or television to help men pass the time.[33]

Since the consent decree effectively governed expenditures for support for the homeless, it acted as a brake on innovative alternatives to shelters, though that was not Hayes's intention. Koch was constantly at loggerheads with Governor Hugh Carey because the governor (along with Hayes) wanted smaller, community-based institutions with more rehabilitation programs to induce more men to come in off the streets.[34] But the mayor had to face angry communities wherever and whenever he tried to site a homeless facility, small or large, and the courts insisted on immediate provision of emergency shelter. So the administration preferred larger and fewer facilities to reduce the neighborhood opposition and increase the likelihood that capacity could be added quickly. From this perspective alternative schemes with a longer-term impact seemed utopian.[35]

Carey blamed homelessness on the Koch administration and its support for tax abatements, claiming that city officials "unfairly linked" the increase in homelessness to deinstitutionalization of mental patients. Koch administration officials challenged the report on which Carey based his statements, branding it irresponsible and "a lot of rhetorical hodgepodge."[36] "We need more analysis," Barbara Blum, the state social services commissioner, told a reporter, supporting the position of her boss, the governor: "Some of these people are young, vigorous and troubled, others have problems with alcohol and drugs. Others, particularly women, are simply bereft of family and income support. We have been treating the homeless as one great glob of humanity." She criticized the centralized shelter scheme for isolating the homeless and making them permanent wards of Ward's Island, with little possibility of finding long-term stable housing and employment.[37] Her agency offered to pay half the cost of such smaller-scale shelters, but the plan was politically unrealistic. Shelters were proposed for quiet middle-class neighborhoods, like Father Cappodano Boulevard near the beach in Staten Island, Ditmas Park in Brooklyn, and Riverdale, a wealthy enclave in the Bronx, all places with the political clout that would make Board of Estimate approval virtually impossible. Even relatively isolated locations for shelters, such as Ward's Island in the East River or the barracks at the old naval air station at Floyd Bennett Field on Jamaica Bay, drew lawsuits and political challenges.[38]

City officials tried almost everything to expand the amount of temporary shelter, but many promising ideas proved difficult to implement. For example, a developer proposed to house displaced families on a cruise ship, an idea that was politically advantageous because a ship is not located in a neighborhood that might oppose the shelter. But the buildings department maintained that the density of twenty-seven hundred residents needed to justify the upfront costs ($8 million a year for five years) would be excessive, especially given the narrow stairs and small residential rooms. The fire department also reported huge safety problems, including the lack of interior fire alarm and sprinkler systems.[39]

Even the most liberal neighborhoods did not want to deal with incontinent drug-dependent or mentally ill homeless men and women as part of their daily routine. But the old, more authoritarian, tools for dealing with such disorders had broken down. Public intoxication was no longer a crime by the mid-1970s, and the police tended to see vagrancy as a problem for social service agencies, which did not have the money to help significant numbers of people with health care, housing, and jobs that would help them reconstruct their lives.[40] Many middle-class citizens nostalgically remembered a time when the police could arbitrarily roust the poor from their neighborhoods and began to call for more coercive solutions. Few knew or cared that the vagrancy laws had been used after the Civil War to effectively re-enslave blacks or arbitrarily imprison and harass them. The insistence that crimes had to be defined by criminal acts rather than social status was an integral part of the civil rights revolution that ensured equal protection of the law to all Americans, regardless of race or class position.

But living in the midst of the homeless was no small burden on neighborhoods. Residents of Murray Hill complained to the Board of Estimate about the effect of a program that provided meals and counseling at the First Moravian Church at Thirtieth and Lexington. Gertrude Huston, secretary of the local community planning board, painted a picture of a neighborhood transformed into a Hieronymus Bosch hell: "Since the program opened, this has been a disaster area. Our brownstone steps, doorways and vestibules have been invaded by derelicts and bag people—and their urine and their feces. Some of us have been attacked by the more violent of the church's clients. A bag person couple were seen fornicating on the church steps one afternoon. Some of the male clients lie on our sidewalks exposing their genitalia."[41]

Koch often voiced the frustration of many middle-class New Yorkers at such public smells and spectacles and attempted more coercive policies.⁴² But he ran smack up against the *Papachristou* decision and a developing body of law on the freedom to refuse medical treatment, which, like deinstitutionalization, was a reaction to the authoritarian abuses of some lobotomizing and electroshocking psychiatrists of the 1950s and 1960s. At the dedication of the Antonio G. Olivieri Center for the Homeless on West Thirtieth Street, in the spring of 1981, the mayor declared that he favored state legislation allowing the police to collect homeless people in vans and hold them without their consent for seventy-two hours "to give them food, a bath and medical attention." The mayor was advised that such a program would be unconstitutional. If so, Koch declared, "then the Constitution is dumb."⁴³ Later, however, Corporation Counsel Schwartz convinced Koch to support a measure that was limited to picking up people who were evidently a danger to themselves or incompetent. This pickup policy would become one of the most controversial of his second and third terms. Koch, who was usually a strong advocate of civil liberties, defended it because he was deeply concerned that some people might freeze to death in the winter.⁴⁴

It was painfully clear that homelessness was increasing by the end of Koch's first term. The Community Services Agency estimated that New York contained as many as thirty-six thousand homeless people, a figure that Koch disputed. "We have done the best we can," the mayor told a state assembly committee, but he continued his squabble with the governor about which jurisdiction had responsibility for the problem: "It is time for New York State to reassume the burden it so cavalierly dumped on local governments when it stopped providing care for a substantial portion of the mentally ill population." At the same time Koch denied charges that his economic development policies involving the SROs had contributed to homelessness. A few days later he offered a plan to meet the growing demand for shelter by putting beds in city armories; it was not clear whether the facilities would be adequate. Just before Christmas 1981 he also appealed to religious groups to take the homeless into churches and synagogues, but the request fell flat.⁴⁵ Koch would continue to wrestle with the problem of making New York a middle-class public space for the rest of his mayoralty. Powerful interests and market forces would support him, but fiscal constraints, constitutional concerns, police enforcement styles, and lack of staffing would limit his progress, as would the ballooning numbers of people living on the street.

After the distraction of his unsuccessful 1982 gubernatorial campaign, Koch resumed the role of mayor-adventurer, watching from behind a "magic window" in a subway station barbershop as transit officers swept men and women from the subway station at Forty-second Street and Eighth Avenue in the middle of the night. On other nights he visited homeless people on the cold winter streets.⁴⁶ He took regular tours with homeless outreach teams. When a homeless woman died in Penn Station, he carefully followed all the details of the case, including the autopsy report, and asked aides to prepare a summary (with names changed) "to show legislators what we are up against" when homeless people refused treatment.[47] On one such trip, at about 11 P.M. on February 4, 1982 (before the gubernatorial campaign got underway), he rushed down to Grand Central Station with welfare commissioner James A. Krauskopf after a television reporter alerted them that a woman lying in the station was "undernourished and covered by sores." She was probably suffering from gangrene. Koch and Krauskopf tried to talk the woman into accepting care and failed. They then awakened Charles H. Gay, the director of the office responsible for service to homeless people. Gay went to Grand Central and got a psychiatrist to examine the woman, Mary O'Hanlon, who was committed on the spot and sent to a hospital. (Later that night Gay died of a heart attack.)[48]

Changes in state law had made it easier to pick up people who were in danger and commit them for seventy-two hours, with a judge and a court-appointed attorney to assure them due process. By the winter of 1982 outreach crews were using the law more and more. In 1985 Koch announced that on cold winter nights the police would begin taking people to shelters, by force if necessary, declaring that he did not care what it cost or how many people would have to be sheltered. "What this is about is saving lives," he insisted.[49]

Conservative critics and some Koch administration officials have attributed both fiscal crisis and homelessness to an excess of municipal generosity, but significant evidence exists that European social democracies have been far more successful in dealing with homelessness in part because of their superior welfare systems and greater reserves of "social housing." A comparative study that included New York, London, and Hamburg also concluded that the superior, nationally funded social safety nets in the United Kingdom and Germany forestalled the explosion of homelessness experienced by New York in the 1980s. The problem was not too much generosity but too little social welfare.[50]

The full brutality of a New York winter hit hard in January 1985, with the temperature sometimes reaching well below zero and a wind chill off an icy river deep-freezing bodies lying outside on heating grates. People had always lived on New York's streets, even during its deadly cold winters. But anyone shivering down Gotham's streets that winter did not need a government report to know that the homeless population had reached "the highest figure since the Depression."[51] Koch repeatedly toured the frigid city and talked to the homeless and the employees assigned to aid them. He could not fathom why they would not come in from the cold.

One March night Koch went to Alphabet City in a social service van. But as he followed a shy, fleeing man (known to social workers as John Doe Plastic Cap), telling him, "I won't hurt you. I'm the mayor and I want to help you," Koch probably seemed more like an apparition than a savior. Who expects the mayor to talk to a homeless person on a freezing New York night? Koch finally did persuade one of three people he approached to take shelter. But he was increasingly uneasy about the morality of the law that said that they could not be forced into shelter merely because their own lives were in jeopardy, unless they were a danger to others.[52]

Not everyone agreed with this position. In the late 1980s a mobile intervention unit picked up a forty-year-old woman who called herself "Billie Boggs" (her name was actually Joyce Brown), who lived on the sidewalk in front of a hot air duct at Swensen's restaurant at East Sixty-fifth Street and Second Avenue. Before she was picked up, Koch had spoken personally to her on one of his tours with outreach workers.[53] According to an appellate court opinion, she used the area in front of Swensen's "as her bedroom, toilet, and living room." Brown had repeatedly run out into traffic and would ridicule people who gave her money unsolicited by ripping up the bills. She had refused psychiatric help several times, and on October 28, 1987, a psychiatrist working with Project HELP decided that she was in need of immediate hospitalization. She was involuntarily committed to Bellevue. She filed for release, and the New York chapter of the American Civil Liberties Union eventually took up her cause. The trial court, faced with six psychiatrists who were split down the middle on the question of whether Boggs was "a danger to herself or others," freed her, in part because of the coherence of her own testimony. The Appellate Division reversed the trial court and sent Billie Boggs back to the hospital, though two judges dissented. As one of the dissenters, Judge E. Leo Milonas noted, the case put a constitutional spotlight on Koch's policy of taking homeless people off the street. The judge characterized the high-profile case as "a classic confrontation between the rights of a citizen against a governmental authority trying to confront and remedy a pervasive societal problem." Milonas ruled that even though the evidence showed that Brown had mental problems, and was defecating in her pants, she was not a danger and had a right to remain on the street.[54]

Joyce Brown was released from the hospital a few days after she was committed, having refused antipsychotic drugs. By February 1988 she had become a "media star" who "received half a dozen movie and book offers," ate dinner at Windows on the World, the restaurant atop the World Trade Center, and went on a shopping spree paid for by television shows on which she appeared. Brown even spoke at Harvard Law School.[55] Ronald Reagan cited her case to Mikhail Gorbachev as an exemplar of freedom, still implying that homeless people were on the streets as a matter of choice.[56] As one scholar noted, "Perhaps the most damaging news coverage of the Brown affair was the way it discredited Mayor Koch, who had played an important role in the earlier stages of the homeless narrative as an outspoken critic of Reaganomics."[57] Brown's good fortune did not last, though she did manage to stay off the street. In the fall of 1988 she was arrested and charged with buying a small amount of heroin and possessing hypodermic needles. Brown was in and out of the shelter system and was involuntarily committed to a hospital again in 1993 and 1994 for a period of six months.[58]

Koch continued to focus on the homeless though the winter holiday season, and when he reiterated his call for churches and private charities to help more, many replied that it was government that was falling down on the job. At the seventy-fifth anniversary of the Stephen Wise Free Synagogue he pointedly noted that, while sixteen churches had answered his call to open their rooms to homeless people, no synagogues did. The next day the New York Board of Rabbis said that three synagogues would add beds but claimed that the decision had been in the works before the mayor's browbeating.[59]

The mayor later explained that he would provide religious groups with bedding and other supplies and affirmed that the basic responsibility for housing the homeless was the government's. The reason he wanted churches and synagogues to house the homeless was not a lack of city-sponsored shelters because they could better help "people like the bag-ladies who are too fearful of large institutions to come into our regular facilities."[60] While some clergy continued to criticize him for putting moral responsibility on churches and synagogues, both because they lacked the resources and because they were not responsible for the economic policies that cast the socially and psychologically marginal out into the streets, Koch pressed the matter.[61] After all, Koch himself had been close to the poverty line—when his own family doubled up with relatives in a two-bedroom apartment with eight people during the Depression, they would have met some recent legal definitions of homelessness.

Koch found continued resistance in neighborhoods to plans for decentralizing care for the homeless. Local residents who had dealt with a decade of declining neighborhoods failed to warm to the idea of a shelter next door. He appealed to the community boards to find places in their neighborhoods for shelters on city property, and he denounced them when the response was meager. Only six of the fifty-nine boards had responded after sixty days, though he did get suggestions for a few sites worth exploring, such as the vacant part of a cruise ship terminal and an abandoned Masonic temple.[62]

Despite its vast holdings of real estate seized at tax foreclosures, New York did not have enough real estate that was suitable for shelters.[63] Later in 1983 the Department of Housing Preservation and Development did tackle the easiest part of the homeless problem—that of displaced families (the least likely to become chronically homeless) by providing $28 million from a jobs fund to renovate apartments as transitional housing. "The idea is to use the unemployed to build homes for the unhoused," declared city housing commissioner Anthony Gliedman.[64] But the program to renovate 1,264 apartments was tiny in proportion to the problem. The homeless and housing programs "were not about politics," according to Abraham Biderman, who served as housing commissioner in Koch's last term.[65] Koch was willing to work with political opponents, such as the Reverend Calvin Butts. The administration cooperated closely with Butts's plan for a transitional shelter for the homeless.[66]

The intractability and emotionality of the homelessness issue did, however, offer many opportunities for grandstanding and clashes of egos. As the religious institutions were showing their reluctance, Donald Trump offered to house homeless people in a building on exclusive Central Park South. City officials did not take him up on it, seeing the invitation as a tactic to harass and scare off existing tenants. Trump actually wanted to demolish the building and put a hotel on the site. When the International Rescue Committee suggested using the space for newly arrived Polish refugees who had fled their home country because of the crackdown on the trade union Solidarity, Trump's offer evaporated, and, according to the *New York Times* columnist Sydney H. Schanberg, Trump was suddenly and atypically unavailable to the press.[67]

Homelessness did become a political battleground between Koch and his old rival Mario Cuomo. Governor Cuomo leaked a state study claiming that child malnutrition was widespread among those living in city-inspected welfare hotels. After the health department conducted medical examinations of seven thousand children in the hotels and shelters, this proved to be an exaggerated claim, though they agency found several individual cases of mistreated children.[68] Koch, in turn, attacked the state's mental health policies as "vile, cruel and heartless." While deinstitutionalization had stopped, Koch faulted Cuomo, as he had criticized Carey, for failing to provide sufficient community-based care. This forced the governor to reverse proposed budget cuts in state funds to help its mentally ill population. Koch made scarce city funds available, he said, as "a response to the state not doing its job and the city doing it for them."[69] Cuomo first moved to limit the damage, making an agreement with Koch to provide two thousand more beds, many of them at the Creedmoor Psychiatric Center in Queens, though many of those beds turned out not to exist when officials actually took homeless people there. But Koch and Cuomo now needed each other to create a record of success, and on this and many other issues the two men created a strange modus vivendi. Eventually, Cuomo restored the mental health programs to the budget, implicitly acknowledging that Koch was right.[70]

Koch's best efforts to emulate La Guardia, albeit on his own and with no Roosevelt, put him in the position of being unfairly compared in public with Herbert Hoover. When New Yorkers moved into the streets during the Depression, their shantytowns were called "Hoovervilles." In June 1988 an impromptu demonstration by homeless people at city hall turned into the "Kochville" encampment in City Hall Park. Though the mayor had declared that he would close it when the weather got too cold to camp outside, Kochville ran itself as an autonomous community, most often with about thirty-five residents protesting city homeless policy round-the-clock. The camp disbanded on its own without interference from the police on Christmas Eve 1988.[71] While the reproach nettled Koch, his toleration of the encampment for more than six months was extraordinary (especially compared with Hoover, who failed to prevent General Douglas MacArthur from dispersing a similar encampment of Bonus Marchers in Washington, D.C., with bayonets). Kochville is a reminder that City Hall Plaza was an open and unique center of city political life, until Rudy Giuliani fenced it off, years before 9/11, on the pretext of a terrorist threat while deploying programs that moved homeless people from the streets to the jails.[72] Political freedom in New York City has never been quite the same since.

19 THE KOCH HOUSING PLAN (1986–89)

I used to get on my bike and ride [from the North Bronx] . . . down the South Bronx, over in to Harlem on Sunday morning, and ride back up. There used to be times when—it was like a joke with me—I could start from my house, and after my house I could go block after block almost for ten miles without finding another resident. If you knew how to do it, you hit all the bad places. You can't do that today. In fact, it just doesn't exist.

—FORMER DEPUTY MAYOR ROBERT ESNARD

In his 1985 "State of the City" message, Mayor Koch announced the most ambitious plan of his political career: a five-year $4.4 billion city-financed program to build or rehabilitate 100,000 low- and moderate-income housing units. The idea took off, and several weeks later he more than doubled that goal, expanding it to 252,000 units, with a revamped ten-year plan, revised once again in 1989, that committed $5.1 billion to finish building the 252,000 units by 1996.[1] It was an extremely risky move. Some experts said at first that Koch's goal was "inspirational rather than realistic." At first, no one in his administration knew exactly where the money would come from. But Koch and his aides managed to pull it off, and the housing plan became his most enduring achievement.

The plan began modestly enough during a lunch of senior administration officials at Junior's, a landmark known for its overstuffed pastrami sandwiches and the best cheesecake in Brooklyn. Abraham Biderman, then a housing adviser to the mayor who later served as housing commissioner, recalled that they sketched out the first draft of one of the largest housing investments in New York's history on the back of a napkin.[2] They realized that New York was facing an affordable housing crisis. Between 1978 and 1981 the number of apartments renting for $200 month declined by 43 percent, with 67 percent of renters spending more than 35 percent of their income on rent. And in Koch's first term eighty-one thousand units of housing stock, mostly at the lower end of the scale, disappeared.[3]

"No other city before or after has committed to building as much housing as we did, moderate and low-income housing," said Biderman, who helped shepherd housing through convoluted bureaucratic pipelines first as a mayoral aide, then as commissioner of finance, and eventually as housing commissioner. "At that time the city population was growing, the jobs were growing, but there was no housing being created for all sorts of reasons, and this was the critical linchpin to the whole city economy, not just the housing industry," he recalled.

THE NEW YORK HOUSING TRADITION

The new housing program broke with Reaganism but was very much in the tradition of the public agencies, workers cooperatives, and public-private partnerships that were building housing for low- and middle-income people in New York since the 1920s.[4] The most unprecedented element of the Koch plan was that while it would be financed with cross-subsidies from luxury projects, and from state entities such as the Battery Park City Authority, the bulk of the money came from the city's capital budget. "We quickly realized that if we wanted to have a real program, a meaningful program, that we needed to start spending a lot of our own capital dollars. This was a very novel idea because I don't think that any other city had ever spent money of any consequence on that kind of a program," Biderman recalled.[5]

Public housing had a bad name in many parts of the country because it was often badly managed by political hacks, and it was seen as a dumping ground for the poorest of the poor. But twentieth-century New York had a long tradition of public housing that was well maintained by civil servants. "The city administration and the city council generally [were] supportive of public housing, more so than most big cities in the United States," according to John Simon, general manager of the New York City Housing Authority.[6] By the 1960s, however, the housing authority had been forced to cut rents and accept a larger proportion of people on welfare, while lawsuits diluted the authority's ability to regulate tenants' conduct or refuse to rent because of a prospective tenant's past misconduct.[7]

Despite these problems, the housing authority had continued to provide quality housing, even during the fiscal crisis, when money for maintenance was increasingly hard to come by. But Koch chose a very different model for his housing program. After the debacle of the grandiose Charlotte Street project in the south Bronx during his first year as mayor, Koch had little interest in building new high-rise projects (see chapter 12). Federal funding had disappeared, but that was not the only reason for the decision in 1985–86 to build subsidized private housing, rather than large-scale public housing projects on the housing authority model. Housing officials understood that one reason for the relative success of New York's public housing was adequate expenditures on maintenance, and they were loath to undertake any housing project that would permanently increase the expense budget. So the plan was generous with capital funds, but officials hoped that private and nonprofit ownership would shift most maintenance expenses to private owners. The city also aided this goal with tax subsidies designed to subsidize maintenance and improvements.[8]

Public housing was not the only model Koch had for his new initiative. The most important initiatives in affordable housing for the poor in Koch's first two terms came from neighborhood organizations, though the Koch administration assisted. One of the earliest successful housing schemes during the Koch administration was the Nehemiah Plan, named for the biblical prophet who rebuilt Jerusalem. Promulgated by a group of thirty-six religious leaders from eastern Brooklyn, including the Reverend Johnnie Ray Youngblood and Roman Catholic Bishop Francis J. Mugavero of Brooklyn, with initial community organizing expertise from the Industrial Areas Foundation, the international network of community organizations founded by Saul Alinsky, the plan proposed to build five thousand homes and offer them to qualified buyers at the cost of construction if the Koch administration would provide no-interest financing. "No group has ever come to us like that before. Basically, they said, 'We've got our $12 million; what have you got?'" said Charles Reiss, a city housing official.[9] Ultimately, city subsidies totaled $20 million, including the provision of public amenities such as sewer connections. Even though the group included political opponents of the Koch administration, the Industrial Areas Foundation persuaded the Department of Housing Preservation and Development to contribute free land and a $10,000 subsidy for each house, along with tax abatements for the buyers. The organization sold the two- and three-bedroom homes for $43,500, their cost, allowing an affordable mortgage payment of $300 for a family earning $20,000 a year.[10]

The group's first project has been a huge success, and it has continued to build low-cost housing into the twenty-first century.[11] Nehemiah was a model for community response in the neoliberal era, rebuilding areas where multiple dwellings had been destroyed as the industrial economy shrank. The project's lower-density subsidized housing bridged the gap into home ownership for the lower -middle class. But building housing for the lower middle class and the working poor would expand in Koch's last term into his largest response to the housing crisis.

By 1985 Koch wanted to go beyond the limits of Nehemiah housing. He realized that New York had a unique opportunity to restore the vast amounts of degraded housing stock that the city had acquired in lieu of taxes. Much of this property could be renovated or, in the case of vacant land, built up. Koch's Panel on Affordable Housing, which included representatives of the real estate industry, argued that the most successful moderate-income housing would be lower-density projects, such as the old-fashioned three-family frame house and the six-story semi-fireproof apartment building with a resident owner.[12] And like the original goals of the housing authority, the focus of the new plan was on housing for a mix of working poor and low-to-moderate income residents. Such rehabilitation and smaller-scale construction avoided the destruction of neighborhoods by large-scale urban renewal of the Robert Moses type, which had been denounced so effectively by Jane Jacobs. The new projects were largely free of the difficult political issues raised by NIMBY (not-in my-back-yard) opposition, in part because most of the construction was in devastated neighborhoods where community groups had been working hard to win more development.

PUTTING MEAT ON THE BONES

The program quickly advanced beyond the napkin-scratching stage. The scale and complexity of the various programs that made up the Koch housing initiative were breathtaking. The plan had four main goals: gut renovation of all suitable city-owned vacant buildings; moderate renovation of all occupied city-owned buildings; promotion of below-market-rate loans and tax breaks to encourage owners of low- and middle-income housing to renovate; construction of new homes for owner-occupants. These units would be located all over the city but were particularly concentrated in the south Bronx, Harlem, and central Brooklyn.[13]

Soon after announcing the housing program, Koch changed housing commissioners. Tony Gliedman was in many ways an effective commissioner, untouched by scandal, but he was closely associated with the Brooklyn regular Democrats, an involvement that was reflected in the subordinates he chose and in the way he ran the agency. Because of the numerous scandals that touched the administration early in 1986 (see chapter 22), Koch had to distance himself from the regulars. To Gliedman's dismay the mayor made a surprise announcement of his departure, along with that of Jay Turoff, the disgraced Taxi and Limousine commissioner who also was a Brooklyn regular.[14]

Paul Crotty, the incoming housing commissioner, was not a housing expert but was respected as a "Mr. Clean"—which was important in a post that was now responsible for dispensing billions. Crotty, who had been city finance commissioner, was a distinguished lawyer from a political family—his father had been Erie County Democratic chair and his brother was on Governor Cuomo's staff. Paul Crotty later went on to serve as city corporation counsel under Giuliani, then became a federal judge. Crotty got along better with housing activists than Gliedman had, "introducing a new tone of respect," according to one activist.[15]

The new commissioner chopped heads in the normally sedate housing agency, eliminating four of the six deputy commissioners soon after taking over. "Tony Gliedman was really very angry because he felt it was some kind of reflection on his judgment. But if I was going to spend the $4.2 billion and spend it wisely, I wanted to have my own people," Crotty said. He was committed to selecting developers strictly on the basis of their track record and appropriateness to the program, recalling: "We weren't going to handcraft particular projects for particular developers. We had a program that we wanted to work on a cookie-cutter basis."[16] But not everyone liked this mass-production approach. Both Kathryn Wylde, president of the Housing Partnership, the prominent nonprofit started in 1982 by David Rockefeller to build low- and middle-income homes, and politicians such as David Dinkins and Charlie Rangel complained as Crotty's agency began to play a larger role in developer selection, although most of those wrinkles were eventually smoothed out.[17]

In New York supporting affordable housing is, in theory, as safe an issue as opposing littering. In practice the mayor got flak for his program from both the Left and the Right. The Right wanted an unregulated private housing market, arguing that market forces would lead to the construction of more affordable housing. Herbert London, an aspirant for the Republican mayoral nomination in the 1989 primary, called for the voucher program touted by the Reagan administration instead of subsidized construction and claimed that "the reason we have a housing crisis in New York is that we won't let markets work."[18]

At the same time Koch's program came under fire from housing advocates on the left, who had become more concerned about redistribution and homelessness than about class and racial integration. Ironically echoing the means-testing Reaganites, they deplored Koch's decision to build significant amounts of middle-income housing, demanding that the needs of the poor should come first. Bonnie Brower, the executive director of the Association of Neighborhood and Housing Development, argued that the Koch housing program did not sufficiently address the needs of low-income householders. "If they want to build middle-income and upper-middle-income housing, let them at least call it by its right name, and let us deal with it on its merits," Brower commented.[19]

Manhattan Borough President David Dinkins and James Dumpson, former commissioner of the Human Resources Administration, also criticized Koch because the city was not renovating enough housing for the poorest New Yorkers. At Dinkins's behest Dumpson wrote a report titled "A Shelter Is Not a Home," calling for the city to double production of housing units affordable by the homeless from four thousand to eight thousand a year and to institute a two-tier welfare shelter allowance, with additional money going to families whose rents had been raised as a result of moderate rehabilitation by private landlords.[20]

Koch dismissed these proposals as too expensive, though Dumpson disputed the administration's estimates. But there was a deeper discussion. The Koch housing program was primarily an economic development program, not a welfare program. Koch aimed to rebuild areas devastated by abandonment and neglect into neighborhoods that were viable and self-sustaining without continuing cash subsidies or maintenance expenses that would have to be paid from the expense budget. Stan Brezenoff wrote Dumpson insisting that "we cannot preserve the City's long-term health if we do not address the needs of the middle class by putting public resources into creating housing for this group. If we don't, who will be here to fill the jobs and pay the taxes that support services and housing creation for the poor?"[21] The practicality of Dumpson's proposals may be judged by the limited implementation they received from Dinkins two-and-a-half years later, when he became mayor: he moderately increased the allocation of housing to the homeless but retained the goal of building primarily for people with low and moderate, but steady, incomes.

Dinkins did not move to build housing for the homeless exclusively, because it would have conflicted with the goal of stabilizing neighborhoods. Low-income subsidy projects cost more, which meant fewer renovations could be undertaken with the funding available, leaving more holes. An exclusively subsidized program would also tend to create ghettos of low-income families who had the least social stability, a particularly questionable idea in 1986 at the height of the crack epidemic.[22] Housing commissioner Paul Crotty was impatient with complaints from "ideologues and advocates" that most of the housing was aimed at middle-income residents who could afford to buy housing in the $25,000 to $40,000 range or pay equivalent rent in proportion to their income. He kept telling them, "Not every program can meet all the income targets. There's lots of notes on this organ; you have to hit all the notes."[23]

REPOPULATING NEW YORK

Such a complicated set of programs, with so many sources of funding, posed daunting obstacles to construction. "The hardest thing to get built is housing," a frustrated Koch told the press after a year and a half of trying to cajole the bureaucracy into building buildings.[24] Complicated financing and regulation, the impact of scandals, and the need to create effective bureaucratic channels between a hodgepodge of agencies all militated against the will to build.

Koch had a lifelong interest in housing issues. He had been a tenant lawyer in Greenwich Village and had jockeyed himself onto the subpanel of the House Banking and Currency Committee that dealt with federal housing programs. As he moved into his third term as mayor in 1986, he recognized that the timing was perfect for a housing initiative: New York was back in the bond markets, and it was sitting on thousands of tax-delinquent properties it had acquired during the fiscal crisis. Pressure from housing groups to stem rising homelessness was seconded by business groups that recognized that affordable housing was essential to the economy.

Koch's attitude toward public housing was shaped by his experience in the 1973 Forest Hills controversy that he had called his Rubicon. In his second year as mayor, he wrote housing commissioner Nat Leventhal, soon to become one of his principal deputies: "I take it as a basic premise that a middle class area should not be grossly impacted by adding low income projects to it where such projects already exist in reasonable numbers."[25] Koch's emphasis on home ownership and neighborhood stabilization eased fears that publicly funded housing would bring crime. By privatizing future maintenance costs, home ownership programs created less of an obligation for the city than did city-owned rental units. In completely destroyed areas, previous attempts to restore housing had been stymied by continued abandonment, but after 1986 economic conditions had changed for the better, so that efforts to restore and preserve neighborhoods had more staying power than previously.[26]

Until the mid-1980s New York's housing stock did not grow significantly. In 1983, for example, the addition of 11,251 newly built or renovated units was offset by the loss of 11,133 units through demolition and conversion to nonresidential uses—a net gain of only 118. Administration officials viewed the small net increase as a hard-won victory: they had managed to reverse a steady decline in the number of units available. Housing commissioner Crotty later suggested that those numbers for units renovated might have been a bit high: "[Former housing commissioner] Tony [Gliedman] was playing this game of massaging numbers. . . . If he put a roof on a fifty-apartment house, a fifty-unit house, he claimed fifty units. If the next year he came back and put a boiler in the same house, he'd claim another fifty units."[27]

Nonetheless, there seems little question that Koch administration policies and an improving economy began to turn the shrinking city back into a growing one, though the administration does bear responsibility for its slow action on single-room-occupancy hotels (SROs). Once the recession ended in 1984, losses of housing slowed to a trickle, and the combination of private and public construction led to a net gain of thirty-seven thousand units by 1987, boosting public confidence in Koch's new expanded housing program.[28]

After 1986 there was much more local control over the kinds of projects that were built, because the housing initiative was using mostly city and state money. The designs could be much more site specific when they were carried out by local development groups in accordance with neighborhood concerns, avoiding Forest Hills–type controversies. Local control and the continuing destabilization of neighborhoods had made construction of affordable housing popular again. Much like Don Elliott and Leticia Kent, the original promoters of the Forest Hills project, Tony Gliedman, who was housing commissioner up to 1986, when the program was in its planning stages, looked to the Upper West Side, where he had lived when he attended Columbia Law School, as a highly desirable model of diversity—"I believe very firmly that the strongest neighborhoods are those that are a combination of rich and poor, black and white, Catholic, Jew, Moslem and Protestant, and homeowner and renter. I thought one of the things that is wonderful for a neighborhood is to have that mix, so in neighborhoods that were essentially homeowner neighborhoods we built some rental housing."[29]

The program shifted the goals for government housing programs from a welfare model primarily interested in housing the poorest to a more racially and income diverse affordable housing model, presaging a similar shift in public housing projects. "We definitely wanted to have a mix. We would have neighborhoods where it was working people, it would be just people who were unemployed, etc. . . . So it's a combination that we strove for, including the working poor and a little bit of middle class," Biderman recalled.[30]

The availability of housing programs also helped Koch engage African American community leaders in tense neighborhoods like Crown Heights. The Reverend Clarence Norman, for example, promised the mayor "a working meeting, without any confrontations or arguments. . . . We will seek the Mayor's support and commitment for a program that will move toward rebuilding our neighborhood."[31] Even Koch's controversial initiative to reform the community development corporations in his first term paid off years later when it came to housing construction, because the reformed CDCs were more efficient at restoring neighborhoods, especially with technical support from corporate-sponsored nonprofits, such as the Local Initiative Support Corporation (LISC). That organization, which had been started in 1980 by Mitchell Sviridoff, a former Ford Foundation vice president who was the mentor of several senior Koch administration officials, including First Deputy Mayor Stan Brezenoff and Herbert Sturz., chair of the city planning commission.[32]

LISC and Enterprise (a similar national nonprofit) helped community groups navigate the legal and bureaucratic requirements for administering housing programs legally, efficiently, and with sufficient technical skill. "If I could get HPD out of dealing with these groups that was a good thing to do," Crotty said, because nonprofits were often mistrustful of city officials but would listen when LISC explained the rules. The housing commission delegated the selection of community groups to these national intermediaries, which helped depoliticize the process. Some critics evaluating the program have complained that newly expanded and bureaucratized

CDCs pushed out more grassroots and participatory efforts to build housing, but following the rules also prevented corruption.[33]

The ten-year plan faced financial obstacles from the start, and it was remarkable that Koch overcame them and brought it to fruition. Originally, most of the financing was supposed to come from tax-exempt bonds floated by the Housing Development Corporation (HDC). That part of Koch's initial proposal was scotched by the federal Tax Reform Act of 1986, which eliminated the tax exemption for the HDC bonds, along with a number of other tax shelters. Budget director Alair Townsend warned Koch early on that she feared that "the funding sources are so insecure for the $4.5 billion program as to raise questions immediately about the likelihood of implementation."[34] The plan's initial fuzziness made some experienced policy wonks suspicious. Roger Starr, a former developer and housing commissioner, who then sat on the editorial board of *New York Times,* told Crotty just before his appointment: "Paul, this is not really a housing program. This is just a budget document, isn't it?" Crotty replied, "Of course it's a budget document. But now we're going to put meat on the bones here, Roger, and you've got to start someplace."[35]

So where did the new money come from? Cobbling the complicated financial package together took significant politicking at the state level. Most of it came from the city's capital budget, after the legislature freed up billions of borrowing capacity by creating a separate Municipal Water Finance Authority for the enormous Third Water Tunnel project.[36] More money came from various state agencies that had surpluses or that owed the city money, including the refinancing of Municipal Assistance Corporation bonds (MAC), a $200 million payment in lieu of taxes from the World Trade Center (less than Koch had hoped), $3.2 billion in increased borrowing by the Housing Development Corporation, and approximately $400 million from the Battery Park City Authority, which was borrowing against anticipated revenues from the World Financial Center. Interestingly, Mayor Koch saw the transfer of Battery Park City Authority funds to low-income housing as a way to justify state subsidies for a luxury downtown development that generated a positive cash flow. But the bulk of funds came from the capital budget, up to the limits of what New York could prudently borrow.[37]

Progress was slow for the first two years following the initial announcement of the housing program in January 1985, despite the labors of Esnard, Biderman, and Crotty, the program's private-sector and nonprofit partners, and the staff of the new Mayor's Office of Housing Coordination, which was created in May 1986 to speed housing construction. The fallout from the Manes and associated scandals made the task of creating new shortcuts around bureaucracy even tougher (see chapter 22). Auditors and prosecutors monitored every city transaction, subpoenas disrupted the normal work of agencies, and anticorruption procedures increased paperwork in a system that was already drowning in it. Koch and Brezenoff courageously refused to allow the scandals to halt the processes of city government. But in a scandal-free atmosphere the results might have been quicker and more dramatic, with more ribbon cutting on actual units.

The administration also announced two other new programs through the Human Resources Administration. The city first offered vacant buildings for sale to developers and nonprofits on condition that they renovate and rent them to families with incomes of less than $32,000. In the poorest neighborhoods rents in such buildings were capped at $350, low enough for a family with an annual income of $14,000. Another new program, the Construction Management Program, was designed to quickly renovate large derelict buildings, to "really make an impact on a neighborhood," Crotty said.[38] Crotty hired major construction managers, such as Tishman in Harlem and Lehrer McGovern in the south Bronx, to rapidly rehabilitate buildings containing a total of two thousand units. Both projects would be funded by the Battery Park City Authority.[39]

Bronx Borough President Fernando Ferrer welcomed the big project just off the Grand Concourse, but the Harlem leadership tried hard to steer the business for the 145th Street project to John Edmonds, a builder in Harlem, even though he was not a construction manager. The contract went instead went to Tishman. Controversy arose again after Tishman failed to use enough minority subcontractors, despite an agreement between the mayor and Manhattan Borough President Dinkins to use 20 percent local contractors.[40]

Crotty speculated that the Harlem initiative, which circumvented Koch's objections to racial quotas by specifying quotas by locality instead, failed because "Tishman wasn't as good at breaking down . . . the work so that smaller contractors could bid on them," and also perhaps "because the contractors in Harlem were expecting way too much." During a 1992 interview Crotty added that he thought "Koch would still be the mayor if he had played the games they wanted to play up in Harlem. There were certain contractors, if you took care of those certain contractors, everything would be hunky dory. If he had done that and not picked on Jesse Jackson in 1988, he'd still be the mayor."[41]

The Construction Management Program was a mixed success. Crotty recalled: "It was way too expensive, which is kind of interesting, because that's the only program we allowed the OMB [the city's Office of Management and Budget] to participate in, OMB, the keeper of the king's purse, the queen's purse. But, it did allow for advanced planning of social needs, it did allow for commercial development, it did provide for day care and a lot of other things that go into a major development. So, I thought it was a terrific program," though it was neither fast nor inexpensive.[42]

By the end of 1987 the city had managed to increase both direct and indirect capital budget support for housing, though turning that money into occupied units was more difficult than Crotty had anticipated. Almost immediately, the transportation department was able to start upgrading streets and infrastructure near affordable housing project sites. The greatest holdup were the bureaucratic hurdles involved in disposing of city property: The housing commission could provide city-owned land for only about three thousand new units. Other measures that the administration was able to push through Albany before groundbreaking lowered the cost of construction by permitting wider use of manufactured housing and allowing the Housing Partnership and other housing construction entities to form tax-exempt corporations. But construction was still limited.[43]

The Reagan administration, which by 1984 had cut federal budgetary authority for housing to one-third of its 1980 levels, actively disliked government housing construction programs.[44] The Reagan administration decreased funding of housing programs by almost 70 percent, from $30 billion to $8 billion between 1981 and 1987, a loss estimated by Felice Michetti, who served as Dinkins's housing commissioner, at $16 billion for the entire decade of the 1980s. Reductions in federal aid to cities began under the Carter administration, but conservatives hastened the process, eager to fund tax cuts for the wealthy by reducing the social wage of the middle class and working poor. Federally funded gut rehabs and new housing starts in New York City plunged from sixty-five hundred in 1983 to fewer than five hundred by 1988.[45]

Using means testing to determine who got federal aid was a conservative strategy to undermine the welfare state and racialize its image. But the Reaganites' alternative "safety net"—rental assistance for the desperately poor through vouchers paid to private landlords—was unworkable in a city with a shortage of habitable apartments because most rentals cost more than the program's ceiling, except for those that were already heavily subsidized.[46] Despite these policies, David Rockefeller was able to get some startup money from the U.S. Department of Housing and Urban Development for the Housing Partnership from HUD secretary Samuel Pierce, a New Yorker and the only African American in Reagan's cabinet. Pierce was also persuaded by Senator Alphonse D'Amato to phase out some of New York's federal housing programs rather than hit them with sudden cuts. But by 1986 almost all that money was gone, and the only assistance Washington offered Crotty was the badly conceived and ideologically driven voucher program.[47]

The public-private hybrids that actually constructed much of the housing did not always work smoothly. Some were disasters, such as Tibbets Gardens, the failed four-year effort with the Real Estate Board of New York to build housing in the Kingsbridge neighborhood of the Bronx. The Manhattan real estate professionals were used to working on a large scale and "just couldn't adapt their overhead and their whole method of operation, including the nature of the subcontractors that they used and the cost of those subcontractors, to the environments that we were working in," Biderman explained.[48]

Others flourished. From the Mid-Bronx Desperadoes to the well-heeled, Rockefeller-sponsored Housing Partnership, nonprofits managed to transform the streets of once-decimated neighborhoods. Andrew Cuomo's Project Help, which built transitional and permanent housing for homeless families, was one of the most successful, in part because it benefited from the generous funding that the son of a sitting governor was able to obtain.[49] And despite the difficulties and delays, Koch's program of decentralized public investment stimulated private developers in the Bronx to build new structures on undeveloped land within a few months of his initial announcement.[50]

City projects also improved in quality during Koch's third term. Deputy Mayor Robert Esnard, an architect by profession, believed that aesthetic appeal and amenities were key to successful public housing construction, even for the homeless. He convinced the prominent architectural firm Skidmore, Owings, and Merrill to design apartment blocks that each contained twenty-four units of transitional housing for homeless families, with counseling and recreation facilities on the first floor and the apartments above. The first one, an unobtrusive three-story hundred-unit building at 346 Powers Avenue, near 141st Street in the Bronx, was completed in 1990, with ten more sites under construction or approved by the Board of Estimate.[51] The firm earned nothing for the design itself, except the promise of good publicity and a discounted fee if the projects came to fruition.[52]

New York Times architecture critic Paul Goldberger described a prototype as "an impressive building, at once sensible and humane," noting particularly the apartment design of "eight single rooms around double height living rooms."[53] Esnard recalled, "They built some beautiful buildings, and the people that lived in them loved them." This was part of a larger Koch administration commitment to buildings that were beautiful as well as functional. Esnard believed that "public buildings, instead of the worst building in the neighborhood, should be the best building, like the library, the church, the school. They are the key buildings in a place . . . so that the homeless buildings were better than the residential buildings around them." The housing commission's programs did more for homeless families than single adults, who needed more intensive social services. In a 1992 interview finance commissioner Abe Biderman said, "We created so many new apartments in the occupied stock, or through the special initiatives program and the construction housing program. We almost came to the point where we eliminated the [welfare] hotels [as temporary housing for homeless families] altogether but unfortunately, since then, they have begun to grow again."[54]

Housing advocate Kathryn Wylde chafed at the relatively slow pace of completion, especially during those first two years. Wylde argued that New York's bureaucratic delays and paperwork made the cost of delivering a manufactured house to moderate-income home buyers in New York 30 percent higher than for the same house in New Jersey. But the Koch administration argued that progress was remarkable given the slow paper flow though primitively computerized agencies, the distractions of subpoenas, and the proliferating new safeguards against corruption. Biderman recalled, "Given the bureaucracy, our responsiveness was relatively high . . . but not fast enough for Kathy."[55]

Koch and Crotty began to take Wylde's complaints more seriously when the *Daily News,* in an editorial probably inspired by Wylde, described the "nightmarish" and "Kafkaesque" bureaucracy required to build new housing in New York City. "If Koch can just put a stop to the shoe-box filing systems and candy store bookkeeping—if he can get the city to operate at half the efficiency of a normal business—it will sharply reduce the costs and time that housing now requires." To drive home the point the *News* illustrated its editorial with a diagram of the thirty-five pieces of paperwork required to complete an apartment rehab, noting that "printing the diagram for a major project—say, a new apartment house—would require a *Playboy*-style foldout."[56] Housing commissioner Crotty replied at Koch's behest that the "editorial ignores the many actions taken by the city to streamline the process" and challenged the accuracy of the diagram, which he said "confused the approval process with the construction process." He also wrote a personal note to *Daily News* editor Gil Spencer complaining about the paper's failure to cover press conferences announcing progress on the housing program. Crotty later recalled, "Miss Wylde, she'd tell you, 'Paul, this is a test of your ability to deliver.' You'd move heaven and hell to deliver what was supposedly the impediment, then nothing would happen" because of a lack of financing or other delays that were the responsibility of the Housing Partnership. Later, deputy commissioner Mark Willis speeded things up at the housing commission by assigning project managers who worked each case from start to finish.[57]

Still, bureaucratic absurdities abounded. "Different agencies didn't want to be pushed into different things . . . so we were always in a state of mini-war with agencies," Biderman remembered.[58] Financing sometimes failed to materialize, and in July 1986, when Koch and Crotty announced the second phase of the MAC housing plan, it came out at the press conference that only one 16-unit building on Eastern Parkway in Brooklyn had been completed under the first phase, with a second building underway on Staten Island. Instead of the eight hundred units for $20 million first contemplated for phase 1, the project had been scaled back to 450 units with a budget of $15 million.[59] Crotty, confronted with statistics from Comptroller Jay Goldin showing that only 54 percent of funding for fiscal 1987 had been committed, confessed, "For capital spending, HPD is somewhat behind projections," attributing the lag to the housing agency's inexperience with the requirements for spending bond money, which had been authorized only since passage of the Housing New York Act by the legislature in January 1986.[60]

Though bureaucrats make good scapegoats for delays, it is important not to forget that cutting back on regulation has consequences. One area that scared the bureaucrats was the innovation of public-private partnerships, which sometimes crossed then-sacred legal boundaries between public and private. Deputy housing commissioner Charles Reiss, speaking at a 1984 conference, called the Housing Partnership's New Homes program "the hardest and most difficult to get going, and to follow though to construction and occupancy" of all the city's housing ventures. City bureaucracies were woefully limited by technology and rudimentary computers. In an age with only primitive word processors, Reiss cited as the primary obstacle to housing construction the glacial production of legal papers, a process that "seems to take longer than the actual construction of the houses." Reiss also feared that housing built on vacant city land in bad neighborhoods might not be marketable, creating a huge budgetary risk.[61]

The 1986 city corruption scandals made it harder to give away city property for fear of impropriety, even for the laudable purpose of building affordable housing. The administration responded by setting up a high-level committee under Robert Esnard to value the land for each project. Housing activists and developers like Wylde complained that the committee greatly increased their paperwork, but such painstaking preparation in the first two years of the housing initiative paid off. "This was one of the major public works programs which was never tainted by scandal, kickbacks, shoddy work. And to get that done we had to get all the right systems in place. And it took time. But once they were in place, it definitely began to move," according to Biderman. By FY1988 the pace of construction began to pick up. Housing completions went 12,763 in FY1987 to 15,388, a 17 percent increase and the most since 1976—nearly two-thirds of the units in the outer boroughs. Between FY1987 and FY1990, annual expenditures under the housing program went from $62 million to $340 million.[62]

In the early 1980s Koch was widely mocked for putting window decals of Venetian blinds and potted plants on abandoned buildings overlooking the Cross-Bronx Expressway in a vain attempt to make them look better.[63] He claimed the idea was his own. Far-fetched as it sounds, it may have been a peculiar extension of his only patented invention—the Boxmobile, the set of decals intended to turn a cardboard box into a toy car.[64] By the 1989 mayoral campaign he was able to break ground on a project to renovate those same buildings, and the mayor traveled to the Bronx to remove the first one himself. Biderman commented, "The decals were an emblem of a lack of hope. Their removal symbolizes the rebirth of these buildings and of these neighborhoods."[65] By the time Koch left office, the housing program alone had renovated three thousand apartments, with thirteen thousand more under construction and design work started on an additional twenty thousand.[66] Crotty was particularly proud of the emphasis on rehabilitation, which, he argued, allowed his department to create thousands more apartments than would have been possible with new construction.[67]

"My plea is to the next mayor: Don't undo the housing efforts of the Koch administration," wrote Willa Appel, executive director of the Citizens Housing and Planning Council shortly after Koch's defeat in 1989.[68] The Dinkins and Giuliani administrations continued to build housing under Koch's ten-year plan, using the bureaucratic pathways he had bushwhacked, though Dinkins increased the subsidies and numbers of apartments built for the poorest families. Giuliani eventually decreased annual capital expenditures to $235 million in 1998, about one-third of what Koch had spent at the program's peak. In those ten years New York spent a total of $4.4 billion on the housing program—a step forward but less than needed.[69]

From the perspective of 2009, more than two decades after the program was announced, Koch's initiative has generally been viewed as the greatest success of his twelve-year mayoralty. The housing he built did not end homelessness but did help rescue New York. Vacant abandoned houses are no longer a common sight, and the value of homes remained more stable than in most other areas of the United States during the general housing contraction that began in 2007. When the program started, the city owned about five thousand vacant buildings with about fifty thousand units of abandoned housing. By 1993, according to then-housing commissioner Michetti, "42,000 of those units have either already been rebuilt, [were] currently undergoing rehabilitation, or are in the preconstruction development stage." In total, between 1987 and 1993 more than 100,000 units were renovated or constructed.[70] Overall, however, the cost of housing in the city remained high, and would continue to increase, in part because the population increased from 7.5 million in the Koch years to more than eight million in 2008 and was projected to reach more than nine million by 2030.[71]

The Koch housing program contributed significantly to the repopulation of New York. As Charles Orlebeke has observed, there was a "confluence of forces," that worked in favor of cities over the long run, notably the Community Reinvestment Act of 1977, which put an end to federal support for private disinvestment in urban neighborhoods. The decline in crime rates and an improved city economy also had a lot to do with the eventual success of the program.[72]

In 1998 borough president Fernando Ferrer invited Koch to the Bronx to see the fruits of his success. *Times* reporter David Gonzalez was present and rhapsodized that as a result of Koch's ten-year housing plan, "entire blocks have come buzzing back, with children and families living in new town houses and renovated apartment buildings."[73] Koch has frequently been criticized, sometimes with justification, for being a crisis-oriented mayor—governing through short-term responses to the day's headlines. But his major strategic decisions—the restoration of New York's credit and the ten-year housing program—were exceptions that put the city on an upward curve for the next generation. The city became such a magnet, requiring more and more housing, that even after 9/11 Mayor Michael Bloomberg was moved to announce a second ten-year housing program in 2002, patterned on the initial Koch program.[74]

20 AIDS

Before the Center for Disease Control identified Acquired Immune Deficiency Syndrome and gave AIDS its name in 1982, the illness was so little understood that it some called it "gay pneumonia." One year earlier, in July 1981, the *New York Native*, a leading gay newspaper, had published the first credible report linking the disease to sex. Dr. Lawrence Mass warned gay men that frequent sex with many partners placed them at risk for a mysterious set of diseases, including Kaposi's sarcoma (KS), a cancerous skin lesion. "Many feel that sexual frequency with a multiplicity of partners— what some would call promiscuity—is the single overriding risk factor for developing infectious diseases and KS," Mass wrote.[1]

Mass's alarming news met with silence. Perhaps because the implications were so frightening few gay readers publicly reacted to his article. Mainstream papers showed themselves unwilling to cover gay issues of any kind. The *New York Times* had an excruciatingly slow start on the biggest health story of the decade. The paper ran only one story on the disease in the crucial months between Mass's article in July 1981 and May 1982, and it did not cover AIDS regularly until almost two years after the outbreak. Only the tragedy of the escalating epidemic and the rage of activists chanting "SILENCE = DEATH" finally made articles about gay people fit to print.

Just after the *Native* article, Koch gave a speech to the Greater Gotham Business Council, a group of gay businessmen.[2] Health issues were not on the group's agenda, but Koch's speech should have been big news anyway: it was the first time a sitting mayor had addressed an openly gay group. Nothing appeared in the papers, even though reporters attended. Koch predicted as much and told his gay listeners that it was not his fault. Singling out a *Times* reporter in the audience, he remarked, "You can't blame me if there's not a story tomorrow. I brought the reporter here and that's all I can do."[3]

Koch's defense—"You can't blame me"—is ironic, considering how the gay community judging his handling of the developing AIDS crisis. While Koch counted himself a loyal ally and had fought for gay rights since entering politics, his record on AIDS would lead thousands of gay New Yorkers to blame him for both silence and inaction. In the case of AIDS Koch acknowledges making big mistakes, but he was acutely sensitive to criticism precisely because he felt he had supported gay causes at great risk to his own career. Just a few weeks before the Mass article in the *New York Native*, Koch was interviewed in the same publication and poured out "his feelings about what it cost him, as a single man, to be vocal on gay rights, the steps he feels he has taken to fulfill his commitment to gays."[4]

One gay man who was not impressed by Koch's sacrifices was Larry Kramer, who would become a bitter enemy. A firebrand who helped change the face of gay politics, Kramer charged that the mayor ignored the epidemic until far too late, dooming hundreds to needlessly painful deaths. Kramer proved himself more than a match for Koch in political acumen, lung power, and self-righteous zeal. If Koch was always the smart aleck who had to have the last word, Kramer had the added edge of literary brilliance. With devastating attacks in print and on stage, backed up with the militant style of gay protest he helped invent, Kramer knew how to hit Koch where it hurt. Long after leaving the mayoralty Koch's comments about Kramer would veer from remorse to rage. For his part, Kramer to this day blames the mayor for callous indifference to human suffering.

When Kramer emerged as a leader, he was already notorious because his recent novel, *Faggots,* disparaged gay promiscuity. By the end of the summer of 1981, Kramer teamed with Mass and others to form the nucleus of Gay Men's Health Crisis (GMHC), the first nonprofit in New York devoted to providing services to people with AIDS. Kramer published an appeal to New York's gay community, urging residents to raise and contribute money for research and treatment, reporting that 120 men had presented symptoms of KS—a worrisome tripling of cases in only one month: "We're appalled that this is happening to them and terrified that it could happen to us."[5]

Kramer accused Koch of not listening, or caring, early on, when the epidemic might have been contained. At the end of 1981 Kramer complained publicly that the mayor's liaison to the gay community, Herb Rickman, never returned his calls. Certainly Kramer himself was hard to deal with; he fought so hard with his own allies that they eventually ousted him from GMHC. But it is also clear that Koch put too much confidence in Rickman, an openly gay international lawyer who was in over his head when the crisis broke. As head of the Mayor's Ethnic Advisory Council, Rickman was Koch's liaison to a wide variety of gay and ethnic groups, which meant he was overextended. Gays started criticizing Rickman even before the AIDS crisis, which demoralized him. Rickman's strength lay in public relations activities, such as "Fragrance Day" at the Garment Center, but he could not handle the raw feelings and political complexities of gay New York at the outset of the AIDS epidemic.

When the AIDS crisis hit, and Kramer and others became louder and more adamant, Rickman withdrew and became even more remote.[6] Lee Hudson, Rickman's deputy in those years, said her boss saw his job as "controlling the message that went to the mayor," rather than ensuring that gays had access, so Rickman became more of a barrier than a conduit between gays and the mayor.[7] Attending gay functions and parties became tense and unpleasant, so Rickman turned his attention to his other duties, which further isolated him from gay concerns.[8] He appeared to be hoping that AIDS would just go away Instead of recognizing the importance of Larry Kramer's warnings, Rickman refused to return the activist's increasingly furious phone calls.

Rickman's failure to establish a rapport with gay activists was not the only obstacle that isolated the Koch administration from an increasingly worried gay community. The new health commissioner, Dr. David Sencer, first expressed little alarm at the increasing rate of Kaposi's sarcoma, listing it as the city health department's fourth priority, behind an outbreak of hepatitis at Elmhurst Hospital, drug-resistant gonorrhea, and the first case of botulism from intravenous drug use, in an update to the mayor early in February 1982. The commissioner did note that the health department, in cooperation with the U.S. Center for Disease Control, was launching "a major investigation," noting that over half the 225 cases of Kaposi's sarcoma in the United States by January 1982 were in New York.[9]

Sencer's experience may have taught him to be cautious. As the former head of the CDC, Sencer had persuaded the Ford administration to take on a huge, costly, and unpopular program of vaccination for a swine flu pandemic that never materialized. In dealing with the AIDS crisis in New York, Sencer advocated a limited, low-profile role for his agency, saying the health department should act only as "the skeleton, with the muscle coming from the community." Nowhere did he explain why this was a good idea, other than that it cost less than providing "muscle." Sencer resisted substantial spending or involvement in prevention even when the crisis was acute and the city council was pressing money on him to do more. But the AIDS crisis hit just as the mayor was trying to bring the FY 1982 budget into true balance. Sencer told him that the city did not need to increase spending to deal with the epidemic—which was just what the mayor wanted to hear.[10] To be fair to Sencer, Dr. Mathilde Krim, a noted cancer researcher at Memorial Sloan-Kettering Cancer Center who pushed the city to respond to the crisis, said that her attempts to get support from Carol Bellamy and Andrew Stein for a coordinated city response to AIDS were just as fruitless as her approaches to Sencer and Koch himself.[11]

In the spring of 1982 Sencer told Mass that gay health would soon be his top priority but insisted on keeping the focus on preventive medicine; he did not consider KS important enough to ask for additional funds. Hudson recalled that she would ask Sencer, "'How can you say we only need $1 million in front of the City Council? They're trying to give you more money!' He sat right there and said, 'No, that's enough. That's all we need.'"[12] Not until April 1982 did the health commissioner decide that KS was "reaching serious proportions," after he attended the first citywide meeting of KS researchers. But he still limited his department to gathering epidemiological information and convening meetings that "the Health Department can provide with no budgetary impact." Sencer left most education and public health efforts in the hands of private organizations, such as Gay Men's Health Crisis. What Sencer saw as organizational imperative, most activists considered dangerous inaction and a failure to lead that put New York behind other jurisdictions in its response to the crisis.[13]

Rickman's and Sencer's slow response frustrated gay leaders in New York, who saw West Coast activists getting more action from their elected officials. Representative Henry Waxman of California held congressional hearings on the federal government's lack of action on Kaposi's sarcoma, concluding that "if the same disease had appeared among Americans of Norwegian descent, or among tennis players, rather than among gay males, the responses of both the government and the medical community would have been different."[14]

RUNNING SCARED? CUOMO VERSUS KOCH AND THE GAY VOTE

In the spring of 1983 Larry Kramer's essay "1,112 and Counting," published in the *Native,* shocked Koch into the realization that AIDS had become one of the great humanitarian issues of his mayoralty and that he was not doing enough. The essay is one of the most withering attacks ever launched against the mayor: "If this article doesn't scare the shit out of you, we're in real trouble. If this article doesn't rouse you to anger, fury, rage and action, gay men may have no future on this earth. " Kramer warned that the city health department's program of AIDS education was almost totally ineffective. The greatest sadness and outrage were reserved for what Kramer saw as Koch's aloofness: "I sometimes think Koch is so protected and isolated by his staff that he is unaware of what fear and pain we're in. No *human* being could otherwise continue to be so useless to his suffering constituents. . . . With this silence on AIDS, the mayor of New York is helping to kill us."[15]

Rickman took Kramer's remarks as a personal attack, however, and isolated the mayor even more from Kramer. Koch and Kramer knew each other and had previously exchanged friendly letters, according to Hudson, who succeeded Rickman as liaison to the gay community. When Koch prepared a reply to Kramer, which might have dispelled the image of a cold uncaring mayor, Rickman counseled him not to send it.[16] Koch did not contact Kramer, but he did start making changes. He tried to score points with the gay community for appointing Dr. Roger W. Enlow, one of the founders of the AIDS Network, a coalition of AIDS organizations, as director of the new Office for Gay and Lesbian Concerns. Some activists criticized Enlow's civil libertarian, privacy-based view of the epidemic. He opposed separate hospital wards for AIDS patients as "leper colonies" and disagreed with Koch's decision to close the gay bathhouses. Enlow's civil libertarian views reflected Koch's general approach to gay rights and contrasted with Kramer's, which was based on forthright pride in queer identity. Kramer's approach also proved that confrontation, not a bland plea for liberty, was key to prying loose money to fight the epidemic, and ultimately to press the larger issue of equality for gay, lesbian, and transgendered people.[17]

As a result of Kramer's criticism, Koch also ordered Sencer to assume "a more aggressive posture" toward the disease, including testing all donated blood, determining the precautions needed for medical personnel who might be exposed to the disease, and ensuring a sufficient number of intensive care beds and special wards for patients. Koch personally instructed Sencer to call a Board of Health meeting within the next two weeks "to review how we have handled the matter to date, to consider the questions I have raised as well as any others, and to promulgate regulations where appropriate."[18] In addition, Koch committed the administration to educating health personnel about AIDS, examined problems involving the privacy of AIDS patients, and agreed to investigate the possibility of a city-run hospice for the terminally ill. These promises effectively overruled Sencer's cautious strategy, and represented a departure from Koch's usual decentralized management style. He rarely gave commissioners such direct and specific orders. Moreover, the unwieldy processes of city government delayed spending for two or three years even on housing, where he had unambiguously ordered them to move as fast as possible. Publicly, Koch acknowledged that his critics were "probably correct" that the government needed to do more, but he still had a tight budget and an intractable bureaucracy.[19]

Koch met with the AIDS Network in the Blue Room at city hall. The meetings excluded Kramer, presumably because of the intensity of his anti-Koch rhetoric, but David Minnos of the AIDS network termed the sessions "highly cordial." With the deaths of more than a thousand New Yorkers and Kramer's allegations in the background, Koch discussed his efforts to mobilize agencies to fight AIDS but refused to agree to "any demand which would cost the mayor money, such as providing for housing needs for AIDS patients, or the donation of a city-owned building on Thirteenth Street to AIDS organizations." Koch soon changed his mind about the building and sold it to the AIDS groups on "favorable terms."[20]

Once again an ineffectual federal government, which was ignoring AIDS, impeded the efforts of local officials, and Koch called for more federal money to fight the epidemic. In June Koch joined San Francisco mayor Dianne Feinstein, Washington mayor Marion Barry, and New Orleans mayor Ernest Morial to push a resolution through the U.S. Conference of Mayors calling for "government assurance of adequate medical, hospital and hospice care and housing for victims of AIDS" as well as more funds for medical research.[21] The four big-city mayors fought off opposition from three cabinet members dispatched by the Reagan administration to oppose the resolution and declare AIDS a local responsibility. Within two months the federal government reversed course. Margaret Heckler, secretary for the U.S. Department of Health and Human Services, appeared with Koch to announce her support for transferring $40 million in federal funds to AIDS research. She singled out Koch because by 1983, 42 percent of reported cases were in New York City.[22] Scientific advances made the path clearer, if not easier. By 1984 and 1985 a reliable way to test for the virus that causes AIDS had been created. While scientists knew that the virus was spread through the exchange of bodily fluids and was not highly infectious, like influenza, some of the public still panicked. Alarmism and homophobia were increasing.

Koch came up for reelection in 1985. Movie idol Rock Hudson died of AIDS that October. The revelation that Hudson was gay forced mainstream media to report on AIDS far more assiduously, but much of that reporting promoted panic and homophobia.[23] Koch faced a political dilemma. His conservative outer-borough constituents had become fearful of AIDS in the public schools and, as with the homeless, did not want social services or housing for people with AIDS in their neighborhood. He also felt increasing pressure from gay supporters to do more to help people with AIDS, especially as city revenues increased during the mid-1980s boom.

THE NORMAL HEART ATTACK

In April 1985 Joseph Papp mounted Larry Kramer's play *The Normal Heart* at the Public Theater. It dramatized the beginning of the AIDS epidemic, satirizing Koch and Rickman as callous bureaucrats. Kramer subjected Koch to a force of ridicule as intense and memorable as Thomas Nast's famous denunciatory cartoons of Boss Tweed. In the play Koch behaves cravenly because he is closeted and afraid to be associated with AIDS.

The play hit its mark. Instead of denouncing Kramer, Koch responded by claiming that the city was spending $31 million a year on AIDS (most of that money paid for care for AIDS patients in city hospitals and did not represent new spending), and he announced a $6 million increase in city AIDS funding, with new programs for subsidized housing, home care, added resources for acute care at hospitals, better coordination of medical teams, an educational program, hospice care, and more research funding.[24] To make sure the bureaucracy did not drag its feet, First Deputy Mayor Stan Brezenoff assigned the political pit bull Victor Botnick to monitor implementation and report to him at the end of the month and every thirty days thereafter. Brezenoff also made Botnick cochair, with David Sencer, of the AIDS Policy and Planning Committee, another indication that Koch no longer trusted Sencer. And when Botnick balked at transferring funding from the Red Cross, which had proved unable to spend city funds effectively, to GMHC, Koch overruled him.

Kramer never forgave Koch, however, and the years never softened his contempt. In the nineties, after Koch left Gracie Mansion, Koch and Kramer found themselves living in the same building on Washington Square (oddly enough, Bella Abzug was also a resident). Kramer recalled running into Koch in the building's lobby as they were picking up the mail: "He was trying to pet my dog Molly and he started to tell me how beautiful she was. I yanked her away so hard she yelped, and I said, 'Molly, you can't talk to him. That is the man who killed all of Daddy's friends.'"[25]

For his part, Koch told an interviewer in 2002 that Kramer was a genius for founding GMHC and ACT UP and said that one of his biggest regrets was that he did not sit down with Kramer and other activists early in the crisis, presumably because Rickman advised against it. But Koch was still furious with the playwright, shouting: "He blames *me* for the deaths of his friends. I just looked at the figure today. It's something like 40 or 50 million people have H.I.V. I'm responsible? I mean, people who know they shouldn't fuck without a rubber and nevertheless do—*I'm responsible for that?*"[26]

Because of Kramer and Shilts, many older gays in New York still believe that Koch did great damage to AIDS sufferers because he was in the closet. The argument is not persuasive. Koch never avoided other gay issues, despite his need to appeal to Catholics, Hasidim, and conservative outer-borough whites. In fact, during the gubernatorial race in 1982, Koch and Cuomo both fought hard to win the New York gay vote. Each purchased full-page ads in gay newspapers. Neither took a stand on KS, which even within the gay community was not yet a key political issue—which undermines Kramer's thesis. In addition, Koch had a long and solid record on gay rights. He had even cosponsored a federal gay rights bill with Waxman. As mayor

Koch issued a broad antidiscrimination order as one of his first acts and wrote President Carter urging him to do the same. Koch also publicly condemned Anita Bryant and other high-profile homophobes, promoted affirmative action for gays and lesbians in city government, including the police department, and started the first lesbian and gay advisory panel on police problems.

None of this is consistent with the theory that he was running away from gay issues because he was closeted. Because Cuomo had limited power as lieutenant governor, his actions on behalf of gay causes were minor in comparison. "When you look at the record, the choice is clear," a Koch ad insisted, noting the endorsement of GLID, the Gay and Lesbian Independent Democrats.[27]

But Cuomo did have some significant gay support, such as Ken Sherrill, a professor of political science at Hunter College, then one of the few openly gay Democratic assembly district leaders. Sherrill, like Kramer, was frustrated by Rickman's intransigence and felt that Koch had not done as much as Feinstein and Waxman had done on behalf of their gay constituents. While Koch was once in the forefront, some gay activists concluded that "his position on gay issues is now pretty much the mainstream view."[28]

RISKY POLITICS, SAFE SEX, AND CLEAN NEEDLES

AIDS became one of the biggest issues in Koch's 1985 reelection campaign. The fear surrounding the epidemic led to a backlash. Reports of violence directed at gays specifically because of their sexual orientation more than doubled in 1985.[29] In the days immediately before the primary, Koch visited a nursing home in Neponsit, Queens, that was scheduled to take in some AIDS patients. While there he talked to elderly residents who were so upset, despite his assurances that the AIDS patients were no danger, that he cancelled the program, convinced that some of the elderly would die of heart attacks if it went ahead.[30]

He initially bowed to the demands of worried parents, declaring that schoolchildren with AIDS should be kept entirely out of the public schools unless a medical panel determined that it was safe. Koch told the panel, "I don't believe you can establish that."[31] But when the doctors' panel found that it was safe to have HIV-positive children in school with other children, Koch did not hesitate to act on the basis of their findings, even though it was the last week of the primary campaign. He moved to quiet parents' fears. Then a health department panel approved the registration of an HIV-positive child, and parents boycotted schools in two Queens districts. Even though it was the day before the mayoral election, Koch sided with the health professionals, telling his constituents: "This child is no danger—no danger—to other children. You can panic if you want to, but I hope you won't."[32]

After the election Koch and Governor Cuomo moved to close the gay bath-houses. As Koch aide Lee Hudson explained, "An elected official doesn't want to stand up there and talk about these clubs in the first place, least of all the details of what is going on there," but Koch, pressed by safe-sex groups, felt it was his duty to take action. In consultation with gay activists Koch began to accumulate evidence of unsafe sex by sending in inspectors—carefully chosen from the Department of Consumer Affairs, not a police agency—and seeking voluntary compliance from bath-house owners. Not mincing words, the mayor asked them to state "precisely what steps you have already taken and what further steps you will take to assure that nei-ther anal intercourse nor fellatio takes place in your establishment." He received some detailed replies. The New St. Marks baths, pointing to the $50,000 it had con-tributed to AIDS causes, argued that closure would not slow the spread of AIDS in New York and cited health statistics suggesting that "practices are getting safer." The bathhouse had also erected signs encouraging safe-sex practices, made patrons sign a pledge to engage in safe sex, and handed out safe-sex literature, while "patrolling all open areas to be sure that only safe sex is being practiced." The heterosexual "couple's club" Plato's Retreat, pointedly included on the list to show that not only gay bath-houses were targeted, replied more matter-of-factly, with generalizations about signs, distribution of flyers, and "adequate security." But when health department reports and some AIDS activists made it clear that attendance at the bathhouses was still contributing to the epidemic, Koch moved to close them.[33]

Closing the bathhouses was easy enough, but some of the health department's other ideas for fighting the epidemic were far more inflammatory politically, particu-larly the needle exchange program. Needle exchanges halt the spread of blood-borne disease by supplying addicts with clean needles in exchange for dirty ones.[34] Studies subsequently proved that providing addicts with clean needles slows the spread of the HIV virus and other diseases. Opponents claimed, without evidence, that it would also spread drug addiction.[35]

Koch had great respect for science, but it took him some time to come around politically. When Sencer first suggested the needle exchange, Koch tested the politi-cal waters by asking the opinion of the district attorneys in all five boroughs and Ru-dolph Giuliani, the U.S. attorney for the Southern District of New York. But even the most liberal prosecutors, such as Robert Morgenthau and Elizabeth Holtzman, de-clined to support the measure, so Koch concluded that it would never pass the state legislature. Despite the political risks, he launched a pilot needle exchange program in November 1988, which was subsequently cancelled by Mayor David Dinkins, who believed that free needles would lend legitimacy to drug use—an analogue to the subsequently discredited idea that promoting the use of condoms promoted sex.[36]

Outreach to religious groups on AIDS prevention and care was another political balancing act. When the mayor offered the archdiocese money to house AIDS patients in Manhattan, instead of the Neponsit site, the Coalition for Lesbian and Gay rights protested the deal: "It is preposterous to award the sole contract for this kind of service to an agency that has a declared policy that it won't hire openly gay people," declared one coalition activist. Koch did not enhance his own or the archdiocese's reputation for sensitivity by labeling the protesters at the news conference as radicals and screwballs. But Richard Dunne, then executive director of GMHC, reserved judgment, saying that in fact the Catholic Church ran "terrific programs, and I believe there are good individuals in the Roman Catholic clergy who can provide appropriate and sensitive care."[37]

The Catholic Church, along with some Orthodox Jews, successfully pressured local media executives to refuse television and radio ads that explicitly urged the use of condoms.[38] When Bishop Edward M. Egan, then the vicar for education in the Archdiocese of New York, objected to commercials urging heterosexual women to get their partners to use condoms, Koch pushed a new set of ads advocating abstinence, assimilating the position of the Catholic hierarchy against advocating the use of condoms because they only reduce risk but do not eliminate it. Thus Koch temporarily advocated abstinence as if that was the only moral choice or an effective strategy for saving lives. Abstinence commercials were not likely to slow the spread of the virus. "It's not reasonable to expect children reaching the point of sexual experimentation to not have sex," responded John Gamrecki, of the organization People with AIDS. He continued: "Efforts would be better directed toward telling adolescents if they're going to practice sex, they should practice safer sex."[39]

In Koch's third term an energetic new health commissioner, Stephen C. Joseph, took a more activist stance than his predecessor had. Joseph wanted more public education and more spending, striking a new pose of action: "The fact that [the AIDS epidemic] is very gloomy and keeps getting worse all the time does not mean we're powerless. Quite the opposite. We really know how to help people protect themselves."[40] Joseph's activism was lauded, but the contrast with his predecessor's comparatively low-key style probably increased the appearance that the administration had taken too long to act.

Two months after Joseph took office in 1986, a panel appointed by Koch issued a five-year plan for dealing with the epidemic, proposing increases in funding for care for the sick and counseling for all directly affected by the epidemic.[41] The panel also recognized that AIDS was not primarily a gay issue, shifting governmental emphasis to the growing numbers of cases spread through heterosexual contact with intravenous drug users, calling for wider availability of free confidential testing.[42]

Critics inevitably argued that San Francisco was doing a better job. One of the most knowledgeable was Dunne, the executive director of GMHC. In an exchange of letters with Koch, Dunne argued that even though New York had spent eight times as much money as San Francisco with only three times the number of cases, it had failed to adopt the kind of "comprehensive, integrated approach" in service delivery or AIDS education that evolved on the West Coast. New York, Dunne felt, spent too much on hospital care and not enough on home care, and education.[43] Koch responded with a handwritten note: "There are too many hostile people out there—We should be working together." He insisted that his programs, such as the special anti-AIDS discrimination unit at the city's Human Rights Commission, had gone far beyond those mandated by the state and federal governments.[44]

Commissioner Joseph also replied to Dunne, pointing out that the number of long-term-care beds had expanded from twenty-four to fifty-two, which he believed was sufficient, and pointed out that the AIDS populations in New York and San Francisco were in face quite different. Many AIDS sufferers in New York were IV drug users, who often needed more intensive care for longer than gay men who contracted the disease, he asserted. Sixty percent of municipal inpatients in New York were IV drug users, compared with 1 percent in San Francisco. Moreover, New York's much larger programs were harder to coordinate than San Francisco's because "the AIDS population served by NYC is larger, more likely to be homeless, and has fewer social and financial resources." Joseph insisted that both cities tried to keep people in their homes for as long as possible.[45]

Larry Kramer still thought that the government could do much better. Forced out of GMHC because of his confrontational style, he helped found the AIDS Coalition to Unleash Power (ACT UP), whose vociferous and aggressive style of protest gave currency to the phrase "in your face." It held its first demonstration on Wall Street on April 24, 1987. ACT UP demanded a comprehensive national AIDS policy, streamlining of the drug approval process, affordable AIDS drugs, and an end to "cruel double blind studies" that gave placebos to dying people.[46]

More than a protest group, these activists created a unique countercultural political force that transformed the medical and public health system. Their protests encouraged the U.S. Food and Drug Administration to speed up approval of AIDS drugs. ACT UP carried out scores of demonstrations over the next five years, including shutting down trading on the New York Stock Exchange, after which Burroughs Wellcome significantly reduced the price of the AIDS drug AZT. The group's tactics included blocking traffic and access to building, and much smaller demonstrations called "zap attacks." These could be personalized. One AIDS researcher was confronted at a conference by ACT UP activists who compared him with the Reverend Jim Jones, the cult leader and murderer. Another zap attack targeted the promoter of a comedian who made tasteless jokes about AIDS, and Koch himself was a favorite villain, as ACT UP plastered the subways with small red-and-black posters of the mayor bearing the legend "10,000 NYC AIDS Deaths. How'm I Doin'?"[47]

Some ACT UP members steeped themselves in the scientific details of therapies, so they could argue with scientists and bureaucrats, and convinced the government that AZT was effective in smaller doses. That reduced both costs and toxicity to people taking the drug. Other notable victories included changes in FDA procedures that greatly speeded the flow of experimental drugs to control the disease.[48] Protesters also directly challenged the homophobia of the Catholic Church. ACT UP's largest demonstrations on March 28, 1989, surrounded city hall with three thousand protesters (two hundred of whom were arrested) and marshaled forty-five hundred demonstrators in front of St. Patrick's Cathedral, where 111 were arrested as they protested the church's opposition to safer sex education and its continued homophobia.[49]

Koch was not unique in responding slowly to the AIDS epidemic before 1983. The whole country did. Once he realized that Commissioner Sencer was overly cautious about spending money on AIDS programs, partly because of the mayor's general budgetary mandates, Koch took the lead, under intense pressure from Larry Kramer and other activists. Usually, the mayor denounced radical political opponents, but in this case he bitterly regretted taking Rickman's advice to stay away from them. Koch tended to see himself as their ally and even used the protests to catalyze government action.[50] For a mayor who prided himself on letting his commissioners run their departments, his interventions in the details of AIDS policy were extraordinary.

When Koch ran for reelection in 1989, opponents criticized his slow initial response to the epidemic eight years before, a meme that Larry Kramer's dramas seared into the public consciousness. But aside from complaints about the needle exchange program, which was unpopular but effective, none of Koch's challengers argued that they could improve the AIDS programs in place by 1989.

21 CRIME AND POLICE ISSUES (1978–84)

Wars on crime—no matter how terrific your effort—are going to be lost because crime is going to be there after you're finished. You mislead the public by letting them believe that you can reduce it by dramatic amounts easily.

—RUDOLPH W. GIULIANI, ASSOCIATE U.S. ATTORNEY

When Ed Koch ran for mayor in 1977, he did so as a law-and-order candidate, calling for reinstatement of the death penalty and harsh action against looters during the blackout. But he really did not know much about crime or criminal justice issues at the time. In his campaign he offered little besides a promise of toughness and a vague plan to put more officers on the street by hiring civilians to do department paperwork.

Fiscal constraints determined all policy in Koch's first term, limiting his ability to reform the police and the criminal justice system. Despite his law-and-order rhetoric, Koch made it clear that until the budget was balanced—and even if crime increased—he would hire teachers before hiring more police, and he got more police on the street by making clerical jobs in the police department civilian jobs.[1] Surprisingly, the voters cut him slack. They had long ago discarded expectations that New York's gravely wounded government could cope with the increasing disorder, and those who could afford it began spending more, and more often, on private security.

Koch also picked a sophisticated liberal police commissioner—not what one would expect, given Koch's rhetoric. Robert McGuire was an unusual choice for the job. He was not exactly an outsider to the New York Police Department—his dad had been deputy chief inspector, and the younger McGuire claimed "an intuitive understanding of how the Police Department functioned" from "the experience of living in a cop's home" and growing up around many senior police officers.[2] But his only real credential in New York law enforcement was a stint working for Robert Morgenthau at the U.S. Attorney's Office. McGuire then spent a year in the 1960s in an MIT-sponsored Peace Corps–type program in Mogadishu, Somalia, serving as an adviser to the local police force. When he returned, he took a job with the Louis Nizer law firm. After becoming thoroughly immersed in the firm's pro bono work, he took a leave to set up the foundation-funded nonprofit Community Law Offices for the poor in East Harlem, using Wall Street lawyers working pro bono to represent his impoverished clients.

McGuire's most interesting qualification was that, after returning to private practice, he represented, for free, David Durk and Frank Serpico in their epic exposure of police department corruption—as their whistleblower status left them vulnerable to retaliation, including violence, or being framed as participants in the corruption they were trying to stop. When the pair decided to sell their story to the media, McGuire quit, convinced that Durk and Serpico would hurt the larger anticorruption cause by giving ordinary cops reason to doubt their motives. Perhaps he also felt that if his clients were making big money, he deserved payment for his legal work. McGuire then represented a number of cops accused of corruption during the Knapp Commission probe instigated by Serpico and Durk.

Appointing McGuire commissioner gave Koch extra protection against the unpleasant surprise of a major police scandal. McGuire, as he himself put it, "knew where the bodies were buried," and the whole department knew that he knew. Nothing privileged had to be disclosed, but his knowledge could guide him as he made his appointments.[3]

The new commissioner, facing a 24 percent increase in corruption allegations at the time he took over, focused on weeding out bad cops. He ordered the chief of inspectional services (responsible for internal investigations) to report directly to him instead of to the first deputy chief.[4] McGuire's job had been made easier by Commissioner Patrick V. Murphy (1970–73), who had wrought a cultural revolution in the department after Serpico blew the whistle. The force became less tolerant of corruption and somewhat more accepting of good cops who turned in those on the take.[5]

At the same time there was a certain temperance in dealing with old sins. First Deputy Chief Joseph Hoffman continued a policy of fines instead of dismissal for officers from Harlem's Twenty-eighth Precinct who admitted accepting bribes several years before. Special prosecutor John Keenan declined to prosecute the cases because the only evidence was the officers' own testimony. "The objective has been to rid the department of corruption without installing a reign of terror," Hoffman told the press.[6] Firing officers who voluntarily came forward to report corruption, even if they themselves were tainted, would only promote more corruption and a culture of secrecy about it.

Corruption was not the only difficult issue. McGuire had become commissioner at a daunting time. Morale was at rock bottom. His predecessor, Michael J. Codd (1974–77), was the first police commissioner in modern history who had to lay officers off. Just sixteen months before McGuire took over, angry off-duty cops had protested poor working conditions. Mutinous gangs of off-duty officers beat up a squad of top brass who tried to disperse the crowd in a riot outside Yankee Stadium on the day of the Muhammad Ali–Ken Norton championship fight. The disgruntled officers then held a raucous 2 A.M. demonstration at Codd's home in a quiet Queens neighborhood, as well as numerous nonviolent pickets throughout the city.[7]

Officers worked in dismal conditions. A patrol officer responding to a code 13 emergency (officer in need of assistance) might step on his radio car's accelerator only to have the pedal fall off. McGuire recalled: "We had precincts that you wouldn't walk into, that had holes in the roof; rain came in, they should have been condemned. We had no money, no capital monies to spend, no money to give raises to cops who were vastly underpaid at the time." When retirements and resignations started to deplete the force even more than was planned by budget cuts, the department was required to rehire cops who had been laid off under Beame. Many were less valuable than rookies; they were angry, disillusioned, and had lost the knack for police work in their years off the force. And they probably hated McGuire for making them walk beats instead of riding in radio cars.[8]

Crime kept rising and the force kept dwindling—from about thirty-one thousand before the 1975 fiscal crisis to fewer than twenty-two thousand in 1981. Despite their unpleasant working environment, cops had to work harder and make more arrests. As late as 1980 Koch said to reporters asking about rising subway crime: "We laid off 2,200 teachers. I am not prepared to lay off additional teachers to have more cops."[9]

McGuire did not even dream of dramatically reducing crime. His job was crisis management: "By and large it was smoke and mirrors. . . . I remember [First Deputy Commissioner] Bill Devine calling me and saying, 'We have no radio cars in Queens on the late tour.' And that was a petrifying thought for a police commissioner. I just sent a duty captain from Manhattan to cover Queens. The entire borough. One radio car. We had no backup." Early in his term McGuire submitted a report to Koch entitled "Agenda for Change"; among its priorities were "reducing street crime," increasing efforts against organized crime, and improving community interaction, but how those goals could be accomplished was not clear, given the department's strained resources.[10]

Despite these daunting difficulties, Koch at first chose to continue reductions in the force through attrition rather than by laying off officers. Budget chief James Brigham advised that five hundred more uniformed police could be lost while maintaining patrol strength at 6,636 by turning desk jobs over to civilians.[11] Block associations and businesses began to hire more private security guards and to invest in iron gates, better locks, and security devices. One butcher even started selling bulletproof vests to the other merchants on his block.[12]

Patrol strength is a fraction of the total uniformed force because of the need for command, support, specialized units, detective squads, and duties, such as testifying in court. Divided into three shifts, only two thousand officers were available to cover New York City's 322 square miles at any given time in the late 1970s and early 1980s, and the actual number was often significantly less.[13]

Civilianization—shifting clerical jobs to lower-paid civilian employees—was supposed to put more cops on the street. But the change took years to complete, even though it had been an important Koch campaign promise. McGuire also tried to deploy one-officer patrol cars, as many cities do, theoretically doubling patrol visibility. But this outraged many officers, who felt it placed their lives in greater jeopardy. The sanitation department had successfully reduced truck crews from three people to two, but union opposition, and the frequent backup required, killed the one-officer patrol car.[14]

Reforming the 911 emergency call system was McGuire's other priority in his first year. The 911 system had a variety of problems. The facility that housed the system was dilapidated, even by the very low standards of the NYPD in the 1970s. During the Beame administration austerity had forced the department to use federally funded workers who were "hardcore unemployed" to fill posts at the emergency response network. Few of these workers had appropriate training or education. For example, witnesses called 911 when a woman was snatched from her car and hauled into an abandoned brownstone off Columbus Avenue, where she was raped and burned to death. The police responded quickly, but the poorly trained 911 operator gave them the wrong address, even though she had correct information. The case spurred a horrified commissioner to reform the system.[15] "We've got to put a permanent cadre of qualified civilians down there with some police officers," the commissioner told the press at the end of his first year.[16]

The 911 system had become too successful: the shrinking police force had to respond to 6.6 million calls every year. Only about 20 percent dealt with serious crime. The other 80 percent were mostly routine service calls for ambulances or cats in trees. Problems other than medical emergencies, fires, or crimes in progress were put on a waiting list. Some callers waited days for a response. The department stopped responding to most burglaries unless the loss was greater than $5,000. Disorderly conduct also got short shrift. These policies allowed burglars to ply their trade with greater impunity and increased the sense of disorder on the streets.[17]

McGuire restaffed 911 with higher-paid, better-trained operators and improved the selection of officers in the calling pool, formerly a dumping ground for "all the walking wounded who could not carry a gun, or drive a radio car," McGuire said. The department also consulted industrial psychologists and fixed up 911's ramshackle offices, adding basic amenities such as vending machines.[18] But improving 911 was only one small part of the problem the NYPD faced in the 1970s and 1980s.

HOW WELL DID THE POLICE FIGHT CRIME?

Despite mountains of detailed statistics, estimating police productivity is difficult, and that was even truer in the 1970s and 1980s before the New York police force was computerized. Firefighters respond to every significant fire, but the police do not solve every crime, so their effectiveness is much harder to measure.

The first statistics kept by the NYPD were notoriously unreliable. Former police commissioner Vincent Broderick (1965–66) remembered one of his predecessors' asking for the latest crime stats. "Sure, commissioner," replied his deputy. "How do you want them, up or down?"[19] Reporting became somewhat more reliable by the Koch era, with the institution of statistical cross-checks. Assistant Chief Anthony M. Voelker, director of the NYPD's Office of Management Analysis, acknowledged that in "the dim past" precinct commanders fudged their numbers but in 1982 insisted that "our policy is absolute honesty."[20] But even honest statistics may underestimate crime, because many crimes are not reported to the police. And computerization was still too rudimentary to marshal the kind of crime statistics on a block-by-block basis that would prove so useful a decade later in finding and targeting the shifting areas of high criminal activity.

Homicide statistics are the most accurate way to measure police effectiveness. The police attend to almost every one, and the reported rate can be cross-checked with the medical examiner's body count. Murder rates closely parallel the rates for auto theft, the most accurately reported property crime, suggesting that the same forces affect the level of both violent and property crimes.[21]

During the Koch years New York's murders evidenced three trends:

- a sharp increase from 1978 to 1981
- a sharp decrease from 1981 to 1985
- a sharp increase from 1985 to 1990, a period of increasing violence related to the crack epidemic[22]

Reported felonies rose in 1979, by 8.9 percent, after a two-year decline. The increase was actually slightly less than the national increase of 9 percent but had disturbing implications for New York's economic viability. Crime was moving uptown to wealthier neighborhoods, and violence was increasing. The robbery rate was the highest in the nation in 1979 at an astounding 1,103.6 per 100,000 people, meaning that more than 1 percent of the population of New York City was getting mugged every year—and that's counting only *reported* robberies. Although New York's overall crime rate ranked thirteenth among the rates for large U.S. cities in 1979, the city had been in fifteenth place only the year before. In mid-1980 it moved to ninth place, with the crime rate increasing by 15.9 percent from the year before and 60 percent higher than the rest of the nation.[23] Philip McGuire, director of the NYPD's crime analysis unit, told the *New York Times* that the Koch administration was "conducting a vast social experiment. . . . 'How far can you cut back your police force before crime runs rampant?'"[24]

Most of Koch's anticrime initiatives were reactive and limited in their effect, because the city had no money for sustained action.[25] One of Koch's most famous and futile rhetorical attacks on crime was a broadcast he ordered WNYC to make. It was called "The John Hour," although reading one week's list of men convicted of patronizing prostitutes took only one minute. Reviewed by the *Times* as "a shabby show, in no way redeemed by its brevity," it was cancelled after the first episode. (Koch still defended the idea years later, when New York governor Eliot Spitzer resigned after admitting trysts with prostitutes.)[26]

Another of the administration's less effective responses was a crackdown on subway crime, which preyed on the public mind out of proportion to its actual prevalence. Subway crime was rare: in January 1979, a month that saw more than ninety million riders, only 1,180 felonies were reported. That was much lower than the citywide robbery rate. Subway crime tripled between 1972 and 1982, and eight murders occurred in the subways in the first quarter of 1979 after none in the first quarter of the previous year, but the subways were still vastly safer than the streets above.[27]

After the New York City Transit Authority, the subagency of the Metropolitan Transportation Aauthority (MTA) that runs the subways, announced an 83 percent increase in robberies, the mayor promised a crash program to stop them. William McKechnie, head of the union representing the transit police, called the program a "Band-Aid approach to fighting crime," a response to the latest headline, not a long-term strategy.[28] Koch agreed that the media exaggerated subway crime but asserted, "The newspapers have not made this up out of whole cloth. Crime is up and we are going to try to bring it back to an all-time low."[29] Crime reduced ridership, reducing the take at the farebox, and it drew the attention of public officials.

The mayor wanted quick action, so instead of taking time to find a new idea, the Transit Authority dusted off an unsuccessful program from the 1960s. Its strategy put all transit police, including those in plainclothes, back on the beat, assigning an officer to each station and every train between the high crime hours of 6 P.M. and 2 A.M. Previously, only stations had been patrolled. To get more transit police on the trains, the NYPD would share patrol of the stations, and all law enforcement officers would be given free passes to encourage their use of the trains while off-duty.[30] This looked good on paper, but NYPD radios did not work underground and could not communicate directly with transit officers, sharply limiting their effectiveness. Of course, the police had no money to buy new radios.[31]

Amid a controversy about whether Sanford D. Garelik, chief of the transit police and former city council president, had properly interpreted the statistics, the transit police reported a 40 percent decline in subway crime in the program's first week. After six months the statistics fluctuated. The actual number of arrests in the transit system was down, perhaps because of the shift of detectives to patrol duty. Koch was spending $8.6 million—enough money to hire a hundred patrol officers—on a program that had little effect on the overall crime rate. The subway crime program began to unravel by the fall of 1979 because of its inefficiency. By October the MTA had suspended free rides for off-duty officers—the eight arrests a month were not worth the five thousand daily fares that the program cost the authority. By December Koch had withdrawn the transit police officers who had been patrolling above-ground stations—they still lacked radios for calling the NYPD. The chief shifted his detectives back to plainclothes. Six months later subway crime was up again, but the mayor reduced the costly overtime patrols. In fourteen months the subway crime crackdown cost $18 million, and when it ended, subway crime was, by some measures, at a higher level than when it started.[32]

At the beginning of his first "war on crime," an optimistic Koch had declared that, where security was concerned, fiscal considerations could not be paramount. The following year, with the deep cuts that Koch made to balance the budget a year early, New York was gripped by a wave of thievery that was impossible to ignore.

THE ROBBERY CRISIS

In the summer of 1979 New York had twenty-five bank robberies in one day. By mid-August 590 banks had been robbed since the beginning of the year—1979 ultimately saw a 36 percent increase over 1978. Part of the problem was design; new customer-friendly banks lacked the barriers and security of the past. The Banco de Ponce in Rockefeller Plaza, New York's largest Puerto Rican bank, even posted a sign to inform robbers that the employees spoke only Spanish and requesting patience so the bank could get an interpreter to allow the robbery to proceed.[33]

The Koch administration's response to the spate of bank robberies did have an enduring effect, which was not the case with many short term, high-profile efforts to clean up New York. When Koch and Police Commissioner McGuire announced a special bank robbery task force, the mayor declared: "We're going to make it difficult for anyone to rob banks."[34]

Prodded by the task force, the police responded faster, and banks increased security, placing tellers behind bulletproof plastic. Amazingly, the banks were reluctant to isolate the tellers, fearing the tyranny of consumer taste more than bank robbers. But where the barriers went up, robberies dropped 79 percent.[35]

A task force that focused on robberies of individuals also succeeded. In 1979 half of the record 860 robbery cases were unsolved; two years later the NYPD declared 80 percent of robbery cases had been cleared in 1981. Robberies declined 13 percent to 748 in 1980 and continued to decline sharply despite increases in the general crime rate. McGuire would later establish similar joint task forces on auto theft, terrorism, and organized crime, the latter helping with some of the spectacular federal prosecutions during Rudolph Giuliani's term as U.S. attorney.[36]

The 120-member robbery unit formed in 1981 dedicated twenty-four hundred detectives and uniformed officers to catching muggers.[37] The new unit patrolled shopping areas using decoys, electronic stakeouts, and mounted police. With no computers for assistance, members of the unit searched voluminous crime reports and stuck pins in wall maps to correlate the spatial patterns of robberies with modus operandi. The maps helped pin several crimes on the same perpetrator. Multiple charges made for stronger cases, surer convictions, and heavier sentences for career criminals. The department also made an effort to solve burglaries—it had previously almost eliminated investigations of burglaries—with specialists trained in latent fingerprinting techniques. Each precinct had to have a squad "devoted exclusively to investigating residential or small commercial burglaries."[38]

Special citywide "homicide apprehension" teams aided local detectives, raising the solution rate for murders from 57 percent to 69 percent. While McGuire and the detectives deserve credit for the improvement, failure to solve 31 percent of homicides cannot be called a success. A killer had a pretty good chance of getting away with murder during the 1980s. Police and prosecutors blamed each other, but surely a lack of funding contributed to the problem.[39]

Efforts at improved detection dented the general crime rate—by 1981 the number of reported robberies and burglaries grew much more slowly than other crimes, and robbery actually decreased if the first three months of 1981, before the task force went into operation, are discounted. The next year serious crime dropped by 9.4 percent, with burglary, robbery, and car theft leading the decline. Causation is always tricky with crime statistics, but there was a case to be made that McGuire's initiatives, made possible by a $4.5 million budgetary allowance for extra overtime, were working.[40]

GUN CONTROL

Ed Koch strongly supported passage of a new gun control law that would carry a mandatory one-year jail term for carrying an unlicensed pistol and a mandatory additional penalty of five years for anyone convicted of using a gun in a crime. "You're not a nice guy if you have a gun, even if you are a nice guy," Koch exclaimed.[41] The legislature eventually passed a bill providing for the one-year sentence for carrying a loaded gun on the street but gave judges discretion to waive the penalty so it was not really mandatory, a loophole Koch later denounced as fatal. The mayor raised private funds to pay for television commercials warning citizens not to violate the law. The commercials showed him "walking along a row of empty jail cells and sternly warning: 'If you get caught carrying an illegal handgun, you'll go to jail for one year. No plea bargaining. No judges feeling sorry for you. Just one year in jail.'"[42]

Mandatory jail sentences did not staunch the flow of guns from outside the state. In 1981, as Koch was running for reelection with law-and-order rhetoric, handgun homicides went up 25 percent, according to NYPD figures.[43] Fewer than half the defendants received the mandatory term, leading Koch to attack judges for their sentencing decisions.[44]

THE WAR ON GRAFFITI WRITERS

Koch looks uncharacteristically pensive and sad in a picture snapped as he rode the Lexington Avenue IRT on his way to lunch with Zimbabwe president Robert Mugabe. Koch had long since given up riding the subway to city hall every day, settling for occasional trips to check out the subways. This Lexington Avenue car was in horrific shape. Every inch was covered in unreadable black scrawls, a scene familiar to all New Yorkers in this era. Accomplished graffitists called this "bombing," and some claimed to condemn it. Almost every car on the IRT had been bombed faster than transit workers, already behind on basic maintenance, could undo the damage.

Koch emerged from the train and announced that he would pressure the Metropolitan Transportation Authority to fence subway yards and protect the cars with unescorted guard dogs, which would presumably solve the problem by eating any graffiti writers who hopped the fence to paint a train or two. "If I had my way, I wouldn't put in dogs, but wolves," Koch declared.[45] Koch deployed dogs to guard the subway cars, an effort endorsed by the *Times*'s editorial board, after a satiric debate over the merits of wolves.[46]

The dog and fencing plan was not new—the MTA itself had proposed it in 1974, just before it was engulfed by the fiscal crisis. At that time the *Times* had complained that spending the large sums required for dogs was at best a misplaced priority. The *Times*'s editorial board suggested that the MTA should instead try to improve the level of service "to the level of the transit system in Baghdad or Kabul."[47] Six years later the paper found that spending $5 million to repaint all 6,424 subway cars (which only provided the graffitists with new blank canvases) "may be the cheapest way to fight back," even though graffiti did not delay a single subway train.

Why did graffiti suddenly become a greater priority than broken subway doors, cracked undercarriages, or deteriorated tracks and signals, all of which were far more directly related to degraded service? The reasoning of graffiti opponents was emotional and aesthetic, according to the *New York Times* editorial board: "A subway atmosphere of insistent squalor, unpunished criminality and contempt for the public breeds a sense of helplessness."[48] True enough, but straphangers felt far more helpless when their trains abruptly stopped in the middle of dark tunnels for thirty minutes with no explanation.

Some art critics, such as the cultural historian Joe Austin, have portrayed graffiti writers as antistatist heroes defying the MTA's attempts to strangle their masterpieces. Few of these critics had to ride the subways every day in the late 1970s and early 1980s. Austin sees graffiti as "perhaps the most important art movement of the late twentieth century." What he dismissively characterizes as nostalgia for "the New Rome"—a better-functioning American empire—was merely straphangers' disgust at what they considered a vulgar art form that symbolized the breakdown of government services and a hostile act against social solidarity.[49]

Since its eradication on the subways, graffiti has had its defenders as a revolutionary assertion of identity by young people of color that evolved in conjunction with hip-hop. According to the artist Lady Pink, "the only hint of life and energy and spirit was on the colorful trains coming out of the Bronx and Brooklyn. . . . New York was being crushed. And the young people just would not die."[50] And graffiti helped drive the culture industry—a far more significant segment of the economy than most writers have previously suggested. Graffiti allowed some people an escape from corporate modes of expression by imposing their own identity on the citizenry, but paradoxically it also created wealth as corporations and wealthy art dealers assimilated and commodified its aesthetic.[51]

But tagging and bombing also drove riders from the subway, and for those who remained graffiti underlined the general neglect and disrepair of the subways. While graffiti on train exteriors was sometimes good art, most of its target audience loathed it, especially the ugly tagging of the interior of trains. Graffiti might not have been as important a political issue if the trains had run on time. But in the early 1980s, before it became possible to raise capital funds to pay for real improvements in service, getting graffiti off the trains was the best Koch could do to create a sense of order among the majority of New Yorkers of all ethnicities who were not part of the graffitists' culture.

THE "QUALITY OF LIFE"

In the spring of 1982 Ed Koch read an article in the *Atlantic Monthly* by two criminologists, James Q. Wilson and George L. Kelling, who argued that incident-oriented policing alone could not reduce crime. They later suggested that control of the physical environment, or at least the appearance of control, could reduce crime: "If the first broken window in a building is not repaired, then people who like breaking windows will assume that no one cares about the building and more windows will be broken. Soon the building will have no windows. Fixing what is wrong with the city sends a message that the authorities are in control and that increases the power of authority to maintain order."[52]

Some sociologists have since argued that crime actually correlates to the level of poverty in an area, rather than its level of disorder, and Wilson and Kelling's theory remains controversial in the discipline.[53] But at the time Koch thought the idea was brilliant and sent McGuire a memo suggesting that he implement it as a policing strategy.[54] But fiscal austerity, the center of Koch's long-term strategy, was the leading cause of broken windows as well as "graffiti-bombed" subway cars, vacant lots full of abandoned cars, and garbage and other signs of disorder that accompanied the fiscal crisis and the increasing crime rate. Koch himself saw austerity only as a temporary measure to get back to a point where he could spend money to clean up the terrible mess created by the continuing budget cuts. But he never had the resources that real broken-windows policing requires.

Wilson and Kelling used the graffiti on the New York subways as a prime example of "a sign that an important public place is no longer under public control. If graffiti painters can attack cars with impunity, then muggers may feel they can attack the people in those cars with equal impunity." They noted that the solution had not been more policing or arresting kids with spray cans but a commitment by the management of the MTA to secure, clean, and paint cars.[55]

So why didn't McGuire implement broken-windows policing? He agreed that reducing crime requires "letting the world know that the government exists and that it's going to not only repair the window and keep the graffiti off the public school wall and keep the prostitutes out of the neighborhood, but it's going to protect you when you go out at night." Looking back, he regretted that "we were unable to protect people in my era" because "I didn't have any cops." Dealing with minor offenses was almost impossible, though McGuire did make a limited effort to oust pushers and prostitutes from parks and other public places.[56]

Even this limited effort at improving "quality of life" proved unsuccessful because relatively few arrests, even for serious offenses, translated into conviction and punishment. The criminal justice system was overloaded, underfunded, and poorly managed. One day a judge even asked the police commissioner whether there was a "way of stopping cops from arresting people in the streets; we really have no place to put them." McGuire was outraged but recalled, "That was the reality that we lived in those days."[57]

Only 1 percent of criminals who committed felonies were sent upstate to the penitentiary, and of those a majority served less than two years.[58] Felons were unlikely to be arrested unless caught in the act. When the police department finally computerized its arrest records in 1982, Barbara Basler of the *Times* got the data tapes for August and ran her own analysis. For serious felonies the rate of arrest was murder, 58 percent; rape, 38 percent; robbery, 22 percent; assaults, 45 percent.[59] Just 1 out of every 668 people arrested on a charge of auto theft went to prison for more than a year, according to a 1982 study.[60]

McGuire and Robert Morgenthau, the Manhattan district attorney, ran a joint study with district attorneys and police department lawyers to determine why cases were dropped. The panel examined three thousand felony cases and found that 51 percent had been reduced to misdemeanors. Cops tended to blame prosecutors for being soft, while prosecutors complained that cops were careless about making their cases. The study showed, however, that police and prosecutors disagreed with the reductions in only 8.5 percent (257) of the cases surveyed, a category of cases in which the prosecutors said the evidence was insufficient, but police lawyers thought the district attorneys could make it stick if they were more aggressive.[61]

In addition to McGuire's efforts, Koch's criminal justice coordinators at city hall tried to stiffen the back of the system. One reform the administration backed was the institution of an improved speedy trial act providing for strict time limits for prosecutions.[62] The mayor also had John F. Keegan, a well-known prosecutor (and later a federal judge), come up with a "master plan" for reforming the criminal justice system.[63] Most of Keegan's recommendations focused on streamlining the state court system along the lines of the federal courts, urging the questioning of prospective jurors by the trial judge instead of by the lawyers for the parties, and more nonjury trials for misdemeanors. The suggestions were unpopular with the bar and so never had a chance in the legislature.[64]

Court administrators and judges disliked other proposed reforms, even some that were commonplace in other jurisdictions, such as adopting a calendar for each courtroom. This "would expose weak and ineffective judges to public scrutiny" and took years to implement. But Koch had little real power over the criminal justice system, which was funded municipally but managed by the state.[65] Even the seemingly simple expedient of appointing more Supreme Court justices to relieve severe clogging of the courts required an amendment to the state constitution, a cumbersome procedure.

The one power Koch did have was to appoint municipal criminal court judges. Koch's reforms depoliticized the judicial selection process and significantly improved the selection of city judges. He introduced independent screening panels to send him candidates for judicial appointments, insulating city judges from the influence of party leaders.[66] But he also denounced judges whose decisions he did not like. While Koch kept his promise to reappoint them if the panel approved of them, even if he disagreed, the judges Koch criticized felt their independence was nonetheless compromised.

Despite these reforms, the criminal courts did not convey a sense of public order. The courtrooms were "filthy and dilapidated," and clerical work was disorganized. Judges were unable to enforce bench warrants for minor offenders. "Unpredictable and unfair" outcomes contributed to crime, confirming criminals' perception that no one was in control. Backlogs continued to grow in part because many lower court judges had been transferred to act as Supreme Court judges to deal with felonies.[67] But as one judge observed, even "if you made the system vastly more efficient, what would we do with these people?"[68]

Kenneth Conboy, then the mayor's criminal justice coordinator, argued that judges, prosecutors, and defense lawyers had to take a more collegial approach, a position that would require considerable changes in the culture of an adversarial system. Judges seldom imposed serious sanctions, and the criminal justice system had become largely administrative rather than adjudicatory, "thereby robbing the process of its ethical legitimacy," Conboy complained. According to him, New York's criminals committed an estimated one million felonies in 1979, but only ninety-four thousand were arrested. Of those, a mere sixteen thousand were indicted, and only five thousand were convicted and sentenced to more than one year in prison— about one half of 1 percent. The failure of the system to punish and reduce crime, Conboy feared, would lead to the privatization of personal security, including self-arming and vigilantism.[69]

Koch favored preventive detention for those accused of violent felonies, requiring judges to provide a written explanation if they did set bail for people accused of such crimes. He attacked judges who applied the law then current, which made the defendant's community ties, and the likelihood that she or he would appear for trial, the only criteria considered for bail. The case of Jerome Singleton, accused of slitting the throat of an undercover police officer, was one of Koch's most famous interventions in the judicial process, and it proved embarrassing.

Singleton appeared before Judge Bruce M. Wright on April 11, 1979. Wright noted that Singleton, an African American, was married, had two children, no prior convictions, and was a student at Manhattan Community College. Over the objections of the district attorney's office, Wright properly applied the law, finding that Single-ton was likely to appear, and freed him on his own recognizance. Because the victim was a police officer, the tabloids quickly dubbed Wright "Turn 'em Loose Bruce."[70]

Koch denounced Wright's action as bizarre and demanded he be investigated by the Commission on Judicial Conduct.[71] The next day Supreme Court Judge James J. Leff, who had once represented Carmine De Sapio in his election case against Koch, ordered Singleton rearrested and held on $10,000 bail, which Singleton raised.[72] Sin-gleton did appear and was not retried after a jury hung 11–1 in favor of acquittal, vin-dicating Wright's decision.[73]

Koch tried to back up his criticism of Wright with a bail plan that would have in-augurated a form of preventive detention but soon withdrew it after criticism from legal experts.[74] "Turn 'em Loose Bruce," anathema to some, was a hero to many blacks and white liberals and became a political power to be reckoned with. One of the few candidates capable of fully mobilizing black voters, he pioneered the black grassroots activism that would eventually unseat Koch. Wright won election to Civil Court in 1979 and to the New York State Supreme Court in 1982.[75]

High-profile attacks on judicial discretion and sudden enforcement crackdowns were part of an uneven and crisis-driven response to crime. Koch often reacted swiftly to press criticism, as if he were still a member of the House of Represeatives. And crime went down and (mostly) up largely independent of anything the mayor did or said, which was frustrating and difficult to accept.

Koch thoroughly reformed the appointment process for criminal court judges, one of the most important elements in his attempts to contain crime. It is the single reform of his mayoralty of which he is proudest. The new system took control of judgeships from the Democratic county leaders, eliminating patronage and party politics as considerations in judicial appointments. But Koch could not take politics out of the picture entirely, as crime and race remained as background issues in every appointment. In the case of "Turn 'em Loose Bruce" Wright, Koch believed that he had license to criticize judges precisely because the appointment process was suffi-ciently independent that judges should not see his comments as a threat to their tenure. But the Wright case foregrounded issues of racial balance in judicial appoint-ments, often with a similar subtext about the toughness of judges on crime.

Screening panels became more controversial as affirmative action issues heated up. The first judicial screening panel chair, William Leibovitz, had been a public de-fender and civil liberties lawyer. He was succeeded in 1983 by David G. Trager, a Republican former U.S. attorney; perhaps Koch used his appointment to send a message that he wanted more conservative appointments. In the middle of a contro-versy involving Koch's decision to appoint Robert F. Wagner Jr. to be schools chan-cellor over a minority candidate, Koch appointed six white men, all recommended by the screening committee, to the bench. Noting the requirement that judges have a minimum of ten years' legal experience, Trager noted that "ten years ago the bar included 2% minorities and 5% women. Within a couple of years the pool to pick from should be different."[76]

A group of senior black judges, including state Supreme Court justices Fritz W. Alexander, William C. Thompson, and Edward R. Dudley, confronted the mayor with his record of judicial appointments of African Americans: two black men, and no black women, to the 107-member criminal court bench. Koch repeated Trager's argument that the pool was just too small, to which Justice Thompson responded, "That's nonsense. We've got all the names he could want." They accused Koch of applying a double standard, rejecting black nominees who lived in the suburbs while accepting Herbert J. Adlerberg, a white suburbanite, on condition he move to New York City before taking office.[77]

Trager countered that 18 percent of Koch's judicial appointees had been minorities and 33 percent women, even though only 3 percent of the lawyers eligible by experience were minorities and only 5 percent were women. Trager also noted several black appointees who got the job even though they lived in the suburbs when they applied.[78]

Although Koch pronounced himself annoyed by the senior black judges, Koch tried to establish his bona fides as an advocate of appointing minorities by picking a very public fight with Justice Francis T. Murphy, presiding justice of the Appellate Division of the Supreme Court, First Department (Manhattan and the Bronx). As a presiding justice, Murphy had the power to appoint six of the twenty-seven lawyers on the screening panel and had appointed only white lawyers in the five years since the committee was formed. After a heated public exchange, Murphy capitulated and agreed to replace one of his expiring appointments from a list of six candidates that included minorities.[79]

Murphy then slapped Koch in the face by appointing Herman Badillo, who had become a vocal critic of the mayor's. Murphy told a reporter, "I resent the fact that I've been drawn into this. The entire matter has been caused by two things, and everyone knows it: the elections in Chicago and Philadelphia," referring to the election of African American mayors Harold Washington and Wilson Goode in those cities. Koch rejoined that "the correspondence on Judge Murphy's record of appointments speaks for itself. I am surprised that it took six years for him to find qualified persons in the Bronx of all categories to sit on that committee. I know if he had tried he could have done it in a day."[80]

CRIME AND RACE

McGuire had been considering resigning for some time before he finally quit in 1983. The job was emotionally taxing—during his term he attended thirty funerals for police officers killed in the line of duty—and was paid far less than he could earn as a lawyer. With cuts in federal aid continuing, Koch offered little prospect for funding to bring the force back to the staffing levels it had enjoyed before the fiscal crisis levels.[81] And the frustration of African American leaders with the police was compounded by slow progress in hiring a more diverse force.

The last straw was hearings on brutality in the NYPD held by a House subcommittee chaired by Representative John Conyers. Anger at police racism had risen once again after officers stopped the Reverend Lee Johnson, a thirty-two-year-old student at the Union Theological Seminary, while he was driving in Harlem, supposedly because his front license plate had fallen off his vehicle. Officers asked Johnson for his license. When an officer insulted him with a "racial epithet," Johnson asked him to show "proper respect" to a minister. Instead of apologizing, the officer arrested and beat him. Johnson called Calvin Butts, pastor of the Abyssinian Baptist Church, Harlem's biggest congregation, for advice. Butts called Conyers, who convened the hearings. Koch claimed Butts hoped the hearings would weaken Koch politically and increase prospects for a black mayor in 1985. The Manhattan district attorney eventually dismissed charges against Johnson and ended a grand jury investigation into the officers' misconduct after Johnson and other witnesses refused to cooperate. A year later the Harlem precinct in which he was arrested had a new African American commander. Johnson himself was invited to Brooklyn's Seventy-ninth Precinct in Bedford-Stuyvesant to address one of the department's new regular "sensitivity sessions."[82]

The Johnson case was no isolated incident. Police officials pointed to New York's ranking of forty-eighth out of fifty-four big-city police departments in fatal shootings per capita, according to the Police Foundation. But that did not mean that racism was not a problem. Formal complaints of racial bias against the police had climbed 38 percent, from 3,801 in 1981 to 5,255 in 1982.[83]

Overflow crowds gathered outside the first hearing held by Conyers's subcommittee, at the Harlem State Office Building. The mayor, Commissioner McGuire, and former chief of patrol William Bracey, who was one of the highest-ranking African Americans on the police force, waited as Representative Major Owens of New York denounced brutality and the lack of police protection given to minority communities. He was interrupted by a woman shouting, "You killed my son." The crowd started shouting and Conyers, unable to contain the disorder, abruptly canceled the meeting. Koch got considerable mileage out of the incident. The papers reported that he had prepared an unusually contrite and conciliatory speech that he had drafted himself. "You can't get any closer to the heart, my heart, than I got with that speech," he told the press.[84]

After that the mayor felt secure in boycotting the next set of hearings, scheduled for an armory in Harlem, on the ground that it would again be a "circus" atmosphere, though in fact it was orderly. McGuire also avoided that hearing. He was exhausted from defending his reputation and his department. He served as commissioner for six years—longer than anyone except La Guardia's police commissioner, the re-doubtable Lewis J. Valentine. The veteran reporter Sam Roberts observed that "serving as such a visible target for all of society's complaints about crime is no mean feat."[85] One of McGuire's last major initiatives was to increase the staff of the department's internal Civilian Police Complaint Review Board by 25 percent, to deal with a complaints backlog that had been growing since the congressional hearings began.[86] In October McGuire announced his resignation, effective at the end of the year.[87] The same black leaders who had called for the congressional investigation praised McGuire. Even the Reverend Herbert D. Daughtry, chair of the Black United Front and one of Brooklyn's more radical community leaders, remarked that "McGuire was a decent chap."[88]

Koch did testify at a third hearing, after announcing that McGuire would be succeeded by New York's first African American police commissioner, Benjamin Ward. The mayor challenged Conyers to "produce so much as a scintilla of evidence" that New York suffered from systemic police violence and forced Conyers to temporarily back off his earlier declaration. The final report of the subcommittee, issued a year later, did not find a systemic problem of violence but focused on three issues: discourtesy to black citizens, the weakness of the Civilian Complaint Review Board, which it said had improved in the past year (as a result of McGuire's reforms), and employment discrimination against African American officers, which the Ward appointment was also designed to address. Koch denounced some allegations as "as a smokescreen by the guilty or as a slander by inveterate critics of the police who were not present." But he did concede that, "on the other hand, . . . this certainly does not mean that charges of illegal use of force by the police are unworthy of attention by responsible officials." Koch seemed callous and high-handed after a day of testimony by clergy, professionals, and African American police officers about instances of brutality and discrimination. But far more than his rhetoric, his choice of Ben Ward as McGuire's successor would reveal how damaging the charges were.[89]

22

THE WARD YEARS

Police, Crime, and Police Crimes (1984–89)

After weeks of bad publicity from the Conyers hearings about racism on New York's police force, Koch made city corrections commissioner Benjamin Ward New York's first black police commissioner. The appointment raised hopes that Koch would change the department's culture, reduce brutality and discourtesy, and increase the trust of African Americans in the NYPD. Despite his repeated denunciation of race-based quotas, Koch made no bones about the political benefits of his new appointee's skin color. Patting Ward on the shoulder, he told the press: "He's black. There is no question about that. If that is helpful, isn't that nice?" He took to repeatedly referring to Ward as "the most qualified" candidate, which betrayed the mayor's own anxiety about appearances. Ward proved to be an energetic reformer who was lousy at public relations and ineffective at stemming violent crime, whether committed by crack addicts or his own police force. During his tenure the annual number of murders increased about 20 percent, part of a national trend of increasing crime during the Reagan years. But Koch stood by Ward, more out of expediency than friendship. When Ward died in 2002, Koch tastelessly told one obituary writer that "the fact that he was black was an extra plus."[1]

More than most New Yorkers, Ben Ward was a complex person whose personal history could not be reduced to stereotypes. For one thing, he spoke fluent Yiddish. He was born in the integrated Weeksville section of Brooklyn, the tenth of eleven children. His father was an Irishman whose light complexion and snow white hair earned him the sobriquet "Santa Claus." Ward's mother was an orphan who had been brought up by a German Jewish family. Ward later remembered that "when she got angry she would just drop into Yiddish altogether." He added that "it was kind of funny to see her. She's a great big black woman, a very proud individual, speaking Yiddish." Ward's parents had met when both were in show business on a minor song-and-dance circuit. So New York's "first black police commissioner" was half-Irish and had a background in Jewish culture and show business.[2]

In high school Ward excelled at his studies, winning a Police Athletic League essay contest that made him "police commissioner for a day," forty years before his appointment. He remembered sitting "behind Teddy Roosevelt's desk as the Police Commissioner while they took pictures of me."[3] He was drafted at age eighteen and married before he left home. In Europe he served as an MP, not far from where Sergeant Koch was serving in postwar Bavaria, and, like Koch, Ward could understand the lingo because the local dialect was related to the Yiddish he had learned at home. The army was his first real experience of segregation. In New York, Ward remembered, segregation "meant don't go to Manhattan Beach and don't spend too long in Brighton Beach, but I could surely go to Coney Island. Even the Jewish population didn't go into Manhattan Beach in those days." But "down South it hits you—Bang! Get in the back of the bus."[4]

After working as one of New York's Strongest, as sanitation workers are called, he joined the NYPD as a traffic cop in the early 1950s, after placing third out of seventy-eight thousand applicants on the police civil service exam and graduating in the top tenth of his class at the Police Academy. He was no stranger to police racism. In his first three-year assignment, to Brooklyn's Eightieth Precinct, the white officers would not even give him a locker and made him walk the beat while white cops with equal seniority rode in radio cars. Instead of complaining, Ward went back to school after seven years on the beat and obtained an undergraduate degree from Brooklyn College and a law degree from Brooklyn Law School. The law degree qualified him for several senior administrative positions in the NYPD, and he was appointed traffic commissioner in the Lindsay administration. Governor Hugh Carey made Ward state corrections commissioner in 1975. Ward gained a considerable reputation in Albany for cleaning up the mess left by the Rockefeller administration in the wake of the 1971 Attica prison uprising, and he prohibited corrections officers from joining the Ku Klux Klan.[5] Koch initially appointed him chief of the Housing Authority Police, and, after a year improving its administration, he went to the Vera Institute for Criminal Justice, where he met Herbert Sturz, who served in the Koch administration as deputy mayor for criminal justice and chair of the city planning commission.

McGuire had opposed the choice of Ward to succeed him. The *Times* editorial board, and several advisers, including Corporation Counsel F.A.O. "Fritz" Schwarz, had persuaded McGuire and that New York needed a black police commissioner, but McGuire feared that Ward's drinking habits and other personal problems "really disqualified him to be police commissioner."[6] McGuire thought that the city should have conducted a national search for his successor and that it could have recruited a stronger black candidate. Koch never asked McGuire's opinion and believed that it was preferable for the first black commissioner to come from within the ranks of the NYPD. Presented with a fait accompli, the incumbent commissioner, unfailingly loyal to Koch, publicly supported the mayor's appointment.

The Police Benevolent Association did not trust Ward because of his role in a notorious case that involved Black Muslims and the death of a police officer in East Harlem. At the time Ward was deputy commissioner for community affairs. On April 14, 1972, someone phoned in a false "10-13" call to the precinct, meaning an officer was in need of immediate assistance, perhaps having suffered serious injury. Police rushed to a building on East 116th Street, unaware that it was the well-known mosque of the Nation of Islam, where Malcolm X had preached. Mayor Lindsay had previously agreed to prohibit the police from entering the mosque without permission, so the police failure to identify the building suggests that the officers involved lacked familiarity with Harlem. A few officers entered and encountered approximately twenty armed men. Two officers were wounded, and one was shot dead at point-blank range. Police arrested two men from the mosque; one had allegedly been standing over the body of the officer who had died. Ward and Chief of Detectives Albert Seedman arrived soon after. So did Louis Farrakhan, the minister of the mosque, and Representative Charles Rangel, who urged the police to release the two men who had been arrested and warned that widespread violence might ensue if they were not released. One of Seedman's superiors, possibly Police Commissioner Patrick V. Murphy, ordered the prisoners released after Farrakhan promised that they would voluntarily report to police headquarters the next day. (They never showed.) White officers at the scene later criticized Ward for excluding all whites, including ballistics detectives, from the mosque and charged that he had acted as part of a cover-up by police brass in the killing of a police officer. Ward's public statement that the cops had no right to enter the mosque and his public apologies to Farrakhan also rankled.[7]

Yet despite Ward's unpopularity with some on the force because of the mosque shooting, Koch chose him because his outlook fit well with the mayor's own middle-class-oriented neoliberalism. When Koch announced the appointment, Ward told the press, "I'm very, very liberal when it comes to race relations, but when it comes to law enforcement, I am very, very conservative. I certainly believe the bad guys belong in jail." The *New York Times* and Governor Cuomo applauded the appointment. The strongest criticism came from the New York chapter of the American Civil Liberties Union, which felt that Ward had been insufficiently responsive to civil liberties concerns as corrections commissioner.[8]

Ward inherited a department that was still struggling to cope with the damage caused by austerity. The force remained the youngest in history through Koch's last two terms, its demographics shaped like a dumbbell: heavy on senior officers and young inexperienced officers, with few of the midcareer people necessary to manage such a large organization. Koch never had enough money to restore staffing to pre-1975 levels, despite skyrocketing crime in the late 1980s. The short Reagan-era boom of 1985–87 temporarily eased some of New York's financial problems, allowing Koch to spend money on the police at the outset of Ward's term. The expansion of the trade in crack cocaine and other drugs, and an accompanying boom in homicide, could not be concealed from the middle classes, who heard some of the gunfire from their windows and sometimes witnessed crimes or saw dead bodies on the street.

Police Commissioner Ward wanted to be seen as a tough taskmaster who demanded the highest standards of integrity for his force, though the Mollen Report in the early 1990s revealed that his methods allowed considerable corruption to continue. Telling a class of recruits that his own son had resigned from the NYPD when he was facing departmental charges for chronic lateness and other deficiencies, the commissioner exclaimed: "Imagine how sympathetic I'm going to be if you don't come up to the standards." But Ward's own conduct raised questions about his fitness to maintain disciplinary standards.[9]

OFF TO A ROCKY START

Ward's first two years were "incredibly rocky" and "demoralizing to the police department," according to his predecessor McGuire.[10] Ward brought disgrace on himself and the force in October 1984, when two scandals emerged, one from his days as corrections commissioner, when he "used his office for after-hours assignations with a woman friend" and had, as police commissioner, appeared drunk at a police convention. Because Koch never confronted Ward with the report, the *Times* editorial board charged that the mayor was allowing "the political value of appointing a black commissioner [to] cloud his administrative judgment" but stopped short of calling for Ward's resignation.[11] In April 1984 Ward could not be found for three days while the police struggled to investigate what the *Times* said was "the largest mass murder in New York City's history," with ten bodies—six of them children's—found in a two-family home in East New York. Ward never gave a satisfactory account of his movements but made amends by promising to install a radio in his car. Both Koch and Manhattan District Attorney Robert Morgenthau defended the commissioner, and a second *Times* editorial demanded that Ward "give a public account of his problems and how they've been resolved."[12] Koch's repeated expressions of confidence kept Ward in the job even after these revelations, but the reports aroused suspicions, warranted or not, that Koch was giving him special treatment because he was black. Throughout his term Ward reinforced the mayor's tendency to react to crises by initiating more reforms than he could effectively administer, especially because he rarely instituted mechanisms for properly evaluating their effectiveness.

Even when Ward was right, his confrontational style often boomeranged. When he banned the hog-tying of prisoners after a prisoner died in custody while tied up, Phil Caruso, head of the Patrolmen's Benevolent Association (PBA), scheduled job actions to insist on the right to hog-tie suspects. Ward publicly asserted that the union leader needed to "be brought up short to let him know that he is not running the Police Department." Koch settled the row by meeting with the two men at Gracie Mansion, later recalling: "I brought the two of them together and we reminisced how each of us—Ward, a black; Caruso, an Italian; and me, a Jew—had overcome prejudice. It was not easy."[13]

Although the PBA and the rank and-file did not trust Ward at first, he supported pay increases and gradually became more popular within the ranks. He increased productivity of both the uniformed force and detectives to cope with the drug epidemic, but despite increased arrest and incarceration rates, the crack epidemic abated only when drug users began to avoid it and it fell out of fashion.[14] Under Ward the diversity of the police force increased somewhat, with the percentage of women rising to almost 12 percent from 7 percent, and the percentage of Hispanics going up from about 8 percent to a little more than 11 percent. The percentage of African Americans on the force, however, rose by less than one percentage point, to 11 percent. Ward's requirements of greater education for the police had the greatest effect, doubling the percentage of people with both two-year and four-year college degrees. "What we were going to do was get less uneducated, suburban dropouts, in effect, from society. The worst kinds of policemen we were getting at that time were the white males from suburbia," Ward recalled. He argued strongly that requiring more education did not slow minority recruitment because, with open admissions at City University, New York had a large pool of eligible minority college students. His requirements gave them an advantage over more poorly educated white suburbanites applying to the force. He also started a program that officially hired minorities while they were still students, so that when they graduated they were being promoted instead of hired. That gave them an additional advantage under the existing civil service law.[15]

Ward's modest achievements were overshadowed, however, by the defects of his own personality, which was ill suited to dealing judiciously with citizens worried about police and crime. He loved to shoot from the hip, a terrible trait for an official in his highly sensitive position. Aware that he rankled many with his outrageous statements, which he called "Wardisms," he professed not to care: "I'm blunt and I'm black." At a community forum in Forest Hills the commissioner decided he'd heard enough from a woman concerned about a rapist who had attacked women in her neighborhood. When she said she was afraid to go out at night, Ward riposted that she couldn't be that scared, since she had shown up for the meeting. As the horrified audience gasped, he added: "You're the kind he's looking for—under 30, beautiful, and blonde."[16] Ward characterized the incident as overblown, but he hated Koch's "raucous" town meetings, which he was forced to attend. "If I had been a little more sophisticated than that, and not so annoyed at the whole format to begin with, then I probably would have said something else," he recalled.[17] His apology to the woman, which included his excuse that asthma medication "may hype me up," was hardly reassuring.[18]

Ward took an aggressive stance toward members of a Hispanic group who sought to air their grievances, saying, "Tell your relatives to be careful where they buy their drugs—we don't want to confiscate their cars." He held a second meeting to make amends. When someone asked him why there were not more Hispanics in high positions in the NYPD, Ward said it reminded him of a "story among whites in South Africa. . . . Don't give the Zulu white bread, give them black bread, because if you give the Zulu white bread, tomorrow they will want butter too." One Hispanic spokesman, the Reverend Ruben Diaz, replied, "I guess we are moving up in the world because at the last meeting we were drug addicts and drug pushers—now we are Zulus."[19]

Though Ward quickly apologized, the group went over his head to Koch, who was more sympathetic to their grievances and publicly promised to meet some of their demands. But more than a few New Yorkers thought Koch would have fired a white police commissioner who had referred to African Americans or Hispanics as drug users and admonished them with Afrikaner proverbs. The editorial board of the *Times* condemned the mayor for "applying a double standard" to Ward.[20] After all, Koch had quickly fired head of the Health and Hospitals Corporation, Dr. Abraham Kauvar, after he complained in public that government critics "were always looking for a nigger in the woodpile" (see chapter 13).

POLICE BRUTALITY: "IT'S LIKE THE SAVAK, FOR GOD'S SAKE"

Many hoped that as the first African American police commissioner, Ward would be able to bring police brutality under control and avert racial confrontations between citizens and police. Instead, racial polarization intensified. Brutality cases often went on for years, reminding African Americans at every turn how easy it was to get killed by the police and how hard it was for the survivors to get justice. Faced with the stories of horrifying abuses of power, Ward offered bland statistics showing that "the NYPD's fatal police shootings per 100 officers [and per citizen] is the model for the nation." It was true that New York tied San Diego for the lowest rate of fatal police shootings per citizen, at the rate of 0.48 police shootings per 100,000 in population, but in New York that meant, on average thirty-five dead people every year, compared with approximately four deaths a year in San Diego.[21] In other words, more than a hundred New Yorkers were killed by the police during Ward's five-year tenure.

Police shootings were merely the most visible aspects of a grim picture. During Ward's tenure so much police brutality, sadism, and corruption came to light that public confidence in the force plummeted. "It's like the SAVAK for God's sake," exclaimed Koch's criminal justice coordinator, Kenneth Conboy, comparing the spate of allegations of NYPD misconduct in the spring of 1985 to the shah of Iran's infamous secret police. Perhaps the most heinous case was that of eighteen-year-old Mark Davidson, who was beaten and tortured with a taser in the 106th Precinct house in Queens by officers who had reportedly been drinking in the stationhouse. Davidson had more than sixty burn marks on his body. The papers soon dubbed the 106th the "torture precinct." In addition, New York saw several fatal shootings by police that year, and in March a patrol car hit-and-run killed two people.[22] In 1988 the NYPD's Internal Affairs Division caught thirteen officers in Brooklyn's Seventy-seventh Precinct (Bedford Stuyvesant–Prospect Heights–Clinton Hill) who enriched themselves by robbing addicts and dealers of their drugs and money.[23] After the Queens revelations Ward addressed three hundred of his top commanders, informing them of his intention to tighten police procedures and ban alcohol from stationhouses. Mayor Koch wanted to go further, calling for a ban on private sales of stun guns and asking that the U.S. Justice Department conduct a national review of stun gun use.[24]

Ward's warnings, moreover, seemed to do next to nothing to stop some rank-and-file cops who continued to use excessive force. Some deaths drew high-profile protests. One famous case, memorialized in Michelle Shocked's song "Graffiti Limbo," was the death in police custody of Michael Stewart. Stewart was a young African American artist, arrested at around three in the morning on September 15, 1983, as he was coming home from a club where he used to work. According to police, he had been scrawling graffiti with a felt-tip pen in the First Avenue Station of the Fourteenth Street BMT line. While in custody, Stewart became unconscious—he had been hogtied—and there was significant evidence that he had been beaten and choked to death by transit police. Both the officers' defense attorneys and the family in the Stewart case accused Dr. Elliott Gross, the medical examiner, of bias, and the doctor's credibility was undermined by his shifting and contradictory testimony. He first claimed that the cause of death was cardiac arrest but offered no opinion on why the twenty-five-year-old Stewart's heart had stopped. Then Gross's final autopsy report stated that a spinal cord injury was the cause of death, which would have been more consistent with a beating. At trial Gross said he had no opinion as to why Stewart had died and that the spinal cord injury had actually occurred after death.[25] A mayoral commission chaired by Arthur Liman, a lawyer, investigated Gross and exonerated him of intentional wrongdoing but found that he had waffled on the results in several cases, including Stewart's. In 1987 Koch finally fired Gross "for poor management."[26] The way the city handled the case exacerbated the growing sense that, for African Americans, the criminal justice system posed a dangerous threat rather than a means of ensuring public safety. The legal proceedings in the Stewart case were unusually convoluted, even by New York City standards. The initial indictment was dismissed, and six transit officers were reindicted on charges of manslaughter and perjury but not homicide.[27] The case finally went to trial in June 1985. More than twenty students from the Parsons School of Design testified that they had observed police officers beating Stewart from their dormitory but were unable to identify the officers or clearly agree on their actions. The prosecution did not need to present so many witnesses, and it proved to be a miscalculation that fatally weakened the case.[28] Defense lawyers were able to impeach prosecution witnesses with inconsistencies and police testimony that Stewart was crazy and aggressive—they had merely restrained a suspect who was struggling and out of control. The prosecution also presented a series of experts who offered different opinions about the significance of the medical evidence.[29] The jury acquitted the defendants on all counts, because of the inconsistencies and vagueness of the Parsons students and the conflicting medical testimony.[30]

Koch ordered any further investigation to be conducted by a special counsel he appointed rather than internally by the Transit Authority. "Every legitimate avenue of investigation should be pursued," the mayor declared.[31] The report, by Harold R. Tyler Jr., a retired federal judge, criticized both the police officers and the leadership of the transit police but did not find sufficient evidence to proceed against the officers for use of excessive force. Transit Police Chief James B. Meehan then resigned, but the officers involved were acquitted of the departmental charges brought against them by the Metropolitan Transportation Authority.[32] Seven years after Michael Stewart's death his family received a $1.7 million wrongful death settlement from the Transit Authority, the officers, Gross, and other defendants in the civil case, none of whom admitted liability. The settlement was paid by the Transit Authority.[33]

As the Stewart case was unfolding, a grand jury was also investigating whether Gross had mishandled the autopsy report in the death of Eleanor Bumpurs, a sixty-six-year-old African American woman who had been diagnosed with mental illness. In 1984 she was shot dead after wielding a kitchen knife at officers who were trying to evict her for nonpayment of her token rent of $88 a month in a housing project in the High Bridge section of the Bronx.[34]

Nothing was more predictable than that Bumpurs would point a knife at police or anyone else entering her apartment. An investigation by mayoral aide Victor Botnick revealed that, a few weeks before her eviction, Bumpurs had pointed a knife at the Housing Authority's manager for the complex, who responded to her claim that her apartment needed repairs. When he arrived, the manager found that she was collecting cans of excrement in her bathroom that she said had been put there by "President Reagan and his people," who had "come through the walls and done it."[35] She also pointed a knife at the inexperienced social worker and the Park Avenue psychiatrist who together made the fateful decision that she should be evicted, then hospitalized. In calling for her eviction, they had ignored welfare department procedure, which normally would have paid her back rent and kept her in the apartment until the agency devised a plan for her treatment and recovery. But the eviction proceeded, and the officers from the special Emergency Services Unit said that they broke down the door to the apartment because they believed that Bumpurs was boiling lye to throw at anyone who tried to remove her. The rumor may have been spread by city marshals after a previous unsuccessful attempt at ejecting Bumpurs. But the officers, who should have been warned, asserted that they were surprised that she had a knife in her hand, despite the earlier incidents.[36]

The aftermath brought new notoriety to Gross. As in the Stewart case, Gross's handling of the autopsy of a black victim generated a scandal. The *New York Times* alleged that he had falsified autopsy reports to cover for police officers, but Gross was exonerated after an investigation by a state special prosecutor and by the U.S. Attorney's Office. The officer who fired the shots that killed Bumpurs was indicted on manslaughter charges. Five thousand officers marched in protest of his indictment by the Bronx County district attorney, and the officer was later acquitted in a bench trial.[37]

At a crowded town meeting in Harlem, Mayor Koch announced that "the City of New York accepts the responsibility because we believe that city personnel failed to comply with the procedures that were put into place." He supported the demotion of two regional social services officials for not taking care of Bumpurs's rent. He then declared, "I know there will always be the question of whether, if she were white, would she have been subject to the same acts." Members of the audience shouted, "No, no!" and Koch said, "We will never know." Underlining the gulf between the mayor and his audience, some of his constituents responded, "WE know."[38] Koch visited the Bumpurs family on Thanksgiving. Though Eleanor's daughter Mary had strongly criticized the police, declaring that she believed her mother would not have been killed by the white officers if she had been white, the visit was cool but correct. Under Koch's successor, David Dinkins, the city settled the wrongful death suit brought by Bumpurs's family for $200,000, much less than the settlement in the Stewart case.[39]

After the Bumpurs shooting Ben Ward announced a change in policy for evictions—that unless a disturbed person being evicted was an imminent threat, a duty captain or precinct commander should be called to determine how to restrain the person. Ward banned the use of shotguns against an emotionally disturbed person who did not have a firearm and ordered the police to use hostage negotiation techniques to talk a person out of the apartment, for example, and, if that failed, to use "existing non-lethal equipment, such as mace, tear gas, nets, restraining bars, plastic shields and fire extinguishers." Some of this equipment, like the nets, Ward developed himself, directing officers to use them for nonlethal restraint.[40]

Many of the "new" policies announced by Ward had been put in place by his predecessor Robert McGuire but were never fully implemented. Under McGuire the shooting of a deranged man named Luis Baez, who had been threatening to kill his mother with a pair of shears, had also caused a change in policy. Baez charged a police officer with the scissors and was felled in a hail of twenty-four bullets fired by the officers at the scene. McGuire recalled that he "went crazy. How could we treat a sick person like a criminal and shoot them like a dog?" Like Ward, McGuire decided that "we're going to start treating them [mentally ill people posing a threat] the way we treat hostage situations. We're going to have language people; we're going to have hostage negotiators, we're going have mace, stun guns, whatever it takes short of lethal weapons. We're changing the jargon, we're no longer calling these people psychos, which was the common jargon inside the police department. . . . EDP, emotionally disturbed person, [became] the new term of art."[41]

McGuire soon learned that changing police culture was not as easy as issuing orders. A few months later he was sitting in the back of his car with his former law partner when a call came over the radio about an EDP. His partner said, "What's an EDP?" McGuire proudly asked his driver to tell the partner what an EDP was. "Emotionally disturbed psycho," the driver replied. McGuire realized "this culture change has not exactly trickled down to this whole department."[42]

NEW YORK'S DEATH WISH

Crime in New York City flits between real tragedy and the world of myth and legend. Some of the crime fictions embody history and some create it. The movie *Death Wish* (1974), starring Charles Bronson, portrays a mild-mannered architect, Paul Kersey. When Kersey's family is murdered in its apartment by a group of Hispanic thugs who spray-paint the flat's white walls, he becomes a vigilante, roaming New York and "taking over where the police left off" by murdering muggers with his .44 magnum. New Yorkers had something of a primal fear of the graffiti-strewn, urine-smelling subways, and in the most memorable scene in *Death Wish* Kersey shoots two muggers in a subway car.

On the Saturday before Christmas 1984, a subway rider opened fire on four black teenagers after they surrounded him in a subway car and asked him for five dollars.

Darryl Cabey was paralyzed from the waist down, Barry Allen suffered a gunshot wound to the back, Troy Canty was wounded in his chest above the heart, and James Ramseur was shot in the chest. The shooter managed to get out of the car and escaped by fleeing through the subway tunnels.[43]

Mythmaking took over, quickly followed by politicking. The pallid, slight man in glasses who put a crowd of subway riders at deadly risk by shooting four young men was dubbed the "*Death Wish* vigilante," and Mayor Koch announced that "vigilantism will not be tolerated in this city." Yet hundreds of phone calls supporting the gunman, and even offers to pay for his defense, flooded in to a hotline that police had set up in the hope of learning his identity. On New Years Day 1985 New Yorkers learned that Bernhard Goetz had walked into a police station in Concord, New Hampshire, and confessed that he was the subway gunman.[44]

Koch decided to forget his initially stern denunciation of vigilante justice. Instead, his antennae throbbing with election-year sensitivity, he played to white voters, praising the initial decision of the grand jury to indict Goetz only on relatively minor gun possession charges rather than any homicide charge, a position publicly opposed even by Ward, Koch's police commissioner. Koch also questioned the indictment of a white officer in the shooting of Eleanor Bumpurs.[45] His position was supported by Republican senator Alphonse D'Amato, who asserted the view that "the issue is the four men who tried to harass [Goetz]. They, not Mr. Goetz, should be on trial."[46]

Manhattan District Attorney Robert Morgenthau reconvened the grand jury, presented the evidence, and secured an indictment against Goetz on charges of attempted murder and assault in March 1985, only to see the trial judge dismiss the charges. Half a year later the charges were reinstated, and Goetz faced a jury trial. On June 16, 1987, Goetz was convicted on a gun charge but acquitted of attempted murder and assault. After Morgenthau's office prevailed over Goetz in the Court of Appeals, Goetz received the mandatory one-year sentence for possessing an illegal gun.[47] In 1996 a civil jury found him liable for damages of $43 million in the suit brought by Darrell Cabey, whom he had paralyzed for life.[48]

Racist violence followed the Goetz case and became all too familiar in New York. The outpouring of sympathy for Goetz, which Koch encouraged by approving the vigilante's acquittal of attempted murder, created an atmosphere that tolerated violence. In the mid- and late 1980s the most heinous racist acts—such as the notorious Howard Beach and Bensonhurst affairs—had significant support from many neighborhood denizens (see chapter 24), and police brutality was actively encouraged in some neighborhoods: "We'd rather have the police be too brutal than too easy," said one Queens resident, applauding a local crackdown on drug dealers.[49]

Goetz himself remained notorious, emblematic of the Koch era. The case received worldwide publicity, and twenty years later the editorial board of the *Daily News* recalled the time "when Bernie Goetz was New York City" and that "he forced us to look deep into our souls and confront the evils that were festering there." Goetz even ran for mayor of New York City in 2001, receiving 1,049 votes. When Charles Bronson died in 2003 at the age of eighty-one, *Death Wish* was his most famous role, and one of his obituaries examined whether the film had stimulated Goetz's actions.[50]

PLAYING DIRTY IN TOMPKINS SQUARE PARK

The feeling that Ward was not in total control of the force increased after the police unleashed a bloody onslaught of violence in Tompkins Square Park during the summer of 1988. Tompkins Square Park is a ten-acre plot between Seventh and Tenth Streets and Avenues A and B on the Lower East Side, named for Daniel Tompkins, the New York governor (and U.S. vice president under James Monroe) who, after his election in 1807, pushed through a law committing the State of New York to abolish slavery by 1827. One of New York's most contested spaces, the park has been the scene of six riots since 1874, when the police charged a group of peaceful unemployed workers while they waited to be addressed by the mayor. In 1967 cultural conflict between neighborhood Ukrainians and hippies who had been living in the park and playing loud music led to a head busting crackdown. Similar conflicts, intensified by gentrification of the neighborhood, where the wealthy live in renovated tenements originally built as slums, occurred in 1988.[51]

Violence exploded on a warm August evening when police tried to enforce a curfew and someone responded by throwing a bottle at the officers. The park had been closed periodically during the last three weeks of July 1988, when a green police captain, Gerald F. McNamara, intermittently tried to impose a 1 A.M. curfew instituted by the community board. By the 1980s the neighborhood was one of the world centers of the postpunk scene, and gentrifiers were squaring off against the artists and musicians whom the wealthy were rapidly crowding out of the neighborhood. The gentrifiers also were seeking to evict an encampment of nearly 150 homeless people struggling to deal with the summer heat.[52]

On a Friday night the police cleared the park without incident, confining the homeless to one corner but not arresting them or kicking them out. At about 11:30 P.M. the next night, August 6, approximately 150 demonstrators, whose banners read "Gentrification Is Class War," blocked traffic. A videotape showed that, though no violence had yet occurred, many police had already taken off their badges or obscured their badge numbers with black tape, in order to prevent identification of officers using excessive force. At about 12:30 A.M., near the protesters' blockade at Avenue A and St. Marks, someone threw a bottle at the police. The police arrested one man and put him in the back of a squad car. Then the crowd surrounded the patrol car, a police line formed outside the crowd, and more bottles were thrown, some hitting mounted officers.[53]

No one knows who, if anyone, ordered police reinforcements, including some on horseback, to charge into the crowd and to sweep through the park swinging billy clubs at about 12:55 A.M. "Officers, on foot and horseback, repeatedly massed, advanced, retreated and then charged into the crowds, often running past superiors who called vainly for them to stay back," according to an investigation by the *New York Times*. "They were fighting very dirty, slamming my head against the ground," said Dean Kuipers, a reporter for *Downtown* magazine who was grabbed by police while walking down St. Marks Place and away from the park. Kuipers was clubbed after he turned around upon hearing an unidentified officer shouting at Kuipers's friend, Tisha Pryor, who is black, to "move along, black nigger bitch."[54]

After some officers radioed that they had been injured, more and more units— about four hundred officers in total—arrived from different commands with little coordination. At about 1:20 A.M. the police entered buildings surrounding the park to look for bottle throwers as helicopter searchlights scoured the roofs for the source of the missiles. About forty minutes later mounted and foot patrol units of the police, many with their badge numbers concealed, sealed off both First Avenue and Avenue A between Seventh and Ninth streets and violently dispersed protesters who had regrouped in Avenue A. Then the police turned the corner and swept down St. Marks Place swinging their nightsticks at both pedestrians and protesters. Between 2 and 4 A.M. about two hundred more protesters showed up. The police charged the crowd twice more, responding to the occasional thrown bottle and again when someone pushed a shopping cart full of flaming trash toward the police line. Sporadic protests continued until 6 A.M. This police riot received an especially large amount of media attention because some of the victims were journalists. By August 28 the NYPD's Civilian Complaint Board had received more than one hundred complaints, including one filed by Angel Franco, a photographer for the *New York Times* who was attacked with nightsticks and observed many other victims at the hospital. Eighteen officers were reported injured; the number was later revised to thirteen.[55]

Ward seemed to discipline the officers responsible, including a police commander who, at a crucial time, left the park to return to the Manhattan South precinct house more than ten blocks away. The commander retired but denied reports that his main reason for leaving the park was to go to the bathroom. Captain McNamara received a slap on the wrist, his precinct command taken away temporarily while he underwent additional training.[56] Ward also sent narcotics units to deal with the drug problems in the park without imposing a curfew and changed training regimens for younger officers.[57]

But despite reforms the "blue wall of silence" prevented the identification and punishment of all but a few of the officers who had used excessive force that day. And when the Civilian Complaint Review Board, which had been criticized as stacked in favor of the cops, actually showed some independence and vigorously pursued what cases it could in the face of limited cooperation from the officers at the scene, Ward deprived it of the power to recommend specific disciplinary action against officers who used excessive force. Ward did not even give the board advance notification of his decision.[58] Ultimately, the complaint board, almost powerless to obtain testimony during its eight-month investigation, named only seventeen officers, although the board received 121 complaints. The board was independent enough to argue that police dominance of the investigation had hampered the identification of most of the officers involved, despite extensive photographic and video evidence.[59]

The ineffectual investigation ultimately led Koch, who was running for reelection against David N. Dinkins, to promise a revised and more independent Civilian Complaint Review Board. But Ward's undercutting of the board contributed mightily to the public perception that Koch had allowed the police to get out of control and that the police had let the streets get out of control.

THE CRACK EPIDEMIC: ENTREPRENEURS IN ACTION

Crack—the street name for smokable cocaine—was a perverse entrepreneur's dream. But it was a nightmare for New Yorkers and residents of most other big cities. Described as perhaps "the most addictive narcotic ever sold," crack sometimes hooked people from the first nearly orgasmic high. They quickly developed a tolerance, and their entire lives eventually revolved around obtaining the drug, which seemed at first affordable as a one-off but was, in fact, an expensive and demanding addiction. Making it required little capital, because it could be cooked up in a microwave oven from readily available ingredients. The culture that grew up around the drug reflected the paranoia it engendered. When it first hit New York's streets in a big way in 1985–86, the murder rate increased more than 50 percent in twenty-one of New York's seventy-five police precincts—those where crack was taking root. Murders increased in those areas even though overall crime was up only 2 percent. In four of those precincts the number of murders doubled in 1986.[60]

The narcotics and quality-of-life task forces that Ward put in place to confront the crack epidemic were the forerunners of those used by Commissioner William Bratton in the 1990s to shut down outdoor drug dealing and start "broken windows" policing. Ward introduced sixty-seven specific initiatives between 1984 and 1987 that modernized the NYPD—from intensive neighborhood crackdowns, such as Operation Pressure Point, to digital license checks during traffic stops and expansion of the mounted units.[61] Ward could point proudly to hundreds of arrests in crackdowns, such as the one launched between September 1986 and June 1987 at New York City Housing Authority projects that netted sixteen hundred arrests and confiscated approximately $678,477 in contraband. But the raids had little long-term effect. The drug trade merely flowed into other neighborhoods from the neighborhoods where Ward applied pressure, and in 1988 drug-related homicides substantially increased.[62]

Koch's contention that the problems of crime and drugs in general, and of public order and the crack epidemic in particular, could not be solved without a more serious assistance from the federal government has merit, just as it does in regard to many other problems that New York faced. "We all know that the real answer to the problem lies in increased federal enforcement," Koch declared, though his notion of federal action had a strong military emphasis. "Drugs—and the criminals who make, smuggle and sell them—should be treated like any other hostile invader," he insisted, floating the fiction that the United States could seal its borders. But the type of militarized response he wanted was hardly more realistic than his call to deploy the National Guard during the 1977 blackout. He asked the feds to use the military to interdict drugs and to provide more funding for the Coast Guard. At one point he approached Attorney General Edwin Meese and Treasury Secretary James Baker with a creative initiative to deputize NYPD officers as customs agents so that they would have the power to board ships in the harbor using NYPD boats. This would have speeded and expanded searches, but customs officials refused to allow it, unless the cops were under control of customs personnel.[63] Koch also proposed recalling all hundred-dollar bills and replacing them with new currency to make drug deals more difficult by invalidating all the currency held by dealers and forcing them to use twenty-dollar bills, which would increase the bulk of the cash that would have to be smuggled. He also called for the death penalty for drug dealers who kill law enforcement officers. Neither of these was within his power to make happen, so his speechifying amounted to little beyond tough talk to a city yearning for order.[64]

OPERATION PRESSURE POINT

Ward focused more on the nitty-gritty of police work, reacting vigorously to the new threat to public safety posed by widespread crack dealing. His predecessors, concerned about corruption, had prohibited beat cops from making narcotics arrests on the street. Narcotics officers concentrated on nailing the higher-ups in the drug trade, but market demand was so strong that even kingpins were quickly replaced. Soon after taking office, Ward decided to attack again at the street level, which was being transformed by the unstemmed crack trade. On his way to work when he first took office in 1984, he would drive by "a hundred people, lined up, to purchase drugs." At Tompkins Square Park (this was years before the police riots), the lines were even longer, part of an organized system, "with runners and controllers of these lines, like you were going to a supermarket someplace," he recalled. What jarred him the most was seeing foreign news crews taking footage of an "open air drug bazaar."

The commissioner's first attempt to take dealers off the streets of the Lower East Side was called Operation Pressure Point.[65] Ward described these efforts to an international audience at a conference in the England, saying,

> I decided that the best police approach was to "retake the streets" through a highly visible, highly publicized effort. We mobilized helicopters, drug sniffing dogs, police officers on mounted patrol, scooters, multiple passenger police vans, marked and unmarked police cruisers to guarantee a tangible presence of uniformed officers. We mobilized the Transit Authority Police Department that patrol our "undergrounds." We mobilized the Housing Authority Police Department that police our public housing complex which houses about one million people, many of whom lived in the target area. We mobilized the specially trained drug sniffing dogs of the Department of Correction and we mobilized our special task force of the Federal Drug Enforcement Administration agents and the New York Police Department detectives. We placed the entire task force under a deputy chief of police.[66]

Ward was quick to point out that Operation Pressure Point was but one part of a multifaceted approach that included the assignment of community patrol officers, an effective civilian review board for handling complaints about police brutality and abuse of power, and a strong affirmative action program, so that the department would be fielding "police officers from all segments of the community served by the police."[67] The allied Total Patrol Area Concept (TOPAC) program also deployed massive police resources in a neighborhood to make arrests for minor "quality-of-life" offenses and to make communities feel like the city was finally fighting the crime on their streets.

Ward brought Koch to watch a Pressure Point operation through a concealed periscope in an undercover surveillance vehicle. According to Ward, Koch "was shocked by it. He never knew it was like that." Koch gave his go-ahead, although he was initially skeptical, telling Ward: "It's not going to work. You're going to lock them up, the courts are going to let them go, and they're going to be right back out there."[68] Despite inadequate staffing levels, Ward tried to keep the pressure on. The program did produce results so long as the cops kept up the pressure, as they did on the Lower East Side. Even there the neighborhood was not uniformly grateful; some accused the Koch administration of intensifying enforcement there to promote gentrification.[69]

Though Koch at first touted the NYPD's short-term success by citing large numbers of arrests and drugs confiscated, both he and Deputy Mayor Stan Brezenoff were well aware that these programs were not going to end the street selling of drugs, especially given the department's relatively weak patrol strength at the time. Both programs were often justified (even by the mayor) on the basis of the number of arrests, rather than on an empirical assessment of whether they were stopping crime. Brezenoff wrote Ward that he had great hope that the program would "incrementally change perceptions about crime and fear, and, consequently, attitudes toward the police," but he insisted that Ward develop better measures of its effectiveness. "One idea might be to develop a statistically accurate method to capture community perceptions," Brezenoff suggested, though Ward never really implemented this directive.[70] When Carol Bellamy, the city council president, later asked how the police were going to move beyond the Pressure Point strategy, police brass lamely pointed to the rising rate of arrests, without any attempt to assess whether the arrests actually reduced drug dealing.[71]

Despite the lack of rigorous evaluation, New Yorkers saw some signs of success. Henry Stern, the parks commissioner, described an operation in Central Park in June 1985, with twenty officers assigned to beef up the usual park patrol for an "intensive crackdown on drug trafficking and other quality of life violations," which was "only part of an overall strategy for strict enforcement of quality of life regulations." Between June 14 and July 6, Stern reported, the police made fifty-five arrests for "narcotics and other violent felonies," and wrote 197 summonses for possession of marijuana and many other summonses for violation of "park rules, possession of alcohol, noise, public urination, littering and disorderly conduct." Stern declared himself "impressed with the police response to the problem, it has resulted in a perceivable difference in the park's atmosphere," though both he and Brezenoff were concerned that the enforcement strategy merely displaced crime rather than controlling or preventing it.[72]

Despite the new efforts to pressure the drug trade, and the economic upswing of 1985–86, crime began steadily and unexpectedly to rise after July 1985, increasing Koch's and Brezenoff's skepticism about these programs. At the end of 1985 Brezenoff eyed the rising robbery and burglary rates in particular, wondered whether officers in the TOPAC program should be reassigned. He also pressed Ward for information about the success of strategies for fighting the increase in robberies, such as the Computer-Assisted Robbery System, which kept track of the techniques used by robbers citywide in an effort to identify their modus operandi. The police also used their new closed computer network to put booking data on-line so that it would be easily available at police precincts across the city. ("On line" was computer jargon long before the internet was established). But Ward did not seem to grasp Brezenoff's key point: that the police collected the wrong sorts of data on the illicit drug industry, so they had no inkling whether their enforcement programs reduced the crack trade that was destroying lives.[73] In May 1986 Ward reported that crime was up 18 percent for January and February and that preliminary statistics indicated that the increase was continuing through the spring. Frustrated at being unable to stem crack, police turned to a far easier target, small marijuana dealers and buyers. In June police made almost the same number of arrests for marijuana as for cocaine, although more than 40 percent of drug complaints to the police involved crack. Ward defended his record—the national jump in crime was higher than that in New York City, which Ward attributed to "being out front on the drug issue."[74]

Ward formed a 101-officer team to deal with the low- and midlevel crack trade on the street. He had already mobilized the police citywide to raid ordinary candy stores and newsstands that were selling drug paraphernalia. Police also confiscated the cars of even small drug buyers under the federal forfeiture laws, though drug crimes seemed to increase even without the paraphernalia (a crack addict could make a pipe from a cardboard tube and aluminum foil, so the clearing of head shops had little effect on the drug trade). At a press conference to display the take, Ward groaned, "Can you believe it?" as he showed reporters a small crack pipe with "I LOVE New York" emblazoned on it.[75] Despite the lack of evidence that they reduced the use of drugs, seizures increased as a result of the federal Comprehensive Crime Act of 1984, which allowed police agencies to keep a portion of the dollar value of whatever cash or equipment they confiscated, a significant financial incentive for strapped bureaucracies that may have diverted resources from police actions that might have been more effective at reducing crime.[76] Despite Ward's claim of success, in 1988 the *Times* reported that "the city's police have all but conceded the fight to abolish trafficking in the drug [crack], saying its virulent growth has overwhelmed traditional law-enforcement tactics."

Instead, the police fell back to the lowest threshold of public order, "keeping some neighborhoods from descending into outlaw rule by drug dealers or gangs." While addressing a department promotion ceremony, Ward himself declared that New York "was in the midst of a drug epidemic."[77] He later said that success depended on whether there "were areas that still had social and religious institutions in place that could help you take control" of the neighborhood.[78] Koch called for a city income tax surcharge to pay for more police in tactical narcotics teams, which he made a priority, despite the severe budget tightening after the 1987 stock market crash.[79]

The tactical narcotics teams were similar to Koch's earlier crime initiatives, such as the crackdown on subway crime: showy but effective only temporarily. They filled the jails. But as Koch himself had predicted, they were ineffective at stopping crack dealers, who often returned once the special team finished its three-month stint in a neighborhood. Low-level dealers were easily replaced. One police inspector noted that his 360 officers had arrested 13,200 sellers between May 1986 and June 1988, but they still did not stop drug dealing in East Harlem. Conviction rates did go up, and the mayor congratulated both Ward and Morgenthau, but the number of actual convictions was tiny compared with the 150,096 felonies reported in Manhattan in 1987, although by 1989 the United States had the highest rate of incarceration of any country in the world. The district attorney reported that, as of June 1989, he had obtained 561 felony convictions from the seventeen hundred arrests by the narcotics teams, a rate of 33 percent. Of those, only 170 defendants ultimately went to state prison. Often, the drug teams might clear a block or two, but New Yorkers did not have to walk far to get drugs, even after what was considered a successful sweep.[80]

The ineffectiveness of New York's police was apparent even with a significant presence deployed in relatively well-heeled neighborhoods. By 1986 Washington Square Park, which borders the main buildings of New York University, had become a drug fair for suburbanites whizzing in through the nearby Holland Tunnel from New Jersey. *New York Times* reporter Peter Kerr observed, "Every day dozens of drug dealers stand on street corners and the park's walkways, soliciting almost all passers-by. They remain there despite years of protests by the university, the community and highly influential residents, despite thousands of arrests by the police, despite promises of help from a host of city leaders."[81]

NYU president John Brademas appealed directly to Koch, writing that "faculty who live in apartments facing the Park are witnesses to [drug] sales day and night. So am I." He painted the situation as a dire indicator of future disorder on a larger scale: "If we cannot solve the Park's problems, there is little hope we can solve the larger problems that plague New York." Brademas enclosed a copy of a letter from a parent worried about the harassment of students by drug dealers. Noting that NYU was then the fourth-largest employer in New York City, Brademas declared that "if word gets around that NYU students are exposed to the kind of street conditions described, . . . our efforts to enroll students will be seriously undermined." He demanded more order in the park and specifically asked for police booths in the area where drug dealers "are most obvious."[82]

When Koch turned to Ward, he learned that the park was already staffed by "25 uniformed Police Officers who work between the hours of 7 am and midnight and two uniformed officers after midnight to ensure that the park remains closed between midnight and dawn," plus eight officers from the Organized Crime Control Bureau, and additional K-9 and mounted units. Ward also detailed for Koch the usual meaningless arrest statistics. Though the police had had little success, Ward maintained that patrols needed to be mobile and denied that a substation would be of any use. Koch had to order him to try the substation, if for no other reason than to give the community the feeling that the police commissioner was doing what he could.[83] In addition, Ward mounted an Operation Pressure Point drive in the park, which resulted in the arrest of a major crack dealer. In making the announcement a police spokesman acknowledged that the drive had not stopped the crack trade, which had simply moved a few blocks west to Sixth Avenue. So why continue the operation? a reporter asked. "We disrupt them, harass them and make life hard as hell," maintained Deputy Chief Francis Hall.[84]

After all this effort, the city had assigned nearly one officer per quarter-acre in Washington Square Park. Yet drug dealers still prevailed and in the very neighborhood where Koch had built his political career and still had an apartment. The crack epidemic continued to rage there, as in other parts of the city. Koch and Ward failed to halt it for many reasons, some out of their control. To a certain extent the drug epidemic simply was not a problem that governmental diligence alone could solve. Despite all the publicity and enforcement efforts, the street price of crack actually dropped between 1986 and 1988, indicating that enforcement efforts were not reducing the supply.[85]

Like so many of Koch's other anticrime efforts, the narcotics team was underfunded and not systematic. Given the existing corruption problem, Ward's reluctance to allow regular beat cops to make narcotics arrests was understandable, but it also impeded enforcement, allowing drug dealing to continue with impunity in many public spaces. Koch and Ward's programs tended to coalesce around generating statistics about arrests and citations and simply did not or could not provide enough courts, prosecutors, computers, or even sufficient enforcement personnel to pick up people on warrants if they failed to show up for court. Nor was there much intelligence gathering, and police of the Ward era evidently knew little about the organization of dealing at the street level. The feds, who did prosecute more efficiently, disdained to go after street dealers. Dealing became substantially less ubiquitous when the Giuliani administration arrested people in the park for drug or other minor offenses if they could not produce identification, instead of the older practice of issuing tickets. But such arrests required many more personnel and a beefed-up law enforcement system, which Koch could not afford.[86]

Another reason that Koch and Ward failed to make much of a dent in the drug trade was that prosecutors and the courts did not have enough money to process the huge increase in the number of people who had been arrested on drug charges. In Brooklyn caseloads had gotten so heavy that, according to Brooklyn District Attorney Elizabeth Holtzman, each of her assistants was assigned 120 cases, and each criminal court judge was responsible for as many as four hundred cases. "The Criminal Court is in absolutely desperate condition" as a result of the narcotics team arrests, declared court administrator Matthew Crossen.[87]

Koch appointed Benjamin Ward in the hope that he would possess both the technical skill and energy to reform the police department, continue to reduce crime, and defuse the perception among many African Americans that the NYPD was a white army of occupation. After a rocky start he proved an energetic reformer and pioneered some programs, such as TOPAC, that his successors would draw upon. But Ward reinforced Koch's tendency to react to crime, rather than to build effective long-term strategies. The inability of the police to control the streets in the face of the crack epidemic, increased homelessness, and the continuing instability of city revenues in the wake of the 1987 Wall Street crash contributed to the increasing sense of disorder in Koch's third term.

23

DON'T FOLLOW COUNTY LEADERS, AND WATCH YOUR PARKING METERS (1986)

If a sparrow has a heart attack in the City of New York, I'm responsible. If my commissioners do something right, I flaunt it. If they fail, I accept it.

—ED KOCH

On the night of January 11, 1986, Parks Commissioner Henry Stern shut off the lights in city parks so New Yorkers could more easily see Halley's comet. Koch, fashionably turned out in an aviator jacket, joked that since he'd still be mayor on the comet's next pass in 2061, "I could possibly see it again." Koch discounted the comet's reputation as a harbinger of disaster, although it had served as an augury of William the Conqueror's invasion of England in 1066 and the Great Fire of London in 1666.[1]

No one had any reason to connect Halley's comet with the next morning's top news story: Donald Manes, the Queens borough president, had been found in his car with his wrists slashed, almost dead. He claimed he had been kidnapped and assaulted, but his story was weak, and many believed he had attempted suicide. Few expected that the Manes story would precipitate a corruption crisis that Koch later said "diminished my reputation, my effectiveness, and my usual enthusiasm . . . and almost cost me my life."[2]

A week later the newspapers revealed that Manes was the subject of a federal investigation of corruption in New York City's Parking Violations Bureau.[3] The lurid story prompted a series of loosely linked investigations and brought the Koch administration under suspicion. Manes, along with officials he had planted in the bureau, had instigated a scheme to extort millions of dollars in kickbacks in return for data-entry contracts, and, along with Bronx Democratic chair Stanley Friedman, in illegally obtaining a $22 million contract from the agency for a portable computer that would issue parking tickets.[4]

THE TONY AMERUSO PROBLEM

Manes was an elected official, not a Koch appointee, but the Parking Violations Bureau was under the control of Koch's pliant transportation commissioner, Anthony Ameruso. While he had nothing to do with the ticket bureau scandal, Ameruso had asked few questions about those he had placed in high-level jobs at the request of Donald Manes. Earlier, Brooklyn Democratic leader Meade Esposito had persuaded Koch to promote Ameruso, a Beame appointee, from highway commissioner to commissioner of transportation. Ameruso lasted longer than any other commissioner in the Koch administration—from 1978 until the scandal forced him to resign in 1986. Subsequently convicted of perjury, Ameruso served sixteen weekends at Rikers Island for concealing a $250,000 investment with a real estate company linked to Angelo Ponte. In 1995 Tom Robbins reported in the *Daily News* that "city police and the FBI list [Ponte] as a Genovese crime family associate, a relationship they say dates back more than 30 years." Other investors in the company included a former judge, William C. Brennan, who had been convicted of bribery; Joseph Martuscello, a business partner of Meade Esposito's; and Anthony Vaccarello, a former sanitation commissioner who had been replaced in the first year of the Koch administration.[5]

To this day Koch vehemently defends his retention and promotion of Ameruso.[6] Ameruso's obituary in the *New York Times* quoted Koch as saying that "to tie [Ameruso] in to the P.V.B. corruption would simply be outrageous," though it was not clear why Koch thought a commissioner should not be held responsible for wrongdoing at an agency he ran for almost a decade, especially when the wrongdoing was perpetrated by a party leader who had protected Ameruso in his job.[7]

According to Koch press secretary George Arzt, appointing someone like Ameruso is "like having a bad child. There are fathers who say for the rest of their lives, 'What could I have done?' and blame themselves, but say to others, 'Well, he was that way from birth.' In this case, they knew that Ameruso was a bad administrator."[8] Arzt, a former city hall reporter for the *Post*, thought there was "a failure of [the Department of Investigation] . . . a failure of City Hall staff, a failure of the media, and I include myself," to look into Ameruso's dealings before they became a problem.[9]

Ameruso did not actually steal from the government, but he did undermine Koch in his last term through a combination of lackadaisical management and bad associations. According to Stan Brezenoff, Commissioner Ameruso "resembled the character in the musical *Oklahoma* who sings, 'I'm just a girl who can't say no.'" Worse, Brezenoff said, Ameruso was a "weak commissioner" who "thought his job was to avoid giving bad news."[10]

Brezenoff's predecessor as deputy mayor, Nat Leventhal, had tried to deal with Ameruso's shortcomings as a manager by installing a deputy, Larry Yermack, to run the transportation department. But Ameruso, though a poor manager, easily bypassed Yermack. Bobby Wagner had warned Koch about Ameruso, but the warning went unheeded because Koch had become overly concerned with maintaining good relations with the Brooklyn and Queens Democratic Party leaders.[11]

Brezenoff did his best to protect the mayor. Manes approached Brezenoff and asked him to replace Yermack with Lester Shafran, the head of the Parking Violations Bureau, and to promote Geoffrey Lindenauer to replace Shafran at the bureau. After Brezenoff chose instead an experienced administrator to succeed Yermack, "Manes went crazy and stormed into my office," said Brezenoff, who told Manes, "I don't know what you're so upset about. Nobody made a commitment to you." When Shafran suddenly resigned, Manes, in a fury, demanded that Lindenauer take his place. After Brezenoff rejected the idea, Manes "went nuts" and had "a major screaming match" with Koch, but the mayor backed Brezenoff. If he had not, the scandals might have done Koch far more damage than they did. "There would be no explaining. It would appear to have been a reward for Manes, an absolute unconcern for integrity and—conversely—it was very useful" when Koch testified before a state commission investigating the scandals, "because he could tell the story about Lindenauer and Shafran and how we did things on the merits. It was sort of on the merits, but it was also very lucky. Very lucky," Brezenoff said.[12] Koch's refusal certainly did not play well with the Queens machine. Lindenauer complained, in a tape played at one corruption trial, "There's no such thing as loyalty or friends."[13]

Koch's headaches with his transportation department kept getting worse. Corruption and mismanagement are often compared with diseases sapping the body politic, but when it came to rusting infrastructure, the metaphor became dangerously literal. Two years after Ameruso's inglorious departure, corrosion under the approaches to the Williamsburg Bridge forced the closing of the entire bridge to traffic for six weeks in the spring of 1988. Regular subway service over the bridge was not restored until that August. The new deputy transportation commissioner, Samuel I. Schwartz, said he decided to recommend the drastic step of closing the span when, during an inspection that day, he heard what the *Times* described as "a squealing or screeching sound which was then abruptly cut off and followed by a bang." Schwartz told the press: "That was one of the most frightening things, it was the sound of something going."[14]

Such problems went undiagnosed for years because city officials had been more worried about corrosion in the cables that might cause the span to fail than they were about the bridge's approaches. And when a city program to repair the bridge with federal funds got stalled in the U.S. Department of Transportation, which wanted to build an entirely new bridge, Ameruso failed to get the project back on track, and Koch's critics pounced. In 1985 mayoral candidate Carol Bellamy toured the bridge during her campaign and blasted Koch for not fixing it. "I'm not an engineer, but you could just point to the holes," she told reporters.[15]

Ross Sandler, Ameruso's successor as transportation commissioner, completely reorganized the maintenance systems of the transportation department after his appointment in 1986. He worked with Sam Schwartz to confront and solve the bridge problems. Brezenoff then reviewed all the annual reports (not the engineering reports) on the condition of the city's bridges that Ameruso had submitted to city hall since 1978. "There was not a clue" in Ameruso's departmental reports that the bridges had major problems that should have been brought to the attention of the mayor.[16] Suggestions by reporter Jack Newfield and others that Koch should have known about Manes's racket amount to 20–20 hindsight. But it's fair to say that for a decade Koch tolerated a lower level of performance from Ameruso than he would have accepted from almost any other commissioner.[17]

By the June 1988 reopening of the bridge, Koch had temporarily stopped defending Ameruso. The commissioner's deficiencies had become evident. It was small political recompense that the diligent Sandler and Schwartz were able to complete the bridge repairs on schedule by August, despite much greater deterioration than originally believed, and Koch's opponents cited the bridge closing in the 1989 campaign.[18]

Koch had run on a pledge that he would be a "competent" mayor and would appoint better people than Beame had. And, by and large, Koch did. He had a certain amount of Teflon that allowed him to shrug off the continuation of dirty streets and high crime because people felt he was doing the best that anyone could, given the city's fiscal problems. The scandals of his last term wore that Teflon thin. The Williamsburg Bridge crisis reminded people that Koch had retained a barely qualified transportation commissioner from the Brooklyn machine. While it would be inaccurate to say that Koch tolerated corruption, the personal sympathy he showed for some corrupt politicians even after they were caught was strange for a committed reformer.

SCANDAL AND TRAGEDY: THE MANES DEBACLE

The first time Koch met Rudolph Giuliani was at the trial of U.S. Representative Bertram L. Podell, convicted in 1974 of taking $41,350 in fees and campaign contributions from an airline that he represented as a lawyer, lobbying federal agencies while still a member of Congress.[19] Giuliani was the prosecutor, and Koch was a character witness for the defendant, a role he also had fulfilled for another corrupt Brooklyn representative, Frank Brasco.[20] Koch testified for the two because he considered them friends and wanted to help. (In 2004 he wrote a letter in support of releasing on parole former Bronx state senator Guy Velella, who had been convicted on a bribery charge.)[21] Testifying on behalf of Podell and Brasco cost Koch little at the time, and he won points with the Brooklyn Democratic organization. When Koch needed regular support in the 1977 mayoral runoff, his testimony in the two cases was partly why Stanley Friedman, then Beame's deputy mayor, had advised Esposito that Koch would be a more tractable mayor than Cuomo. Perhaps it led Friedman and Esposito to expect that they could get away with more than Koch intended.

There were trouble signs: "I remember Donny [Manes] coming in to me and being concerned about the very agency [the Department of Transportation] that went bad," recalled David Brown, deputy mayor for administration in the first year of Koch's mayoralty.[22] Brezenoff had thought of Manes as "street smart, good for a few laughs, basically shrewd in understanding his constituents and ready to make a political deal, but not just for his own interests. It turned out not to be true."[23]

Reporters, such as the New York Post's long-time city hall correspondent, George Arzt, had no suspicions about Manes at the time of Manes's January 1986 suicide attempt. Arzt recalled, "The Daily News headline that day was 'PVB Investigation.' No names, no anything." Then Arzt ran into U.S. Representative Mario Biaggi. "Biaggi puts down the paper in front of me and says, 'That's it.' I'm trying to watch the Superbowl. This guy is putting down this paper. 'That's it.' 'What's it?' 'Manes.' And I said, 'What are you talking about?' He said, 'PVB and Manes.'" Arzt ran back to his newsroom and called a source at the FBI, who would not deny that Manes, Shafran, and Lindenauer were under investigation. Arzt said the Post's libel lawyers told him he did not have enough information on the record to print names, so the story referred to two officials under investigation.[24]

At a city hall press conference Brezenoff confirmed that Shafran and Lindenauer were being investigated in connection with a kickback scheme for parking bureau collections contracts. The connection to Donald Manes made the story. Arzt recalled calling some friends in Queens politics and asking, "'Who the hell is Geoffrey Lindenauer?'" They replied, "'Hey he's the fat guy that runs around with Donny.'" It all suddenly clicked into place: "Much like 9/11, everyone says, 'Oh, right, the signs were all there,' but no one could put it together beforehand."[25]

One of the signs was that Manes had been behaving strangely in the days before his suicide attempt. When Arzt saw him at city hall, Manes had been "white as a sheet."[26] Peter Vallone, a city council member from Queens, wondered why the borough president was so hoarse, spacey, and distracted during negotiations with Bronx boss Stanley Friedman over the vote to install Vallone as the city council's next leader. Vallone also thought it curious that Manes was reading a Chicago paper (Manes's extortion racket had come to light when a businessman who had been paying kickbacks in the Windy City mentioned that he'd been doing similar business in New York). According to Vallone, "Corruption or criminal behavior still seemed to me the least likely cause for what was happening to Donald, even a few days later when Geoffrey Lindenauer . . . was charged with extortion. . . . Rumors had floated about Friedman or Esposito, but not Donald."[27] Something clearly was bothering Manes. At his inauguration ceremony at the Queens borough hall the day before his first suicide attempt, Manes "looked ill; he kept putting his whole hand into his mouth—not his fingernails, but his entire fist," Vallone recalled. Vallone thought at the time that the Queens leader might be dying of cancer.[28]

Political interest and politesse combined to form the strong disinclination of Koch and of his political adviser John LoCicero to believe the signs that the county leaders of Kings, Queens, and the Bronx were up to no good. Interviewed a few months after the scandals broke, former deputy mayor Robert F. Wagner said, "I think in some ways that naivete—that not really relating to and understanding this political world, and moving from a very negative view of the world of county leaders to essentially discovering they're nice guys—was part of the problem." Though Koch had devoted his life to city politics, he simply "didn't know that other world and what was going on," Wagner said.[29]

Should Koch have realized that the county leaders were corrupt? One incident that should have given him pause was the dinner Manes arranged for Koch with T. C. "Eddie" Chan, whom the Queens leader later tried to get appointed to the city Youth Board. Afterward, Police Commissioner Robert McGuire, Manhattan district attorney Robert Morgenthau, and John LoCicero all warned Koch that Chan was "a major underworld figure with whom he and Manes should not socialize," LoCicero said. Two years earlier law enforcement officials had testified before the President's Commission on Organized Crime that Chan was a leader of organized crime in Chinatown. Chan, who was never convicted, vigorously denied any links to the underworld but disappeared shortly after he was named in the hearings. Koch probably assumed that Manes's interest in Chan derived from his aboveboard campaign contributions to Queens politicians. It did not lead Koch to doubt Manes's honesty.[30]

After Manes's initial suicide attempt, Koch was solicitous, called Manes his dear friend, and kissed him at the hospital. As questions arose about Manes's bizarre tale of being kidnapped by a black man with white hands, Koch clumsily tried to distance himself, describing the stricken politician as " a close friend—in the abstract."[31] As more incriminating details about the extent of Manes's corruption leaked out, Koch made a rapid and unseemly U-turn, telling the press in late January that Manes was a crook.[32] Koch even tried to pose as Manes's biggest victim, vainly hoping to play on public sympathy. "I feel violated. I feel as though a friend had assaulted me physically," Koch ghoulishly told the *Washington Post*.[33]

Manes was more intent on doing harm to himself. The borough president's psychiatrists had disagreed as to whether he was better off at home or in a mental hospital. His wife, Marlene, decided to bring her husband home. As a teenager Donny had discovered his father's body after his suicide and had sworn that he would never do that to his children. Marlene may have thought that was one reason home would be a safe and healing place. Tragically, family history repeated itself. Manes's daughter Lauren found him lifeless, with a knife through his heart, at 9:50 P.M. on March 12, 1986. Marlene tried vainly to resuscitate her husband as Lauren called 911.[34]

The situation called for the mayor to take a low profile until the investigation played out. Instead, Koch displayed an irrepressible tactlessness. Dan Wolf and David Garth callously told reporter Joyce Purnick the day after Manes died that his death signaled the end of the scandal period of the Koch administration and that they would be getting back to business. Koch appeared at the St. Patrick's Day luncheon of the Queens Chamber of Commerce that day. Purnick reported that Koch began with a serious remembrance of Manes, whose funeral had not yet been held, and "then he turned to comedy," crassly polling the audience (many of whom were friends of Manes's) on his own popularity, while others on the dais with him were visibly wearing symbols of mourning.[35]

At his press conference the day after the luncheon, Koch apologized for his harshness and announced that he would attend the funeral, though he had not been invited. Pressing Marlene Manes for permission to attend, he said, "I want us to be friends."[36] Marlene was well liked and was regarded as an innocent victim. She was later spared from poverty by a generous settlement worked out by Corporation Counsel F. A. O. "Fritz" Schwarz that allowed her husband's estate to make restitution to the city by paying $301,000 to City Meals on Wheels, half of it from Manes's campaign funds and half from his estate. Marlene Manes was able to keep the remainder of her husband's $1 million estate.[37]

At the funeral, however, Koch created the impression that he was dancing on Manes's grave. The mayor set up a microphone stand after the funeral and held what looked like a press conference, a move he later called a "foolish mistake." He later explained that "Cuomo just walked past these reporters, without comment, but I could never do that." This remark betrayed a compulsiveness about his political style that even he realized came off badly.[38]

The scandals did not disappear with Manes's death, as new corruption involving Bronx Democratic chair Stanley Friedman began to surface days after Manes's first suicide attempt and more and more evidence emerged in subsequent weeks. A cigar-chomping professional politician of the old Tammany school, Friedman kept himself busy dealing in favors and profiting from opportunities gleaned from inside information about city government. He had come up as an assistant Bronx district attorney; served as counsel to David Ross, the vice chair of the city council in the 1960s; and then was groomed as Pat Cunningham's successor as Bronx leader. Friedman was a gifted and wily fixer. Abe Beame made him deputy mayor, and the Bronx boss later brokered the crucial endorsements of Koch by Abe Beame and Meade Esposito after Koch won the 1977 runoff, putting Koch forever in Friedman's political debt.

In 1984 Friedman, Manes and Lindenauer became partners in a complicated scheme designed to turn political influence into cash. The complex scheme was the brainchild of Marvin Kaplan of Datacom, the most successful and innovative of the parking bureau's ticket collectors. Datacom made millions by entering parking violation data into computers and took a percentage of what was collected.[39] Kaplan wanted to control the manufacture of hand-held computers to preserve his profitable enterprise as mainframes and punch cards, the mainstays of his business, were becoming obsolete. If the city adopted a hand-held computer terminal like that offered by Motorola—it would hook directly into a central computer by radio—the city would no longer need Datacom. Kaplan founded Citisource to sell hand-held computers to the city and thereby preserve his business. But Citisource's products were inferior, and the company could succeed only through flexing political muscle.[40]

Kaplan, who had already been paying kickbacks as part of his PVB business, realized that he could buy the city's hand-held computer contract by giving Manes and Lindenauer stock in Citisource. Once it had a contract with the city, the three would take the company public and walk away with the profits. But either they underestimated the difficulty of developing the technology or figured that they would leave the public stockholders holding the bag.[41]

Lindenauer was an obese unlicensed therapist who owned a private Manhattan clinic called the Institute for Emotional Education. He seemed like a character from a detective novel. Lindenauer admitted under oath that he had had sex with four patients and testified that patients at the clinic sometimes had sex with each other and with therapists. When asked by a defense attorney during the bribery trial whether he had "knowingly encouraged" patients to have sex, Lindenauer replied, "I don't recall." When the lawyer asked if he had problems with his memory, the witness rejoined, "I don't recall having any problems with my memory," finally acknowledging that he had permitted but "didn't encourage" sexual relations.[42]

Manes had invested $25,000 in the clinic, and Marlene Manes became its codirector. Her husband's role in the bribery scheme may have been a way to recoup this investment.[43] Lindenauer's father had been a criminal lawyer who, like Manes's father, committed suicide. After the institute folded in the 1970s, Manes promised to find Lindenauer a city job, and took him to Friedman, Beame's deputy mayor, who arranged matters.[44] Ameruso later hired Lindenauer as deputy director of the parking bureau on Manes's recommendation after Lindenauer was fired from another city job. At the parking bureau Lindenauer served as Manes's bagman, collecting kickbacks from the collection agencies, like Kaplan's, that pursued parking ticket payments.[45]

The parking bureau scandal grew when the papers reported that Lindenauer had awarded a $20 million contract for a wireless hand-held parking enforcement computer called SIDNEY—Summons Issuing Device for New York—to Citisource, a company with no working hardware, software, or qualification other than its political connections. As a parking bureau official, Lindenauer could not legally award a contract to a company he partly owned. Manes, who would be voting on the contract as a member of the Board of Estimate, had a similar conflict of interest, so he suggested that Friedman could be their partner and front man, holding the stock for them to hide Manes's and Lindenauer's ties to the company.[46]

Lindenauer drew up contract specifications that would disqualify other companies. He bullied subordinates into awarding the contract to Citisource over bids by established firms, such as McDonnell Douglas or Motorola. The latter had a working system in production. Somehow Lindenauer managed to override a finding by the bureau's own research division that the Motorola bid was technologically superior to that of Citisource.[47] The bureau paid for Friedman's "vaporware," even though Motorola had submitted a bid based on a working system that was already in use.[48]

Computerization was a major money-saving strategy of the Koch administration, but it was running in the background. Few senior officials at city hall were technologically savvy, and general knowledge of computer technology had not permeated society the way it would a decade later. Brezenoff, the deputy mayor, was aware of only minor routine objections to the terms of the contract, when Friedman, acting as Citisource's lawyer and concealing his status as a stockholder, lobbied city hall to speed up contract approval by the Board of Estimate.[49]

Friedman's stockholdings first became known as early as October 1984, when the editor of a local Brooklyn paper asked Koch about the deal at a luncheon honoring the mayor. Koch defended the county leader, saying, "The fact that it's Stanley Friedman, you know, it's so easy to libel people and that's what I perceive the implication of what you're saying, intended or otherwise. . . . I don't, do you, know of any criminality on his part? If you do, don't answer. If you do, rush to the DA, because if you don't, how dare you say those terrible things about him?"[50] If it had not been for the small-time bribery allegations involving parking ticket collections that first raised suspicions about the parking bureau, Lindenauer, Friedman, and Manes might have gotten away with their stock fraud. Or perhaps they would have blundered onto a serviceable, if inferior, device and made their money semilegitimately.[51]

Brooklyn boss Meade Esposito had played an indirect but crucial role in the parking bureau scandals. By the 1980s Esposito was a slightly stooped, paunchy man with a fringe of white hair and a raspy voice. He was given to regaling interviewers with self-serving confidences. He was also politically liberal and enjoyed shattering the stereotype of bossism by reminiscing about his strong support for George McGovern and the help that Eleanor Roosevelt and Herbert Lehman had given Esposito when he was starting out.[52] His powerful Thomas Jefferson Democratic Club, which included state assembly speaker Stanley Fink, a noted civil libertarian, was a force for liberalism and tolerance in an increasingly conservative political environment in Canarsie, Esposito's largely Italian and Jewish neighborhood.[53]

Esposito boasted of picking more than forty judges, and his insurance company profited from his close relationship to government, without ever, he hoped, "denting the cherry" by incurring criminal charges. Esposito would later be convicted of giving an unlawful gratuity—a free trip to Florida—to Biaggi and his mistress.[54]

The Manes and Friedman scandals had national political implications. Queens lawyer John Zaccaro, husband of Geraldine R. Ferraro, the 1984 Democratic nominee for vice president, was accused but later acquitted of charges stemming from what prosecutors said was a million-dollar bribe for Manes from a cable television company.[55] Another borough president close to Friedman, Stanley Simon of the Bronx, was prosecuted and later convicted of taking a $50,000 bribe to influence the award of leases of city property to a south Bronx defense contractor. Wedtech, which had been a symbol of the economic revival of the south Bronx, tarnished the reputations of Attorney General Ed Meese and Reagan aide Lyn Nofziger, who had played a role in steering the no-bid contracts to the company. Both were forced to resign. Meese was never charged, and Nofziger's conviction was reversed on appeal. Meese's closest friend, San Francisco attorney E. Robert Wallach, was convicted of using his relationship with Meese to aid Wedtech, though the conviction was reversed on appeal and a second trial ended in a hung jury. U.S. Senator Alphonse D'Amato of New York was often mentioned as a leading advocate for Wedtech in Washington but never was charged with wrongdoing.[56] None of these imbroglios involved Koch's own people.

The first scandal to touch Koch's inner circle broke in May 1986 and involved Victor Botnick, whom the mayor had appointed to head the Health and Hospitals Corporation despite his lack of credentials. Botnick, thirty-two, had grown up in an Orthodox Jewish family in Peter Cooper Village in Koch's congressional district. Botnick had gone to Jewish high schools and worked for Koch his whole working life, starting as a volunteer on Koch's 1972 congressional campaign. Botnick and Koch became friends, and Botnick left college to work in Koch's congressional office in 1975.[57]

If Koch and Botnick were like father and son, as reporters tended to portray their relationship, their archetypal myth might be Daedalus and Icarus. Koch gave his protégé the wings that led to Botnick's fall—the younger man was not up to the challenge, with too many enemies and not enough skill to fly through the shrapnel of city politics.[58] The HHC job called for managerial and political skills—Stan Brezenoff was one of the rare administrators who had survived the agency for any length of time with his reputation intact. Though Botnick had had one or two good ideas about health care, the heavy-handed apparatchik lacked the cultivated brilliance of some other senior Koch appointees.

Botnick was a dutiful factotum and fact-gatherer, but he was in over his head at Health and Hospitals. Sometimes his reports were hard hitting, detailed, and useful, as in the Bumpurs case and during the AIDS epidemic. The first sign that Botnick was in trouble came with a leak to the *Times* in February 1986 that he was a scofflaw and owed $270 for five parking tickets. The report was an outgrowth of the audits of the parking bureau, which gave an especially bad odor to his failure to pay.[59] Botnick was involved in another investigation, as a prosecution witness against John J. McLaughlin, former president of HHC, who was acquitted of taking a bribe from an HHC contractor called Nu-Med. He was convicted in August 1986 of lying on financial disclosure forms and stealing from former law clients unrelated to his government services.[60] Botnick's testimony revealed that he had made several trips to California to visit Nu-Med officials, at a cost to the agency of more than $21,000. Botnick's relationship with the company was already politically messy—in 1983 he had solicited a $5,000 campaign contribution from the company that Koch had returned after a newspaper found out about it a year later, shortly after HHC awarded a hospital management contract to Nu-Med.[61]

Although Botnick did nothing criminal in connection with Nu-Med, and the parking tickets were a small infraction, the mud stuck. He had less leeway in the public's eyes when other small improprieties turned up, such as his failure to disclose his wife's employment at New York University Medical Center when his agency was negotiating the city's $31 million contract with the facility. Then there was the physical altercation between Botnick and Dr. Barry Liebowitz, the head of the Doctors' Council, which represents HHC doctors, in regard to Botnick's secret sessions of the

HHC board, which Liebowitz contended were illegal. After the shoving match, Koch reiterated his "full confidence" in Botnick.[62]

Koch continued his loyalty to Botnick even after journalists noted that accounts in the *New York Daily News* and the *New York Post* differed about where Botnick had obtained his undergraduate degree.[63] Pressure on Botnick to resign was increasing. In early June 1986 the *Times* ran an editorial, "The Botnick Principle," that argued that Botnick was an embodiment of the Peter Principle, implying that Koch had promoted Botnick to his level of incompetence. Koch's response to Botnick's apparent lies about his college attendance was to order Botnick to do community service as a hospital orderly working with AIDS patients—a slap on the wrist that nonetheless infuriated Botnick.[64] A week later it was revealed that he had submitted a false résumé to the Health Systems Agency, a federally mandated planning agency that oversees the HHC. The *New York Times* reported: "When asked about his education on the questionnaire, he first wrote, 'B.A.,' and then wrote over it, 'B.S.'" But the coup de grâce came after Morgenthau made Koch aware of his dissatisfaction with Botnick's cooperation in the McLaughlin case because the Koch aide was now useless as a witness, having demolished his own credibility in public, which may have resulted in McLaughlin's acquittal on the HHC-related charges against him. The next day Koch reluctantly fired Botnick. The mayor told reporters that he'd been through "the most painful period I've ever been through in my life" the weekend he decided to let Botnick go.[65]

A devastated Botnick, who had devoted his entire adult life to Koch, withdrew from contact with the mayor for a while. After a time he occasionally accompanied the mayor on official functions. He completed his bachelor's degree in biology after his resignation, but his life became progressively more tragic. Botnick tried to kill himself twice in the 1990s and was tried but acquitted for the planting of stink bombs on two separate TWA flights in 2000. He died of gastrointestinal bleeding at the age of forty-seven while on trial in a federal court in New Jersey, accused of stealing $200,000 from his former employer, the Cathedral Health Care System.[66]

THE BESS MESS

The Botnick case lent the Koch administration the air of a soap opera, but the revelations involving Bess Myerson, the commissioner of cultural affairs, proved even more melodramatic. "The Bess Mess" was catnip for gossip columnists as well as political reporters, dripping with obsession, sex, money, bribery, the mob, and truths stranger than fiction. Myerson and Koch had been each other's route to political power. Despite misgivings about his difficult and demanding ally, Koch had backed Myerson in a 1980 primary race for Jacob Javits's seat in the U.S. Senate. Myerson lost decisively to the Elizabeth Holtzman, who in turn lost in November to Republican

Alphonse D'Amato. In the wake of her loss, Myerson persuaded Koch to appoint her commissioner of cultural affairs in 1983, despite warnings from Police Commissioner Robert McGuire that the former Miss America had been stalking her former boyfriend, the investor John R. Jakobson, and had allegedly sent threatening letters to herself, then falsely complained about them to the police.[67]

Koch ignored the danger signs. Both he and his aide Herb Rickman were close enough to Myerson that they probably knew by 1983 that she was romantically involved with a much younger married city construction contractor, Carl A. "Andy" Capasso, a sometime tennis partner of Manes's and Friedman's.[68] Manes had introduced Capasso to Myerson at a Queens Democratic fund raiser. At the time Marlene Manes was one of Nancy Capasso's best friends.[69] Then Andy Capasso raised money for Myerson's Senate bid and soon became a loving and generous paramour. When he was out with Bess, Andy gave Nancy the colorful excuse that he was spending his evenings with their neighbor Matty "The Horse" Ianniello, whom Jack Newfield and Wayne Barrett described as "an interesting, well-read Mafia capo who controlled large portions of the construction, concrete, and pornography industries."[70] Given that the major source of Capasso's wealth was from city construction contracts, a newly appointed city commissioner might have seen fit to list gifts such as a $41,000 Mercedes, expensive jewelry, and a new fur coat on her financial disclosure form. But Myerson did not do so.[71]

Capasso eventually divorced Nancy Capasso, who sued for most of his wealth. Within a month of her appointment as a commissioner, Myerson began to seek a way to help Capasso and hurt his ex-wife by reducing the divorce award. Capasso consulted Myerson on the details of the divorce, even on strategy and the wording of legal papers submitted to the judge, Hortense Gabel. Myerson saw an opportunity when she heard that Judge Gabel was trying to find a position for her troubled daughter, Sukhreet, who held a doctoral degree from the University of Chicago and had recently been hospitalized for acute depression.[72]

Myerson had known Gabel and her husband for years; they were both part of the fabric of municipal government, but theirs was the casual acquaintance of people who attended the same parties and fund raisers. Suddenly, Myerson began lavishing attention on the Gabels. Accompanied by mayoral aide Rickman, Myerson started taking the Gabels out to dinner, going to the Gabels' house for dinner, and taking Sukhreet Gabel out, courting her so successfully that "her mother said that Sukhreet had 'a crush' on Myerson."[73] Myerson offered Sukhreet a job, which she accepted on August 22, 1983. Two weeks later Judge Gabel reduced Nancy Capasso's temporary maintenance payments from $1,500 to $500, and Rickman warned Myerson that she was in dangerous territory because of her hiring of Sukhreet.[74]

Just as the Botnick affair was ending in May 1986, the stories about Myerson's using her power to help Capasso hit the papers. Koch stood by Myerson, who neglected to tell him that she had taken the Fifth Amendment when called to testify before a federal grand jury investigating Capasso. He had come to the attention of federal investigators because of his daily phone calls and visits to Donald Manes between the Queens leader's attempted suicide and his death. Capasso was not indicted until January 1987 and soon after pleaded guilty to tax evasion charges.[75]

In the meantime Koch had pledged to fire any city commissioner who failed to cooperate with corruption investigations, and the mayor was privately furious that Myerson had not told him in advance about her grand jury appearance. Still, he allowed her to take a ninety-day leave of absence while the allegations about Myerson's behavior in connection with the Capasso divorce were investigated by a retired federal judge, Harold Tyler. Tyler concluded that "Ms. Myerson's employment of Sukreet Gabel was intended to, and did, improperly influence Justice Gabel in the conduct of the divorce proceeding."[76] That week Andy Capasso pleaded guilty to income tax evasion, thinking he'd get a light sentence. Instead, he got four years in prison.[77]

On October 7, 1987, Rudolph Giuliani, then U.S. attorney for the Southern District of New York, announced the indictment of Myerson, Judge Gabel, and Andy Capasso on a variety of charges stemming from the hiring of Sukhreet. But Giuliani ultimately failed to convince the jury. The prosecution's use of testimony and recordings made by Sukhreet to try to convict her own mother did not help the feds' case, and the jury voted to acquit. "We all felt she was a brilliant girl, but she contradicted herself too much for her testimony to have credibility," one juror observed.[78]

During the Myerson inquiry, rumors spread that Koch himself was under investigation, according to former Koch press secretary George Arzt.[79] In his biography of Giuliani, Wayne Barrett reports that the U.S. attorney assigned an IRS agent, Tony Lombardi, to check out a story that Koch had had an affair with health policy analyst Richard Nathan.[80] When the story first surfaced in the heat of the 1993 mayoral race, Giuliani had insisted that such charges were "'totally untrue,' 'baseless' and 'disgusting' and a 'tissue of fabricated little facts put together.'"[81]

The investigation of Koch was fueled by AIDS activist Larry Kramer, who thought that the mayor was underfunding city AIDS programs because showing too much sympathy might lead people to believe that he was in the closet.[82] When Kramer had dined with Nathan, a respected health-care consultant who had been part of Koch's inner circle in 1978, Nathan had said that he was considering outing Koch. Nathan reconsidered after a conversation with the mayor's friend Dan Wolf and did not further participate in Kramer's outing attempt. Kramer, however, repeated the rumor to every reporter he could think of. The columnist Jack Newfield, hoping to undermine Koch's reelection chances, promoted the story to other reporters, though it never caught on because Newfield provided no hard evidence.[83]

After working on Koch's 1977 mayoral campaign and on his Health Care Task Force after that, Nathan moved to California. From there he did some minor consulting for the Health and Hospitals Corporation, and Victor Botnick met with him on one of his junkets to Los Angeles on HHC business, which brought Nathan's name to the attention of the U.S. Attorney's Office. The first indication that Koch had of Giuliani's investigation was when Herb Rickman, himself a former assistant U.S. attorney, told press secretary George Arzt that he, Rickman, was cooperating with Giuliani in the Myerson case. During that conversation "Rudy's people told me that they're going to go after Ed next," Arzt recalled. "I said, 'Who's going to go after Ed next?' He said the reporters. I said on what? He said, on his sex life."[84]

The rumors spread when reporters started calling Arzt, who became convinced that it was Lombardi, the IRS agent, who was pushing the story.[85] According to Arzt, Lombardi tried to pressure Nathan about his $12,000 contract to do for a report for the Health and Hospitals Corporation and then started asking him about Koch. Nathan, who had never come out to his own family, refused to talk, declaring, "My private life is private." He recited his qualifications, including his Harvard degree and the substantial work he had done for $12,000. Arzt then tried to get a copy of Nathan's report—he "called up Health and Hospitals, and they said he did produce a report, but it's missing." He called Nathan and had him send a copy, which Arzt forwarded to HHC. Arzt thought "it was obviously a perfect setup. Someone had taken the report [out of the files] and said [Nathan] never produced a report."[86]

Clearly, Nathan's compensation was legitimate. He was a respected policy analyst who had performed such studies for HHC for years before Koch was elected mayor.[87] But if it was a setup, it was not merely about outing Koch as gay—which likely would not have surprised most New Yorkers; it was an attempt to frame Koch for supposedly having given a male lover a $12,000 no-show contract, which would have been a felony.

Moreover, Nathan, who by this time had hired the former Koch press secretary Maureen Connelly to advise him about how to deal with the press, had firmly decided not to substantiate Kramer's allegations. Nathan died in 1996 without ever publicly commenting on the story.[88] Newfield actively pushed the Nathan-Koch tryst story to the mainstream media, after getting the *Voice*'s sister paper in LA to run it, but no one picked it up. "Reporters came down to me and said, 'We're not touching it,'" Arzt recalled.[89]

As usual, Koch was ready for battle. In a draft marked "This was never released," the mayor denounced Kramer for believing "that somehow or other it is intimidating to call someone else a homosexual. . . . But I have realized over the years that by defending myself against the accusation, I was in effect acceding to homophobic behavior by some heterosexuals and self-hate by some homosexuals." Finally, he asserted, "At age 62 I don't care whether people think I am a homosexual or a heterosexual. I am going to do my job as Mayor and I am not going to be intimidated."[90]

The scandals took a toll on Koch.[91] At a forum on AIDS in early August 1987, Koch gave a great performance, then rushed off to the opening of a welfare center in Harlem. While they were driving uptown, Koch put his hand to his head and slumped down. "And Ed taps the guy in front [the driver], and says, 'My speech is slurred, I think I'm having a stroke. Turn the car around and go to Lenox Hill [hospital].' When he arrived, he could barely get out of the car." Arzt recalled cops shouting into the phone, "Phoenix is down! Phoenix is down!" The next thing Arzt remembers is that "I was holding his pants" while talking on the phone to the first reporter on the story. . Koch suffered further episodes that night and was moved to Columbia-Presbyterian Hospital.[92]

Koch had suffered a "transient ischemic attack," a sudden, temporary contraction of a cerebral artery that caused his speech to slur and impeded his muscular coordination. When doctors later reclassified the blockage as a "trivial stroke," "neurologically equivalent to breaking his toe," a recovering Koch riposted, "Trivial to you!" But there was no lasting damage.[93]

A more serious health episode might have hurt the mayor politically, but the "trivial stroke" marked the end of a period dominated by scandal. Instead, the media reported avidly on the famous people, including Mario Cuomo, who were visiting the mayor's sickbed. When the governor asked politely if he could do anything, Koch asked him to veto the pension supplement bill, which was going to cost the city a mint. "We gave you a book and cookies," Cuomo replied, jokingly skirting the issue. Cuomo did veto the bill but signed it the next year anyway.[94]

Koch played up a new religious piety that followed this confrontation with his mortality, educating the press about the Jewish concept of *b'sherrt,* or the acceptance of fate. This religious turn led Koch to announce that he and Cardinal John J. O'Connor were writing a book together.[95] "I happen to believe in the power of prayer," Koch said on leaving the hospital after a four-day stay. "I'm someone who believes in God, and I'm convinced that helped me."[96] A week after his stroke, Koch was back at city hall when Mother Teresa came for a surprise visit.[97] And his first political challenge, brokering a deal among the five boroughs for the locations of homeless shelters and a jail, came off by a 6–5 vote in the Board of Estimate that left even the mayor's critics admitting that he still had clout.[98]

Before the stroke Koch was depressed, even suicidal, and was terrified of false accusations. "After all, I was the big fish, the mayor of the city of New York; it was only natural that they came after me. On an irrational level, though, I was scared to death. Really, I was petrified. I knew that under the rules of evidence in a federal court, corroboration isn't needed to make a case. All that's required is for the jury to decide who is telling the truth." Feeling that "it was like being in a Kafka novel," Koch feared that Lindenauer or "one of the others would perjure themselves and implicate me in exchange for a lesser sentence, even though I wasn't involved at all."[99]

By the fall of 1987 the mayor had emerged from the scandals with his popularity only dented. Meanwhile, his political fortunes had improved along with his health, and he pulled out of the deep depression he had labored under for a year and a half. "I felt that they [the voters] were disappointed out there," he said. "It just crushed me a little that they would be disappointed in me."[100] Alair Townsend, the deputy mayor for finance, recalled that the "two years of hell," from 1986 to 1987, "started to alleviate by 1988." The scandals made officials "very timid in terms of making decisions and second-guessing everything." The investigations also took enormous amounts of senior officials' time because of the scope of document requests, she recalled: "Remember, every district attorney, every federal person, every newspaper was on a fishing expedition . . . it just seemed like all you were doing was responding to that kind of thing."[101]

"GOVERN OUR WAY OUT"

But the government kept functioning because of the level-headedness of Stan Brezenoff, who recalled the period as "total warfare . . . and this will sound perverse, as the greatest success of my career." Brezenoff got up at 5:30 every morning to be at city hall before the mayor, ready to brief him on how to get through the day. "I remember saying to him many times, 'the only thing we can do, Ed, is govern our way out of this. We've got to run the city every day.'"[102]

Koch did run the city. Any mayor would envy the accomplishments of Koch's last term: enactment of the gay rights bill, creation of a civilian review board for the police, public financing for campaigns for city offices, and a charter revision commission that would ultimately abolish the Board of Estimate. The city continued the $5.7 billion, ten-year housing program that reinvigorated the outer boroughs. All helped Koch remake New York. They also structured the mayoralties of his successors.

Ironically, enactment of the gay rights bill was a by-product of the last big political deal between Donald Manes and Stanley Friedman, to replace Thomas Cuite, the retiring majority leader of the city council, with Manes's protégé, Peter Vallone. Vallone made a distinguished record as the council's first Speaker under the new city charter, seeing the city council through a difficult transition when it became a more important body after the abolition of the Board of Estimate in 1989. The city council in those days was a dictatorship of the majority leader, as it had been back when Koch was on the council. Cuite, working closely with the Catholic hierarchy, had refused to allow a vote on the gay rights bill for a dozen years. The proposed law— unique among antidiscrimination laws—contained exceptions for companies with fewer than four employees, religious organizations, and landlords of owner-occupied apartment buildings.

Koch had been campaigning for a gay rights bill for years, passing out copies of a sympathetic gay novel and screening the documentary *The Life and Times of Harvey Milk* (1984) for council members. Koch was finally able to get some leverage, extracting Vallone's promise to allow a vote in return for the mayor's help in becoming Speaker.[103]

Lee Hudson, Koch's liaison to the gay community, helped devise a new strategy, bringing experienced gay political operatives, including Ethan Geto and Thomas Stoddard, on board. Eventually, Corporation Counsel Schwartz also played a major role. They shortened the text of the bill, so that no one could claim not to have read it in order to squirm out of taking a stand.[104]

Vallone personally opposed the bill, but his larger objective was to abolish the Board of Estimate. That could not be done unless the hitherto farcical city council became a respected and fair body that could be entrusted with real power in the new charter. So Vallone allowed the gay rights bill to come to a vote.[105] Catholics, Jews, and evangelical Christians screamed their furious opposition to the measure. When Koch entered the council room to testify, dozens of Hasidic men in black hats stood up and turned their backs to him. The bill's leading opponent on the council, Noach Dear, from the Orthodox Jewish neighborhood of Borough Park, Brooklyn, claimed that the bill "could open up a Pandora's box of other lifestyles, like bestiality."[106]

When Joseph Papp, the head of the New York Shakespeare Festival, testified about the long history of homosexuals in the arts, someone screamed, "I hope you die of AIDS." Papp replied that he had been a friend to Rabbi Menachem Schneerson, the Lubavitcher rebbe, and noted that the Nazis had targeted gays and Gypsies for extermination along with Jews.[107]

Despite pressure on the council from powerful religious and political forces, the gay rights bill passed easily, 21–14. Koch personally lobbied for the measure. Some feared the political consequences, but the mayor personally assured council members that if anyone used their vote against them, he would provide personal and material support in "both primary and general election, regardless of party."[108] Koch left his office and walked up to the city council chamber to announce that he would sign the bill, savoring a triumph for his besieged administration. Koch later reassured New Yorkers that "the sky is not going to fall. There isn't going to be any dramatic change in the life of this city."[109] But change did come. While homophobia was far from eliminated, the city became significantly more tolerant, and the bill stands as one of Koch's most important legacies.[110]

The most important structural change in city government under Koch was the new city charter, a revision prompted by a 1986 U.S. federal district court decision, later upheld by the U.S. Supreme Court, that declared the Board of Estimate unconstitutional because its districting system gave Staten Island voters 78 percent more power on the board than voters from Manhattan.[111]

The new charter abolished the Board of Estimate, to the horror of most of the incumbent borough presidents. But many New Yorkers agreed with the famed political scientist Richard C. Wade, who termed the board "a theater of corruption," not an unreasonable assessment. Two of the five borough presidents, Stanley Simon of the Bronx and Donald Manes, had resigned for profiting from awards of city contracts in the months before the charter revision process started.[112]

The new charter promised a stronger mayor and a more effective city council, enlarged from thirty-five to fifty-one members to increase minority representation. Formerly the butt of jokes that it was not even a rubber stamp, "because a rubber stamp leaves an impression," the council would now have power over the budget, local laws, and land-use decisions, which would be made in the first instance by an expanded city planning commission, reviewable within fifty days by the council. The idea was to let the executive branch handle routine applications but to let controversies be decided by democratically elected representatives.

In practice, power shifted to the mayor. The borough presidents lost their sweeping power to spend money and to approve budgets, contracts, franchises, and land use. They were left with small discretionary funds, the authority to reassign service-delivery personnel, and limited participation in decisions about situating city buildings and services.[113]

Voters approved the charter overwhelmingly despite a campaign financed by the borough presidents and real estate interests that featured an image of worms coming out of a can. "Charter revision is a sneak attack on our neighborhoods," said the voiceover. "It's bad government and a big mistake. It's a can of worms that'll make New York worse."[114] The anticharter coalition also included grassroots campaigners such as Marcy Benstock, a leading opponent of Westway who feared that the fifty-day limit on bringing land-use decisions to the city council would prevent elected officials from vetting them.[115]

The mayor endorsed the charter revision in most aspects, but after the election he criticized the provision requiring minority representation on the reapportionment commission as "imposing quotas." He was also skeptical about the land-use provisions. He assumed that the council would be controlled by its Speaker and therefore worried that the Speaker would have complete control over land-use decisions. Speakers turned out to have less power than Koch feared, especially after subsequent charter revisions limited the mayor and council members to two terms. The mayor now dominates land-use and zoning decisions.[116]

The Police Civilian Review Board was another important reform. Despite the political capital Koch put into passing it, the project ultimately fizzled. As a middle ground between the Police Benevolent Association, which opposed civilian review, and civil rights groups, which wanted an entirely civilian board, six members would be appointed by the police commissioner from within the department; the other six would be appointed by the mayor and confirmed by the city council—with one appointee from each borough and one member representing the city at large. Unlike the unsuccessful Lindsay measure of 1966, no majority of outsiders would judge the police.[117]

But the police union was furious. The board would "make every cop duck for cover to protect his or her back," claimed Phil Caruso of the PBA, who also asserted that Koch was accommodating "radical elements." The council approved the measure establishing the board by a vote of 27–7. Eventually, Police Commissioner Benjamin Ward significantly weakened the board by taking away its power to recommend specific disciplinary action against officers and starving it of investigatory resources. Consequently, even in blatant cases, such as the 1988 Tompkins Square riot (see chapter 22), the board failed to deter police brutality or increase public confidence in the police. In 1989 Koch's primary opponent, David N. Dinkins, would call for a fully independent civilian oversight board as originally proposed by Lindsay, which was enacted in 1993.[118]

The scandals of 1986–87 might have been avoided if Koch had maintained a healthier skepticism about the character of the outer-borough county leaders. He needed them politically, to deliver votes, especially with the city council. In reassessing and rejecting parts of his Manhattan reformer past, he decided that the reformers had been exaggerating the criminality of the county leaders. It was easy to conclude, as Koch observed in 1988, that "most people" though of Donald Manes as a future mayor and that "most people thought Stanley Friedman was an honest rogue . . . he'd walk up to the line, but he'd never cross the line of criminality."[119] It turned out that the old reformer was wrong. But Koch could never fully assimilate his errors in judgment. He continued to defend the appointment of Anthony Ameruso, because Koch had to convince himself that it was on the merits, the way he usually tried to do business, and evidence that it was not is considerable. Ameruso lied under oath, broke bread with racketeers, and lacked the competence of most Koch commissioners, a lack underlined by the parlous state of the Williamsburg Bridge, which came to light only after he left office. If the county leader scandals were a product of Koch's naïveté, the Botnick and Myerson scandals owed to his strong loyalty to friends who had been strongly loyal to him, and who were both eccentric and self-centered.

The conventional interpretation of Koch's third term is that scandals paralyzed the administration. Certainly, the demands to produce documents and new procedures implemented to discourage corruption did slow agencies down. And Koch's misjudgments lessened his influence with other politicians and added to voter fatigue with his administration, making him easier to beat in 1989. But Koch was able to manage major accomplishments, notably the gay rights bill in 1986, and the $5.1 billion, ten-year housing program that began in late 1986. Charter reform was another major accomplishment. But Koch had worn out his welcome with many voters.

24 KOCH'S ENDGAME (1988-89)

Vigilante violence erupted in some white neighborhoods even as the crack epidemic ravaged some black neighborhoods from the mid-1980s. Mayor Koch described the beating of two black men in Howard Beach, Queens, on December 1986, as "the most horrendous" display of racism since he had become mayor. The naked brutality of the Howard Beach gang highlighted New York's continuing racial divisions, despite perceived progress in education and employment. "As a black, you can have a summer house in Sag Harbor, you can have an I.R.A., you can have all the material things. But you still can't walk through Howard Beach. It takes something like that to smack you in the face," observed Mark Washington, an employee of the Mayor's

Office of Construction.[1] Far more than the transportation department scandals, a political storm that had largely blown over, the beatings in the segregated Queens neighborhood at the city's edge marked a turning point: even some former supporters questioned Koch's leadership, despite his sympathy for the victims; eventually, what happened in Howard Beach and its aftermath led many African Americans and white liberals to leave the Koch coalition.

Howard Beach, an Italian and Jewish area near John F. Kennedy International Airport, achieved infamy early on the morning of December 20, when a gang of white men beat twenty-three-year-old Michael Griffith and his friend Cedric Sandiford with fists and baseball bats and chased them from the New Park Pizzeria on Cross Bay Boulevard, shouting "Niggers, you don't belong here." As Koch vividly described it: "The survivors were chased like animals through the streets, with one of them being killed on the highway."

The two men had walked three miles to the pizza parlor after their car had broken down on Cross Bay Boulevard in a desolate area near the beach neighborhood of Broad Channel. Griffith's pursuers forced him to run onto the Shore Parkway, which, as the main road to the airport, is one of the busiest expressways in New York, where he was struck and killed.[2] That same night some of the same youths beat up a firefighter, John Gerig, and broke his leg in four places. Yet another group of youths beat two other men, Raphael Gonzalez and Greg Torres, who happened to be in the neighborhood that night. Gonzalez and Torres managed to get into a taxi and escape, though one of them was later hospitalized for a concussion. Two seventeen-year-olds, Jon L. Lester and Scott Kern, and sixteen-year-old Jason Ladone were arrested and charged in the beatings of Griffith and Sandiford.[3]

Koch immediately met with a group of twenty-three black leaders, most of whom, he was advised by James H. Harding, special adviser to the mayor on minority affairs, "are in support of your position." Koch and the group then issued a joint New Year's Day statement condemning "pervasive and systemic" racism. Harding suggested that the mayor reiterate the steps he had taken to catch the culprits: posting a $10,000 reward, reassuring the black community that the police department was strongly pursuing the case, visiting local white churches to enlist their help in calming violent whites, and coordinating a Board of Education teach-in on racism while beefing up security for the reopening of the schools for the spring term. But some vocal leaders of New York's black community were not satisfied with the mayor's meeting with a select group of sympathetic black leaders. Attorney Alton Maddox charged that Koch had "inflamed the passions of the lynch mob" and the reverends Al Sharpton and Calvin Butts blasted Koch for consulting with only relatively moderate black leaders such as the Reverend Floyd Flake, Police Commissioner Ben Ward, and U.S. Representative Charles Rangel.[4]

When Koch remarked that the Howard Beach beating "is the sort of thing that you would expect to happen in the deep South," he inadvertently pointed out that

New York had become more violent than much of the Deep South. He was severely censured by a group of five Mississippi mayors, some of them African American, including Dale Danks of Jackson, Mississippi; James Trotter of Columbia, South Carolina; Charles Evers of Fayette, Arkansas; and William Burnley of Greenville, South Carolina. While some of the mayors were only trying to make clear that they had brought an end to white terrorism in their own cities, the comments of one mayor, W. W. Godbold of Brookhaven, Mississippi, reminded the nation of the prevalence of prejudice: "That Jew bastard. I believe Jews like him who get in this office don't know the what hell they are talking about. It opens up wounds when he persists that the South has problems like this. Especially when he has murders up there every minute and he compares New York to Mississippi. The trouble we had in the '50's wouldn't have happened unless people like him came down here and stirred things up." Godbold later said that he did not mean to smear all Jews. "I have some very good friends who are Jewish," he remarked.[5]

Eventually, Lester, Kern, and Ladone were convicted of second-degree manslaughter and first-degree assault, both felonies, in the Howard Beach case, while the jury found Lester and Kern not guilty of second-degree murder. Several other defendants were convicted in separate trials on a variety of misdemeanor charges, mostly those connected to rioting.[6] Koch, Governor Cuomo, and Manhattan Borough President David Dinkins, who had emerged as a leading black spokesman, cautiously praised the verdict. Both Koch and Charles Hynes, the special prosecutor appointed by the governor, called for the maximum sentence of ten to thirty years. All three received substantial prison terms—Lester, who was seen as the instigator, did receive the maximum sentence, while Ladone was sentenced to five to fifteen years and Kern to six to eighteen.[7]

Less than a month after Griffith was killed in December 1986, a furious crowd had greeted Koch with cries of "Resign!" and "Go home!" when he addressed a predominantly white audience at Our Lady of Grace Roman Catholic Church in Howard Beach, Queens, not far from where the beatings had occurred. "We are not a racial community, but you labeled us," Howard Beach resident Mary Slater shouted at the mayor. The crowd complained of murder and rape in the neighborhood and was infuriated when Koch, shocked back into a more liberal rhetoric, talked about the need to combat the racism endemic in society. Koch later enjoyed a much more friendly reception at a black church in the Caribbean American neighborhood of St. Albans, Queens, evidence of the work that his administration had done to keep and expand ties with politically moderate and middle-class blacks.[8]

Demonstrations in Howard Beach resulted in verbal and physical violence against peaceful demonstrators and revealed the utter and total racism that had taken root in the neighborhood, despite residents' denials. Rev. Al Sharpton, who organized the protests, recalled one particularly vivid incident: "We got to one corner, and there was these little kids. I don't think they were teenagers. And they were yelling the n-word over and over again. And [Police Commissioner] Ben Ward was standing on the corner, obviously disdaining our march. And he looked at these little white kids and said, 'All right, all right, enough of that.' And one of the white kids looked up and said: 'Who are you talking to? You're nothing but a nigger yourself.' And, I remember, I looked at Ben Ward, and his eyes kind of dropped. I think he was hurt and stunned, and I think the reality of who he was dealing with came home."[9]

Two years later racial politics dominated the New York presidential primary, a contest labeled by the newscaster John Chancellor as "the Okefenokee swamp of American politics." Massachusetts governor Michael Dukakis, the frontrunner by the time of the 1988 New York primary, was a cool technocrat whose principled stand against negative campaigning convinced even some Democrats that he might be too nice to be president. Koch's candidate was Al Gore. Gore was running as the most conservative of the candidates, and, as a southerner, he had little natural support in the Empire State. Dukakis was so dry that Gore seemed charismatic in comparison. The only engaging speaker among the Democratic candidates was the Reverend Jesse Jackson, who made Dukakis and Gore seem listless.

Koch had lit into Jackson in 1984 over Jackson's refusal to repudiate Black Muslim minister Louis Farrakhan, who had made numerous anti-Semitic remarks and had threatened the family of an African American reporter who had reported overhearing Jackson characterize New York City as "Hymietown." But in 1988 Jackson had categorically repudiated Farrakhan and criticized the Palestinian leader Yasser Arafat. Jackson also called for a negotiated end to the Arab-Israeli conflict in an effort to court Jewish liberals. And this time around, Jackson had the support of virtually every major African American elected official in New York City.[10]

Indeed, by 1988 Jackson had solidified his identification as the leader of the black community and the best qualified man to be president in the minds of a majority of blacks and of many white liberals, to an extent that no other leader had since Dr. Martin Luther King. The solid organizational work that Jackson's campaign did in minority communities—the campaigns of Sutton and Dinkins were feeble—reached across the boroughs, despite the perpetual Harlem-Brooklyn rivalry, still almost as strong as in 1977, when the Harlem leaders backed Koch and the Brooklyn leaders mostly backed Cuomo. The devotion of Jackson's supporters made him more than an ordinary presidential candidate, more than someone who would be forgotten once he had lost the nomination, as inevitably he would. At the grassroots level Bill Lynch, a brilliant organizer, had significantly increased the base of registered minority voters in New York City, fundamentally altering its political landscape.

At first Koch moderated his tone, as David Garth had advised him to do, and jumped into the fray on Gore's behalf. Noting a "more populist" trend in the electorate, Koch said that he'd like to run for reelection with black or Hispanic running mates (to which Rangel sarcastically rejoined that he was "overwhelmed and pleased to hear that when Ed Koch runs, he will run with a Hispanic and a black. I am confident there will be a spot for Koch either as president of the City Council or comptroller"). Garth, who had engineered Koch's slight tilt away from conservatism, as suggested by his New Year's Day statement on Howard Beach, remarked, "The very fact he's thinking in these terms is the most helpful thing I've heard this year."[11]

"THE BIGGEST HIP-SHOOTER IN THE COUNTRY"

Something had clicked in Koch's mind. Perhaps he was getting sick of the job; perhaps it was the emotional stress of the scandals, of almost getting outed, of seeing Auschwitz during his trip to Poland. But on April Fools Day 1988, Ed Koch wasn't fooling when he declared that Jews had "to be crazy" to vote for Jesse Jackson, "in the same way that they'd be crazy if they were black and voted for someone who was praising Botha and the racist supporters of the South African administration." Koch then went on to say that if Jackson were elected president, "the country would be bankrupt in three weeks." The mayor was not misquoted—Koch reiterated his remarks a week later. Garth, always preparing for the next election cycle and therefore forever seeking to control his candidate, now wearily commented that the stroke had stoked the mayor's ego: "By coming through a life-threatening experience, you start to believe that you are invulnerable. Plus, his political health recovered by a tremendous percentage. That gave Ed a high. When Ed gets high, he gets confrontational. He becomes the impartial arbiter of life. He does his quote-unquote thing, which I think does not serve him well."[12]

Stan Brezenoff recalled lying in bed on a Sunday morning with coffee and a croissant as he watched Koch make these remarks on a television show. He was appearing as a stand-in for Al Gore, whom he was supporting for president, along with Jackson's campaign manager and Representative Charles Schumer, who was there for Michael Dukakis. What Brezenoff saw appalled him: "They couldn't restrain Ed. He sort of leaped out of his chair in response to a question about Jesse Jackson, and didn't respond directly to the question which had something to do with his quality as a candidate, and he repeated the things that he had been saying all along, but he came across as some wild person. I spilled everything."[13] Brezenoff feared Koch's emotional intensity about Jackson "called into question [Koch's] ability to govern in New York with 25% of the population black. This doesn't mean that he has to be hypocritical about his points of view. He can express his points of view. But he's the mayor first." Brezenoff knew there would be political consequences. Until Koch's denunciation of Jackson, David Dinkins was not even mentioned as a candidate for mayor.[14]

A few days later Jackson received a hero's welcome when he visited New York to commemorate the twentieth anniversary of King's death on April 10. Many New Yorkers agreed with Brezenoff that the mayor had gone too far. One voter, Fred

Monderson of Brooklyn, told the *Times* that he had started a movement for next year's mayoral election: "You'd be crazy if you vote for Ed Koch."[15] Norman Mailer, who had been a Koch supporter, wrote that Koch "may have succeeded in blasting the last rickety catwalk of communication between Jews and blacks in this city."[16] Koch had managed to focus all the energy of Jackson's Rainbow Coalition on sweeping him out of Gracie Mansion as its next natural political goal. Hulbert James, Jackson's New York campaign manager, said that at Jackson's packed meetings, "People are asking: 'What if we could keep this together?' into the 1989 mayor's race."[17]

Police Commissioner Benjamin Ward, a supporter of Jesse Jackson's, declared: "Whatever the mayor thought he was doing about what he did, I'm here to tell him, and I think the whole city community—black and white—are saying, that it didn't come out right, Ed, and it has a divisive tone to it."[18] When Jim Harding warned Koch that one of his closest black allies, U.S. Representative Edolphus Towns, had complained about the flak that he was getting from other black elected officials, the mayor told Harding, "There is little that I can do, because I do have a position with which they would not be in accord," but Koch agreed to raise the matter at his next breakfast with a group of black politicians.[19] Koch had no choice but to back down, although he did so only partially. He responded apologetically that "it was never my intent to reject or insult the black community. . . . Be assured that I realize my obligations, both as a mayor who must represent all the people and as an individual who has invested his entire life in public service and who must be true to himself. The challenge comes in striking the right balance." But it was too late.[20]

Koch had endorsed Al Gore for president, probably at the behest of Garth, who was managing Gore's New York effort. Gore had won some southern primaries but needed a solid northern showing to challenge Dukakis. Gore, Koch maintained, was "committed to an urban agenda" and "would be like a rock in supporting Israel," but the mayor characterized his support of Gore's faltering bid as "quixotic," not exactly a ringing endorsement.[21]

Even more embarrassing for Gore, who was trying to be particularly gracious to his opponents in the interest of party unity, Koch continued his attacks on Jackson as a liar regarding his actions on the day King was shot. Nor was Koch's endorsement particularly effective. He asked his commissioners to tell him who they supported for president with a show of hands—and far more supported Dukakis and even Jackson than Gore.[22] Koch hurt Gore's candidacy in other ways—the association probably damaged Gore with African Americans, and Koch constantly upstaged the presidential hopeful, as at the Salute to Israel parade, where Gore was ignored by the journalists swarming around the mayor. Finally, the controversy energized Jackson voters: "[Koch] is the best get-out-the-vote apparatus we've had," remarked one Jackson campaign worker.[23]

The results of the primary were a disaster for Koch and a something of a victory for Jesse Jackson. Though Dukakis carried the New York primary with votes from upstate, Jackson carried New York City, with an election day organization of as many as ten thousand volunteers. Since Koch's endorsement, Gore's polling numbers had barely moved, laying bare Koch's political weakness.

The week after Koch's nasty jibes at Jackson and at his supporters, Koch's old adversary from the Village Independent Democrats, Wilbert Tatum, now editor of the *Amsterdam News,* had begun running weekly front-page editorials headlined "Koch Must Resign" and continued them until Koch lost the mayoralty. And Jackson campaign workers were hopping mad at the mayor—not even Jackson himself could quiet his local supporters' shouts of "Koch is a crook" and "Down with Koch" on primary night.[24]

Exit polls showed that 60 percent of voters in the Democratic presidential primary thought that Koch should not run for reelection the next year. Koch remained outwardly optimistic about his chances, but even he acknowledged, "It's not going to be as easy as it was last time." Seasoned urban political scientists like Charles Hamilton, Martin Kilson, and John Mollenkopf gave Koch more of a chance, figuring the Jackson organization was unlikely to maintain an effective coalition for the next mayoral election.[25]

Ironically, there was one precedent for activists from a presidential campaign to stay together to transform local politics—the 1956 Adlai Stevenson campaign. Just as reformers like Koch had gone into local politics to change a system that they believed had made the election of good candidates like Stevenson impossible, so Jackson's Rainbow Coalition would stick around because its activists believed that the system had made the election of good candidates like Jesse Jackson impossible. And their Carmine De Sapio was Ed Koch.

Koch's remarks about Jackson had turned the mayor from New York's brassiest satirist into an object of ridicule. Upon meeting New York's mayor, Mayor Sonny Bono of Palm Springs, California, pronounced himself thrilled to meet "the biggest hip-shooter in the country."[26] Given Bono's mouthy reputation, this was like being described by Bill Clinton as promiscuous. As Howard Kurtz of the *Washington Post* observed, "Koch tried the public's patience once too often, crossing some kind of invisible line beyond which people are less willing to tolerate his histrionics."[27]

A week later Koch managed to outrage voters once again, inexplicably declaring himself in favor of the British troop deployment in Northern Ireland. Koch, who was visiting Ireland at the time, did not stop there, insisting that the British "were no longer an occupying force" but "are safeguarding the peace, by preventing what, if these people were Jewish, would be called pogroms." Koch's bombshell infuriated Irish Catholics back home, and they had been among his most loyal supporters.[28]

When he returned to New York, Irish American members of his administration, including Paul Crotty, protested his statement. Crotty asked the mayor, "'How can you equate 3 years of being good with 800 years of oppression?" which convinced him to reverse course.[29] The mayor issued a "rare formal apology," broadcast on radio station WINS, and denounced the British as occupiers. But even the efforts of Cardinal John J. O'Connor could not entirely undo the damage—Koch seemed to be completely out of control.[30] His efforts to recover from all these gaffes appeared frantic. Attempting to repair relations with blacks on an issue that resonated with his civil libertarian instincts, the mayor defended Louis Farrakhan's right to freedom of speech at a kosher catering hall and was forced, for the sake of party unity in the upcoming presidential campaign of Governor Michael Dukakis, to hold a humiliating meeting with Jesse Jackson.[31]

The meeting was originally Cuomo's idea, but Koch agreed to it—he got Jackson's home number from David Dinkins. Koch called first thing in the morning and woke Jackson up. Jackson agreed to the meeting and delegated Dinkins to work out the details. At the governor's New York office at Two World Trade Center, Cuomo sat between a "beaming" Koch and a "stern-faced" Jackson, who gave "one brief, slight smile" only after Koch promised that he would not use pictures from the fence-mending session in his reelection campaign literature. Jackson looked reluctant when the mayor shook his hand but spoke more generously, saying that Koch had nothing to apologize for. Both men pledged support for Dukakis.[32]

Jackson gave Koch not one inch of ground or one ounce of political comfort, emphasizing that the serious racial crisis in the New York metropolitan area and citing the case of Tawana Brawley, a black teenager in Orange County who claimed to have been raped and abused by a gang of white men; the recalcitrance of the City of Yonkers regarding school desegregation; and the Howard Beach and Goetz cases.[33]

UNIFYING THE OPPOSITION

The impact of Koch's strident criticisms of Jackson was devastating. Among blacks Koch's approval had plummeted from 59 percent in 1986 to 17 percent in mid-1988. By then only 8 percent of New York's African Americans favored Koch's reelection and 76 percent wanted someone else to take over, according to a New York Times/CBS poll taken in late June 1988, before the meeting with Jackson.[34]

Koch's rhetoric had hurt him almost as badly among the entire electorate. The poll showed his favorable rating was down to 36 percent, with 34 percent unfavorable. Worse yet, from his perspective, 58 percent wanted a new mayor, while only 27 percent favored his reelection. His only consolation was that when respondents were asked to name a candidate whom they would support, none of the potential challengers, including Manhattan Borough President David N. Dinkins, was cited by more than 3 percent.[35]

Dinkins, despite his low-key style, and the undeniable problem of having failed to file income tax returns for several years in the late 1960s and early 1970s, would be a far more formidable opponent for Koch than Percy Sutton or Herman D. "Denny"

Farrell. Dinkins had positioned himself carefully with a cohesive bloc of black support that no other previous African American candidate had enjoyed. He also appealed to many white voters, stressing his strong support for Israel, his early condemnation of Farrakhan, and his willingness to criticize the more radical reverend Al Sharpton. In the campaign Dinkins seemed an ideal bridge between blacks and Jews because of his long history in black politics and willingness to openly defend the Jewish community at a time when many black leaders would not.

Dinkins was forming a strong coalition and by May 1989 had received the endorsement of District Council 37 of the American Federation of State, County and Municipal Employees (AFSCME), the largest municipal employee union, and would continue to rack up endorsements from important unions, including the Teamsters, the United Federation of Teachers, and the Service Employees International Union. Dinkins also had nearly unified support among black elected officials. Charles J. Hynes, an Irish American who was popular in the black community for his successful prosecution of the Howard Beach cases, declared that he would stay out of the race if Dinkins ran.[36] This time it was the white vote that split, among Koch, developer Richard Ravitch, and comptroller Harrison J. Goldin, though neither challenger ultimately got much traction.

Koch's principal managers, Garth and Crotty, tried to rein him in, to project a "kinder, gentler" mayor. Said Crotty: "The big challenge for the mayor is to have voters separate their personal feelings about Koch from his record. We think a lot of the negatives are associated with the mayor's personality, not his accomplishments." And while in previous campaigns the main message was that Koch was good for business, in 1989 the Koch campaign stressed the success of his housing program and plans to spend more on drug treatment, AIDS, and measures he had supported to alleviate the misery of the poor. Fearing he would be seen as polarizing, Koch avoided attacking Dinkins and refused to run negative ads because he believed that a nasty campaign would hurt New York and taint his legacy. Koch confined himself to criticizing the borough president for his well-known failure to file his income tax returns nearly twenty years previously.[37]

Koch tried to shore up his base in various ways; one significant gesture was the publication of *His Eminence and Hizzoner*, a book of essays on moral issues written jointly with Cardinal O'Connor. And, for the first time in a campaign, Koch directly asserted that he was heterosexual—perhaps a response to Giuliani and Kramer's attempts to out him. But gay votes were very much in play, and Koch appealed to the gay community by recognizing domestic partnerships for municipal employees, increasing AIDS funding, and reminding gay voters of his role in shepherding the gay rights bill through the city council.

Aide Jim Harding even encouraged Koch to try to trim Dinkins's margin of African American voters, but Koch's reaction betrayed a certain weariness that was far from the energetic enthusiasm of the candidate he was in 1977, when he would do almost anything that was legal and ethical to get elected. A usually deferential but increasingly frustrated Harding thought at the outset of the campaign that Koch needed to spend more time attending meetings in the black community: "While the polls indicate that David Dinkins controls a large percentage of the Black vote, there is a unique opportunity for us to capture some of it." Harding urged Koch "to accept these invitations while they are still being offered," as he expected that "they may cease as we near the election due to pressure put on the Black community by the Dinkins campaign." But Koch refused to give up his Friday nights off in order to attend more meetings in the black community. And those meetings he did attend not did not always go well, especially after Koch's statements about Jackson.[38]

Shortly after the Jackson affair Harding bluntly told the mayor that he was inappropriately loquacious at a meeting of black clergy: "The ministers should have had more of an opportunity to express their views," to allow the mayor to "hear their concerns and to see how we can be of assistance and, thereby, continue to improve relationships with the Black community." When Koch demanded to know why Harding had booked him at relatively small churches, rather than churches with memberships of more than one thousand, his aide explained that they had to stick to smaller churches because "churches with larger congregations are usually the political base for ministers who have different views from the administration."[39]

The June 1989 polls showed Dinkins leading among registered Democrats with 37 percent. Koch polled 24 percent, a three-point decline since April. Goldin had 9 percent, and Richard Ravitch mustered 6 percent. Significantly, among white Democrats, Koch led Dinkins by only 7 percent, hardly a large enough margin to offset Dinkins's huge majority among blacks.[40] And the survivor of the Democratic primary would face a tough campaign against Republican-Liberal Rudolph Giuliani.

The scandals were pretty much over by the beginning of 1989, except for the investigation by the New York State Commission on Government Integrity, and later by a grand jury, of the Talent Bank, a clearinghouse for résumés for city jobs that operated out of the basement of city hall and the Tweed Courthouse, with the stated purpose of promoting minority hiring. In fact, 66 percent of the people hired through the Talent Bank were minorities, but these were mostly low level. Most of the high-paying jobs for which the Talent Bank had made a recommendation had gone to whites with political connections.

The mayor's people had also put the résumés of people with political rabbis in folders with special colors that announced their need for special handling. [41] This was not in and of itself illegal or unusual; it became politically embarrassing, however, because Koch had denounced such political patronage in his books and public statements, so the hypocrisy undermined his credibility as a reformer. But as budget director Paul Dickstein recalled, "The irony of the corruption scandal was that, of all the politicians in the United States, Koch had less patronage than anyone, and he got painted as somebody who had a lot of it."[42]

The Talent Bank scandal embarrassed Koch because he had been under fire for not promoting affirmative action in both municipal hiring and contracting, which led to the widespread perception—which Koch believed was unfair—that he was more interested in protecting white privilege than promoting minorities into the middle class. The mayor's own Commission on Black New Yorkers was a political disaster for the him, heavily criticizing the Talent Bank in its November 1988 report and calling for exactly the kinds of affirmative action and minority set-asides that Koch condemned. So did *Crain's New York Business,* which satirized the mayor with a cartoon showing three tall white guys with sacks full of contracts walking away from Gracie Mansion and a short black guy with a sack labeled "minority firms" who is talking to Koch, who says, "Sorry, no more treats." More seriously, a *Crain's* editorial charged that Koch was "contributing to a climate that simply prevents the emergence of more black companies into the corporate mainstream." An outraged Koch contemplated a splenetic response that was never published. If it had, it would only have contributed to his image as a polarizing figure, for he wanted to tell the publication: "Your comments are outrageous, indeed despicable. It is clear to me that Crain's is suffering a failure of nerve. I truly doubt whether it hires its people on the basis of racial quotas."[43]

When the political commentator William Schneider, in the wake of the Jackson debacle, maintained that "Edward Koch has been elected and re-elected mayor of New York by appealing to racial resentment," the mayor attacked it as a "false and outrageous statement." Schneider even claimed that Koch's attacks on Jackson were calculated "to provoke the black community into running a Jackson-endorsed black candidate against him for mayor next year." But Koch's outburst was not calculated at all—it was an unwise emotional outburst spurred by the fear that Jackson would succeed in turning the Democratic Party away from supporting Israel. Koch himself acknowledged he "should have said the same things in a less strident way." The damage was irreparable, not because it was a calculation gone wrong, but because it revealed so plainly what Koch really thought.[44]

When the Talent Bank investigation began, Joe DeVicenzo, the office's director, managed to turn a nonissue into a crime by panicking and destroying agency records. After retiring early to save his pension, DeVicenzo was indicted on a charge of perjury related to his testimony before a state commission in August 1989 during the last few weeks of Koch's primary battle for reelection. DeVicenzo did far more damage by trying to hide the truth than if he had just acknowledged that he was a patronage dispenser, which was not in itself illegal. The issue continued to hurt Koch's re-election bid, and DeVicenzo pleaded guilty to the perjury charge and received five years' probation.[45]

Tragedy struck Brooklyn late that election summer with the murder of Yusuf K. Hawkins by a gang of white teenagers on Bay Ridge Avenue in Bensonhurst on the evening of Wednesday, August 20.[46] Hawkins, a sixteen-year-old African American, and three friends were on their way to look at an '83 Pontiac that had been advertised for sale when they were accosted by a mob of at least ten or more white kids, yelling, "Let's club the fucking nigger!" Another shouted: "No, let's not club, let's shoot one." Brezenoff went to Bensonhurst with Koch, just as he had gone to Howard Beach. They were struck by the sadness of what had happened but could not ignore its political implications: "Both of us knew that this would reenergize the—remind people, give some pause to even white voters who would worry about racial conflict in the city," Brezenoff recalled.[47]

Koch later termed it "the turning point of the campaign," a deep human tragedy, the shedding of the blood of innocents. To some African Americans it seemed as if they were reliving a century of rule through terror.[48] As the columnist Clarence Page observed, the killing "meshes neatly with the frictions that sparked George Bush's 'Willie Horton' commercials or neo-Klan leader David Duke's successful campaign for the Louisiana legislature," the deep and resurgent racism of George H.W. Bush's America.[49] The events in Bensonhurst underscored the arguments of Dinkins's supporters, that New York needed a mayor who would confront racism and reduce racial tension. Dinkins himself declared: "These young people set upon the victim because they fit the mould. It wasn't mistaken identity. It was a case of any nigger will do."[50]

Koch then did himself more political injury by trying to prevent Al Sharpton from leading a march into Bensonhurst. Koch later recalled telling the marchers, "There is nothing wrong or illegal about a protest march. . . . The question is, do you want to be helpful in reducing the tensions, or do you want to escalate those tensions?"[51] From the perspective of Sharpton, who continued to organize nonviolent marches in Bensonhurst for months and who was later stabbed there by a white counterdemonstrator, Koch was abandoning the legacy of the civil rights movement—the tradition of using nonviolence to confront and unmask the violence of racism. "So how do you tell us don't do King tactics in Howard Beach and in Bensonhurst and then go speak at the King Day memorial? It was the most amazing contradiction I ever saw in my life," Sharpton declared. He regarded Koch's objection to the marches as hypocritical: "You can't brag about going to Selma, Alabama, and then tell people fifty years later, 'Don't go to Bensonhurst.' I mean, you can't. Because even though you may be looking at it differently because you're the mayor now, you are inadvertently emboldening guys that are throwing watermelons at us [by] saying you shouldn't be in the neighborhood. You should be in any neighborhood. And you should be able to protest in any neighborhood where a crime has been committed."[52]

Hawkins's funeral on August 31, less than two weeks before the primary, turned into a political free-for-all. The Black Muslims provided security, and Louis Farrakhan's men kept Mayor Koch and Governor Cuomo waiting for an hour in the hot sun before admitting them to the church, to put them in their place. Koch was roundly booed. The proud mayor, who had once declared that he would always leave through the door he entered, took the advice of Al Sharpton and Hawkins's father, Moses Stewart, and prudently left by a side door to avoid further disruption of the funeral. Koch told the press that Stewart had been "kind and generous" and had courageously offered to help the mayor get out of the church.[53]

Stewart, who deplored the attempts to exploit his grief for political ends, was approached by both Dinkins and Koch. Stewart actually in some ways preferred Koch to Dinkins. The mayor, he declared, had "offered me the services of his office and those he knows. Money for the funeral. Police protection. A job interview. He called my aunt and sent flowers to my mother in the hospital. He offered those things that any person in any kind of political status who really cared would have offered. No one else did that, except Al Sharpton and Louis Farrakhan. Dinkins didn't even say to me, 'Mr. Stewart or Miss Hawkins, I am going to do this or that to see that your son's death is not in vain.' Dinkins came to me to campaign."[54] This occurred in the last two weeks of the mayoral campaign, which continued, as hot and heavy as the late summer days.

Koch himself thought it unlikely that he'd recoup and win the Democratic primary. According to Stan Brezenoff, the last polls showed clearly that "unless there was some kind of lightning striking certain neighborhoods in the city we were going to lose this election."[55] Nonetheless, the mayor fought hard to the end, still able to raise more money than any other candidate, raising more than $800,000 in August, twice as much as Dinkins, though that may have cemented Koch's reputation as the candidate of rich developers. He still got the endorsement of the *New York Times* and of the Queens Democratic chair, Tom Manton, who recognized that Ravitch's candidacy was going nowhere. Such mystique surrounded these efforts that the *Washington Post* declared the race a cliffhanger, despite the late summer poll numbers. [56]

When the results came in, Dinkins had won a resounding victory. The vote totals were:

David N. Dinkins	537,887	50.7%
Edward I. Koch	445,941	42%
Richard Ravitch	48,289	4.6%
Harrison J. Goldin	28,792	2.7%[57]

Koch's total primary vote dropped about 20 points, from the 63.3 percent he had won in the 1985 Democratic primary. His most precipitous losses were among blacks and Latinos—a decline of more than a 30 percent in black, mixed minority, and Latino districts. Koch also lost many votes from his base of white Catholics and Jews. He was down 7.1 percent among white Catholics, 10.4 percent among outer-borough Jews, and a whopping 13.2 percent among white liberals.[58]

Dinkins fared dramatically better in minority communities than Denny Farrell had in 1985. Dinkins's base of success was the extraordinary support he received from blacks, 94.2 percent, and from 57.5 percent of Latinos. And he had added a considerable base of white support: 24.6 percent of Jews, 47.9 percent of white Protestants, and 62.7 percent of nonreligious whites.[59] Even more significant was that Dinkins's support for moderation and condemnation of anti-Semitism also had made him significantly more popular among New York's white voters than Jesse Jackson. White liberals had given Jackson 29 percent of their votes in the 1988 New York Democratic primary; a year later 46.5 percent of white liberals wanted Dinkins as their mayor.[60]

Koch decided to give an early concession speech, "to give Dinkins the spotlight for the balance of the evening. It would be good for him, and for the party, to be on the eleven o'clock news."[61] Koch had become so identified with the mayoralty that friends worried that he would have trouble adjusting to life as a private citizen. But Koch, who had given little thought to what his new private life might be like, told supporters that night, "I want you not to feel sorry for me. Believe me, there is life after the mayoralty."[62]

Koch still had a bit more than three months left in his term, and lame duck status did not quiet him down. The mayor decided to take a stand against the repression of demonstrators in Tiananmen Square that fall. Koch renamed the street across from the Chinese mission to the UN "Tiananmen Square," after the site of the massacre, and insulted the Chinese ambassador, telling him "to defect and seek asylum here in the United States and then to tell the truth." Ambassador Weng Fupei asserted that renaming the street and Koch's statements were "a gross insult to the dignity of the Chinese diplomats and an unreasonable provocation against the Chinese people," yet gleefully Koch retorted that the ambassador's remarks "one step short of a declaration of war."[63]

Still, despite public denials, Koch was sad to leave the mayoralty. He said to city council Speaker Peter Vallone: "What am I going to do? My whole life has been the city." A few days after Koch moved out of Gracie Mansion, Vallone saw him again, hale and hearty. Koch "said something to me like, 'You know this morning, some guy came over and said 'I'm glad you lost, you son of a bitch.'" Koch then told the guy to go fuck himself, telling Vallone, "It felt so good. I could never do that when I was mayor."[64]

25 EPILOGUE

On the evening of December 9, 2004, a glamorous party was in full swing in the Blue Room of Gracie Mansion. Glasses started clinking loudly, signaling the main event. All eyes turned to the rostrum. Mayor Michael Bloomberg was flanked by New York's two senators, Charles Schumer and Hillary Rodham Clinton, and the evening's honoree, Edward Irving Koch, whose eightieth birthday had prompted this display of power and pomp. Bloomberg craned his neck to gaze up at Koch, whose height allows him to dominate even a star-studded scene. "When I was just a lowly millionaire in the 1970s, I wanted to be like Koch if I went into politics," said Bloomberg. "I'd be tall, I'd be loud, and I'd be both a Democrat and a Republican." The crowd guffawed.[1]

Clinton took the stage and declared that she owed her election to her old friend Ed Koch, who had helped line up Jewish support in her new home state. Schumer followed. His friendship with Koch was of more recent vintage. Six years previously Koch had opposed Schumer in the senate race in favor of Republican incumbent Al D'Amato. But while Koch threw his support behind D'Amato, he would not cover up for him. When news got out that D'Amato had called Schumer a "putzhead" in a closed meeting with a Jewish group, Koch confirmed the story. Backlash may have helped Schumer come from behind in the polls to win by a 10-point margin, despite polls less than a week before the election that showed the race tied.[2] The centrist Schumer and Koch soon made full amends. By 2004 Schumer was triumphantly re-elected with a record 70 percent of the vote, and he glowingly described how Koch had been a political role model since 1974, when Schumer at age twenty-three had won election in 1974 as the state's youngest assemblyman since Theodore Roosevelt.

Then Governor George Pataki waltzed in late. He had his hands full at the time because he was running for president, a bid that was widely ridiculed as near-delusional. With an unerring sense of political timing, he chose to praise the ex-mayor by saying he, Pataki, knew that he could go to bed early on election night because Ed Koch had been campaigning in Florida for George W. Bush. The almost entirely Democratic audience gaped at him, stunned. A few tense moments passed. Then Koch grabbed the microphone, declaring, "Wrong audience, Governor!" The crowd erupted into relieved laughter at the hapless Pataki, though Koch says he was actually trying to save the governor from embarrassing himself further.[3] Koch had endorsed Bush for reelection, which horrified many of his closest friends, but Koch was still Koch.[4]

By the time Koch left the mayoralty in 1990, his life had been centered on politics for almost thirty of his sixty-five years, most of them spent in an incessant, if not permanent, campaign for office. He had not consciously decided to stay in politics when he left office. His first thought, he said, was keeping busy and earning a living. Making money came to him surprisingly easily and in ways that kept him in the public eye. By 2007 he had amassed a fortune of almost $10 million. His last financial disclosure form before he left the mayoralty showed a net worth of only $740,757, mostly earned from his best-selling books.[5]

Shortly after Koch's primary loss in 1989, his former partner, Allen G. Schwartz, met with him to discuss the future. Schwartz recommended that Koch join a law firm. Koch had thought of becoming a member of Proskauer, Rose, Goetz, and Mendelson, a major corporate law firm that had advised management during the 1980 transit strike. Then Schwartz spoke with an old friend, James Gill, who had been an assistant district attorney with Schwartz in Frank Hogan's legendary shop. Gill convinced Koch that he'd be happier in Gill's smaller, more personal firm, Robinson, Silverman, Pearce, Aronsohn and Berman, a respected midsize midtown firm that later merged with the very large firm of Bryan Cave LLP. Koch acknowledged that he has not generated much business for the firm, but he did increase its visibility, consulting with other partners "on matters relating to city government or ordinances" and meeting "with prospective clients of other partners."[6]

With a midtown office to serve as a base of both income and operations, Koch turned to other ventures. These made money, but he undertook most for fun and to remain in the public eye. He hit the speaking circuit hard, making fifty-five speeches a year. As mayor, Koch was always talking about his weight. So it was a natural when the UltraSlimFast diet program hired him as a spokesman and offered him a large sum to lose forty pounds. He did it and went on television, telling his friends that he now looked "like a Greek god." In the perverse logic of the advertising world, his fame for dieting led him to do commercials for Dunkin' Donuts, and he also did commercials or ad endorsements for HIP Health Insurance, Citibank, General Tire, Snapple, and FreshDirect. He also did some television and movie cameos, famously strutting down a fashion runway in an episode of HBO's *Sex and the City*.[7]

Shortly after he made the UltraSlimFast deal, a radio executive approached Koch in a restaurant and offered him $150,000 to do a five-minute, five-day-a-week commentary on WNEW. In 1992 WABC signed Koch for a weekly talk-radio show that he could do from his office. Koch's tagline was "The Voice of Reason," and he was paid $300,000 a year. This was the job he loved most, engaging with callers on the radio, and he was rather sad when he was pushed aside seven years later by the new owners of the station for an extra hour of *Dr. Laura*. Regular newspaper columns in the *New York Post* and the *Daily News* (Koch switched back and forth), and a Sunday morning talk show on CBS that Koch says was cancelled after he criticized Charlie Rangel, a powerful member of the Ways and Means Committee, and the network feared Rangel would retaliate by causing it tax headaches. Koch even began doing movie reviews for the throwaway *West Side Spirit*.[8]

He published books with a with a variety of coauthors, beginning a cottage industry of recycling bits and pieces of his life in print, starting with his autobiography, *Citizen Koch*. Koch is undoubtedly the only major politician in history ever to write mystery novels (four of them) featuring *himself* as the mayor-detective and has produced two illustrated children's books about incidents in his childhood: *Eddie, Harold's Little Brother*, about a boy who is bad at sports but defended by his athletic brother and eventually finds himself by joining his school debate team, and *Eddie's Little Sister Takes a Splash*, about rescuing his sister when she jumped into a lake in the Catskills without knowing how to swim. In all he has produced about a dozen books, plus the three he published while in office: *Mayor, Politics*, and *His Eminence and Hizonner*, coauthored by Cardinal John J. O'Connor.

One of Koch's most visible and profitable stints was as a judge on *The People's Court* for which he earned $1 million for each of the two years he was on television. But the sensationalism of the television cases did not sit well with the former mayor. His most memorable case involved Tawny Peaks, a stripper whose act had involved pounding the head of a customer with her huge breasts. The customer sued her, claiming her rock-hard breasts had given him whiplash. Koch Solomonically dispatched a female court officer to the bathroom with Peaks, and the report came back that the body parts in question were soft and weighed about two pounds each. Judgment for the defendant. Despite these entertaining incidents, Koch was eventually replaced by Judge Judy Sheindlin (whom, ironically, Koch had originally appointed to the real bench). Judge Judy browbeat her litigants and outdid Koch's ratings 3:1. Koch took judicial demeanor seriously, contrary to the idea that on "reality" television, the objective is to turn court into a circus.[9]

In his postmayoral life Koch reconciled with a number of people with whom he had feuded in recent years. Most dramatically, he joined with Reverend Al Sharpton to push a plan that Koch worked out with Harvard Law professor Charles Ogletree to rehabilitate nonviolent former offenders. The program would provide drug treatment, job training, and educational opportunities, and if the participants stayed out of trouble for five years, their felony records would be expunged. A form of their proposal became state law in 2009 over strong Republican opposition.[10] Koch and Sharpton turned all the heads in New York's Four Seasons restaurant when they walked in together. Koch asked Sharpton to support the plan and urged him to repudiate the Tawana Brawley hoax, which resulted in a judgment for defamation against him. But Sharpton, though he has maintained a friendship with Koch, never took his advice, to apologize for his role in the Brawley affair.[11]

Koch also reconciled with former Carl McCall, one of Koch's principal antagonists in the Sydenham Hospital controversy, when they were both in New York's delegation to the 1995 funeral of Israeli president Yitzhak Rabin. Snubbed by then-mayor Rudolph Giuliani, they spent a lot of time together during the visit and sat next to each other on the eleven-hour flight back. McCall remembered, "We talked about a lot of things, including some of the battles that we'd had before that I didn't even remember." The two men began to "understand that we had a lot in common and that our views were not so separate." And the next year, when McCall was running for reelection as comptroller, Koch made television commercials for him, an important asset for an African American candidate who was running statewide and seeking white votes. McCall won.[12]

Koch buried the hatchet with some but kept it razor-sharp for others. He supported David Dinkins, the Democratic nominee, in his general election race against Giuliani. But as a radio and newspaper commentator Koch barraged Dinkins from the beginning of his successor's mayoralty with criticism of a boycott by some blacks of a Korean grocery in Brooklyn. Koch also blasted Dinkins's record on crime, an issue where Dinkins was ultimately more successful than Koch. Koch was a key endorser of Giuliani in his 1993 bid against Dinkins, which Giuliani won by less than 3 percent of the vote. As with Lindsay, Koch's help had made it more acceptable for Democrats to vote for a Republican mayor. But Giuliani showed even less gratitude than Lindsay in his determination to overshadow Koch's mayoralty. Koch began to sour on Giuliani a year after the election, when the new mayor overruled screening panels for city judgeships, although Koch subsequently endorsed him for election to a second term.[13]

Koch began to doubt that Giuliani had consistently told him the truth in their personal conversations. When Giuliani came to him for an endorsement, Koch had asked whether Giuliani had told Sukhreet Gabel to record her conversations with her mother, Judge Hortense Gabel, and turn her in to the feds. Koch was appalled that a prosecutor would recruit someone to spy her own mother. Giuliani had told Koch "that he told [Sukhreet] not to but that she inadvertently pressed the wrong button and taped her." Giuliani then told Koch that he had explained that to the judge at the arraignment. Koch believed him at the time but eventually spoke to the arraignment judge, who denied the story. Koch believes that Giuliani lied to him about this and about his role in handcuffing stockbrokers in their offices while they were being arrested in front of television cameras. Like Hortense Gabel, the brokers were later acquitted.[14]

In part, Koch and Giuliani's dispute involved differences about dissent and liberty—not so far from the old fault lines between Jews and Catholics that emerged in the 1960s.[15] Koch's greatest criticisms of Giuliani, collected in Koch's 1999 book *Giuliani: Nasty Man,* mostly amount to what Koch called hubris. Some of this had to do with Giuliani's desire to run a hierarchical government in a style similar to that of George W. Bush—one that did not tolerate deviation from talking points or engage with empirical information at variance with the mayor's view of reality. Koch alleged that Giuliani axed midlevel city bureaucrats who said something "off agenda" without consulting the commissioners whose agencies were involved.[16]

Giuliani's firing of Police Commissioner William Bratton for taking credit for New York's decrease in crime (the ideas were almost all Bratton's) reflected Giuliani's management style of undemocratic centralism. Giuliani vindictively barred Bratton from appearing at a police conference to discuss the methods the commissioner had pioneered.[17] Giuliani's authoritarianism stuck in Koch's craw. "People were finding out that you cannot have an honest disagreement with Rudy. If you disagree with him he scorns you as dishonest, stupid, or a hypocrite. We also learned that Rudy believes he is responsible for every single one of his administration's achievements. Apparently, no one else has contributed," Koch wrote.[18]

Koch was furious at Giuliani for abolishing Koch's reform of the judicial appointment process, thereby threatening the independence of the city's judiciary. Giuliani refused to reappoint two incumbents declared qualified by the screening board in order to replace them with two hacks—one of whom had flunked out of law school twice and had no law degree; the other was a well-connected Brooklyn assistant district attorney who had tried only seven cases in six years.[19] Koch criticized Giuliani for his vindictive attempt to force the Campaign Finance Board out of its Manhattan office to Brooklyn and for attempting to take away its funding after the nonpartisan commission fined Giuliani's campaign nearly $243,000 for violating campaign laws in the 1997 elections.[20] Koch's reforms and the substance of his housing program were reinstated by Mayor Michael Bloomberg.

Koch also thought that Giuliani had grossly mishandled the almost universal outrage that followed the killing of Amadou Diallo, a young unarmed African immigrant. Diallo was mistaken by the police for a rape suspect and killed in a hail of bullets by an elite (and, according to critics, trigger-happy) Street Crimes Unit. Giuliani rebuffed minority leaders after Diallo was slain, instead telling Representative Floyd Flake, Giuliani's chief black supporter, that to reach out to black elected officials "would look like he was basically kowtowing to them."[21] When Koch suggested a way for the mayor to meet with Al Sharpton without issuing an embarrassing invitation, Giuliani chose to ignore his advice. Koch had even planned to get arrested, along with Dinkins, at the Diallo protests at One Police Plaza to protest Giuliani's failure to talk to black leaders following the shooting. Koch was prevented from going after he suffered a sudden drop in blood pressure and had to be rushed to the hospital in an ambulance.[22]

Koch was released from the hospital that night. He never did get arrested, because Giuliani had met his demand that he meet with at least some black political leaders, but Koch was scandalized that the police handcuffed David Dinkins on television when they arrested him, especially because they did not handcuff most of the protesters. Koch believed the handcuffing of Dinkins was personally orchestrated by Giuliani to harass the former mayor.[23]

Although as mayor Koch had pressed for more order on the streets and in parks, he found Giuliani's attitude toward the First Amendment reprehensible. Giuliani banned protests on the city hall steps—one of New York's prime spaces for political speech—and eventually fenced off city hall itself in a fearful response to the threat of terrorism. City hall was no longer a building that members of the public could enter without an invitation or a permit to rally, and it remains fenced under Bloomberg. Giuliani's policy was a marked departure from that of Koch, who commented: "With me, people could always picket. It was a point of pride."[24]

At times Giuliani's overreaction to criticism seemed ridiculously petty, but it could lead to serious breaches of civil liberties. Giuliani had the Metropolitan Transit Authority sue New York Magazine to prevent it from running ads on the sides of buses proclaiming that the magazine was "possibly the only good thing in New York Rudy hasn't taken credit for," a rather mild attention-getting satire. The MTA got three hired guns from the top-flight firm of Skadden, Arps, Slate, Meagher, and Flom to take the case, which put taxpayers on the hook for $500 an hour to defend Rudy from a minor slight to his ego. The MTA lost and had to pay the magazine's legal fees of $190,000. Giuliani also lost 90 percent of the thirty-six free speech lawsuits brought against him, wasting an estimated $5 million in his efforts to censor his critics.[25]

Koch thought Giuliani had completely crossed the line when he threw Yasser Arafat out of a theater at Lincoln Center at an event jointly sponsored by the city and the UN. Koch had been ferociously critical of the UN, and even more critical of Arafat, but he had always honored the rules allowing all participants in UN meetings to go to UN functions without interference, as required by treaty and international law. Koch had even defended the rights of the Libyans and Palestinians to build UN missions, despite protests from neighbors. "I only felt ashamed that Giuliani had disgraced our city—and his office—with his discourtesy to an invitee of the United Nations," Koch wrote.[26]

By the end of Giuliani's second term, Koch's criticism was becoming hardened political opposition. In 1999 Koch wrote a column for the *Daily News* in which he urged Hillary Rodham Clinton to run for the U.S. Senate. The Republican candidate was widely expected to be Mayor Giuliani. Giuliani subsequently pulled out of the race for health reasons and was replaced by state senator Rick Lazio.

Most of the time Koch believed that endorsements do not matter. But just as he was important to Giuliani in his 1993 run against Dinkins, Koch was a crucial bridge for Hillary Clinton, who was initially unpopular with some Jewish voters because of her public support for a two-state solution and her willingness to talk to Palestinians. Less than a month before the election, Clinton was booed and taunted with shouts of "hypocrite" at a pro-Israel rally attended by fifteen thousand, who cheered her opponent. Clinton countered with ad that featured Koch saying, "Rick, stop the sleaze." Then Koch, defending Clinton against charges that she had been too friendly with opponents of Israel, referred to a picture of Lazio shaking Yasser Arafat's hand. "It's a great smile, but what? . . . This means Lazio supports terrorism? Come on." Clinton won the election with 56 percent of the vote.[27]

Koch had stayed out of the Democratic mayoral primary scheduled for Tuesday, September 12, 2001, which was postponed because of the attack on the World Trade Center. But he vehemently opposed Giuliani's attempt to have his term extended for three months past its expiration on January 1, supposedly because he was indispensable. When one of the Democratic candidates in the subsequent runoff, Mark Green, endorsed Giuliani's plan to stay in Gracie Mansion, Koch, whose backing the *Daily News* called "perhaps the most important endorsement up for grabs in the runoff," decided to support Green's opponent, Fernando Ferrer. "Why Mark Green would be terrified and afraid to [oppose Giuliani] is beyond me. But on the other hand, sometimes people under pressure lose the ability to make a responsible, reasonable judgment," Koch declared, dripping with sarcasm.[28] Green won the runoff anyway, and

Koch, with noticeably more enthusiasm than he had mustered for Ferrer, declared his support for Michael Bloomberg, on whose network he was a commentator.[29]

After the 9/11 attacks Koch became a vociferous and unsubtle war hawk, urging Defense Secretary Donald Rumsfeld in April 2003 "to declare Baghdad a 'non-defended locality,'" and give the inhabitants forty-eight hours to evacuate before the city was completely destroyed. Though Rumsfeld did not follow Koch's strategy, the former mayor had made his mind up to support George W. Bush and the war.[30] "While I don't agree with Bush on any domestic matters, there's only one matter that's important in this race, and that relates to standing up to international terrorism, taking it on—and George Bush has established that he is willing to do that," Koch declared.[31] He actively campaigned for Bush in Florida and other states, coordinated volunteers, and spoke at the Republican National Convention, which was held in New York, the city covered with billboards of Koch declaring, "The Republicans are coming. Make nice."[32] Outside the convention the crowds that jammed the streets to protest the Republican conclave in their midst jeered Koch's smiling face. Inside, Koch was a centerpiece at the convention, along with another "Democrat for Bush," former Georgia governor Zell Miller.

Koch's decision to endorse Bush appalled many of his oldest and closest friends at a time when even Joe Lieberman supported John Kerry, the Massachusetts senator who was the Democrats' nominee in 2004. Koch's explanation smacked of tunnel vision. He said he disagreed with Bush on virtually all matters of domestic policy, yet he chose to support him because of the need to get tough on terrorism: "I've never before supported a Republican for president, but I'm doing so this time because of the one issue that trumps everything else: international terrorism. In my judgment, the Democratic Party just doesn't have the stomach to stand up to the terrorists. But Bush is a fighter."[33] Despite Koch's support the vast majority of Jewish voters, perhaps as many as 80 percent, even in Florida, voted for Kerry. Nonetheless Koch's campaign in Florida conceivably had an effect—according to a postelection poll conducted by a Republican pollster, in 2004 Bush more than doubled the number of Jewish votes he received in the state in 2000.[34]

The episode hurt Koch less than might be imagined—in the presidential campaign of 2008 both parties vied for his endorsement. For a man in his eighties Koch still wielded enviable political clout. During the primary season he endorsed Senator Clinton for the Democratic presidential nomination but hinted that he might consider supporting a third-party bid by New York mayor Michael Bloomberg if he were to run. Through his column broadcast on Bloomberg Radio and e-mailed to a large readership, Koch kept people guessing about his endorsement for the general election until after the Republican National Convention. Early in fall 2008 Koch endorsed Barack Obama and campaigned actively for him in Florida.

Before he officially declared his support for Obama, Koch showed his hand by attacking his old enemy Giuliani, who took the stage at the Republican National Convention to mock Obama. In his column Koch zeroed in on a "verbal tic" in

Giuliani's delivery—"a kind of maniacal laugh appearing before or simultaneously surfacing as he delivered his slashing attack on Senator Obama." Koch compared Giuliani with actor Richard Widmark in the film *Kiss of Death,* in which Widmark "pushed a wheelchair in which an old woman was sitting and, laughing maniacally, shoved it off the top of the stairs with its occupant still in it." Koch suggested that someone wean Giuliani of the habit before he makes a run for higher office.[35]

When he endorsed Obama, Koch maintained that he had no regrets about endorsing Bush four years earlier, because he had not trusted Kerry to "combat international Islamic terrorism." Now, in 2008, the situation was different because Koch trusted both candidates to do so. His rationale was contorted, to say the least. Koch asserted that Obama had a greater recognition than Kerry had had of the need to fight terrorism and to support Israel. Koch also went back to his pre-Bush views on the public good: "Protecting and defending the U.S. means more than defending us from foreign attacks. It includes defending the public with respect to their civil rights, civil liberties and other needs, e.g., national health insurance, the right of abortion, the continuation of Social Security, gay rights, other rights of privacy, fair progressive taxation and a host of other needs and rights." Koch also acknowledged that "it would scare me" if McCain's vice presidential choice, Alaska governor Sarah Palin, succeeded to the presidency.[36] After Obama's election Koch rethought his commitment to the wars in the Middle East, calling for immediate withdrawal from both Iraq and Afghanistan, a position to Obama's left.[37]

For a politician who spent his life as a liberal who loved to flirt with conservatism, such a shift is not so surprising. What was out of character was his newfound willingness, at the age of eighty-two, to forgive and forget. In 2006 Andrew Cuomo called Koch to ask for his endorsement when running for New York State attorney general, a bold move since Koch had just declared in public that he would never support Cuomo.[38] Koch and his friends had blamed Andrew for years for the infamous "Vote for Cuomo, Not the Homo" ads in 1977—at the time the nineteen-year-old Cuomo was campaigning for his father. More than one friend of Koch's swore they would never vote for Andrew Cuomo for anything.

Koch had other grievances against Andrew Cuomo, going back years, and they talked them all out. Koch considered Cuomo's answers, asking himself, "Why am I carrying on my anger with him and with Mario? Both say they did not initiate the 'Vote for Cuomo, Not the Homo,' but they acknowledged that somebody did and that they were sorry about it. It only makes you less able when your anger can dominate." So Koch reversed his decree and endorsed Cuomo. It was hardly crucial, as Cuomo was heavily favored to win. But it was a very changed Ed Koch who could allow that such grudges might be a burden, remarking, "I don't need that limitation. It's over. What's the sense of carrying it to my death?"[39]

CONCLUSION

"Koch? I hope you get him!" declared a colleague at the American Historical Association convention several years ago when he learned I was writing this book. Harsh criticism of Koch among academics is not limited to comments in the hallway. In a 1999 survey of urban scholars asking them to judge mayors, La Guardia won by a landslide, with 61 of 69 naming him as the best big-city mayor in American history. The one mayor no one could agree on was Koch: he drew 14 negative votes and 8 positive ones, ranking as the fifteenth-worst American mayor of all time. Because of this radical split Koch actually finished below Abe Beame and just above John Lindsay—an astonishing result for a mayor *New York Magazine* described in 1980 as "the most popular mayor within memory," and who won reelection twice by huge majorities.[1] The survey of historians was probably made too early for an assessment of the long-term effects of Koch's policies, but it does show that Koch left office with strong negatives.

More recently, a political scientist, Lynne A. Weikart, delivered this blistering evaluation: "The city was in a mess in the 1980s under Koch's watch, a fact seldom acknowledged. . . . Since Mayor Koch is an entertaining fellow and has had years after office to create a record, he appears to have weathered any criticism of his time in office. Later historians may not be so kind."[2] But an alternative and much more positive narrative, exemplified by the title of a 2005 exhibit at the Museum of the City of New York, "New York Comes Back," credits Koch for New York's revival and for rebuilding from the days before he was mayor, when it was shrinking.[3] Still, the perceptual gap between the Ed Koch who supposedly saved New York and the Ed Koch who allegedly "balanced the budget on the backs of the poor" needs explanation.[4]

Probably the best way to evaluate elected officials is to focus on whether they accomplished what they intended. Did Koch build the New York he wanted to build, and where did he fall short? Were his aims beneficial to most New Yorkers? What were the difficulties he had to overcome? Was his success undermined by his bad judgment or by external forces out of his control? Were his innovations worthwhile and enduring?

Koch faced challenges greater than any New York mayor of the twentieth century and met many of them. He laid the foundations for the city's recovery, although that recovery indisputably benefited the rich more than the poor. When he took office in 1978 New York was in deep crisis, its credit shot, its infrastructure decaying. One section of the south Bronx had been reduced to such a charred shell that a German film used it as a location for the firebombing of Dresden. Because it had deindustrialized by the 1970s like other cities, New York had few economic prospects, and no one really knew what strategy could pull it back from the edge of the fiscal abyss. Fundamental changes in the world economy had eroded the city's economic raison d'être. By the 1970s the United States had declined as an industrial power relative to Asia and Europe, in part because of cold war policies that financed the development of foreign nations to the detriment of its own industrial base. In the national context, suburbanization and the development of the South and West shrank New York's share of the national economy. And even in its region its importance relative to the suburbs declined.

The fiscal emergency forced Koch to go hat in hand to Washington and Albany. He desperately needed to get loan guarantees from a national government that hated New York and had little belief in the city's ability to right itself. Moreover, the city's influence in Albany and Washington had significantly declined during the preceding two decades, proportionate to its decline in population. His "to do" list in New York was even more daunting. Koch set about to secure support for unpopular budget cuts. He would restore New York's credit by imposing austerity and building a gentrified, economically viable city, with an expanding tax base and rehabilitated housing stock, while reducing what he claimed was excessive liberality to the poor. As a moderate liberal, he wanted to finance city services, public works, and wealth redistribution by spurring new economic growth. In his view promoting and investing in the finance, insurance, and real estate sectors seemed the only way for New York to claw its way back to its status as a world city, as it had been at the end of World War II, when New York was a regional, national, and global center of economic power.

Certainly Koch's decisions are open to criticism. It is not true, as Margaret Thatcher said, that "there was no alternative" to an economic strategy that increased income inequality and real human suffering. Many alternatives to the redistribution of wealth to the wealthy might have been more successful and less harmful to the most vulnerable people in society. But the alternatives at the local level, those available to a mayor, were severely circumscribed by state and federal mandates and limitations on municipal power. He was also hampered by having inherited a budget system in chaos. For three years before Koch became mayor, New York was run badly by the Emergency Financial Control Board and by Mayor Beame, who retained a residue of power and often worked at cross-purposes to the board. The loose coalition of creditors that governed the city through the control board engaged in across-the-board budget cutting that jeopardized the functioning of many agencies and damaged the physical plant. Ill-considered layoffs and grinding austerity had brought New York to the brink of disaster but failed to balance its budget. Little was done to halt arson. New York was surviving but just barely, and many thought it could never reclaim its former glory. Creditor rule, with its focus on financial solvency, had increased the risk of a physical collapse.

Koch's tireless and personal lobbying campaign for federal loan guarantees, along with other management reforms, led to a balanced budget by 1981—quite simply the greatest turnaround accomplished by any New York mayor in the twentieth century, including Fiorello La Guardia. When Koch promised Congress in 1978 that he would balance New York's budget, few believed he would accomplish what the Emergency Financial Control Board had been unable to do, much less do it one year early. When he left office, debt service costs were reduced to about 11 percent of the city budget, down from 25 percent at the height of the fiscal crisis.[5] Despite many missteps and limitations, Koch laid the foundations of municipal government and political economy for the next twenty years, rebuilt areas of the city destroyed by fire and abandonment, and exceeded expectations when he took office. If he had not succeeded, the cancerous erosion of neighborhoods would have continued, and today New York might resemble other deindustrialized, segregated, Rust Belt hulks like St. Louis or Detroit, where attempts at "renaissance" have failed.

Koch's restoration of New York's credit, followed by the construction of more than 150,000 units of low- and middle-income housing, largely with funds from the newly revived capital budget, have resurrected neighborhoods that were once fields of rubble. The only other mayor who faced such challenges was Abe Beame, who failed to meet them. La Guardia had faced bankruptcy, but in his day New York had a stronger economy than many other places, and he had a great deal of help from President Franklin D. Roosevelt. Rudolph Giuliani took office in a city that still had trouble paying its bills, but he inherited a relatively well-managed system for balancing budgets, with access to credit and the first sympathetic government in Washington in twenty-five years. New York had been repairing its infrastructure and increasing its population. And many of these good things resulted from the structures that Koch had put in place.

Koch's strategic initiatives also created the post–fiscal crisis structure of municipal government by introducing computerization and sweeping management reforms such as on-time payment of bills in a city that had kept its past-due bills in shoeboxes. The appointment of city criminal and civil court judges was taken out of the hands of county leaders and placed in the hands of nonpolitical screening panels, significantly improving the quality of the municipal judiciary. One seemingly arcane but far-reaching policy called "co-terminality" matched the response areas for subunits of police, fire, sanitation, and other agencies to the boundaries of each community planning board. District cabinets of officials in charge of local services then reported to each board, giving it much more leverage over those agencies. New public-private partnerships, such as the Central Park Conservancy, reaped substantial criticism, on the ground that they eventually privatized public space, but they also rebuilt major parks that the Beame administration and the creditor regime had neglected. Compared with Bloomberg's and Giuliani's cavalier attitudes toward political protest, Koch's record on civil liberties was exemplary, for example, permitting demonstrations of hundreds of thousands of people, such as the huge June 12, 1982, antinuclear rally in Central Park. The Times Square rejuvenation plan, though delayed until the 1990s because of the Wall Street crash in 1987, was another major achievement.

While Koch was impressively effective in many spheres, his policies did not always have the outcomes he desired. His reforming spirit could produce disasters as well as triumphs. He closed down Harlem's Sydenham Hospital on what he saw as the merits and mocked his opponents for obstructing what he regarded as common sense. Closing Sydenham made sense as a managerial decision, but Koch failed to understand its tremendous significance as the first hospital in the city to give black doctors admitting privileges, and he ended up sounding racially divisive—a political loss that he later acknowledged was not worth the administrative and budgetary gains. His positions on affirmative action, which he saw as principled and others saw as ethnocentric, reinforced the perception that he did not care what the black community thought. Koch often tried to offset the paucity of African Americans in his inner circle by citing statistics about how he had increased minority hiring, but the recitation often rang hollow, since his inner circle remained almost entirely white. Nevertheless, the persistent idea that the mayor had little or no black support was an exaggeration, if not a myth, and he garnered sizable numbers of votes from blacks until the 1989 election. Another serious mistake with long-term consequences was his failure to halt or slow the conversion of single-room-occupancy hotels into tax-subsidized upscale housing without providing inexpensive alternatives for the displaced tenants. He took no action until the city had lost 100,000 of these low-cost units. Many of those hotels had been islands of disorder in middle-class neighborhoods, such as the Upper West Side, but they were the only affordable shelter for many people. Closing them did not make the streets more orderly, as apartment dwellers still had to deal the increasing number of disorderly homeless people.

Washington's failure to construct a financially viable national health-care system meant that New York's budget, which was closely tied to the business cycle, was difficult to stabilize over the long term, even after Koch's reforms. The cost of caring for the uninsured through Medicaid and the operations of the Health and Hospitals Corporation usually equaled one-third to one half of the annual budget gap and exceeded it in 1979 and 1987. Under such circumstances a balanced budget guaranteed the perpetual inadequacy of basic city services, to say nothing of social welfare, jobs, and mental health-care programs for the poor. Koch had to bring wages under control and often blamed overly generous union contracts for New York's financial troubles. But he avoided layoffs, reducing agencies by attrition. While he bargained hard, he also bargained in good faith. He did not try to bust public employee unions, as Reagan had in the 1981 air traffic controllers strike.

Scandals marred Koch's last term, largely in the city Department of Transportation, one of the few places where he suspended his usual reform criteria for appointing the commissioner. As a result the Democratic county leaders ran amok. Koch's personal integrity was unquestioned, however, and it would be utterly inaccurate to imply, as some have done, that corruption was endemic to his administration. But his reputation as a reformer was jeopardized, diminishing his political capital. Some politicians would lapse permanently into defensive mode after such problems. Koch suffered a period of depression but then tried to govern his way out of them.

To his credit, the scandals did not stop him from racking up substantial achievements in his last term, including the ten-year housing program. He also shepherded the gay rights bill through the city council, a major breakthrough in civil liberties, and led the way internally in mobilizing a reluctant city bureaucracy on AIDS issues, in part because of the pressure exerted by Larry Kramer's incendiary satire. The usual fiscal pressures, and his reliance on the expertise of an imprudent adviser and an overcautious health commissioner, slowed Koch's initial response in 1982; he bears responsibility for trusting them for too long and for listening to advice that he wanted to hear because it fit with his fiscal goals. But there is little, if any, evidence that he ever failed to help AIDS sufferers for fear of being outed as gay, as Kramer and others alleged. When Koch left office on January 1, 1990, New York had yet to recover from the 1987 stock market crash. While the finance, insurance, and real estate sector sent tremendous tax revenues to city hall and helped balance the budget, Wall Street's periodic gyrations meant it could not generate the stable revenue stream the city needed, and Koch had to make painful budget cuts once again in his final months as mayor. New York still suffered from severe problems with drugs, violence, and a decaying infrastructure, all of which cried out for attention.

Nonetheless, New York continued to grow, with an estimated 578,000 new immigrants choosing to settle in the city from 1980 to 1986.[6] That growth can in large measure be attributed to Koch's initiatives and his unparalleled energy. His four most important reforms—fiscal integrity, management reform, the promotion of the finance, insurance, and real estate sector, and the ten-year housing program—made the city a flourishing magnet again, against all expectations. Some faulted Koch for dismantling the old model of "socialism in one city," claiming that he was a conservative, perhaps because he was nationalistic, anticommunist, procapitalist, and had an exaggerated dislike for radicals.[7] But at least on domestic policy, Koch tried to mediate pragmatically between liberalism and neoliberalism. He consistently and strongly condemned Ronald Reagan's urban policies, called for a national health-care system, built housing, vigorously pursued gay rights legislation, and tried his best to reinstate necessary government services when money was available. No one claims that David Dinkins was a conservative, but his slightly more redistributive fiscal policies did not in the main depart from Koch's blueprint or end homelessness and poverty. Nor has Bill Clinton ever been considered a conservative, despite positions on the death penalty and welfare that are quite similar to Koch's.

So why does Koch's name evoke such heat, even today? One answer might be found in Koch's conception of the public interest. Voters could mark this as early as the 1977 mayoral runoff. The New York Times ran two "Quotations of the Day," one from each of the candidates. Mario Cuomo's rhetoric was conventionally liberal, and he gave New Yorkers the slogan that David Dinkins used to defeat Koch in 1989: "What we have in this city is a magnificent mosaic and it must be harmonized. Abrasiveness must be avoided." Where Cuomo was pacific, Koch was pugilistic, saying, "I don't believe what the City of New York wants is compromise—someone who cuts the baby in half, but rather someone who will distribute services equally and on merit."[8]

As one historian, writing about the 1968 teachers' strike, observed, "The question of how to define the words 'equality,' 'racism,' and 'merit' divided largely along racial lines," creating "two hostile, culturally separated New Yorks," with some white liberals identifying with blacks.[9] Koch did little to heal the schism. For many African Americans and some liberals, Koch's continual assertions that all his positions were unbiased and in the neutral public interest were intensely irritating, especially during the rash of hate crimes by whites in his last term. His in-your-face brand of humor, such as his assumption of the sobriquet "Mayatollah," only further divided his audience, as did his direct attacks on some of them as wackos. Koch's cockiness and his racial divisiveness are often exaggerated, but they do help explain why he made some people so angry.

But that anger should not be allowed to obscure his accomplishments. Koch bravely faced one of the worst crises in New York's history, restructured the city with minimal help from the federal government, and kept it solvent and growing for a generation.

NOTES

Unless otherwise stated, citations to the Koch Papers are to the departmental correspondence series, which is on microfilm and available at both the New York City Municipal Archives and the La Guardia and Wagner Archives at LaGuardia Community College. Finding aids for the Koch papers that have been processed are available online at www.laguardiawagnerarchive. lagcc.cuny.edu/. The citation form for this series is three numbers, as in, for example, EIK to Dinkins, April 10, 1987, enclosing "An Analysis of the Report Prepared by the Manhattan Borough President's Task Force on Housing for Homeless Victims," 4–10–8, Koch Papers. The first number is the reel of microfilm, the second is the box number, and the third number is the folder number. Other series include the congressional series, subject files series, and speeches series, all on paper at the La Guardia and Wagner Archives. The citation form for these papers specifies the box number, followed by the folder number. Finally, one collection, Haskell Ward's papers, was not processed at the time I examined it. It is available upon advance request at the New York City Municipal Archives, and its citation form is Allen G. Schwartz to Haskell G. Ward, June 11, 1979, Haskell Ward series, box 3 (unprocessed), Koch Papers, Municipal Archives. Oral histories from the Koch Collection at the Columbia University Oral History Research Office are cited as they are cataloged in CLIO, the on-line catalog of the Columbia University Libraries.

1.   Andy Logan, "Around City Hall," *New Yorker*, December 26, 1977. David Rockefeller, *Memoirs* (New York: Random House, 2002), 395.

2.   William Sites, *Remaking New York: Primitive Globalization and the Politics of Urban Community* (Minneapolis: University of Minnesota Press, 2003), 46–47. John C. Teaford sees Koch as a prototypical "messiah mayor" in *The Rough Road to Renaissance: Urban Revitalization in America, 1940–1985* (Baltimore: Johns Hopkins University Press, 1990), 255–57.

3.   Kansas City, Kansas, had a population of 168,213 in 1970 and 143,801 in 2006; Detroit reached a peak of 1,849,568 in 1950 and declined to 871,121 in 2006, according to the U.S. Census (http://quickfacts.census.gov; "Population of Cities with at Least 100,000 Population in 1990: 1790–1990," Series Aa832–1033, Historical Statistics of the United States, online edition). See also Jon C. Teaford, *The Metropolitan Revolution: The Rise of Post-Urban America* (New York: Columbia University Press, 2006), 126–39.

4.   John Mollenkopf, *A Phoenix in the Ashes: The Rise and Fall of the Koch Coalition in New York City Politics* (Princeton, N.J.: Princeton University Press), 54.

5.   Evelyn Diaz Gonzalez, *The Bronx* (New York: Columbia University Press, 2004), 120–24.

6.   Alex. S. Vitale, *City of Disorder: How the Quality of Life Campaign Transformed New York Politics* (New York: New York University Press, 2008), 109.

7.   Lynne A. Weikart, *Follow the Money: Who Controls New York City Mayors?* (Albany: State University of New York Press, 2009), 59.

8.   U.S. Census, http://quickfacts.census.gov, and "Population of Cities with at Least 100,000."

9.   The definition of neoliberalism is from David Harvey, *Neoliberalism* (Oxford: Oxford University Press, 2005), 2; also see 18, 159–64.

10. Joshua B. Freeman, *Working Class New York: Live and Labor since World War II* (New York: New Press, 2000), 299–305 (Freeman also provides the best description of the city's industrial, Fordist incarnation); Judith Stein, *Running Steel, Running America* (Chapel Hill: University of North Carolina Press, 1998), 317–21; Robert Fitch, *The Assassination of New York* (London: Verso, 1993), 235, 237; Saskia Sassen, "Cities, Foreign Policy, and the Global Economy," in Margaret E. Crahan and Alberto Vourvoulias-Bush, eds., *The City and the World: New York's Global Future* (New York: Council on Foreign Relations, 1997), 176; Saskia Sassen, *The Global City: New York, London, Tokyo*, 2d ed. (Princeton, N.J.: Princeton University Press, 2001), 204–14.

11. Mollenkopf, *A Phoenix in the Ashes*, 9. Black and Hispanic employment in construction rose more than 50 percent between 1970 and 1980. See Thomas Bailey and Roger Waldinger, "The Changing Ethnic Division of Labor," in John H. Mollenkopf and Manuel Castells, eds., *Dual City: Restructuring New York* (New York: Russell Sage, 1991), 43–78, 60–70. On abatements see Vitale, *City of Disorder*, 111–12.

12. The historian is William Bryk, quoted in John Strausbaugh, "From Wise Guys to

Woo-Girls," in Marshall Berman, and Brian Berger, eds., *New York Calling: From Black-out to Bloomberg* (New York: Reaktion Books, 2007), 57.

13. John Flynn, dir., *Out for Justice,* 1991, IMDB, www.imdb.com/title/tt0102614/ (November 13, 2007).

14. Ester R. Fuchs, *Mayors and Money: Fiscal Policy in New York and Chicago* (Chicago: University of Chicago Press, 1992), 96.

15. "Mayor Michael Bloomberg's State of the City Address," Brooklyn Botanic Garden, January 23, 2003, http://home.nyc.gov/portal/site/nycgov/menuitem.b270a4a1d51bb 3017bce0ed101c789a0/index.jsp?pageID=nyc_blue_room&catID=1194&doc_name= http%3A%2F%2Fhome.nyc.gov%2Fhtml%2Fom%2Fhtml%2F2003a%2Fstate_city_2003 .html&cc=unused1978&rc=1194&ndi=1 (December 11, 2008). See also Julian Brash, "Invoking Fiscal Crisis: Moral Discourse and Politics in New York City," *Social Text* 21, no. 3 (2003): 59–83, 61.

16. "Democratic Party Platform of 1980," August 11, 1980, The American Presidency Project, www.presidency.ucsb.edu/ws/index.php?pid=29607 (October 13, 2009); *New York Times,* October 22, 1980.

17. Martin Shefter, *Political Crisis, Fiscal Crisis: The Collapse and Revival of New York City* (New York: Basic, 1985), 182.

18. Nicholas Freudenberg, Marianne Fahs, Sandro Galea, and Andrew Greenberg, "The Impact of New York City's 1975 Fiscal Crisis on the Tuberculosis, HIV, and Homicide Syndemic," *American Journal of Public Health* 96, no. 3 (March 1, 2006), www.ajph.org/ cgi/content/abstract/96/3/424 (December 17, 2007). A syndemic is defined by the Centers for Disease Control and Prevention as "two or more afflictions, interacting synergistically, contributing to excess burden of disease in a population. Related concepts include: linked epidemics, interacting epidemics, connected epidemics, co-occurring epidemics, co-morbidities, and clusters of health-related crises" (www.cdc. gov/syndemics/definition.htm [December 11, 2008]).

19. EIK, interview by author, March 18, 2000.

20. *New York Times,* May 22, 1980.

21. Ibid., September 2, 1977.

22. *New York Times,* March 28, 1987; Bob Kappstatter, "Anti-Poverty Baron Ramon Velez, 75," *New York Daily News,* December 1, 2008; *New York Times,* December 3, 2008.

23. Ibid., September 26, 1983; Gillian Sorensen, interview by author, April 19, 2005.

24. *New York Times,* May 31, 1984.

25. Jonathan Soffer, "Mayor Edward I. Koch and New York's Municipal Foreign Policy," in Shane Ewen and Pierre Yves Saunier, eds., *The Other Global City: Transnational Municipal Trails in the Modern Age (1850–2000)* (New York: Palgrave 2008), 119–34 (some material from this chapter is incorporated here and elsewhere as noted, with the permission of the publisher); Saskia Sassen, *Cities in a World Economy* (Thousand Oaks, Calif.: Pine Forge, 1994), 1–4.

26. *New York Times,* January 2, 1986; *New York Times,* December 20, 1987; Peter Solomon, interview by author, November 12, 2004. *New York Times,* December 21, 2003.

27. Michael Goodwin, introduction to Michael Goodwin, ed., *New York Comes Back: The Mayoralty of Edward I. Koch* (New York: Museum of the City of New York, 2005), 15.

28. For a full account of the I ♥ NY campaign, see Miriam Greenberg, *Branding New York: How a City in Crisis Was Sold to the World* (New York: Routledge, 2008), 193–225.

29. Arthur Browne, Dan Collins, and Michael Goodwin, *I, Koch: A Decidedly Unauthorized Biography of the Mayor of New York City, Edward I. Koch* (New York: Dodd, Mead, 1985), 163–69.

2. STRUGGLING TO BE MIDDLE CLASS: ED KOCH'S EARLY LIFE

1. Edward I. Koch, with Daniel Paisner, *Citizen Koch: An Autobiography* (New York: St. Martin's, 1992), 7.

2. Reminiscences of Harold Koch, 1994, Columbia University Oral History Research Office Collection (hereafter Columbia), 1–2.

3. Deborah Dash Moore, *At Home in America: Second Generation New York Jews* (New York: Columbia University Press, 1981), 66, 73.

4. Harold Koch interview, Columbia, 1–2.

5. Louis Koch, interview by Pat Koch Thaler, Harold Koch, and Jared Koch, May 1975, tape recording in possession of Pat Koch Thaler. The geographic information also based on the 1882 Austrian map of Galicia, http://feefhs.org/maps/AH/ah-galic.html (April 26, 2008).

6. John-Paul Himka, "Ukrainian-Jewish Antagonism in Galicia," in Peter J. Potichniyj and Howard Aster, eds., *Ukrainian-Jewish Relations in Historical Perspective,* 2d ed. (Edmonton: Canadian Institute of Ukrainian Studies Press, 1990), 111–58, 115, 121–34.

7. Louis Koch interview.

8. Ibid.

9. Arthur Kurzweil, "Hizzoner's Roots," *New York Magazine,* October 28, 1979, 46–48. This somewhat doubtful story about the Koches' gangster connections in the old country is based on a statement by an aged landsman from Usciesko, who later retracted it.

10. Himka, "Ukrainian-Jewish Antagonism," 111–58, 115, 121–34.

11. Edward I. Koch, with Raphael Medoff, *The Koch Papers: My Fight against Anti-Semitism* (New York: Palgrave Macmillan, 2008), 89; A. Lichtblau, "The Jews' Search for Zugehörigkeit in Austria up to 1938," *Histoire Sociale–Social History* 33, no. 66 (November 2000): 236, 245.

12. Louis Koch interview.

13. Ibid.

14. Pat Koch Thaler, interview by author, May 23, 2001.

15. Passenger Record for Louis Koch, Statue of Liberty–Ellis Island Foundation, www.ellisisland.org/search/passRecord.asp?MID=10860352970054622528&FNM=GRUEL&LNM=GODEL&PLNM=GODEL&first_kind=1&last_kind=0&RF=1&pID=101644150629 (October 17, 2009). See also EIK, *Citizen Koch,* 3.

16. Ibid.

17. "Genealogy" document in the personal files of Pat Koch Thaler; Louis Koch interview; EIK, *Citizen Koch*, 2–4.

18. EIK, *Citizen Koch,* 3–4.

19. Ibid.; Arthur Browne, Dan Collins, and Michael Goodwin, *I, Koch: A Decidedly Unauthorized Biography of the Mayor of New York City, Edward I. Koch* (New York: Dodd, Mead, 1985), 25.

20. EIK, interview by author, March 19, 2000; Pat Koch Thaler, interview by author.

21. EIK, *Citizen Koch,* 8.

22. Harold Koch, interview by Sharon Zane, March 23, 1994, Columbia, 18.

23. Pat Koch Thaler, interview by Sharon Zane, March 21, 1994, Columbia, 1–9.

24. EIK, interview by author, March 23, 2000; Browne, Collins, and Goodwin, *I, Koch,* 27.

25. Edward I. Koch, with Daniel Paisner, *I'm Not Done Yet! Keeping at It, Remaining Relevant, and Having the Time of My Life* (New York: William Morrow, 2000), 25.

26. Ibid., 28.

27. Pat Koch Thaler, interview by author.

28. Ibid.

29. Ibid.; EIK, *Citizen Koch,* 11.

30. Harold Koch interview, Columbia, 4.

31. EIK, *Citizen Koch,* 4.

32. EIK interview, March 23, 2000.

33. Pat Koch Thaler, interview by author; Harold Koch interview, Columbia, 4.

34. Harold Koch interview, Columbia, 8.

35. EIK, *Citizen Koch*, 15; Browne, Collins, and Goodwin, *I, Koch,* 27–28.

36. EIK interview, March 23, 2000.

37. Ibid.; Pat Koch Thaler, interview by author.

38. EIK, *I'm Not Done Yet,* 3; Browne, Collins, and Goodwin, *I, Koch,* 31. See also Edward I. Koch, Pat Koch, and James Warhola (illustrator), *Eddie: Harold's Little Brother* (New York: Putnam Juvenile, 2004), 1–32; EIK, *Citizen Koch,* 18–19.

39. Pat Koch Thaler interview, Columbia, 3.

40. Browne, Collins, and Goodwin, *I, Koch,* 32–33.

41. EIK interview, March 23, 2000.

42. EIK, *Citizen Koch,* 24.

43. Ibid., 24; Pat Koch Thaler, interview by author.

44. EIK, *Citizen Koch,* 27–29; Koch and Medoff, *Koch Papers,* xi, xii.

45. EIK, *Citizen Koch,* 32.

46. Ibid., 32–38.

47. Leo A. Hoegh and Howard J. Doyle, *Timberwolf Tracks: The History of the 104th Division* (Washington, D.C.: Infantry Journal Press, 1946), 34–38.

48. Ibid., 40.

49. Ibid., 43–44.

50. EIK, *Citizen Koch,* 33–34.

51. Ibid., 35. Koch and Bolechowski were not "close friends," as claimed in Browne, Collins, and Goodwin, *I, Koch,* 46 (EIK interview, March 23, 2000).

52. EIK, *Citizen Koch,* 35–37; Browne, Collins, and Goodwin, *I Koch,* 47. The quote is from *Stars and Stripes,* December 6, 1944, www.104infdiv.org/QUOTES.HTM (December 12, 2008).

53. EIK interview, March 23, 2000.

54. EIK, *Citizen Koch,* 40–41.

55. Pat Koch Thaler, interview by author; EIK, interviews by author, March 18, 2000, and May 12, 2001.

56. EIK, *Citizen Koch,* 39–45.

57. Browne, Collins, and Goodwin, *I, Koch,* 52.

58. EIK, *Citizen Koch,* 45; EIK interview, March 18, 2000.

59. EIK, *Citizen Koch,* 46; reminiscences of Pat Koch Thaler, March 21, 1994, Columbia, 21–24.

60. EIK interview, May 12, 2001.

61. Allen G. Schwartz, interview by author, December 21, 2000.

62. Browne, Collins, and Goodwin, *I, Koch,* 72–73; "Simulated Toy Vehicle," U.S. Patent no. 3099443, applied for March 13, 1961, issued July 1963, available for download on Google Patent search.

63. EIK, *Citizen Koch,* 48–49; United Synagogue of Conservative Judaism, "Standards for Congregational Practice," http://web.archive.org/web/20080408210854/http://uscj .org/Revised_Congregation5973 (accessed April 28, 2010).

64. EIK interview, March 18, 2000; EIK, *Citizen Koch,* 48–49; Pat Koch Thaler, interview by author; EIK, interview by author, June 8, 2002.

65. EIK, interview by author, May 12, 2001; Lary May, *Recasting America: Culture and Politics in the Age of Cold War* (Chicago: University of Chicago Press, 1989), 118.

66. EIK, *Citizen Koch,* 49–50.

67. Ibid., 51.

68. *Brooklyn Eagle,* October 8, 1953, quoted in Chris McNickle, *To Be Mayor of the City of New York: Ethnic Politics in the City* (New York: Columbia University Press, 1993), 106.

3. IT TAKES A VILLAGE (1949–58)

1. Edward I. Koch, interview by author, March 18, 2000.

2. Caroline F. Ware, *Greenwich Village, 1920–1930* (1935; repr. Berkeley: University of California Press, 1994), 480–81.

3. Edward I. Koch, with Daniel Paisner, *Citizen Koch: An Autobiography* (New York: St. Martin's, 1992), 52.

4. Ibid., 52–53; EIK, interview by author, March 18, 2000.

5. John Lankenau, interview by author, May 22, 2001.

6. Stanley Geller, interview by author, March 9, 2001; Ware, *Greenwich Village*, 9–16.

7. Jan Seidler Ramirez, "Greenwich Village," in Kenneth T. Jackson, ed., *Encyclopedia of New York City* (New Haven, Conn.: Yale University Press 1995), 507–509.

8. "Can Reform Unseat Tamawa Incumbent?" *Village Voice*, July 26, 1962.

9. Arthur Browne, Dan Collins, and Michael Goodwin, *I, Koch: A Decidedly Unauthorized Biography of the Mayor of New York City, Edward I. Koch* (New York: Dodd, Mead, 1985), 69.

10. EIK, *Citizen Koch*; EIK, interview by author, May 12, 2001. The series came to an abrupt end and Koch severed his connection with the group when it was taken over by a group that advocated man-boy love.

11. Seymour Krim, "Revolt of the Homosexual," *Village Voice*, March 18, 1959.

12. EIK, interview by author, May 12, 2001.

13. See, for example, Fred I. Greenstein, *The Hidden Hand Presidency* (New York: Basic, 1982), xvii–xviii.

14. Porter McKeever, *Adlai Stevenson: His Life and Legacy*, 1st ed. (New York: William R. Morrow, 1989), 247.

15. Ibid., 335.

16. EIK, interview by author, May 12, 2001.

17. Edward I. Koch, with William Rauch, *Mayor* (New York: Simon and Schuster, 1984), 14–15; Miki Wolter, interview by author, March 2, 2001; Ed Gold, interview by author, March 5, 2001.

18. Constitution of the Village Independent Democrats, 1957, www.villagedemocrats.com/vid_constitution.htm (May 17, 2001).

19. Gold interview.

20. EIK, interview by author, May 12, 2001.

21. EIK to author, June 18, 2002.

22. EIK, *Citizen Koch*, 54.

23. Browne, Collins, and Goodwin, *I, Koch*, 65; EIK, interview by author, May 12, 2001; EIK, *Citizen Koch*, 54–55.

24. Constitution of the Village Independent Democrats.

25. Gold interview; Carol Greitzer, interview by author, October 23, 2001.

26. Chris McNickle, *To Be Mayor of the City of New York: Ethnic Politics in the City* (New York: Columbia University Press, 1993), 57, 83–84; Warren Moscow, *The Last of the Big-time Bosses: The Life and Times of Carmine de Sapio and the Rise and Fall of Tammany Hall* (New York: Stein and Day, 1971), 63; Selwyn Raab, *Five Families: The Rise, Decline, and Resurgence of America's Most Powerful Mafia Empires* (New York: St. Martin's Griffin, 2006), 106–107.

27. McNickle, *To Be Mayor*, 105.

28. Moscow, *Last of the Big-time Bosses*, 120–21.

29. Ibid., 14.

30. Ibid., 121.

31. Ibid., 132–34; *New York Times,* July 26, 1957; "National Affairs: A New Kind of Tiger," *Time,* August 22, 1955.

32. Moscow, *Last of the Big-time Bosses,* 143–53.

33. Ibid., 159–61.

34. "Primary Box Score," *Village Voice,* September 23, 1959.

35. Moscow, *Last of the Big-time Bosses,* 165.

36. McNickle, *To Be Mayor,* 145–46.

37. Moscow, *Last of the Big-time Bosses,* 168–69; Geller interview.

38. Moscow, *Last of the Big-time Bosses,* 170.

39. Wolter interview; Geller interview.

40. Ibid.

4. "RHYMES WITH NOTCH" (1959-64)

1. Pat Koch Thaler, interview by author, May 23, 2001; Edward I. Koch, with Daniel Paisner, *Citizen Koch: An Autobiography* (New York: St. Martin's, 1992), 54–62.

2. EIK, *Citizen Koch,* 54–62; death certificate, Joyce Koch, 080057:2, Koch Papers, La Guardia and Wagner Archives.

3. EIK, *Citizen Koch,* 63.

4. William Honan, "Ed Koch: The Man behind the Mayor," *New York Times,* February 1, 1981.

5. EIK, *Citizen Koch,* 64–66.

6. Ed Gold, interview by author, March 5, 2001.

7. Arthur Browne, Dan Collins, and Michael Goodwin, *I, Koch: A Decidedly Unauthorized Biography of the Mayor of New York City, Edward I. Koch* (New York: Dodd, Mead, 1985), 74.

8. Warren Moscow, *The Last of the Big-time Bosses: The Life and Times of Carmine de Sapio and the Rise and Fall of Tammany Hall* (New York: Stein and Day, 1971), 170.

9. Ibid.

10. Chris McNickle, *To Be Mayor of the City of New York: Ethnic Politics in the City* (New York: Columbia University Press, 1993), 169.

11. Ibid., 167.

12. Miki Wolter, interview by author, March 2, 2001.

13. Village Independent Democrats, fact sheet, n.d. (probably 1961), VID Papers, www.villagedemocrats.org/ (October 22, 2009).

14. Carol Greitzer, interview by author, October 23, 2000.

15. Stanley Geller, interview by author, March 9, 2001.

16. "Lanigan Picked by Reformers to Stop Tammany's De Sapio," *Village Voice,* April 6, 1961.

17. Ibid.

18. "Ban Holds on Singers in Square: Rally Planned," *Village Voice*, April 6, 1961.

19. "Reaction Mixed over Square," *Villager*, April 13, 1961; J. R. Goddard, "Right to Sing Rally Scores Ban by Morris; Ready to Fight," *Village Voice*, April 20, 1961; Mary Perot Nichols, "Morris Ban on Singers in Sq. Divides Village," *Village Voice*, April 27, 1961.

20. Dan Drasin, *Sunday*, 1961, a film about the Washington Square Park sing-in, courtesy Immy Humes.

21. Nichols, "Morris Ban on Singers"; Paul Hoffman, "Folksingers Riot in Washington Square," *New York Times*, April 10, 1961; Drazin, *Sunday*; *New York Times*, May 11 and 23, 1961. See also Immy Humes's documentary *Doc*, a biography of Doc Humes that graphically tells the story of the Washington Square sing-in, and EIK, *Citizen Koch*, 66–70.

22. J. R. Goddard, "Mayor Relents, Opens Square to Folksingers," *Village Voice*, May 18, 1961; EIK, *Citizen Koch*, 66–70.

23. J. R. Goddard, "Reform Clubs Line Up behind Wagner Drive," *Village Voice*, July 27, 1961.

24. "Wagner Pops Up at Tammany Home Base," *Village Voice*, July 27, 1961.

25. Mary Perot Nichols, "VID: Insurgents No More; De Sapio: The Last Hurrah," *Village Voice*, September 14, 1961.

26. Browne, Collins, and Goodwin, *I, Koch*, 79.

27. EIK, *Citizen Koch*, 66.

28. Mary Perot Nichols, "VID Takes Tough Line on Democrat Reform," *Village Voice*, January 11, 1962; Stanley Geller, interview by author, March 3, 2001.

29. Greitzer interview; Geller interview by author, March 9, 2001; EIK, interview by author, May 12, 2001.

30. Greitzer interview; Village Independent Democrats, advertisement in *Village Voice*, October 22, 1958.

31. "Reform Leader Ready to Oppose Passannante," *Village Voice*, May 10, 1962.

32. EIK, *Citizen Koch*, 70; Greitzer interview; Geller interview by author, March 9, 2001; EIK, interview by author, May 12, 2001.

33. Greitzer interview.

34. Koch leaflets, 1962, VID Papers.

35. "Passannante Wins CU Okay, Liberals Back Kupferman," *Village Voice*, August 16, 1962; EIK, *Mayor*, 16.

36. "Self-Respect and Politics: An Editorial," *Village Voice*, September 6, 1962; EIK, *Citizen Koch*, 70.

37. Ibid., Geller interview by author, March 9, 2001.

38. *New York Times*, September 7, 1962.

39. Ibid.; Stephanie Gervis, "Passannante Wins with 57.5% of the Vote," *Village Voice*, September 13, 1962.

40. EIK to Eleanor Roosevelt, September 7, 1962, VID Papers; *New York Times*, February 1, 1981.

41. Costikyan appointment book, box 7, "Behind Closed Doors" materials, Edward N. Costikyan Papers, Columbia University; Mary Perot Nichols, "Third Democratic Force? Lanigan Is Ready to Go," *Village Voice,* November 29, 1962.

42. "Lanigan Appointment Hints Blessing from City Hall," *Village Voice,* April 18, 1963.

43. Gold interview.

44. Mary Perot Nichols, "Militant Reformers Retain Power among Village Democrats," *Village Voice,* January 10, 1963.

45. Gold interview.

46. Greitzer interview.

47. Browne, Collins, and Goodwin, *I, Koch,* 75; Wolter interview; Gold interview.

48. EIK interview.

49. *New York Times,* December 18, 1996.

50. Mary Perot Nichols, "Reform Discord over Drive to Jettison Passannante," *Village Voice,* May 31, 1962.

51. "Fourth Dimension Added to Village Democratic Chaos," *Village Voice,* March 21, 1963.

52. Wolter interview.

53. *New York Times,* July 22, 1963; "Koch on 'Searchlight,'" *Village Voice,* July 25, 1963; Susan Goodman, "Lehman Gets behind Koch, Asks Defeat of De Sapio," *Village Voice,* August 15, 1963.

54. "Koch on 'Searchlight'"; "Lehman Gets behind Koch."

55. "Lehman Gets behind Koch."

56. "De Sapio Is Humanitarians' Choice for Brass Cat," *Village Voice,* August 29, 1963.

57. Browne, Collins, and Goodwin, *I, Koch,* 81.

58. *Villager,* June 6, 1963.

59. Ibid., August 22 and September 5, 1963.

60. Ibid., August 22, 1963, "Two Rallies on VID Schedule," *Village Voice,* August 29, 1963, See also *Village Voice,* September 5, 1963; Koch-Greitzer advertisements in *Village Voice,* August 29, 1963, September 5, 1963, and *Villager,* September 5, 1963.

61. Greitzer interview.

62. Jane Jacobs, interview by author, July 22, 2000.

63. EIK, *Politics,* 43.

64. *Villager,* August 29, 1963.

65. EIK, letter to the editor, *Villager,* August 29, 1963.

66. "Edward I. Koch, A Militant 'Reformer,'" *Villager,* August 29, 1963.

67. EIK to author, June 18, 2002.

68. Gold interview.

69. *New York Times,* September 6, 1963; Susan Goodman, "Last Hurrah for Tamawa! Village Is Reform Country!" *Village Voice,* September 12, 1963; EIK, *Citizen Koch,* 76–77.

70. Goodman, "Last Hurrah for Tamawa!"; EIK, *Citizen Koch,* 75–76.

71. *New York Times,* September 13, 1963; Goodman, "Last Hurrah for Tamawa!"; EIK, *Citizen Koch,* 76–77.

1. "Democratic Leaders Welcome Mrs. LBJ," *Village Voice,* January 23, 1964.

2. The motion to censure Evens passed the New York State Commission on Judicial Conduct despite several dissenting votes, one of them Victor Kovner's. See *In re* Lester Evens, a Judge of the Civil Court of the City of New York, New York County, September 18, 1985, www.scjc.state.ny.us/Determinations/E/evens.htm, www.scjc.state.ny.us/Determinations/E/evens.htm (April 26, 2008).

3. Allen Schwartz, interview by author, December 16, 1992, Columbia University Oral History Research Collection (hereafter Columbia), 3, 10–12.

4. Allen Schwartz, December 16, 1992, Columbia, 10–11.

5. Allen G. Schwartz, interview by author, December 21, 2000.

6. Ibid.

7. Schwartz interview, December 16, 1992, Columbia, 11–13; Schwartz interview by author, December 21, 2000; *New York Times,* December 22, 1964.

8. Schwartz interview, December 16, 1992, Columbia, 11–13; Miki Wolter, interview by author, March 2, 2001.

9. John Lankenau, interview by author, May 22, 2001.

10. Ibid.

11. Ibid.; Victor Kovner, interview by author, June 25, 2001.

12. Congress Project, questionnaire 1971, 080063:05, Congressional Files, Koch Papers, La Guardia and Wagner Archives.

13. Edward I. Koch, with Daniel Paisner, *Citizen Koch: An Autobiography* (New York: St. Martin's, 1992), 78–79.

14. *New York Times,* April 3, 1964; "Koch Seeks Senate Post," *Village Voice,* March 26, 1964; "De Sapio Is In—So Koch Is Out and In," *Village Voice,* June 24, 1965.

15. *De Sapio v. Koch,* 14 N.Y.2d 735 (1964).

16. EIK, interview by author, May 12, 2000; Edward I. Koch, with William Rauch, *Politics* (New York: Simon and Schuster, 1985), 54; *New York Times,* May 15, 1964.

17. Mary Perot Nichols, "The Reformer Must Work the Village's Sidewalks," *Village Voice,* May 28, 1964.

18. Mary Perot Nichols, "Blow to De Sapio: Passannante Goes Reform, Joins Ex-Foes at VID," *Village Voice,* March 19, 1964.

19. Ibid.; Susan Goodman, "Bizarre Asks Variance: Enforcement of Zoning Threatens Coffee Houses," *Village Voice,* June 25, 1964; Stephanie Gervis Harrington, "De Sapio Nowhere: Koch Enlists City Aid on M'Dougal St. 'Mess,'" *Village Voice,* July 2, 1964.

20. EIK, *Politics,* 48.

21. Susan Goodman, "Post-Election Switch: South Villagers Cheer Koch Move on MacD. St.," *Village Voice,* July 30, 1964.

22. EIK, *Politics,* 50.

23. Goodman, "Post-Election Switch."

24. *New York Times,* March 31, 1965; "No More Parking: City Cools the Crowds on Mac-Dougal Street," *Village Voice,* May 27, 1965; Vincent J. Cannato, *The Ungovernable City: John Lindsay and His Struggle to Save New York* (New York: Basic, 2001), 141–42.

25. David Carter, *Stonewall: The Riots That Sparked the Gay Revolution* (New York: Macmillan, 2004), 42; *New York Times,* October 7, 1964.

26. *New York Times,* May 13, 1964.

27. Susan Goodman, "Moses Retreats from Plan to Renovate Washington Sq.," *Village Voice,* May 28, 1964.

28. *New York Times,* May 28, 1964; "Mayor to See Greitzer, Koch on Square," *Village Voice,* May 28, 1964; *New York Times,* October 28, 1964 .

29. "Mr. Morris, Is He or Isn't He?" *Village Voice,* September 9, 1965.

30. Theodore H. White, *The Making of the President, 1964* (New York: Atheneum, 1965), 221–22.

31. Ibid., 242.

32. James Yates, letter to the editor, *Village Voice,* March 19, 1964.

33. EIK, letter to the editor, *Village Voice,* March 12, 1964.

34. Michael W. Flamm, *Law and Order: Street Crime, Civil Unrest, and the Crisis of Liberalism in the 1960s* (New York: Columbia University Press, 2005), 76–82.

35. EIK, *Politics,* 74. For a full account of the Civilian Complaint Review Board referendum, see Cannato, *Ungovernable City,* 155–87.

36. Susan Goodman, "Liberal Dilemma on Rights in Wake of Goldwater," *Village Voice,* July 23, 1964.

37. Ibid.

38. Ibid.

39. EIK, letter to the editor, *Village Voice,* July 30, 1964.

40. Name Withheld, Harlem, letter to the editor, *Village Voice,* August 13, 1964.

41. EIK, *Politics,* 84–88.

42. Ibid.

43. Ibid.

44. Ibid., 130; Joseph Rauh, "Department of Amplification," *New Yorker,* October 1, 1979, 128--29.

45. Jerald E Podair, *The Strike That Changed New York: Blacks, Whites, and the Ocean Hill–Brownsville Crisis* (New Haven, Conn.: Yale University Press, 2002), 14.

46. Jack Newfield, "Marching to Montgomery: The Cradle Did Rock," *Village Voice,* April 1, 1965.

47. "VID Hits Wagner for Manipulating Borough Presidency," *Village Voice,* March 4, 1965.

48. "New Districting Plan Splits Village in Two," *Village Voice,* April 29, 1965.

49. Ronald Sullivan, "Jones Says Koch Wanted Italians Gerrymandered," *New York Times,* May 7, 1965; Mary Perot Nichols, "Jones Says Koch Wanted Fewer Italians in District," *Village Voice,* May 13, 1965.

50. John C. Walter, *The Harlem Fox: J. Raymond Jones and Tammany, 1920–1970* (Albany: State University of New York Press, 1989), 188.

51. Wolter interview.

52. Ibid.

53. EIK, *Politics,* 52–53.

54. "De Sapio Is In."

55. Susan Brownmiller, "DeSapio Blows Quiet Bugle in Second Comeback Try," *Village Voice,* August 5, 1965.

56. "Koch: De Sapio Is Ahead, He Can Win in September," *Village Voice,* August 19, 1965.

57. EIK, *Citizen Koch,* 85.

58. Joshua M. Zeitz, *White Ethnic New York: Jews, Catholics, and the Shaping of Postwar Politics* (Chapel Hill: University of North Carolina Press, 2007), 176–87, argues that the Lindsay campaign exaggerated Procaccino's conservatism in the 1969 mayoral race.

59. Cannato, *Ungovernable City,* x, 579.

60. EIK, *Citizen Koch,* 86; Cannato, *Ungovernable City,* 65.

61. Mary Perot Nichols, "Pro-Lindsay Move Shakes Up Dems," *Village Voice,* November 4, 1965.

62. EIK, *Politics,* 68–69.

63. *New York Times,* November 19, 1965.

64. Mary Perot Nichols, "Democrats: The Little Expulsion That Fizzled," *Village Voice,* November 25, 1965.

6. A REBEL WITH REASON

1. "Former Opponents Working for Koch," *Villager,* September 15, 1966.

2. Stephanie Harrington, "Koch-Kingman: It's Close in Doubtful District," *Village Voice,* October 20, 1966.

3. "Former Opponents Working for Koch"; Edward I. Koch, with William Rauch, *Politics* (New York: Simon and Schuster, 1985), 73.

4. "Liberals Go All Out for Koch," *Village Voice,* April 14, 1966; "Koch Wins Mayor Backing; Schiff Scores Liberals," *Village Voice,* April 21, 1966; Harrington, "Koch-Kingman: It's Close."

5. Jack Newfield, "Runnin' Scared," *Village Voice,* September 20, 1966; Edward I. Koch, with Daniel Paisner, *Citizen Koch: An Autobiography* (New York: St. Martin's, 1992), 90–93.

6. Edward I. Koch, with William Rauch, *Mayor* (New York: Simon and Schuster, 1984), 19–20; *Villager,* November 10, 1966.

7. EIK, *Politics,* 76.

8. EIK, *Citizen Koch,* 94.

9. "Bob Price Wows 'Em in the Lion's Den," *Village Voice*, March 3, 1966.

10. Warren Moscow, *The Last of the Big-time Bosses: The Life and Times of Carmine de Sapio and the Rise and Fall of Tammany Hall* (New York: Stein and Day, 1971), 199.

11. David Gurin, "MacD: A Losing Battle with a Turned-on Street," *Village Voice*, March 24, 1966.

12. EIK, letter to the editor, *Village Voice*, March 31, 1966.

13. Sidney E. Zion, "Lindsay Placates Coffeehouse Set," *New York Times*, May 3, 1966; Stephanie Harrington, "He Shall Return—The Mayor Comes to MacDougal St.," *Village Voice*, May 3, 1966.

14. "It's Open and Ready for Business: Little City Hall Is Set Up Here at 83 MacDougal Street," *Villager*, February 9, 1967. On the limitations of such "little city halls," see Ira Katznelson, *City Trenches* (New York: Pantheon, 1981), 141–43.

15. Leticia Kent, "500 Mass against Mess on MacDougal Street," *Village Voice*, June 1, 1967.

16. Arthur Browne, Dan Collins, and Michael Goodwin, *I, Koch: A Decidedly Unauthorized Biography of the Mayor of New York City, Edward I. Koch* (New York: Dodd, Mead, 1985), 97.

17. EIK, *Citizen Koch*, 94–95.

18. *New York Times*, December 21, 1966; Woody Klein, "Out of the Woods," *Villager*, January 26, 1967. Klein was Mayor Lindsay's press secretary.

19. See Craig Steven Wilder, *A Covenant with Color: Race and Social Power in Brooklyn* (New York: Columbia University Press, 2000), 175–218.

20. See Roger Sanjek, *The Future of Us All: Race and Neighborhood Politics in New York City* (Ithaca, N.Y.: Cornell University Press, 2000), 41–45.

21. *New York Times*, June 30, 1968.

22. Ibid., September 27, 1967.

23. EIK, letter to the editor, *New York Times*, July 21, 1968.

24. Browne, Collins, and Goodwin, *I, Koch*, 97.

25. *New York Times*, February 9, 1966.

26. Ibid., January 25, 1968.

27. "Koch Wins VID, Liberal Backing," *Village Voice*, March 28, 1968.

28. Theodore H. White, *The Making of the President, 1968* (New York: Pocket Books, 1970), 115.

29. "Reformers Re-Reassess: Stay Clean for Gene," *Village Voice*, April 4, 1968; Sarah Kovner, interview by author, June 27, 2001.

30. Leticia Kent, "Koch: No to Humphrey, Strongly Backs O'Dwyer," *Village Voice*, September 5, 1968.

31. "Reformers Re-Reassess."

32. "3-Way Race in the 17th," *Village Voice*, May 30, 1968.

33. *New York Times*, June 19, 1968; "Koch and Seymour Win," *Villager*, June 20, 1968; *Village Voice*, June 27, 1968; Joe Pilati, "Tough Race in the 17th," *Village Voice*, October 24, 1968.

34. "Koch Deplores Neutralism, Backs McCarthy," *Village Voice*, June 27, 1968.

35. "17th C.D. Candidate Koch: I Can't Support Humphrey," *Villager*, September 5, 1968.

36. Ibid.; Leticia Kent, "VID, Quoting Camus, Endorses Humphrey," *Village Voice*, October 31, 1968.

37. Brown to Lankenau, September 1, 1968, 080062:6, Congressional Files, Koch Papers, La Guardia and Wagner Archives.

38. Ibid.

39. Brown to Lankenau. On Eisenhower's national security policy, see Jonathan Soffer, *General Matthew B. Ridgway: From Progressivism to Reaganism, 1895–1993* (Westport, Conn.: Greenwood, 1998), 175–92.

40. Brown to Lankenau; Pilati, "Tough Race in the 17th."

41. Brown to Lankenau.

42. Pilati, "Tough Race in the 17th."

43. EIK, *Citizen Koch*, 99.

44. Pilati, "Tough Race in the 17th"; EIK, *Citizen Koch*, 98; EIK to author, June 18, 2002.

45. Pat Jennings, clerk of the House of Representatives, "Statistics of the Presidential and Congressional Elections of November 5, 1968," U.S. Government Printing Office, Washington, D.C., 1969, 20.

7. KOCH'S CORRIDOR (1969–76)

1. "List of Jews in Congress," n.d., 80062:2, Congressional Files, Koch Papers, La Guardia and Wagner Archives.

2. Robert A. Caro, *The Years of Lyndon Johnson: Master of the Senate* (New York: Random House, 2002), 103.

3. Edward I. Koch, with Daniel Paisner, *Citizen Koch: An Autobiography* (New York: St. Martin's, 1992), 110.

4. Ronay Menschel, interview by author, November 6, 2000.

5. "Business Breakfast, Lunch and Dinner Expenses," 1970, 1971, 80057:6, Congressional Files, Koch Papers.

6. Edward I. Koch, with William Rauch, *Politics* (New York: Simon and Schuster, 1985), 183–84.

7. EIK, interview by author, June 8, 2002.

8. Ibid.

9. "No Apologies for Israel," draft for projected book on ethnic politics in Congress, n.d. (probably 1974), 80062:2, Congressional Files, Koch Papers. For the full story of the prayer breakfast, see EIK, *Politics*, 184.

10. Pirkei Avot, chap. 1, Mishna 14, as quoted in EIK staff paper, "Interesting Quotes," 80062:2, Congressional Files, Koch Papers.

11. Deuteronomy, as quoted in EIK staff paper "Interesting quotes."

12. Talmud, Baba Batra 90b, as quoted in EIK staff paper, "Interesting Quotes."

13. EIK staff paper, "Interesting Quotes."

14. EIK, interview by author, June 8, 2002.

15. EIK, interview by author, telephone, September 17, 2002.

16. EIK interview, June 8, 2002; Koch/Arlt Itinerary, n.d. (October–November 1973); draft of constituent letter on trip to Israel, 80058:5, Congressional Files, Koch Papers.

17. EIK interview, June 8, 2002.

18. Ibid; Koch/Arlt itinerary; draft of constituent letter on trip to Israel.

19. EIK interview, June 8, 2002.

20. Ibid.

21. *New York Times*, November 19, 1973.

22. Al Kamen and Peter Perl, "Three Cleared in Justice Probe of Drugs on Hill," *Washington Post*, July 28, 1983; George Crile, *Charlie Wilson's War* (New York: Grove Press, 2003), 25, 249.

23. *New York Times*, November 27 and 29, 1973; EIK telephone interview.

24. EIK, "Encounter: A Synagogue in Damascus," *New York Times*, November 9, 1975; EIK, *Politics*, 185–90.

25. EIK, "Encounter"; EIK, *Politics*, 185–90.

26. EIK interview by author, June 8, 2002.

27. See EIK, Bloomberg Radio commentary, January 4, 2003; EIK, e-mail to author, December 31, 2002.

28. EIK to Nimetz, June 1, 1972, 80057:7, Congressional Files, Koch Papers.

29. Arthur Browne, Dan Collins, and Michael Goodwin, *I, Koch: A Decidedly Unauthorized Biography of the Mayor of New York City, Edward I. Koch* (New York: Dodd, Mead, 1985), 271.

30. EIK, *Politics*, 170.

31. Victor Kovner, interview by author, June 25, 2001.

32. *New York Times*, October 14, 1975. See also Edward I. Koch, with William Rauch, *Mayor* (New York: Simon and Schuster, 1984), 24.

33. EIK, *Politics*, 171.

34. Ibid.

35. Ibid., 203–206.

36. EIK, interview by author, June 8, 2002.

37. EIK to Archbishop Iakovos, October 7, 1974, 80058:3, Congressional Files, Koch Papers.

38. Diane Coffey, interview by author, May 22, 2001; EIK interview, June 8, 2002.

39. EIK, *Mayor*, 26. See the biography of Robert N. Giaimo that accompanies the finding aid to his papers, www.lib.uconn.edu/online/research/speclib/ASC/findaids/Giaimo/MSS19800003.html (April 26, 2008).

40. James Capalino, interview by author, June 6, 2002.

41. *New York Times*, October 14, 1971; *New York Times*, September 11, 1976.

42. EIK, *Citizen Koch*, 111; Browne, Collins, and Goodwin, *I, Koch*, 102.

43. *Congressional Quarterly Almanac* 25, second supplement, 3, 91st Cong., 1st sess., 1969.

44. *Village Voice,* February 13, 1969.

45. "Koch: Let Resisters Come Home," *Village Voice,* January 29, 1970.

46. Questionnaire for Congress Project, 1970 or 1971, 0080063:5, Congressional Series, Koch Papers.

47. Ibid.

48. *New York Times,* May 5, 1974; Charles Kaiser, *The Gay Metropolis* (Boston: Houghton Mifflin, 1997), 215.

49. Michael Barone, Grant Ujifusa, and Douglas Matthews, *The Almanac of American Politics, 1974* (Washington, D.C.: Gambit Press, 1975), 691.

50. *New York Times,* October 8, 1973.

51. *New York Times,* May 17, 1975.

52. *New York Times,* November 10, 1975; Alexander Burns, "Former GOP Senator, Vet, Backs Obama," *Politico,* October 26, 2008, www.politico.com/news/stories/1008/14963.html (December 16, 2008).

53. Coffey interview.

54. Cummins to EIK, November 16, 1974, 80058:11, Congressional Series, Koch Papers.

55. EIK to Cummins, November 20, 1974, 80058:11, Congressional Series, Koch Papers.

56. Cummins to EIK, November 22, 1974, 80058:11, Congressional Series, Koch Papers.

57. EIK, *Citizen Koch,* 112.

58. Questionnaire for Congress Project.

8. "A LIBERAL WITH SANITY": KOCH AS THE ANTI-BELLA

1. Bella S. Abzug, *Bella! Ms. Abzug Goes to Washington,* ed. Mel Ziegler (New York: Saturday Review Press, 1972), 3.

2. Sarah Kovner, interview by author, June 27, 2001.

3. Edward I. Koch, interview by author, June 8, 2002.

4. This account of Abzug's life relies heavily on Blanche Wiesen Cook, "Bella Abzug," in Paula Hyman and Deborah Dash Moore, eds., *Jewish Women in America: An Historical Encyclopedia* (New York, Routledge, 1997), 1:5–10.

5. Ibid., 7.

6. James Capalino, interview by author, June 6, 2002.

7. Cook, "Bella Abzug," 8.

8. Ibid.

9. Capalino interview.

10. Cook, "Bella Abzug," 8.

11. Ibid., 9.

12. Nick Browne, "The Bella Blitz: 'I'm Going to Washington,'" *Village Voice,* July 2, 1970.

13. Ibid.

14. "Antibella," *Village Voice,* July 9, 1970; Edward I. Koch, *All the Best: Letters from a Feisty Mayor* (New York: Simon and Schuster, 1990), 203.

15. Bella Abzug, letter to the editor, *Village Voice,* July 23, 1970.

16. Thelma Horowitz, letter to the editor, *Village Voice,* July 30, 1970.

17. *Village Voice,* October 29, 1970; *New York Times,* October 30 and November 4, 1970; EIK, interview by author, May 12, 2001; EIK, *All the Best,* 203.

18. Capalino interview.

19. "Bellacose Abzug," *Time,* August 16, 1971.

20. Abzug, *Bella!* 29.

21. "Village Politics," *Villager,* January 28, 1971.

22. *Villager,* February 18, 1973; "Bellacose Abzug."

23. Capalino interview.

24. Ibid.

25. Ibid.

26. Ibid.

27. Abzug, *Bella!* 13.

28. Capalino interview.

29. Ibid.

30. Abzug, *Bella!* 125–27.

31. Jack Newfield and Mary Perot Nichols, "Runnin' Scared," *Village Voice,* February 12, 1970.

32. Mary Perot Nichols, "Runnin' Scared," *Village Voice,* July 2, 1970.

33. W. Pat Jennings, clerk of the House of Representatives, "Statistics of the Presidential and Congressional Election of November 5, 1968," U.S. Government Printing Office, Washington, D.C., 1971, 23.

34. Phil Tracy, "Bella & Bill," *Village Voice,* June 8, 1972.

35. Mary Perot Nichols, "Runnin' Scared," *Village Voice,* December 16, 1971.

36. Anthony E. DeCarlo, letter to the editor, *Village Voice,* March 30, 1972.

37. Alan Wellikoff, letter to the editor, *Village Voice,* April 6, 1972. According to Koch, who was present, Dellums actually said, "You white motherfucker, don't you ever talk to me like that again" (EIK, interview by author, December 27, 2007).

38. Susan Braun Levine and Mary Thom, *Bella Abzug: An Oral History* (New York: Farrar, Straus and Giroux, 2007), 112–13.

39. EIK, interview by author, February 1, 2008; *New York Times,* June 21 and September 18, 1972.

40. Mary Perot Nichols, "The Ryan-Abzug Race: Who'll Run the City?" *Village Voice,* October 5, 1972.

41. "VID Backs Bella Abzug," *Village Voice,* April 13, 1972; Mary Perot Nichols, "Runnin' Scared," *Village Voice,* May 11, 1972. Also see Koch's remarks in Levine and Thom, *Bella Abzug: An Oral History,* 114.

42. Levine and Thom, *Bella Abzug: An Oral History,* 114.

1. David Brown to Edward I. Koch, "Between Now and Then," November 4, 1970, 80062:3, Congressional Files, Koch Papers, La Guardia and Wagner Archives.

2. David Brown to John Lankenau, September 1, 1968, 080062:6; Brown to EIK, "Between Now and Then." 80062:3, both in Congressional Files, Koch Papers.

3. Alfred Dixon Speech Systems, "Tonal drill," n.d., box 80057:6, Congressional Files, Koch Papers.

4. John LoCicero, interview by author, October 25, 2000.

5. Ibid.

6. Michael Barone, Grant Ujifusa, and Douglas Matthews, *The Almanac of American Politics, 1974* (Washington, D.C.: Gambit Press, 1975), 691.

7. See Judith Stein, *Running Steel, Running America: Race, Economic Policy, and the Decline of Liberalism* (Chapel Hill: University of North Carolina Press, 1998), 87, 316–18.

8. John Mollenkopf, *A Phoenix in the Ashes: The Rise and Fall of the Koch Coalition in New York City Politics* (Princeton, N.J.: Princeton University Press, 1992), 7–18, 82.

9. Richard Scammon and Ben Wattenberg, *The Real Majority* (New York: Primus, 1992), 3, 20.

10. Richard M. Nixon, *The Memoirs of Richard Nixon* (New York: Grosset and Dunlap, 1978), 490–91; Scammon and Wattenberg, *Real Majority*; Bella S. Abzug, *Bella! Ms. Abzug Goes to Washington,* ed. Mel Ziegler (New York: Saturday Review Press, 1972), 3.

11. EIK to Matt Nimetz, June 1, 1972, 80057:7, Congressional Files, Koch Papers.

12. *New York Times,* May 2, 1972; Edward I. Koch, with William Rauch, *Politics* (New York: Simon and Schuster, 1985), 131.

13. Michael V. Gershowitz, "Neighborhood Power Structure: Decision-Making in Forest Hills" (Ph.D. diss., New York University, 1974), 34, 54. On the history of Brownsville, see Wendell E. Pritchett, *Brownsville, Brooklyn: Blacks, Jews, and the Changing Face of the Ghetto,* Historical Studies of Urban America (Chicago: University of Chicago Press, 2002), and Eli Lederhendler, *New York Jews and the Decline of Urban Ethnicity, 1950–1970,* Modern Jewish History (Syracuse, N.Y.: Syracuse University Press, 2001).

14. Herbert Kaufman and Wallace S. Sayre, *Governing New York City: Politics In the Metropolis* (New York: W. W. Norton, 1965), xlvii, xii.

15. Jewel Bellush and Dick Netzer, "New York Confronts Urban Theory," in *Urban Politics, New York Style* (London: M. E. Sharpe, 1990), 13; Donald H. Haider, "Sayre and Kaufman Revisited: New York City Government since 1965," *Urban Affairs Review* 15, no. 2 (December 1, 1979): 123–45, 132–33. See also Vincent J. Cannato, *The Ungovernable City: John Lindsay and His Struggle to Save New York* (New York: Basic, 2001), 506, 509–15; Daniel A. Wishnoff, "The Tolerance Point: Race, Public Housing and the Forest Hills Controversy, 1945–1975" (Ph.D. diss., City University of New York, 2005), 233.

16. EIK, *Politics,* 131–32.

17. Ibid.; Wishnoff, "Tolerance Point," 302.

18. Sarah Kovner, interview by author, June 27, 2001.

19. Nat Hentoff to EIK, December 14, 1971, box 080057 :5, Congressional Files, Koch Papers; *Village Voice*, December 16, 1971.

20. Paul Cowan, "'Them' in Forest Hills," *Village Voice*, December 23, 1971; Roger Starr, "The Lesson of Forest Hills," *Commentary*, June 1972, 45–49. Kahane was quoted in the *New York Times*, November 21, 1971, as cited in Wishnoff, "Tolerance Point," 232.

21. Herman Badillo, "The Forest Hills Affair: Beyond Stereotypes," *Village Voice*, December 2, 1971.

22. Nat Hentoff, "Bringing the Constitution to Forest Hills," *Village Voice*, December 30, 1971.

23. EIK to Margot Mindlich, December 7, 1971, box 80057:4, Congressional Files, Koch Papers; Wishnoff, "Tolerance Point," 288; EIK, *Politics*, 132.

24. *New York Times*, August 20, 1972.

25. Ibid., October 22, 1995; Cannato, *Ungovernable City*, 515.

26. *New York Times*, October 22, 1995.

27. Ibid., November 4, 1971, and February 19 and October 4, 1972.

28. Ibid., August 16, 1973.

29. Ibid., May 24, 1970.

30. Ibid., April 8, 1970, and May 14, 1975.

31. Edward I. Koch, with Mervyn Kaufman, "Burning the Litmus Paper: Enlightened Liberalism," 1975, manuscript, p. 44, 80062:3, Congressional Files, Koch Papers.

32. *New York Times*, October 19, 1976; Office of the Clerk, U.S. House of Representatives, "Statistics of the Presidential and Congressional Election of November 2, 1976," comp. Benjamin J. Guthrie, U.S. Government Printing Office, Washington, D.C., 1977, http://clerk.house.gov/member_info/electionInfo/index.html (March 19, 2009).

33. Edward I. Koch, with William Rauch, *Mayor* (New York: Simon and Schuster, 1984), 13.

34. On the national nature of the urban crisis, see, for example, Jon C. Teaford, *The Rough Road to Renaissance: Urban Revitalization in America, 1940–1985* (Baltimore: Johns Hopkins University Press, 1990), 4–5.

35. Stein, *Running Steel*, 4, 197–252.

36. Raymond D. Horton, "People, Jobs, and Public Finance in New York City," *City Almanac* 12, no. 2 (August 1977); Lynne A. Weikart, *Follow the Money: Who Controls New York City Mayors?* (Albany: State University of New York Press, 2009), 37–38.

37. Ester R. Fuchs, *Mayors and Money: Fiscal Policy in New York and Chicago* (Chicago: University of Chicago Press, 1992), 87–89; Jac Friedgut, "The Role of the Banks," *City Almanac* 12, no. 1 (June 1977): 3.

38. *New York Times*, May 12, 1975.

39. Ibid., April 7 and May 16, 1975; Weikart, *Follow the Money*, 46, 49.

40. Friedgut, "Role of the Banks"; Weikart, *Follow the Money*, 2–3, 43.

41. Fuchs, *Mayors and Money*, 96.

42. For works arguing for structural causes of the fiscal crisis, see Fuchs, *Mayors and Money*; Martin Shefter, *Political Crisis, Fiscal Crisis: The Collapse and Revival of New York City* (New York: Basic, 1985); and Roger Alcaly and David Mermelstein, eds., *The Fiscal Crisis of American Cities: Essays on the Political Economy of Urban America with Special Reference to New York* (New York: Vintage, 1977).

43. Shefter, *Political Crisis, Fiscal Crisis*, xi–xiv, 10; Fred Siegel, *The Future Once Happened Here: New York, D.C., L.A., and the Fate of America's Big Cities* (New York: Encounter, 2000), 30–31.

44. Fuchs, *Mayors and Money*, 95–109.

45. Kim Moody, *From Welfare State to Real Estate: Regime Change in New York City, 1974 to the Present* (New York: New Press, 2007), 50–51.

46. Fuchs, *Mayors and Money*, 106–109.

47. Moody, *From Welfare State to Real Estate*, 53.

48. Ibid., 58–60.

49. *New York Daily News*, October 30, 1975; *New York Times*, October 14, 1975.

50. See Kimberly Phillips-Fein, *Invisible Hands: The Making of the Conservative Movement from the New Deal to Reagan* (New York: W. W. Norton, 2009), xi, 166–211, 245.

51. Ibid., 245–46. Richard Shinn, CEO of Metropolitan Life and chair of the Mayor's Management Advisory Committee (the Shinn Commission), also joined the Executive Advisory Group.

52. Carol Doeringer, "Ten Questions to Ask before Making a Seasonal Loan," *RMA Journal*, May 1, 2007, 34–35, 37–39, www.proquest.com/ (October 24, 2009); Fuchs, *Mayors and Money*, 91.

53. Weikart, *Follow the Money*, 43; *New York Times*, March 13, 1976.

54. *New York Times*, September 2., 2000.

55. Gordon Davis, interview by author, February 18, 2005.

56. Fuchs, *Mayors and Money*, 125, 133; *New York Times*, September 14, 1975.

57. *New York Times*, July 17, 1976.

58. "Holloman Calls Koch a Racist, Leaves Hearing," *New York Amsterdam News*, November 27, 1976; "View Koch and Badillo as Betraying Holloman," *New York Amsterdam News*, October 23, 1976.

59. EIK, *Mayor*, 13–14.

10. THE 1977 MAYORAL ELECTION

1. James Capalino, interview by author, June 13, 2002.

2. Ibid.

3. Ibid.

4. John LoCicero, interview by author, October 25, 2000.

5. Ibid.; Maureen Connelly, interview by author, June 10, 2003.

6. Robert S. McElvaine, *Mario Cuomo: A Biography* (New York: Scribners, 1988), 228.

7. *New York Times,* January 30, 1977.

8. Geoffrey Stokes, "Mayoralty '77: Is the Race Already Over?" *Village Voice,* January 24, 1977; McElvaine, *Mario Cuomo: A Biography,* 234.

9. David Garth, interview by author, October 31, 2000.

10. Ibid.

11. Andy Logan, "Around City Hall," *New Yorker,* December 26, 1977.

12. Ibid., September 5, 2001, 79.

13. Reminiscences of Maureen Connelly, 1992, Columbia University Oral History Research Collection (hereafter Columbia), 18; LoCicero interview.

14. Garth interview.

15. Jerry Skurnik, interview by author, June 4, 2002.

16. *New York Times,* July 25, 1977.

17. Ester R. Fuchs, *Mayors and Money: Fiscal Policy in New York and Chicago* (Chicago: University of Chicago Press, 1990), 4, 9.

18. "Sutton-Dinkins Drive Heats Up," *New York Amsterdam News,* August 27, 1977; Carlos E. Russell, "We Can Win with Percy," *New York Amsterdam News,* September 3, 1977; Jon Ciner, "Percy Sutton: A Campaign's a Test of Political Strength," *Villager,* September 1, 1977; "Mr. Sutton's 'True Picture,'" editorial, *New York Times,* January 28, 1977.

19. Mary Connelly, "Who's Who of Donors to Mayoral Candidates," *New York Post,* August 15, 1977; *New York Times,* September 4, 1977.

20. *New York Times,* July 13, 1977; campaign speech, n.d., series 2, box 1066 (NYC Mayoralty 1977), folder "Bella's speeches," Bella S. Abzug Papers, Rare Book and Manuscript Room, Butler Library, Columbia University.

21. Abzug mayoral campaign leaflet, n.d. (1977), series 2, box 1066 (NYC Mayoralty 1977), folder Economic Development, Abzug Papers.

22. Leaflet from race against Bill Ryan, 1972, series 2, box 1070 (NYC Mayoralty 1977), Abzug Papers. See also Geoffrey Stokes, "Hats and Minds: Bella Abzug Runs a Cautious Race," *Village Voice,* August 22, 1977.

23. Mary Connelly, "Beame Backers' Stake in Election," *New York Post,* September 7, 1977.

24. *New York Times,* August 11, 1977.

25. Connelly, "Who's Who of Donors"; Maurice Carroll, "How Backers Line Up in the Mayoral Race," *New York Times,* September 4, 1977.

26. Mario M. Cuomo, op-ed, *New York Times,* August 18, 1977.

27. *New York Times,* May 20, 1977.

28. Ibid., May 20, August 15 and 13, 1977.

29. Ibid., April 3, 1977.

30. Edward I. Koch, with Daniel Paisner, *Citizen Koch: An Autobiography* (New York: St. Martin's, 1992), 104.

31. Jon Ciner, "Ed Koch: Emerging as a Fiery Old Testament Prophet," *Villager*, September 1, 1977; Garth, interview.

32. Koch press release, March 4, 1977, box 0080063:3, Koch Papers, La Guardia and Wagner Archives; *New York Times*, March 5, August 10 and 12, 1977.

33. Garth interview; Ciner, "Ed Koch."

34. Martin Shefter, *Political Crisis, Fiscal Crisis: The Collapse and Revival of New York City* (New York: Basic, 1985), xix; Arthur Browne, Dan Collins, and Michael Goodwin, *I, Koch: A Decidedly Unauthorized Biography of the Mayor of New York City, Edward I. Koch* (New York: Dodd, Mead, 1985), 135–36, 139–40.

35. *New York Times*, May 22, 1977.

36. Jerry Skurnik, interview by author, June 4, 2002.

37. *New York Times*, July 13, 1977.

38. The best narrative history of the blackout is Jonathan Mahler, *Ladies and Gentlemen: The Bronx Is Burning: 1977, Baseball, Politics, and the Battle for the Soul of a City* (New York: Farrar, Straus, Giroux, 2005).

39. "Black Opinion Mixed on Looting; Merchants, Politicians Outraged," *New York Amsterdam News*, July 23, 1977; editorial, *New York Amsterdam News*, July 30, 1977.

40. *New York Times*, August 18, 1977.

41. Ibid., July 30 and July 19, 1977.

42. Mahler, *Ladies and Gentlemen*, 228.

43. Ibid.; *New York Times*, July 19 and August 24, 1977.

44. *New York Times*, July 30, 1977.

45. Ibid., July 31, 1977.

46. Ibid., July 19, 1977.

47. Ibid., July 31 and August 24, 1977.

48. *New York Post*, August 17, 1977.

49. Although his autobiography suggests that this was done on the phone, Murdoch actually set up a meeting attended by Koch, Garth, Murdoch, and Costikyan at which they agreed to the arrangement (EIK to author, March 19, 2004).

50. "The Post Endorses Ed Koch for Mayor," editorial, *New York Post*, August 19, 1977.

51. *New York Post*, August 22, 1977.

52. "Page Six," *New York Post*, August 25, 1977.

53. Lee Dembart, "Beame Assails 'Vicious Document'; Reactions of Primary Rivals Vary," *New York Times*, August 27, 1977; "Beame Conned the City," *New York Post*, August 26, 1977.

54. *New York Times*, August 31, 1977. See also "Yippie Has Fling at Mayoral Debate," *New York Post*, August 31, 1977.

55. *New York Times*, August 15, 1977.

56. Ibid., September 2, 1977.

57. Ibid.

58. McElvaine, *Mario Cuomo: A Biography,* 249.

59. Joy Cook, "And the Cool Koch Relaxed," *New York Post,* September 9, 1977.

60. "Congressman Is Out and Campaigning in Brooklyn after Three Hours' Sleep," *New York Times,* September 10, 1977.

61. Reminiscences of James Capalino, 1994, Columbia, 18.

62. Ibid., 18, 24–35.

63. Ibid., 22–23.

64. LoCicero interview.

65. David Brown, Koch's former chief of staff, said that Koch's testimony for Brasco and Podell was "an outreach kind of politics to the regulars" (Brown, interview by author, November 1, 2000).

66. LoCicero interview.

67. *New York Times,* September 17, 1977; Capalino, interview by author, June 6, 2002.

68. Capalino interview by author, June 6, 2002.

69. Ibid.

70. Edmund Newton, "Blacks Weigh Effect of Sutton, Dinkins Defeats," *New York Post,* September 9, 1977.

71. Editorial, *New York Amsterdam News,* September 17, 1977.

72. H. Carl McCall, interview by author, February 15, 2005; Basil Paterson, interview by author, February 14, 2005.

73. *New York Times,* September 18, 1977.

74. *New York Amsterdam News,* September 17, 1977; EIK to author, March 19, 2004; McCall interview; Paterson interview.

75. *New York Times,* September 10, 1977; Capalino interview, Columbia, 17; "Koch and Cuomo Battling It Out for the Big One," *New York Post,* September 9, 1977.

76. Browne, Collins, and Goodwin, *I, Koch,* 54; Garth interview.

77. *New York Times,* September 10, 1977.

78. Ibid., October 27, 1977; Jane Perlez, "Koch: The Media Whispers," *Soho Weekly News,* November 10, 1977.

79. *New York Times,* September 10, 1977; Perlez, "Koch: The Media Whispers."

80. Alexander Cockburn and James Ridgeway, "Sex and the Single Politician," *Village Voice,* November 21, 1977.

81. Jack Newfield and Wayne Barrett, *City for Sale: Ed Koch and the Betrayal of New York* (New York: Harper and Row, 1988), 125.

82. McElvaine, *Mario Cuomo: A Biography,* 254–55; *New York Times,* November 10, 1977.

83. *New York Times,* November 6, 1977. See also McElvaine, *Mario Cuomo: A Biography,* 254–55.

84. Geoffrey Stokes, "Smear News Is No News," *Village Voice,* November 7, 1977.

85. Capalino interview by author, June 12, 2002.

86. LoCicero interview.

87. David Garth, interview by author, October 31, 2000.

88. Ibid.

89. Edward I. Koch, with William Rauch, *Mayor* (New York: Simon and Schuster, 1984), 35–36; *New York Times*, November 22, 1977.

90. John Mollenkopf, *A Phoenix in the Ashes: The Rise and Fall of the Koch Coalition in New York City Politics* (Princeton, N.J.: Princeton University Press, 1992), 105–107.

91. *New York Times*, September 23, 1977; *New York Post*, September 21 and 22, 1978.

92. *New York Times*, October 18, 1977.

93. Ibid., October 17, 1977. On the importance of union campaign contributions to the Cuomo campaign, see *New York Times*, October 3, 1977.

94. Capalino interview by author, June 12, 2002; *New York Times*, November 6, 1977.

95. Andy Logan, "Around City Hall," *New Yorker*, October 3, 1977.

96. EIK, *Mayor*, 96; *New York Times*, October 6, 1977.

97. This paragraph from my essay "Mayor Edward I. Koch and New York's Municipal Foreign Policy," in Shane Ewen and Pierre Yves Saunier, eds., *The Other Global City. Transnational Municipal Trails in the Modern Age (1850–2000)* (New York: Palgrave Macmillan, 2008), 119–20, is reprinted by permission of Palgrave Macmillan.

98. *New York Times*, October 4, 1977. On the 1977 mayoral race see Mollenkopf, *A Phoenix in the Ashes*, 105–107.

99. EIK, *Mayor*, 96.

100. Rita Delfiner and Joy Cook, "Storm Cuts Vote in Half," *New York Post*, November 8, 1977.

101. Mollenkopf, *A Phoenix in the Ashes*, 106–108. For a different view see the op-ed by Koch's pollsters, Mark J. Penn and Douglas E. Schoen, *New York Times*, November 9, 1977.

102. *New York Post*, November 9 and 26, 1977.

103. *New York Times*, November 9, 1977.

104. Capalino interview by author, June 12, 2002.

105. *New York Times*, November 26, 1977.

106. Jack Newfield and Geoffrey Stokes, "Runnin' Scared," *Village Voice*, December 5, 1977; *New York Times*, January 28, 1993.

107. EIK, *Mayor*, 47.

11. THE CRITICAL FIRST TERM (1978–81)

1. *New York Times*, January 2 and January 9, 1978.

2. Edward I. Koch, letter to author, December 27, 2007.

3. *New York Times*, January 1, 1978; EIK, interview by author, September 22, 2004.

4. *New York Times*, January 2, 1934.

5. Ibid., January 2, 1978. Although Koch approved and edited his first inaugural speech, it was probably written by Clark Whelton.

6. All quotations are from "Text of Koch Inaugural Address," *New York Times,* January 2, 1978.

7. George Lakoff, *Don't Think of an Elephant! Know Your Values and Frame the Debate* (White River Junction, Vt.: Chelsea Green Press, 2004), 9–12.

8. "Text of Koch Inaugural Address."

9. Peter W. Colby, *New York State Today: Politics, Government, Public Policy* (Albany: State University of New York Press, 1989), 54–56.

10. *New York Times,* January 2, 1934.

11. Edward I. Koch, with Daniel Paisner, *Citizen Koch: An Autobiography* (New York: St. Martin's, 1992), 161.

12. The Catholic Church, whose influence had kept gay rights legislation bottled up in the city council for years, later successfully sued to invalidate Koch's order. Koch responded by pushing a bill through the city council that became law in 1986.

13. *New York Post,* January 3, 1978.

14. *New York Times,* November 27, 1976, January 2, 1978; Herbert Daughtry, *No Monopoly on Suffering: Blacks and Jews in Crown Heights and Elsewhere* (Trenton, N.J.: Africa World Press, 1997), 65–67.

15. Daughtry, *No Monopoly on Suffering,* 65–67.

16. Beth Fallon and Vincent Cosgrove, "Mayor Gets a Taste of Brooklyn Bile," *New York Daily News,* January 2, 1978.

17. Daughtry, *No Monopoly on Suffering,* 29.

18. Reminiscences of Harold Koch, 1994, Columbia University Oral History Research Collection (hereafter Columbia), 31.

19. *New York Post,* January 18, 1978; *New York Times,* March 24, 1982.

20. Maureen Connelly, interview by author, June 10, 2003; Nat Leventhal, interview by author, October 8, 2004.

21. *New York Times,* January 11, 1978.

22. David Brown, interview by author, September 27, 2004.

23. *New York Daily News,* January 1, 1978.

24. Reminiscences of James Brigham, 1992, Columbia, 16.

25. Reminiscences of Maureen Connelly, 1992, Columbia, 95.

26. David Brown, interview by author, September 27, 2004.

27. Office of Strategic Planning, Health and Hospitals Corporation, "NYC Medically Uninsured Summary Data," December 1988, City Hall Library, 2.28. 1980 Democratic Platform, www.presidency.ucsb.edu/showplatforms.php?platindex=D1980 (viewed April 27, 2008); "Transcript of Welcome by Koch at Convention," *New York Times,* August 12, 1980.

29. See Max Page, *The City's End: Two Centuries of Fantasies, Fears and Premonitions of New York's Destruction* (New Haven, Conn.: Yale University Press, 2008), 20, 38.

30. Denis Hamill and Ken Lerer, "The Congressman from Disney World," *New York Magazine,* January 9, 1979, 10.

31. EIK, interview by author, September 22, 2004.

32. Andy Logan, "Around City Hall," *New Yorker,* May 1, 1978.

33. *New York Times,* November 10, November 11, and December 2, 1977, and May 19, 1978.

34. Andy Logan, "Around City Hall," *New Yorker,* January 23, 1978; *Fiscal Observer,* January 19, 1978; *New York Times,* January 5, 1978.

35. Logan, "Around City Hall," January 23, 1978.

36. *New York Times,* January 17, 1978; *Fiscal Observer,* February 2, 1978, 10–11.

37. *New York Times,* January 16, 1978.

38. Ibid.

39. Ibid. and January 20, 1978.

40. Ibid., January 21, 1978; *Fiscal Observer,* February 2, 1978, 1–2.

41. *New York Times,* February 7, 1978.

42. Ibid., March 1 and 3, 1978.

43. James L. Rowe Jr., "House Panel Votes New York City Aid Plan," *Washington Post,* April 27, 1978; "Banking Unit Approves N.Y. Loan Program," *Washington Post,* May 4, 1978.

44. Jack Egan, "Proxmire Cancels Hearing on N.Y.C. Finance Plan," *Washington Post,* May 24, 1978. Proxmire also demanded more definite commitments from Albany that it would provide the aid it had promised.

45. Connelly interview, Columbia, 2–78.

46. *New York Times,* May 11, 1978; Eagan, "Proxmire Cancels Hearing."

47. *Fiscal Observer,* March 16, 1978, 7.

48. *New York Times,* April 2, 1978; Andy Logan, "Around City Hall: Stopping the Clock," *New Yorker,* April 1, 1978.

49. Andy Logan, "Around City Hall," *New Yorker,* May 1, 1978.

50. Basil Paterson, interview by author, February 14, 2005; reminiscences of David Margolis, 1994, Columbia, 39.

51. *New York Times,* June 3, 1978; Jack Eagan, "NYC Is Still Deadlocked with Unions," *Washington Post,* June 3, 1978.

52. *New York Times,* June 3, 1978.

53. Ibid., June 6, 1978.

54. Margolis interview, Columbia, 42; reminiscences of Victor Gotbaum, 1994, Columbia, 4–5.

55. Senate Committee on Banking, Housing, and Urban Affairs, *Hearings on Aid to New York City,* 94th Cong., 2d sess., 1978, 1–15.

56. Ibid., 14–18.

57. Ibid., 22.

58. Ibid., 28.

59. Ibid., 78.

60. Jack Egan, "Loan Guarantee Plan Supported by Blumenthal," *Washington Post,* June 8, 1978.

61. Jack Egan, "Proxmire Softens Anti-New York Stance," *Washington Post,* June 7, 1978.

62. Senate Banking Committee, *Hearings on Aid,* 292–96.

63. Edward C. Burks, "House Votes 247 to 155 to Approve Loan Guarantees" *NYT,* June 9, 1978.

64. *New York Times,* June 9, 1978.; Jack Egan, "Senate Approves $1.6B New York City Aid Bill; Senate Votes $1.68 Aid Bill for New York," *Washington Post,* July 28, 1978; Fred Barbash, "Thousands See Carter Sign NY Aid Bill," *Washington Post,* August 9, 1978.

65. Reminiscences of Abraham Biderman, 1992, Columbia, 6.

12. THE POLITICS OF RACE AND PARTY

1. Reminiscences of David Margolis, 1994, Columbia University Oral History Research Collection (hereafter Columbia), 37.

2. Brooklyn County leader Clarence Norman was convicted of extorting money for judgeship nominations. See *New York Times,* February 24, 2007.

3. Edward I. Koch, interview by author, September 22, 2004.

4. James Capalino, interview by author, June 13, 2002; *New York Times,* February 1 and January 31, 1978.

5. EIK interview.

6. Capalino interview by author.

7. EIK interview.

8. David Brown, telephone interview by author, September 27, 2004.

9. Ibid.

10. Haskell Ward, interview by author, January 3, 2007.

11. Maureen Connelly, interview by author, June 1, 2003.

12. Brown interview.

13. Reminiscences of Robert F. Wagner Jr., August 18, 1992, Columbia, 76.

14. Reminiscences of James Capalino, July 13, 1994, Columbia, 69–70; "New York State Commisson of Investigation," Administrator–CriminalDivision.com, August 20, 2007, http://criminaldivision.com/articles/34/1/New-York-State-Commission-Of-Investigation/ CommissionContinued.html (September 17, 2009). The CriminalDivision.com appears to be devoted to security matters; see also the posting by the State of New York at www. sic.state.ny.us/ (September 17, 2009), which announces that the commission ceased operations on March 31, 2009, "as required by legislation passed in 2008."

15. Brown interview; reminiscences of Anthony Gliedman, 1994, Columbia, 6.

16. *New York Amsterdam News,* January 7 and January 21, 1978.

17. Allen G. Schwartz, interview by Ellen Kastel, May 23, 1996, La Guardia and Wagner Archives. See also reminiscences of Allen G. Schwartz, January 6, 1993, Columbia, 153.

18. *New York Times,* May 25, 1978.

19. Reminiscences of Maureen Connelly, Columbia, 1992, 60.

20. Robert F. Wagner Jr., interview by Chris McNickle, September 9, 1991, La Guardia and Wagner Archives.

21. Herman Badillo, interview by author, June 3, 2003.

22. Basil Paterson, interview by author, February 14, 2005.

23. Wagner interview by McNickle.

24. Margolis interview, Columbia, 35.

25. Doug Ireland, "Blacks: Koch Isn't Beautiful," *Soho Weekly News*, February 2, 1978.

26. Ward interview.

27. H. Carl McCall, interview by author, February 15, 2005.

28. Badillo interview.

29. Flake is a former president of Wilberforce University and a senior fellow of the Manhattan Institute. He endorsed Republican mayor Rudolph Giuliani for reelection and chaired the unsuccessful campaign of the conservative Republican Ken Blackwell for governor of Ohio but supported Barack Obama in 2008.

30. Connelly interview, Columbia, 60.

31. Brown interview.

32. EIK to Pinckett, May 18, 1978; Pinkett to EIK, May 25, 1978, both in 4–28–11, Koch Papers. Koch's letter was dated about two months after the meeting.

33. Roger Wilkins, "Black Leaders Are Critical of Some of Koch's Policies," *New York Times*, June 9, 1978.

34. Michael Kramer, "The National Interest," *New York*, September 8, 1980,10.

35. *New York Times*, December 8, 1979.

36. Ward interview.

37. EIK interview.

38. *New York Times*, February 12, 1979.

39. Ibid., February 3, 1978.

40. Ward interview.

41. *New York Times*, January 19, 1978.

42. Ibid., May 25, 1978.

43. Ward interview.

44. Ibid. On Ward's working-class background, see *New York Times*, January 20, 1979.

45. *New York Amsterdam News*, April 1, 1978.

46. Stephen M. David, "Welfare: The Community-Action Program Controversy," in Jewel Bellush and Stephen M. David, eds., *Race and Politics in New York City: Five Studies in Policy-Making* (New York: Praeger, 1971), 25.

47. On the ways in which antipoverty programs diverted the discourse about poverty from one about job creation to "sociological discourse," see Judith Stein, *Running Steel, Running America* (Chapel Hill: University of North Carolina Press, 1998), 70, 87.

48. James Jennings, *Persistent Poverty Project, Understanding the Nature of Poverty in Urban America* (Westport, Conn.: Greenwood, 1994), 31–32.

49. Edward C. Sullivan, interview by author, February 8, 2005.

50. David, "Welfare," 38; Susan Abrams Beck, "The Limits of Presidential Activism: Lyndon Johnson and the Implementation of the Community Action Program," *Presidential Studies Quarterly* 17, no. 3 (Summer 1987), 545, 546.

51. David, "Welfare," 46–51.

52. Martin Shefter, *Political Crisis, Fiscal Crisis: The Collapse and Revival of New York City* (New York: Basic, 1985), 90.

53. Charles V. Hamilton, "The Patron-Recipient Relationship and Minority Politics in New York City," *Political Science Quarterly* 94 no. 2 (summer 1979): 212–13, 216, 222–24.

54. *New York Times*, March 7, 1978, and March 9, 1979.

55. Ward interview; *New York Times*, November 22, 1978.

56. *New York Times*, February 2, 1979.

57. Ibid., February 2 and 5, 1979.

13. SHAKE-UP (1979–80)

1. Andy Logan, "Around City Hall," *New Yorker*, December 31, 1979.

2. Jimmy Carter, "Energy and National Goals Address to the Nation," July 15, 1979, *Public Papers of the Presidents*, Jimmy Carter, book 2, American Presidency Project,www.presidency.ucsb.edu/ws/index.php?pid=32596&st=&st1= (October 26, 2009); *New York Times*, October 22, 1979.

3. *New York Times*, October 22 and May 3, 1979.

4. Michael Rosenblum, "First Cut: Across the Airwaves," *Soho Weekly News*, August 2, 1979.

5. *New York Times*, September 18, 1979.

6. Doug Ireland, "Sizing Up Koch," *Soho Weekly News*, January 4, 1979.

7. *New York Times*, September 28, 1979.

8. Herman Badillo, interview by author, June 3, 2003.

9. *New York Times*, November 3, 1979.

10. Ibid., November 12, 1980.

11. Robert F. Wagner Jr., interview by Jonathan Soffer, August 18, 1992, Columbia University Oral History Research Collection (hereafter Columbia), 98.

12. Jill Jonnes, *South Bronx Rising: The Rise, Fall, and Resurrection of an American City* (New York: Fordham University Press, 2002), 341.

13. Richard Plunz, *A History of Housing in New York City* (New York: Columbia University Press, 1990), 162.

14. Evelyn Gonzalez, *The Bronx* (New York: Columbia University Press, 2004), 109, 116.

15. *New York Times*, February 7, 1970. Both men were convicted (*New York Times*, July 28, 1971).

16. *New York Times*, September 2, 1974.

17. Gonzalez, *Bronx,* 120.

18. Ibid., 125.

19. Ibid., 125–26.

20. Ibid., 125. See Deborah Wallace and Roderick Wallace, *A Plague on Both Your Houses: How New York Was Burned Down and National Public Health Crumbled* (London: Verso, 1998), xv–xvi. While this study may make too much of some specific causal connections, it is generally correct about the relationship of cuts in fire service and prevention programs, the burning of neighborhoods, and the fallacies of the RAND Corporation studies that justified the cuts, as well as the other ill effects of austerity on the health of New Yorkers.

21. *New York Times,* May 18, May 22, and July 13, 1975.

22. Ibid., October 25, 1977.

23. Ibid., November 12, 1980; Michael Jacobson and Philip Kasinitz, "Burning the Bronx for Arson," *Nation,* November 15, 1986, 512–15.

24. Gonzalez, *Bronx,* 126, 207n63; Jacobson and Kasinitz, "Burning the Bronx for Arson"; *New York Times,* November 12, 1980.

25. Herbert Sturz to EIK, December 15, 1978, 49–115–2, Koch Papers, La Guardia and Wagner Archives; *New York Times,* March 29, 1979, and July 1 and November 10, 1980.

26. John P. Engel (Arson Strike Force) to Francis A. McGarry, February 15, 1980, 115–245–05, Koch Papers.

27. Wilfredo E. Morales to EIK, n.d. (September 1981), 107–229–12, Koch Papers.

28. *New York Times,* November 21, 1982.

29. Ibid., March 22, 1982; Anthony Gliedman, "Analysis of Arson in Residential Buildings," New York City Department of Housing Preservation and Development, November 1, 1983, 78–176–6, Koch Papers.

30. Kenneth Conboy to EIK, August 17 1984, 51–199–5, Koch Papers.

31. Gonzales, *Bronx,* 124.

32. EIK to Angelo Pisani (arson strike force coordinator), May 28, 1985; "NYC Anti-Arson Update," *Arson Strike Force Newsletter,* winter/spring 1985, both in 66–151–7, Koch Papers.

33. Jonnes, *South Bronx Rising,* 318–19.

34. Badillo interview; Jonnes, *South Bronx Rising,* 319.

35. Stephanie Ebbert, "Logue Recalled as Reinventor of Boston" *Boston Globe,* January 29, 2000; Edward Driscoll, "Edward Logue Is Dead; Gave Boston New Face," *Boston Globe,* January 28, 2000; Jonnes, *South Bronx Rising,* 319.

36. Gonzalez, *Bronx,* 130.

37. Ibid., 132; *New York Times,* November 6, 1983; Ward Morehouse III, "Grassroots, Not Politics, Stirs Hopes in South Bronx," *Christian Science Monitor,* October 20, 1980.

38. Jonnes, *South Bronx Rising,* 364.

39. Ibid., 321–22; Gonzalez, *Bronx,* 130–32.

40. Jonnes, *South Bronx Rising,* 321–22; Gonzalez, *Bronx,* 130–32.

41. Wagner interview by Soffer, Columbia, 99.

42. Ibid.; Badillo interview.

43. Edward I. Koch, with William Rauch, *Mayor* (New York: Simon and Schuster, 1984), 129.

44. Wagner interview by Soffer, Columbia, 100.

45. EIK, *Mayor,* 132–33.

46. *New York Times,* February 9, 1979.

47. EIK, *Mayor,* 130; *New York Times,* February 9, 1979.

48. Wagner interview by Soffer, Columbia, 102.

49. *New York Times,* March 19, 1983.

50. *New York Times,* October 7, 1979; Wagner interview by Soffer, Columbia, 97–98; EIK, *Mayor,* 135; prices, www.nytimes.com, October 29, 2009.

51. *New York Times,* March, 19, 1989; October 5, 2007.

52. Jack Deacy, "The Koch Watch: Politics and Public Relations," *New York,* March 6, 1978, 14.

53. *New York Times,* April 8, 1978.

54. David Brown, interview by author, September 27, 2004.

55. Edward I. Koch, with Daniel Paisner, *Citizen Koch: An Autobiography* (New York: St. Martin's, 1992), 168.

56. *New York Times,* August 3, 1979.

57. EIK, *Mayor,* 156–57.

58. *New York Times,* October 7, 1979.

59. Nat Leventhal, interview by author, January 8, 2004.

60. EIK to Deputy Mayors, July 2, 1979, 13–31–8, Koch Papers.

61. Allen G. Schwartz, interview by Ellen Kastel, 1996, La Guardia and Wagner Archives; Leventhal interview by author, January 8, 2004.

62. EIK, *Mayor,* 156.

63. Badillo to EIK, August 20, 1979, 13–31–8, Koch Papers.

64. *New York Times,* August 3, 1979.

65. Ibid.

66. Ibid.

67. *New York Times,* May 3, 1972.

68. Michael Rosenbaum, "Koch's Main Man," *Soho Weekly News,* September 20–26, 1979.

69. Ibid.

70. Leventhal interview by author, October 8, 2004.

71. *New York Times,* October 31, 1980.

72. Nat Leventhal to EIK, October 15, 1979, 26–65–1, Koch Papers; *New York Times,* October 13, 1979.

73. Leventhal to Koch; *New York Times,* October 13, 1979.

74. Leventhal to Koch.

75. Alexandra Altman, interview by Ellen Kastel, 1996, LaGuardia and Wagner Archives, 5.

76. Wagner interview by Soffer, Columbia, 44–45; Schwartz interview by Kastel.

77. Joseph P. Fried, "City's Housing Administrator Proposes 'Planned Shrinkage' of Some Slums," *New York Times,* February 3, 1976. See Michael Rosenbaum, "Shrinking the City," *Soho Weekly News,* August 9,1979.

78. *New York Times,* October, 31, 1980.

79. Draft Executive Order, December, 1979, 26–64–2, Koch Papers.

80. Leventhal interview by author, October 8, 2004.

81. EIK, interview by author, February 1, 2008.

82. Leventhal interview by author, October 8, 2004.

83. Ibid.

84. *New York Times,* October, 31, 1980.

85. EIK, letter to author, December 27, 2007.

86. Basil Paterson, interview by author, February 14, 2005; H. Carl McCall, interview by author, February 15, 2005.

87. *New York Times,* June 12, 1979; Simon Anekwe, "Koch Kicks Poor," *New York Amsterdam News,* June 16, 1979; Michael Rosenbaum, "Koch's Political Health," *Soho Weekly News,* June 21, 1979.

88. *New York Times,* June 21, 1979, September 18, 1980, and November 2, 1979. See also Charles Tejada, HEW Civil Rights Division, to Francis Morris, NYC Law Dept., December 17, 1979, and Charles Tejada, HEW Office of Civil Rights, to Joseph C. Hoffman, December 17, 1979, both in 13–32–5, Koch Papers.

89. John O'Shea, "Louis T. Wright and Henry W. Cave: How They Paved the Way for Fellowships for Black Surgeons," *Bulletin of the American College of Surgeons* 90 (October 2005), 25, www.facs.org/fellows_info/bulletin/2005/oshea1005.pdf (January 7, 2010).

90. Wagner interview by Soffer, Columbia, 126.

91. Paterson interview; EIK, interview by author, March 11, 2007.

92. B. Drummond Ayres Jr., "On the Issues: Senator Edward M. Kennedy," *New York Times,* March 20, 1980.

93. Allen G. Schwartz to Haskell G. Ward, June 11, 1979, Haskell Ward Series, box 3 (unprocessed), in Koch Papers, Municipal Archives.

94. The impact of HHC expenditures and the Medicaid share in the context of the entire city budget is discussed in chapter 11. These figures are taken from table 2.

95. See Charles Brecher and Diana Roswick, "The City's Role in Health Care," in Raymond D. Horton and Charles Brecher, eds., *Setting Municipal Priorities, 1980* (New York: Universe Books, 1979), 134–70. See also table 2.

96. Brecher and Roswick, "The City's Role in Health Care," 134–170, 143; EIK, *Mayor,* 149.

97. Ester R. Fuchs, *Mayors and Money: Fiscal Policy in New York and Chicago* (Chicago: University of Chicago Press, 1990), 5.

98. *New York Times,* December 24, 1978; EIK, *Mayor,* 146; *New York Times,* March 9, 1979.

99. Haskell Ward, speech to City Club, n.d. (ca. 1979), Haskell Ward Series, box 3, Koch Papers, Municipal Archives.

100. *New York Times,* June 12, 1979; Wagner interview by Soffer, Columbia, 126–29; Haskell Ward, interview by author, January 3, 2007.

101. EIK, *Mayor,* 147; Michael Rosenbaum, "Ward's Fate," *Soho Weekly News,* August 23–29, 1979.

102. "Logan Closes Despite Protest," *New York Amsterdam News,* February 10, 1979.

103. *New York Times,* June 22, 1980.

104. Alexander B. Grannis to Haskell Ward, June 25, 1979, Haskell Ward Series, box 3, Koch Papers, Municipal Archives.

105. Vanessa Northington Gamble, *The Black Community Hospital: Contemporary Dilemmas in Historical Perspective* (New York: Garland, 1989), 66, 72. See also David Barton Smith, *Health Care Divided: Race and Healing a Nation* (Ann Arbor: University of Michigan Press, 1999).

106. Gamble, *Black Community Hospital,* 192

107. Vanessa Northington Gamble, *Making a Place for Ourselves: The Black Hospital Movement, 1920–1945* (New York: Oxford University Press, 1995), 64–68 (Du Bois is quoted on p. 64); Smith, *Health Care Divided,* 34.

108. Ebun Akinwayo Adelona, "The Social Relations of Health," PhD. diss., Columbia University, 1998, 194.

109. Bruce Gantt to Haskell Ward, Note to File, Meeting with Health Committee of the 100 Black Men, July 11, 1979, Haskell Ward Series, box 3, and Victor Botnick to EIK, draft op-ed on hospital closings, July 31, 1979, both in 13–32–2, Koch Papers, La Guardia and Wagner Archives.

110. Zambga Browne and Wista Johnson, "Hospitals Closing: 15,000 at City Hall Rally," *New York Amsterdam News,* May 5, 1979.

111. Ibid.

112. Al Vann to Ward, February 21, 1979, Haskell Ward Series, box 3, Koch Papers, Municipal Archives.

113. EIK, *Mayor,* 208.

114. *New York Times,* April 30, 1977.

115. Adelona, "Social Relations of Health," 280–81.

116. Wagner interview by Soffer, Columbia, 129.

117. *The City Worker* (1980), quoted in Adelona, "Social Relations of Health," 270–71.

118. Victor Botnick to EIK, May 24 1979; Botnick, draft op-ed on hospital closings.

119. Ward interview; reminiscences of Victor Botnick, 1993, Columbia, 2–58.

120. *New York Times,* August 10, 1979; Nat Leventhal, Stanley Brezenoff, and John LoCicero, interview by author, February 20, 2008.

121. Arthur Browne, Dan Collins, and Michael Goodwin, *I, Koch: A Decidedly Unauthorized Biography of the Mayor of New York City, Edward I. Koch* (New York: Dodd, Mead, 1985), 209.

122. Ken Auletta, "Profiles: The Mayor I," *New Yorker*, September 10, 1979, 116–17 (Gault defined "top-level" as deputy mayors, commissioners, administrators, directors, and deputy commissioners or administrators); *New York Times*, September 7, 1979.

123. *New York Times*, September 7, 1979.

124. Ibid.

125. Auletta, "Profiles: The Mayor I," 114–15.

126. *New York Times*, September 7 and 15, 1979.

127. EIK, *Mayor*, 154.

128. *New York Times*, September 9, 1979.

129. EIK, *Mayor*, 155.

130. *New York Times*, September 16, 1979.

131. Ibid., May 22, 1980.

132. Robert Wagner Jr., interview by Chris McNickle, September 9, 1991, La Guardia and Wagner Archives.

133. Adelona, "Social Relations of Health," 275.

134. EIK, *Mayor*, 206.

135. Adelona, "Social Relations of Health," 282.

136. *New York Times*, September 17 and 18, 1980.

137. Ibid., September 18, 1980.

138. Wagner interview by Soffer, Columbia, 129.

139. *New York Times*, September 18, 1980.

140. Ibid., September 17, 1980.

141. EIK, interview by author, March 11, 2007.

142. John LoCicero, interview by Jonathan Soffer and Richard K. Lieberman, March 14, 2007, La Guardia and Wagner Archives.

143. Edward C. Sullivan, interview by author, February 18, 2005.

144. *New York Times*, September 20, 1980; EIK, *Mayor*, 212.

145. EIK, *Mayor*, 212.

146. Sullivan interview; Paul L. Montgomery, "30 Hurt as Police and Protesters Clash outside Sydenham," *New York Times*, September 21, 1980.

147. *New York Times*, September 23, 1980.

148. Ibid., September 22 and 25, 1980.

149. Ibid., September 26, 1980.

150. Ibid., November 21, 1980.

151. Botnick to EIK, May 24, 1979; Botnick, draft op-ed on hospital closings; Adelona, "Social Relations of Health," 301; Anna Robaton, "Hospital Health Centers Shift to Unlikely Spaces," *Crain's New York Business*, October 16, 2000.

152. *New York Times*, September 29 and October 21, 1980.

153. Ibid., March 10, 1981.

154. Judith Stein, *Running Steel, Running America: Race, Economic Policy, and the Decline of Liberalism* (Chapel Hill: University of North Carolina Press, 1998), 70.

155. EIK, *Mayor*, 206; Jim Sleeper, *Closest of Strangers* (New York: W. W. Norton, 1991), 108–109; Stanley Brezenoff, interview by Richard Lieberman, June 14, 1995, La Guardia and Wagner Archives.

14. CONTROLLED FUSION: OR, TO KOCH OR NOT TO KOCH (1980–81)

1. *New York Times,* February 1, 1981.

2. Nat Leventhal, interview by author, January 8, 2004.

3. An example of Koch's support from the economic elite was the Citizen of the Year award he received from the business-oriented Citizens Budget Commission (*CBC 1980 Annual Report,* Bobst Library, New York University).

4. Tom Boast, "Fiscal Update," *City Almanac* 14 (January 1980): 10–11.

5. Leventhal interview; Leventhal to EIK, January 20, 1980, 3, 25–64–6, Koch Papers, La Guardia and Wagner Archives.

6. Sidney Schwartz, "New York City's Fiscal Crisis: How It Developed, Why It Persists," *City Almanac* 15, (October 1980): 1.

7. Jimmy Carter, "State of the Union Address, 1980," January 23, 1980, www.jimmycarterlibrary.org/documents/speeches/su8ojec.phtml (October 30, 2009); Bruce J. Schulman, *The Seventies* (New York: DaCapo, 2002), 133; Judith Stein, talk to the Twentieth-Century Seminar, November 28, 2006, Columbia University.

8. Ronald Smothers, "Koch Budget Gives Schools $91 Million Previously Cut," *New York Times,* May 9, 1990; Stanley Littow and Robin Willner, "A Budget Strategy for the Board of Education," *City Almanac* 14 (April 1980): 6.

9. *New York Times,* January 10, 1980; "New York City Tells Union Chiefs of Plans to Cut 10,000 Jobs," *Wall Street Journal,* January 9, 1980.

10. Unlike the transit workers, AFSCME and the uniformed services unions negotiated their contracts with the mayor's office, under Koch's direct supervision.

11. "State Panel Questions New York City's Plan for Balanced Budget," *Wall Street Journal,* May 28, 1980; Boast, "Fiscal Update," 11.

12. *New York Times,* January 18, 1980.

13. Ibid., January 19 1980.

14. Ibid., March 9, 1980.

15. Ibid., January 18 and 20, 1980.

16. Ibid., January 30, 1980.

17. Ibid., January 18, 1979.

18. Ibid., May 10, 1980.

19. Ibid., May 28, 1980.

20. Ibid., April 21, 1980.

21. Ibid., August 10, 1979.

22. Ibid., June 3, 1980.

23. Terry L. Posner, "Fiscal Update," *City Almanac* 15 (August 1980): 13; Charles Brecher, Herbert J. Ranschburg, and Larry J. Silverman, "Fiscal Update," *City Almanac* 15 (December 1980): 8–9.

24. Koch discusses his view of the strike in detail in Edward I. Koch, with William Rauch, *Mayor* (New York: Simon and Schuster, 1984), 169–205.

25. Victor Gotbaum, interview by author, October 4, 2004; Meyer S. Frucher, interview by author, May 14, 2007; *New York Times,* May 11, 1981. On the Stevens boycott see EIK to Jean Larkin, June 6, 1979, 32–81–2, Koch Papers.

26. On WNYC see Peter J. Solomon to EIK, January 22, 1979. See also Solomon to EIK, September 24, 1979, urging sale; and EIK to Solomon, October 3, 1979, all in 32–80–21, Koch Papers.

27. *New York Times,* January 2, 1980.

28. Ibid., February 20, 1980.

29. *New York Times,* January 2, 1980; Geoffrey Stokes, "Runnin Scared," *Village Voice,* March 31, 1980. Ravitch, who would later become New York's lieutenant governor, was in no sense a hard-right union buster—in 2006 he chaired the AFL-CIO Housing Investment Trust's board of trustees, along with AFL-CIO president John Sweeney. See www.afl-cio-hit.com/wmspage.cfm?parm1=629 (October 30, 2009).

30. *New York Times,* March 23, 1980.

31. Ibid.

32. Ibid., March 20, 1980.

33. Ibid., May 4, 1980. I would like to thank my student Emily Allen, whose research for an undergraduate seminar contributed to my understanding of Koch's bicycling policies.

34. Ibid., March 25, 1980, 1; "Text of New York City's Plan in Case of a Strike by Transit Workers on April 1," *New York Times,* March 25, 1980.

35. *New York Times,* May 7, 1980; Richard Ravitch, interview by author, September 27, 2004.

36. Ravitch interview.

37. Edward I. Koch, with William Rauch, *Mayor* (New York: Simon and Schuster, 1984), 174; *New York Times,* April 2, 1980.

38. *New York Times,* April 9, 1980.

39. Ibid., April 3, 1980.

40. Ibid., April 1, 1980.

41. Koch, *Mayor,* 174.

42. Ibid., 175.

43. Koch, interview by author, May 11, 2007; Leventhal interview.

44. *New York Times,* April 2, 1980.

45. Ibid., April 6, 1980.

46. Ibid., April 2, 1980.

47. Leventhal interview.

48. *New York Times,* April 8, 1980.

49. Ibid., April 6, 1980; Leventhal interview.

50. Frucher interview.

51. *New York Times,* April 4, 1980.

52. *The Oxford English Dictionary* lists a document from the 1980 New York City transit strike as the first recorded use of the term *gridlock.*

53. *New York Times,* April 4, 1980.

54. Ibid.

55. Ibid.

56. Koch, *Mayor,* 190; Ravitch interview.

57. *New York Times,* April 6, 1980.

58. Ibid.

59. Ibid., April 8, 1980.

60. Ibid., April 7, 1980.

61. Frucher interview.

62. *New York Times,* April 7, 1980.

63. Ibid.

64. Ibid., April 9 and 10, 1980.

65. Koch, *Mayor,* 192–93.

66. Ibid., 193–95.

67. *New York Times,* April 10 and 11, 1980; Wayne Barrett and Joe Conason, "Running Scared," *Village Voice,* April 14, 1980.

68. Office of Economic Development, Industry Survey, April 9,1980, 33–81–14, Koch Papers.

69. Reminiscences of James Brigham, 1992, Columbia University Oral History Research Collection (hereafter Columbia), 33–34.

70. Koch, *Mayor,* 195. See also 195–201.

71. *New York Times,* April 13, 1980; Ravitch interview.

72. "Labor Leaders Talk about the Upcoming Negotiations: Conversations with Michael Oreskes," *City Almanac* 16 (March 1982): 14.

73. Koch, *Mayor,* 201.

74. *New York Times,* April 12, 1980.

75. Ibid.

76. Ibid., April 13, 1980.

77. Ibid., April 12, 1980.

78. Ibid., June 28, 1980.

79. Ibid., July 3, 1980.

80. Leventhal interview.

81. *New York Times,* December 23, 1980; Andy Logan, "Around City Hall," *New Yorker,* May 18, 1981, 158.

82. *New York Times,* March 17, October 16, and April 28, 1980.

83. Ibid., August 15, 1980.

84. Ibid., August 4, 8, and 10, 1980.

85. Ibid., August 12, 1980.

86. Ibid., August 12 and 17, 1980.

87. James L. Rowe Jr., "Koch's New Fiscal Plan Slaps at Carter, Congress," *Washington Post*, August 12, 1980; *New York Times*, August 12, 1980.

88. *New York Times*, September 30, 1980.

89. Associated Press, "Koch Says Reagan Would Win New York City If Election Held Now," April 7, 1980, Nexis.

90. *New York Times*, September 27 and 30,1980.

91. Ibid., September 30, 1980.

92. Ibid., October 22, 1980.

93. Ibid., October 16, 1980.

94. Ibid., October 26 and 27, 1980.

95. Ibid., October 30, 1980; EIK, letter to author, December 27, 2007.

96. Andy Logan, "Around City Hall: Contention," *New Yorker*, September 22, 1980, 128.

97. *New York Times*, January 8, 1980.

98. Ibid., July 3, 1980.

99. Ibid., June 7, 1980.

100. See William E. Simon and John M. Caher, *A Time for Reflection: An Autobiography* (Washington, D.C., Regnery, 2004), 150; Kim Phillips-Fein, *Invisible Hands: The Making of the Conservative Movement from the New Deal to Reagan* (New York: W. W. Norton, 2009), 245–56.

101. *New York Times*, June 6, 1980.

102. Ibid., December 23 and October 18, 1980.

103. Brigham interview, Columbia, 38–39.

104. Michael Kramer, "The National Interest," *New York*, November 10, 1980; *New York Times*, October 16 and September 26, 1980.

105. *New York Times*, September 23, 1981.

106. Ibid., November 6, 1980.

107. Ibid., November 7, 1980.

108. Ibid., September 4, 1980; Katherine Tate, *From Protest to Politics: The New Black Voters in American Elections* (Cambridge, Mass.: Harvard University Press, 1994), 72; Samantha Luks and Laurel Elms, "African-American Partisanship and the Legacy of the Civil Rights Movement: Generational, Regional, and Economic Influences on Democratic Identification, 1973–1994," *Political Psychology* 26, no. 5 (October 2005): 735–54.

109. John Lennon, interview for KFRC RKO Radio, December 8, 1980, quoted in Christopher Denny, "The Double Fantasy of John and Yoko: Milk and Honey Revisited," *Black and White*, January 17, 2002, www.bwcitypaper.com/Articles-i-2002-01-17-29350.111115-The_Double_Fantasy_of_John_and_Yoko.html (October 30, 2009).

110. *New York Times*, December 13, 1980; Pamela Allen Brown, interview by author, August 13, 2004.

111. *New York Times*, May 13 and 18, 1981.

112. Ibid., May 18, 1981.

113. Christian Williams, "Stop the Movie—We Want to Get Off!" *Washington Post,* May 4, 1980; *New York Times,* February 15, 1981.

114. Abe Beame, letter to the editor, *New York Times,* February 16, 1981; *New York Times,* March 7, 1981.

115. *New York Times,* May 18, 1981.

116. Ibid., March 7, 1981.

117. Marilyn Rubin, "The Anatomy of Fiscal Recovery," *City Almanac* 15 (April 1981): 2–5.

118. *New York Times,* January 17, 1981.

119. Ibid., January 17 and June 18, 1981.

120. Ibid., January 17, 1981.

121. Ibid., May 7, 1981.

122. Ibid., January 17, 1981. On Reagan see *New York Times,* March 15, 1981.

123. *New York Times,* May 6, 1981.

124. EIK to author.

125. *New York Times,* June 5, 1981.

126. Ibid., September 23, 1981.

127. Ibid.

128. Ibid., October 18, 1981; Godfrey Sperling Jr., "Democrats Still Can't Learn Right Lines for Their Role as Nay-sayers," *Christian Science Monitor,* October 19, 1981.

129. "Totals by Assembly District in Citywide Elections," *New York Times,* November 5, 1981.

130. Ibid., December 2, 1981; Ward Morehouse III, "New York Mayor Koch Joins in Criticism of Reagan, but in a 'Civil' Way," *Christian Science Monitor,* December 30, 1981.

131. *New York Times,* December 2, 1981.

132. Koch to Soffer, December 27, 2007.

133. *New York Times,* October 20 and December 10, 1981.

15. GOVERNOR KOCH? (1982–83)

1. *New York Times,* January 2, 1982.

2. Albert Camus, *The Myth of Sisyphus,* trans. Justin O'Brien (New York: Vintage, 1991), 121.

3. *New York Times,* January 1, 1982.

4. Ibid., January 2, 1982.

5. Ibid., January 22, 1982.

6. See Domecq Sherry Company, Jerez, Spain, January 21, 1982, photo 08.001.0011, Koch Papers, La Guardia and Wagner Archives.

7. See "Mayor Koch Visits the Ancient Shlomo Ben Adret Synagogue," Barcelona, Spain, January 1982, photo 08.001.0317, Koch Papers.

8. *New York Times,* January 27, 1982.

9. Ibid., February 8, 1982; Edward I. Koch, interview by author, January 31, 2006.

10. Arthur Browne, Dan Collins, and Michael Goodwin, *I, Koch: A Decidedly Unauthorized Biography of the Mayor of New York City, Edward I. Koch* (New York: Dodd, Mead, 1985), 248–49.

11. *New York Times,* February 4, 1982.

12. Ibid., February 23, 1982.

13. Browne, Collins, and Goodwin, *I, Koch,* 252.

14. *New York Times,* July 17, August 21, September 19, and October 31, 1982.

15. Ed Koch, interview, *Playboy,* April 1982, 70, 98; *New York Times,* February 24, 1982.

16. Koch *Playboy* interview, 98.

17. Ibid., 68; G. Barry Golson, *The Playboy Interview II* (New York: Perigee, 1983), 481.

18. Browne, Collins, and Goodwin, *I, Koch,* 244.

19. Evan Cornog, interview by author, May 29, 2007.

20. Browne, Collins, and Goodwin, *I, Koch,* 254–55.

21. *Rochester Times-Union* editorial, quoted in *New York Times,* March 1, 1982.

22. Browne, Collins, and Goodwin, *I, Koch,* 255, 258.

23. *Syracuse Herald American,* quoted in *New York Times,* March 1, 1982.

24. *New York Times,* August 6, 1982.

25. Ibid., September 12 and August 13, 1982.

26. Ibid., August 21, 1982.

27. Martin Schram, "Koch, Cuomo Race an Electric Battle of Conservative vs. Liberal," *Washington Post,* August 7, 1982; Ward Morehouse III, "Candidate Koch Takes His New York City Show on Road," *Christian Science Monitor,* July 26, 1982.

28. *New York Times,* August 11, 1982.

29. Morehouse, "Candidate Koch."

30. Schram, "Koch, Cuomo Race an Electric Battle."

31. *New York Times,* September 24 and 25, 1982.

32. Ibid., September 24, 1982.

33. Ibid., January 16 and 19, 1982.

34. Ibid., July 17, 1982.

35. Ibid., October 20, 1982, and November 17, 1980; Charles Brecher and Raymond D. Horton, interview by author, March 12, 2008. Brecher was an associate professor at New York University's Graduate School of Public Administration, and Horton was an associate professor at Columbia University's Graduate School of Business. Their study is published as Charles Brecher and Raymond D. Horton, *Setting Municipal Priorities FY 1981* (Montclair N.J.: Allanheld, Osmun, 1980).

36. *New York Times,* February 18 and November 18, 1982.

37. Ibid., November 19, 1982.

38. Ibid., and December 15, 1982.

39. Ibid., April 27, 1983.

40. Ibid., September 26 and December 17, 1982, and February 8, 1984.

41. Ibid., March 29 and March 24, 1983.

42. Edward I. Koch, letter to the editor, *New York Times,* April 11, 1983.

43. *New York Times,* April 10, 1983.

44. Ibid., June 16, 1983.

45. Ibid., July 11, 1986.

46. Ibid., March 8 and 23, and May 13, 1984; "N.Y.C. School Chief Steps Down before Hearings," *Christian Science Monitor,* May 14, 1984.

47. Reminiscences of Stanley Brezenoff, 1992, Columbia University Oral History Research Collection (hereafter Columbia), 11–18.

48. Ibid., 4.

49. "Picketing by CORE Stirs Riot in Bronx," *New York Times,* July 7, 1963; Martin Arnold, "Neo-Nazis Seized with Arms Cache in Bronx Dispute," *New York Times,* July 15, 1963.

50. Brezenoff interview, Columbia, 14–15.

51. Ibid., 15, 21–24, 35–48.

52. Ibid., 20; see also 35–48.

53. Ibid., 62–63.

54. Ibid., 62, 66.

55. *New York Times,* February 10, 1984.

56. Brezenoff interview, Columbia, 114.

57. EIK to Nat Leventhal, April 19, 1983, 27–67–16, Koch Papers.

58. Fritz Schwarz to EIK, June 14, 1983, 27–67–23, Koch Papers; *New York Times,* April 25, 1989.

59. Brezenoff to EIK, April 28, 1983, 27–67–23, Koch Papers.

60. EIK to Leventhal; Alair Townsend to EIK, April 5, 1983, 27–67–16, Koch Papers.

16. LARGER THAN LIFE (1984-85)

1. Edward I. Koch, "Remarks in Interview in *Public Opinion* Magazine," *Washington Post,* November 27, 1983.

2. *New York Times,* January 8, 1984.

3. Ibid., March 20, 1984.

4. James F. Gill, *For James and Gillian: Jim Gill's New York* (New York: Fordham University Press, 2003), 121–22.

5. Bill O'Shaughnessy, *More Riffs, Rants, and Raves* (New York: Fordham University Press, 2004), 107.

6. Gill, *For James and Gillian,* 122.

7. *Under 21 v. City of New York,* 65 N.Y.2d 344 (1985); David W. Dunlap, "Archdiocese Seeks Accord with City," *New York Times,* June 18, 1984. On Executive Order 50 see *New York Times,* June 18, 1984.

8. Mark Penn, telephone interview by author, January 21, 2005.

9. Reminiscences of Stanley Brezenoff, 1992, Columbia University Oral History Research Collection (hereafter Columbia), 103.

10. *New York Times,* January 10 and 15, 1984.

11. Ibid.

12. Ibid., June 25, 1985.

13. Ibid., February 26, 1984.

14. Margot Hornblower, "Koch Lets Hair Down in Biography 'Mayor,'" *Washington Post,* February 2, 1984.

15. *New York Times,* April 16, 1985.

16. Ibid., January 20, 1984.

17. George Will, "Koch's Brawl in Hardback," *Washington Post,* March 18, 1984.

18. Edward I. Koch, with Leland T. Jones, *All the Best: Letters from a Feisty Mayor* (New York: Simon and Schuster, 1990), 203.

19. *New York Times,* February 19, 1985; "20 Questions with Ricky Skaggs," CMT News, November 24, 2004, www.cmt.com/news/articles/1494136/11242004/skaggs_ricky.jhtml (November 1, 2009).

20. *New York Times,* May 12, 1985.

21. Ibid., May 14, 1985.

22. Charles Strouse et al., *Mayor—The Musical,* 1985 original off-Broadway cast, audio CD 2001; Margot Hornblower, "Celebrating Chutzpah; in New York, a Witty 'Mayor, the Musical,'" *Washington Post,* May 14, 1985.

23. *New York Times,* March 19, 1984.

24. Martin Schram, "Garth to Create Ad Campaign for Mondale's New York Drive," *Washington Post,* March 21, 1984.

25. *New York Times,* January 29, 1984. For an example of Jackson's comments, see Don Oberdorfer, "Jackson, Back from Mideast, Wants PLO Policy Changed," *Washington Post,* October 9, 1979.

26. *New York Times,* February 20, 1984; James R. Dickenson and Kathy Sawyer, "Jackson Admits to Ethnic Slur; Candidate Makes Conciliatory Stop at Synagogue," *Washington Post,* February 27, 1984.

27. *New York Times,* May 3, 1984.

28. Eleanor Randolph, "Meeting Urged with Reporter; Jackson Calls Farrakhan Threat 'Wrong,'" *Washington Post,* April 4, 1984.

29. *New York Times,* May 3, 1984.

30. Associated Press, "Koch: Farrakhan Cast Shadow across Campaign," April 15, 1984, Nexis; *New York Times,* April 13, 1984.

31. *New York Times,* July 2, 1984; Walter Pincus, "Libya Lobby Bid Touched Members of Congress, Other Leaders," *Washington Post,* August 9, 1980.

32. *New York Times,* January 29, 1984.

33. Ibid., July 14, 1984.

34. Ibid., July 16, 1984.

35. Ibid., April 5, 1984; Margot Hornblower, "Black Vote Resounds in New York City; Mondale Was Victor, But to Jackson Go the Spoils," *Washington Post,* April 5, 1984.

36. *New York Times,* April 5, 1984; Hornblower, "Black Vote Resounds."

37. *New York Times,* April 5, 1984; Hornblower, "Black Vote Resounds"; editorial, *New York Times,* April 5, 1984.

38. *New York Times,* September 29, 1984; Basil Paterson, interview by author, February 14, 2005.

39. *New York Times,* January 16, 1985.

40. Carol Bellamy, interview by author, April 25, 2007.

41. For details on the Goetz and Bumpurs cases, see chapter 22.

42. *New York Times,* December 27, 1985, and January 18, 1986.

43. Edward I. Koch, "What Insensitivity to Minority Concerns?" *New York Times,* January 5, 1985; EIK to Stan Brezenoff, April 26, 1985, May 17, 1985, 20–50–9, Koch Papers.

44. Jim Harding to EIK, April 15, 1986, 23–56–22, Koch Papers; Harding to EIK, May 11, 1987, 23–56–26, Koch Papers.

45. *New York Times,* January 17, 1985.

46. Ibid., January 30, 1985.

47. This section on divestment was previously published in Jonathan Soffer, "Mayor Edward I. Koch and New York's Municipal Foreign Policy," in Shane Ewen and Pierre Yves Saunier, eds., *The Other Global City. Transnational Municipal Trails in the Modern Age (1850–2000)* (New York: Palgrave 2008), 119–33 and 129–33 (reprinted by permission of Palgrave Macmillan).

48. "Turning the Tables," *Washington Post,* February 16, 1984; *New York Times,* February 16, 1984. John Sears, Ronald Reagan's former campaign manager, was senior partner in Baskin and Sears. In the postapartheid era Dumisani Kumalo became South African ambassador to the UN.

49. *New York Times,* May 31, 1984.

50. "Posturing over Pretoria," *New York Times,* June 1, 1984.

51. Ibid.

52. *New York Times,* October 6, 1985.

53. Ibid., July 14, 1984.

54. Crotty to Mulhern re Banking Commission Local Law 19, August 13, 1985; Crotty to EIK, August 27, 1985, both in 29–74–20, Koch Papers.

55. *New York Times,* June 22, 1986.

56. Ibid., September 20, 1985; "Surprise Serve for Soviets as NY Mayor Lashes Apartheid," *(Brisbane, Australia) Courier Mail,* September 21, 1985; *New York Times,* October 6, 1985.

57. *New York Times,* January 31, 1985.

58. Penn interview.

59. *New York Times,* August 15, 1985.

60. Ibid., August 27, 1985.

61. Ibid.

62. Ibid., July 13, 1985.

63. John Hull Mollenkopf, *A Phoenix in the Ashes: The Rise and Fall of the Koch Coalition in New York City Politics* (Princeton, N.J.: Princeton University Press, 1992), 165–66, 170; *New York Times*, September 12 and 29, 1985.

64. "Mayoralty," in Kenneth T. Jackson, ed., *Encyclopedia of the City of New York* (New Haven, Conn.: Yale University Press, 1995), 743.

65. *New York Times*, November 7, 1985.

17. A NEW SPATIAL ORDER: GENTRIFICATION, THE PARKS, TIMES SQUARE

1. Blake Fleetwood, "The New Elite and an Urban Renaissance," *New York Times Magazine,* January 14, 1979.

2. Sharon Zukin, "Gentrification: Culture and Capital in the Urban Core," *Annual Review of Sociology* 13 (1987):132–33.

3. Ibid., 131.

4. Neil Smith, *The New Urban Frontier: Gentrification and the Revanchist City* (New York: Routledge, 1996), 30, 43.

5. Fleetwood, "New Elite and an Urban Renaissance."

6. Robert F. Wagner, *New York Ascendant: Report of the Commission on the Year 2000*, June 1987 (New York: HarperCollins, 1988), 7; On rebranding, see Miriam Greenberg, *Branding New York: How a City in Crisis Was Sold to the World* (New York: Routledge, 2008), 12.

7. *New York Times*, March 2, 1982.

8. Ibid., November 1, 1981.

9. Ibid., June 8, 1979.

10. Ibid.

11. Saskia Sassen, *Cities in a World Economy* (Thousand Oaks, Calif.: Pine Forge, 1994), 116–17.

12. Robert C. Smith, Héctor R. Cordero-Guzmán, and Ramón Grosfoguel, "Three Social Facts about Transnationalization, Immigrant Incorporation and the Changing Ethnic Structure and Political Economy of New York City," in Robert C. Smith, Héctor R. Cordero-Guzmán, and Ramón Grosfoguel, eds., *Migation, Transnationalization, and Race in a Changing New York* (Philadelphia: Temple University Press, 2001), 2.

13. See Craig Wilder, *A Covenant with Color: Race and Social Power in Brooklyn, 1636–1990* (New York: Columbia University Press, 2001), 210–12.

14. Fleetwood, " New Elite and an Urban Renaissance."

15. Lance Freeman, *There Goes the 'Hood: Views of Gentrification from the Ground Up* (Philadelphia: Temple University Press, 2006), 189–210.

16. *New York Times*, July 13, 1980.

17. Lynne B. Sagalyn, *Times Square Roulette: Remaking the City Icon* (Cambridge, Mass.: MIT Press, 2001), 70.

18. Reminiscences of Robert Esnard, 1995, Columbia University Oral History Research Collection (hereafter Columbia), 2–3.

19. *New York Times,* July 23, 1980; Susan S. Fainstein, *The City Builders: Property Development in New York and London, 1980–2000,* 2nd ed. (Lawrence: University Press of Kansas, 2001), 38.

20. Alex. S. Vitale, *City of Disorder: How the Quality of Life Campaign Transformed New York Politics* (New York: New York University Press, 2008), 93–94.

21. *New York Times,* May 28, 1978.

22. Ibid., March 29, 1987.

23. Ibid., July 26, 1981.

24. Ibid., October 16, October 1, and July 18, 1981.

25. Ibid., July 18 and April 18, 1979.

26. Ibid., September 22, 1980.

27. Ibid., October 19, 1980.

28. Harry Hurt III, *Lost Tycoon: The Many Lives of Donald Trump* (London: Nicolson and Weidenfeld, 1993), 109–10; *New York Times,* August 26, 1980.

29. *New York Times,* August 26., 1980.

30. Donald Trump and Tony Schwartz, *Trump* (Random House, 2004), 6; *New York Times,* July 6, 1984.

31. Hurt, *Lost Tycoon,* 123.

32. Edward I. Koch, with Daniel Paisner, *Citizen Koch: An Autobiography* (New York: St. Martin's, 1992), 193.

33. Ibid., 193.

34. Esnard interview, Columbia, 9–10.

35. Ibid., 10–11.

36. Trump and Schwartz, *Trump,* 6.

37. Esnard interview, Columbia, 46; Esnard, interview by author, May 26, 2006.

38. Arthur Browne, Dan Collins, and Michael Goodwin, *I, Koch: A Decidedly Unauthorized Biography of the Mayor of New York City, Edward I. Koch* (New York: Dodd, Mead, 1985), 193–94.

39. Hurt, *Lost Tycoon,* 174; Trump and Schwartz, *Trump,* 6.

40. Gordon Davis, interview by author, February 18, 2005.

41. Ibid.

42. Ibid.

43. Michael Goodwin and Anna Quindlen, "Paradise Lost? New York City's Parks," three-part series, *New York Times,* October 13–15, 1980.

44. Ibid.

45. Ibid.

46. Ibid.

47. Ibid.; Charles Brecher, Raymond D. Horton, Robert A. Cropf, and Dean Michael Mead, *Power Failure: New York City Politics and Policy since 1960* (New York: Oxford University Press, 1993), 309.

48. Davis interview; Brecher et al., *Power Failure,* 309.

49. *New York Times,* August 16, 1980.

50. Ibid.

51. Elizabeth Blackmar, "Appropriating 'the Commons': The Tragedy of Property Rights Discourse," in Setha Low and Neil Smith, eds., *The Politics of Public Space* (New York: Routledge, 2006), 49–77.

52. Ibid., 62.

53. *New York Times,* December 20, 1981.

54. Davis interview.

55. Henry J. Stern, interview by author, January 26, 2009; Sam Roberts, "Metro Matters; For Parks Chief, Offbeat Charm Is His Signature," *New York Times,* October 3, 1988.

56. *New York Times,* October 23, 1966.

57. Ibid., February 15 and March 16, 1983.

58. Ibid., March 18 and 27, 1983.

59. Ibid., November 28, 2002.

60. Stern interview.

61. New York City Department of Parks and Recreation, www.nycgovparks.org/sub_about/about_parks.html (November 1, 2009); *New York Times,* January 19, 1984; "Text of Mayor La Guardia's Report on 1934 Administration," *New York Times,* January 11, 1935.

62. *New York Times,* July 24, 1988; Stern interview.

63. *New York Times,* July 22 and 26, 1983.

64. Ibid., June 27, 1985, and March 24, 1986.

65. Ibid., March 31, 1986.

66. Ibid., May 20, 1987.

67. Ibid., April 21 and April 29, 1989; Joan Didion, "New York: Sentimental Journeys," *New York Review of Books* 38, no. 1 (January 17, 1991), www.nybooks.com; Harold L. Jamison, "Leaders Temper Anger with Caution," *New York Amsterdam News,* April 29, 1989.

68. *New York Times,* December 6 and October 5, 2002. An internal "rebuttal" report by the New York Police Department claimed that the police had acted properly in arresting the boys (*New York Times,* January 28, 2003).

69. *New York Times,* April 21 and April 29, 1989; Didion, "New York: Sentimental Journeys." For the 1990 crime statistics see Police Department, City of New York, *CompStat: 22nd Precinct,* December 21–27, 2009, "Historical Perspective" table, www.nyc.gov/html/nypd/downloads/pdf/crime_statistics/cs022pct.pdf (June 11, 2009).

70. *New York Times,* February 10 and 16, 2001.

71. Cindi Katz, "Power, Space and Terror: Social Reproduction and the Public Environment," in Low and Smith, *Politics of Public Space,* 112–17.

72. Ibid., 112–17.

73. Lisa Keller, *Triumph of Order: Democracy and Public Space in New York and London* (New York: Columbia University Press, 2009), 234–36.

74. Ibid.; Blackmar, "Appropriating 'the Commons'"; Oliver Cooke, "A Class Approach to Municipal Privatization: The Privatization of New York City's Central Park," *International Labor and Working-Class History* 71, no. 01 (2007): 123–27.

75. *New York Times,* May 21 and July 23, 1978.

76. Ibid., July 23, 1978.

77. Ibid., August 1, 1978.

78. Ibid., June 29, 1984, and August 7, 1987.

79. Sagalyn, *Times Square Roulette,* 64.

80. Ibid., 58; *Papachristou v. Jacksonville,* 405 U.S. 156 (1972).

81. Sagalyn, *Times Square Roulette,* 19; *Papachristou v. Jacksonville*; Vitale, *City of Disorder,* 119.

82. Sagalyn, *Times Square Roulette,* 48.

83. Ibid., 62–64.

84. Ibid., 63.

85. Ibid., 66.

86. James Traub, *The Devil's Playground: A Century of Pleasure and Profit in Times Square* (New York: Random House, 2004), 138; Merrill Brown, "N.Y.'s Times Square to Get Face-Lift; Developer, City Officials Announce $1.6 Billion Office Complex," *Washington Post,* December 21, 1983.

87. Meyer S. (Sandy) Frucher, interview by author, May 14, 2007.

88. Sagalyn, *Times Square Roulette,* 190–93.

89. Traub, *Devil's Playground,* 141–42.

90. Ibid., 144, 148.

91. Sagalyn, *Times Square Roulette,* 194; Thomas Bender, "Ruining Times Square," *New York Times,* March 3, 1984.

92. Traub, *Devil's Playground,* 146.

93. Sagalyn, *Times Square Roulette,* 119–20, 128.

94. Traub, *Devil's Playground,* 155–56.

95. Ibid., 159.

96. Sagalyn, *Times Square Roulette,* 12.

97. Traub, *Devil's Playground,* 164.

18. HOMELESSNESS

1. Richard Reeves, *President Reagan* (New York: Simon and Schuster, 2005), 212.

2. Donna Wilson Kirchheimer, "Sheltering the Homeless in New York City: Expansion in an Era of Government Contraction," *Political Science Quarterly* 104, no. 4 (winter 1989–90): 607–609.

3. Joel Blau, *The Visible Poor: Homelessness in the United States* (New York: Oxford University Press 1992), 133–34.

4. Alex S. Vitale, *City of Disorder* (New York: New York University Press, 2008), 27.

5. Blau, *Visible Poor,* 137–38. See also Neil Smith, *The New Urban Frontier: Gentrification and the Revanchist City* (New York: Routledge, 1996), 18.

6. Smith, *New Urban Frontier,* 67–69.

7. *New York Times,* May 26, 1979.

8. Vitale, *City of Disorder,* 93.

9. Edward I. Koch to Laurence Klein, March 5, 1979, 25–63–11, Koch Papers, La Guardia and Wagner Archives.

10. Klein to EIK, February 15, 1979 25–63–11, Koch Papers.

11. Ibid.

12. Ibid.

13. Ibid.

14. Ibid.

15. Kim Hopper, *Reckoning with Homelessness* (Ithaca, N.Y.: Cornell University Press, 2003), 64–65, 115.

16. Michael Goodwin, "S.R.O. Hotel: Rare Species: Curbing Conversions Proving Difficult Task," *New York Times,* November 20, 1981; James D. Wright and Beth A. Rubin, "Is Homelessness a Housing Problem?" *Housing Policy Debate* 2 no. 3 (1991): 948.

17. Klein to EIK, July 3, 1979, 25–63–11, Koch Papers.

18. *New York Times,* June 28, 1981.

19. Ella Howard, "Skid Row: Homelessness on the Bowery in the Twentieth Century," Ph.D. diss., Boston University, 2007, 307–10.

20. Martha Burt, Laudan Y. Aron, Edgar Lee, and Jesse Valente, *Helping America's Homeless: Emergency Shelter or Affordable Housing?* (Washington, D.C.: Urban Institute Press, 2001), 241–42.

21. Wright and Rubin, "Is Homelessness a Housing Problem?" 939.

22. Blau, *Visible Poor,* 86.

23. *New York Times,* December 8, 1980.

24. Ibid.

25. Ibid., January 4, 1980.

26. Hopper, *Reckoning with Homelessness,* 65.

27. Reminiscences of Stanley Brezenoff, 1992, Columbia University Oral History Research Collection (hereafter Columbia), 2–54.

28. The text of orders and briefs in *Callahan v. Carey* may be found at www.escr-net.org/caselaw/caselaw_show.htm?doc_id=399028 (April 28, 2008); Glenn Fowler, "Koch Pays Visit to New Shelter on Wards Island," *New York Times,* January 4, 1980.

29. Brezenoff interview, Columbia, 54–55.

30. Hopper, *Reckoning with Homelessness,* 186.

31. *New York Times,* January 4, 1980.

32. Ibid., August 27, 1981.

33. Hopper, *Reckoning with Homelessness,* 91.

34. *New York Times,* August 27, 1981, and December 29, 1980.

35. Hopper, *Reckoning with Homelessness,* 186; David Schoenbrund and Ross Sandler, "Government by Decree," *City Journal,* December 1994, www.city-journal.org/article01.php?aid=1430 (April 28, 2008).

36. *New York Times,* December 29, 1980.

37. Ibid., September 18, 1981.

38. Ibid., December 20, 1980, and October 8 and August 14, 1981.

39. Margaret Boepple to EIK, July 19, 1985, 13–31–29, Koch Papers.

40. Robert McGuire, interview by author, May 22, 2006, See also Botnick to EIK, May 16, 1983, 14–33–9, Koch Papers.

41. *New York Times,* June 28, 1981.

42. Vitale, *City of Disorder,* 80.

43. *New York Times,* March 27 and 28, 1981.

44. Ibid.

45. Ibid., November 20, 1980, and December 1, 11, and 28, 1981.

46. Ibid., October 5, 1982.

47. EIK to Brezenoff, November 4, 1985, 15–37–12, Koch Papers; EIK to Patrick Mulhearn, January 8, 1985, 29–74–17, Koch Papers.

48. *New York Times,* February 5, 1982. For Koch's personal interest in the case of Judy Engle, a clearly delusional woman who was accorded the constitutional right to refuse treatment and returned to the streets, see EIK to Sara Kellermann, December 20 1984, 29–74–17, Koch Papers.

49. *New York Times,* January 23, 1985.

50. Brendan O'Flaherty, *Making Room: The Economics of Homelessness* (Cambridge, Mass.: Harvard University Press, 1996), 276–78.

51. *New York Times,* January 23, 1985.

52 Ibid., March 25, 1983.

53. Ibid., November 3, 1987.

54. *In re* Billie Boggs, 132 A.D.2d 340, 347 (1987).

55. *New York Times,* February 15, 1988.

56. Associated Press, "Reagan's Remarks on Homeless Cause Controversy," June 1, 1988, Lexis-Nexis Academic.

57. Jimmie L. Reeves, "Re-Covering the Homeless: Hindsights on the Joyce Brown Story," in Eungjun Min, ed., *Reading the Homeless: The Media's Image of Homeless Culture* (Westport, Conn.: Greenwood, 1999), 59.

58. *New York Times,* September 8, 1988, and November 10, 2002.

59. Ibid., January 23, 1985.

60. Ibid., February 26, 1983.

61. Ibid., January 29, 1983.

62. Ibid., January 27, 1983.

63. Ibid., February 19, 1983.

64. Ibid., July 19, 1983.

65. Abraham Biderman, interview by author, June 10, 2009.

66. Calvin Butts to EIK, June 2, 1987, 23–56–26, Koch Papers.

67. *New York Times*, August 2, 1983.

68. Ibid., August 23 and 25, 1983.

69. Ibid., November 23, 1983.

70. Ibid., November 24 and December 6 and 9, 1983.

71. John Jiler, *Sleeping with the Mayor* (St. Paul, Minn.: Hungry Mind Press, 1997), 289. This is an astonishing booklength account of Kochville by a journalist who lived nearby.

72. Vitale, *City of Disorder*, 88.

19. THE KOCH HOUSING PLAN (1986–89)

1. *New York Times*, January 31, 1985; "Text of Address Delivered by Mayor Koch at his Third Inauguration," *New York Times*, January 2, 1986; Susan D. Wagner to Robert Esnard, "Status of the Recommendations in the Report by the Mayor's Panel on Affordable Housing and the Blue Ribbon Panel Report," January 12, 1987, 21–52–14, Koch Papers, La Guardia and Wagner Archives; *New York Times*, April 30, 1986, and June 11, 1989; New York City Department of Housing Preservation and Development, "The Ten-Year Housing Plan: Fiscal Years 1989–1998," n.d. (1989?), New York City Municipal Library.

2. Abraham Biderman, interview by author, June 10, 2009.

3. Yvette Shiffman and Nancy Foxworthy, "Producing Low-Income Housing in New York City," typescript, Community Service Society of New York, January 1985, Bobst Library, New York University, 2–3.

4. Richard Plunz, *A History of Housing in New York City* (New York: Columbia University Press, 1990), 151–63.

5. Biderman interview by author.

6. Nicholas Dagen Bloom, *Public Housing That Worked: New York in the Twentieth Century* (Philadelphia: University of Pennsylvania Press, 2008), 218.

7. Richard Plunz, *A History of Housing in New York City* (New York: Columbia University Press, 1990), 151–63; Bloom, *Public Housing That Worked*, 5–10.

8. Biderman interview by author.

9. *New York Times*, June 30 and July 30, 1982.

10. Ibid., February 21, 1984, and November 21, 1985.

11. Samuel Friedman, "This Partnership of Government and Faith Succeeds," *USA Today*, August 20, 2001.

12. *New York Times,* April 17 and May 3, 1986.

13. Felice Michetti, "The New York City Capital Program for Affordable Housing," in Jess Lederman, ed., *Housing America: Mobilizing Bankers, Builders and Communities to Solve the Nation's Affordable Housing Crisis* (Chicago: Probus, 1993), 201–203; reminiscences of Abraham Biderman, 1992, Columbia University Oral History Research Collection (hereafter Columbia), 42, 45.

14. *New York Times,* February 28, 1986.

15. William Sites, *Remaking New York: Primitive Globalization and the Politics of Urban Community* (Minneapolis: University of Minnesota Press, 2003), 87.

16. Reminiscences of Paul Crotty, 1992, Columbia, 66–67.

17. Wagner to Esnard, "Status of the Recommendations"; Sturz to EIK, February 20, 1985; EIK to Esnard February 25, 1985, 21–52–4, Koch Papers; Charles J. Orlebeke, *New Life at Ground Zero: New York, Home Ownership, and the Future of American Cities* (Albany, N.Y.: Rockefeller Institute Press, 1997), 125; Crotty interview, Columbia, 71–72.

18. *New York Times,* April 30, 1989.

19. Ibid., December 4, 1986.

20. Ibid., April 30, 1989; David Dinkins to EIK, May 11, 1987; EIK to Dinkins, April 10, 1987, enclosing "An Analysis of the Report Prepared by the Manhattan Borough President's Task Force on Housing for Homeless Victims," 4–10–8, Koch Papers.

21. Stan Brezenoff to Jane Dumpson, June 26, 1987, 4–10–10, Koch Papers; Biderman interview, Columbia, 42, 45.

22. *New York Times,* April 17, 1987.

23. Crotty interview, Columbia, 127–28.

24. *New York Times,* July 30, 1986.

25. EIK to Nat Leventhal, December 5, 1978, 25–63–31, Koch Papers.

26. For Koch's earliest inquiry about promoting home ownership, see Leventhal to EIK, August 23, 1979, 25–63–31, Koch Papers.

27. Herbert Sturz to EIK, "Mayor's Monthly Report for Period Ending March 7, 1985," March 15, 1985, 6, 39–94–11, Koch Papers; Crotty interview, Columbia, 62–63.

28. *New York Times,* November 15, 1987.

29. Reminiscences of Anthony Gliedman, 1994, Columbia, 34.

30. Bloom, *Public Housing That Worked,* 5; Biderman interview by author.

31. Norman to Harding, May 19, 1987; Crotty to Harding, July 16, 1987, both in 23–57–1, Koch Papers.

32. *New York Times,* October 23, 2000.

33. Crotty interview, Columbia, 113; Janice L. Bockmeyer, "Devolution and the Transformation of Community Housing Activism," *Social Science Journal* 40, no. 2 (2003), 185.

34. Townsend to EIK, January 23, 1985, 8–18–17, Koch Papers.

35. Crotty interview, Columbia, 60–61.

36. Ibid., 180–81.

37. See Esnard to EIK April 4, 1985, 21–52–6, Koch Papers; "Excerpts from Text of the May-

or's State of the City Message," *New York Times,* January 31, 1985; Biderman interview, Columbia, 43; "Cuomo Signs Bill to Build New Housing Using Excess Funds from 2 Authorities," *Bond Buyer,* April 11, 1986; David L.A. Gordon, *Battery Park City: Politics and Planning on the New York Waterfront* (Amsterdam: Gordon and Breach, 1997), 91–93; *New York Times,* October 9, 1988.

38. See Crotty interview, Columbia, 191–94.

39. Koch press release, December 23, 1986, 23–56–27, Koch Papers.

40. Crotty interview, Columbia, 195; *New York Times,* September 17, 1987.

41. Crotty interview, Columbia, 191–94.

42. Ibid., 194.

43. Wagner to Esnard, "Status of the Recommendations"; Orlebeke, *New Life at Ground Zero,* 124–27; *New York Times,* November 15, 1987.

44. Elizabeth A. Roistacher, "A Tale of Two Conservatives," *Journal of the American Planning Association* 50, no. 4 (1984): 488; Norman J. Glickman, "Economic Policy and the Cities: In Search of Reagan's Real Urban Policy," *Journal of the American Planning Association* 50, no. 4 (1984): 475–76.

45. Bloom, *Public Housing That Worked,* 218–19; Michetti, "New York City Capital Program," 200; New York City Department of Housing Preservation and Development, "Ten-Year Housing Plan."

46. Biderman interview, Columbia, 42, 45; Crotty interview, Columbia, 116–17.

47. Orlebeke, *New Life at Ground Zero,* 46, 85; Crotty interview, Columbia, 116–17.

48. Biderman interview by author.

49. Sam Howe Verhovek, "Cuomo Son Plans Units for Homeless," *New York Times,* October 31, 1988; Crotty interview, Columbia, 61–64; Biderman interview, Columbia, 68–69.

50. *New York Times,* June 8, 1986.

51. Ibid., April 8, 1990.

52. Ibid., June 18, 1987; reminiscences of Robert Esnard, 1995, Columbia, 28.

53. *New York Times,* March 27, 1988.

54. Esnard interview, Columbia, 28; Crotty to EIK, n.d. (1986), 82–183–2, Koch Papers; *New York Times,* August 2, 1988; Biderman interview, Columbia, 52.

55. Orlebeke, *New Life at Ground Zero,* 125–26, 135. See Wagner to Esnard, "Status of the Recommendations."

56. Editorial, *New York Daily News,* February 13, 1987.

57. EIK to Crotty, February 17, 1987; Crotty to editor, *New York Daily News,* February 20, 1987; Crotty to Spencer, February 20, 1987, all in 82–183–8, Koch Papers; Crotty interview, Columbia, 128.

58. Biderman interview, Columbia, 17.

59. *New York Times,* July 30, 1986.

60. Crotty to EIK, January 8, 1987, 82–183–7, Koch Papers; *New York Times,* November 15, 1987.

61. Orlebeke, *New Life at Ground Zero,* 102–104.

62. Ibid., 126; Michael H. Schill, Ingrid Gould Ellen, Amy Ellen Schwartz, and Ioan Voicu, "Revitalizing Inner-City Neighborhoods: New York City's Ten-Year Plan," *Housing Policy Debate* 13, no. 3 (2002):536; Biderman interview by author.

63. *New York Times,* December 1, 1989.

64. Ibid., November 12, 1983.

65. Ibid., July 12, 1989.

66. Ibid., December 1, 1989.

67. Crotty interview, Columbia, 60–61, 180–81.

68. *New York Times,* October 10, 1989.

69. Ibid., March 18 and May 17, 1990.

70. Michetti, "New York City Capital Program," 203, 211.

71. Office of the Mayor, Historic and Projected Populations, New York City, 1950–2030, "PLANYC," n.d., www.nyc.gov/html/planyc2030/html/challenge/openyc.shtml (November 4, 2009).

72. Orlebeke, *New Life at Ground Zero,* 179; *New York Times,* October 30, 1987.

73. *New York Times,* September 2, 1998.

74. Ibid., January 5, 2009.

20. AIDS

1. Lawrence Mass, M.D., "Cancer in the Gay Community," *New York Native,* July 27–August 9, 1981.

2. Brandon Judell, "Koch on Homophobia: 'It's a Matter of Conscience,'" *New York Native,* May 18–31, 1981; Lawrence Mass, M.D., "Cancer in the Gay Community," *New York Native,* July 27–August 9, 1981.

3. Larry Bush, "Koch's Accomplishments: The Debate Continues," *New York Native,* September 7–20, 1981.

4. Larry Bush, "King Koch Talks to the Native," *New York Native,* October 5–18, 1981.

5. Larry Kramer, "A Personal Appeal from Larry Kramer," *New York Native,* August 24–September 2, 1981.

6. Lee Hudson, interview by author, December 11, 2009.

7. Ibid.

8. Bush, "King Koch."

9. Bush, "Koch's Accomplishments"; Bush, "King Koch."

10. Randy Shilts, *And the Band Played On: Politics, People and the AIDS Epidemic* (New York: St. Martin's, 2000), 379–80; D. J. Sencer, "Major Urban Health Departments: The Ideal and the Real," *Health Affairs* 2, no. 4 (1983): 93; Hudson interview by author.

11. Shilts, *And the Band Played On,* 380.

12. Hudson interview by author.

13. David Sencer to Nat Leventhal, April 20, 1982, 74–168–6, Koch Papers, La Guardia and Wagner Archives; Shilts, *And the Band Played On,* 279. I would like to thank Steven

Levine and Douglas DiCarlo of the La Guardia and Wagner Archives for sending me the document cited.

14. *New York Native,* April 26–May 9 and May 10–23, 1982.

15. Larry Kramer, "1,112 and Counting," *New York Native,* March 14–27, 1983. The essay politicized so many gay readers that the playwright Tony Kushner wrote that "1,112 and Counting" "changed the world for all of us" (Michael Specter, "Larry Kramer, the Man Who Warned America about AIDS, Can't Stop Fighting Hard and Loud," *New Yorker,* May 13, 2002).

16. Hudson interview by author; reminiscences of Lee Hudson, December 10, 1993, Columbia University Oral History Research Collection (hereafter Columbia), 22.

17. Richard Kaye, "Anatomy of a Smear: Making Hay with Homophobia," *New York Native,* September 13–26, 1982; Shilts, *And the Band Played On,* 246, 248.

18. EIK to Sencer, May 5, 1983, 74–168–07, Koch Papers; James D'Eramo, "Not a Bureaucrat," *New York Native,* May 9–22, 1983.

19. Larry Bush, "Notes from a Symposium," *New York Native,* May 9–22, 1983.

20. Kaye, "Koch Meets with AIDS Network." On building reversal see Steven C. Arvanette, "Koch Relents on 13th Street Building," *New York Native,* June 20–July 3, 1983; EIK to Sencer, May 5, 1983.

21. Bush, "Notes from a Symposium"; Howard Kurtz, "Mayors Call for Action on AIDS; Government Asked to Guarantee Care for Its Victims," *Washington Post,* June 13, 1983.

22. Kurtz, "Mayors Call for Action"; "Mrs. Heckler Asks More AIDS Funds," *New York Times,* August 18, 1983; Lawrence K. Altman, "Fewer AIDS Cases Filed at End of '83," *New York Times,* January 6, 1984.

23. Gregg Bordowitz, interview by Sarah Schulman, December 17, 2002, ACT UP Oral History Project, interview #004, www.actuporalhistory.org (April 28, 2008); Edward Alwood, *Straight News: Gays, Lesbians, and the News Media* (New York: Columbia University Press, 1996), 235.

24. Jesus Rangel, "City Expanding Its Plan to Help Victims of Aids," *New York Times,* March 30, 1985.

25. Michael Specter, "Larry Kramer, the Man Who Warned America about AIDS, Can't Stop Fighting Hard and Loud," *New Yorker,* May 13, 2002, 63.

26. Ibid.

27. Shilts, *And the Band Played On,* 109, 181; *New York Times,* April 18, 1984.

28. Richard Kaye, "Anatomy of a Smear: Making Hay with Homophobia," *New York Native,* September 13–26, 1982.

29. *New York Times,* March 8, 1986.

30. Ibid., September 4, 1985; Koch to author, January 23, 2008.

31. *New York Times,* September 2, 1985.

32. Ibid., September 25 and September 9, 1985.

33. EIK to Sencer, October 4, 1985, AIDS, subject files series 80049–3, Koch Papers; *New York Times,* October 31, 1985; and Koch to Everard Spa, November 7, 1985; New St. Marks Baths to EIK, November 14, 1985; Plato's Retreat to EIK, November 14, 1985, all

in AIDS, subject files series 80049–3, Koch Papers; Hudson interview, Columbia, 26–27.

34. *New York Times,* October 4 and 5, 1985; Hudson interview, Columbia, 26–28.

35. S. F. Hurley, D. J. Jolley, and J. M. Kaldor, "Effectiveness of Needle-Exchange Programmes for Prevention of HIV Infection," *Lancet* 21, no. 349 (June 21, 1997): 1797–800.

36. EIK to Barbara Starrett, M.D., February 3, 1986, subject files series 800949–4; EIK to All District Attorneys, August 20, 1985; Elizabeth Holtzman to EIK, September 20, 1985, AIDS, subject files series 80049–3, all in Koch Papers; *New York Times,* November 8, 1988, and January 30, 1989.

37. *New York Times,* September 6, 1985.

38. Harding to EIK, November 17, 1987, 23–57–3, Koch Papers.

39. *New York Times,* June 8, 1987.

40. Ibid., May 25 and October 10, 1987.

41. Ibid., May 25, 1987; EIK to Brezenoff, January 6, 1987, and Joseph to EIK, December 9, 1986, subject files series 80049–5, Koch Papers.

42. *New York Times,* May 25, 1987.

43. Jones to EIK, June, 24, 1987; EIK to Dunne, July 1, 1987; Dunne to EIK, July 9, 1987, all in AIDS, subject files series 80049–5, Koch Papers.

44. EIK to Dunne, August 4, 1987; Joseph to EIK, August 4, 1987; Stephen Joseph, "AIDS: A Tale of Two Cities: A Report to the Mayor, October 19, 1987," all in AIDS, subject files series 80049–5, Koch Papers.

45. Joseph, "AIDS: A Tale of Two Cities."

46. First flyer from ACT UP Wall Street demonstration, ca. April 1987, reproduced at www. actupny.org/documents/1stFlyer.html (April 28, 2008).

47. Paula Span, "Getting Militant about AIDS; ACT-UP's Mission and the Escalating Protest," *Washington Post,* March 28, 1989.

48. ACT UP Capsule History, www.actupny.org/documents/capsule-home.html (April 28, 2008). See also Larry Kramer, interview by Sarah Schulman, November 15, 2003, and Bordowitz interview.

49. Ibid.

50. Hudson interview, Columbia, 22.

21. CRIME AND POLICE ISSUES (1978–84)

1. *New York Times,* January 1 and 31, 1978.

2. Reminiscences of Robert McGuire, 1992, Columbia University Oral History Research Collection (hereafter Columbia), 18.

3. Robert McGuire, interview by author, May 22, 2006; see also McGuire interview, Columbia, 29.

4. *New York Times,* May 18, 1978.

5. Ibid., December 9, 1979.

6. Ibid., July 1, 1978.

7. Ibid., April 16, 1978.

8. McGuire interview by author.

9. *New York Times,* September 5 and October 25, 1980.

10. McGuire interview by author.

11. *New York Times,* April 15, 1979.

12. Ibid., January 12, 1978, and April 4 and May 4, 1981.

13. Charles Brecher, Raymond D. Horton, Robert A. Cropf, and Dean Michael Mead, *Power Failure: New York City Politics and Policy since 1960* (New York, Oxford University Press, 1993), 280.

14. Ibid., 277–81.

15. McGuire interview by author.

16. *New York Times,* December 17, 1978.

17. Ibid., June 7, 1981, and December 17, 1978.

18. Ibid.; McGuire interview by author.

19. Vincent Broderick, interview by author, Wagner Oral History Project, La Guardia and Wagner Archives, 22–23.

20. *New York Times,* March 6, 1982.

21. Andrew Karmen, *New York Murder Mystery: The True Story behind the Crime Crash of the 1990s* (New York: New York University Press, 2000), 19, 21.

22. Ibid., graph 1.1, "Trends in Murders, New York City, 1955–1998," 17.

23. *New York Times,* January 26, 1978, December 7, 1980, and November 18, 1980.

24. Ibid., November 18, 1980.

25. Ibid., August 18, 1979.

26. See Allan Wolper, "From De Sapio to Big Ed," *Soho Weekly News,* October 18, 1979; editorial, *New York Times,* October 26, 1979; Edward I. Koch, "Out the Johns and Bring on the Shame," *New York Daily News,* March 16, 2008 (March 18, 2009).

27. *New York Times,* March 17 and 20, 1979.

28. Ibid., June 15, 1979.

29. Ibid., March 17 and 20, 1979.

30. Ibid., March 17, 1979.

31. Ibid., September 11, 1979.

32. Ibid., March 28, September 8, October 13, and December 30, 1979, and May 29, 1980.

33. Ibid., August 18 and 23, 1979.

34. Ibid., August 18, 1979.

35. Ibid., July 19, 1981; McGuire interview by author.

36. *New York Times,* July 5, 1981, and January 30, 1983.

37. See McGuire to EIK, July 27, 1981, 107–229–6, Koch Papers, La Guardia and Wagner Archives.

38.   *New York Times,* March 5 and July 16, 1981.

39.   Ibid., January 4, 1981.

40.   Ibid., July 1, 1981, and August 6, 1983.

41.   Ibid., February 22, 1980.

42.   Ibid., April 11, 1982.

43.   Ibid.

44.   Ibid., June 11, 1980, and March 21, 1981.

45.   Ibid., August 27, 1980.

46.   Ibid., August 27 and July 31, 1980, and October 18, 1981.

47.   Ibid., August 5, 1974. See Joe Austin, *Taking the Train* (New York: Columbia University Press, 2001), 82–83.

48.   *New York Times,* July 30, 1980.

49.   Austin, *Taking the Train,* 6, 13. While Austin's book has much valuable oral history and analysis of masterpiece graffiti as art, he romanticizes graffiti.

50.   Miriam Greenberg, *Branding New York: How a City in Crisis Was Sold to the World* (New York: Routledge, 2008), 63, 148–49.

51.   Elizabeth Currid, *The Warhol Economy: How Fashion, Art and Music Drive New York City* (Princeton, N.J.: Princeton University Press, 2007), 1–16.

52.   James Q. Wilson and George L. Kelling, "Making Neighborhoods Safe: Sometimes 'Fixing Broken Windows' Does More to Reduce Crime Than Conventional 'Incident-oriented' Policing," *Atlantic Monthly,* February 1, 1989, 48; James Q. Wilson and George L. Kelling, "Broken Windows," *Atlantic Monthly,* March 1, 1982, 29–38. For an excellent critique of broken windows policing, see Alex. S. Vitale, *City of Disorder: How the Quality of Life Campaign Transformed New York Politics* (New York: New York University Press, 2008), 46–50.

53.   Vitale, *City of Disorder,* 49.

54.   McGuire interview by author.

55.   Wilson and Kelling, "Making Neighborhoods Safe," 49.

56.   McGuire interview by author.

57.   Ibid.

58.   Ibid.

59.   *New York Times,* September 18, 1982.

60.   Commanding officer, Auto Crime Division, to Chief, Organized Crime Control, n.d. (1983), 29–74–10, Koch Papers.

61.   *New York Times,* February 12, 1982.

62.   Kevin Frawley (deputy coordinator, criminal justice) to EIK, April 21, 1983, 29–74–10, Koch Papers.

63.   *New York Times,* June 30, 1983.

64.   John F. Keenan to EIK, August 4, 1981; EIK to Mulhearn, August 8, 1983, both in 29–74–10, Koch Papers.

65.   Keenan to EIK, August 4, 1981, 29–74–10, Koch Papers.

66. *New York Times,* November 23, 1980.

67. Ibid., June 30, 1983.

68. Ibid., July 2, 1983.

69. Conboy to EIK, June 1, 1981, 107–229–11, Koch Papers.

70. *New York Times,* April 12, 1979.

71. Ibid., April 13, 1979.

72. Ibid., April 14, 1979.

73. Ibid., December 1, 1979.

74. Ibid., May 9, 1979.

75. Ibid., March 26, 2005.

76. Ibid., April 19, 1982, and February 8, 1983.

77. Ibid., February 27, 1983.

78. Ibid., March 4 and 23, 1983.

79. Ibid., December 8, 1983.

80. Ibid., December 31, 1983.

81. McGuire interview by author.

82. *New York Times,* July 17, 1983, and July 25, 1984; House Subcommittee on Criminal Justice, Committee on the Judiciary, *Report on Hearings in New York City on Police Misconduct,* 98th Cong., 2d sess., 1984, Committee Print 19, 1–18, www.lexisnexis.com/congcomp/getdoc?CRDC-ID=CMP-1984-HJH-0015 (viewed January 11, 2010).

83. *New York Times,* July 17, 1983.

84. Ibid., July 21, 1983.

85. Ibid., October 13, 1983.

86. Ibid., September 16, 1983.

87. Ibid., October 13, 1983. McGuire served from January 1, 1978, to December 31, 1983, a total of six years.

88. Reminiscences of Benjamin Ward, 1992, Columbia, 100.

89. *New York Times,* September 15 and 20, and November 29, 1983, and November 15, 1984; and Subcommittee on Criminal Justice, *Report,* 17–21.

22. THE WARD YEARS: POLICE, CRIME, AND POLICE CRIMES (1984–89)

1. Owen Moritz, "Ex-Top Cop Ward Is Dead," *New York Daily News,* June 11, 2002; *New York Times,* June 11, 2002; Christopher Reed, "Benjamin Ward: As New York's First Black Police Chief, He Mixed Fairness with Conservatism," *(London) Guardian,* June 12, 2002; Andrew. Karmen, *New York Murder Mystery: The True Story behind the Crime Crash of the 1990s* (New York: New York University Press, 2000), 17.

2. Reminiscences of Benjamin Ward, 1992, Columbia University Oral History Research Collection (hereafter Columbia), 9–13.

3. Ibid., 37.

4. Ibid., 23–24.

5. Moritz, "Ex-Top Cop Ward Is Dead"; *New York Times,* June 11, 2002; Reed, "Benjamin Ward."

6. Reminiscences of Robert McGuire, 1992, Columbia, 85.

7. Vincent Cannato, *The Ungovernable City* (New York: Basic, 2002), 484–91.

8. *New York Times,* November 8, 1983.

9. Ibid., October 19, 1984, and May 24, 1988.

10. McGuire interview, Columbia, 85.

11. *New York Times,* October 20, 1984.

12. Ibid., April 16, October 20, 23, 25, and 26, 1984.

13. Ibid., March 16, 1987; Associated Press, "P.B.A. Drops Expulsion Plan," March 27, 1987, Nexis; *New York Times,* March 31, 1987; Edward I. Koch to author, December 27, 2007; *New York Times,* October 2, 1989.

14. Andrew Karmen, *New York Murder Mystery: The True Story behind the Crime Crash of the 1990s* (New York: New York University Press, 2000), 118, 145, 150.

15. *New York Times,* October 2, 1989; Ward interview, Columbia, 148.

16. *New York Times,* July 29 and 30, 1987.

17. Ward interview, Columbia, 203; Moritz, "Ex-Top-Cop Ward Is Dead."

18. *New York Times,* July 30, 1987.

19. Ibid., February 1, 1989.

20. Ibid., February 13 and October 1, 1989.

21. Ward to EIK, September 7, 1984, and Robert J. Johnston, Jr. to Ward, September 19, 1984, both in 108–230–8, Koch Papers, La Guardia and Wagner Archives; Samuel Walker, *The New World of Police Accountability* (Thousand Oaks, Calif.: Sage, 2005), 43.

22. Melinda Beck, with Martin Kasindorf, Anne Underwood, and Shawn Doherty, "New York's Bad Apples," *Newsweek,* May 6, 1985, 31; Victoria Irwin, "Brutality Charges Spark Concern for Police Behavior in New York," *Christian Science Monitor,* April 30, 1985.

23. *New York Times,* September 24, 1986.

24. Ibid., April 25 and 28, 1985.

25. Ibid., October 18 and October 13, 1985.

26. Ibid., April 25, April 30, and August 1, 1985; John Shanahan, Associated Press, "Mayor Fires Medical Examiner for Poor Management," October 30, 1987, Nexis.

27. *New York Times,* February 22 and 23, 1985.

28. Ibid., October 9, 1985.

29. Ibid., August 8 and 13, 1985.

30. Ibid., November 25, 1985, and January 4, 1986.

31. Ibid., November 26, 1985.

32. Ibid., January 24, February 3, and March 28, 1987.

33. Ibid., August 29, 1990.

34. Gary Langer, Associated Press, "Woman with Knife Killed by Police Officer during Eviction," October 29, 1984, Nexis; Dan Collins, United Press International, "Federal Grand Jury to Investigate Gross' Office," February 1, 1985, Nexis.

35. Botnick to EIK, November 9, 1984, 14–33–21, Koch Papers.

36. Ibid.; Dr. Robert John to EIK, November 15, 1984, 14–33–24, Koch Papers.

37. *New York Times,* January 27, 1985; May 9, 1986; and February 27, 1987.

38. Ibid., November 21, 1984.

39. Ibid., November 23, 1984, and March 29, 1991.

40. Ibid., November 2, 1984; Ward to EIK, November 8, 1984, 14–33–21, Koch Papers; Ward interview, Columbia, 177–78; NYPD press release, February 1, 1985, 108-230-9, Koch Papers.

41. Robert McGuire, interview by author, May 22, 2006.

42. Ibid.

43. *New York Times,* December 24, 1984; Margot Hornblower, "Selection Begins for the Goetz Jury; Attempted Murder Trial Underway," *Washington Post,* March 24, 1987; *New York Times,* December 30, 1984. See the case study in Joel Samaha, *Criminal Law* (Stamford, Conn.: Thomson Wadsworth, 2004), 201–205.

44. *New York Times,* January 1, 1985; Hornblower, "Selection Begins for the Goetz Jury"; *New York Times,* December 30, 1984; United Press International, "Goetz Trial Adapted for Public TV," October 21, 1987, Nexis; *New York Times,* December 25, 1984.

45. *New York Times,* February 22 and February 9, 1985.

46. Ibid., February 1, 1985.

47. Ibid., March 28, 1985, and June 17, 1987.

48. Ibid., April 28, 1996.

49. Beck et al., "New York's Bad Apples"; Irwin, "Brutality Charges Spark Concern."

50. "2001 General Election Statement and Return of the Votes for the Office of Mayor," New York City Board of Elections, November 28, 2001, http://vote.nyc.ny.us/results. html (November 6, 2009); "When Bernie Goetz Was New York City," editorial, *New York Daily News,* December .19, 2004; Bill Hutchinson, "Actor Bronson Dies at 81," *Daily News,* September 1, 2003.

51. Esther Mipaas, "Tompkins Square Park," in Kenneth T. Jackson, ed., *The Encyclopedia of New York City* (New Haven, Conn.: Yale University Press, 1990), 1190. In 1991 the park was closed for an extended period for reconstruction, resulting in the final victory of the gentrifiers.

52. *New York Times,* August 14, 1988.

53. Ibid.

54. Ibid.

55. Ibid. and August 12, 1988; "N.Y. Officers Disciplined over Handling of Riot," *Washington Post,* August 25, 1988; *New York Times,* January 2, 1989.

56. "N.Y. Officers Disciplined."

57. *New York Times,* September 8, 1988.

58. Ibid., January 2 and March 24, 1989.

59. Ibid., April 19, 1989.

60. Ibid., March 24, 1987.

61. See Ward to EIK, June 8 1987; Ward to EIK, June 9, 1987, 12–30–2, Koch Papers.

62. *New York Times,* October 1, 1989, and March 23, 1988.

63. EIK to Conboy, October 1, 1985, 108–231–1, Koch Papers; Ward to EIK, April 28, 1986, 108–231–3, Koch Papers.

64. Gray to EIK, n.d. (1984), 23–56–6, Koch Papers; Clark Whelton to EIK, enclosing speech to National Organization of Black Law Enforcement Executives, June 27, 1988, 080077–5, speeches series, "blacks" files, Koch Papers; remarks by Mayor Edward I. Koch at Operation Pressure Point II press conference, January 26, 1985, 080077–8, speeches series, "Criminal Justice," January–October 1985, Koch Papers.

65. Ward to EIK, February 7, 1986, 108–231–1, Koch Papers.

66. "The United States Police/Public Consultation: A Perspective from Police Commissioner Benjamin Ward," in "Models of Police/Public Consultation in Europe," Cranfield-Wolfson Colloquium, 1984, Cranfield Institute of Technology, Cranfield Bedford, United Kingdom, 1984, 108–230–10, Koch Papers.

67. Ibid.

68. Ward interview, Columbia, 110–11.

69. Ibid., 112–13.

70. Ward to Brezenoff, October 9, 1984; Brezenoff to Ward, October 24, 1984, 108–230–8, Koch Papers.

71. Brezenoff to Ward, July 18, 1985, 108–230–11, Koch Papers.

72. Stern to Brezenoff, July 12 and 17, 1985; Brezenoff to Ward, July 19, 1985, all in 108–230–11, Koch Papers.

73. Ward to EIK, February 7, 1986, 108–231–1, Koch Papers, ; Brezenoff to Ward, December 13, 1985, 108–231–11, Koch Papers.

74. Ward to Brezenoff, May 23, 1986; Deputy Police Chief Frances C. Hall, "Crack: Briefing for the Mayor," July 23, 1985, 108–230–10, Koch Papers; *New York Times,* April 20, 1988, and January 7, 1991.

75. *New York Times,* June 27, and August 5 and 22, 1986; Brademas to EIK, October 9, 1986, 108-231-6, Koch Papers.

76. Bruce L. Benson, David W. Rasmussen, and David L. Sollars, "Police Bureaucracies, Their Incentives, and the War on Drugs," *Public Choice* 83, no. 1 (April 1, 1995): 39.

77. *New York Times,,* June 24, 1988.

78. Ward interview, Columbia, 119.

79. *New York Times,* June 24, 1988.

80. Ibid.; Morgenthau to Ward, July 12, 1989, 12–30–24, Koch Papers.

81. Brademas to EIK, October 9, 1986, 108–231–6, Koch Papers; *New York Times,* January 12, 1987.

82. Ibid.

83. Benjamin Ward to EIK, January 6, 1987, 108-231-7, Koch Papers.

84. *New York Times,* June 7, 1987.

85. Ibid., June 24, 1988.

86. Ibid., June 24, 1988, and March 6, 1996.

87. Ibid., April 4, 1989. See also Karmen, *New York Murder Mystery,* 160–84.

23. DON'T FOLLOW COUNTY LEADERS, AND WATCH YOUR PARKING METERS (1986)

1.   *New York Times,* January 12, 1986.

2.   Edward I. Koch, with Daniel Paisner, *Citizen Koch: An Autobiography* (New York: St. Martin's, 1992), 203.

3.   Jack Newfield and Wayne Barrett, *City for Sale: Ed Koch and the Betrayal of New York* (New York: Harper and Row, 1988), 59.

4.   Ibid., 45–55; *New York Times,* March 14, March 27, and May 23, 1986.

5.   *New York Times,* February 19, 1986, and October 7, 1987; Newfield and Barrett, *City for Sale,* 282, 300; Tom Robbins, "The Kings of Trash: The City's Garbage Honchos' Reputed Mob Links Have Been Anything but a Waste," *New York Daily News,* December 17, 1995; Barbara Ross and Tom Robbins, "Carted Off to Prison, Trash Bigwig Gets 2 Years, 7.5m Fine," *New York Daily News,* January 28, 1997.

6.   John LoCicero, interview by author, October 25, 2000.

7.   *New York Times,* May 12, 2006.

8.   LoCicero interview; George Arzt, interview by author, June 1, 2007.

9.   Arzt interview.

10. Stanley Brezenoff, interview by author, May 23, 2006.

11. Reminiscences of Stanley Brezenoff, 1992, Columbia University Oral History Research Collection (hereafter Columbia), 109–10; Arzt interview.

12. Brezenoff interview, Columbia, 110–11; Brezenoff interview by author.

13. *New York Times,* October 10, 1986.

14. Ibid., April 14, 1988.

15. Ibid., June 10, 1988.

16. Brezenoff interview, Columbia, 109.

17. *New York Times,* May 9, 1988.

18. Ibid., June 10 and August 9, 1988; Sullivan, letter to the editor, *New York Times,* September 10, 1989.

19. Ibid., September 26, 1974; "Convicted Politician Bertram Podell, 79," *Washington Post,* August 22, 2005.

20. *New York Times,* September 26, 1974; Wayne Barrett, *Rudy: An Investigative Biography of Rudolph Giuliani* (New York: Basic, 2000), 86–87.

21. Associated Press, "A List of People Who Wrote Letters Supporting the Ex-senator Jailed at Rikers," November 4, 2004, Nexis.

22. David Brown, interview by author, September 27, 2004.

23. Brezenoff interview by author; Brown interview.

24. Arzt interview.

25. Ibid.

26. Ibid.

27. Peter F. Vallone, *Learning to Govern: My Life in New York Politics, From Hell Gate to City Hall* (New York: Chaucer Press, 2005), 112.

28. Ibid., 98.

29. *New York Times,* April 22, 1986.

30. Newfield and Barrett, *City for Sale,* 87–88; LoCicero interview, June 1, 2007; President's Commission on Organized Crime, *Organized Crime of Asian Origin: Record of Hearing III, October 23–25, 1984, New York* (Washington, D.C.: Government Printing Office, 1985, 93–94; Peter Kwong, *The New Chinatown* (New York: Macmillan, 1996), 118–20; *New York Times,* October 25, 1984, September 2, 1990, and January 6, 1991.

31. *New York Times,* January 16 and 22, and February 24, 1986.

32. *New York Times* January 27, 1986.

33. "Mayor Koch Favors Jailing 2 in Growing Bribery Scandal," *Washington Post,* January 27, 1986.

34. Newfield and Barrett, *City for Sale,* 100–101; *New York Times,* March 15, 1986; Robert D. McFadden, "Manes Is a Suicide, Stabbing Himself at Home in Queens," *New York Times,* March 14, 1986.

35. Newfield and Barrett, *City for Sale,* 102; *New York Times,* March 17, 1986.

36. Koch, *Citizen Koch,* 211.

37. *New York Times,* January 15, 1987.

38. Koch, *Citizen Koch,* 211.

39. Newfield and Barrett, *City for Sale,* 244–50; *New York Times,* March 27, 1987; *U.S. v. Kaplan,* 886 F.2d 536 (2d Cir. 1989).

40. *U.S. v. Kaplan.*

41. Newfield and Barrett, *City for Sale,* 244–50; *U.S. v. Kaplan.*

42. *New York Times,* October 8, 1986; United Press International, October 7, 1986, Nexis.

43. *New York Times,* October 13, 1986.

44. Seena Gressin, United Press International, October 1, 1986, Nexis.

45. *New York Times,* October 8, 1986; Newfield and Barrett, *City for Sale,* 36, 89–91; Larry Elkin, Associated Press, "City Official Pleads Guilty to Payoff Charges," March 10, 1986, Nexis; Larry McShane, Associated Press, "Former City Official Tells of Splitting Bribes in Bathroom," October 8, 1986, Nexis.

46. Newfield and Barrett, *City for Sale,* 246–47; *U.S. v. Kaplan.*

47. Newfield and Barrett, *City for Sale,* 244–50; *U.S. v. Kaplan.*

48. *New York Times,* June 25, 1984, and January 28, January 21, and March 11, 1986; Newfield and Barrett, *City for Sale,* 93–96, 244–57.

49. Newfield and Barrett, *City for Sale,* 244–50.

50. Stanley Penn, "Tainted City—Above It All: New York's Scandals Don't Seem to Harm Mayor Edward Koch—His Popularity Is Enormous," *Wall Street Journal,* April 30, 1986.

51. Newfield and Barrett, *City for Sale,* 249–57.

52. Meade Esposito, interview by Jonathan Soffer, May 15, 1991, Robert F. Wagner Oral History Project, La Guardia and Wagner Archives.

53. See Jonathan Rieder, *Canarsie: The Jews and Italians of Brooklyn against Liberalism* (Cambridge, Mass.: Harvard University Press, 1985), 52.

54. Newfield and Barrett, *City for Sale,* 303–343; *New York Times,* September 4, 1993; Esposito interview.

55. *New York Times,* October 5, 1987.

56. Barrett, *Rudy,* 16–171. On D'Amato's involvement with Wedtech, see Leonard Lurie, *Senator Pothole* (Secaucus, N.J.: Carol Publishing, 1994), 326–34. I have standardized the eccentric trial lawyer's moniker, e. Robert Wallach. *United States v. Simon,* 909 F.2d 662 (2d. Cir., 1990), affirmed Simon's conviction and describes Simon's criminal activities in detail.

57. *New York Times,* October 17, 2002, and June 12, 1986.

58. Ibid., June 12, 1986.

59. *New York Times,* February 22 and 23, 1986.

60. Marianne Yen, "Who's Who in the New York City Corruption Scandals," *Washington Post,* August 26, 1987.

61. *New York Times,* May 6, 1986.

62. Ibid., May 6, 15, and 31, and June 4, 1986. On Botnick's allegation of a "vendetta" against him by *New York Times* reporter Josh Barbanel, see reminiscences of Victor Botnick, 1993, Columbia, 159.

63. Newfield and Barrett, *City for Sale,* 296.

64. "The Botnick Principle," *New York Times,* June 8, 1986.

65. Ibid., June 10, 1986; Newfield and Barrett, *City for Sale,* 297.

66. "Victor Botnick Dead," *New York Daily News,* October 17, 2002; *New York Times,* October 17, 2002.

67. Newfield and Barrett, *City for Sale,* 389, 394–95; *New York Times,* June 20, 1987. See Shana Alexander, *When She Was Bad: The Story of Bess, Hortense, Sukhreet and Nancy* (New York: Random House, 1990), 127–32, 193.

68. Newfield and Barrett, *City for Sale,* 391; William Neuman, "Cancer Kills 'Bess Mess' Big Capasso at Age 55," *New York Post,* March 15, 2001; John Hanrahan, United Press International, "House Burglar Triggers Sweeping New York Corruption Probe," May 17, 1987, Nexis.

69. Alexander, *When She Was Bad,* 13, 134.

70. Newfield and Barrett, *City for Sale,* 391; Alexander, *When She Was Bad,* 156; Neuman, "Cancer Kills 'Bess Mess' Big Capasso."

71. Newfield and Barrett, *City for Sale,* 395; Alexander, *When She Was Bad,* 172, 183; *New York Times,* June 11, 1987.

72. Newfield and Barrett, *City for Sale,* 396–98; Alexander, *When She Was Bad,* 161–91.

73. Harold R. Tyler Jr., "Report to the Mayor on the Investigation of Bess Myerson, Commissioner of Cultural Affairs," New York City Municipal Library, 5. This report, originally held as confidential, was made public by the mayor on June 10, 1987, after the *Village Voice* published excerpts.

74. *New York Times,* June 11, 1987.

75. Alexander, *When She Was Bad,* 193–95; *New York Times,* January 23, 1987.

76. EIK to Peter Zimroth, June 10, 1989, 12–30–16, Koch Papers, La Guardia and Wagner Archives; Tyler, "Report to the Mayor," 5.

77. *New York Times,* June 12, 1987.

78. Barrett, *Rudy,* 160–61; *New York Times,* December 23, 1988.

79. Arzt interview.

80. Barrett, *Rudy,* 175–88.

81. *New York Times,* October 7, 1993.

82. Barrett, *Rudy,* 188.

83. Ibid., 178–88; Arzt interview.

84. Arzt interview. On Rickman see reminiscences of Lee Hudson, 1993, Columbia, 4–5. See also Barrett, *Rudy,* 183.

85. Arzt interview.

86. Ibid.

87. The 1976 Nathan study is discussed in Charles Brecher and Diana Roswick, "The City's Role in Health Care," in Raymond D. Horton and Charles Brecher, eds., *Setting Municipal Priorities, 1980* (New York: Universe Books, 1979), 134–70.

88. Barrett, *Rudy,* 175–88.

89. Arzt interview.

90. Undated press release (1987) bearing legend "This was never released," 80049:6, Koch Papers.

91. Barrett, *Rudy,* 175.

92. Arzt interview.

93. *New York Times,* August 8, 1987.

94. Ibid.; Koch, *Citizen Koch,* 225.

95. Associated Press, "Mayor and Prelate to Pen Joint Book," August 23, 1987, Nexis.

96. *New York Times,* August 10, 1987.

97. Associated Press, "Mother Teresa Visits Koch."

98. *New York Times,* August 21, 1987.

99. Koch, *Citizen Koch,* 209, 214.

100. *New York Times,* August 24, 1987.

101. Alair Townsend, interview by author, May 23, 2006.

102. Brezenoff interview by author.

103. Hudson interview, Columbia, 16–20.

104. Ibid., 20.

105. On Catholic and Orthodox Jewish opposition, see Margot Hornblower, "Gay-Rights Bill Roils New York; Catholics, Hasidic Jews Opposed Discrimination Ban," *Washington Post*, March 11, 1986; *New York Times*, August 12, 1986.

106. Hornblower, "Gay-Rights Bill Roils New York."

107. Ibid.

108. EIK to author, December 27, 2007.

109. *New York Times*, March 21, 1986.

110. By 2008, 53 percent of New York State residents supported same-sex marriage, and, given the partisan breakdown of the poll, the figure was much higher for the heavily Democratic city (Quinnipiac Poll, June 12, 2008, http://www.quinnipiac.edu/x1318.xml?ReleaseID=1184 [April 27, 2008]).

111. *Board of Estimate of City of New York v. Morris*, 489 U.S. 688 (1989).

112. Vallone, *Learning to Govern*, 123; *New York Times*, November 21, 1986.

113. Joan Lebow, "New York City Charter Stirs Controversy—Developers Fear Revision Will Bind Them in Red Tape," *Wall Street Journal*, November 13, 1989; *New York Times*, November 8, 1989.

114. *New York Times*, November 1, 1989.

115. Ibid., November 6, 1989.

116. Ibid., April 23, 1990; Vallone, *Learning to Govern*, 156–70.

117. *New York Times*, October 22, 1986.

118. Ibid., October 22, 1986, and December 18, 1992.

119. *New York Magazine*, April, 11, 1988, 96.

24. KOCH'S ENDGAME (1988–89)

1. *New York Times*, March 29, 1987.

2. Ibid., December 21, 1986.

3. Ibid.

4. Jim Harding to Edward I. Koch, December 30, 1986, 23–56–24, Koch Papers, La Guardia and Wagner Archives; press release, December 31, 1986, 23–56–25, Koch Papers; *New York Times*, January 1, 1987.

5. *New York Times*, December 25, 1986.

6. Ibid., December 22, 1987.

7. Ibid., December 29, 1987, and January 21, January 23, and February 12, 1988.

8. Ibid., December 29, 1986.

9. Al Sharpton, interview by author, June 6, 2007.

10. Thomas Edsall, "Jackson's New Coalition and Koch's '89 Race: Can City Hall Balance of Power Be Altered?" *Washington Post*, April 14, 1988.

11.   *New York Times,* March 10, 1988.

12.   Ibid., March 14, April 2, and April 9, 1988.

13.   Reminiscences of Stanley Brezenoff, 1992, Columbia University Oral History Research Collection (hereafter Columbia), 123–24.

14.   Ibid., 126.

15.   *New York Times,* April 11, 1988.

16.   Ibid., April 18, 1988.

17.   Edsall, "Jackson's New Coalition."

18.   *New York Times,* May 1, 1988.

19.   EIK to Harding, April, 14, 1988, 23–57–5, Koch Papers.

20.   *New York Times,* May 1, 1988.

21.   Howard Kurtz, "Koch Endorses Gore, Jackson Parries Critics," *Washington Post,* April 15, 1988.

22.   *New York Times,* April 24, 1988.

23.   Kurtz, "Koch Endorses Gore."

24.   *New York Times,* April 20, 1988.

25.   Ibid.; Edsall, "Jackson's New Coalition."

26.   *New York Times,* July 19, 1988.

27.   Howard Kurtz, "New York to Koch: Clam Up! The Mayor May Be Unbeatable But He Is No Longer So Lovable," *Washington Post,* May 29, 1988

28.   *New York Times,* July 19, 29, and 30, 1988.

29.   EIK to author, January 23, 2008.

30.   Kurtz, "New York to Koch"; *New York Times,* July 19, 29, and 30, 1988.

31.   *New York Times,* May 21, 1988.

32.   Ibid., August 1, 1988; Howard Kurtz, "Jackson, Koch Meet to Mend Fences; Conciliatory Mayor Gets Cool Response," *Washington Post,* August 31, 1988; *New York Times,* September 1 and 2, 1988.

33.   Ibid.

34.   *New York Times,* July 1, 1988.

35.   Ibid.

36.   Ibid., July 30, 1988, and May 9, 1989.

37.   Howard Kurtz, "On Talk Show, N.Y. Mayor Koch Declares Candidacy for 4th Term," *Washington Post,* July 14, 1989.

38.   Harding to EIK, May 20, 1988, 23–57–5, Koch Papers; Harding to EIK, April 5, 1989, 23–56–11, Koch Papers; Harding to EIK, March 3, 1989, 23–57–12, Koch Papers; EIK to Harding, April 11, 1989, 23–57–13, Koch Papers.

39.   Harding to EIK, May 20, 1988, 23–57–5, Koch Papers; Harding to EIK, April 5, 1989, 23–56–11, Koch Papers; Harding to EIK, March 3, 1989, 23–57–12, Koch Papers; EIK to Harding, April 11, 1989, 23–57–13, Koch Papers.

40.   *New York Times,* June 22 and 23, 1989.

41.   Ibid., January 13, 1989.

42.   Reminiscences of Paul Dickstein, 1992, Columbia, 103.

43. "How Koch Can Really Help Black Business," *Crain's New York Business,* October 24, 1988; EIK to Robert Esnard, October 28, 1988, 21–52–32, Koch Papers.

44. William Schneider, "An Insider's View of the Election," *Atlantic Monthly,* July 1, 1988, 29–57; EIK, letter to the editor, *Atlantic Monthly,* n.d., 800077–5, speeches series, "blacks" folders, Koch Papers.

45. "Ex-aide to Koch Indicted," *Washington Post,* August 5, 1989; *New York Times,* August 5, 1989, and April 5, 1991.

46. *New York Times,* August 25, 1989.

47. Brezenoff interview, Columbia, 127.

48. Mimi Hall and Bruce Frankel, "NYC Killing May Affect Vote; City Mayoral Election Just 19 Days Away," *USA Today,* August 25, 1989; Edward I. Koch, with Daniel Paisner, *Citizen Koch: An Autobiography* (New York: St. Martin's, 1992), 231.

49. Clarence Page, "New Yorkers Voted with Their Fears," *Chicago Tribune,* September 17, 1989.

50. *New York Times,* August 25, 1989.

51. EIK, *Citizen Koch,* 231.

52. Sharpton interview.

53. *New York Times,* August 31, 1989; EIK to author, January 23, 2008.

54. *New York Times,* September 28, 1989.

55. Brezenoff interview, Columbia, 132.

56. *New York Times,* September 2 and 3, 1989; Howard Kurtz, "N.Y. Mayoral Primary Is Cliffhanger; Pollsters, Papers Split over Koch, Dinkins," *Washington Post,* September 7, 1989; *New York Times,* September 6, 1989. On Dinkins's public image and the media, see Wilbur C. Rich, *David Dinkins and New York City Politics* (Albany: State University of New York Press, 2007), 124–30.

57. *New York Times,* September 14, 1989.

58. John Hull Mollenkopf, *A Phoenix in the Ashes: The Rise and Fall of the Koch Coalition in New York City Politics* (Princeton, N.J.: Princeton University Press, 1992), 170.

59. Ibid., 178.

60. Ibid., 179.

61. EIK, *Citizen Koch,* 234.

62. Ibid., 235.

63. *New York Times,* October 29, 1989.

64. Peter F. Vallone, *Learning to Govern: My Life in New York Politics, From Hell Gate to City Hall* (New York: Chaucer, 2005), 170.

25. EPILOGUE

1. Maggie Haberman, "Ed's Doin' Fine at 80," *New York Daily News,* December 10, 2004; Jonathan Soffer, notes on EIK's eightieth birthday, Gracie Mansion, December 9, 2004, in author's possession.

2. "Charles Schumer," *Almanac of American Politics,* http://nationaljournal.com/pubs/almanac/2000/people/ny/nys2.htm (November 25, 2007).; *New York Times,* November 2 and 4, 1998.

3. Edward I. Koch to author, January 23, 2008.

4. Soffer, Koch birthday notes.

5. Edward I. Koch and Christy Heady, *Buzz: How to Create It and Win with It* (New York: Amacom, 2007), 19; *New York Times,* April 15, 1989.

6. Edward I. Koch, with Daniel Paisner, *I'm Not Done Yet! Keeping at It, Remaining Relevant, and Having the Time of My Life* (New York: William Morrow, 2000), 35–38.

7. EIK, *Buzz,* 12–14, 19.

8. EIK, *I'm Not Done Yet,* 40–55.

9. Stephen Schaelfer, "Neck Injury Case Is a Bust," *USA Today,* July 9, 1998.

10. Associated Press, "Rockefeller Rollback; Agreement by Paterson, Legislative Leaders Would Dial Down Drug Law Penalties," *Newsday,* March 28, 2009.

11. EIK, *I'm Not Done Yet,* 147–49; "Winning the War on Drugs: A 'Second Chance' for Nonviolent Drug Offenders," *Harvard Law Review* 113, no. 6. (April 2000): 1485–1502; Edward I. Koch, interview by author, February 25, 2008. Sharpton was the principal adviser to Tawana Brawley, a fifteen year old from Newburgh, New York, who was found November 28, 1987, wrapped in a garbage bag, covered in feces, with racist slogans written on her chest. A grand jury later found her claim of rape by a white police officer, and that the whole affair was a hoax. In 1998 an assistant district attorney, whom Brawley supporters had accused of kidnapping, raping, and abusing Brawley, won a defamation suit against, and an award of $345,000 in damages from, Sharpton, Brawley, and attorneys Alton Maddox and C. Vernon Mason (Dorian Block, "Twenty Years Later Tawana Brawley Has Turned Back on the Past," *New York Daily News,* November 18, 2007; William Saletan, Ben Jacobs, and Avi Zenilman, "The Worst of Al Sharpton: A Troubling Tale from His Past," *Slate,* September 8, 2003, www.slate.com/id/2087557/ [January 12, 2010]).

12. H. Carl McCall, interview by author, February 15, 2005.

13. *New York Times,* September 13, 1990. On Giuliani's conservatism see David Greenberg, "Rudy a Lefty? Yeah, Right," *Washington Post,* October 28, 2007.

14. Edward I. Koch, *Giuliani, Nasty Man* (New York: Barricade Books, 1998), 8, 111–12.

15. Joshua M. Zeitz, *White Ethnic New York: Jews, Catholics, and the Shaping of Postwar Politics* (Chapel Hill: University of North Carolina Press, 2007), 2.

16. EIK, *Giuliani, Nasty Man,* 36.

17. John Marzulli and Alice McQuillan, "Bratton's Blackballed," *Daily News,* April 25, 1997.

18. EIK, *Giuliani, Nasty Man,* 11.

19. Andrew Kirtzman, *Rudy Giuliani: Emperor of the City* (New York: Perennial, 2001), 156.

20. EIK, *Giuliani, Nasty Man,* 18.

21. David Saltonstall, "He Burned His Bridges with Blacks; Little Help for Mayor after Series of Slights," *New York Daily News,* March 28, 1999.

22. EIK, *Giuliani, Nasty Man,* 21; EIK, *I'm Not Done Yet,* 105–11.

23. EIK, *I'm Not Done Yet,* 105–11.

24. Ibid., 142, 169–70.

25. EIK, *Giuliani, Nasty Man,* 89; Michael Daly, "Federal Case to Cost Taxpayers a Bundle," *New York Daily News,* December 3, 1997; David Lefer, "Rudy's Losing Causes Costly; Taxpayers Foot Bill in Free-Speech Cases," *New York Daily News,* November 28, 1999.

26. EIK, *Giuliani, Nasty Man,* 13.

27. Joel Siegel, Joe Mahoney, and Edward Lewine, "Rick and Hil: Attack, Attack, Attack: Competing Ads Bring out Bile between Them," *New York Daily News,* November 5, 2000.

28. Celeste Katz and Joel Siegel, "Leaping off Fence, Koch Lands on Ferrer's Side," *New York Daily News,* October 3, 2003.

29. Michael Saul, "Koch and Carey Backing Bloomy in Slap at Rival," *New York Daily News,* November 2, 2001.

30. Melissa Radler, "A Proud Jewish Democrat," *Jerusalem Post,* April 18, 2003.

31. "Koch: I Support Bush, His Stance on Iraq," AP Online, August 22, 2004, Nexis.

32. Michael Saul, "Koch Helping Republican Party," *New York Daily News,* April 22, 2004.

33. Jeff Jacoby, "Why Koch Is in Bush's Corner," *Boston Globe,* August 29, 2004.

34. The poll was conducted by Fabrizio, McLoughlin and Associates and reported in Jonathan Singer, "Parties Target Fla. Jews Who Switched to Bush," *Hill,* June 28, 2005; "Poll Shows Significant Increased Jewish Voter Turnout in Florida for Bush-Cheney Ticket," PR Newswire, December 6, 2004.

35. Ed Koch Commentary, Bloomberg Radio and e-mail, September 8, 2008, e-mail in possession of author; Alex Koppelman, "Koch: Giuliani Looks Like He'd Kill Old Woman in Wheelchair," *Salon,* September 6, 2008 www.salon.com/politics/war_room/2008/09/08/koch_giuliani/ (June 15, 2009).

36. Jennifer Siegel, "Koch on Bloomberg: He'd Be a Fine President," *Jewish Daily Forward,* June 20, 2007; *New York Times,* September 14, 2008; Koch Presidential Endorsement, EIK to author (and his e-mail list), September 9, 2008, e-mail in author's possession.

37. Ed Koch Commentary; EIK to author (and his e-mail list), March 30, 2009.

38. Joe Mahoney, "Koch Rips Andy over 'Homo' Flap," *Daily News,* January 27, 2006.

39. EIK, interview by author, November 28, 2007.

CONCLUSION

1. Melvin G. Holli, *The American Mayor: The Best and the Worst Big-City Leaders* (University Park: Pennsylvania State University Press, 1999), 24–25, 177–78; Rinker Buck, "How'm I Doing? An In-depth Look at Mayor Koch's Record," *New York Magazine,* September 8, 1980. On the problems of Holli's methodology from the standpoint of historians, see Neil Larry Shumsky's review of Holli's book for H-Net (Humanities and

Social Sciences) Online, October 11, 1999, http://h-net.msu.edu/cgi-bin/logbrowse. pl?trx=vx&list=h-review&month=9910&week=b&msg=8PGrwXRmSXdlChrxqr7Ch A&user=&pw= (November 18, 2009).

2. Lynne A. Weikart, *Follow the Money: Who Controls New York City Mayors?* (Albany: State University of New York Press, 2009), 139.

3. The exhibit was curated by Sarah Henry, Greg Dreicer, and Charlotte Brooks and financed in part by donations, largely from Koch's friends and former appointees. I served without compensation on the exhibit's advisory board, comprised of approximately twenty scholars, former officials, and curators, but I did not control the content of the exhibition and did not participate in writing the catalog, which was edited by the columnist Michael Goodwin.

4. Charles Brecher and Raymond Horton, interview by author, March 12, 2008; *New York Times,* November 17, 1980.

5. "The American Dream, the American Nightmare," *Economist,* October 7, 1989.

6. Ibid.

7. For examples see John Mollenkopf, *A Phoenix in the Ashes: The Rise and Fall of the Koch Coalition in New York City Politics* (Princeton, N.J.: Princeton University Press, 1992), 15, 17, and François Weil, *A History of New York,* trans. Jody Gladding (New York: Columbia University Press, 2004), 284.

8. *New York Times,* September 10, 1977.

9. Jerald E. Podair, *The Strike That Changed New York* (New Haven, Conn.: Yale University Press, 2004), 48.

INDEX